1991

# WORLD CINEMA SINCE 1945

# WORLD CINEMA
# SINCE 1945

## Edited by WILLIAM LUHR

UNGAR ▪ NEW YORK

1987

The Ungar Publishing Company
370 Lexington Avenue
New York, NY 10017

Printed in the United States of America

*Library of Congress Cataloging-in-Publication Data*

World cinema since 1945.

   Includes bibliographical references and
index.
   1. Moving-pictures—History. 2. Moving-picture
industry—History. I. Luhr, William.
PN1993.5.A1W67      1987      791.43′09      86-24981
ISBN 0-8044-3078-0

# Contents

v

ILLUSTRATIONS for each national cinema covered in this volume start on the following pages:

# Introduction

*World Cinema since 1945* surveys significant developments in the major national or regional cinemas since the end of World War II and seeks, not only within the individual essays, but cumulatively, to place those cinemas within a global context.

World War II brought fundamental change to many countries, although its influence varies with individual cases. It provides, however, a useful starting point for recent film history as well as one that in many cases saw genuine new directions, even new beginnings. The contributors to this book have traced the main developments of their respective cinemas over the past four decades; they have indicated ways in which the cinema they review is unique, as well as ways in which it resembles and has influenced others. As with the effects of the war, the issues raised differ in each case, and they are not limited to aesthetic concerns. They extend to government financing and policy toward national cinema—in fact, it has been said that the history of postwar cinema is the history of government funding. Market shifts, shifts in national taste, changes in technology, quotas, political imperatives, the valorization of modes of filmmaking and of genres (documentary as opposed to fiction; "quality" films as opposed to mass entertainment), international co-production, and the influence of broadcast television and video are some of the major areas of exploration aside from, as is traditional, the careers of individual filmmakers and filmmaking combines.

The Hollywood cinema remains a dominating fact of the world scene, both as an industrial presence and as a style. The passion with which many national cinemas have defined themselves in opposition to it—viewing it as supremely decadent and culturally corrosive—should not obscure the fact that, institutionally, it is the dominant cinema, nor that, as Bruce Kawin indicates here, assaults on and alternatives to it have developed not only from without but from within the United States.

Its influence, however, is not monolithic. Some cinemas have developed largely outside of not only the Hollywood model but also many of the more visible alternatives to it. India, for example, which dominates the world in feature production, remains for complex reasons isolated from the Western marketplace. India's mainstream cinema, Rosie Thomas points out, itself provides a paradigm against which much of its alternative cinema revolts, but that paradigm is very different from the Western one. Other cinemas constantly lock horns with the Western one.

Certainly one of the most influential alternatives to the classical Hollywood model has been that of Italian neorealism. Using visual and narrative styles, and production modes severely deviating from those associated with Hollywood, it not only gave Italy great visibility on the international market, but has also itself provided a still viable stylistic and production model for cinemas as diverse as those of South America, Africa, Czechoslovakia, India (primarily Satyajit Ray), Cuba, Mexico, Spain, Portugal, and Poland.

But Italian neorealism is not postwar Italian cinema, although the two are often conflated, and Peter Bondanella points out that during the 1945–1953 period most commonly associated with neorealism, only ten percent of Italian features could be so classified. That same is true of popular perceptions of German cinema. Eric Rentschler contends that it is simplistic to view German film as a single unit that emerged from a postwar abyss only with the New German Cinema. Furthermore, Germany belies the very notion of a unified national cinema since there are two Germanies and two very different cinemas. Esther Yau reveals a comparable diversity in Chinese cinema, as does Andrew Horton with Yugoslavian film. For most countries or regions, what is perceived as a national or a regional style is simply the most visible of a cluster of often competing, varied impulses, and the essays here pay as careful attention as space permits to the complex forces involved in that contention.

One alternative to the widely admired, quasi-documentary norms of neorealist cinema is what Dudley Andrew points to as the French notion of "quality" cinema—often using fictional materials, but carefully distinguishing itself from the traditions of Hollywood filmmaking. This had a strong influence on the French New Wave, which in turn influenced cinemas such as those of Cuba, Brazil, Czechoslovakia, Hungary, Germany, Israel, Greece, Portugal, and Sweden.

Much of Third World cinema has evidenced profound ideological concerns. But instead of producing a reactionary cinema to promote these concerns, as in the Soviet Union under Stalin, it has, in films from Cuba and Africa, for example, shown great interest in experimental techniques, in contemporary women's issues and in critiquing the macho ethic.

One of the areas of fascination of national surveys is in seeing styles and tastes shift, seeing, for example, many of the directors of Italian neorealism, or of the British kitchen-sink era of the late 1950s and early 1960s, who began with gritty, low budget, quasi-documentary films, now doing lavish, technicolor productions that seem initially at variance with presumptions of their earlier work.

Many national cinemas achieved visibility when creative artists began to assume production responsibility and take over the modes of production, as happened with the New German filmmakers or in the New Greek cinema. On a parallel track, nationalism has been a strong imperative behind the development, often through government funding and direction, of many national cinemas. Some countries, such as Canada, developed formulas encouraging productions employing indigenous workers or dealing with national themes; others set up quotas to restrict the importation of foreign films, particularly those from the United States, in an attempt to encourage greater home support for domestic productions; many Third World countries encourage domestic cinema as an important route to international visibility.

A counter tension has developed through growing recent tendencies toward international co-production. Furthermore, the great economic drawing power of Hollywood remains such that, as in the 1920s, artists who had achieved international renown within a national cinema are drawn to the often greater resources of Hollywood; examples are Milos Forman, Roman Polanski, Bruce Beresford, Peter Weir, among many others. And in contradistinction, sometimes those resources are used within a national cinema, as with the Hollywood funding that enabled Akira Kurosawa to make *Kagemusha* and *Ran* in Japan.

Television is likely to alter the world picture radically and has already had a profound influence on many national cinemas. Theater attendance has consistently declined in many instances, funding priorities are in many cases shifting, artists like Ingmar Bergman have recently done much of their work in television, and the technology of the industry is changing. Video further complicates things, often creating an important presence in countries without significant broadcast capabilities.

These essays are individual ones and reflect their authors' perspectives. Since the book is published in English, we have presumed the primary audience to be English-speaking and have placed either the English-language release title or a literal translation of the film's title first, accompanied by its original, sometimes transliterated, title in parentheses, as well as the date of the film's release. For the sake of consistency, we have maintained this policy, although in some cases the reader will more readily recognize the non-English title. The essays are of necessity surveys, introductions to much more complex issues, and selected bibliographies are provided at the end of the essays for further investigation.

Finally, this project was started by Stanley Hochman, and a good deal of work on it was continued by Evelyn Erlich. Much of the credit for what is good in it goes to them.

William Luhr

NOTE: In the photocaptions we have generally used only English-language titles, which may be more familiar to the English-speaking reader. The original titles of foreign-language films can readily be found in the text, where they immediately follow the English version. See also index of film titles.

# AFRICA
## The Last Cinema

CLYDE TAYLOR

More than ninety nations have gained independence since World War II, and most of the African nations among them date their independence from 1960. The furling of the European flags coincides with the first films made by Black Africans. The building of African cinema in the decades since reflects a painful stretching away from the cramped restrictions of the past and the persisting mechanics of domination; it presents a tense examination of decolonization.

The meaning of cinema for preindependence Africans is captured in a character sketched by African filmmaker Ousmane Sembène: "She lived in a kind of separate world; the reading she did, the films she saw, made her part of a universe in which her own people had no place, and by the same token, she no longer had a place in theirs." Commercial narrative fantasies had intimated the "lack of civilization" of her own people. "When N'Deye came out of a theater where she had seen visions of mountain chalets deep in snow, of beaches where the great of the world lay in the sun, of cities where the nights flashed with many-colored lights, and walked from this world back into her own, she would be seized with a kind of nausea, a mixture of rage and shame." Through the education of colonial schools and such movie theaters, she "knew far more about Europe than she did about Africa."

The experience of Africa with motion pictures for six decades had been one of existential distress. In relation to this magical instrument, blacks in Africa were locked into colonial silence for a term far longer than any comparable population. They were forced to watch in fascination worlds sharply different from the ones they knew, even when the films were putatively about their homeland, in which successions of Trader Horns and Tarzans cavorted among them with glamorized animation, all the more to signify their own unreality. African intellectu-

als were pained to watch Paul Robeson, whom they knew as a champion of liberated art and liberated Africa, betrayed by devious direction
into the ignominy of *Sanders of the River* (1935). As Bosambo (son of
Sambo?), the camera frames him shuffling and grinning obsequiously
to "Sandi," the representative of the British crown, who alone is able to
restore order out of chaotic rebellion and install him as king of the river
people.

Today's African filmmakers who watched *Sanders* and the like as
youths have evolved in a steadily shifting environment for cinema. This
has been mainly a shift from colonialism to neocolonialism, for from direct domination from Europe to indirect domination from Europe and
the United States. During the same time America has become a super-
power in film as well as in global politics. Africa stands today at the
other end of the scale from Hollywood. Americans view cinema from the
center of profitable, monopolistic production and distribution. Africa
provides a laboratory for the study of film's relation to society from the
viewpoint of the exploited.

Because Hollywood after the war began to depend on foreign distribution for more than half its profits, the gross caricatures of foreign
peoples, routine in earlier times, were muted. In the 1950s the Motion
Picture Producers Association began systematically previewing scripts
to eliminate potentially offensive materials. The most recent television
episodes of Tarzan now transpire in some anonymous, tropical land,
populated by vaguely equatorial people. The results of these modula-
tions have been limited. According to a 1968 study cited in *Africa on
Film and Videotape 1960–1981*, "More twelfth graders (percentage in
parentheses) than seventh graders assigned the following stereotypical
terms to Africa: witch doctors (93%), wild animals (91%), drums (91%),
spears (90%), savages (88%), tribe (88%), natives (86%), cannibals
(85%), pygmies (84%), poison darts (82%), naked (78%), huts (69%), superstition (69%), primitive (69%), missionaries (52%), strange (44%),
backward (43%), illiterate (42%), no history (38%)." A reasonable explanation of this shift between seventh and twelfth grades is the cumula-
tive impact of television and movie watching.

Far more important to Africans as filmmakers were the shifts in the
contexts of production and distribution, with little relief for their aspirations. What gives emerging African cinema a highly charged political ambience is the realization that political and cinematic independence are closely linked. The number of films produced by colonized
nations universally has been negligible (Hong Kong being a special exception). But those who set out to frame authentic African images after
the flag-lowering ceremonies soon found that the necessary material resources were almost entirely out of African hands and were organized
to resist the growth of indigenous film industries.

When independence came, two French companies, SECMA and

COMACIO, dominated francophone distribution through a dual monopoly. They dealt with theater owners on an all or nothing basis, allowing them no choice in selecting films, and traditionally giving them only the trashiest of movies, failed films seldom seen on the Continent. This, in turn, discouraged African film production because monopolistic distributors could "dump" films made elsewhere at rentals far lower than domestic films could afford to charge.

Upper Volta moved against this one-sided situation in 1970 by nationalizing its cinemas. The French conglomerate immediately imposed a boycott, closing down its theaters. A valiant effort to secure films from other sources was not able to fill the gap and a compromise was struck, effectively leaving film selection still in the hands of the French companies. Other efforts to nationalize distribution have met with similar results, with the exception of Guinea which, under a Marxist-Leninist government, was able to withstand the monopolies.

The controlling distribution cartel in English-speaking Africa is the American Motion Picture Export Company of Africa (AMPECA). AMPECA differs from the French distribution combine in not owning a network of theaters. Another American association, AFRAM (Afro-American Films, Inc.) controls the distribution of American films in francophone countries. In an interesting collision with the French combine, AFRAM also used the tactic of boycotting until it got what it wanted—distribution on a percentage basis instead of outright sale of films.

An indication of the resistance to a self-motivated African film industry came in the tour of Eric Johnston of the Motion Picture Producers Association in 1960, the same year most African nations became independent. The reason for his tour, according to *Variety*, was the example of governments either nationalizing or protecting national film enterprises by taxing foreign imports. "The Johnston tour is designed to check this situation, if possible, before it starts."

The lopsided film situation in sub-Saharan Africa today is implied in the yearly production of less than a dozen African features, while in 1976 Tanzania imported 160 features, Kenya 219, Senegal 248, and Uganda 936. In 1979, according to the *United Nations Statistical Yearbook*, Nigeria imported 105 features, all of them from the United States.

The African film market is small by Western standards, but this does not make it unimportant. In societies where literacy rates are low and where several languages coexist within national borders, the communications potential of cinema for informational and intellectual development is compelling. Ousmane Sembène sees cinema as "the night school of my people." The role films could play in developing a sense of national identity where such identity is now fragile equals the place once held by epics in the oral tradition. And while this is a secondary consideration to most African directors, the production and worldwide distribution of African films promises a needed enrichment of human culture.

"Cinema is a conversation I hold with my people," says Sembène. Many African film artists see film as such a conversation through which fundamental questions may be settled. Some recent features obviously bid for commercial success, but the overwhelming preoccupations of African filmmakers are marked by a sincerity, dedication, and commitment that draw their works into considerations of art and social thought, and away from the entertainment for profit that is the dominant concern of the major film powers. Moreover, the communal role of art in traditional Africa and the critical pressure of public realities combine to invest the space usually occupied by artistic and intellectual cinema with cultural and political awareness. To be both African and a filmmaker is to be cut off from the usual grounds of complacency. The dialogue that is wanted with an African audience (which might begin with the question, What does it mean to be an African in these times?) is crudely interrupted by the clanking machinery of white male adventure thrillers, kung fu operas from Hong Kong, and convoluted Indian melodramas which hold African audiences in prolonged captivity.

Thus Africa's cinema has been called a "cinema of hunger," an accurate enough description in terms of material resources. The available technical equipment in most countries is less than in some American film school departments. Film stock has been rare, unselected and often defective. Most West African films are processed and finished in European laboratories. By the time the director sees developed footage, the production team can seldom be reassembled for retakes. The ratio of footage exposed to footage used in the final print often approaches one to one. There are few trained African actors or technicians. Electricity is not always available.

The environment for making films with any accountability to local reality is more constrained than in any other area. Though African filmmakers mostly understand the pressures ranged against them, it must often seem as though nobody wants the truths their films would willingly bring. Leaders of African governments are wary of the kind of critical inquiry into national conditions the filmmaker is likely to stimulate. The economic weaknesses of the continent, problems of drought, famine, disease, ignorance, wars and interethnic conflicts make the filmmakers' bid for scanty resources seem impudent.

To this position the filmmaker makes two cogent replies. First, the resources needed are already present in the sums Africans presently spend to see mind-wasting films. Second, the perspectives brought by his or her film can have an impact on such calamities as drought, famine, disease, and ignorance by clarifying their causes and solutions. An African elite that mainly sees its salvation in its ties to the economic ally troubled over the ordeal of ritual scarification, who is treated without success by Western psychotherapists and finally receives solace through traditional healing practices.

Frequently in African films, women who respect the old ways are juxtaposed with those attracted to Western aesthetics, morals, and consumerism. This paradigm coexists with films where a new examination is made of old social attitudes, as when chauvinist males limit their women's freedom or when old caste and class barriers stand in the way of young lovers and wider social harmony.

Not surprisingly, these themes percolate in the work of Ousmane Sembène, perhaps the best-known African film director, and legitimately considered one of the century's major artists. *God's Bits of Wood*, his second novel, is a masterpiece of African and world literature. Yet he turned almost immediately from this success toward film, realizing that the political awakening of his people, his chosen vocation, would be better served by film than fiction in Senegal, where the majority are unlettered.

The language and communications predicaments of powerless Third World people are the subject of Sembène's second feature, *The Money Order* (*Mandabi*, 1968), based on his novella *Le Mandat*. It deliberately shadows Dieng, an illiterate, unemployed Dakar workingman, into the city center, as he seeks to cash a money order sent to him by his nephew in Paris. This African everyman daily encounters a ritualistic succession of tricksters from both the Westernized African elite and once-traditional Africans corrupted by city living, until he is fairly plucked clean of the hopes the money order had brought him. Not only is his quest symbolic, but the money order itself can be read as a metaphor for the paper independence recently granted from the "mother country." The allegory beneath Sembène's naturalistic portrayal has less to do with the handicaps of analphabetism than with the politics of information, whether "linearized," "commoditized," and made coefficient with wealth by the West, withheld for a bribe by the domestic educated class, or twisted into begging lies by Dieng's neighbors.

In Sembène's third feature *God of Thunder* (*Emitai*, 1972) unequal conflict brews between the villagers of the Casmance region and the French colonizers descending upon them during World War II to take first their young men for military service and then the rice crop they depend on for survival. This dilemma is background to the search for salvation by the elders through consultation with ancestral gods, and to the more practical and tough-minded resistance organized by the village women.

*Curse of Impotence* (*Xala*, 1974) is another of Sembène's comic-satiric essays on neocolonialism. Its principal is El Hadj, one of the bureaucrat-businessmen who collect the charter for political independence above the table and attaché cases full of multinational bribe money under it. Straightaway from this independence ritual, El Hadj is driven to his wedding to a third wife. As young as his daughter, this third wife is testimony of his overweening drive toward conspicuous consumption, for which prideful action he is attacked by *xala*, the curse of impotence, preventing fulfillment of his bridal night duties. His own frantic quest, in his Mercedes cooled with imported bottled water, is to find a solution for this well-publicized embarrassment. It leads him finally to a ritual of abject humiliation at the hands of the dregs of the society he has betrayed.

In many ways Sembène's next feature, *Ceddo* (1978), is the summation of his progress toward filmic decolonization. Whereas *Black Girl* was filmed in French at the insistence of its financial supporters, *Mandabi* was made in two versions, one in French (and in black and white), the other in Wolof, a Senagalese language, (and in color). *Emitai* uses the language of the Diola people among whom the historical events it builds on took place. In *Xala* the predominant Wolof of the Dakar setting is interrupted by French mainly to underscore the cultural subservience of its speakers. *Ceddo* was not only filmed in Wolof, but Sembène wrote the novel on which it is based in his personal reconstruction of ancient Wolof.

Set in an unspecified colonial past, *Ceddo* explores colonialism, slavery, and domination as historical typologies. The *ceddo* of the village, literally the common people seen as pagan outsiders, are aroused to resistance when one of their numbers kidnaps the king's daughter. Rivalries are sparked at the court among the different, self-interested advisers to the king. As one after another of the would-be suitors fails to recover the princess, the powerful imam, or muslim teacher, asserts his influence over well-placed converts, assassinates the king, makes captives of the remaining *ceddo*, and finally engineers the death of the solitary kidnapper. On the fringes of this court struggle, angling to take advantage of it, skulk a European slave trader and a Catholic missionary. The drama is resolved when the princess, awakened to the plight of her people by the example of her captor, slays the imam and frees the *ceddo* from their subjection.

While all of Sembène's films have been warmly received in Senegal (except *Ceddo*, which is banned) and abroad, admirers are split evenly when choosing favorites. The power of his filmic art is muted for Western spectators of his first three features on whom his subtle Marxist dialectic and layered significances are often lost in the restraint of his cinematic style—his stationary camera, infrequent close-ups, long silences, and deliberate, ritualistic pacing. Like his literary style, his film technique builds on an immanent realism where the surface of everyday, prosaic reality is simultaneously the scene of less obvious resonances, metaphors, and symbols. Teshome Gabriel likens it to the lost wax method of making African gold sculpture.

The same observation of immanent symbolic riches breaking through the unsuspecting plane of surface reality holds true for Sembène's work as a whole. *Xala* and *Ceddo* direct their political points more explicitly than the earlier films and carry more dramatic confrontations likely to hold audience interest. Sembène's conviction that African women remain unacknowledged as keepers of African tradition and as the more progressive force toward African liberation is more boldly voiced in each successive film. For these reasons, *Ceddo* forms a kind of paradigm of the definitive elements of Sembène's work in cinema.

The path of Med Hondo (Mohamed Abid Hondo; Mauritania) into cinema runs some parallels to Sembène's. Like Sembène, he discovered his creative vocation in France. After working as a jack of all trades, including docker, he became an actor and formed his own group, Shango, in Paris in 1966, to present plays of the Black African diaspora. Because of French indifference to his theater productions and their small chance of reaching black audiences, he widened his scope to include films. But unlike Sembène, he remained an expatriate in France.

The deep sense of estrangement and alienation Hondo experienced in France has been the driving energy behind his films. Through his Marxist dialectic, he finds that estrangement parallels the severance of Africa from its own values under imperialism. The expression of this theme, he feels, demands the search for an undominated African film language, and he has carried this search into a style more disruptive and nonlinear than Sembène's.

Hondo's first feature, *O Sun (Soleil-O*, 1970; after a lament from a song of Africans transported to the West Indies), uses estrangement as both theme and technique. Its protagonist, an accountant living in France, is nameless, like the central character of Ellison's novel *Invisible Man*. After the opening—a cartoon behind the titles showing an African placed in power through foreign military intervention, only to have that power reneged—this ambivalent hero, a composite of personal experiences, including some of Hondo's, moves through a succession of episodes more modular and metaphoric than sequential and representational. The many frameworks of his appearances, with the broom of a Parisian street sweeper, in a classroom, conversing with an executive about capitalism, all stress his essential alienation and ambiguous identity. He is traumatically and climactically shocked by the waste of food of a French family lunching at its country villa. Fleeing into the forest, he falls at the gnarled roots of a tree, his mind spinning with images of Third World revolutionaries—Patrice Lumumba, Che Guevara, Malcolm X—his ears echoing machine gun fire.

According to critic Francoise Pfaff, Hondo's film style shows the influence of the disruptive literary technique (and values) of Frantz Fanon, Leon Damas, and Aimé Césaire, and the militant anticlassicism of Godard and avant-garde theater, as well as African oral tradition,

Conspicuous consumption highlights a bureaucrat's wedding to a girl as young as his daughter, in Ousmane Sembène's comic satire *Curse of Impotence* (*Xala*, 1974).

A princess is kidnapped, a king assassinated, a villainous imam slain in *Ceddo* (1978), Sembène's powerful film on colonialism and slavery, based on his own novel.

Haile Gerima's *Harvest: 3000 Years* (1975) used nonprofessional actors in a black-and-white film about the injustices of feudal oppression.

A coproduction by Egypt and Algeria, Youseff Chahine's *The Sparrow* (1973) probed the corruption held partly responsible for Egypt's defeat in the 1967 Mideast war.

the precedent that Hondo most emphatically cites. These influences penetrate the documentaries he made after *Soleil-O*. *Dirty Arabs, Dirty Niggers, Your Neighbors* (*Les bicots-nègres, vos voisins*, 1973) critiques at length the abusive use of North African and Black African workers in France. *We'll Have All Death To Sleep* (*Nous aurons toute la mort pour dormir*, 1977) follows with sympathy the freedom fighters of the Polisario liberation movement.

*West Indies* (1979) is an extraordinary African film, both by virtue of its cost ($1.35 million) and its pictorial and dramatic spectacle. Based on a play by Daniel Boukman, a Martiniquan, it is a magnum opus, a cinematic opera set on a gigantic slave ship, said to have been staged in a huge, abandoned Citroen factory. This colorful music/dance epic links the past and present oppression of West Africans through their endurance first of venal African kings who sold their countrymen into slavery and then of their modern counterparts, the elite African collaborators with French neocolonialism.

Haile Gerima, another expatriate African, repatriated the alienation and outrage of his sojourn in America in a remarkable film, *Harvest: 3000 Years* (1975), made in his native Ethiopia. Gerima considers himself self-taught, despite several years as a film student at UCLA. Unlike Med Hondo, the several films Gerima made outside Africa are not usually considered to be African cinema, but part of the independent Black American film movement. These include *Bush Mama* (1975), *Child of Resistance, Wilmington Ten: USA 10,000* and *Ashes and Embers* (1983).

*Harvest*, which has won many festival prizes, was shot in Ethiopia in a few weeks, cost $20 thousand, and had a shooting ratio of nearly one to one. Using nonactors, including members of his family, Gerima captures as in a timeless documentary the unchanging reality of feudal oppression. A peasant family endures an overbearing landlord while a canny, deranged veteran declaims the injustice of the social order. The veteran finally kills the landlord who had confiscated his land while he was at war.

The commentary of Ahmed el Maanouni is worth quoting: "The peasant is doubly enslaved—by the earth and by the landowner . . . the yoke of serfdom is clearly represented by the death of the young peasant girl, carried away by the torrent while trying to save the landowner's cow from drowning. . . . While the peasants go out to work the land, the landowner goes to church. The religion is from outside and an image of power like western clothing worn over traditional dress. Foreign domination is also indicated by the frequent passing of lorries along the road—technology at the same time present and yet out of reach."

Gerima's slow-paced, black-and-white staging transports his spectacle beyond neorealism into a timeless collective memory. The grace and elegance of the peasants' movements, the unalienated, unsentimental firmness of their love for each other, the eloquent testimony of their faces in this nearly silent film, the spirituality of their daily culture impart to their story an antiquity of biblical resonance. The peasant father's long trek uphill to bow to the rebukes of the landlord seated atop his domain, the dream sequence of the daughter in which she and her parents are driven through the fields, yoked like oxen to a plow, a whip cracking overhead, are unforgettable. Such moments make *Harvest* more convincing than fact or fiction.

Another sort of expatriate film is *Sambizanga* (1972), made by Sara Maldoror, born in Paris of Guadaloupian parents. Drawn from *The Real Life of Domingos Xavier*, by Angolan novelist Luandino Vieira, it frames the beginning stages of the Angolan revolution (although actually shot in Guinea-Bissau). When Maria's husband is arrested and imprisoned by the Portuguese, she sets out on the road with her baby to find where he is, hoping her inquiries will protect him from official indifference. Important lessons are unobtrusively conveyed along the way: her husband dies of torture rather than betray his white comrade, while she is aided on her pilgrimage by a network of party members. The storming of the prison where Domingos died, not shown in the film, is said to have moved the revolution to the open level of combat where it found success.

The films of Souleymane Cisse of Mali, trained in Moscow (like Sembène and Sara Maldoror), have found a form between the extended parables of Sembène and the disrupting strategies of Med Hondo and Haile Gerima. His two most recent and popular films, altogether free of the cliche devices of Western cinema, wind naturally and therefore surprisingly through many lives, but get their centralizing spark from idealistic young people trying to bring change to a society where inequality of wealth and poverty is protected by powerful elders.

*The Porter (Baara*, 1979) follows an itinerant worker, much like the driver in *Borom serrett*, through the diverse daily rounds of Bamako, until he is befriended by a countryman, a young engineer who gives him a job in his factory. The owner of the factory later murders his wife for infidelity and simultaneously has the young engineer assassinated for his attempts to unionize the plant. In *The Wind (Finye*, 1982), two young students disturb their elders and the general peace, not only because their love crosses class lines but also because of their common fight, with other students, against inequality. Their love and commitment are only strengthened by their imprisonment.

The search for a genuinely African film language remains a common pursuit of Africa's leading filmmakers, While this search has already born fruit in films that look like those of no other culture, it has also turned most of them, including those already discussed, to African oral tradition as a creative matrix. This tradition has informed films focusing on pastoral settings, village-city transitions, and explorations, sometimes caustic, of the old ways.

Safi Faye of Senegal opens her most recent film *Grandfather* (*Fad jal*, 1979) with the now famous words, "In Africa, an old man who dies is a library burned to the ground." As the narrator relates the history of his village to the young boys of his family, events are reenacted. Simultaneously, questions arise concerning the village's relation to the state in land ownership and control. Similar questions preoccupy the village elders in her first feature, *Letter from a Village* (*Kaddu-beykat*, 1976), in which two lovers separate when the young man ventures to find work in the city.

"While studying African rites and customs," she notes, "apart from their problems of religion, people always ended up talking to me about their current problems which were, rather, ones of economics." Thus her films, which have been characterized as documentary and ethnographic, hold social relevance as well. The particular mix of elements in her films, their peaceful movement, the sensitive incorporation of ritual, make a distinctive contribution to African film grammar by the first Black African woman director.

*One Man, Many Women* (*Sey seyti*, 1980), by Ben Diogaye Beye, ties the loose interconnections of oral narrative to the problems of polygamy. Some of these problems befall Nder, a muslim with two wives, the younger, misled by a marabout, suspecting the other of causing the illness of her child. In another scramble of relationships, Fatou, who promises her lover to divorce the husband forced on her by her parents, announces a new day after her lover marries another and invites her to become his second wife. Ben Beye's is a witty, diverting, and thought-provoking film, however much controversy it has aroused for his treatment of a subject demanding much sensitivity.

More in the nature of an exposé is *Njangaan* (1974; Senegal) perhaps the best-known film of Mahama Johnson Traore. The title refers to a Koranic schoolboy subjected to abuse by a corrupt marabout who profits from his students' labor while only teaching them to recite verses of scripture they cannot read. This moving and well-coordinated study ends in the anguish of the boy's flight to the city where he is killed by the auto of an indifferent bureaucrat.

Discussions of oral tradition in African cinema must give special attention to *Jom* (1981; Senegal), Ababacar Samb's second major film after *Kodou*. Samb brings oral tradition into the foreground with a *griot*-narrator who articulates, sometimes directly to the camera-audience, the virtues of *jom*, a Wolof concept loosely translated as the dignity, respect, and courage without which a man is not a man. Declaiming to a group of fellow striking workers fractured by dissidence, he makes vivid and relevant the issue of *jom*, illustrated through two stories re-enacted through flashbacks to the 1900s and the 1930s.

A different contribution to African film language through oral tradition is made by *The Gift of God* (*Wend kuuni*, 1982); Upper Volta, by Gaston Kabore. Beautifully shot pastoral village scenes provide the setting for the story of a young boy who wanders out of the forest, unable to speak as the result of a traumatic experience. He is taken in by a family whose daughter patiently helps him recover his reality. Placed in a time before European presence, *The Gift of God* is remarkable for its simple originality and its filmic poetry. Like *Jom* and other works of the eighties, it noticeably widens the understanding of what an African film can be.

Just barely submerged beneath these explorations of oral tradition as foundation for cinema is an implicit contestation with the ethnographic visualization of Africa, most particularly identified with the work of Jean Rouch. A major pioneer in both *cinéma vérité* and ethnographic filmmaking, Rouch's films about Africa are free of the enthusiastic racism of earlier treatments. But according to René Vautier, another French filmmaker and one of the founders of Algerian cinema, Rouch's kind of film remains propaganda against a colonized people. Rouch's ethnographies, in fact, do little to disturb the stereotypic thinking reflected in the study cited of twelfth- and seventh-grade American school children.

The heart of the difficulty is the anthropological project itself, the preservation of the single view of Africa as the Africa of the past. Moreover, Rouch has difficulty explaining why Africans in his films never speak for themselves. To his credit, Rouch makes a point of training African technicians, and several African directors have worked with him, including Mustapha Alassane and Oumarou Garde of Niger, Desiré Ecare of the Ivory Coast and Safi Faye of Senegal. But do these directors subsequently need to de-Rouchify themselves? As much is implied in Safi Faye's positive response to rural villagers' concern with present economic issues.

Vautier likens ethnographic films about Africa to an amateur film made by his aunt featuring Bretons circling a mountain on their knees. In fact, African filmmakers have occasionally chosen to reverse roles and become occidentalists. In this frame of mind, Inoussa Ouseini of Niger follows a naive itinerant African worker to the outskirts of Paris where he is victimized by the deceit of both blacks and whites, particularly a French prostitute whose friendliness he mistakes for friendship. Poorer but wiser, he sends home a postcard whose message gives this short film its ironic title, *Paris Is So Pretty* (*Paris, c'est joli*, 1975). Kwate Nee-Owoo of Ghana turned his camera on the African art treasures in the British Museum; he then took it down into the basement where, amid surprised museum officials, he trained them on more Afri-can religious artifacts heaped about like junk. *You Hide Me* is a rough, *cinéma vérité* expression of culture outraged.

The point is that a truer, more complete ethnography is recorded by the ninety-one film directors treated in Guy Hennebelle's *Cinéastes d'Afrique noir* than in the special, curio films of anthropologists. It is a more valid ethnography, not only because through it Africans speak for themselves, from both sides of the camera—a circumstance that Jean Rouch applauds—but also because these films do not delete the press-ing considerations of politics and economics, the lack of which makes portrayals of Africa mere souvenir gathering. It is a more accurate ethnography because through it these films delineate Africa's transit among the Fanonian stages toward decolonization.

Fanon also offers the strategic link between sub-Saharan and North African cinema, as well he might, having been the principal ideologist of the Algerian revolution. Of the films made in Algeria after indepen-dence from France in 1962, Ahmed Rachedi's *The Dawn of the Damned* (*L'aube des damne*, 1965), an indignant documentation of revolution-ary struggle from Angola to Vietnam, owes an obvious debt to *The Wretched of the Earth*. Also in 1965, Lakhdar-Hamina won a prize at Cannes with *Wind from Aures* (*Le vent des Aures*). Considered by some the finest of Algerian features, it movingly depicts a mother's search for her son as both are caught up in the revolution. *Chronicle of the Years of Embers* by Hamina is another landmark of Algerian cinema, win-ning an award at Cannes in 1975. One of the most ambitious of Third World films, it is a sweeping analysis of the background to the Algerian revolution from 1939 to 1954, when open resistance broke out.

Algeria's nationalized film industry, which produces about five or six features and sixty to eighty shorts a year, has seen a brief epoch of hymns to battle films reflecting the history of the revolution, finally re-jected by their audiences as incompletely felt heroics, and a later period of more commercial, even Hollywoodlike efforts. This demonstrates that the coming of socialism does not freeze the oscillation among the phases outlined by Fanon.

One of Algeria's several successful coproductions (*The Battle of Al-giers* was another) was *The Sparrow* (*Al-asfour*, 1973), directed by You-seff Chahine, one of Egypt's and the world's major filmmakers. Probing through several well-drawn characters the inner corruption partly re-sponsible for the failures of the June 1967 war, *The Sparrow* reaches an unforgettable climax, based on historical fact, when Behelja, after watching Nasser offer his resignation on television, is the first of thou-sands to walk into the streets singing and marching in a remarkable spontaneous demonstration of national spirit, persuading Nasser to re-main.

*Cairo Station* and *The Land* are two other celebrated Chahine films.

*Cairo Station* (1958) is a marvel of neorealism, capturing the tangle and tragedy of lives intersecting at the railway station, some of them totally foiled by the society's repressive sexual codes. *The Land* (1969) is an even more complex, epic narrative of a Nile-bordering village in the 1930s, in which a powerful landowner is able to call in the army against the poor and helpless.

*Night of the Counting Years* (1969), by Shadi Abdelsalam, stands out as another masterpiece of Egyptian cinema. It plays the dialogue between old and new against the splendidly portrayed visual riches of Egyptian antiquities. Two brothers are shocked to discover that the economic life of their tribe relies on knowledge of secret burial places of pharaonic treasures, and must choose whether or not to inform the investigating authorities.

These most notable Egyptian films are part of a body of artistic and intellectual works that stand apart from a developed entertainment film industry that has earned Egypt the name of the Hollywood of the Arab world. This handful of Egyptian and Algerian films are cited merely to suggest some of the ways North and sub-Saharan Africa relate to each other. One mark of the cultural development of filmmakers from both worlds is the conscious effort to keep alive the spirit and practice of cooperation and mutuality between the two regions.

The biannual Festival of Carthage, Tunisia, first opened in 1966, is a major locus of this cooperation. The other major recurring festival is FESPACO, the Pan-African Festival of Cinema, at Ouagadougou, Upper Volta. Somalia hosts MOGPAFIS, Mogadishu Pan-African Film Symposium, first held in 1981 and promising to become a regular event. All three gatherings observe African-Arab cooperation while favoring their local regions.

If Egyptian cinema otherwise deserves its characterization as the Arab Hollywood, the similarities come from priorities placed on commercial success, superstars, and formula fantasies. We could celebrate this commercially successful industry as an example of creative independence and national ingenuity if it were not for the reality that almost from the beginning the goal, as in India and Hong Kong, was to reproduce the values of Western movies as closely as local taste made profitable. Such industries represent the domestication and internalization of Western mass culture, not its transformation or transcendence. A close look at their history and development reveals a Hollywood with a non-Western face.

Two sub-Saharan films reflect a recent inclination to move in this direction, without descending to the level of exploitation cinema: *Love Brewed in the African Pot* (1980) and *Kukurantumi* (1983), both made by Ghanaian directors. Typical of this trend, themes familiar in serious decolonization cinema are given a more popular turn. Kwaw Ansah in *Love Brewed*, for instance, stages the by now familiar story of class-

crossed lovers pressured apart, he to the city and she into mental de-
rangement. The film achieves fairly high production values, solid performances, and, in playing the theme for laughs, irrelevant songs and
tear-jerking pathos, instead of reflective inquiry. King Ampaw's *Kukurantumi*, partly set in a village of that name, adopts the same theme
but handles it with greater seriocomic realism, interesting rather neorealistic settings and camera movements, and a deeper than typical examination of the girl's bus-driver father. Far from a cheap distraction,
its roots are still traceable, though not as much as in *Love Brewed*, to
formulas nurtured by Egyptian popular films more than to African
films of commitment.

These are two of the few features made by English-speaking film directors. The pronounced domination in African cinema of the formerly
French colonies may be explained partly by the more assimilationist
cultural policy of the French, compared to the British inclination toward indirect control. The British influence, through the little training
and development assistance they have made available, has been toward
documentaries and television. Significantly, Ansah was trained in the
United States, Ampaw got West German help in making *Kukurantumi*,
and Ola Balogun, the most prolific film director from Nigeria, was
trained in France. Whatever the explanation, decolonization of cinema
has moved forward with more energy where the French rather than the
British did the colonizing.

Southern Africa is not surprisingly the source of the most repressed
and the most militantly liberationist films of Black Africa, the first and
third of Fanon's phases. In Azania, South Africa, the majority black
population is denied the training and opportunity to make films reflecting their embattled reality by the democratic fascist system of apartheid. According to Molefe Pheto, exploitative gangster and adventure
movies are made for black audiences by white film groups, using black
actors to front as directors. He reports that playwright Gibson Kent
was put into solitary confinement for six months as producer of an innocuous film to be made from his play *How Long*. At the same time,
aware of the importance of visual media, Black South Africans continue to prepare scripts and train themselves as best they can, both inside the nation and in exile.

Many features and documentaries have been made about the South
African situation, but not by South Africans. An important exception
is *Last Grave at Dimbaza* (1975), shot clandestinely and codirected by
Nana Mahomo, a South African exile living in England. Justly celebrated, *Last Grave* launches from consideration of the graves of infants
dead from malnutrition in the barren "homelands" where many South
Africans have been dumped by apartheid policies. It makes an impressive indictment of South Africa's totalitarian scheme of white domination.

A film industry does exist in South Africa, but strictly for the commercial benefit of white South Africans. It produces about twenty-five features a year, of consistent mediocrity. Not one of them has ever received international recognition. The industry benefits from heavy government subsidy, and is sporadically riddled by disclosures of financial corruption. Some of the mishandled funds came from the Department of Information, part of the Muldergate exposé. Government funds have been channeled into movies like *The Wild Geese*. Widely distributed in the West, these films use internationally known stars as mercenaries and present antiliberation propaganda as pure entertainment.

The playwright and actor Athol Fugard has written the filmscripts for *Boesman and Lena* (1974) and *Marigolds in August* (1980), both directed by Ross Devenish, subjectivist ruminations on the outskirts of political emergency. Eleven stories of Nadine Gordimer have been translated to film, but are ambiguously South African, being made for German television by international crews. They come, however, from a more serious level of consciousness than most liberal humanist thought on apartheid.

Angola and Mozambique offer revolutionary views from the other side of fallen Portuguese colonialism. Said to be the better equipped and more productive of the two, Angola has shown little interest in displaying its films outside its borders. The Angolan revolution thus remains best known in film through *Sambizanga*.

Mozambique formed a modest but determined film institute shortly after independence, and has produced several short documentaries and two features, *These Are the Weapons* (1979) and *Mueda* (1980). The first is a compilation documentary of the overthrow of colonialism. It includes fascinating stock footage of colonized Mozambique and footage of the revolution in action, secured from Robert Van Lierop, the Black American director who made *The Struggle Continues* (*A luta continua* 1971) and *The People Organized* (*O povo organizado*), among other films. *These Are the Weapons* is a moving recovery of contemporary history, singular in being a representative depiction made by Black Africans of their successful liberation.

*Mueda* is an unusual film of special significance. Ruy Guerra, Brazilian veteran of *cinema novo*, directed the filming of a folk play staged annually in the village of Mueda where the reenacted events took place. Just before the armed revolution broke out, politicized Mozambiquans entered this village near the border of recently independent Tanzania, demanding their own independence, only to be jailed by the local Portuguese colonial administrators. They kept coming, raising the consciousness of the villagers who finally rose up against the colonizers, only to be massacred. But their rebellion added a spark to the liberating eruption to come.

*Mueda* offers a provocative vision of what a people's cinema or a revolutionary folk cinema can be, freed entirely of the pandering styles of entertainment for profit. Humble in production values (it has been described as more gray and white than black and white), it captures stunning distanciation effects lodged in the folk play. Interviews with participants of the original events intertwined with the reenactments, help achieve an unheralded model of the demystifying cinema that progressive Western filmmakers have stumbled desperately to discover.

The fate of African cinema hangs on the outcome of persistent organizing to design remedies for problems of economics, underdeveloped infrastructure and distribution—an organizing that is highly strategized in the Naimey resolutions of 1983. These remedies stress regional cooperation in production, postproduction, and distribution that will demand a new level of enlightened self-interest among national governments. But whatever the fate of future production and distribution—which could conceivably get worse—Africa is no longer the cinematic desert Georges Sadoul saw twenty-five years ago. The problems and resilient solutions African films have posed are more apposite to other societies than intellectual fashion allows us to recognize. Even if they were not, African films make an invaluable addition to human culture.

Still another question is whether African filmmakers can wed engagement with the perennial public desire for fascinating spectacle. When given a fair hearing, the films of Sembène, Hondo, Gerima, and Cisse have won large and enthusiastic audiences. Whether or not films of this sort can win sustained followings in competition with exploitation films, the battle lines are so clearly drawn, the alternatives are so sharply marked, and the space for growth, experimentation, and human-spirited use of films is so vast that Africa remains the last hope for film to play the role of inspirer and enlightener that the inventors of cinema first had in mind.

## SELECTED BIBLIOGRAPHY

*Africa on Film and Videotape, 1960–1981: A Compendium of Reviews.* East Lansing: African Studies Center, Michigan State University, 1982.

Boufhedir, Ferid (dir.). *Caméra d'Afrique, 20 Years of African Cinema.* (85 min., 16 mm, color, 1983) Distributed by Mypheduh Films.

Gabriel, Teshome. *Third Cinema in the Third World: Aesthetics of Liberation.* Ann Arbor, MI: UMI Research Press, 1982.

Hennebelle, Guy and Catherine Ruelle, eds. *Cinéastes d'Afrique noire. CinemAction* (special edition), no. 49 (1979).

Martin, Angela, ed. *African Films: The Context of Production.* London: British Film Institute, 1982.

Pfaff, Françoise. *The Cinema of Ousmane Sembène: A Pioneer of African Film.* Westport, CT: Greenwood Press, 1984.

Sadoul, Georges. *The Cinema in the Arab Countries*. Beirut: UNESCO, 1966.

Salmane, Hala, Simon Hartog, and David Wilson, eds. *Algerian Cinema*. London: British Film Institute, 1976.

Vieyra, Paulin Soumanou. *Le cinéma africain: des origines à 1973*. Paris: Presence Africain, 1975.

The majority of the African films discussed here and available in the United States are distributed by Mypheduh Films, Inc., 48 Q Street, N.E., Washington, D.C. 20002, and New Yorker Films, 16 West 61st Street, New York, NY 10023.

story by the writer Jorge Luis Borges had been adapted for the screen. *Days of Hatred* (*Días de odio*, 1954) is the tale of a woman's vengeance for her father who was framed for theft by, in turn, framing her enemy for rape, after giving herself to an unknown sailor. The picture largely failed, ruined by having had to be stretched to feature length, when the other parts of a projected omnibus failed to materialize. But Torre Nilsson achieved striking stylistic flourishes in the depiction of the woman's solitude, which interested him more than the plot itself.

Torre Nilsson came fully into his own with his eighth picture, *The House of the Angel/End of Innocence* (*La casa del ángel*, 1957), an adaptation of a story by his novelist wife, Beatriz Guido. (Beatriz Guido would thereafter be involved in the scripting of virtually every one of his films.) The angel in the film's title is an architectural adornment in the house where the young heroine (played by Elsa Daniel) is kept in a state of exaggerated sexual repression by her "old money" family: statues are covered up and the girls must bathe with clothes on so as not to see their own bodies. In this memorably depicted claustrophobic world of the Argentine plutocracy, the heroine—eventually—ends up in the bed of a house guest, a politician (Lautaro Murúa) who is to fight a duel in the morning.

*The House of the Angel* established the Argentine cinema's beachhead in the festival circuit. Torre Nilsson took it to Cannes, where it was hailed as "the revelation of the festival" (André Bazin) and "the best South American film since the cinema exists" (Eric Rohmer).

Torre Nilsson followed this success with such films as *The Fall* (*La caída*, 1959), *The Party Is Over/The Blood Feast* (*Fin de fiesta*, 1960), and *The Hand in the Trap* (*La mano en la trampa*, 1961). In *The Fall* a student from the provinces (Elsa Daniel) boards with a nightmarish family where the talk is about a faraway uncle (Murúa); when he turns up, she precipitously ends up in his arms. In *The Party Is Over*, which registers a political rather than a social critique, a young male innocent (Leonardo Favio) is the grandson of a murderous political boss, against whom he rebels. In *The Hand in the Trap*, a Spanish coproduction, Elsa Daniel is again the heroine, who discovers that a mysterious retarded stepbrother, whom her mother and aunt claim to have living upstairs in their once-splendid mansion, is in reality another aunt. This aunt locked herself up, many years before—while pretending to have gone to live in the United States—to avoid the shame of being jilted by a rich landowner. The heroine engineers a confrontation between landowner and aunt, causing the death of the latter—and ends up as the kept woman of the former.

*The Hand in the Trap* was not only honored at the festival of Santa Margherita-Ligure, Italy, but made off with the FIPRESCI prize at Cannes. It was followed, however, by a set of less prepossessing coproductions, including two filmed in Puerto Rico with U.S. financial backing. Next, Torre Nilsson entered what might be called a Cecil B. De Mille phase. It began with *Martín Fierro* (1968), a spectacle based on Argentina's national epic (a lengthy poem by José Hernández on the life of a downtrodden gaucho plainsman) and continued with the screen biographies of two Argentine national independence heroes. Argentina's top male star, Alfredo Alcón, led the casts of all of the Torre Nilsson epics, as well as of most of his later works.

With *The Mafia* (*La Maffia*, 1972), a story of Argentine organized crime, Torre Nilsson entered a final period of synthesis, putting out six films combining some of the psychological probing and sociological portraiture of his early period with some of the popular elements of his epic period. Of note was *The Seven Madmen* (*Los siete locos*, 1973), based on two novels by the writer Roberto Arlt which, despite some flaws, memorably sketches a group of amoral (and ineffectual) social misfits and conspirators.

Documentaries occupy an especially important place in Argentine cinema history. the first landmark is the work of Fernando Birri. With film school students, Birri created a signal short, the neorealistic *Throw a Dime (Tire dié,* 1958), showing slum children besieging long-distance trains, seeking passengers' coins. "One must place oneself face to face with reality with a camera," he declared, "and document it, document underdevelopment. . . . Cinema which makes itself an accomplice of that underdevelopment is sub-cinema."[2] Birri next directed the feature-length *Flood Victims* (*Los inundados*, 1961), a mixture of documentary and fiction, showing people coping with a natural disaster and displaying luminous dashes of humor. It earned the *opera prima* prize in Venice in 1962.

Despite some technical shortcomings, particularly in the area of sound, the two Birri pictures are generally recognized as being among the most important output of the Argentine cinema. Yet this policy of openly "documenting underdevelopment" was not universally popular in Argentina: Birri came to find the working atmosphere untenable and left for Italy.

The other noteworthy name from the same years is that of director Fernando Ayala, with two films which unmask the flaws of certain types of leaders: *The Boss* (*El jefe*, 1958) and *The Candidate* (*El candidato*, 1959). In later years, his best work was arguably a comedy, based on a stage hit, *Laziness* (*La fiaca*, 1968)—a mild, funny social satire about a worker who flatly refuses to go to work.

Around 1960 there coalesced, stimulated by the example of Torre Nilsson and the French New Wave, a movement of new Argentine directors, sometimes referred to as the New Argentine Cinema, but more generally known as the 1960 Generation. The most notable of this new crop of directors included David Kohon, Rodolfo Kuhn, Lautaro Murúa, Simón Feldman, José Martínez Suárez, Manuel Antín, and, stretching chronology a bit, Leonardo Favio (he made a short in 1960, but didn't release his first feature until 1965).

The 1960 Generation was to a large extent a short-lived phenomenon, in part because a revolution in 1962, which overthrew the elected government of President Frondizi, worsened the cultural climate.

Many believe the two best directors of the group to be Lautaro Murúa and Leonardo Favio, both of whom were originally actors. Chilean-born Murúa started out in direction with *Shunko* (1960)—its title taken from the name of one of its principal characters—about a forgotten provincial community and the teacher who works with the townspeople to awaken their own sense of worth. It was shot in a style akin to Birri's, on location and with the villagers playing themselves. Murúa followed this with *A.k.a. Little Gardel* (*Alias Gardelito*, 1961), a masterfully caustic story of the hard climb to fame of a social upstart in a corrupt, manipulative world.

Leonardo Favio showed himself to be in possession of the most brilliant directorial talent of his generation—and, arguably, of all Argentine filmmaking history. His second feature was as good as anything that his mentor Torre Nilsson ever did. However, Favio also displayed a character as turbulent as it was gifted, and his zig-zag career included not only film acting and directing but also a relatively brief but successful stint as pop singer.

Favio's first feature, the partly autobiographical *Chronicle of a Boy Alone* (*Crónica de un niño solo*, 1965), depicted the sad and solitary odyssey of an urchin finding himself on the wrong side of the law. Unsentimental, vivid, and skillfully told, the film is from a script by Favio and his brother Zuhair Jury.

Favio's second and best work is the lengthily titled, *This Is the Romance of Aniceto and Francisca, of How It Was Cut Off, Sadness Began . . . And a Few Other Things* (*Este es el romance del Aniceto y la Francisca, de cómo quedó trunco, comenzó la tristeza . . . y unas pocas cosas más*, 1966); in general use, it is shortened to *The Romance of Aniceto and Francisca* (*El romance del Aniceto y la Francisca*). Beginning with the title, which is read by an off-screen voice, Favio displays a knack for cinematographic expression with a self-assuredness bordering on exultation. The story was written by Jury; it is melodrama about barren provincial existences, starring Federico Luppi and Elsa Daniel. Favio juggles daringly with the tempi. Fittingly, he keeps much of the film at the painfully slow pace of the portrayed lives themselves—yet he can challenge expectations with a sudden jump in narrative time. This burnished black-and-white film (its cameraman, Juan José Stagnaro) is lyrical and filled with empathy.

Among the other most significant films of the 1960 Generation are: Manuel Antín's *The Odd Number* (*La cifra impar*, 1961), an intellectual game about the "reality" of a character's supposed death, based on a story by the Argentine writer Julio Cortázar; José Martínez Suárez's *The Ace* (*El crack*, 1960), a (somewhat theatrical) exposé of corruption in the world of soccer, and *Face the Music* (*Dar la cara*, 1963), the story of three young men facing the first difficulties of adulthood; Rodolfo Kuhn's *Little Bird Gómez* (*Pajarito Gómez*, 1964), a bitter exposé of the entertainment industry; Simón Feldman's *Those of Table 10* (*Los de la mesa 10*, 1960), about the troubles of a young couple, compounded by their differing social class; David Kohon's *Prisoners of One Night* (*Prisioneros de una noche*, 1960), a doomed romance against the background of night-time Buenos Aires; and *Three Times Ana* (*Tres veces Ana*, 1961), three romantic stories about young women in a harsh world. If there is a common thread to these films, it is one of disenchantment. The disbanding of the Generation showed that the lack of optimism was not unfounded.

Nevertheless, in later years, the movement's graduates did occasionally manage to return with a noteworthy work. Such is the case of Kohon's *Brief Sky* (*Breve cielo*, 1968), another fragile romance against a sharply-etched portrait of Buenos Aires—a city whose strong character has been a constant Kohon concern. Antín fashioned the most sensitive and polished screen depiction of gaucho life, *Don Segundo Sombra* (1969), with an inspired palette by cinematographer Miguel Rodríguez. The film is based on a book of the same name, written by Ricardo Güiraldes, which is to gaucho prose what *Martín Fierro*, filmed by Torre Nilsson, is to gaucho poetry.

Favio himself, who followed *The Romance of Aniceto and Francisca* with *The Clerk* (*El dependiente*, 1967, another view of stunted small-town lives, also entered the gaucho world with *Juan Moreira* (1971). Neither of the later films, though, managed to consistently sustain the high level of its best moments.

Just after the student uprisings of May 1968 in France, one Argentine film generated considerable worldwide attention (in Argentina itself, it was banned for years, although it was shown at numerous clandestine screenings): *The Hour of the Furnaces* (*La hora de los hornos*, 1968). It is a long (four hours and twenty minutes), flashy documentary which fitted the overheated, and perhaps less than wholly rational, temper of the times. It won awards at festivals in Italy, Venezuela, West Germany, and Britain.

The film's creators, Fernando Solanas and Octavio Getino, were founding members of what they called the Liberation Cinema Group. The subtitle to the three-part work is *Notes and Testimonies on Neo-Colonialism, Violence and Liberation*. The film combines newsreel footage, reenacted material, printed slogans, and other ingredients in a mixture which is often cinematographically potent.

The first section was the most often shown, and it is the best of three parts. It ends with a celebrated five-minute-long still close-up of the

Hugo Fregonese's solid thriller *Merely a Criminal* (1949) stands out in a dismal cinematic era with its account of a released swindler trying to protect the loot he had hidden away.

Honored at the Cannes Film Festival, *The Hand in the Trap* (1961) was one of many successful films of director Leopoldo Torre Nilsson.

Part documentary, part fiction, Fernando Birri's striking *Flood Victims (Los inundados,* 1961) was awarded a top prize in Venice but was only moderately successful at home.

The multitalented Leonardo Favio's first directorial feature was the partly autobiographical *Chronicle of a Boy Alone* (1965), an unsentimental look at a young boy in trouble with the law.

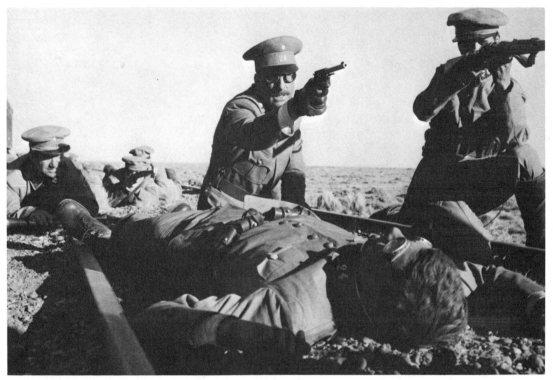

Anti-British sentiments before the Falklands (Malvinas) war: Hector Olivera's *Rebellion in Patagonia* (1974) accused British farm owners in Argentina of encouraging a massacre of striking farmhands.

In the late sixties young directors from the Group of Five adapted flashy advertising techniques to largely experimental films, one of which was Ricardo Becher's *A Shot of Grace* (*Tiro de gracia*, 1969).

dead Che Guevara. *The Hour of the Furnaces*, the filmmakers indicated, was not intended as art but as a revolutionary tool. Politically, it attempted to marry a left-wing outlook to admiration for the then-exiled General Juan Perón. Sophisticated, hard-hitting montage techniques and the records of real underdevelopment and exploitation were put at the service of simplistic sloganeering—for example, that all the media in Latin America are controlled by the CIA.

Another member of the Liberation Cinema Group was Gerardo Vallejo, maker of another prizewinning work: *The Road Towards Death of Old Reales* (*El camino hacia la muerte del viejo Reales*, 1969), which achieved dignity in a study of a family of exploited rural workers, with whom Vallejo lived during the filming.

The same year of *The Hour of the Furnaces*, the Argentine cinema also yielded another pivotal picture: Hugo Santiago's *Invasion* (*Invasión*, 1968). Based on a story by Jorge Luis Borges and Adolfo Bioy Casares, on whose screenplay Borges himself collaborated with Santiago, it is a cryptic film about a city which in many ways feels intensely like Buenos Aires, but strangely rearranged, in which a shady invading force wages a murky battle with unidentified defenders. It is darkly sparkling, stimulating—and more than a little premonitory, with regard to some aspects of the sordid civil struggles which Argentina would endure in later years.

Contemporary with the Liberation Cinema Group was the Group of Five, hailing from the world of advertising. For the most part, each of the members of the Group of Five (Raúl de la Torre, Alberto Fischerman, Juan José Stagnaro, Ricardo Becher, and Néstor Paternostro) was able only to apply the flashy techniques of the commercial (which is very advanced in Argentina) once—in interesting, largely experimental films—before vanishing from the scene. Some did manage to resurface much later.

Such was not the case, however, of de la Torre, the most distinguished of the Five's alumni. De la Torre shone with a consistent series of motion pictures which were simultaneously glossy and thoughtful, and accessible. Almost invariably they were about a woman, whose mind would be intelligently studied; more often than not she was upper-class; and she was usually played by Graciela Borges. Important works include: *Juan Lamaglia and Wife* (*Juan Lamaglia y señora*, 1969); *Chronicle of a Lady* (*Crónica de una señora*, 1971); *Heroine* (*Heroína*, 1972), possibly the best of the lot; and *Alone* (*Sola*, 1976).

Eight years before the war in the Malvinas (Falklands), two well-made films coincidentally displayed anti-British stances, chronicling British misdeeds in Argentine history. One was Héctor Olivera's *Rebellion in Patagonia* (*La Patagonia rebelde*, 1974), which narrates an outrage from the 1920s, when British farm owners in southern Argentina encouraged the army to massacre farmhands striking against abominable conditions. It starred one of Argentina's most talented actors in recent years, Héctor Alterio, as the army officer who realizes too late who has been pulling the strings. The other film was Ricardo Wülicher's *Quebracho* (1974), with Lautaro Murúa in a leading role, which described more recent episodes involving workers' near-slavery and the turning into a desert of a large tract of the Argentine north by a British lumber company.

Nineteen seventy-four was also the first year that saw an Argentine film selected as one of the five candidates for an Oscar in the foreign-language category: *The Truce* (*La tregua*, 1974), an office-worker melodrama (*Amarcord* got the Oscar). Also starring Alterio, it was directed by Sergio Renán, himself a noted actor.

Likewise earning attention was Juan José Jusid's *The Jewish Gauchos* (*Los gauchos judíos*, 1975), about the Jewish immigrants who headed for the Argentine pampas, a picture which rather overemphasized farcical elements. A musical, it had some surprising plot parallels with *Fiddler on the Roof*, though based on local historical incidents: it even included a character lurking on rooftops! (In this case, he lurks to drive a widow out of her mind.)

*The Power of Darkness* (*El poder de las tinieblas*, 1979) was a disquieting story about a conspiracy among the blind, based by its director, Mario Sábato, on a tale by his well-known novelist father, Ernesto Sábato. Also of international stature were Alejandro Doria's *Infamy on Trial* (*Proceso a la infamia*, 1978), a gangster story, marred by censors' cuts, and Oscar Barney Finn's *Broken Comedy* (*Comedia rota*, 1978), a probe, not unreminiscent of de la Torre, of the ennui of an idle rich woman.

To have three generations of directors in one family is unusual in any country in an art form as young as the cinema. Javier Torre, grandson of Leopoldo Torres Ríos, son of Leopoldo Torre Nilsson, made his debut with *Yellow Fever* (*Fiebre amarilla*, 1982), a tale of Buenos Aires under a plague in the last century. There was widespread agreement that it was an inauspicious start. Torre was working from a much-rewritten script which his father had been unable to film because of censorship problems.

The late 1970s and early eighties saw disastrous economic conditions paralyzing most of the Argentine cinema. The director who stands head and shoulders above the rest of his colleagues in this time is Adolfo Aristarain. He showed himself to be in possession of an unaffected, solid talent, in such works as the compelling *The Lion's Share* (*La parte del león*, 1978), a hard-nosed, mature, *noir* thriller, and *Time for Revenge* (*Tiempo de revancha*, 1981), a cynical, ambiguous parable of a crooked worker who feigns an industrial accident in order to get back at an equally crooked company.

Especially when writing the scripts himself, or having a hand in them, Aristarain displayed a knack for firm plotting, believable dialogue, and gifted handling of actors, as well as a healthy dose of wry wit.

A decisive change—quickly reflected in the country's cinema—took place in 1983 with the replacement of military rule by a democratic government. One of the latter's priorities was the dismantlement of the censorship of film exhibition and production. As a result, exiled talent returned from abroad and domestic filmmakers hurried to explore the newly liberated territories of the mind, soon winning international recognition that culminated in the 1986 foreign-language Oscar.

Not surprisingly, Argentine cinema of the new era concentrated most of its best efforts on an examination of the country's central political circumstance—its grisly recent past, in which thousands of people were made to vanish to face torture and death. The Oscar-winning *The Official Story* (*La historia oficial*, 1985), directed by Luis Puenzo and based on a script by Puenzo and Aída Bortnik, describes the growing suspicions of a woman (played by Norma Aleandro) that her adoptive daughter may be the offspring of parents who were kidnapped and murdered for political reasons. The film also won a Golden Globe award and a Cannes prize for Aleandro, while other Argentine movies were also garnering laurels at international festivals. *Tangos, The Exile of Gardel* (*Tangos, el exilio de Gardel*, 1985), a fictional piece written by Fernando Solanas and directed by him in a glossy style far removed from that of his *Hour of the Furnaces*, tells about Argentine political exiles in Paris. Starring Marie Laforet, it is an Argentine-French example of the field of co-productions that Argentina was beginning to take growing advantage of; its prizes included trophies from Venice, Biarritz, and Havana. Héctor Olivera's *Funny, Dirty Little War* (*No habrá más penas ni olvido*, 1983; Berlin Silver Bear, Cartagena, Biarritz), with Federico Luppi, is a bitter comedy of warfare between political factions in an Argentine microcosm. María Luisa Bemberg's *Camila* (*Camila*, 1984; Karlovy-Vary, Havana, an Oscar nomination), with Susú Pecoraro, told a period story of forbidden romance and political-ideological repression —taken from Argentina's nineteenth-century history—with resonances of more modern persecutions. There were also plaudit-earning documentaries on Argentine historical events and on the organization of mothers of vanished people, e.g., Rodolfo Kuhn's *Only Emptiness Remains* (*Todo es ausencia*, 1983) which spearheaded resistance to the military dictatorship.

In the mid-1980s most of the major works of this Argentine renaissance, though discussing the key Argentine subject matter, centered on the impact of the dictatorship's atrocities on the victim's relatives, or else dealt with the violence in a period context (*Camila*) or through a farcical prism (*Funny, Dirty Little War*). It appears to be too soon for face-on inquiries into the fate of the actual victims and, *a fortiori*, into the crucial question of how the country allowed itself to degenerate into a fetid replica of the European extermination arenas of the '30s and '40s. The corollary would appear to be that even more formidable works could perhaps be expected from Argentina if and when it decides to let its cameras delve squarely into its tortured (and torturing) soul.

## NOTES

1. The others named were Luis Buñuel, Ingmar Bergman, Andrzej Wajda, Michelangelo Antonioni, Federico Fellini, Alain Resnais, François Truffaut, Tony Richardson, Akira Kurosawa, and Satyajit Ray.
2. Birri, Fernando. *La escuela documental de Santa Fe.* Buenos Aires: Instituto de Cinematografía de la Universidad Nacional del Litoral, 1964.

## SELECTED BIBLIOGRAPHY

Abel Martin, Jorge. *Los Films de Leopoldo Torre Nilsson.* Buenos Aires: Ediciones Corregidor, 1980.

————. *Cine Argentino '76–'82.* Buenos Aires: Ediciones Metrocop, 1977–1982.

Astray, Daniel. *El Cine en la Argentina—Anuario '81, '82, '83, '84.* Buenos Aires: Helguero-Villalba Editores, 1985.

Chanan, Michael, Editor. *Twenty-five Years of the New Latin American Cinema*, Manifestoes of Fernando Birri, Fernando Solanas, Octavio Getino and others. London: British Film Institute and Channel Four Television, 1983.

Couselo, Jorge. *Historia del Cine Argention.* Buenos Aires: Claudio Espana et al., 1984.

Cozarinsky, Edgardo. *Borges y el Cine.* Buenos Aires: Editorial Sur, 1974.

Di Nubila, Domingo. *Historia del Cine Argentino* (2 vol.). Buenos Aires: Ediciones Cruz de Malta, 1959–1960.

dos Santos, Estela. *El Cine Nacional.* Buenos Aires: Centro Editor de America Latina, 1971.

Mahieu, Agustin. *Breve Historia del Cine Nacional.* Buenos Aires: Alzamor Editores, 1974.

# AUSTRALIA

## NEIL McDONALD

Although the Australian feature film industry virtually ceased to exist between 1945 and the mid-sixties, what films were made displayed a sophistication and adventurousness that marked a significant advance on the achievements of the 1930s. The era began promisingly with the release in 1946 of *Smithy*, a "bio-pic" about the pioneering Australian aviator Sir Charles Kingsford Smith. Although financed by Columbia, the film was made wholly at Cinesound, the major Australian studio of the thirties, by the company's producer-director, Ken G. Hall. In the thirties Hall had copied American models for action adventures such as *Lovers and Luggers* and *Thoroughbred*, as well as directing a string of successful folk comedies like *Dad and Dave Go to Town* and *Mr. Chedworth Steps Out*, which were often quite sensitive to tensions in Australian society. However, for *Smithy* the veteran director devised a unique synthesis of American and Australian narrative conventions. Instead of climaxing the film with Smith's historic Pacific crossing, as his American backers wanted, Hall widened the scope of the film to explore the psychology of the central character in relation to that combination of idolatry and denigration Australians bestow upon their national heroes. The film is also noteworthy for its attention to historical authenticity; Smith's plane, *The Southern Cross*, was restored to operation and flown; and Cinesound's newsreel library was ransacked for actuality footage of Smith's arrivals and departures, which was skillfully matched by editor Terry Banks with Hall's reenactments of the same events.

Equally impressive were two films by Hall's great rival, Charles Chauvel. *Sons of Matthew* (1949), a pioneering epic about three generations of an Irish family who settled the Cullenbenbong Valley and the Lamington Plateau in Queensland, comes as close as an indigenous film to portraying an Australian Manifest Destiny; indeed, Chauvel's exploitation of the south Queensland landscape and his superb low angle shots of the clearing of the forest invest the attempt by the five sons of Matthew to find their own land with a grandeur that makes the idea of their fulfilling some higher purpose quite plausible. Certainly the matching of studio shot exteriors and location footage is at times clumsy, and the story—a love triangle—all too predictable, but Chauvel more than compensates with his sophisticated staging and expert handling of the epic plot, replete with natural disasters such as bushfires, stampeding horses, and a climactic cyclone.

Chauvel's last film, *Jedda* (1955) was supposedly precipitated by a Universal executive's suggestion that someone make a film about aborigines. Nevertheless, it was a return to themes the director had tackled nineteen years earlier in *Uncivilised* (1936). *Jedda* is a far more accomplished work, in which the conflict between assimilation and the tribal culture is given powerful expression through a plot involving the adoption of an orphaned oboriginal girl, Jedda (Ngarla Kunoth), by a white family. When she reaches adulthood, the girl is kidnapped by a tribal murderer, Marbuck (Robert Tudwali). Chauvel's treatment of this material is curiously ambivalent. The arguments for assimilation are forcefully presented, but what dominates the film is the director's fascination with aboriginal ritual and the magnificent presence of Robert Tudwali as Marbuck. While his fight with a crocodile may echo the Tarzan movies, the scenes between Tudwali and Kunoth, a superlative natural actress, have considerable sexual and emotional force, making their double suicide at the end genuinely tragic.

Sadly, these films proved to be isolated achievements. What work there was came mainly from the documentaries being made at the Commonwealth Film Unit (Film Australia) and the Shell Film Unit, as well as from overseas companies who used Australia as just another exotic location. These foreign films ranged from travesties such as Lewis Milestone's *Kangaroo* (1952; the script for which was so bad that the director, to his credit, tried to persuade Twentieth Century-Fox to allow him to adapt two Australian novels of convict life instead) to genuine attempts to come to terms with Australian culture, such as Harry Watt's splendid *The Overlanders* (1946), Ralph Smart's *Bush Christmas* (1947) and *Bitter Springs* (1950), and Fred Zinneman's superb *The Sundowners* (1960), which prefigured such distinctively Australian films as *Sunday Too Far Away* and *The Last of the Knucklemen*.

Australians had little opportunity to see their own culture on film. Exhibition was dominated by American and British interests, while the attitude of the government under Prime Minister Menzies to an Australian film industry ranged from indifference to outright hostility. Some idea of the problems that faced an Australian filmmaker in the fifties may be gathered from an examination of the all too brief career of Cecil Holmes. His first feature, *Captain Thunderbolt* (1953), was a return to the bushranger genre of the silent era (a bushranger is an outlaw who makes the bush his hide-out), except for the fact that Holmes made a conscious attempt to portray the hero as a victim of the class struggle. Though it recovered twice its cost from overseas sales, *Captain Thunderbolt* was given only limited exhibition in Australia.

Holmes's next film, *Three in One* (1956), was much more ambitious. It consisted of three stories, "Joe Wilson's Mates," "The Load of Wood," and "The City." The unifying theme, stated in a rather patronizing narration by expatriate Australian actor John McCallum, is mateship and workers' solidarity. Very little happens in the first episode. An unknown drover, identified only by his union card, is buried by a group of "mourners" largely recruited from the local pub. But as the dead man's "mates" stop for a drink, listen to a few bush songs, and push the hearse up the hill to the graveyard, in a quite unself-conscious way, Holmes makes his point about the value of solidarity and mateship. Much blacker is the second episode, "A Load of Wood," a depression story about the theft of a load of firewood from a local skinflint during the bitter winter of 1930. The sequences showing the cutting down of the tree have a force out of all proportion to the events themselves, attributable to the moody low-key lighting of the night scenes and Jerome Levy's vigorous performance as a burly revolutionary. The final segment, "The City," strongly influenced by the Italian neorealists, is the slight story of two lovers (James Vicary and Joan Lander) who are unable to consummate their relationship because of economic circumstances and the oppressive sexual morality of the period, but are saved by the intervention of their mates. Once again, in spite of the excellence of the film, Holmes failed to get anything like adequate distribution in Australia, and the film only recouped half its costs.

Somewhat more successful, but far less concerned with interpreting national life or character than Holmes, Chauvel, or Hall, was the partnership of Lee Robinson and Chips Rafferty. Realizing that local features would only get token distribution in Australia, they directed their output (which included *The Phantom Stockman* (1953), *King of The Coral Sea* (1954), and *Walk Into Paradise* (1956) to the overseas B-picture market. When television rendered supporting features obsolete, their company collapsed.

It is, of course, unfair to blame the foreign control of exhibition in this country entirely for the inability of talented filmmakers to create an Australian industry. This virtual conspiracy against the local product was possible because of public and governmental indifference.

Just why Australians came to support the idea of a local industry in the 1960s is difficult to determine. Certainly it coincided with an upsurge of nationalism in the theater, painting, and literature. As well, the issue of foreign ownership of Australia's resources (an important preoccupation of the period) was easily extended to a concern for the film industry.[1] Coinciding with this was the emergence of a sophisticated film culture, sustained by a vital film society movement (particularly in Sydney and Melbourne) and the vast collections of American films from the thirties and forties that were originally imported for television but later exhibited theatrically by the National Film Theatre.[2] As a result, articles in journals such as *FilmDigest, Masque* and the *Sydney University Film Group Bulletin* anticipated many of the "discoveries" of overseas critics. There also emerged in Sydney and Melbourne an exciting experimental film movement which developed alternative distribution through film societies and university campuses.

Although films of this "underground" movement, like Albie Thoms and Bruce Beresford's *It Droppeth as the Gentle Rain* and Thoms' solo effort, *The Spurt of Blood*, may have drawn their inspiration from European trends such as surrealism and the Theater of Cruelty, would-be Australian filmmakers desperately wanted to create their own narrative forms which, while borrowing from American or European sources, would still embody a distinct national identity.

Many of the attitudes that underlay these beginnings of what David Stratton has termed "the last new wave" can be seen in Tim Burstall's first feature, *Two Thousand Weeks* (1968). The script was based on interviews with Burstall and cowriter Patrick Ryan's contemporaries, and rather obsessively dwells on many of the preoccupations of Australian intellectuals in the sixties such as the generation gap and open relationships. As one might expect with a first feature, the direction is labored and the dialogue somewhat stilted. Nevertheless, in its concern with class attitudes and the nuances of personal relationships, Burstall's film prefigures the achievements of David Williamson in plays like *A Handful of Friends* and *The Perfectionist*, and of writer-director John Duigan in *The Trespassers* and *Winter of Our Dreams*. In spite of the poor reception of *Two Thousand Weeks* in its own country, Burstall was able to crystallize in one exchange between Noel (David Turnbull) and Will (Mark McManus) all the frustration creative Australians had felt for thirty years at the deification of the expatriate and the cultural and economic dominance of Britain and of America. When told that no one has heard of him in England, Will replies, "Why should they? I work in Australia." It was one of the first expressions of film of the nationalism that is the basis of the New Wave Australian cinema.

The commercial and critical failure of *Two Thousand Weeks* caused Burstall to abandon the audience of middle-class intellectuals, for whom his first feature was intended, and to direct his work to a public that would not, he believed, betray him. In the process he began the cycle of films which can be grouped under the heading of the Australianism *ocker*, denoting both the "archetypal uncultivated working man" and the word's even wider application to the "uncouth chauvinistic Australian." The "ocker" comedies celebrated the often deplored aspects of Australian male behavior, such as beer drinking, sexual prowess (real and alleged), and colorful language freely sprinkled with four letter words. The first of these, Tim Burstall's *Stork* (1971), was based on a David Williamson play, *The Coming of Stork*, first performed at the La Mama theater in Melbourne. In spite of excesses such as a revolting vein of lavatory humor and a disgusting trick when the leading character disrupts an art show by stuffing an oyster up his nostril, the film is often perceptive and witty. Bruce Spence, Jackie Weaver, and Graham Blundell contribute splendid comic performances and the film became the first box-office success for the new Australian cinema.

Burstall followed *Stork* with a less critical celebration of male sexual fantasies. *Alvin Purple* (1973) is essentially a one joke film, in which the bumbling and average Alvin (Graham Blundell), for no obvious reason finds himself irresistible to women. In spite of some predictably terrible reviews, the film proved to be immensely successful, partly because Graham Blundell and the bevy of nude and semi-nude beauties who, in the words of the advertisements, "did it for Alvin," were all expert comic performers.

Whatever one thinks of *Alvin Purple* or its sequel, *Alvin Rides Again* (1974), they were quite amiable. Far blacker are Bruce Beresford's *Barry Mackenzie* films. These were based on Barry Humphrey's comic-strip character who first appeared in the British satirical magazine *Private Eye* in 1964. For the first film, *The Adventures of Barry Mackenzie* (1972), Beresford and Humphreys devised a series of loosely connected comic episodes built around the culture clash between an Australian innocent abroad, Barry (played by singer/comedian Barry Crocker), and the British. Its parody "ocker" is antiintellectual, obsessed with beer and sex, and speaks outrageously crude dialogue. The film is better paced than Burstall's efforts, but the climax which involves Barry exposing himself on "live" television, then vomiting over his assailants, reached a nadir of bad taste without parallel in any other Australian comedy. *The Adventures of Barry Mackenzie* and its less effective sequel, *Barry Mackenzie Holds His Own* (1974), were very successful both here and in Britain. Indeed, in Australia, screenings of *The Adventures of Barry Mackenzie* were often accompanied by behavior only marginally less offensive than that portrayed and, purportedly, satirized in the film.

In his indispensable *The Last New Wave*, David Stratton endeavors to defend at least *The Adventures of Barry Mackenzie* as "a worthy if vulgar successor to Dad and Dave and George Wallace." While one can respect Stratton's motives, this kind of argument demeans the achievements of a great tradition of Australian folk comedy. Ken G. Hall's films certainly relished Dad's redneck obtuseness and Wallace's bumbling naivety, but throughout there was a genuine affection for these characters, who were never allowed to lose their basic dignity, whereas the dominant characteristic of a Barry Mackenzie is that he has no dignity at all. A far more valid defense of the form is that Australian filmmakers went on to make works which portrayed in depth the very characteristics which had previously been exploited.

The key figure in what became a critical examination of the ocker is playwright and screenwriter David Williamson. As early as 1973 he scripted a disturbingly black episode, "The Family Man" for the film *Libido*. In this Jack Thompson plays Ken, the family man of the title who, together with his mate Gerry (Max Gillies), picks up a pair of girls at a pub and brings them home while his wife is in the hospital having a baby. The episode begins as ocker comedy, but Williamson, although clearly critical of the girls' brinkmanship, skillfully introduces disturbing hints of violence and even possible rape into the group's sexual fencing. Although John Murray's direction is only competent, Thompson and Gillies superlatively document the aggressiveness and violence that is too often a part of Australian sexual politics.

Even more interesting was Williamson's script for Tim Burstall's *Petersen* (1974) which is, in the words of the writer, "a sympathetic portrait of an ocker confronted by the only form of class distinction remaining in Australian society, university education."[3] Jack Thompson once again plays a tradesman seeking to better himself by attending university part time. Regrettably, Burstall's direction is, at times, indistinguishable from that of the *Alvin Purple* films. Bare bodies and ribald sex scenes abound and even though the director's handling of sequences like the invasion of a North Shore party by a gang of thugs is masterly, the film's tone is, on the whole, uneven. What saves *Petersen* is the high quality of the script and performances. Actresses Wendy Hughes, as Petersen's tutor at university, and Jackie Weaver, as his wife, provide Burstall with sensitive, believable characterizations. As well, Jack Thompson expertly conveys the insecurity and vulnerability which underlies Petersen's aggressiveness and sexual prowess.

The most significant film to emerge from the ocker cycle is Bruce Beresford's *Don's Party* (1976). Based on a play by David Williamson, who also scripted the film, it examines the brutal vulgarity of ocker behavior when adopted by the middle-class intellectual. As Don's premature party to celebrate the Labour "victory" of 1969 degenerates into boozy self-revelation and near violence, the exposure of the essential shallowness of the characters and the futility of their aspirations reflects not just the disappointments of 1969 but the despair following the dismissal of the Whitlam government in 1975. If anything can be said to redeem the excesses of the *Barry Mackenzie* films, it is the unsparing honesty Beresford brought to his direction of *Don's Party*. This in effect marked the end of the ocker cycle. Beresford's next collaboration with

Williamson, *The Club* (1980), had some ocker characteristics but emphasized power games within a Melbourne football club, while, on the other hand, a film version of Jack Hibberd's broad comedy *Dimboola* (1979) directed by, of all people, John Duigan, proved to be an artistic and commercial failure.

Closely related to the ocker cycle have been a series of what can best be regarded as "outback" (or back country) films. These have explored themes such as the passing of old traditions, mateship, and the tensions within all male groups isolated by the nature of their occupations from mainstream society. The first of these films was by no means strictly Australian. *Wake in Fright* (1971) was an American-Australian coproduction directed by Canadian Ted Kotcheff. But in spite of this foreign involvement and the presence of the cast of British actors Gary Bond and Donald Pleasance, the film was a genuine attempt to come to terms with the mores of outback society. The plot is deceptively simple: a schoolteacher (Bond) is drawn into the boozy mateship and mindless brutality of Bundanyabba, a thinly disguised portrait of a mining town in New South Wales, Broken Hill. This process enables Kotcheff to paint a terrifying picture of the dark side of such cherished activities as two-up (in which bets are placed on the simultaneous toss of two coins), the shout (paying for a round of drinks), and mateship itself, which in this context becomes stultifying and oppressive. What makes the film so fascinating is that Gary Bond's schoolteacher, for all his contempt for outback life and his dreams of being a journalist in London, really wants to be drawn into the *'yabba's* (Broken Hill's) mindless conviviality. The climax, a pointlessly brutal kangaroo hunt, is as powerful an indictment of the ocker mythology as exists in any Australian film.

Far less bleak, but just as perceptive and honest, is Ken Hannam's *Sunday Too Far Away* (1974), an exploration of the values and relationships of a group of shearers in the mid-1950s. As originally conceived by screenwriter John Dingwall, the film was about three generations, a boy, Michael (Gregory Apps), who wants to emulate the top shearer, Foley (Jack Thompson), and old Garth (Reg Lye), an alcoholic representing what Foley could become. According to producer Gil Brealey, Ken Hannam's version incorporating these themes, which ran about two hours, was unreleasable.[4] Consequently, the film was cut to ninety-three minutes, which had the effect of making Foley the virtual hero, and while Garth's tragedy remains significant, Michael's relationship with Foley is now only suggested. Nevertheless, unlike Jerry Bresler's vandalization of Sam Peckinpah's *Major Dundee* or Warner Brothers' truncation of George Cukor's *A Star Is Born*, Brealey's cut of *Sunday Too Far Away* works superbly. The climax where Foley reaffirms his solidarity with the other shearers as they prepare to strike is as powerful an affirmation of the ideal of mateship as was *Three in One* nearly twenty years earlier.[5]

Less complex, but equally compelling, is Tim Burstall's *The Last of The Knucklemen* (1979), an adaptation of John Powers's play. In filming this story of the power struggle between the devious Pansey (Mike Preston) and the aging knuckleman (or foreman) Tarzan (Gerard Kennedy) for the leadership of a gang of miners in an isolated camp, Burstall wisely employs only very few location shots to open out the action. Instead, he concentrates on the confrontations and relationships in the scenes set in the men's cramped living quarters. As a result, the film has considerable dramatic tension and marked the coming of age of a director to whom the Australian industry owes a great deal.

Recently the cycle of outback films has become much more benign. John Dingwall's script for Arch Nicholson's *Buddies* (1983) about a pair of sapphire miners (Colin Friels and Harold Hopkins) in Central Queensland, whose way of life is threatened when the big operators try to muscle in certainly has external conflict aplenty but lacks any real thematic or dramatic tension. Far more effective is Howard Rubie's underrated *The Settlement* (1983). Unlike *Buddies*, this is a period piece, set during the shearers' strike in the mid-fifties and exploring the tensions that arise in a small town when a pair of seasonal outback workers set up a *ménage à trois* with the local barmaid. The film has a genuine feeling for the Australian countryside and meticulously recreates the sexual oppressiveness of Australia in the 1950s, which is the source of most of the dramatic conflict. Bill Kerr, John Jarrett, and Lorna Leslie are splendid as the unconventional threesome, while Tony Barry gives a sensitive performance as the likeable, but basically corrupt local policeman. Rubie directs with a pleasantly light touch, which easily encompasses the shifts from comedy to drama in Ted Roberts's literate screenplay.

So far there have been only a few isolated attempts to revive the outback genres of the twenties and thirties. Phillipe Mora's bushranger film, *Mad Dog Morgan* (1976), which, like *Captain Thunderbolt*, portrays its hero as the victim of a repressive colonial administration, failed at the box office because of its reputation for excessive violence. Similarly, Mark Egerton's *The Winds of Jarrah* (1983), a reworking of themes from successful thirties' films like *The Squatter's Daughter*, *Tall Timbers*, and *Rangle River*, had difficulty finding a distributor in spite of impeccable period atmosphere and fine performances by Terry Donovan, Harold Hopkins, and Susan Lyon.

On the other hand, both Donald Crombie's *The Irishman* (1978) and George Miller's *The Man from Snowy River* (1982) made self-conscious attempts to create a new, distinctively Australian cinematic mythology. *The Irishman* concentrated on the passing of the old order, represented by the replacement of bullock teams by motor transport. Crombie also contrasted the main character's legendary stature as the representative of an older Australia with the "reality" of his weakness and irresponsibility. In spite of superb photography (by Peter James) that evokes the styles of *Sons of Matthew* and *The Squatter's Daughter*, the film's potential is dissipated by some clumsy scripting (by Crombie himself) that leaves key dramatic issues undefined.

The problems that afflict *The Man from Snowy River* are quite different. The script builds upon suggestions in A. B. ("Banjo") Patterson's famous poem to create a narrative that portrays the rite of passage whereby "the stripling" of the poem (called "Jim" in the film) overcomes both the cattle baron, Harrison (Kirk Douglas), and the stallion who leads the wild horses. Criticism of the film in Australia has concentrated on the use of veteran American actor Kirk Douglas in the key roles of Harrison and his twin brother Spur, and on the combination of plot devices derived from the Western with "authentic" Australian material.[6] However, to an unprejudiced eye the combination works extremely well; as for Kirk Douglas, he is hardly comparable with the overseas nonentities who have all too often been forced on Australian producers. Indeed, director George Miller insists Douglas became a considerable asset to the film. "He is such a powerful Harrison that when Jim overcomes him, by Jesus, you know he has become a man."[7] In addition, his contribution is matched superbly by Tom Burlinson's sensitive portrayal of "the stripling" and Jack Thompson's impersonation of the "living legend," Clancy of the Overflow. What has been the source of the film's great success in Australia and overseas, however, is the climactic pursuit of the wild horses, a tour de force of superb photography and stunt riding that more than equals Chauvel's classic charge of the Australian Light Horse in *Forty Thousand Horsemen* (1940).

Even before the success of *The Man from Snowy River*, historical films had dominated the public's perception of the "new" Australian cinema both here and overseas. This concentration on the past has been severely criticized by Australian writers as an escape from "difficult" contemporary issues. These attacks, however, are repudiated by the filmmakers themselves. Writer-producer Joan Long points out that when she was scripting *Caddie*, the problems of single parents were almost identical to those confronting her heroine of the depression era.[8] Also, *Kitty and the Bagman*'s portrayal of corruption in Sydney of the 1920s became disturbingly relevant when similar allegations surfaced in State Parliament and on the A.B.C. (Australian Broadcasting Corporation) just after the film's release in 1983. Certainly the cycle of Australian historical films is, on the whole, meticulously researched and recreates authentic period attitudes, but as often as not the issues these films address are believed by their creators to be of continuing relevance to contemporary audiences.

A good example of this relevance comes from one of the earliest of the historical cycle, Mike Thornhill's *Between the Wars* (1974). The hero, Edward Trenbow (Corin Redgrave), is a recessive personality who, because of a stubborn basic integrity, finds himself in the center of controversies that reflect some of the issues that divided Australia in the thirties and forties. He opposes the right-wing New Guard and is accused of being a leftist. Later, because of his opposition to Australia's involvement in World War II and his championship of the cause of a colleague who has been interned as an alien, Trenbow becomes isolated even from his own family, which regards him as a traitor. Although these conflicts are based on period issues and are superbly recreated as such by Thornhill and the author of the screenplay, the famous short story writer Frank Moorhouse, they had their counterparts in Australia of the late sixties and early seventies. By the time the film was released, the Labour government's modest program of social reform under Prime Minister Whitlam had already provoked hysterical right-wing opposition, while those who had initially opposed Australia's involvement in Vietnam felt as isolated as Trenbow does in the film when, in 1966, the conservative Harold Holt (author of the phrase "all the way with L.B.J.") was returned to power as prime minister by an overwhelming majority.

Equally relevant to the mid-seventies, although even more meticulous in its recreation of the sights and sounds of the 1930s, is Donald Crombie's *Caddie* (1976). Viewed today it remains as impressive as ever, with some splendid photography and a superbly detailed performance by Helen Morse in the title role. However, the heroine's predicament as a single mother in the depression era seemed particularly apposite in 1976 as Australia moved from prosperity to recession. Even her problems over child minding had a contemporary application with the Whitlam government's support for preschool facilities. It was not that Crombie or producer Tony Buckley were endeavoring to create some kind of contemporary allegory. Rather, they were endeavoring to tell a good story which proved to be relevant to the audience who made *Caddie* a box-office success.

The best examples of authentic recreation of period attitudes finding modern parallels are Bruce Beresford's *Breaker Morant* (1980) and Peter Weir's *Gallipoli* (1981). *Breaker Morant* was based on a cause célèbre of the Boer War, where two officers of the Australian army, Lieutenants Morant and Handcock, were court-martialed and executed by the British for shooting Boer prisoners. Beresford based the screenplay on Kenneth Ross's play about the court-martial, but also interpolated material from Kit Denton's fine novel *The Breaker* that had revived public interest in the case. In addition, Beresford commissioned his own research in Australia and at the Army Museum in London. Consequently, much of the darker side of Morant and Handcock, which had been ignored in the novel and play, was incorporated in the film. It is, for example, made quite clear that Handcock was guilty of murdering a German missionary. Although in every respect a period piece, the comparison between the Boer War and Vietnam is obvious, while the parallels between Morant's and Handcock's execution of their prisoners evokes memories of Lieutenant Calley and the My Lai massacre. But what dominates the film is a deeply felt resentment at the hypocrisy of the British High Command, who use Australian soldiers as scapegoats for their own violations of the rules of war. The period recreation reflects contemporary Australian resentment at being subordinate not only to Britain but also to the United States. None of this would have been as effective if *Breaker Morant* had not been arguably the best film to emerge to date from the Australian New Wave.

If anything, Peter Weir's *Gallipoli* is even more bitter about the way Australians have been exploited by the great powers. The theme was, once again, derived from sources of the period, this time from C. E. W. Bean's official history of the Gallipoli campaign. In it the scriptwriter, David Williamson, perceived a thinly disguised resentment of the way Australian troops had been used to serve British interests.[9] This became the basis for one of the film's most telling scenes, where the British are described as sitting on the beach drinking tea while the Australians are dying in the "diversionary attack" on Lone Pine. Although *Gallipoli* is flawed by Weir's characteristic reluctance to take full advantage of the dramatic potential of Williamson's screenplay, it is still a powerful film. The mateship of the two main protagonists may be idealized, but becomes unbearably poignant as Mel Gibson's Frank runs desperately back with the order postponing the attack as Mark Lee's Archie "goes over the top" to certain annihilation. These sequences are made even more effective by the fact that Weir and his cameraman, Russell Boyd, based many of their compositions on the Gallipoli paintings by G. W. Lambert in the Australian War Memorial. *Gallipoli*'s greatest achievement in the Australian context is that it embodies a major revision of one of the most deeply felt of national myths. For Peter Weir and David Williamson the Gallipoli landings were not, as generations of schoolmasters insisted at Anzac (a soldier in the Australian and New Zealand Army Corps) Day ceremonies, the birth of a new nation, but a national tragedy. The events at Lone Pine become an emblem not just of the futility of war, but a reminder to Australians still enmeshed in one-sided overseas alliances of how they have been exploited in the past.

This kind of vigorous reinterpretation of national myths is exactly what is absent from a later historical epic, Graeme Clifford's *Burk and Wills* (1985). Based on events well known to every Australian school child, of a doomed attempt to reach the Gulf of Carpentaria by a lavishly equipped exploring expedition (led by the Burk and Wills of the title), the film displays little grasp of character and offers no interpretation of the social and historical context. Instead, *Burk and Wills* concentrates wearisomely on the details of the journey itself. The usually

reliable Jack Thompson (as Burk) is encouraged to overplay outrageously, and although Nigel Havers (as Wills) is genuinely moving as
the shy Englishman who accompanies Burk against his better judgment, the fascinating story of their true relationship remains untold.
The only redeeming feature is the superb photography by Russell Boyd,
who displays a genuine feeling for the vastness and mystery of the Australian outback.

This tendency to reinterpret the past in the light of modern problems
is also a feature of one of the best films to be made about the immediate
postwar era, Phil Noyce's *Newsfront* (1978). On one level it is an affec-
tionate celebration of the immediate past of the Australian film industry. Cinesound becomes Cinetone; its managing director during most
of the period, Ken G. Hall, becomes A. G. Marwood; and the Maguire
brothers (played by Bill Hunter and Gerard Kennedy) are based on the
cameramen Ross and Syd Wood. The film actually incorporates newsreel footage from the period, moving from color to black and white to
make the transitions more effective. According to Phil Noyce, the style
of the newsreels dictated that of the film as a whole.[10] Telephoto shots
were avoided because newsreel cameramen of the forties and fifties did
not use them; medium-range lenses and balanced, classically composed
framing were employed throughout. As a result, *Newsfront* looks like
the kind of film Ken G. Hall or Chauvel might have made in the fifties
had they been able to secure the backing.[11] But the film is more than a
tribute to veteran filmmakers. Bob Ellis's script, pared down by Phil
Noyce, concentrates on the political divisions of the 1950s, raising in
that context issues about the treatment of news that were even more
relevant in the Australia of Prime Minister Malcolm Fraser. The richness and complexity of *Newsfront* can best be appreciated when it is
compared with another film about the film industry, John Power's *Picture Show Man* (1976). Although scripted and produced by Joan Long, a
recognized authority on the history of the Australian cinema, it is little
more than a recreation of the period when private exhibitors, or picture
show men, traveled the outback screening silent films in country
towns.

A very different aspect of Australian society in the 1950s is portrayed
in Fred Schepisi's semiautobiographical *The Devil's Playground* (1974)
which is based on his own experiences in a Roman Catholic school preparing boys for the priesthood. Given that Schepisi, like Tom the film's
hero, rejected the Catholic tradition, he treats the priests and brothers
with remarkable tolerance and compassion. Even the obsessed Brother
Francine (Arthur Dignam), with his dreams of naked women threatening his chastity, is all too sadly believable. Shot in muted Eastmancolor
by Ian Baker, the low key lighting emphasizes the oppressiveness of the
unnatural environment against which the irrepressible Tom, splendidly portrayed by Simon Burk, finally rebels. In charting the hero's

gradual alienation from school and church, Schepisi never caricatures the teachers or priests, as has been done all too often in Australian theater. All of which makes the film's scathing indictment of the system itself so effective. Schepisi's next film, *The Chant of Jimmy Blacksmith* (1978), used the true story of an aboriginal murderer to make a pointed comment on white Australia's treatment of the indigenous inhabitants. It is a worthy film, but Schepisi's heavy-handed direction, in marked contrast to that of *The Devil's Playground*, along with its reputation for excessive violence, caused it to fail at the box office.

The period films that have dominated the perception of Australia's New Wave here and overseas, however, have been the series of women's pictures set in a turn of the century colonial environment. The origin of this cycle is usually thought to be Peter Weir's *Picnic at Hanging Rock* (1975). But although it lovingly recreates Victorian trappings, it is best understood in terms of its director's preoccupation with fantasy and mysticism.

Actually, the beginnings of this cycle lie in one of the best television series ever produced by the A.B.C., Ron Way's *Seven Little Australians* (1973). Based on a novel by a famous children's writer, Ethel Turner, the series portrayed the clash between wilful tomboy heroine Judy (Jennifer Cluff) and her well-meaning but unbending father, Captain Woolcott (Leonard Teale). Eleanor Witcomb, who is the key figure in the development of this series, having scripted both *The Getting of Wisdom* and *My Brilliant Career*, included in her adaptation of the novel all the essentials of the cycle that was to follow: a careful recreation of the turn of the century period and a strong heroine in rebellion against a male-dominated establishment.

The problems confronting Laura (Susannah Fowle), the heroine of Bruce Beresford's *The Getting of Wisdom* (1977), are more complex than those of *Seven Little Australians*. In the setting of an upper-class ladies' college, the film portrays Laura's desperate attempts to belong to this world by inventing a fantasy romance with a local clergyman, having an affair with an older girl, and finally asserting her independence by playing a piece other than the one announced at her final school assembly. Bruce Beresford deftly handles Eleanor Witcomb's sharply observed scenes of schoolgirl cruelty and elicits superb performances from Sheila Helpmann as Miss Gurley, the fearsome headmistress, and Patricia Kennedy as her more compassionate deputy. But dominating the film is Susannah Fowle's portrait of Laura, which achieves under Beresford's direction just the right combination of wilfulness and sensitivity.

Along with *Picnic* and *The Getting of Wisdom*, the final work of this virtual trilogy is Gillian Armstrong's *My Brilliant Career* (1979). Based on an autobiographical novel by Miles Franklin, the film traces its heroine's continual assertion of independence from her family, suitors,

Ron Randell as pioneering aviator Charles Kingsford Smith, and World War I Prime Minister W.M. Hughes as himself in Ken G. Hall's *Smithy* (1946), which combined American and Australian approaches to the true story.

The still from Beresford's *Don's Party* (1976) with Ray Barrett and John Hargreaves captures something of the film's critique of "ockerism."

Barry Crocker in the title role of Bruce Beresford's *The Adventures of Barry Mackenzie* (1972), based on a comic-strip character. The shot skillfully encapsulates the film's raucous vulgarity.

Sigrid Thornton and Tim Burlinson in a shot that expresses superbly the romanticism of George Miller's *The Man from Snowy River* (1982).

Bruce Beresford's *Breaker Morant* (1980) was the best of the Australian New Wave. The still, with Edward Woodward and Jack Thompson, captures much of the tension of the court martial scenes.

Judy Davis (left), Aileen Brittan (center), and Sam Neill (right) in Gillian Armstrong's *My Brilliant Career* (1979), which had an international success.

Barry Otto and Kerry Walker in Ray Lawrence's uneven but original *Bliss* (1985), which successfully blended surrealism and social satire.

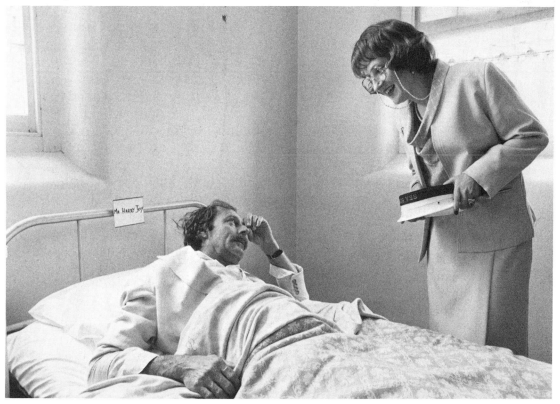

and, above all, the role she is supposed to play as a woman in Australian society of the 1900s. Beautifully played by a cast including Wendy Hughes, Patricia Kennedy, and Aileen Brittain (whose career in Australian film went back to Ken G. Hall's *Tall Timbers* of 1937), the film includes the most detailed portrayal to date of the mores of Australian society in the 1900s. *My Brilliant Career*'s major flaw is that in the episode when heroine Sybylla, in order to pay off her father's debts, is forced to act as a bonded schoolteacher to an outback family, Gillian Armstrong allows what should have been one of the most powerful sequences in the film to degenerate into backwoods comedy. Once again, Eleanor Witcomb's script makes no attempt to gloss over Sybylla's less attractive qualities, and these opportunities are seized by Judy Davis to give perhaps the most richly detailed performance of the cycle. *My Brilliant Career* seems to have marked the end of the women's period films for the time being. *We of The Never Never* (1982) attempted to extract drama from a newly married couple's reaction to outback life in Central Australia, but neither its director, Igor Auzens, nor its scriptwriter, Peter Shreck, were sufficiently alert to the possibilities of the subject and the film degenerated into a sumptuously photographed bore.

However, two recent releases testify to the continuing vitality of the Australian period film itself. Carl Schulz's *Careful He Might Hear You* (1983), the story of a custody battle between two sisters in the Sydney of the 1930s, displays a lively awareness of the class divisions of the period and includes some fine acting by Robyn Nevin, Wendy Hughes, Peter Whitford, and John Hargreaves. Carl Schulz elicited from Nicholas Gledhill the finest child performance in any Australian film. *Careful*'s main weakness is that its visuals, with their silken tracking shots, the low angle set-ups to suggest the child's perspective and the elaborate design are rather too inflated for the subject matter. A very different kind of film is Simon Wincer's *Phar Lap* (1983), the story of a legendary racehorse of the depression era. Most criticism here has tended to dismiss the film because of the "obvious" commercial calculation that went into its making. What has been ignored is the way David Williamson's script underscores the class conflict of the period by emphasizing how Phar Lap was the people's horse and by highlighting the hostility of the Melbourne Jockey Club. About Phar Lap's mysterious death in America, Williamson, while leaving the matter open, clearly implies that the horse was poisoned by the mob. Not unexpectedly, the film exploits the glamor of the turf in the 1930s, and the races themselves were superbly shot by veteran cameraman Russell Boyd in clean, sharp visuals which make the most of Phar Lap's legendary red colors as the horse moves through the field.

Given the New Wave's origins in film criticism of the sixties, it is not surprising that there have been a number of attempts to rework American film genres. Bruce Beresford's *Money Movers* (1978) was essentially a "big caper" movie, while Dinny Lawrence's and Bob Ellis's script for Carl Schultz's *Goodbye Paradise* (1982) simply transposed "private eye" situations into a Queensland setting. Both Phil Noyce's *Backroads* (1976) and Esben Storm's *In Search of Anna* (1978) exploited quite self-consciously the "road" format of films like *Two Lane Backtop* and *Vanishing Point*, while Donald Crombie's *The Killing of Angel Street* (1981) and Phil Noyce's *Heatwave* (1982), which were based on the events surrounding the mysterious disappearance of publisher Juanita Neilsen when she was in the middle of a campaign against a development project in the Kings Cross area of Sydney, borrowed heavily from *film noir*.

But the most complex *manipulation* of overseas forms is embodied in the three "Mad Max" films. *Mad Max* (1979) is a profoundly disturbing vision of the future. Sadistic "bikie" gangs roam the highways, hunted by a near psychopathic police force, who are only marginally less brutal than their quarry. Its treatment of violence draws on director Dr. George Miller's experiences of motor accidents while working in a Melbourne hospital and are the most sickening, both in terms of what is shown and implied, ever seen in an Australian film. But even though *Mad Max* is a darkly misanthropic work (reflecting a difficult shoot), there is no denying the power of its vision of people in extreme situations and the sheer kinetic energy of the action sequences. The extraordinary worldwide success of this small-budget film is the reason for the very different tone of its sequel, *Mad Max II* (American title, *The Road Warrior*) (1982). By now Miller was collaborating with former journalist Terry Hayes, who profoundly changed his outlook.[12] Both of them came to believe that the totally unexpected success of the earlier film was because they had tapped into some kind of unconscious need for a mythical hero figure. Consequently, whereas *Mad Max* was for Miller simply a "combination of the bikie film with the horror genre," the sequel draws on a much wider range of influences. The bleak landscape, which is the setting for the confrontation between Max and the marauders, was influenced by Kurosawa's *Yojimbo*, while the portrayal of the hero figure derived from the Western. *Mad Max II*, while possessing if anything even more kinetic energy than its predecessor, is a richer, more complex work. Terry Hayes's script skillfully "places" the violence of the marauders in a more humane context and provides a leavening of wit and humor. Although the mythic dimension of Max's character is enlarged, he is also given a bizarrely comic companion, the Gyro Captain (Bruce Spence). Furthermore, instead of the mindless violence of the final sequences of its predecessor, *Mad Max II* concludes with the creation of a new community made possible by its hero's courage and resourcefulness.

These elements become more pronounced in *Mad Max III Beyond the Thunderdome*. Here the nameless hero is confronted by two communities: Bartertown, a grotesque parody of the consumer society, and the tribal culture of the lost children waiting for Captain Walker. The film traces the destruction of the false myth of the return of the dead Captain Walker and its substitution by a new legend of sacrifice and redemption involving Max himself. Although lacking the intensity of its predecessors, *Mad Max III* is perhaps the richest film of the cycle, encompassing a wide range of allusions to myth, popular culture, and other films, most noticeably *Lawrence of Arabia*.

An even more complex *assimilation* of overseas influences marks the cycle of fantasy/horror films. Richard (*Psycho II*) Franklin's *Patrick* (1978) and *Roadgames* (1982) may be heavily indebted to Hitchcock's *Psycho* and *Rear Window* respectively, but they are equally influenced by the hospital melodrama in the case of *Patrick* and Peckinpah's *Convoy* in the case of *Roadgames*. Similarly, while *The Birds* is clearly the inspiration for Colin Eggleston's *Long Weekend* (1979), it also includes a complex portrayal of the disintegration of a marriage.

The director who has worked most consistently in the fantasy/horror format is Peter Weir. His first effort, the short film *Homesdale* (1969), seems in retrospect to be impossibly clumsy. Even the climax, involving a severed head, is deprived of any real shock value because of inept framing. Only slightly more competent is Weir's first feature *The Cars That Ate Paris* (1974). Certainly the basic situation of an outwardly respectable country town living off the proceeds of deliberately contrived car wrecks is promising enough, and Weir is very good at suggesting the menace beneath the mundane surface. But as if in distrust of his central theme, he piles on a series of extra effects that not only strain credibility but soon become simply ludicrous. Whether *Picnic at Hanging Rock* (1975) is any more successful is still debated. Certainly the teaming of Weir with cameraman Russell Boyd resulted in the creation of a superbly accomplished visual style. Once again Weir is fine at suggesting nuances in this story of the disappearance of a party of schoolgirls at Hanging Rock and the effect of this on all those with whom they have been in contact. A whole range of solutions are hinted at, ranging from kidnapping to the supernatural, but ultimately Weir does not even define his ambiguities. As David Ansen commented in *Newsweek*, "There is something hollow at the core, an unearned sense of importance, a reliance on mere word to suggest mystical depths."[13]

Weir's next film, *The Last Wave* (1977) also began its life as a mystical fantasy, this time about an imaginary link between the Incas and Australia. But as the script was being developed by the director himself, he approached veteran screenwriter Tony Morphett to give the characters dimension.[14] This collaboration resulted in some of the best sequences in *The Last Wave*. The portrait of the upper-middle-class world of its barrister hero (Richard Chamberlain) and the uncertain response of his wife to having one of his aboriginal clients to dinner is as fine a piece of social observation as exists in any Australian film. The hints of impending catastrophe are also very well done. Particularly effective are the scenes of a hailstorm pelting down out of a clear sky on an outback school. But ultimately the resolution of the film, with the hero discovering Inca artefacts in a Sydney sewer, followed by a vision of a wave about to engulf the city (actually a shot borrowed from a surfing film), is neither emotionally nor intellectually satisfying.

One need have no such reservations, however, about Weir's only telemovie to date, *The Plumber* (1979). This story of a middle-class couple (Judy Morris and Robert Colby) who are persecuted by an eccentric plumber (Ivar Kants) enables the director to exploit his ability to convey intimations of menace in ordinary circumstances. Essentially the film is about evasion itself. The wife initially will not acknowledge her distaste for tradesmen, while the plumber, perhaps sensing this, persecutes her by taking an inordinate time about his tasks, hinting at an imaginary criminal past and imposing his company on her at the slightest opportunity. Relieved of the need to stage open confrontations, Weir uses this indirection to generate considerable dramatic tension and to make some pointed social comment. He is aided by a fine performance from Judy Morris, who superbly conveys the sense that her character has been reduced to a subhuman level and is prepared to use any means to defend herself. Equally impressive is Ivar Kants, who expertly conveys the plumber's paranoia beneath a facade of geniality.

Significantly Weir's only U.S. film to date, *Witness* (1985), is remarkably consistent with his Australian work. Certainly the script by William Kelley and Earle Wallace is in the best tradition of American narrative cinema, but Weir's treatment of these materials remains characteristically oblique and impressionistic. The tensions and conflicts in the Amish community in which detective John Bock (Harrison Ford) takes refuge from his corrupt superiors are touched on but remain unexplored. The urban imagery too, especially when it is viewed from the perspective of a small child, is redolent with the magic and mystery that characterized *The Last Wave*. In the scenes preceeding the climax, as Bock's enemies in the police department close in on the Amish settlement, Weir and his cameraman, John Seale, duplicate set-ups from *The Cars That Ate Paris*. *Witness* has made its director an international figure, but from an Australian perspective what makes the film so fascinating is the tension between Weir's style and preoccupations and the demands of the genre within which he has chosen to work.

Although the period and fantasy cycles have attracted the most attention here and overseas, the Australian New Wave has produced far more films dealing with urban life than most people realize. These cover a wide range and while the themes and narrative structures are far too diverse for any group to be regarded as a genre, they do fall into a number of reasonably distinct categories.

The prototype for what can be termed the "street" film is Bert Deling's *Pure S*—— (1976).[15] Built around a frantic search for heroin by a group of users, the film employs an open structure whereby the viewer is plunged into the world of the drug addict. It makes few concessions: characters wander in and out of the story; much of the dialogue (modeled on Howard Hawks's *His Girl Friday*) is frenetic, and there is an abrupt change of tone in the final sequences, with a hilarious send-up of methodone treatment. It is splendidly shot by Tom Cowan, who complements the narrative with open groupings and lighting derived from American *film noir* of the 1940s. When *Pure S*—— was first released it was attacked because there was no overt condemnation of its characters' lifestyle. In retrospect, it is possible to see that the whole film embodies an implied criticism of the sterility and messiness of their lives.

Partly because of the style of the original novel, Ken Cameron employed a similar narrative structure for *Monkey Grip* (1982). The basic situation is, of course, quite different. A "straight" girl (Noni Hazelhurst) becomes involved with an addict (Colin Friels) only to discover that her relationship with him is as dangerous an addiction as heroin. However, the milieu of the city dwellers who, in the words of the film's narration, are "hovering on the edge of smack" is portrayed in an elliptical style very similar to that of *Pure S*——. This proved to be a mistake, because although the predicament of the main protagonists emerges strongly, there is insufficient development of the subsidiary figures who are left to virtually wander in and out of the story.

In a sense, *Monkey Grip* was a throwback to the mid-seventies, because other directors of street films had already been experimenting with different kinds of narrative. Don McLennan's *Hard Knocks* (1980) traced its delinquent heroine's progress toward rehabilitation by moving backward and forward through time. Consequently, images of her as a street punk are contrasted with incidents where she has a much greater sense of her own personal worth. While this structure is built around a series of contrasts, Tracey Mann's interpretation of the main character is so richly detailed and carefully judged that the device simply acts as a means whereby certain aspects of the heroine's experiences can be emphasized. Unlike *Pure S*—— the condemnation of the system is quite explicit. Particularly effective in this context are Bill Hunter and Max Cullen as a pair of sadistic policemen.

The street film which experiments most freely with narrative is undoubtedly Hayden Keenan's *Going Down* (1983). The film is an extraordinary blend of artificiality and realism. The treatment of the main plot involving the heroine Karli's search for some stolen money through a night of bizarre encounters in the Kings Cross area of Sydney is quite realistic, even though there is a marked contrast between Tracey Mann's incisive underplaying of Karli and Esben Storm's florid perfor mance as her parasitic "friend." On the other hand, these scenes are intercut with shots of Hugh Keyes Byrne riding around the "Cross" on his bicycle, reciting excerpts from *A Midsummer Night's Dream*; and for the climax, where just about everyone rushes to bid farewell to Karli at the airport, Keenan devises a hysterically funny chase sequence that would have done credit to Mack Sennett. It is, of course, doubtful whether all these diverse elements form a coherent whole. Nevertheless, the performances in *Going Down* are uniformly excellent.

In contrast, the best street film to date, writer-director John Duigan's *Mouth to Mouth* (1978), is totally conventional in form and structure. The film is a character study of four unemployed youths, two boys and two girls, who experience fleetingly a measure of emotional security through a mutually sustaining fellowship. With infinite compassion Duigan builds up a contrast between Carrie (Kim Krejus), who has been so bruised by her experiences that she is closed off from any meaningful relationship, and the warmer, more outgoing Jeanie (Sonia Peat). For Duigan it is Jeanie's ability to accept and give fellowship that will ensure her survival, while Carrie's yielding to despair will ultimately destroy her. These relationships are delineated with great sensitivity; throughout there is at once a sense of the characters' potential combined with a passionate indignation that this potential is being wasted by a heedless establishment. Handsomely shot by Tom Cowan, the visuals are consistently subordinated to the development of the characterization. Recently Duigan has taken the street film a stage further in *One Night Stand* (1984) by portraying a group of adolescents confronting nuclear holocaust. Unlike many of the recent American treatments of this theme, the film is basically optimistic, delineating against an often surreal background of implied horror the kind of personal and sexual bonds that could make survival possible in the event of a world conflict.

Closely related to the street films have been a series of quite specific treatments of social problems. Once again these concerns date back to the very beginnings of the new Australian cinema. Esben Storm's *27A* was released in 1974 and dealt simultaneously with an abuse of human rights and the problem of alcoholism. Based on an actual case, when an alcoholic was confined indefinitely in a Queensland asylum under Section 27A of the Penal Code, the film is both an indictment of the system and a detailed portrait of a social misfit, played with great sensitivity and understanding by alcoholic actor Robert McDarra. Equally specific is Stephen Wallace's *Stir* (1980), which follows closely the events of the second Bathurst jail riots. Scripted by ex-convict Bob Jewison, who was in the prison at the time of the disturbances, the dialogue has a documentary realism. Partly because of the careful "workshoping" prior to the shoot, the cast, which includes Bryan Brown, Max Phipps, and

Denis Miller, provides some of the best ensemble playing in any Australian film. Consequently, not only does *Stir* document the conditions that led the Nagle Royal Commission into New South Wales prisons, it is also a powerful portrait of men in extreme circumstances and certainly deserves to rank with such classics of the prison picture as *Brute Force* and *Riot in Cell Block 11.*

Paul Cox, together with John Duigan, are the two directors working in the Australian industry who have succeeded best in portraying personal relationships in a middle-class setting. Cox's finest work to date, *Lonely Hearts* (1982), is a romance, this time between a repressed spinster (Wendy Hughes) dominated by her family and a middle-aged bachelor (Norman Kaye) who has devoted his life to caring for his late mother. The film makes some acute observations about the way lonely people are forced to occupy their time and the often destructive effect of family obligations. Cox's *Man of Flowers* (1983) is much more bizarre. It is the study of a gentle eccentric (Norman Kaye again) who, among other things, pays a model to strip for him to music from Donizetti's *Lucia di Lammermoor* before leaving abruptly to play the church organ, writes letters to his dead mother, and allows himself to be exploited by a psychiatrist who is even more disturbed than he is. Throughout, there is a fascinating tension between the racy allusive dialogue, provided by Bob Ellis (who also plays the psychiatrist), and the measured pace and lush visuals of Cox and his favorite cameraman, Yuri Sokol.

The director's 1984 work, *My First Wife*, proved less successful. An autobiographical story based on his own attempted suicide following the break-up of his marriage after completing *Man of Flowers*, the film fails to relate Cox's deeply felt personal experience to the wider concerns of his audience. Nevertheless, *My First Wife* includes some fine performances from John Hargreaves and Wendy Hughes and splendid photography, again by Yuri Sokol. Moreover, it provides fascinating insight into the creative processes of a man who is by any standards a major director.

On the other hand, John Duigan's two films about the Vietnam generation, *The Trespassers* (1976) and *Winter of Our Dreams* (1981), deal with quite specific social and historical developments. *The Trespassers* focuses on the discrepancy between its characters' entirely admirable politics and the confusion of their personal lives. Set specifically in 1970, Duigan takes a simple triangle situation in which two women, Dee (Judy Morris) and Penny (Briony Behets), share the favors of Richard (John Derum), a radical journalist, and uses it to portray how the political terminology of the period was used to analyze personal relationships. The film is at its best in its treatment of the way the two women, after an embarrassing encounter when Penny discovers Dee emerging from Richard's bedroom, become friends. Cameraman Vincent Monton's clean, sharp visuals are entirely appropriate to the film's relentless examination of the characters' lives and the photography also makes the most of the script's contrast between the rather cramped life of the city, where the film begins, with the open spaces of the country surrounding the lonely farmhouse where Dee takes Penny for a holiday. *Winter of Our Dreams* takes up the story of the generation portrayed in *The Trespassers* ten years later. Rob (Bryan Brown), a former leader of the anti-Vietnam War movement, and Gretel (Cathy Downes), his middle-class academic wife, have settled for affluence when Lou (Judy Davis), a drug-addicted prostitute, enters their lives. As the film unfolds, Duigan builds up a contrast between different ways of living in the world: between someone existing on the fringes of society and those who have achieved a measure of affluence.

But by far the most original film about the Australian middle class is Ray Lawrence's *Bliss* (1985). An uneven work that had to be drastically cut between its disastrous première in Cannes and its triumphant release in Australia, *Bliss* is an exciting blend of surrealism and social satire. Its bizarre basic premise is that an advertising executive (Barry Otto) "dies" briefly, then after he revives believes he is in hell and nothing he finds contradicts this assumption. The film encompasses many shifts in tone, ranging from hilarious slapstick to the measured pastoral quality of *Bliss*'s moving conclusion, that are not fully integrated. But for all its failings *Bliss* has proved an inspiration at a difficult time in the evolution of the Australian industry.

None of the overseas directors who have worked "down under" to date has displayed anything like the understanding of Australian mores of a Fred Zinnemann or a Ted Kotcheff. Werner Herzog's *Where the Green Ants Dream* (1984) proved to be a costly embarrassment, while Dusan Makavejev's *Coca Cola Kid* (1985) failed to assimilate the themes and motifs of its director's European films to the very Australian content of Frank Moorhouse's original stories on which the screenplay was based. On the other hand, Australian directors have been much more successful in adapting themselves to conditions in America. Fred Scepsi's *Iceman* (1984) and *Plenty* (1985) are indistinguishable from the overseas products.

However, Bruce Beresford, working with top Australian cameraman Russell Boyd on Horton Foote's script for *Tender Mercies* (1984), brought a characteristically Australian treatment of space and skyline to the very American theme of a failed country-and-western singer's regeneration and assimilation into family and church. Whereas most American directors dwell on the urbanization of the landscape, Beresford and Boyd chose to emphasize the vast expanse of the Texas countryside, evoking the country-and-western tradition by formal groupings of figures within the frame, influenced by scenes from John Sturges's *Last Train from Gun Hill* and *Bad Day at Black Rock*.

While Beresford's 1985 project, *King David*, seems to have had serious script problems, causing him to shoot the film in a perfunctory style that alternated extreme close-ups with long shots, no such problems afflicted Gillian Armstrong's direction of her first American feature, *Mrs. Soffell* (1985). She brought to the bleakly tragic tale of a doomed jailbreak by two brothers aided by the wife of the prison governor the sensitivity and rich visual style characteristic of her Australian work. Skillfully she uses Russell Boyd's splendid "winter" photography to emphasize the drabness and oppressiveness of the environment against which its heroine rebels. Armstrong also evokes a superbly controlled performance from Diane Keaton in the title role that is matched by Mel Gibson's intense underplaying of her doomed lover.

Since 1970 the Australian cinema has produced a body of work that, in terms of its responsiveness to social change and awareness of the influence of recent history, is comparable with the achievements of the American film industry in the 1930s. There has been a major reinterpretation of recent Australian history, in which films like *Breaker Morant* and *My Brilliant Career* have only been the most noteable. Furthermore, films such as *Mouth to Mouth* or *Stir* have focused on quite specific problems in contemporary Australian society. Equally significant in this context have been two films, Peter Weir's *The Year of Living Dangerously* (1983) and John Duigan's *Far East* (1982), which show Australians confronting the dangerous ambiguities of Indonesian and Filipino politics respectively. Performers like Jack Thompson, Bryan Brown, and Bill Hunter have helped define a quite specific national identity, while actresses like Judy Morris, Wendy Hughes, and Judy Davis have illuminated the problems of women in a country that is still alarmingly sexist. The challenge for the future is to see whether we can build on our reinterpretation of the past, so that we can continue to sharpen our awareness of the problems confronting contemporary Australia.

## NOTES

1. For a full discussion of the administrative and social background to the emergence of the industry in the sixties, see Graham Shirley and Brian Adams, *Australian Cinema—The First Eighty Years* (Sydney: Angus and Robertson and Currency Press, 1983).
2. The MGM and Warners collections survived until the eighties when they were wantonly destroyed in 1981 and 1983, allegedly on instructions from MGM in America.
3. Phone interview with the author.
4. Phone interview with the author.

5. For a full discussion of the dispute over the various versions of *Sunday Too Far Away*, see David Stratton, *The Last New Wave* (Sydney: Angus and Robertson, 1980), pp. 98–105. (Distributed in the U.S. by The Ungar Publishing Company)

6. For a sympathetic, yet critical, account of the film that summarizes the hostile reviews, see Arnold Zable's article in *Cinema Papers*, June 1982.

7. "Interview," Geoff Burrows and George Miller by George Tosi, *Cinema Papers*, June 1982.

8. Interview with the author.

9. Phone interview with the author. This resentment is even more explicit in Bean's diary, which had not been published when Williamson was writing the script. See *Gallipoli Correspondent, The Frontline Diary of C. E. W. Bean*, ed. Kevin Fewster (London: George Allen and Unwin, 1983); also C. E. W. Bean, *The Story of Anzac*, vol. 1 of The Official History (Brisbane: University of Queensland Press and the Australian War Memorial, 1981).

10. Interview with the author.

11. Noyce also credits Ken G. Hall with explaining to him and producer David Elphick how they could shoot the flood scenes, undoubtedly the film's most powerful sequence.

12. Interview with Terry Hayes. This George Miller (a qualified medical practitioner) is called "Dr." to distinguish him from George Miller the director of *The Man from Snowy River*.

13. David Ansen, "Rocky Horror," *Newsweek*, 5 July 1979.

14. Phone interview with Tony Morphett.

15. The original title, *Pure Shit*, was changed because of demands by the censor.

## SELECTED BIBLIOGRAPHY

Baxter, John. *The Australian Cinema*. Brisbane: Pacific Books, 1969.

Hall, Ken G. *Directed by Ken G. Hall*. Melbourne: Landsdown Press, 1977.

Pike, Andrew and Ross Cooper. *Australian Film 1900-1977*. Sydney: Oxford University Press and The Australian Film Institute, 1980.

Shirley, Graham and Brian Adams. *Australian Cinema: The First Eighty Years*. Sydney: Angus and Robertson and Currency Press, 1983.

Stratton, David. *The Last New Wave*. Sydney: Angus and Robertson, 1980. (Distributed in the U.S. by The Ungar Publishing Company)

# BELGIUM

## ELAINE MANCINI

The dominant Belgian cinematic tradition is the documentary film. Features and experimental films are also made, but comprise very small though lively sections of the national cinema.

Undoubtedly the best-known name in Belgian cinema remains that of Henri Storck whose vision has influenced two generations of his native filmmakers and whose dedication to cinema has seen his involvement in many and varied metacinematic activities. Storck earned his reputation long before World War II, most notably for his documentaries *Story of the Unknown Soldier (L'histoire du soldat inconnu,* 1930), *Misery in the Borinage (Borinage* 1932) which he codirected with Joris Ivens, and *Houses of Misery (Les maisons de la misère,* 1938). His intense activity did not lag during and after the war either, beginning immediately with the release of the 113-minute *Peasant's Symphony (Symphonie paysanne,* 1944). This was quickly followed by another feature-length documentary on the life of Father Damien entitled *The Pilgrim of Hell (Le pelerin de l'enfer).* In fact, Storck has made over twenty-five films since the end of the war, including fiction shorts and features.

Storck has consistently rejected the idea that documentary is a purely objective form, emphasizing instead that it depends on artistic temperament, vision, and sensitivity. He has admirably combined this personal approach to the documentary with commissioned projects for various organizations, such as the Department of Information of the United Nations. He has stated, "I have to be very careful to remain small, artisanlike, or else I should change professions and work as a director for a producer and that I've never been able to do. I can never agree with anyone on the conception and direction of a film."[1] His efforts have usually been rewarded with successful distribution and/or critical acclaim. *The Smuggler's Banquet (Le banquet des fraudeurs,* 1951), which he codirected with Charles Spaak, advocating a United States of Europe, proved highly successful. Of the Technicolor film *The Open Window (La fenêtre ouverte,* 1952) fifteen hundred copies were processed in response to distributors' demands.

Storck's trademarks and influence can be seen in most of the work of his documentary colleagues, the most notable of whom are Lucien Deroisy, Frederic Geilfus, Genevieve Grand'ry, Paul Haesaerts, Patrick Ledoux, and Frans Verstreken. Many of these filmmakers have made fiction films as well. Deroisy, for example, made an admirable adaptation of Robbe-Grillet's novel, *The Rubbers (Les gommes,* 1968), and the twenty-minute short *Apolline* about an artist's search for a woman's face, which won the prize for best fiction film at Antwerp in 1960. Ledoux's interests run to the experimental film, a good example of which is his 1963 *The Man on His Own (L'homme seul).*

Storck's interest in cinema goes beyond the limits of his own productions. He founded a film club in Ostend in 1928 and remained active in the management of Belgian film clubs for over five decades. He has also been strongly influential in both film education and in assistance organizations for Belgian film artists. In 1964 he cofounded the International Association of Documentary Filmmakers as well as serving as president of the Association Belge des Auteurs de Films et Auteurs de Télévision for fifteen years. These activities, plus his teaching at the Institute of Communication Arts in Brussels, have paved the way for younger film artists.

The Belgian industry on the whole, however, has never been solvent. As in many European nations after the war, Belgium filmgoers saw mainly Hollywood productions. In 1949, for example, American-made films controlled 80 percent of the market, largely due to a lack of import restrictions. Throughout the 1950s there was virtually no native production and even the dubbing of the imported films into French was handled in Paris. As in every other Western nation, the onslaught of television severely crippled film exhibition. While there had been a yearly attendance of 145 million in 1945, by 1959, when 280 thousand homes owned television sets, the attendance dropped to ninety million. Thus Belgium was hit by doubly crippling phenomena: a battle between television and cinema and a lack of domestic production. In 1960 Belgium produced only five features and sixty shorts for a population of nine million. Not surprisingly, the United States and France accounted for nearly 75 percent of the total box-office receipts. The government seemed to ignore the cultural importance of national production while the filmmakers seemed wary of capitalist financing. Thus the few highlights of Belgian filmmaking after the war were the results of individuals working without an industry to back them. Storck's *Le banquet des fraudeurs* (1951), Roland Verhavert's *The Seagulls Die in the Harbor*

(*Les moueites meurent au port*, 1956), Emile Degelin's (*Si le vent te fait peur*, 1960), Paul Meyer's *Déjà s'envole la fleur maigre* (1960), and Andre Cavens's *There Is a Train Every Hour (Il y a un train toutes les heures*, 1962) remain the testaments of cinema practice before active organization and government financing developed.

Clearly production had to be encouraged. Even though the Ministry of Economic Affairs had created a Production Premium for films in 1952, the amount of monies awarded was too low and too badly managed to be of much assistance. In the 1960s, spurred by the climate of crisis, changes occurred, one of which was the establishment of the National Festival of the Belgian Film in Brussels in 1964. Through this venue distributors and exhibitors and potential producers could at least see recent Belgian productions. In 1964 a film department was established within the Ministry of Culture with a yearly budget of between two and three million French francs. Until 1973, however, the maximum aid per film from this department was 600 thousand francs, enough to subsidize only a small part of the costs.

Another spur to filmmaking in Belgium was film education. The most active schools are the IAD (Institut des Arts de Diffusion), where Henri Storck teaches, the INSAS (Institut National Supérieur des Arts du Spectacle et Techniques de Diffusion), an official establishment where André Delvaux acted as head of the cinema section, and the RITCS (Hoger Rijksinstituut voor Toneel en Cultuurspreiding), an official Flemish organization, where Emile Degelin was director of cinema studies during the 1960s and into the 1970s. Degelin's films include the 1960 *If You Are Afraid of the Wind*, concerning incestuous love between a brother and sister, and *And Tomorrow?* (*Y mañana*, 1966), a burlesque fantasy with almost no dialogue which relates the adventures of a Flemish traffic warden on an ill-fated holiday. In 1969 Degelin made a trilingual film, including Swahili, *Palabre*, about three black students from Zaire and their judgments on Belgium.

From the schools emerged Patrick Ledoux, Christian Mesnil, Benoit Lamy, Jacques Brel, and Harry Kumel. Kumel, in particular, scored a great success. This Flemish television director released *Monsieur Hawarden*, a stunning visual display, in 1968. Later came *Malpertuis* (1972) which, due to Kumel's reputation and its status as a coproduction, became famous as the most expensive film ever made in Belgium, costing one million dollars to produce.

The first tangible result of the attention paid to film education and film financing appeared with the work of André Delvaux. His film *The Man With The Shaven Head* (*L'homme á crane rasé*, 1966), focusing on a psychiatric patient's division between fantasy and reality, proved so successful within and beyond Belgium that it alone caused a resurgence of interest in full-length Belgian films. His other features, such as *Rendezvous at Bray* (*Rendezvous à Bray*, 1971) and *Belle* (1973), an interiorized fantasy filmed in the Belgian Ardennes, received more attention than was usually allotted to the work of a Belgian filmmaker.

In the 1960s, therefore, production began in earnest. Jean Delire released *Chalet 1* (1968), based on two autobiographical novels of André Baillon. Hugo Claus, the Swiss novelist, entered scriptwriting and direction with his 1967 *The Enemies (Les ennemis)* in which three antiheroes speak in English as the only language they can all understand. Herman Wuyts and Roland Verhavert emerge as two of the most important Flemish directors. Wuyts' *Princess* (1968) is a photo-novel and a catalogue of brilliant effects, and Verhavert's *Farewells (Les adieux*, 1966) and his bilingual study of an affair between a Flemish man and a Parisienne, *Story of a Passion (Chronique d'une passion*, 1972), attracted considerable attention. *Farewells*, filmed in Dutch, won special prizes at the Venice Film Festival, the Edinburgh Festival, the Cork International Film Festival, and the Sydney Film Festival.

A fair number of films produced at this time focused on children or teenagers. Louis Grospierre's *Bruno or Sunday's Children* (1969) dealt with children of divorced parents while Etienne Perier's *Boys and Girls* (1968), a French coproduction, deals with the growing pains of ten teenagers who share the costs of a house.

A breakthrough came in 1971 with Fons Rademakers' box-office wonder *Mira*, co-scripted with Hugo Claus. It was a Belgian-Dutch coproduction made for only $324 thousand and seemed to indicate a profitable formula for filmmaking: low budget coproductions.

At this time, successful Belgian producers were needed who understood national identity and who could also guarantee exhibition. Producers had been scarce in the Belgian cinema. Charles Dekeukeleire died in 1971 and Gaston Schoukens and Jan Van der Heyden, who financed folkloric films typical of the 1950s, dropped out of the industry in 1961. New attitudes were evidenced by Jacqueline Pierreux from INSAS, the Flemish Paul Verhavert, and Paul Collet and Pierre Drouot who ran their own production company. Pierreux started in 1970, working occasionally with Paul Danblon of Belgian television. She was determined to counteract what she saw as amateurism in Belgian production. Seeing herself more as an organizer than a financier, she was largely responsible for Jacques Perrin's *Home Sweet Home* (1973), Michel Huisman's antimilitaristic *Over (Ras le bol)*, and Marian Handwerker's *Bear Cage District (La cage aux ours*, 1972). Handwerker and her scriptwriter Paul Paquay wanted to make a political and popular film set in Brussels in which the film public could recognize their situation in the film's story. They described it as a film-manifesto. As the official Belgian entry at Cannes in 1972, it is both a family chronicle and a study of political consciousness.

Throughout the 1970s most filmmakers felt themselves trapped. Production companies lacked sufficient funds. Many features caused so

André Delvaux's *The Man with the Shaven Head* (1966), about a psychiatric patient caught between fantasy and reality, revived international interest in Belgian film and became a cult classic.

Delvaux's *Belle* (1973), filmed in the Ardennes region, also reached a wider audience.

(Right)
Described by its makers
as a "film-manifesto,"
Marian Handwerker's
*The Bear Cage* (1972)
set out to be a popular
family drama and a study
of political consciousness.

(Left)
Chantal Akerman, the
avant-garde writer-
director with an
all-female crew,
deconstructs the
Hollywood-style musical
extravaganza in *The
Golden Eighties* (1983).

much disappointment after they were finished that they were never released. The majority of filmmakers preferred not simply national production, but a national expression of what Belgian culture means made possible by the funds from the Ministry of Culture. Many people felt there was a lack of inventive scripts, especially in terms of dialogue, so in 1972 the Ministry of French Culture started an annual scenario contest that awarded a prize of fifteen thousand French francs. In 1973 subsidies had allowed for nineteen features; in 1974, sixteen features and in 1975, eighteen features—large annual outputs for Belgium. The following year production received one-third of its funds from the government, one-third from private sources, and one-third from coproductions. Although two million homes had television sets in 1975, cinema theaters witnessed an upsurge in attendance. That year a postproduction bonus of roughly one million dollars for some films began. However, Henri-Francois Van Aal, the minister of French culture (1976–77), helped only directors who were their own producers, which caused fly-by-night production companies to be set up by directors. The minister of Flemish culture from 1974 to 1982, Rika de Backer, a Christian Democrat, was estranged from most of the viewpoints of the filmmakers. Even after fifteen years of a resurgence, by the 150 anniversary of Belgian independence in 1980, of the twenty top-grossing films, seven were American and ten were French. Jacqueline Pierreux retired from film and began work as a television producer for the French-language network. The combined ministries gave less than $2 million in 1981, much less than the amount allotted to theater. Since the average Belgian film costs $500 thousand, the subsidies allowed for a total production of three features that year.

Emerging from the revitalized climate of the 1970s and deserving special mention here is the work of Chantal Akerman. Akerman is an avant-garde filmmaker who writes and directs her films and who miraculously finds the small amount of funding she needs for her productions. She also starred in her first film, *I, You, He, She* (*Je, tu, il, elle*, 1974), when she was twenty-four years old. It is a private sexual journey made public, consisting of three parts which become progressively more explicit until the film spectator's gaze (which Akerman sees as the voyeuristic response legitimized) is exhausted. Her masterpiece remains *Jeanne Dielman, 23, Quai du Commerce, 1080, Bruxelles* (1975), where all the important and perhaps even the most interesting facts about the protagonist are supplied in the title. For 198 minutes we watch Jeanne (played by Delphine Seyrig), a housewife, go about her daily chores over a three-day period, which include prostituting herself in the afternoons in order to earn enough money for her and her son to live on. Jacques Doniol-Valcroze, a critic, and Henri Storck play her clients, but the sexual act always occurs behind closed doors. Cinematographer Babette Mangolte and Akerman filmed it in five weeks and completed this 35 mm film on a budget of $120 thousand. There is almost no dialogue although Jeanne sometimes delivers soliloquies to the camera in which she drones on about the frustration and monotony of her life, which consists primarily of cleaning, cooking, ordering, arranging and straightening up around the house. Eventually she is driven to murder one of her clients. The length of the film is perfectly justified because the viewer must experience Jeanne's life and share Jeanne's point of view to the extent that prostitution and murder appear to the viewer as unsensational, almost dull, as they do to the protagonist. In later films such as *Les rendezvous d'Anna* (*Meetings with Anna*, 1978) and *News from Home* (1976), Akerman returned to very personal subject matter although it is always superbly controlled and presented in a detached style. Her latest film, *The Golden Eighties* (*Les annees 80*, 1983), is an ironic deconstruction of a Hollywood-type musical. Aspects of the process of making an extravaganza are analyzed carefully, complete with lyrics written by Akerman. Faithful again to her subject matter, the film runs eighty minutes, as did many of the MGM musicals of the 1940s. Akerman's works attest to the virtues of independent filmmaking, combining rigor of style with freedom of expression, and are among the finest feminist films (her crew is composed mainly of women) and examples of formalist cinema made in the last ten years.

## NOTES

1. Roy G. Levin, ed., *Documentary Explorations: 15 Interviews with Filmmakers*. (Garden City, NY: Doubleday, 1971), p. 169.

## SELECTED BIBLIOGRAPHY

Davay, Paul. "Cinéma de Belgique 1965–1972." *Cinéma 73* (Paris), no. 174 (1973): 68–79.

Levin, Roy G., ed. *Documentary Explorations: 15 Interviews with Filmmakers*. Garden City, NY: Doubleday, 1971. See the chapter on Henri Storck.

Roanne, Henri. "Le 'nouveau' cinéma belge: Intégrer le constat dans une dynamique révolutionnaire." *Cinéma Québec* 3, nos. 9–10 (August 1974): 54-58.

# BRAZIL

## PATRICIA AUFDERHEIDE

"This problem of us not being able to resist asking what the national significance of our culture is—it would have no meaning in the so-called 'mother cultures'," said sociologist Antonio Cândido in some exasperation at a 1977 film conference in Brasília. "You don't even dream of a good novel coming out in France and the critics saying, 'Why, this is a perfectly *French* novel, without foreign cultural impositions.' It is unthinkable. Only some backwater academic or retired army colonel would pose the problem like that. But in Brazil—for us—it is a sad but true fact. Especially in film, we only address the question of culture to find out if it is explaining us or not."[1]

The aesthetic history of Brazilian cinema is intertwined with the questions of cultural nationalism that face developing countries, as much as its production history is interlocked with the tensions of Brazilian politics and economics. The postwar period is marked not only by a lively debate on film culture, but by a wealth of answers. *Cinema novo*, which flourished between the mid-sixties and early seventies, has been best known internationally, but the international successes of such films as *Dona Flor and Her Two Husbands* (*Dona Flor e seus dois maridos*, 1976), *Bye Bye Brazil* (1980), *Pixote* (1980), *Xica* (*Xica da Silva*, 1976), *I Love You* (*Eu te amo*, 1980), and *They Don't Wear Black Tie* (*Eles não usam black tie*, 1980) signal more than a recovery. They testify to the endurance and, indeed, growth of a strong national cinema throughout the postwar era.

The movies in Brazil grew up in the shadow of Hollywood. Brazilian film production was not, however, limited to imitation. By 1945 at least one indigenous style had developed: the *chanchada*, or musical comedy whose flamboyant low comedy style owed something to the popularity of radio programming and something to vaudeville tradition, and even carried the flavor of the *carnaval* street celebrations. The short-lived film studio Cinédia made *chanchadas* a staple.

In the late forties film entrepreneurs, including Luiz Carlos Barretto and Alberto Cavalcanti, founded the film studio Vera Cruz. Modeled on MGM, its aim was to recapture the Brazilian market with high-quality entertainment. The film company produced more than a dozen features, one of which, Lima Barreto's *The Bandit* (*O Cangaceiro*, 1953), won an award in Cannes. But in 1954 the company—which had fatally left distribution of its films in the hands of Columbia Pictures—went bankrupt.

Cinédia and Vera Cruz had tried to make popular movies on a Hollywood model but with a Brazilian flair. In the fifties another film movement emerged—*cinema novo*—which was dedicated to discovering the reality of Brazil, both stylistically and thematically. *Cinema novo* celebrated the individual filmmaker as artist (borrowing from the French New Wave) and valued an artisanlike production process and concern for social relevance (borrowing from Italian Neorealism).

The *cinema novo* movement began in a time of economic boom. It accompanied the upbeat political rhetoric of progress promoted by President Juscelino Kubitschek (1955–60; the founder of Brasília). At the time, artists regarded the creation of an authentically Brazilian film culture to be part of the optimistic national development project. In the same way that Brazil had to find a unique way out of its entangling neocolonial economic arrangements, so it had to discover its authentic cultural voice. As the critic Paulo Emilio Salles Gomes put it, "We are neither Europeans nor North Americans but, destitute of an original culture, nothing is foreign to us because everything is. The painful construction of ourselves goes on in a rarefied dialectic between not-being and being-other."[2]

Marking, in part, the international excitement of art film *internationally* and, in part, the growing self-assertiveness of a Brazilian middle class, a "cinema culture movement" was created in São Paulo and Rio de Janeiro, where cinematheques were also founded. Such critics as Gustavo Dahl, Jean-Claude Bernardet, and Maurice Capovilla, along with veteran cultural critics like Salles Gomes, were active in promoting the new movement. They led discussions of film history and saw both classics and new work on the international film scene. The movement benefited as well from visits by foreign filmmakers like the Italian neorealist Cesare Zavattini and the Argentine neorealist filmmaker Fernando Birri. They and such filmmaker-critics as Leon Hirzman, David Neves, Glauber Rocha, Nelson Pereira dos Santos, Carlos Diegues, and Ruy Guerra were doing more than founding cineclubs. They were laying the foundations for a socially informed film style. These intense young men (the cinema culture movement was largely a male club) were looking for ways to express filmically authentic Brazilian experience.

Some of their themes and vehicles were to become staples of serious Brazilian cinema; some were already staples of self-consciously nationalist drama and literature. Filmmakers in search of their cultural roots seized on Brazil's nonwhite ethnic heritage, stressing (until recently) the period before industrial immigration—its Indian cultures, typically decimated by contact with whites; its black cultures, introduced in the slave trade that fueled sugar production in the colonial era; and the race mixing and culture mixing that surfaced in a racially mixed population and cultural practices such as syncretic religion. In a nineteenth-century cultural nationalist period, writers had created a lyric romanticism of Indian and black cultures, always safely in the past; these filmmakers, and their successors, would take a hard look at racism, oppression, and extermination.

To history, too, they looked for heroic social conflict that would give the lie to a passive and dependent national self-image; slave revolts, colonial-era independence movements, worker protests, banditry. And they drew critically on the folklore that came out of such movements as millennial religions.

They addressed endemic social problems, such as the desperate poverty of the drought-ridden northeast and the urban slums. Sometimes their best sources were works by socially conscious, often leftist authors who flourished in the politicized thirties: Graciliano Ramos, the early Jorge Amado, Guimarães Rosa.

These and later filmmakers regularly resorted to metaphor and allegory. To speak of a Brazilian historical moment, a Brazilian character, a Brazilian institution was to make a statement about what being Brazilian meant. As Nelson Pereira dos Santos (a figure so influential in postwar Brazilian cinema that he is often called "the father of our cinema" by a new generation of filmmakers) said of his *Memorias do Cárcere*, a film of Graciliano Ramos's prison memoirs, "It is a microcosm of all Brazil."

These filmmakers were not satisfied simply to define and describe a Brazilian identity. Seeing Brazil as a country with a colonial past and a neocolonial present, they saw their role as helping to change that reality.

In the first period of *cinema novo* (1960–1964), films drew on the history of popular revolt and the folklore of the poor. Some of these films quickly became classics: Glauber Rocha's *Black God, White Devil* (*Deus e diabo na terra do sol*, 1964), which critiqued the folklore of banditry and millennialism in the northeast; Ruy Guerra's *The Guns* (*Os fuzis*, 1964), a probing dramatic essay on conflicts between peasants and landowners and military; Carlos Diegues's *Ganga Zumba* (1963), about a runaway slave community in the seventeenth century; and Nelson

Pereira dos Santos's *Barren Lives* (*Vidas secas*, 1963), from Graciliano Ramos's realist novel about peasant poverty in the northeast.

Although filmmakers agreed that popular art meant not just box-office appeal but also art that mobilized Brazilian people to social change (the word *revolution* was tossed about freely in those early days) there was little agreement on how to achieve such change. Should one work collectively, as the students who had made the pioneering neo-realist film *Slum, Five Times Over* (*Cinco vezes favela*, 1961) argued? Or should the film artist take his camera into the streets to discover the people's reality with them instead of for them? If the latter, how was one to have an authentic relationship with "the people"? Perhaps the period's most eloquent spokesperson was Glauber Rocha, who in a 1965 essay entitled "An Aesthetic of Hunger" called for a cinema that would spur the downtrodden masses to action. In its ruthless portrayal of social misery it would not only be authentic and true to the violence of reality, but revolutionary, because it would articulate outrage. "Our originality is our hunger," he wrote, "and our greatest misery is that this hunger is felt but not intellectually understood."[3]

Such revolutionary aspirations were not fulfilled, at least not in the short run. For one thing, there was a distribution problem. The sliding-screen circuit that amplified the discussion among energetic, idealistic intellectuals at the cinematheques was spreading rapidly, but it rarely extended beyond a narrow band on the spectrum of social class. Elsewhere, Brazilians were going to American, Mexican, or Italian commercial films, or watching ultra-low-budget Brazilian diversions. As well, *cinema novo* films were often brutally frank, and terribly depressing, depictions of social anguish, not likely to draw Saturday-night crowds of any social class. "The best quality of cinema novo," said *cinema novo* veteran Zelito Viana, "was its worst. It was a cinema of poverty. We were free, then, to say what we wanted—but to whom?"[4]

From 1964 to 1968 *cinema novo* was in a period of reassessment, and not only because of distribution problems. The bubble of developmentalism had burst, and in 1964 the military seized power from an incompetent populist government. The intelligentsia, stunned, analyzed what had gone wrong with the exuberant, often strident populism reflected in film as well as political work. The "intellectual in anguish" became the theme for Rocha in his *Land in Anguish* (*Terra em transe*, 1967), the fevered recollections of a self-styled revolutionary shot down by police; this "petit-bourgeois intellectual" also became the protagonist of Dahl's *The Brave Warrior* (*O bravo guerreiro*, 1968) and Paulo César Saraceni's *The Challenge* (*O desafio*, 1966). Ismail Xavier finds the reflexive film styles of this period appropriate to the doubts raised by a political crisis in filmmakers who had wanted their cinema "to be an instance of popular communion."[5]

Meanwhile, international opinion was catching up to *cinema novo*'s achievements. The French, who at Cannes often showed interest in cinema in the developing world, had been taking note of the film trend. In 1962 *The Given Word* (*O pagador de promessas*, 1962), by Anselmo Duarte, a film version of a play about syncretic religious belief, won the Golden Palm at Cannes. The European vogue for the Brazilians finally caught on with Americans, and in 1968 the Museum of Modern Art in New York ran a major retrospective.

But by that year Brazil was in the midst of a new crisis. The ever-worsening economic situation precipitated a right-wing coup-within-a-coup. Censorship and summary arrests, often followed by torture (always denied at the time), were two of the generals' solutions for querulous intellectuals working in a popular medium. *Cinema novo* entered its third phase, which lasted until about 1972. Filmmakers responded to these cultural dark ages with what Carlos Diegues calls "an aesthetic of silence."[6] Some of them, like Rocha, Ruy Guerra, and Diegues himself, took refuge in exile. Some worked on films that avoided open reference to current politics with elaborate use of metaphor, historical reference—"There was a time when you could only talk about politics if it was in the 17th century," recalls screenwriter-actor Gianfrancesco Guarnieri—and a less didactic exploration of Brazilian culture.[7] For Xavier these strategies were more than mere circumventions; they showed a new willingness to listen and learn from the Brazilian people as well as to talk and educate.

Rocha's operatic *Antonio das Mortes* (1968) made on the cusp of these changes, became an international talisman of *cinema novo* (perhaps thus overstating the tropical expressionism of a movement that even then was marked by diversity of styles). Nelson Pereira dos Santos set to work on a film version of the diary of a sixteenth-century European trader captured by cannibals, *How Tasty Was My Little Frenchman* (*Como era gostoso meu frances*, 1970). Slyly recasting early Brazilian history from the Indians' perspective, it became an enduring success within Brazil. Also a success with Brazilian audiences was Joaquim Pedro de Andrade's *Macunaíma* (1969), an allegorical film made from a famed experimental novel of the twenties. Macunaíma, a black Brazilian Everyman born in the sticks, goes to the city and turns white, and encounters numerous social and political realities, including urban terrorists, along the way. Exploiting flamboyant aspects of popular culture in style and benefiting from the novel's classic reputation, the film put the seal on its Brazilian popularity with star Grande Otelo, a leading figure on Brazilian television.

To get their films made, some filmmakers worked with foreign coproducers. Pereira dos Santos's dark fantasy *Who Is Beta?* (*Quem é Beta?*, 1973), which played off the science fiction genre, was a coproduction with France. Joaquim Pedro de Andrade's *The Conspirators* (*Os inconfidentes*, 1972), about a middle-class rebellion at the end of colonial rule, was backed by Italian television. Jorge Bodanzky, who worked in a *cinéma vérité* style and had experience in documentary work, made *Iracema* (1974) with a West German, Wolf Gauer. Iracema (whose name, an acronym for America, comes from a romantic nineteenth-century novel that became a hallmark of lyric indigenism) is an Indian who becomes a prostitute and, in her travels along the Transamazônica highway sinks ever deeper into the morass of Brazilian development.

Some filmmakers returned to work in the theater, although that arena too was shrinking under political pressure. Others turned to television, where TV Globo was on its way to becoming, as it is now, the fourth largest network in the world and a major source of entertainment for Brazilians who had earlier gone to movies.

Filmmakers were also working for institutions that would guarantee a more secure, less artisan-based future. Independent filmmakers had lobbied heavily for the creation of Embrafilme in 1969. Embrafilme, a government agency, now finances roughly 30 percent of Brazilian features and shorts, distributes and promotes films (including those it did not help make), and even controls some theaters. It also oversees the distribution of funds from the 5 percent of the box-office take that must go to make Brazilian short subjects; enforces a law mandating that theaters show Brazilian films 140 days a year; and sets terms for the amount of money foreign distributors can take out of the country. The agency is funded through a 35 percent cut from box-office receipts. When, in 1973, *cinema novo* veteran Roberto Farias became the head of Embrafilme, the cinema culture movement had moved into the establishment, albeit with caution. At the same time, the old havens of cinema culture, the Rio and São Paulo cinematheques, became places where the recent cinematic heritage was preserved and extended, and younger generations could challenge and learn from veterans.

However, in some ways that debate over the role of the Brazilian cinema, was becoming hermetic, showing signs of strain under political pressure. Experimentation in form and content went on, but the *udigrudi* filmmakers (the word was a corruption of the English word *underground*) often made inaccessible films. The films of Júlio Bressane and Rogerio Sganzerla, among others, registered a desperate but sometimes despairing wit, and so-called garbage aesthetics had little mass appeal. Other filmmakers, like then-student Ana Carolina, were making "guerrilla documentaries" that never surfaced in the censored media.

The Brazilian audience continued to be difficult for filmmakers to reach. When people were not at home watching spectacles and soap operas on television, they were watching American hits or the lowest-common-denominator commercial films made in Brazil, the *pornochanchadas*, or light sex and lifestyle comedies. Some, like Hugo Carvana's excellent lifestyle comedy about Rio de Janeiro, *Go to Work, You Bum* (*Vai trabalhar, vagabundo*, 1973), had populist energy. Most were Brazilian versions of *Beach Blanket Bingo*, with titles like *A Bra for Daddy* and *More or Less Virgin*.

By 1975 the "Brazilian miracle"—a wedding of state control over labor with the expansionist ambitions of multinationals—had definitively failed. The political thaw that ensued was probably the cheapest answer to public unrest. It also meant a freer atmosphere for film production. The relaxing of censorship allowed, among other things, a hit run of *Last Tango in Paris* and Brazilian films have become well ensconced on the national screens. In 1982 two hundred foreign and seventy-nine Brazilian films were shown, and seven of the top ten were national products. The abysmal quality of projection, sound, and ventilation in theaters undercut filmmakers' hopes, however, and encouraged their ever-closer alliance with television projects.

The distinction between commercial and art films, and between popular and political films, has become less stark. Three-quarters of the annual production is lowest-common denominator sex and action films, but the remainder captures a wider market than ever before.

The problem has not gone away. The first Brazilian film to be a national hit in the era of the thaw was *Dona Flor*, directed by the scion of an old line movie family, Bruno Barretto (son of Luis Carlos). The film is taken from a novel by Brazil's most popular novelist, Jorge Amado. Set in Bahia, the colonial capital, a town marked by black culture from its sugar days, the plot is a frothy diversion in which the proper young wife of a sexy philanderer becomes a widow and remarries a conservative dentist, only to have her husband return as a ghost. She thus gets the best of both worlds.

As entertainment it has everything: colorful settings (Bahia is a favored tourist spot), exotic cultural references, and plenty of sex and death. But was it really Brazilian? Some critics found the film too Hollywood in style, noting that Bahian culture was exploited for its folkloric aspects. One point of comparison was Pereira dos Santos's *Tent of Miracles* (*Tenda dos milagres*, 1977), also made from a Jorge Amado novel, in which racial discrimination forms the core of a plot about a black sociologist's attempt to recover the black roots of elite Bahian culture. *Tent* not only focused on a social rather than a personal issue, but its style also allowed for witty social criticism. The story pokes fun at Brazilians' national inferiority complexes and invidious racial attitudes, and even takes a swipe at the bureaucratic snafus at Embrafilme.

Both films were popular nationally, although *Dona Flor* also became an international hit. Their differences bespeak differences within postwar filmmaking history. Barretto's family comes out of the most aggressively commercial tradition. (Barretto went on to direct *Gabriela* for a U.S.-based production company.) Pereira dos Santos, while dedicated to high-quality entertainment, also sees his task as much wider. It is, he said in 1977 "to help create a cinema nourished by popular roots to free the people—strengthening those parts of their behavior which are not bound to the prescribed model of another society. A people going its own way—that is Jorge Amado's secret and that is what Brazilian films should have to be about."[8]

When Pereira dos Santos made *The Road of Life* (*Estrada da vida*, 1980), a comedy starring two popular country-style singers in a road adventure, some asked how its high-energy, low-brow buffoonery answered that goal. Others found it a hopeful example of Brazilian popular culture surfacing in film in its original form (as opposed to the way that bandit legends became raw material for highly stylized personal art in the hands of Glauber Rocha, for example).

Carlos Diegues's merging of the political and the popular also raised debate. One of the hallmarks of his style is the use of the dramatic in pop culture—vaudeville, carnival, street theater. His *Bye Bye Brazil*, about a traveling circus act, makes a knowing critique of Brazilian development through a hapless couple's competition with electronic media. His *Xica* draws from the true story of a slave in eighteenth-century gold rush territory, who became the mistress of a high official and lived extravagantly before he fell from favor and she from privilege. Star Zezé Motta played the slave Xica with great zest, but some said the role bordered on the sexually exploitative and that the approach Diegues took to slavery and oppression was also exploitative. Diegues responded that the story celebrated a utopian vision of freedom and it also made a criticism of achieving that goal through personal means.

Other filmmakers have drawn from the most commercial forms of popular Brazilian film and television to make their own critiques. Joaquim Pedro's *Conjugal Warfare* (*Guerra conjugal*, 1975) is a savage take-off on soap opera-style family drama. Arnaldo Jabor's *Everything Is OK* (*Tudo bem*, 1978) draws its stock characters (a middle-class Rio family) and stock situation (family crisis) from the seemingly bottomless pool of *pornochanchadas*. Jabor, one of Brazil's most intellectually acute, acerbic and angry filmmakers, has long had the pretensions of the middle class as his subject. In this bitterly funny satire the family's ludicrous contretemps expose class and race conflicts, the domination of the economy by multinationals, the lingering heritage of native fascist politics, the prevalence of superstition and syncretism, and other skeletons in the closets of the bourgeoisie.

Jabor, also a critic, screenwriter, and director, has written eloquently on the need for an authentic Brazilian style in the face of international cultural domination. When Jack Valenti visited Brazil in 1977 to lobby against restrictions on foreign distributors, Jabor wrote a now-famous poem called "Jack Valenti's Brazilian Agenda," reading in part, "Under

Glauber Rocha's *Antonio das Mortes* (1968) revealed both his distinctive style and concerns of the *cinema novo* movement: themes of social justice, and a search for authentically popular cinema forms.

Bruno Barretto turned a Jorge Amado novel into a box-office hit, *Dona Flor and Her Two Husbands* (1976), with a Hollywoodian style.

Carlos Diegues's *Xica* (*Xica da Silva*, 1976), starring Zeze Motta, scandalized some with its sensational recapituation of a tale of colonial decadence.

In Diegues's *Bye Bye Brazil* (1980) traveling entertainers discover the high price of development as they barnstorm Brazil's interior.

Nelson Pereira dos Santos's elegant interpretation of Graciliano Ramos's prison memoirs, *Memories of Prison* (1984), demonstrates both change and continuity with his 1938 interpretation of a Ramos novel.

Valenti's non-Brazilian shoes/the red carpets of hospitality will roll/ and no one will see the cinematic crimes in the air . . . purple wounds, pink wounds, rainbow wounds . . . invisible victims of a thousand dazzling fairy wounds/Eastmancolor burns/seven-colored napalm/ kodak-yellow of our hunger. . . ." Jabor's own attempts to use genre critically have been stimulating even when only partially successful. His *I Love You*, starring film-and-television idol Sonia Braga (also star of *Dona Flor*), made use of a familiar marital romance to probe the frustrations of bourgeois marriage. It was only a moderate success; one filmmaker who admires him said lightly, "Poor Jabor—he just doesn't know how to sell out."

Along with the revival of debate on popular culture and the widening of the Brazilian public's interest in national cinema came a return to overt social criticism. Jorge Bodanzsky, still working with Gauer, made a documentary, *Third Millennium (Tercero milénio*, 1980), on the campaign of a dissident oddball politician in the Amazon. Hector Babenco's *Pixote* (Babenco is an Argentine now residing in Brazil) addressed the plight of abandoned children in the cities; Neville de Almeida's *Rio Babylon* (1983) has as its theme homosexual life in Rio. And historical subjects took on a new edge. The winner of the 1982 Gramado Film Festival—one of the biggest film events of the year— was Hermanno Penna's *Sargento Getúlio*, about economic power and police corruption during the Vargas era in the late thirties and forties. Leon Hirzman's *They Don't Wear Black Tie* (1980), a social realist drama about a family torn apart by different attitudes during a strike, recasts in the present a play originally written in the 1960s. Geraldo Sarno's *Colonel Delmiro Gouveia (Coronel Delmiro Gouveia*, 1977) is a case study in the contradictions of modernization for old-fashioned elites; the protagonist, an ambitious entrepreneur at the turn of the century, discovers that paternalist capitalism does not work. One of the most daring historical films recently was *Hooray, Brazil (Para frente, Brazil*, 1982), which Roberto Farias made with Embrafilme about government torture in 1970. Perhaps the greatest synthesis of cinematic art and social commentary in postwar Brazilian cinema was the monumental, three-hour *Memories of Prison*, by Nelson Pereira dos Santos, which won a critics award at Cannes in 1984.

It has not been smooth sailing, however. *Third millennium*, made on a shoestring and looking like it, received a lackluster reception. Other films have run up against government hostility. *Rio Babylon*, for instance, was censored for graphic scenes of sex and violence. *Hooray, Brazil* caused so many waves that the head of Embrafilme, who had authorized its funding, was fired and the film was banned. *Black Tie* was held up for national release until it won the Venice Film Festival award for 1981.

But the diversity of style and subject matter offers some protection as Brazil enters a democratic era. So does the existence of a younger generation of filmmakers, many of whom benefit from *cinema novo* experience. Tizuka Yamasaki, for instance, trained with Pereira dos Santos and with Glauber Rocha before making *Gaijin* (1979). *Gaijin* lightly fictionalizes the story of Yamasaki's grandmother, who left Japan at sixteen to work on the coffee plantations of São Paulo state. Through her experience, the film portrays labor battles and the ways in which employers used the family-oriented Japanese to break strikes. Yamasaki's work boldly critiques the Brazilian version of the "melting pot"; immigrant history may become, for this generation, what the recovery of black and Indian heritages was for an earlier generation.

Yamasaki's transparent, traditional style in *Gaijin* contrasts with the surrealistic, free-associational style of a filmmaker like Ana Carolina, who since her "guerrilla documentary" days has made highly personal feature films. Both *Sea of Roses* (*Mar de rosas*, 1978), a road movie in which a child fatally exposes family hypocrisy, and *Heart and Guts* (*Das tripas coração*, 1982), a dream movie about a Catholic girls school, use stream of consciousness imagery and an urgent, almost hysterical tone to communicate anguish and frustration. The work of Carlos Alberto Prates Correia is also notable for stylistic innovation, as in, for instance, the imagistic *Cabaret Mineiro* (1981), a disjointed series of tableaux featuring archetypal Brazilian characters. Experimental documentary work continues to flourish on the alternative cinema circuit, still strongest in São Paulo and Rio de Janeiro.

The pluralism of style and subject that marks the present era looks to older filmmakers like a transitory phase. As Zelito Viana put it, "We are waiting to see what happens next; we are waiting for *cinema novo* to begin again. The present phase is one of perplexity."[10]

That perplexity was heightened in 1985 when, after the military relinquished power to civilian authority and elections were held, an unstable coalition was further jeopardized by the death of president-elect Tancredo Neves. The political future of civilian rule was then made even hazier by plans for a constitutional convention, in which artistic freedom along with all other kinds became a clause yet to be written. And for filmmakers concerned as much with the economic health of their industry as with its aesthetic direction, the condition of the Brazilian economy was deeply troubling since it was afflicted with a monumental foreign debt and, until Draconian fiscal measures were taken in March 1986, triple-digit inflation.

Such national problems make long-range economic plans chancy, at a moment when the terms of film marketing and new technologies are changing the international context. Still, the business of Brazilian film is rapidly becoming more sophisticated. Foreign sales, often negotiated through Embrafilme, have burgeoned, and Brazil's market is now worldwide. Not only did *I Love You* and *Pixote* each net half a million dollars in U.S. theatrical and ancillary rights, but Embrafilme negotiated a sale of 100 sex comedies to a Hong Kong distributor in the same period, capitalizing on both faces of the current Brazilian cinema.

Since the mid-1970s, Brazilian film has established itself firmly as an industry again in Brazil, no longer a sporadic exercise in cultural imitation and resistance. Several national festivals are held, including the financially beleaguered Rio film festival and the Bahia festival of documentary and alternative films. *Cinema novo* veterans are thriving, with projects that echo and develop longstanding themes. Nelson Pereira dos Santos's *Memories of Prison* (*Memorias do carcere*, 1984) captures on film the memoirs of leftist intellectual Graciliano Ramos, whose *Barren Lives* (*Vidas secas*, 1938) offered Pereira dos Santos the theme of his classic early work. Carlos Diegues's disappointing spectacular *Quilombo* is a commercial remake of his early *Ganga Zumba*. Arnaldo Jabor with *I Know I'm Going to Love You* (*Eu sei que vou te amar*, 1985) manages to marry his rage at the contradictions of middle-class self-realization aspirations of *Everything's OK* (*Tudo bem*, 1977) with the sexual politics of *I Love You* (*Eu te amo*, 1982). Veteran documentarians have undertaken ambitious and commercially viable projects; Batista de Andrade's feature *Open Skies* (*Ceu aberto*, 1985) documents with a critical eye the public rituals surrounding the death of president-elect Tancredo Neves, and Geraldo Sarno is completing a survey of liberation theology throughout Latin America. "Udigrudi" or underground outrage burns on screen with features such as Rogerio Sganzerla's *Not Everything Is True* (*Nem tudo e verdade*, 1985), a film-essay on an aborted film by Orson Welles in Brazil, and Julio Bressane's *Bras Cubas* (1985), an elegant treatment of a novel by iconoclastic classic author Machado de Assis. The *cinema novo* epoch came full circle with Eduardo Coutinho's moving documentary *A Man Marked to Die* (*Cabra marcado para morrer*, 1985), seen in 1984 in the New York New Directors/New Films series. The film was begun in 1964 as a docudrama of a peasant leader's death, and was finished during the political thaw in Brazil, with interviews with the man's widow and children. While the Brazilian filmmaking industry is now quite active, however, its future is uncertain. Young filmmakers now experiment more often in video than in film, and a wide network of alternative video distribution flourishes, while at the same time theatrical exhibition languishes.

If Brazilian cinema still stands in the shadow of American cinema, as do most national cinemas, it is also casting shadows itself. Perhaps the best measures of both its independence and its problem is the growing complexity of the question, "But is it authentically Brazilian?"

## NOTES

1. "Cinema: Trajetoria no subdesenvolvimento," pp. 2–20, *Filme/Cultura* (Embrafilme), July–August–September 1980, p. 17 (author's translation).
2. Quoted in *Filme/Cultura*, op. cit. A key essay by Paulo Emilio, "Cinema: A Trajectory within Underdevelopment," has been translated in Randal Johnson and Robert Stam, *Brazilian Cinema*, East Brunswick, N.J., Associated University Presses, 1982. His film criticism is available in *Critica de cinema no suplemento literario*, 2 vols, Rio de Janeiro: Ed. Paz y Terra, 1981.
3. "An Aesthetic of Hunger," translated in Johnson and Stam, op. cit., p. 70. Rocha has received extensive analysis from critics. A useful point of reference both critically and bibliographically is Ismail Xavier, *Sertao Mar: Glauber Rocha e a estetica da fome*, Sao Paulo: Ed. Brasiliense, 1983.
4. Interview with the author, Toronto Festival of Festivals, September 1982.
5. Julianne Burton, "The Intellectual in Anguish: Form and Ideology in *Land in Anguish* and *Memories of Underdevelopment*," paper presented at Woodrow Wilson International Center for Scholars, Smithsonian Institution, Washington, D.C. 20560, April 26, 1983; Ismail Xavier, "Allegories of Underdevelopment: from the 'Aesthetics of Hunger' to the 'Aesthetics of Garbage,'" New York University Ph.D. Thesis, 1982. University Microfilms International, 300 N. Zeeb Rd., Ann Arbor MI 48106.
6. Interview with the author, Toronto Festival of Festivals, September 1982.
7. Ibid.
8. *Filme/Cultura*, op.cit.
9. Johnson and Stam, p. 111.
10. Interview with the author, Toronto Festival of Festivals, September 1982.

## SELECTED BIBLIOGRAPHY

Aufderheide, Pat. "Will Success Spoil Brazilian Cinema?" *American Film* 8, no. 5 (March 1983): 65f.

*Brazilian Cinema*. ed. Randal Johnson and Robert Stam. NJ: Associated University Presses, 1982.

Burton, Julianne. "The Intellectual in Anguish. Form and Ideology in *Land in Anguish* and *Memories of Underdevelopment*." Paper presented at Woodrow Wilson International Center for Scholars, Washington, DC, 26, April, 1983.

"Discovering the Brazilian Cinema." Rio de Janeiro: Embrafilme Publications.

*Filme/Cultura* (Brazil) July–August–September 1980.

Johnson, Randal. *Cinema Novo X Five: Masters of Contemporary Brazilian Film*. Austin: University of Texas Press, 1984.

Stam, Robert. "Slow Fade to Afro: The Black Presence in Brazilian Cinema." *Film Quarterly* 36, no. 2 (winter 1982–83): 16f.

Variety, annual Latin American issues as well as regular reporting.

Xavier, Ismail. *Allegories of Underdevelopment: From the "Aesthetics of Hunger" to the "Aesthetics of Garbage."* New York University Ph.D. dissertation, 1982 (University Microfilms International, 300 N. Zeeb Road, Ann Arbor, MI 48106).

# CANADA

## PIERS HANDLING

Perhaps the first question to be asked of Canadian cinema is semantic. Can we claim that there is one identifiable, discernible, and visible Canadian cinema, or are there in fact at least two major cinemas in Canada? There are two cultures and two official languages—anglophone and francophone, French and English, Quebec and the rest of Canada — and this fact is basic to Canadian cinema. Quebec has a special status within Confederation; resisting absorption into the rest of North American culture, it has been firecely protective of its rich and vital heritage. Despite these differences however, Quebec and the rest of Canada share a common history. Both were colonies and this colonial past has resulted in a number of conjunctions. Canada is a paradox. There are thematic schemas and artistic concerns mutual to both cultures, yet often these imaginative structures are treated in extremely different ways. The history of cinema in Canada reflects these tensions. It is possible, indeed perhaps inevitable, to want to deal with two cinemas. Yet at the same time, the history of film policy and economics cannot really be divided. The sad lament of production, distribution, and exhibition sectors finds one voice within Canada. The river may have branched out in different directions but it shares a common source.

If the modern Canadian cinema began in the sixties, its context for development goes back decades. The first film screenings took place in 1896 when traveling projectionists brought their flickering, ghostly images to a rapt and eager public. This new invention was being developed simultaneously in the United States and France by Edison and the Lumière brothers respectively, and their films made up the first programs shown in Montreal and Ottawa. It was, ironically, a foreshadowing of the future. A foreign invention bringing foreign material—bathing scenes at Atlantic City and French workers leaving their factories; Canada would become a battleground over which these giants would struggle for economic domination, thrusting its own self-image deep into the shadows. As a colony, lacking the entrepreneurial skills and capital of the great nations, sharing a common, "undefended" border with the United States, Canada was in a particularly vulnerable and disadvantageous position. In hindsight these three facts of its existence have marked every aspect of Canadian society, and nowhere have the implications been realized more completely than in its cinema.

The first significant battle to be decided was an economic one, fought out in boardrooms by businessmen. When, in 1923, a Toronto businessman, N. L. Nathanson, with the backing of Paramount, bought out an independent chain of theaters that the Allen brothers had built up, a pattern of exhibition and distribution was imposed upon the country that essentially remains in effect today. Nathanson's company, Famous Players Canadian Corp., took its orders from New York, unlike the Allens who took their orders from no one. From this moment on Canadians have always remained foreigners within their own cinematic marketplace, their screens dominated by American products, their distribution system predominantly in the hands of the U.S. "majors"—Paramount, Columbia, Universal, Warner Brothers, Twentieth Century-Fox, and United Artists. Even Quebec, with the advantage of a different language did not escape this hegemony. Locked out of its own market, Canada's production sector remains a tenuous, and often nonexistent, practice. The arrival of Odeon Theatres in 1941, a rival chain to Famous, did little to change the situation; it was a British company. There were attempts to resist this stranglehold. In 1930 a combines investigation reported that the Hollywood companies constituted a combine. In a subsequent trial they were acquitted and it would be another fifty years before their grip would be relaxed.[1]

Faced with this reality of the marketplace, but also recognizing the first tremors of nationalist sentiment emerging in the wake of World War I, the government stepped into the fray, beginning a tradition of public involvement in virtually every aspect of Canadian cultural affairs. In 1932 the Broadcasting Act established the Canadian Radio-Broadcasting Commission, the precursor of the Canadian Broadcasting Corporation, and in 1939 the National Film Act created the National Film Board (NFB) of Canada, an organization that was to leave an indelible mark on Canadian cinema.

Until 1939 film production in Canada was sporadic at best, but the creation of the NFB changed all this. It was opportune that the NFB came into existence at a time when public monies were readily forthcoming because of the war effort. John Grierson, the fiery little Scot who ran the NFB, had a golden tongue and a way of maneuvering through the bureaucratic maze which made sure that the NFB never went wanting. But Grierson also left another legacy, a philosophy of filmmaking that has survived for over forty years. He was a propagandist who had great faith in liberal democracy. Somewhat left of center in his politics, Grierson recognized that film had a unique role to play in a modern world rapidly being changed by the new technologies of mass communications. Influenced by Walter Lippman's ideas, Grierson grappled with the question of providing the modern citizen with information that would allow him to intervene in society. Grierson's philosophy of film was primarily functional. Film had a purpose, to educate, thereby giving people an idea of how they fitted into the broader pattern of society. He was also an internationalist, fascinated by the big picture, and the NFB films of the war years were at pains to situate Canada's role in the global conflict.

But first and foremost, Grierson was a great believer in the power of actuality and the documentary film. He turned his back on the escapist entertainments of Hollywood in favor of documenting and reflecting the realities of society and its many peoples. This he did with visible success. An intellectual heir to the cinematic poems of Robert Flaherty and the didactic constructs of Eisenstein, Vertov, and Pudovkin, Grierson's vision was essentially collective and progressive. He believed in communities struggling together to create a better world, and thought that economic development resulted in social health. But above all Grierson believed in the powers of a realist cinema.

Grierson's aesthetic heritage obviously touched a deep, responsive chord in a nation that had an affinity for landscape art and the realist novel. The documentary film became a way of understanding the world and transmitting its truths. There was an almost messianic quality to this belief in the power of the realist cinema. If Hollywood's carefully constructed illusionism pandered to dreams of wealth, happiness, and romantic love through fantasy and artifice, Grierson would show real people in real situations, be they at work or at home.

Grierson's belief in the power of a realist cinema, or as he put it, "the creative treatment of actuality," would become the bedrock of a philosophy of filmmaking that suffused his creation, the National Film Board. It would also provide a touchstone against which the two cultures and their cinemas would measure themselves in quite different ways.

Even as the war was ending though, the Griersonian legacy underwent one last development, totally beyond his control, which would nevertheless have many repercussions. When a Soviet embassy cipher clerk, Igor Gouzenko, defected, the information he brought with him included Grierson's name. Grierson would eventually be cleared but it ruined his career in the United States, and the NFB, because it was so closely associated with his name, was widely thought to be the agent of a foreign power, transmitting evil propaganda. The communist tag was slow to disappear. Three years later, in 1949, a second red scare led to the sacrificial dismissal of three employees, the appointment of a new film commissioner who altered key components in the Film Board's status, and a lasting legacy of a different kind.

During the immediate postwar years the NFB was engaged in making numerous films that explained the immense variety of social reforms that the government was busy enacting. It was a time when many of the great social welfare programs were established. There was an excitement in the air. There were even a few films that dealt with international affairs, a theme dear to Grierson. Despite their conventional paternal tone, extolling the virtues of the democratic system, the NFB was making films that grappled with the problems of an external social world. The red scare changed all this. Fear was pervasive, and the films began in their own way to exclude this world and turn inwards upon themselves. The organization was politically suspect and moves were made to alter this perception. The new Film Act in 1950 effectively removed the NFB from the political sphere in two important ways. A decision was made to move it from the capital city, Ottawa, to Montreal, shifting it away from the political center of the country. Moreover, the close parliamentary association that Grierson had done so much to foster was abruptly fractured when the cabinet ministers who had sat on the board of governors were removed in the new administrative changes. The NFB was very consciously removed from the political firing line, but as a result there was a potential for it to become increasingly marginalized as an organization that would intervene as an instrument for social change.

All this had a significant impact upon the NFB and indeed upon the future of film in the country. It must be remembered that until 1956 the NFB was predominantly an English institution. The red scare and the subsequent organizational shake-up left pyschic scars upon the anglophone filmmaker that became evident in the films that followed.

The NFB at this time consisted of a number of tightly knit film units; one of them began to produce a remarkable body of work, films that still bear close scrutiny and that reveal the true roots of the English-Canadian feature film. The Unit B classics—*Paul Tomkowicz: Street Railway Switchman* (1954), *Corral* (1954), *City of Gold* (1957), *Universe* (1960), *Lonely Boy* (1962)—began an indigenous aesthetic that in some ways was a reaction against the strident Griersonian films of the war years. These works were quieter and more reflective, content to give the impression that reality was revealing itself naturally, as opposed to shaping this reality into predetermined statements. The films were observational in approach and diffuse in structure. Nevertheless, an underlying ideology was apparent, if unconscious. The films were middle class, applauded success, and celebrated the achievements of the individual (Glenn Gould, Paul Anka, and Igor Stravinsky were the subjects of three of the better-known efforts). As Peter Harcourt has pointed out they were also full of a sense of awe and wonder at man and his potential, but they were also distant from their material, maintaining a stance of objective detachment.[2] But what is most striking about the Unit B work are the structured absences in the films, which often point toward tensions in the material and society that somehow escaped any examination. Women and native people are invisible in this work, as is any real sense of a modern society. Common working people are rarely present or safely situated in the past. *Corral* and *City of Gold* look to history; *Universe* to the infinites of outer space; *Lonely Boy, Glenn Gould: Off the Record/On the Record* (1959), and *Stravinsky* (1965) to exceptional individuals rather remote from the problems of society. *Paul Tomkowicz* is the exception but it does not manage to transcend the insular Unit B mentality. It portrays an immigrant Polish worker who sweeps snow off tramcar rails. He is an outsider, visually and verbally separate from the society he lives in, but nowhere is this exclusion examined. Like all the other Unit B classics, conflict, while present, is either ignored or safely resolved.

One filmmaker who strayed into the inner circle at Unit B, Terence Macartney Filgate, had a much more highly developed sense of issues than his colleagues. *The Back-Breaking Leaf* (1959), *The Days Before Christmas* (1958), *Blood and Fire* (1958), and *Pilgrimage* (1958) lack the polish of the rest of the Unit B films but they are not afraid to get their hands dirty, pushing their inquiries out into society, far from the philosophical musings of *Universe* or *The Living Machine* (1962). *The Days Before Christmas*, with its images of guns and police set against the backdrop of the festive season and the continual exchange of money, has a strong sense of coercion and latent violence, as indeed does *The Back-Breaking Leaf*, a film on migrant tobacco workers. But again, tensions are merely suggested, or simply avoided, totally unlike the conflict style documentaries of Robert Drew, Ricky Leacock, and D.A. Pennebaker that were being made at the same time in the United States. Consciously or unconsciously, these films ignored differences and societal tensions to stress the notion of a monolithic society where problems could be safely worked out within the system. The fact that the NFB was a state film organization, whose existence depended on government monies, becomes abundantly clear in retrospect.

However, this did not deter the Quebecois filmmaker. The move of the NFB to Montreal in 1956 turned the organization into a truly bilingual institution. A host of young and energetic filmmakers joined the NFB and turned their backs on the dispassionate, objective anglophone style, with its use of the omnipotent narrator and its attraction to the individual subject. The films they would make were involved, subjective, interested in the collective, and highly mediated in their structure. Reality would not simply yield up its secrets to the camera. There was a deeper, hidden reality, invisible to the camera, that could only be foregrounded by mediation and intervention on the part of the filmmaker. This could take several forms. Unlike their Unit B counter-parts these films were often self-reflexive in their use of the formal properties of film. Conventions of the silent film (music, intertitles) and questions of theatricality inform *Wrestling* (*La lutte*, 1961) as well as a very sophisticated, nonsynchronous soundtrack that forces us to reflect on the rituals we are watching. *Day after Day* (*Jour après jour*, 1962) employs a female narrator and poetic narration, tied to a densely edited image-track, deliberately challenging accepted documentary practice of the period.

These filmmakers saw themselves engaged in a nationalist struggle of self-definition and preservation. *The Snowshoers* (*Les raquetteurs*, 1958) marked the beginnings of a distinct French style at the NFB. *Golden Gloves* (1961), *Wrestling, Quebec USA or the Pacific Invasion* (*Québec USA ou l'invasion pacifique*, 1962), *Day After Day, A Simple Game* (*Un jeu si simple*, 1964), *See Miami* (*Voir Miami*, 1962), and *September Five at Saint-Henri* (*A Saint-Henri le cinq septembre*, 1962) are all as distinctive as the Unit B films. They formulate a unique way of looking at the world, establishing the different cultural perceptions that distinguish the two cinemas in Canada.[3]

If Canada was a colony (it is in an economic sense since about one-quarter of our economy is foreign owned, mainly by U.S. interests; 47 percent of our vital manufacturing sector and 45 percent of our mining, oil, and gas industries are controlled from abroad), Quebec was deter-mined to resist this reality. As the province emerged from the oppres-sive Duplessis years of the fifties into the intensely nationalist spirit of the sixties, its filmmakers illuminated these dreams and provided an album of self-defining family pictures. While the English-Canadian films of the period were self-contained, hermetic artefacts, the Quebec films began to challenge and resist the status quo. Two films, *Normétal* (1959), a critical portrait of the economic and social realities that domi-nated a mining town, and *Manouane River Lumberjacks* (*Bûcherons de la Manouane*, 1962), on the timber industry, ran into trouble and were eventually cut before their release. It was inevitable that the Quebec-ois, struggling for survival against a centralist, federal power, should choose to resist. While the NFB's films had always supported industrial development and the exploitation of our abundant natural resources, *Normétal, Manouane River Lumberjacks* and *Day after Day* called into question prevailing attitudes. This was unthinkable for the anglophone filmmaker at the NFB, who had had to live through the uncertainties of the red scares.

If Grierson's belief in a realist cinema initially defined both cinemas in Canada, it was ultimately a legacy that would evolve in different, di-vergent ways. The anglophone filmmaker was securely centered in the Bazinian tradition, with its belief in the real and its faith in notions of empiricism. The francophone filmmakers would look to another theoretician for their aesthetic guidance—Eisenstein—for they found themselves engaged in much the same struggle as the Soviets: trying to define a new society. Because of its nationalist aspirations as a province, Quebec had begun to question the reality of its situation in a very specific way. Like Marxist materialism, it was interested in examining the underlying forces and relationships which structure human interaction and determine the workings of the social dynamic. For Eisenstein, and other Marxists of the time, it became necessary to displace the real world, which for them was a construct of bourgeois ideology, and to replace it with a range of other possibilities. Only by deconstructing reality and rearranging it could the hidden patterns of reality be revealed *and* a potential for future action be suggested and affirmed. For the francophone filmmaker, realist conventions had to be undermined and subverted.

While the Unit B and French Unit films were classics, they were only miniatures and also only documentaries, no matter how formally inventive. The more ambitious, and culturally acknowledged arena of the fiction feature film was still just a glint in people's eyes. The country had made features in its past, but these efforts were infrequent and lacked imagination. This is not surprising because the economic climate was not conducive to sustained production. Imaginatively Canadian filmmaking may not have been able to handle the complexities of the feature film, but there were other factors at play as well. In 1948 an opportunity was lost to create the potential for a financial arrangement that may have sparked the genesis of an industry. The Canadian Cooperation Project (CCP) was a deal worked out between the Canadian government and the Motion Picture Association of America, designed to let the American majors take their box-office receipts out of Canada at a time when Canada had a severe balance of payments problem with the United States. In return for the flow of money out of the country, short films would be made in Hollywood about Canada which would ostensibly promote its tourist industry! The CCP was an absurd arrangement, indicative of a colony afraid of alienating its powerful neighbor.[4] Who knows what might have happened if Hollywood's money had been frozen in Canada and used to invest in Canadian films. As it was, only *one* English-Canadian feature film was produced in the years between 1937 and 1956, *Bush Pilot* (1946), a rather pedestrian imitation of the Jimmy Cagney effort, *Captains of the Clouds* (1942).

It is true that in a nine-year period after 1944, nineteen commercial feature films were produced in Quebec, largely through the efforts of two companies: Quebec Productions Corporation and Renaissance. The latter was financed by the Catholic Church, intent on using film for its own ends. The films it made—*Father Chopin* (*Le Père Chopin*, 1944), *Big Bill* (*Le gros Bill*, 1949), *Doctor Louise* (*Docteur Louise*, 1949) and *The Lights of My City* (*Les lumières de ma ville*, 1950)—were all highly moralistic and preached the virtues of traditional values. Its competitor, Quebec Productions, was more commercial, but not surprisingly its films reflected a similar self-righteousness. Culturally and politically Quebec was extremely conservative in its attitudes until the death of Duplessis in 1960. The most representative film of this period was *Little Aurore's Tragedy* (*La petite Aurore l'enfant martyre*, 1951), a morbid, masochistic portrait of a young girl victimized by a jealous stepmother. Right and wrong are painted in the broadest possible strokes and the wicked are punished for their sins in true Christian fashion. The most artistically satisfying film made at this time was *Tit-Coq* (*Tit-Coq*, 1953), the story of a conscript who loses his girl to another man while he is at war, but it was to be the last gasp of an industry that would not be revived for another decade. The introduction of television in 1952 satisfied the need for French-Canadians to see their image on a screen, effectively ending this early experiment at creating a national cinema.

Television had an enormous effect on an entire generation of filmmakers. Our best talent, people like Norman Jewison, Ted Kotcheff, Sidney Furie, Silvio Narizzano, and Arthur Hiller, all moved into television, before leaving the country to make their feature films elsewhere. An entire generation of our young filmmakers left due to an unhospitable production climate, leaving a huge gap. The only exception was Sidney Furie, who before leaving in 1959, never to return, made two fresh, low-budget features: *A Dangerous Age* (1957) and *A Cool Sound from Hell* (1959), both dealing with the youth of the beat generation.

If the fifties was a decade of erratic production, magnificent short films, and departing directors, the sixties witnessed the birth of the modern Canadian cinema. This was due to a variety of factors. In the wake of the French New Wave, the neorealist films coming from Italy, an evolving 16mm technology, the changing political and social climate in post-Duplessis Quebec, and the country's deepening sense of itself around the centennial year of 1967, a number of films were made that mark a definite break and a new beginning. In a three-year period a deluge of vital and energetic first features were made, both independently and at the NFB. They were all low-budget productions, and the majority of them were shot on the cheaper and more flexible 16mm film stock. Virtually all of them dealt with the growing pains of adolescents and the passage into adulthood, as if this theme corresponded with the psychic mood of a country moving into full nationhood. *The Bitter Ash* (Larry Kent, 1963), *Take it All* (*A tout prendre*, Claude Jutra, 1963), *The Cat in the Bag* (*Le chat dans le sac*, Gilles Groulx, 1964) *Nobody Waved Good-bye* (Don Owen, 1964), *The Revolutionary* (*Le révolutionnaire* (Jean Pierre Lefebvre, 1965), *Winter Kept Us Warm* (David Secter, 1965), *The Merry World of Léopold Z.* (*La vie heureuse de Léopold Z.*, Gilles Carle, 1965), and *The Luck of Ginger Coffey* (Irvin Kershner,

1964), all centered around male protagonists confused by the world around them. Invariably, Quebecois films dealt with questions of politics. Characteristically, English-Canadian work was more isolated from this context.

The seminal films were *Le chat dans le sac* and *Nobody Waved Good-bye*, both of which grew out of the French Unit and Unit B work.[5] Both deal with questions surrounding the couple (adolescents of about seventeen to twenty), although in totally different ways. The Quebec film features a young man obsessed with politics who is trying to get newspaper articles published. He is living with an English actress, a relationship that resonates with the problems of the country as a whole. *Nobody Waved Good-bye* deals with a middle-class teenager who drops out of school, gets picked up by the police, finds a job in a car lot, and ends up with a pregnant girlfriend. Both Claude and Peter, the respective protagonists of the two films, are rebels but in quite different ways. Peter leaves home, steals a car, rifles a till. His concerns are personal and center around money and cars. Claude abandons the city for the country because he cannot get published, leaves his girlfriend, and indulges in intensive self-questioning. Politics are foregrounded in his life; his concerns are collective and social, and never materialistic. Both films end in escapes and in the separation of the couple, but *Le chat dans le sac* suggests the possibility of a new relationship, this time with a Quebec girl. *Nobody Waved Good-bye* concludes on a rainy highway, with Peter crying as he drives off we know not where, leaving his expectant girlfriend behind on the roadside. So the English film ends on a note of confusion and despair, the Quebec film on a note of reflection and optimism.

But most distinctive are the formal strategies both employ. *Le chat dans le sac* is densely structured, highly mediated, and foregrounds its filmic conventions in a manner similar to Godard. It is also a film of interior monologues, which assume as much importance as the images we are presented with. *Nobody Waved Good-bye* eschews off-camera monologues, is shot like a documentary, and is concerned with constructing a faithful illusion of reality, seemingly free from the filmmaker's intervention. Each film expresses a different view of reality, sensitive to the demands of its culture. Reality is being scrutinized and questioned in the Quebec film, and formally this is incorporated into its structure, while reality is only being mirrored or reflected in the English-Canadian film, so no similar intervention is required.

These characteristics, evident in the short films of Unit B and the French Unit of the NFB, apparent in *Nobody Waved Good-bye* and *Le chat dans le sac*, surface with surprising regularity in the films of our two cultures. *A tout prendre* is as structurally innovative as *Le chat dans le sac*, reveling in the use of jump-cuts, temporal dislocations and visual fragmentation. Film is used like a diary with extensive voice-over communicating inner thoughts. *Le révolutionnaire* follows a small band of harmless Quebec terrorists to their snowy country retreat. It is also a film of invention and formal play, highly stylized in its refusal of the conventional. In all these films there is a pervasive desire to create new forms for self-expression where everything is possible.

*Winter Kept Us Warm*, on the other hand, tells its story of a university love affair using traditional narrative codes. No moments of formal interruption intervene to question the nature of what we are seeing. Reality seems to be transparent and the camera functions as a window that looks out onto the world. This characterizes the anglophone cinema, and has become the central tradition in our fictional cinema. Only two English filmmakers of the time came close to emulating the French challenge. Don Owen moved away from the faithful realism of *Nobody Waved Good-bye* to direct films that became increasingly complex. *Notes for a Film about Donna & Gail* (1966) is split into eight chapters and uses a narrator who calls into question much of what we are seeing, while *The Ernie Game* (1967) deliberately avoids any psychological characterization in a story about a schizophrenic.

On the West Coast Larry Kent was busy developing his own highly personal style. *The Bitter Ash*, another story about disaffected youth, is notable for its arbitrary editing which mirrors the uncertainties of its characters. Kent went on to develop his own authorial style in *Sweet Substitute* (1964) and *When Tomorrow Dies* (1965) before moving to Montreal. *High* (1967), an absurdist and disturbing look at the amorality of the hippy generation, uses colored tints over black-and-white images, interviews, stylzied moments of theatricality, still photographs and extensive jump-cuts. *Façade* (1968) goes even further. In its examination of an unhappy marriage between a college professor and a beautiful model, friends of the couple are interviewed speaking directly to the camera, but more audaciously, split-screen, multiple images (as many as nine at a time) and rear projection are continually employed. It went unreleased and unseen and forced Kent to move into the mainstream. Having made five features over a six-year period in the sixties, Kent has directed three more in the past fifteen years. A similar fate befell Owen. Both men were forced to step back from their innovations.

Concurrent with, and subsequent to the outpouring of creative energy in the mid-sixties, a number of important developments were occurring. Production at the National film Board was formally split along linguistic lines into two production branches. At the same time, Quebec filmmakers at the NFB were testing the limits of the organization's capacity for self-expression. Five of them took the daring step in 1964 of publicly denouncing the NFB in the radical separatist journal, *parti pris*. They argued that it was a huge federal propaganda machine and maintained that its chief tool was the objective documentary, which pretended not to take sides but in so doing supported the status quo.

Within two years the counterrevolution had cleared out the best and the brightest Quebec filmmakers at the NFB. The organization was too small for their aspirations. Most of them wanted to make feature-length fiction films anyway and this would have been extremely difficult to do in a place whose reputation was based on the documentary. They moved into the private sector to make highly distinctive contributions, forming the core of the Quebec film industry. Others, like Gilles Groulx, Denys Arcand, and Pierre Perrault, remained behind and would cause the NFB further embarassment in a succession of censorship scandals that swept the NFB between 1969 and 1972.

The most important initiative of this period was the creation in 1967 of the Canadian Film Development Corporation (CFDC), a federal body designed to foster the growth of an indigenous feature film industry. The CFDC was established in response to a growing need; after all a number of eloquent films were beginning to attract international attention and the momentum needed to be sustained. This new body would assist in the financing of films thereby guaranteeing some kind of production continuity for our best filmmakers. However, its impact was severely limited in one vital way. It could finance films, but it could make no impression in getting these films distributed or exhibited. So, while production began to escalate, there were still enormous difficulties in getting these films into the marketplace where they could be seen by a public who was paying for them in large part. Quotas and levies were discussed as a means of breaking the logjam but the government lacked the political will to impose such draconian (for Canada) measures. The two major theater chains, Famous and Odeon, agreed to voluntary quotas of at least two weeks of screen time for Canadian films in Montreal, Toronto, and Vancouver, quotas they broke and which were eventually abandoned. Even at present this state of affairs has not changed—only 2 *percent* of screen time is devoted to Canadian material. The closest Canada came to getting tough with the Americans was in 1977 when a 10 percent tax on distribution revenues was proposed, with a rebate that would have functioned as a quota for Canadian films. This measure was turned down by the cabinet and has never been implemented. Nevertheless, the CFDC has had an enormous impact on the country's production sector, providing the foundation for a future film industry.

It is erroneous to say that the CFDC created our modern cinema. It acted as a catalyst for a movement that had predated its formation. Larry Kent had made four films in the early sixties. In Montreal a unique experiment in cooperative filmmaking was underway, whereby most of the people involved in the film's production would defer their salaries against future profits. This company, Coopératio, would produce six feature films between 1964 and 1967, including Michel Brault's wistful *Drifting Upstream* (*Entre la mer et l'eau douce*, 1967), a film about a love affair that is abandoned for professional success. Paul

Almond took Geneviève Bujold off to the rugged Gaspé coast to shoot *Isabel* (1968), a gothic tale of a young woman confronting the ghosts in her past. There were also films being made by university students across the country, the most distinguished of whom was David Cronenberg, whose *Stereo* (1969) was a stark introduction to his particular imaginative universe. Denis Héroux already had three feature films to his credit before the CFDC arrived on the scene, including the phenomenally successful *Valérie* (1968), the first soft-core skin flick made in the province. The titillating nudity caused a sensation in Quebec, but despite the apparent rebelliousness of the central character, who is whisked off on the back of a motorcycle from a convent into a life of dissipation and prostitution, traditional morality eventually triumphs as she ends up in the arms of a painter who is also a single parent! The financial success of *Valérie* went a long way toward creating a domestic audience for Quebec films, and the CFDC began to invest in more sex films, until diminishing returns and public criticism ended this flirtation with vice. Jean Pierre Lefebvre had also made four features by 1967, including the remarkable *Don't Let It Kill You* (*Il ne faut pas mourir pour ça*, 1966), and Gilles Carle had moved into the private sector to make the absurdist *The Rape of a Sweet Young Girl* (*Le viol d'une jeune fille douce*, 1968).

There were two major documentary projects of the period and they further illuminate our two cinemas. Pierre Perrault devoted a decade of work to his Ile-aux-Coudres trilogy—*For Those Who Follow* (*Pour la suite du monde*, 1963), *The Times That Are* (*Le règne du jour*, 1966) and *The River "Schooners"* (*Les voitures d'eau*, 1969)—which documented the threatened lifestyle of a community of islanders living in the St. Lawrence River, while Allan King embarked on a less homogenous series of films that dealt with problems of childhood (*Warrendale*, 1966), adolescence (*Come on Children*, 1972), and marriage (*A Married Couple*, 1969). Both filmmakers dealt with similar questions from totally different angles. Both use the present as a touchstone but Perrault goes back to the past to show what is being lost, while King concludes that the present is full of absences and there is no past that can be recovered. In *A Married Couple* King exposes the emptiness of the modern world. A suburban couple live their lives out in an endless round of arguments and trivial disagreements. They have surrounded themselves with objects that they do not use. They sense an absence because they are unhappy but conclude that the problem lies not with society but with themselves. They are isolated, from each other, society, other people, a family, and a culture that could sustain their lives. King gives us a damning portrait of modern marriage and by extension the social system that creates and "supports" this convention. There is no past, no future, only an unhappy, frustrated present.

*Pour la suite du monde* is also concerned with the present but its avenue of access is through the past. It turns to a community that is reviving an old fishing hunt which has not been practiced for thirty years. It is a film obsessed with the rituals that define who and what you are, which in effect connect you to your past and your community. This is lovingly shown through community meetings and gatherings, Lent celebrations, Easter rituals, and the construction of the huge trap to ensnare the beautiful beluga whale. If *A Married Couple* shows a nuclear family, *Pour la suite du monde* unravels all the generational links between grandparents, parents, and children on the island, making it into a huge extended family where everyone seems to be either a Harvey or a Tremblay! They have a unique culture that sustains them but they are also threatened by the modern world, jeopardized by the massive boats that steam past their island and which make their little wooden *goélettes*, or schooners, look like vestiges of another century. But Perrault's film tells us that this community and all it represents must be preserved "for those who follow." After watching both films we feel that our present priorities must be rearranged. Perrault offers us an example of what he thinks should endure (and he has been criticized for being a romantic, naive and politically conservative), while King can only unveil the present and offer no equivalent option.

If the groundwork for a fully developed national cinema was being laid in the sixties, then the seventies would consolidate these activities. The decade started auspiciously with two landmark films appearing almost simultaneously: *Goin' Down the Road* (1970) and *My Uncle Antoine* (*Mon oncle Antoine*, 1971). Don Shebib made the leap from documentaries to fiction with a film that blurs the distinction between the two forms, relying on the predominant realist tradition. *Goin' Down the Road*'s tale of two Maritimers who come to the big city hoping to find a better life is a sobering venture that bears comparison to Brault's *Entre la mer et l'eau douce*. Both films treat men from working-class backgrounds leaving economically depressed areas. Claude sets out from a small North Shore village for Montreal with little more than a guitar in his hands, just like the two Maritimers, Pete and Joey, who arrive in Toronto virtually penniless. Claude, and the two Maritimers, lead a hand-to-mouth existence when they arrive in the city, living in shabby little apartments and finding work where and when it is available. They even end up dating waitresses in both films! But the cultural differences that mark the two cinemas are apparent despite their shared mileu and narrative thrust. Claude stays with his brother, cushioning the shock of adjusting to the city, whereas Pete and Joey are turned away from a relative's house and forced to survive on their own. Claude also lives in a house where one of the tenants is highly politicized, and these issues seem to be a part of daily interchange, floating in the wind. There is no equivalent to this in *Goin' Down the Road*.

Both Claude and Pete feel restless with their lives and in their jobs but this is where the films significantly part company. In the anglo-phone film the city is seen as relentlessly insensitive, capable of crushing its weaker members through a web of fate and circumstance. A girlfriend gets pregnant, marriage follows, jobs are lost and an inevitable descent down the social ladder begins. After a succession of humiliating jobs, the two men rob a grocery store, viciously beat up a clerk, and abandon the wife, as they leave town one step ahead of the police. *Entre la mer et l'eau douce* gives one an entirely different sense of the city. It may be cold and impersonal, but it is never malicious. It never intervenes as a character. Jobs are found. Claude may break with his girlfriend but it is not because he is on the run. He enters a music competition, wins first prize and tumbles into an affair with the wife of a television producer. In *Goin' Down the Road* there is a strong, unspoken sense of not really being able to control one's life. Events conspire to defeat these poor victims. The opposite is true of *Entre la mer et l'eau douce*. Claude eventually makes a success of his new music career. He may regret the implications of what he has done, realizing his mistake in abandoning his waitress-lover, but he is free to make these decisions.

The other major film of the period was Claude Jutra's *Mon oncle Antoine*, another coming of age story set in a tiny Quebec mining village, famous for its strike in 1949. It revolves around a young boy, an orphan, living with his uncle and aunt who own a general store. The adult world, with all its hypocrisies, is gradually revealed to him, the final rite of initiation being a sleigh journey he makes with his uncle to pick up a young boy's corpse. All of the boy's illusions are mercilessly stripped away as a result of this trip but this is not seen simply in terms of loss. The final shot of the film conveys confrontation, of facing up to reality and to choices, that is quite different than the escapes we witness at the end of *Nobody Waved Good-bye* and *Goin' Down the Road*.

The overwhelming paralysis of a film like *Goin' Down the Road* is mirrored in the most important anglophone films of these years. Peter Pearson's *Paperback Hero* (1972), Peter Carter's *The Rowdyman* (1972), Don Shebib's *Between Friends* (1973), and Ted Kotcheff's *The Apprenticeship of Duddy Kravitz* (1974), deal with high-spirited men who are beaten down and defeated in a variety of ways. Rick Dillon in *Paperback Hero* is a small-time hockey hero who emulates the antics of a wild-west marshall, before being gunned down by the police after trying to live out his fantasies. His psychic schizophrenia of confused identity is mirrored in *Between Friends*, where a Canadian is still dazzled by a childhood hero, an American surfer, who reenters his life. They plan a robbery so he can go and live in California, the land of his dreams, but the heist gets confused in jealousies and he is killed. *The Rowdyman* features a wild, gregarious, and totally irresponsible boozer whose high jinks lead to the death of his best friend, and the departure of his girlfriend. Even the energetic, young hustler of *The Apprentice-*

(Above)
Don Owens's portrait of
troubled youth in *Nobody
Waved Good-bye* (1964)
has become an enduring
classic.

(Right)
Irvin Kershner's *The Luck
of Ginger Coffey* (1964)
was a tender examination
of the immigrant
experience.

(Right)
In his exploration of a
tumultuous bilingual
relationship, Gilles
Groulx turned *The Cat
in the Bag* (*Le chat dans
le sac*, 1964) into a
landmark of Canadian
cinema.

(Left)
Richard Dreyfuss (r.)
captured the cocky
arrogance of Ted
Kotcheff's protagonist
perfectly in *The
Apprenticeship of Duddy
Kravitz* (1974).

Marilyn Chambers and
Frank Moore before the
motorcycle accident that
will change their lives in
David Cronenberg's
*Rabid* (1976).

Jean Pierre Lefebvre's remarkable career reached an apotheosis with *The Old Country Where Rimbaud Died* (1977).

Jackie Burroughs and Richard Farnsworth as the unlikely couple—an eccentric suffragette and an American train robber—in Phillip Borsos's evocative period piece, *The Grey Fox* (1982).

*ship of Duddy Kravitz* finds himself all alone, abandoned by his lover after his greed has resulted in the crippling of their best friend. One of the most remarkable films of the period was Bill Fruet's *Wedding in White* (1972), an unrelenting story of gloom that sees a young girl raped by a soldier friend of her brother and ends in an arranged marriage to a disgusting drunk old enough to be her father.

It has been noted that many of these films see the world through the eyes of victims, this being common to a colonized mentality,[6] where people do not see themselves as being forceful, energetic, and successful because they are placed in positions where their resources are looted and plundered by foreigners. They do not control their destiny. It is controlled for them by people from elsewhere. Concepts of "here" and "there" are central to this cinema; "here" being somehow inadequate, "there" surrounded with an aura of glamor. But this colonized mentality manifests itself most visibly in its identification with victims and fringe life. Quebec films display a similar fascination with marginality and many of the films are just as concerned with impotency as their anglophone counterparts. They are full of traditional victim figures—prostitutes, Indians, gangsters, or often just women.

In Gilles Carle's *Red* (1969) an Indian half-breed wanders through the contradictions of his life in white society as a small-time car thief, before being gunned down. Denys Arcand's *Dirty Money* (*La maudite galette*, 1972) follows the mechanics of a petty crime, fashioned like a vignette from Zola, before the protagonist, an unimaginative, uninspired, apparently motiveless laborer, is blown away by a woman he thought he had killed. His *Réjeanne Padovani* (1973) is a tautly controlled, brilliantly executed examination of political corruption in high places, that sees the ex-wife of a highway contractor buried in cement because she tries to return and see her children. André Forcier's *Tavern* (*Bar salon*, 1973) is an uncompromising look at the owner of a small bar whose wife flaunts her affair with their lodger, and whose mistress eventually steals his car before he is forced to close his business. Jean Pierre Lefebvre's *Pigs Are Seldom Clean* (*On n'engraisse pas les cochons à l'eau claire*, 1973), *Ultimatum* (1971–73), and *Wounded Love* (*L'amour blessé*, 1975) are deeply pessimistic statements that reflect the despair in Quebec after the October crisis of 1970. The former deals with an enigmatic undercover policeman. Shot as a *film noir*, it depicts a world of double dealings and betrayals and ends in his unexplained death. *L'amour blessé* is a minimalist exercise that confines a woman to her apartment as she listens to "hotline" radio shows. It is a film of darkness and restriction, where mysterious men are engaged in electronic surveillance and fear pervades every frame. *Ultimatum* is also clouded with overtones of death and incarceration, which intrude into an idyllic countryside where a young couple live out their love affair.

While Quebec cinema has continually resisted the aesthetic and the implications of the realist tradition, it has not escaped this influence entirely. Filmmakers like Lefebvre, Arcand, and Carle may wish to challenge and subvert our filmic expectations, but often what some of these films are saying is not that much different from their anglophone counterparts. Love is impossible, people are isolated, society is unfeeling, change is not visible, everyone is trapped and a victim, death is felt everywhere. However, within Quebec, there are many films that manage to transcend this paralysis, often made by the same directors. Lefebvre's *Those Damned Savages* (*Les maudits sauvages*, 1971), a structurally ambitious, historical analysis of Quebec society that plays freely with time, mixing events from 1670 with those of 1970 (its subtitle is, *Almost an historical film!*), uses an Indian squaw and a boorish French-Canadian trapper to unmask our colonial status. The Indian is exploited, by the chief who trades her for cigarettes and alcohol and by the trapper who gets her a job as a stripper. The trapper is also perceived as a victim, of church and state, but the end of the film, a highly mystical and ambiguous joining of hands across historical generations, suggests the need for the present to understand the past so that its mistakes can be avoided. *The Last Betrothal* (*Les dernières fiançailles*, 1973) meticulously records the last days in the life of an elderly couple. A film about death, its final moments dealing with regeneration and resurrection are full of profound joy. His masterly *The Old Country Where Rimbaud Died*, (*Le vieux pays ou Rimbaud est mort*, 1977) follows a man on a visit to France, the country of his ancestors. He finds that he is completely different from his kinsmen, and after a brief affair with a married woman who carries the fatigue of her civilization in her, returns to Quebec to start a new beginning. In *House of Light* (*La chambre blanche*, 1969) we experience the loving reinvention of a new kind of couple.

Gilles Carle's *The Males* (*Les mâles*, 1970), *The True Nature of Bernadette* (*La vraie nature de Bernadette*, 1971), and *Death of a Lumberjack* (*La mort d'un bûcheron*, 1972) are concerned in one way or another with women trying to escape from the clutches of a male world, and in all three films the escape, a form of liberation, is made. This is also central to Denys Arcand's *Gina* (1974), a disturbing depiction of a stripper who is brutally raped by a gang of snowmobilers, but who decides to exact her revenge, wiping out the entire gang in an orgy of bloodletting.

Even *Orders* (*Les ordres*, 1974), Michel Brault's moving account of the imprisonment of five people during the October crisis of 1970, which concentrates on the hapless victims of this event, manages to transcend the paralytic sense of entrapment and constraint that it depicts so well. Finally, as the five are released, there is the acknowledgment that while history cannot be reversed it must be remembered.

The experimentation of *Le chat dans le sac* was pushed even further by Gilles Groulx in *Where Are You?* (*Ou êtes vous donc?*, 1967–69), *Be-*

*tween You and You* (*Entre tu et vous*, 1969), and *24 Hours or More . . .* (*24 heures ou plus . . .*, 1972–76), which are daring statements with revolutionary overtones to them. In the first film the central character, who wanders in a red space to the sounds of the Internationale, taunts the viewer with his final line, "Where are you then, assholes!" *Entre tu et vous* centers around the couple trying to redefine their relationship and asserts that, "the passive life does not exist." *24 heures ou plus . . .* concludes that everything must change in society.

The seventies also witnessed the emergence of an idiosyncratic film-maker who slowly began to establish an international reputation and a cult following for his work. David Cronenberg seems to fall outside the aesthetic mainstream of Canadian cinema, for his films turn away from the dominant realist tradition. While most English-Canadian films scarcely conceal their documentary roots, Cronenberg was far more interested in that which was concealed. If the anglophone filmmaker accepted the Bazinian notion that reality would yield up its truths, Cronenberg displayed no such trust. He looked beyond mere surfaces and in this way shared some of the interests of Quebec cinema.

The Cronenberg world is markedly different from that explored by most of our cinema. In *Shivers* (1975) a parasite is let loose in an apartment building, releasing a wild sexual energy. *Rabid* (1976) sees a skin-graft operation turn a young woman into a blood-sucking vampire who releases a virulent rabies on an unsuspecting population. It remains Cronenberg's most apocalyptic vision. A woman actually gives her thoughts a physical presence in *The Brood* (1979), a nightmarish look at a disintegrating marriage and a child caught between the warring parents, while in *Videodrome* (1983) a sleazy cable-television owner becomes embroiled in an hallucinatory video world. But does Cronenberg manage to escape from the realist thematic? Most of his protagonists are victims, caught within a vicious web of circumstance. While Cronenberg is fascinated by the subconscious, he remains deeply ambivalent when its forces are released. The subconscious does not liberate or emancipate. The Cronenberg project is a deeply ambiguous one, uncertain of moral imperatives, finding a reason behind all action. It offers no answers, leaves us unclear as to what the future will hold, and baffles us at times with its complexities. And finally, for those people who see the subconscious as a realm where dreams of change and resistance are at least felt as a possibility, Cronenberg holds out little optimism. The liberating potential of the horror film is largely bypassed.

There were other anglophone films made at this time that seemed to resist the darker implications of realism, but they tended to be the exception and not the rule. Shebib, whose *Goin' Down the Road* and *Between Friends* displayed a fine understanding of losers, appeared to be trying to work his way out of this with *Second Wind* (1976) and *Heartaches* (1981). The former deals with a stockbroker who decides to take up running which threatens his marriage, while *Heartaches* returns to the terrain of *Goin' Down the Road*, but this time the city is nowhere threatening. The film that did the most to break away from the fatalism of the realist impulse was Richard Benner's exhuberant *Outrageous!* (1977), a film that celebrates marginality and differences. A psychologically disturbed young woman, recently released from hospital, moves into an apartment with a friend, a female impersonator, who is tired of his life as a hairdresser, and decides to follow his fantasies by going to New York to impersonate for a living. This film showed that it was possible to live out one's dream and that change was possible and indeed desirable.

The filmmakers in English-Canada who were most conscious of their aesthetic roots and were determined to confront what this meant turned to the experimental film. All questioned traditional forms of representation and even the status or ontology of the image itself. Michael Snow's meditations on the physical properties of film and its structural conventions in work like *Wavelength* (1967), *Back and Forth* (1969), *One Second in Montreal* (1969), *The Central Region* (*La région centrale*, 1971), *Breakfast/Table Top Dolly* (1972–76), and *Presents* (1981) forces us to confront the actual medium itself. The extended zoom of *Wavelength* is as much a study of that device as it is of narrative expectancy and structure. David Rimmer's films examine the intricacies of representational imagery by utilizing elaborate optical effects in work like *Variations on a Cellophane Wrapper* (1970), *Surfacing on the Thames* (1970), *Watching for the Queen* (1973), and *Bricolage* (1984), while another west coast filmmaker, Al Razutis, is determined to make us look at the psychedelia of modern life in his massive *Amerika* (1972–83). Bruce Elder has progressed beyond the enclosed world of his first films into deeper reflection on the individual, society, and history. His best work—*The Art of Worldly Wisdom* (1979), *1857 (Fool's Gold)* (1981), and *Illuminated Texts* (1983)—derives from an autobiographical impulse that is then extended into an exploration of the tension between the personal and the collective, the individual and society, past and present, creation and destruction.[7]

The majority of filmmakers functioning within the realist tradition presented a view of the world that was fixed and immutable. When they looked at reality, in their documentaries or their fictions, they saw no real possibility of change. It was left to an emerging generation of talented women directors to really begin to transcend the imaginative constraints of the realist aesthetic. A resistance to the forms and models of conventional (some would say patriarchal) cinema is a predominant quality of virtually all the women's cinema made in Canada. Paule Baillargeon and Frédérique Collin's *The Red Kitchen* (*La cuisine rouge*, 1979) is an uncompromising piece of Brechtian filmmaking that examines the differences between the male and female world through an analysis of three contrasting spaces: the bar, the kitchen, and the garden. The film unwinds around a wedding; the men and women split into separate groups, the men stick to their drinking in the bar while the women move from the madness of the kitchen to the paradise of the garden, where their fantasies are given free rein.

Anne Claire Poirier's *A Scream from Silence* (*Mourir à tue-tête*, 1979) mixes documentary and fiction, a film within a film, and moments of theatrical artifice, to uncover the facts and feelings of rape from the point of view of women. The final moment, which functions almost as a call to arms, is anything but passive. Women may be victims but they can also do something about it. Léa Pool's *The Woman in Transit* (*La femme de l'hôtel*, 1984) explores the act of artistic creation, showing a woman filmmaker opening the central character in her film up to the insights provided by a mysterious woman, close to suicide, who is staying at the same hotel as the crew. It is a film of considerable renewal. The major director whose films do not fit this pattern is Micheline Lanctôt. *The Handyman* (*L'homme à tout faire*, 1980) gently circumscribes an affair between a frustrated middle-class housewife and a laborer who comes to renovate her basement. After her fling she returns to the deadening solace of her marriage. *Sonatine* (1984) is a tautly controlled, formally severe film where two young girls, insulated from the outside world by their Sony Walkmans, gradually drift toward a common suicide amidst a world that is too unfeeling to notice their plea for help. If change is not felt or desired within the film itself, *Sonatine* implies that this society must be changed if we are to avoid similar tragedies.

Not surprisingly, the cultural divisions that mark our cinema are also present in the films that have been made by women filmmakers. Mireille Dansereau's *Dream Life* (*La vie rêvée*, 1972) and Joyce Wieland's *The Far Shore* (1976) view the world from the perspective of women who are placed in a position of subject. Dansereau focuses on two young women, one of whom is infatuated with an older man. *Dream Life* is full of fantasy, dream sequences, and nightmares that continually trouble the narrative surface as a series of interruptions. Reality, and by implication conventional narrative, cannot contain or represent the world of women. By the end of the film, the girl sleeps with her dream man and has her illusions destroyed, enabling her to free herself from the notion of an idealist, romantic love. Even though *The Far Shore* is not as formally adventuresome as *Dream Life*, it nevertheless plays with concepts of dreams and desires, at times within the conventions of the silent film. It is a historical film, set in 1919, and portrays the marriage of a Quebec woman to a Toronto businessman (like the relationship in *Le chat dans le sac*, and a number of other films, a microcosm of our cultural and historical reality). Gradually disillusioned, she falls in love with a Toronto painter (a thinly disguised portrait of the famous landscape painter, Tom Thomson) and runs off with him. But their idyll is short-lived as they are killed by the husband's henchman intent on revenge. Both films share the assumption that society as it is presently constituted has no healthy place for women. But *Dream Life* ends in exhilaration as the two women rip down consumer images of women and couples that decorate their walls, in stark contrast to the nihilism of *The Far Shore*.

The feature film has often been beyond the reach of many women, so they have often turned to the short film. Patricia Gruben's *Sifted Evidence* (1982) uses a number of optical devices to reenact the trip a woman makes to Mexico in search of Mayan ruins. She meets a Mexican who takes control of her holiday because of his access to language, leaving her powerless and inept in her dealings. When he tries to sleep with her she resists and this moment is matched by a growing control that she establishes over her formal positioning in the film itself. Finally she is rid of him. Paule Baillergeon's *Anastastie My Darling* (*Anastasie oh ma chérie*, 1977) is one of the most perfectly realized miniatures made in Canada. A woman has just left her husband to set up in her own gaily decorated apartment. Her husband pleads for her return before sending in the police who dress her up like a mannequin in party clothes before taking her off to see a psychiatrist, a man who is obviously close to a breakdown himself. It deftly probes the nature of patriarchal control (husband, police, doctor) that is brought into play to try and reestablish control over an independent woman. The conventions of narrative expectancy created by the device of cross-cutting are scrutinized in Nesya Shapiro's *Passages* (1978), a film that moves back and forth between a woman taxi driver and a male saxophone player. Their paths crisscross many times and their sexual fantasies create a desire in the audience to see them meet, but when they finally literally bump into each other they simply keep moving on. Kay Armatage uses extremely limited images to suggest a sense of denial, and a complex off-screen aural montage to convey the reality of abortion in *Speak Body* (1980). Her *Storytelling* (1983) tries to probe the origins of narrative.

These women consciously deal with filmic practice and its formal strategies. They question the codes of the dominant narrative cinema which has traditionally fixed women in its gaze as object—of love, lust, violence. In their desire to reposition women as subject they have more often than not found themselves constrained by conventions that are not conducive to this repositioning. They have assaulted the unspoken implications of the realist aesthetic and are determined to fashion their own practice. That this often incorporates the use of dreams or fantasies, and optical devices like rear projection, slow motion, matte photography, is further proof of their wish to deconstruct accepted notions of realism.

The last twenty years has been a period of considerable transition at the National Film Board. Undoubtedly it reached the zenith of its creativity in the decade between 1954 and 1964. After the mid-sixties and the demise of the unit system, English production seemed to lose its way, and began to turn in upon itself. Situated in Montreal, it was in many respects a community in exile, and this distance from the society it was meant to reflect began to show in its work. The Challenge for Change program, designed to create a two-way flow of information by letting the subjects speak for themselves, managed to inject much needed vitality into the NFB, and many of the films that came out of this scheme included some of the best work the NFB had ever done. Many of the films were activist and recorded dissent, a return to the original Griersonian social impulse. Yet it was apparent that by the mid-seventies this energy had been expended.

French production, stimulated by the move to Montreal, was always straining at the constraints of the organization. By the early seventies this had spilled over into open confrontation. In 1971, Denys Arcand's documentary on the textile industry, *On est au coton** (1970) was banned by the film commissioner, and a year later a similar fate befell Groulx's *24 heures ou plus . . .*, causing an enormous uproar. This clampdown effectively limited the amount of self-expression allowed the francophone filmmaker, who then turned away from the NFB as a source of work. Jacques Leduc's *Stories of Daily Life (Chronique de la vie quotidienne*, 1977–78) series was a major work, but increasingly the important documentaries were done outside the purview of the NFB. Arthur Lamothe, who had run into problems in the early sixties with *Manouane River Lumberjacks*, embarked on an ambitious series of films that exhaustively depicted the way of life of the Montagnais Indians of Quebec. This eight-film project, *Carcajou and the White Devil (Carcajou et le péril blanc*, 1974–77) was followed by another extensive series, *Land of Man (Terre de l'homme*, 1980).

Pierre Perrault is the one major documentary figure who has stayed at the NFB. His Ile-aux-Coudres trilogy is a classic of the form, and *A Ridiculous Kind of Country! Or Wake Up, My Friends!!! (Un pays sans bons sens! Ou Wake Up, Mes bons amis!!!*, 1970) ranks among the finest Canadian films. His recent work has been less rewarding although *The Shimmering Beast (La bête lumineuse*, 1982) shows he has lost none of his talent.

The Film Board documentary inevitably mirrored the two cultures as well. For the anglophone filmmaker, society was the creation of individuals: artists, politicians, explorers, sportsmen. History consisted of great events—wars, elections, the building of a railway—and was molded by great people. Consequently the portrait film became the perfect expression for this view of society, and the best-known documen-

*An untranslatable French idiom; some of its flavor is captured in "We're Fed Up."

tary filmmaker at the NFB excelled at this mode. In a film like *The Champions* (1978), Don Brittain reduces the historical tensions between English and French in Canada to the level of personalities, and his finest work concentrates on the exceptional individual.

Quebec filmmakers were far more intrigued by the collective and did not view society and history as the creation of the outstanding person. This kind of documentary does not exist in Quebec. They even avoided the historical documentary, a staple of the NFB's production. For them history is not immutable, locatable, or fixed back there in time. It cannot be dealt with objectively because it is as much a part of the present as the past.

The most significant development at the NFB in the last decade has been the formation of Studio D, a women's unit dedicated to making films for and about women. Bonnie Sherr Klein's examination of pornography in *Not a Love Story* (1981) contains some interesting paradoxes. It focuses on the individual as a point of access: a Montreal stripper becomes our guide into the subterranean world of strip-clubs, peep shows, and porno films. Gradually, we realize that the film is as much about her growing decision to abandon stripping as it is about the wider issue of pornography. Despite its moralizing and reductionist view of a complex problem, Klein has managed partially to work her way out of the realist bind by showing a person who can change her life. The Studio D films in general have a bite and an edge that place them at the forefront of contemporary NFB production.

Documentary filmmaking in the private sector was grappling with similar problems. Laura Sky's *Moving Mountains* (1979) and *All of our Lives* (1984) examined issues of concern to women in a collective manner that also managed to be celebratory at the same time. This is also true of Janis Cole's and Holly Dale's films: *Hookers on Davie* (1984) showed that they had moved beyond the prisons they had documented so well in *P4W—Prison For Women* (1981). Ron Mann's documentaries —*Imagine the Sound* (1981), *Poetry in Motion* (1982), and *Echoes Without Saying*(1983)—eschewed the portrait film in favor of statements that showed a number of artists engaged in the avant-garde of their art: jazz, poetry, or literature.

While the country's filmmakers mirrored the national pysche, the mandarins were grappling with some of the structural problems of an emerging, underdeveloped cinema. By the mid-seventies the CFDC had been around for almost a decade but many questioned the tangible results of its policies. There had been no major commercial successes. A number of low-budget films held out great promise for their directors but the CFDC had not been established as a grant-giving organization. It was expected to invest money, recoup its investment, and then reinvest in other projects. This simply was not happening. The majority of films never returned a cent to the CFDC. Public pressure mounted. In this climate the CFDC began to explore the possibility of coproductions, especially with France. None of the films that came out of this initiative, except for Lefebvre's *The Old Country Where Rimbaud Died*, which didn't make any money, can really be considered a success. They certainly did not result in any financial breakthroughs. A new tack was tried. In 1975 the government passed a law allowing investors to deduct their total investment in the production of feature films for tax purposes. The era of the tax shelter had begun and it would radically alter the production scene for the next decade.

In the absence of a decision to impose quotas or levies the government had to look to other ways of stimulating domestic production. When the proposal to levy a 10 percent tax on American distributors' gross rental revenue was rejected in 1978, other devices had to be found. The Capital Cost Allowance (CCA) program offered a tax write off to investors of 100 percent. The CCA was designed to create an industrial situation conducive to film investment and to manufacture films that would be competitive in the international marketplace. At the same time, important changes were made at the CFDC. Michael Spencer, who had run the corporation since 1967, a man sensitive to cultural as well as commercial imperatives, was replaced by Michael McCabe, whose mandate was obviously to gear up the industry. McCabe had an enormous impact in a very short space of time. He came up with an ingenious scheme to stretch the annual $4 million CFDC budget by not tying it down to actual production financing, but instead rolling it over countless times to provide crucial preproduction bridge financing. The CFDC were now first in and first out, helping productions get started before moving on, and McCabe managed to multiply the impact of his money significantly.

The effect was almost immediate as the following table (taken from CFDC annual reports) indicates:

| ANNUAL YEAR | TOTAL PRODUCTION BUDGETS ($ million) | NUMBER OF FEATURE FILMS PRODUCED |
|---|---|---|
| 1977 | 19 | 29 |
| 1978 | 63 | 17 |
| 1979 | 150 | 70 |
| 1980 | 165 | 50 |
| 1981 | 85 | 37 |
| 1982 | 35 | 17 |
| 1983 | 100 | 34 |
| 1984 | 71 | 27 |

This table becomes even more interesting if figures for the previous decade are included. On the average we produced about twenty-eight theatrical features a year over this period, and combined domestic production budgets *for the decade* ran to about $100 million, or in other words about $10 million per year. As the CFDC pointed out, the combined budgets of the 220 films they had invested in between 1967 and 1977 was $60 million (about $6 million per year), whereas in 1979 alone the organization invested in films with a combined budget of $107 million!

There was a price to be paid for all of this. Production in Quebec virtually withered away and is only now slowly being resurrected; the directors who had burst onto the scene in the sixties were perceived as noncommercial, and consequently McCabe elevated the producer to the position of key creative person; and the independent Canadian distributors, who of course hoped to distribute all of these expensive movies, were ignored in favor of the U.S. majors, creating a crisis of some proportion that many companies did not weather. The need to generate an echelon of competent producers was laudable but the intention never met expectations. Canadian producers and investors went for the deal and the quality of the film itself was ignored. Key creative people— directors, stars, cinematographers, script writers—were imported to make these films, bypassing a generation of indigenous talent. But the most damning indictment was that the films produced through the CCA never accomplished what they had been designed to do: make money. In fact the opposite was true. Many of them were so bad that they were never released. The idea of importing foreign "names" to guarantee market access turned out to be a gigantic mistake. Many films were Canadian in name only. They specifically disguised their locations—license plates were switched, Canadian money was replaced by American money on the screen, and the American flag flew everywhere. Cultural schizophrenia was the order of the day and Quebec directors began to make films in English just so they could continue to practice their craft.

As the figures show, the boom was short-lived. Full employment was followed by massive underemployment. Sensing that another crisis was near the government again stepped into the breach, announcing the creation of the Broadcast Program Development Fund in June 1983. This fund, administered by the CFDC, put aside $175 million for film investment over a five-year period. The creation of the Broadcast Fund implicitly acknowledged that the battle for sovereignty over our own theatrical market had been lost. Television was perceived as the new battleground. Appropriately, the CFDC changed its name to Telefilm Canada. Television was now the tail that would wag the dog. The fund can only be drawn on if a producer raises a third of his budget from the private sector and another third from a broadcaster who would then guarantee a playdate. Only if the broadcaster decides that the film is worthy of investment will it get made. It is still far too early to measure the impact of the Broadcast Fund but it is already having repercussions. Productions are now a hybrid, spawning both a theatrical feature and a television mini-series.

In spite of the CCA years that almost systematically erased anything Canadian from the screen, low-budget, independent production continued to produce interesting work in a beleaguered and fragmented way. Most of it reflected the dark mood that had beset part of the independent production sector, and its concerns and themes were rooted in the dominant aesthetic tradition. Allan Moyle's *The Rubber Gun* (1977), Zale Dalen's *Skip Tracer* (1977), Francis Mankiewicz's *Good Riddance* (*Les bons débarras*, 1979), and Clay Borris's *Alligator Shoes* (1981) are all gritty, uncompromising looks at the underbelly of society. Mireille Dansereau's *Heart Break* (*L'arrache coeur*, 1979), Lefebvre's *To Be Sixteen* (*Avoir 16 ans*, 1979), and Micheline Lanctôt's *The Handyman* shift the focus to the problems of the middle class but are finally no less bleak. Nevertheless, a number of fine films did reflect a sense of renewal and hope. André Blanchard's *Blue Winter* (*L'hiver bleu*, 1979) pointed the way toward political commitment, while Zale Dalen's *The Hounds of Notre Dame* (1980) celebrated the notion of community by looking at a Catholic boarding school on the prairies in the forties. Lefebvre elegantly fashioned a poem to the countryside and the family in *Wild Flowers* (*Les fleurs sauvages*, 1982) and Bill MacGillivray's *Stations* (1983) suggested that a return to one's roots was a return to all that was valuable.

Canadian filmmakers never turned to historical subjects for inspiration, unlike the Australians, until quite recently. Many of these films also used literary sources for their inspiration: *Who Has Seen the Wind* (Allan King, 1977), *Why Shoot the Teacher* (Silvio Narizzano, 1976), *Kamouraska* (Claude Jutra, 1973), *The Plouffes* (*Les Plouffe*, Gilles Carle, 1981), *Maria Chapdelaine* (Gilles Carle, 1983), *The Wars* (Robin Phillips, 1983), *The Tin Flute* (*Bonheur d'occasion*, Claude Fournier, 1983), *Two Solitudes* (Lionel Chetwynd, 1978), and *The Crime of Ovide Plouffe* (*Le crime d'Ovide Plouffe*, Denys Arcand, 1984). But the two acknowledged classics were both made from original screenplays, and instead of differences we are drawn toward their common bases. Jean Beaudin's *J. A. Martin Photographer* (*J. A. Martin photographe*, 1976) and Philip Borsos's *The Grey Fox* (1982) both focus on the couple. Beaudin's film follows a wife who decides to accompany her husband on his annual business trip through the Quebec countryside. It depicts a marriage in crisis that is regenerated and reaffirmed through the shared experiences on the trip.

*The Grey Fox* deals with an oddly mismatched couple—an American train robber who drifts up into Canada and an eccentric suffragette. Borsos lovingly situates his characters against a stunning mountain landscape, and reflects on a couple that is threatened by the Royal Canadian Mounted Police and a Pinkerton detective. The magical union that ends *J. A. Martin Photographer*, as husband and wife fall into the marital bed, is matched by an upbeat ending that we do not see, but which is broadly hinted at, in *The Grey Fox*. These two period pieces point toward another way out of the realist dilemma. By situating their subjects in the past where fiction holds sway, the documentary impulse is completely undermined.

In retrospect this becomes an important distinction when approaching the Canadian cinema. On the whole the documentary is by its very nature passive. It records and observes, and it is surrounded by ethical notions of remaining true to reality, that which is filmed. This has resulted in a detached, observational cinema, content to accept what is observed without insisting that it be changed. Quebec filmmakers immediately saw the limitations inherent in the "objective" documentary because they wanted to radically alter the reality that they saw before them. The same is true of feminist filmmakers. This is why both turned so quickly to the fictive mode; its possibilities allow for the self-expression of persons desperate to communicate their vision of the world. If documentarians allow others to speak for them, filmmakers who work within the fictional mode are convinced that their personal voices are of great importance. This is a necessary arrogance that by and large has escaped the English-Canadian filmmaker.

## NOTES

1. See Kirwan Cox, "Hollywood's Empire in Canada," *Self Portrait: Essays on the Canadian and Quebec Cinemas* (Ottawa: Canadian Film Institute, 1980), for more detail on the American stranglehold over Canadian exhibition and distribution sectors.
2. Peter Harcourt, "The Innocent Eye: An Aspect of the Work of the National Film Board of Canada," *Sight and Sound* 34, no. 1 (Winter 1964–65). Also reprinted in *Canadian Film Reader*, ed. Seth Feldman and Joyce Nelson (Toronto: Peter Martin Associates, 1977). See also Bruce Elder, "On the Candid Eye Movement," in *Canadian Film Reader*.
3. See David Clandfield, "From the Picturesque to the Familiar: Films of the French Unit at the NFB, 1958–1964," *Cine-Tracts* 4 (Spring–Summer 1978). Also reprinted in *Take Two*, ed. Seth Feldman (Toronto: Irwin Publishing, 1984).
4. For more information on the Canadian Cooperation Project, see Pierre Berton, *Hollywood's Canada—The Americanization of Our National Image* (Toronto: McClelland and Stewart, 1975), pp. 169–175; and Maynard Collins, "Cooperation, Hollywood and Howe," *Cinema Canada* 56 (June–July 1979).

5. See Peter Harcourt, "1964: The Beginning of a Beginning," *Self Portrait*.
6. See Margaret Atwood, *Survival* (Toronto: Anansi, 1972).
7. For a more detailed examination of the concerns of the Canadian experimental film see Bruce Elder, "Image: Representation and Object. The Photographic Image in Canadian Avant-Garde Film," *Take Two*.

## SELECTED BIBLIOGRAPHY

Barrowclough, Susan, ed. *Jean Pierre Lefebvre: The Quebec Connection*. London: British Film Institute, 1981.

Bérubé, Renald, and Yvan Patry. *Jean Pierre Lefebvre*. Montreal: Les Presses de l'Université du Québec, 1971.

Brûlé, Michel. *Pierre Perrault ou le cinéma national*. Montreal: Les Presses de l'Université de Montréal, 1974.

Drew, Wayne, ed. *David Cronenberg*. London: British Film Institute, 1984.

Feldman, Seth, ed. *Take Two*. Toronto: Irwin Publishing, 1984.

Feldman, Seth and Joyce Nelson, eds. *Canadian Film Reader*. Toronto: Peter Martin Associates, 1977.

Handling, Piers. *The Films of Don Shebib*. Ottawa: Canadian Film Institute, 1978.

Handling, Piers, ed. *The Shape of Rage: The Films of David Cronenberg*. Toronto: General Publishing, 1983.

Harcourt, Peter. *Jean Pierre Lefebvre*. Ottawa: Canadian Film Institute, 1981.

Hardy, Forsyth. *John Grierson—A Documentary Biography*. London and Boston: Faber and Faber, 1979.

James, C. Rodney. *Film as a National Art: NFB of Canada and the Film Board Idea*. New York: Arno Press, 1977.

Jones, D. B. *Movies and Memoranda: An Interpretative History of the National Film Board of Canada*. Ottawa: Canadian Film Institute and Deneau Publishers, 1981.

Morris, Peter. *Embattled Shadows: A History of Canadian Cinema 1895–1939*. Montreal: McGill-Queen's University Press, 1978.

Véronneau, Pierre. *Cinéma de l'époque Duplessiste*. Montreal: La cinémathèque québécoise, 1979.

———. *Le succès est au film parlant français*. Montreal: La cinémathèque québécoise, 1979.

—— and Piers Handling, eds. *Self Portrait: Essays on the Canadian and Quebec Cinemas*. Ottawa: Canadian Film Institute, 1980.

# CHINA

## ESTHER YAU

Michel Foucault prefaced *The Order of Things* with Borges's exotic view of ancient China, an Other and older civilization highly inscrutable to Western eyes. China in modern times still has the unique integration of disparate entities that fascinated Borges and Foucault. Indeed, a very interesting characteristic of Chinese cinema is the blending together of imported traditions and styles from both Hollywood and Europe with China's own rich literary and theatrical heritage. The pan-Chinese cinema is, furthermore, being produced separately by the world's two most different economic systems, the capitalist and the socialist. Although a recent, perhaps unifying, change in the economic setup of the film industry has begun to take shape, it is still hard to imagine when the pan-Chinese cinema will ever arrive at a stage approximating classical Hollywood homogeneity in modes of production and in the kinds of narratives produced. Hence Chinese cinema offers an interesting case for the study of the relationships between culture and film, and ideology and narrative. This brief account of the last forty years of Chinese cinema will offer a glimpse of how political and ideological changes in China have affected its three cinemas (Chinese Mainland, Hong Kong, and Taiwan).

## Chinese Cinema before 1949

Films were imported into China by European and American businessmen at the end of the nineteenth century. These moving pictures immediately caught the Chinese imagination with their blend of technological novelty and familiar theatricality, and they were fondly called "ying she" or "shadow play." During the first decade of the twentieth century, the Chinese urban moviegoing audience devoured thousands of imported silents from France, the United States, Germany, and England; they learned Western adventures and romances from Chinese "picture-decipherers" who explained the silent spectacles and elaborated on the narratives by citing local idioms.

The indigenous Chinese cinema was started in 1905 with a "filmed theater" called *Ding Jun Mountain* (*Ding jun shan*). In 1913 the first story feature, entitled *The Suffering Couple* (*Nan fu nan qi*), inaugurated the genre of Chinese family melodrama that always contained a mild criticism of traditional feudalism. Between 1910 and 1945 Chinese cinema became a full-grown industry, with studios situated mainly in the large cities along the eastern coast. In Shanghai especially, the influx of trading corporations and opportunists had spurred business in all its aspects, and novice film producers and exhibitors soon learned how to make fast money on this burgeoning entertainment medium that had begun to capture the imagination of the emerging urban bourgeoisie. In the 1920s and 1930s tabloids dealing with films appeared in Shanghai, and sensational stories of stars from both the West and the East became leisure-class gossip. Hollywood-made movies soon predominated in early Chinese cinema, and famous Hollywood figures like Chaplin and Garbo became widely recognized. The early Chinese film industry seemed to be indifferent to the fact that, ever since the mid-1840s, China under Manchurian rule had suffered from unfair treaties imposed on her by nations that had recognized her military weakness, and Chinese films were generally of an escapist rather than a social-realist nature.

In the late 1910s, a literary revolution known as the May Fourth movement was instigated by intellectuals eager to improve the national condition by introducing science and democracy from the West; in this climate, literature and theater became important outlets calling for reformation. This elevating of social and political consciousness did not, however, have much influence on the film industry, which was still profiting from stories of romance and trivia. Sound film came to China in 1929, and by 1931 small studios were experimenting with sound productions. In Shanghai many short-lived companies attempted to make a quick profit with cheap productions; nevertheless, emerging major film production companies (including Ming Xing, Shanghai Yingshe, Xin Ya, Da Zong Hua, and Tien Yi) began to increase their concern with narrative technique and the aesthetic quality of films as well. With the formation of the Luan Hua Studio in 1930, artistic interest became an important agenda for aspiring young directors. Both *The Fisherman's Song* (*Yu guang qu*, 1933), directed by Cai Chusheng of the Luan Hua Studio, and *Twin Sisters* (*Zi mei hua*), directed by Zheng Jingqiu of the Ming Xing Studio, were selected to represent China in the Russian Film Festival of 1934. In general, by the end of the 1930s a film style developed that was an amalgam of imported film narrative techniques, local theatrical performing styles, and story forms of contemporary popular literature.

The Japanese invasion of China during the 1930s and the takeover of Shanghai in 1936 had significant effects both on the industrial and narrative aspects of the Chinese cinema. Japanese bombings and military aggression from the northeast induced the southern migration of the film industry, both to Hong Kong (a British Colony since 1842 under the Treaty of Nanking) as well as to southeast Asia, especially Singapore and Malaysia. During the fall of Shanghai, Hong Kong became the production base for anti-Japanese films, and remained so until the British Colony also fell under Japanese occupation in 1941. The Japanese then took control of film production by organizing the seventy or so small production companies into the Hong Kong Motion Picture Association. Film production was severely affected during wartime and by the aftermath. In particular, the inland migration of the urban population caused temporary evacuation of the cities and a sharp decline in the moviegoing audience.

Beginning with the mid-1930s, a number of important films began to deal with social reality: *The Fisherman's Song* (*Yu quang qu*, 1933) depicted two young fishermen's vicissitudes in prewar Shanghai; *Highway* (*Da lu*, 1934), directed by Sun Yu, incorporated documentary footage in its narration of national sufferings; *Street Angel* (*Ma lu tian shi*, 1937), directed by Yuan Muzhi, and *Crossroads* (*Shi zi jie tou*, 1937) by Shen Xilin called attention to the wasted lives of the young, victimized by a society itself under military and economic stresses. A certain neorealist style accompanied narratives of wartime sufferings, and films produced during this period were marked by a more unified style and subject matter.

When film production fully resumed after the Japanese defeat, two wartime epics became important classics of the 1940s. The best-known, *Spring River Flows East* (*Yi jiang chun shui xiang dong liu*, 1947), written and directed by Cai Chusheng and Zheng Junli, was a Chinese *Gone with the Wind*. Its story of the disintegration of a Chinese family during and after the Japanese invasion plucked at the heartstrings of many who had undergone a similar tragedy themselves, and it remained the most popular, domestic film for a long time. *Eighty Thousand Miles of Clouds and the Moon* (*Ba qian li lu yun he yue*, 1947), written and directed by Shi Dongshan, surveyed the national trauma during wartime through the perspective of a traveling theater group. Throughout the 1940s, the baptism of war had made social criticism and the depiction of human tragedies two consistent subject matters for film, marking a distinct contrast with the romance and trivia of the 1920s and early 1930s. With the onset of the Left-Wing Film movement in the late 1930s, the earlier modes of pure fantasy and sensationalism gradually dissolved into increased moral and political edification. Yet before socialism staked out its claims in China, radical films produced by left-wing sympathizers were heavily censored by the Kuomintang Government on the grounds of political subversion. Even though the Left-Wing Film movement already had a studio base in Yanan in the West, the political and industrial transformation of Chinese cinema in the eastern cities did not take place until after 1949.

## Chinese Cinema after 1949

With the founding of the People's Republic of China and the migration of the Kuomintang Government to Taiwan after 1949, Chinese cinema became separated into three different entities, distinguished primarily by the political regions of the Chinese Mainland, Hong Kong, and Taiwan. Unified by a similar cultural and literary heritage, the three Chinese cinemas undertook different paths, each with its own unique economic infrastructure, aesthetic development, and history. The subsequent divergence of the pan-Chinese cinema resulting from the socialist transformation of the Chinese Mainland has become a prime example of the diverse ways in which art and ideology function under capitalism and under socialism. An historical study of the successes and failures of these three cinemas in political and economic terms should offer enlightenment to any utopian formulation about ideology and culture.

## Mainland Chinese Cinema: 1949-1985

The history of cinema on the Chinese Mainland after 1949 could be largely divided into three distinct spans marked by an anomalous ten-year period of Cultural Revolution. The pre-Cultural Revolution cinema from 1949 to 1966 could be characterized by adjustments made by the film industry to new socialist standards, with film narratives conforming to requirements that arose from national projects and political movements. The ten years of Cultural Revolution, which lasted from 1966 to 1976, brought extensive disruption to all aspects of social and cultural life. Subsequently, film production was virtually stopped for three years as the result of an extremely critical and arbitrary political censorship of films coupled with the deportation of film professionals to the countryside. The post-Cultural Revolution cinema after 1976 showed that a more sophisticated relationship between the film industry and the Party had developed. In the context of modernizing China, a more relaxed policy toward art and literature spurred increasing attempts at eclectic subject matters and styles, and the onset of national television in the early 1980s added more competitive pressure to film production. Largely speaking, the thirty-six-year history of the development of cinema on the Chinese Mainland has been an account of the vying between politics and art.

After 1949, the film industry on the Chinese Mainland fell directly under the purview of the Film Bureau of the Minister of Culture. Cinema had been enlisted as an important tool for mass movements during the earlier years of socialist revolution; hence, after 1949, the Party undertook to construct and finance a national film base, which involved converting all private film-production facilities into state operation. In the context of the socialist reconstruction of "feudal and imperialist" China, the Party and State abolished commercial film production and financed the industry for full technological independence from foreign (except Soviet) assistance. Ten major studios were built in the major cities all over China: in Beijing, the Beijing Film Studio and the August First Film Studio; in the northeast, the Changchun Studio; in the west, the Xian, Tian Shan, Inner Mongolia, and the Emei Studios; and in the south, the Guangxi, Xiaoxiang, and the Pearl River Studios. All of the new studios were state financed, and steady increases in production output were planned. By 1958, this phase of studio construction was completed.

The State also undertook to set up more exhibition units for the masses. Consequently, from 646 theaters in 1949, exhibition units increased up to 20,363 in 1966, with half of these units located in the countryside for the sake of entertaining the peasant audience. Meanwhile, a central distribution operation was set up to arrange for prints of each studio production warranting national distribution. In this manner, the production, distribution, and exhibition of films on the Chinese Mainland became free of commercial influence, and were primarily regulated by the Party and the State.

Within the first few years after 1949, it became clear to the film studios that Chinese cinema, like other art and literary media in socialist China, had been assigned the role of assisting the transition of Chinese society to a socialist state. Under Party imperatives, films (called "Gong Nong Bing Dianying"), were made for the masses, that is, for the workers, peasants, and soldiers. While more serious genres, such as adaptations of May Fourth literary classics or historical adaptations, were added, most narratives did away with any traces of "romance and trivia" that belonged to the "mandarin ducks and butterfly school." In almost all of the productions, whether family melodramas, opera films, espionage films, or adaptations, the dual purposes of preaching to the peasants and to the less-educated masses as well as instilling the socialist world view became the chief aim, replacing commercial constraints and competition. As film messages were given prime attention, experimentation with styles came to be of lesser significance. It was suggested that films should achieve the socialist aesthetic ideal, which combined "revolutionary realism" and "revolutionary romanticism"; however, this area was never too clearly defined. Even though the emerging fourth generation of filmmakers had some problems aligning their aesthetic criteria fully with Party requirements, films began to show simpler plot development and characterization.

From 1949 to 1950, the Northeast Studio (precursor of the Changchun Studio) produced about eighteen films to celebrate the triumph of the socialist revolution, setting the narrative paradigm and tone for the new revolutionary cinema. These films were straightforward and upbeat, the more notable examples including *Boundless Light* (*Guang mang wan zhang*, 1949) directed by Xu Ke, *Daughters of China* (*Zhong hua nu er*, 1949) by Ling Zifeng and Zhai Qiang, *White-Coated Fighter* (*Bai yi zhan shi*, 1949) by Feng Bolu, *Zhao Yi Man* (*Zhao yi man*, 1950) by Sha Meng, and *The White-Haired Girl* (*Bai mao nu*, 1950) by Wang Bin and Shui Hua. In these film narratives, the appearance of the Red Army always signified for the peasants and the proletariat their liberation from oppressive forces in pre-1949 China, and 1949, the year of the socialist takeover, was always the departure line for Chinese history. Character types also emerged from these narratives and became stabilized: the sympathetic peasants, the exploitative landlords, the courageous Red Army, and the corrupt Kuomintang officials filled stock situations about revolutionary success. Under the imperative of an unambiguous extolment of socialism, stories uniformly ended on a positive note with all problems resolved and all loose ends tied,

From 1949 to 1956, newly built studios were steadily producing films that dealt with the theme of new life in the New China. It was quite obvious by then that in the socialist state, Party politics became the leading factor in shaping the development of cinema, subjugating the autonomy of the studios, filmmakers, and audience to national economic plans and political movements. Yet the extent of the implication of cinema in the various phases of these political movements and the subsequent impact on films could not be accurately gauged by either the Party or the filmmakers until it was placed into perspective by the historical circumstances that followed.

From 1956 to 1957, the Hundred Flowers movement was introduced by the Party to invite public criticism of existing weaknesses in her leadership and administration. In such a climate of openness, Lu Ban's *Before the New Director Arrives* (*Xin ju zhang dao lai zhi qian*, 1956) was made. This film carried a mild criticism of cadres, and risked the Party's rebuttal considering the latter's relentless campaign against Sun Yu's *The Life of Wu Xun* (*Wu Xun zhuan*, 1950) four to five years earlier. Chairman Mao promoted the movement to "Let a Hundred Schools of Thought Contend," and the Party encouraged a greater variety of approaches in art and literature in 1956. Subsequently, more "bourgeois-type" adaptations of May Fourth classics that were also more aesthetically oriented were produced, including Sang Hu's *The New Year's Sacrifice* (*Zhu fu*, 1956) and Chen Xihe's *Family* (*Jia*, 1956). The attack on the evils of feudalism in these May Fourth novellas justified the adaptation efforts; nevertheless, new scenes were added to ensure that conflicts between the oppressors and the oppressed were made explicit to the masses.

It appeared that filmmakers who prized their May Fourth heritage found better opportunity in 1956, and a request for more artistic autonomy was voiced. The Russian Zhandovist way of imparting political education through films had been adapted more or less by filmmakers working under the strict revolutionary tradition of Yanan, and was largely continued in major productions after 1949. But in 1956 it was also clear that such a tradition had not been unanimously adopted or accepted, and that there were still some filmmakers who desired art above all else. In 1957, the Anti-Rightist movement hit the film circle, and outspoken filmmakers and actors were ostracized for their "petit-bourgeois" and "antirevolutionary" sentiments. Lu Ban's *Before the New Director Arrives* became a problematic piece, and innocent works like Sun Yu's *Braving Winds and Waves* (*Cheng feng po lang*, 1957) were also cited for criticism. By the end of the Anti-Rightist movement, filmmakers determined that politically sound productions were important for their own good, and they began to exercise their own political judgment in selecting film scripts.

In the two years following the Anti-Rightist movement, two major developments restored the morale of film professionals who had experienced internal uncertainty in political and artistic inclinations. In 1958, the national Great Leap Forward was aimed at stepping up national economic output. In response to the Party's call for a production increase, 229 features and animation films were made during the years 1958 and 1959. In order to create a statistical miracle, studios reduced production budgets and shortened schedules to increase output. Even though a great number of these films had simple stories and straightforward characterization, the psychological freeze that accompanied the Anti-Rightist movement was partially thawed by the Party's encouragement to higher production. A typical case of studio conversion during the Great Leap Forward was the Shanghai Film Studio, which had branched into three smaller studios (Jiangnan, Haiyan, and Tianma) in 1958, and which produced fifty-two features in 1958 and twenty-seven in 1959. Films made during the year were invariably devoted to the subject matter of modernized production; typical examples were Lu Ren's *Steel Man and Iron Horse* (*Gang ren tie ma*, 1958), Zhao Ming's *Loving the Factory as One's Home* (*Ai chang ru jia*, 1958), and *Small Episodes in Gigantic Waves* (*Da feng lang li di xiao gu shi*, 1958). The greater homogeneity and simplicity of films made in 1958 resulted from quota-oriented production. In 1959 failure of the Great Leap Forward productions spurred ambition for better quality works. Thus, in the same year, when the occasion of the tenth anniversary of the People's Republic of China encouraged better productions, Zheng Junli's *Lin Zexu (Lin Zexu*, 1959), Shui Hua's *The Lin Family Shop (Lin jia pu zi*, 1959) and Cui Wei and Chen Huaiai's *Song of Youth (Qing chun zhi ge*, 1959) stood out as successful works of art.

From 1959 to 1964, the film industry experienced less interference from political movements. Further, after a decade of attempts, the socialist Chinese cinema had reached a stage in which politics and art were integrated with more sophistication. The third and fourth generation of filmmakers had learned to come to terms with the dual roles of their cinema, and some devoted themselves to work out a national socialist film aesthetic. Apparently, during this period the filmmakers' artistic aspirations and the audience's interest were better acknowledged both by the Party and the studios themselves, and many of the films produced gained popular reception. Shui Hua's *Revolutionary Family (Ge ming jia ting*, 1960), Ling Zifeng's *Red Flag Chronicle (Hong qi pu*, 1960) and Xie Jin's *The Red Detachment of Women (Hong se niang zi jun*, 1960) fulfilled Party expectations with themes of class struggle, and at the same time were stylistically interesting. As China struggled to be independent of Russian aid in the early 1960s, historical dramas set in pre-1949 China were produced with themes of patriotism, and Zheng Junli's *Lin Zexu* (1959) and Lin Nong's *Naval Battle of 1894 (Jia wu feng yun*, 1962) were two stylistically interesting works that dramatized the imperialist wars at the turn of the twentieth century. In particular, the subtle use of visual imagery in *Lin Zexu* was a cinematic realization of Chinese poetry, and this film remains a masterpiece of the period.

With the revival of interest in the Chinese historical and cultural past in the early 1960s, four sizable adaptations from operas were filmed, each with its unique appeal: Su Li's *Third Sister Liu (Liu san jie*, 1960) is popular due to hilarious folk tunes sung by a vividly portrayed woman; Cui Wei and Chen Huaiai's *Women Generals of the Yang Family (Yang men nu jiang*, 1960) and *Wild Boar Forest (Ye zhe lin*, 1962) celebrated nationalism with well-known narratives of familial and political intrigues, and Cen Fan's *Dream of the Red Chamber (Hong liu meng*, 1962), co-produced with the Hong Kong Golden Sound Motion Picture Corporation, was an elaborate operatic spectacle of the famous literary classic. Of the May Fourth adaptations, *Early Spring in February (Zao chun er yue*, 1963) directed by Xie Tieli and adapted from a novella by Rou Shei, dealt with emotional entanglements, with an open story ending unusual to most Chinese films of that time.

After a decade or so of serious political edification, more lighthearted efforts were found to also be viable in depicting life in new China. Comedies such as Xie Jin's *Fat Li, Young Li and Old Li (Da Li, xiao Li he lao Li*, 1962), Lu Jen's *Li Shuang Shuang (Li Shuang Shuang*, 1962) and Yen Gong's *Satisfied or Not (Man yi be man yi*, 1963) treated the problems of contemporary Chinese life with humorous touches. Films that dealt with minority groups in China, like Wang Jiayi's *Five Golden Flowers (Wu duo jin hua*, 1959) and *Daji and Her Father (Da Ji he ta de fu qin*, 1961), and Liu Qiong's *Ashma (A Shi Ma*, 1964) foregrounded the subject matter of romance and love, which had been regarded as less important in the revolutionary dialects. Together, the films of this period displayed a more mature integration of art, socialist world view, and Chinese culture and society. A number of promising directors began to emerge in the early 1960s, succeeding earlier masters like Sun Yu and Zheng Jinli. The younger directors grew up during Chinese social and political transformations and were witnesses both to the old and the new Chinese society; they contributed much to the more harmonious integration of the different traditions and requirements. Among these directors were Shui Hua, Ling Zifeng, Xie Tieli, and Xie Jin. Xie Jin turned out to be an auteur director who was also a master in screen treatment of women, and his *Stage Sisters (Wu tai jie mei*, 1965) was a finely crafted character study of two female opera singers. In 1962 the first Hundred Flowers Award was set up to enable audiences to vote for their favorite films, and *Li Shuang Shuang* was nominated as the Best Film of the Year. Unfortunately, the second Award that was held a year later turned out to be the last one before the Cultural Revolution, which caused the suspension of popular voting for films for about thirteen years.

From 1966 to 1976, the political upheaval of the Cultural Revolution, provoked by factions in the Party, caused disruption to every social institution in China. The film industry suffered a major blow, with filmmakers dispatched to the countryside to learn from the peasants, and all except a few films produced previously were labeled "poisonous weeds" and withdrawn from circulation. From 1967 to 1969, feature film production virtually stopped, and was only partly resumed when amateurs and the remaining unindicted few were called in by the "Gang of Four" to film stage operas in 1970. The subsequent productions, called "Geming Yangbanxi" or "revolutionary model operas," were glaring socialist agit-prop that took on a militant approach to culture and society consistent with ultraleft tendencies. Some of these productions were: *Taking Tiger Mountain by Strategy (Zhi qu wei hu shan*, 1970), directed by Xie Tieli, *The Red Lantern (Hong deng ji*, 1970), by Cheng Yin, *The White-Haired Girl (Bai mao nu*, 1970), by Sang Hu, and *The Red Detachment of Women (Hong se niang zi jun*, 1971), by Pan Wenzhan and Fu Jie, the latter two being stage opera versions of two films of similar titles made before 1966. Together with opera films such as Xie Tieli and Xie Jin's *The Harbor (Haigang*, 1972) and Xie Tieli's

*Eulogy of the Dragon River* (*Long jiang song*, 1972), these productions formed a genre of their own, characterized by stylized dances and acrobatic performances differentiating good from bad character types without any ambiguities, and often accompanied by grand symphonic music celebrating the triumph of revolution in the end. Toward the latter half of this decade of political extremity, feature film production resumed slowly but steadily, and more and more film professionals were brought back from cadre schools and countryside camps. Between 1973 and 1976, more than eighty films were made, with Changchun, Beijing, and Shanghai Studios bearing most of the productive load. Many opera films based on folklore were made for their safe, nonpolitical quality, yet a good number of them remained unreleased. In spite of the poor entertainment value of the repetitively shown model operas, audiences still attended the theaters and exhibition units for whatever was available, either on a mandatory basis, or because of the dearth of alternatives during this period. In other words, Chinese cinema of that time was completely subjugated to political control, and had little relationship with actual social life or the audience's interest.

Post-Cultural Revolution cinema was gradually rejuvenated after 1978, when filmmakers and screenwriters were largely rehabilitated for work. A policy of relaxation (or "fang") was administered by the Party to art and literature, and other factors of influence set in. The ten years' experience of political persecution and arbitrary censorship nevertheless had some positive effects: filmmakers were extremely eager to make up for the loss of a decade, and they desired more artistic achievement for their films as the political grip loosened, while the audience demanded the removal of unrealistic myths from the screen. A whole new generation of writers who had experienced extremely harsh realities in their youth began to populate the literary scene with novels and short stories written with unusual sensibility, and many well-written stories based on human tragedies during the Cultural Revolution became major sources for screenplays, as adaptation from contemporary literature became a frequent phenomenon in most of the post-Cultural Revolution productions. In the early 1980s, another new generation of filmmakers who had worked on farms and in factories during the Cultural Revolution graduated from the Beijing Film Academy, the only state film school in China, and these young people became a significant impetus for change in the new Chinese cinema.

At the beginning of the 1980s, a new relationship among the Party/State, the film industry, and the audience began to take shape, encouraged by the nation's change to a modified economic policy that allowed more autonomous financial planning. The State withdrew full financial backing of all productions, and made each studio plan its own annual budgets. In this context, audience reception became much more important, as poor box office would jeopardize income to the fixed subsidy,

(Left)
A wedding scene from
Chen Xihe's *Family*
(1956), one of the popular
films of Chairman Mao's
"Hundred Flowers"
movement, which for a
few years encouraged a
freer cinema.

(Right)
With the revival of
interest in the Chinese
historical and cultural
post, film adaptations of
well-known operas
became popular, one of
them *The Wild Boar
Forest* (1962).

(Left)
Kie Jin was one of the
younger directors noted
for integrating different
traditions, as in his fine
character study of two
opera singers, *Stage
Sisters* (1965).

(Right)
A mute tragedy amid festivity: a feudal marriage in Chen Kaigè's masterpiece *Yellow Earth* (1985), which won international praise for its photography and narrative style.

(Left)
Director Ann Hui drew on her strong Hong Kong television experience for *The Boat People* (1982), exploring a visiting photographer's relationship with a Vietnamese family.

(Right)
The ambivalence and cultural conflicts between Hong Kong and the Mainland are at the heart of Yim Ho's *Homecoming* (1984).

The "new wave" of Taiwan's filmmakers concentrated on exploring their cultural identity:
the sorrow of older family members at a family death, or severance from the Mainland,
in *A Time to Live and a Time to Die* (1985).

while popular films could earn money for the studio to finance an additional production. There was an annual moviegoing audience of twenty-seven billion in 1983, but television and imported films had also joined the scene of mass entertainment. The Party had issued calls for films to assist in the new phase of economic development, but the directives became more general in nature. With the traumatic memories of the Cultural Revolution still fresh in people's minds, a more nuanced approach had to be accepted by the Party. In this way, political considerations were gradually relegated to the competing notions between art and popularity, even though the censorship section of the Film Bureau still screened out attempts that were unpalatable for modernization politics.

Post-Cultural Revolution cinema was characterized by two phases: from films that looked back on the woes of the Cultural Revolution, filmmakers moved on to innovative attempts at a variety of subject matters related either to the pre-1949 past or to contemporary living under a changing economy. Most of the films that were adapted from "wound" or "scar" literature were produced before 1983; they focused mainly on the disruption of love relationships and the disappointment of individual devotion to the country caused by unjustified persecution during the Cultural Revolution. In narrating calamities of the past decade, these films used flashbacks and voice-overs as narrative devices; overall, a more poetic, rather than didactic approach was adopted. Compared to films made before the Cultural Revolution, these films were much more outspoken about social reality. For example, Yang Yenpu and Deng Yimin's *Troubled Laughter* (*Ku nao ren de xiao*, 1979) bluntly presented a journalist's frustration under bureaucratic pressure, Xie Jin's *Legend of the Tianyun Mountain* (*Tian yun shan chuan qi*, 1980) presented a relentless picture of the intellectuals' sufferings during the Anti-Rightist movement, and Wu Yigong's *Evening Rain* (*Bashan ye yu*, 1980) contrasted the unsympathetic Red Guard with the human warmth of the common people. In all these films, human calamities during the Cultural Revolution were presented in flesh and blood stories that were familiar to many of the audiences. The inflexible typification of characters according to political dogmas was no longer adopted, and both intellectuals and peasants were shown suffering in quite the same way in Wang Qimin and Sun Yu's *At Middle Age* (*Ren dao zhong nian*, 1982) and in Wu Tianming's *River without Buoys* (*Mei you hang biao de he liu*, 1983). In 1980, the first official Golden Rooster Award for feature films was won by *Evening Rain* and *Legend of the Tianyun Mountains*, indicating that films about intellectuals were not necessarily "petit-bourgeois," and could be just as well received as the "Gong Nong Bing Dianying" (films for workers, peasants, and soldiers). Apparently, the Party also sanctioned stark revelations of recent history to a certain degree. Nevertheless, the genre of "wound" or "scar" films finally ran its gamut, and more optimistic expressions of life in a modernizing China captured the imagination of both screenwriters and filmmakers.

Beginning with Wu Tianming's *Life* (*Ren sheng*, 1984), the phase of one-sided praise of peasants at the expense of intellectuals became a thing of the past on film. *Life* told a sympathetic story of a young intellectual being suffocated in the countryside and of his frustrated attempts to realize his small ambitions. Extensive discussion was subsequently generated in film circles, focusing on the notion that films could provide identification with characters who have more complex psychological make-ups and motivations regardless of their social class. Stereotypes henceforth became much less acceptable, while the urge to depict all walks of life increased. In the spirit of innovation, Chiang Liang used amateur actors and more location shooting in his treatment of the unsuccessful attempts of unemployed youths at private enterprise in *Yamaha Fishstall* (*Yamaha yu dang*, 1984). Chiang Liang's next pursuit of naturalistic performance in *Juvenile Delinquents* (*Shao nian fan*, 1985) caused a sensation by recruiting teenagers serving in juvenile disciplinary centers as chief actors to depict an aspect of Chinese society that had never appeared in films before. On a more grandiose level, Xie Jin staged a spectacular Sino-Vietnamese war front in his award-winning *Garlands at the Foot of the Mountain* (*Gao shan xia de hua huan*, 1984). This tearjerker military film reflected the influence of *Patton* but was outspoken in criticizing the privilege-seeking mentality of high-level cadres. Woman director Lu Xiaoya created an exquisite visual imagery with a delightful interplay of colors in *Girl in Red* (*Hong yi shao nu*, 1985), and showed her support for a young teenager's search for individuality while rejecting the tradition of unquestioning obedience to authorities. The elderly Ling Zifeng made *Bordertown* (*Bian cheng*, 1985); adapted from the May Fourth writer Shen Congwen's modernist novel, the film was a beautiful realization of Shen's subtle metaphors in an extremely picturesque setting.

The fifth and sixth generations of young Chinese filmmakers were even more inquisitive in their search for cultural expression through films. Narrative clichés about the socialist delivery of the old Chinese society were questioned in general, and a more skeptical contemplation of how the poor and feudal village in the Chinese west responded to a Red Army representative came out in Chen Kaige's masterpiece *Yellow Earth* (*Huang tu di*, 1985). The film immediately drew international attention for its astounding cinematographic treatment of the loess (silt) plateau of the Yellow River with the style of a Chinese scroll painting, an unusually sparse use of dialogue, and a narrative structure that effectively interwove four different perspectives. Wang Jianjong's *Good Woman* (*Liang jia fu nu*, 1985) attributed a country divorce to the liberating presence of a Red Army soldier. It is significant for its Freudian handling of the exotic subject matter of child bridegrooms in a re-

mote village, noting the villagers' resistance to women's liberation promoted by the socialists. Director Tian Zhuangzhuang detached himself
from narratives of city life, and offered a poetic treatment of the vast
grasslands in the Chinese west in *On the Hunting Ground* (*Lie chang
zha sha*, 1985), underplaying narrative aspects to such an extent that
no copies of his beautiful study of Mongolian living were being ordered,
yet his film elicited noted documentarist Joris Ivens's exclamation that
"Chinese film has great hope." Tian continued to pursue his obsession
with natural life in the Chinese west in his next film *Horse Thief* (*Dao
ma zei*, 1986).

The sixth and the most energetic generation of directors and cinematographers such as Chen Kaie, Tian Zhuangzhuang, Wu Ziniu, and
Chang Imou grew up in socialist China, yet they embraced not only traditional Chinese culture, but also eagerly studied European, American,
and other foreign cinemas. As young mavericks, their works demonstrated a unique conception of a cinema that encouraged artists' sensitive observations of human life and informed contemplation of culture
and society unmediated by considerations of Party or audience expectations.

As television became popular in Chinese homes in the 1980s, China
Central Television took up the task of instruction and education of the
Chinese people in an era of modernization and change, hence releasing
cinema from the cumbersome duties it had performed in the earlier
years of socialist transition. Cinema's competition with television grew
more rigorous beginning with 1984, and theatrical audiences dropped
slightly, to everyone's speculation and alarm. However, according to
Zheng Dongtian, a director and lecturer of the Beijing Film Academy, it
was important that the Chinese people have more choices in mass entertainment and could learn to be more selective, for it is in such a context of competition that Chinese cinema can make greater strides in the
coming years.

## Hong Kong Cinema before 1949

In 1842 Hong Kong was ceded to Britain as a result of the Opium
War; thereafter, its political and economic administration separated it
from the Chinese Mainland for more than a century. With an economic
development under a capitalist laissez-faire policy administered in the
context of colonial politics, the subsequent cultural development of this
small southern Chinese port took a shape very different from that of the
Chinese Mainland. Generally speaking, Hong Kong cinema was the
outcome of a business enterprise that absorbed pertinent influences
from the Mainland in literary and film traditions, from Hollywood in
commercial practices and narrative techniques, and from subcultures

of southern China. The cinema comprised a dialect film production (Cantonese) and a national language production (Mandarin), reflecting Hong Kong's unique local culture as well as its linkage with the Mainland. In four decades, the Hong Kong film industry has grown into one of the most prolific in southeast Asia, producing melodrama, kungfu, swordplay, and Cantonese musicals for both southeast Asian and overseas Chinese markets.

As early as 1923, a business agent, Li Min Wei, started local film production with the Min Xin Film Company and built the New World Theater. Li was soon discouraged, however, by the dim prospects of the small local market and moved his business to Shanghai in 1925. In the 1920s and early 1930s, film production was sporadic and mostly negligible. After the mid-1930s, two major military and political turbulences on the Mainland (the Japanese invasion of China and the socialist takeover) stimulated investment in the setting up of a production base in Hong Kong. During 1937 to 1941, Japanese military advances in China threatened film production in Shanghai, and filmmakers and producers moved their companies southward to Hong Kong, expecting this British colony to be free of Japanese attacks. At that time, about 60 percent of local productions were taken up by Cantonese operas, swordplay, folklore, and romances, which were basically low-budgeted films made by small production companies. Patriotic and anti-Japanese films made up the remaining 40 percent, enhanced by a Southern China Defense Film Movement mobilized by left-wing directors, including Szeto Huimin, who made *Bloodshed at Po Shan City* (*Xue qian bao Shan cheng*, 1938), and Cai Chusheng, who made *Orphan Island Paradise* (*Gu dao tian tang*, 1939). Themes of resistance and of people's suffering also appeared in films made by nonaligned directors such as Hu Pang's *Morning Clock of the Earth* (*Da di chen zhong*, 1940), Tang Xiao Dan's *Howl of the Race* (*Min zu de hou sheng*, 1941) and Lu Dun's *A Village at War* (*Feng huo gu xiang*, 1941). These films shared a similar outlook with anti-Japanese films made on the Mainland during this period. After December 1941, Hong Kong also fell under Japanese occupation for about three and a half years, during which film production was suspended.

Shortly after the war ended Hong Kong film production quickly resumed. Population had increased considerably during wartime, and the southern migration of small businessmen and filmmakers helped establish a stronger film industry in the late 1940s. Lee Zuyong set up Yong Hua Studio with a production lot and inaugurated an era of Cantonese film production that gained entry to theaters in Mainland Chinese cities. Two expensive palace period classics, *Soul of a Nation* (*Guo hun*, 1948), directed by Bu Wancang, and *Secret History of the Ching Court* (*Qing gong mi shi*, 1949) directed by Zhu Shilin, established the status of Yong Hua and Lee Zuyong, and their box-office and critical success stimulated other entrepreneurs to increase local production.

The second major southern migration of film professionals and capital took place after the socialist takeover of the Chinese Mainland in 1949. Hong Kong became nonsocialist territory for both right-wing and nonaligned filmmakers and businessmen who preferred commercial productions to state-run enterprises. Subsequently, a significant segment of the Shanghai film industry, together with its production companies, directors, and talent, was transferred to Hong Kong. In 1949, film professionals who intended to upgrade the Hong Kong film business started a Southern Film Culture Movement to clean up scandals and corrupt practices, and to encourage artistic emulation of Mainland Chinese cinema. Shortly after 1949, the Mainland Chinese market was closed to Hong Kong films, thus formally separating the film industry in these regions. From then onward, the Hong Kong and Mainland Chinese cinemas had an entirely different economic base as well as a dissimilar political and socio-cultural background, resulting in films that differed greatly in narrative and stylistic terms.

## Hong Kong Cinema from 1949 to 1985

Postwar Hong Kong was still at a preindustrial stage in the 1950s, its economy largely dependent on small businesses set up by new immigrants. Many film production companies were short-lived, single-film companies, and productions were largely low-budgeted "seven-day wonders" except for those of one or two larger studios like Yong Hua, which occasionally had more ambitious productions. About fifty to seventy production companies appeared in the market each year, rendering a steady output of about 150 to 170 films annually throughout the 1950s. However, only about twenty to twenty-five companies stayed in business for more than a year, and a surviving company made an average of about six to eight films each year. The medium-sized companies that emerged in the 1950s formed the "Big Eight" to protect their mutual interest in pricing; they included Da Guan, Xin Lian, Zhong Lian, Hua Qiao, Yong Mao, Da Cheng, Zhi Li and Ling Guang. Dian Mao (Motion Picture and General Investment Company) took over Yong Hua in the mid-1950s, together with Tian Yi (which later changed its name to Shaw Brothers); they became two major studios that owned theater chains both in Hong Kong and in Singapore and Malaysia.

From the 1950s to mid-1960s, family melodrama, Cantonese opera, and swordplay were popular genres with the local audience. Postwar poverty had led to melodramas like Wang Weiyi's *Tragedy on the Pearl River* (*Zhujiang lei*, 1950) and Qin Jian's *Families* (*Jia jia hu hu*, 1954), which depicted lower-class families under the pressure of poverty, unemployment, and generational problems with heart-wrenching scenes. The influx of refugee immigrants who searched for their identity was narrated into films like Li Tie's *In the Face of Demolition* (*Wei lou chuan xiao*, 1953) and *Orchid in the Fire* (*Huo ku you lan*, 1960) and Lu Dun's *Typhoon Signal Number 10* (*Shi hao feng qiu*, 1954), which provided a survey of underprivileged characters struggling together in decaying old buildings. Melodramas produced by left-wing directors usually incorporated strong social critique, while generational problems between in-laws were emphasized by most other filmmakers.

In a more escapist vein, swordplay (wu xia) and martial arts (kung fu) films were made up of narratives of legendary feuds among clans, monks, and swordsmen set in earlier historical times. In the 1950s and early 1960s, Cantonese swordplay films outnumbered their Mandarin counterparts. Adapted from popular pulp novels, they combined narratives of mythical figures with elements of fantasy, and created a bizarre iconography of combats and duels through the use of animation and optical effects. For example, *Strange Hero* (*Jiang hu qi hia*, 1956), directed by Wang Tianlian, and *Burning of the Red Lotus Monastery* (*Huo shao hong lian si*, 1963), by Ling Yun, contained scenes depicting a monk's magical ability, which found parallels in John Carpenter's 1986 Hollywood spoof *Big Trouble in Little China*. On the other hand, films like *Legend of the Brave Archer* (*Shediao ying xiong zhuan*, 1958), directed by Hu Peng, and *Story of the Sword and the Sabre* (*Yi tian tu long ji*, 1963), by Zhang Ying and Cai Chang, carried strong overtones of family melodrama of that decade. The most popular martial art films produced during the 1950s were the Huang Fei Hong series, which portrayed an upright martial arts coach curbing urban crimes with his disciples in the 1920s. There were about forty-seven of these films made in the 1950s, all starring Guan Dexing as the coach, Shi Jian as the gangster lead, and Cao Dehua as Guan's disciple. Altogether, these swordplay and martial art films reworked the Confucian code of filial bondage and social justice as they depicted conflicts between folk heroes and archvillains.

Toward the end of the 1960s, social-problem films typical of the 1950s disappeared, replaced by more lighthearted comedies and urban musicals, while Mandarin "new style" swordplay films, which emphasized tougher martial arts fights and faster editing, became more popular than Cantonese swordplay films, which relied on special effects. As a large urban working class emerged with industrialization, narratives about economic hardships and in-law problems were replaced by those about workplace and coupling problems. Subsequently, the once-popular roles of fierce mothers-in-law played by actresses Wang Manli and Ma Xiaoying and tearful daughters-in-law by actresses Bai Yen and Fang-Yenfen gave way to women of independence played by the youthful and versatile Chen Baozhu and Xiao Fangfang.

During the 1960s, the Shaw Brothers Studio superseded Dian Mou in business and emerged as a major studio with vertical integration of production, distribution, and exhibition in the industry. With a movietown consisting of shooting stages, palace sets, period costumes, as well as film labs, dubbing studios, and training classes for talents, Shaw Brothers became a major supplier of about fifty Mandarin swordplay films and melodramas each year. Out of the studio also emerged such major directors as Li Hanxiang, Chu Yuan, Chang Cheh, and King Hu whose works were mostly genre-based. Li Hanxiang was well known for period drama, his more notable works including a Cannes Festival exhibit *Magnificent Concubine* (*Yang gui fei*, 1961) and a famous adaptation *Love Eterne* (*Liang shanbo yu zhu yingtai*, 1963); later, he added a sideline of soft-porns such as *Legends of Lust* (*Feng yu qi tan*, 1972) and *The Happiest Moment* (*Yi le ye*, 1973). Chu Yuan's two outstanding Shaw productions were *Intimate Confessions of a Chinese Courtesan* (*Ai lu*, 1971), a mystic swordplay melodrama depicting lesbian sexuality, and *The House of 72 Tenants* (*Qi shi er jia fang ke*, 1973), an urban melodrama whose box office success helped revive Cantonese film production in the early 1970s. Chang Cheh specialized in "new style" Mandarin swordplay films, celebrating masculine power and individual heroism, with works influenced by the Samurai tradition like *One-Armed Swordsman* (*Du bi dao*, 1966) and *Golden Swallow* (*Jin yanzi*, 1968). King Hu brought the swordplay genre to its expressionist heights with his "Inn Trilogies" *Come Drink With Me* (*Da zui xia*, 1966), *Dragon Gate Inn* (*Long men ke zhan*, 1967), and *The Fate of Lee Khan* (*Yingchunge zhi feng bo*, 1973), blending Chinese opera and classical painting in a mature stylistic handling of movement and space. His "Buddhist Trilogies" *A Touch of Zen* (*Xia nu*, 1971), *Raining in the Mountain* (*Kong shan ling yu*, 1979), and *Legend of the Mountain* (*Shan zhong chuan qi*, 1979) were produced outside Shaw, and *A Touch of Zen* won the Grand Prix de Technique Superieur at the 1975 Cannes Festival. As an auteur of the genre, King Hu's introduction of philosophical mysticism into the genre won international attention for Hong Kong cinema. With box-office success brought by widescreen color distribution of Mandarin swordplay films, Shaw Brothers took control of most of the southeast Asian markets of Taiwan, Singapore, Malaysia, and Thailand in the 1960s.

In the early 1970s, Mandarin kung fu films earned international recognition through Bruce Lee's quintessential martial arts performances in *The Big Boss* (*Tang shan da xiong*, 1971), *Fist of Fury* (*Jing wu men*, 1972), and *The Way of the Dragon* (*Meng long guo jiang*, 1972). Their box-office success enabled a new independent studio, Golden Harvest, to rise to prominence in southeast Asia like the Shaw Brothers. Tough competition from Mandarin cinema and television caused a sharp decline of Cantonese cinema in the early 1970s, with only two features made during 1971 to 1973. With the sudden death of Bruce Lee in 1974, kung fu film production temporarily slowed down for want of a comparably attractive hero and adequate support from family audiences. Subsequently, the local market reopened for Cantonese productions of melodrama and social satires, out of which the television variety-show host Michael Hui emerged as an auteur comedian, turning out box-office winners for Golden Harvest with *Games Gamblers Play* (*Gui man shuang xing*, 1974), *The Last Message* (*Tian cai yu bai chi*, 1975), *The Private Eyes* (*Ban jin ba liang*, 1976), and *The Contract* (*Mai shen qi*, 1978).

Shaw Brothers continued churning out cheap swordplay and melodrama films in the 1970s, with thirty or so smaller production companies emulating their example of profiteering. On the other hand, Shu Shuen, an independent filmmaker trained in the States, managed to produce a landmark treatment of Chinese feminine sexuality in *The Arch* (*Dong fu ren*, 1970), which remained an isolated work of art. However, her bold exploration of the Chinese identity through a study of Cultural Revolution refugees in *China Behind* (*Zai jian zhong guo*, 1974) was banned from commercial release for chiefly political reasons. While Hong Kong's political stability was shaken by the riots of 1966 and 1967, and its colonial status seriously questioned by joint student movements rallying for the official position of Chinese and anti-corruption, the film business remained fully devoted to quick profits. However, as television came on the media scene in 1967, it quickly took the place of the local cinema in expressing the young generation's search for a contemporary Hong Kong identity in the 1970s.

A significant symbiosis between cinema and television took place in the mid-1970s, first through generic transference from television to cinema, followed by the latter's structural changes. As the television audience's appetite was whetted for urban violence through daily news and local police drama series like *CID* and *Operation Manhunt* (*Da zhang fu*), the crime thriller, responding to pressures of metropolitan living, was added to existing genres with the commercial success of Alex Chang's *Cops and Robbers* (*Dian zi bing bing*, 1979), *Man on the Brink* (*Bian yuan ren*, 1981), Yim Ho's *The Happenings* (*Ye che*, 1980), and Liang Puzhi's *He Lives by Night* (*Ye jing hun*, 1982). Urban comedies became popular with Michael Hui's social satires, which banked on the high ratings of the Hui Brothers' television variety show *Shuang Xing Bao Xi*, conceived during the brief economic depression of the early 1970s. Cinema City Company, another independent studio, quickly captured the television audience's need for high-budgeted spectacles by producing comic melodramas like *Laughing Times* (*Hua ki shi dai*, 1980) and the *Aces Go Places* (*Zui jia pai dang*) trilogies, the commercial success of which enabled Cinema City to become the third major studio backed by a theater chain that competed rigorously with the Shaw Brothers and Golden Harvest.

More significantly, the first generation of young television producers and directors transferred their careers to feature film production and brought a "new wave" to Cantonese cinema characterized by stronger social awareness, bolder treatment of sex and violence, as well as higher aspirations of stylistic sophistication. These more notable filmmakers included Ann Hui, whose international reputation was established by her docudrama approach to *The Story of Woo Viet* (*Hu yue de gu shi*, 1981) and *The Boat People* (*Tou bin hu hai*, 1982); Allen Fong, whose self-reflexive study of family relationships in a changing society in *Father and Son* (*Fu zi qing*, 1981) and cinéma vérité depiction of a fishseller's daughter in *Ah Ying* (*Ban bian ren*, 1982), distinguished his works; She Ke, whose *Butterfly Murders* (*Die bian*, 1979), introduced elements of horror-fantasy and science fiction into the swordplay genre; and Tan Jiaming, whose *Nomad* (*Lie huo qing chun*, 1982), about uninhibited youthful sexuality, alarmed censorship concerns and stimulated a genre of teenager topics. These and other television-turned-film directors brought their training from overseas film schools as well as their experience in commercial and public television drama to Cantonese film production. In addition, as a result of the crossover between television and film, more independent studios sprang up in the early 1980s with ambitious productions, toppling the Shaws' hegemony of the market.

In 1981 the British Government began negotiating with China about returning the colony to the Mainland in 1997. As the issues of political affiliation, cultural identity, and reincorporation policies became major topics in Hong Kong, the film industry appeared largely indifferent and kept turning out entertainment spectaculars or cheap romances, which were more profitable than political allegories like Ann Hui's *The Boat People*. In the mid-1980s, competition between new independents and the majors remained fierce, and the so-called "new wave" cinema turned commercial, staying mostly apart from politics. Ultimately, it was Yim Ho's *Homecoming* (*Shi shui liu ni nian*, 1984) that portrayed the relationship of ambivalence and contradiction between Hong Kong and its cinema and the Chinese Mainland. This prosperous entity, which owed its development to a capitalist ideology under a colonial history, has yet to resolve its split interests between economic wealth and cultural worth.

## Taiwan Cinema

The film industry in Taiwan combined the structural characteristics of both the Mainland and Hong Kong. The state studios, Zhong Ying, Zhong Zhi, and Tai Zhi, were established in 1949 and produced mainly propaganda and social education films. Commercial studios financed by Shanghai emigrants, Hong Kong and local businessmen, and filmmakers began genre film production similar to that in Hong Kong in the

1950s and 1960s. Like Hong Kong, Taiwan cinema also has two dialect productions, the Mandarin and the Taiwanese, both of which include the genres of melodrama, romance, and musicals, whereas swordplay films were mostly Mandarin productions, stimulated by many Hong Kong imports. The Shaw Brothers' command of the Taiwan market encouraged crossovers between Hong Kong Mandarin film directors and Taiwanese actors and actresses, thereby increasing the generic influence in the 1960s and 1970s. In general, however, political and moral film censorship in Taiwan was stricter, and resulted in Hong Kong's producing slightly altered versions of the same films for the Taiwan market.

Beginning in the 1980s, a "new wave" cinema took shape in Taiwan, signifying the maturation of a young generation of filmmakers who affirmed the historical and cultural value of their country. These films differed from earlier lavish studio productions by adopting a low-budgeted look, and focused on the process of growing up in Taiwan with narratives that placed stylistic emphasis before plot complexity. The more notable directors included Chang I, Chen Kunhou, Hou Xiaoxian, and Yang Dechang, whose *Kwei Mei, a Woman* (*Wo zheyang guolao yisheng*, 1985), *Marriage* (*Jie hun*, 1984), *The Boys from Fengkuei* (*Fengkuei lai de ren*, 1984), and *A Time to Live and a Time to Die* (*Tongnian wang shi*, 1985) won international acclaim and gave Taiwan a very promising future.

## SELECTED BIBLIOGRAPHY

Berry, Chris, ed. *Perspectives on Chinese Cinema*. Ithaca, New York: Cornell University Press, 1985.

Cheng, Jihua, Li Xiaobai, Xing Zuwen. *History of the Development of Chinese Cinema*, Vols. I & II. Beijing, China: China Film Press, 1963.

Jarvie, I.C. *Window on Hong Kong*. Hong Kong: University of Hong Kong, 1977.

Leyda, Jay. *Dianying: Electric Shadows, An Account of Films and Film Audiences in China*. Cambridge, Massachusetts: MIT Press, 1972.

Rayns, Tony, and Scott Meek, eds. *Electric Shadows: 45 Years of Chinese Cinema*. London: British Film Institute, 1980.

### Journals and Special Issues

*China's Screen*. Beijing: China Film Import and Export Corporation, published quarterly in both Chinese and English.

*Contemporary Cinema*. Beijing: China Film Art Research Center, published bi-monthly in Chinese only.

*Hong Kong International Film Festival Monographs*. Hong Kong: Urban Council, special topics on Hong Kong cinema published annually from 1978 to 1984.

*Jump Cut*, 31, March, 1986, Special section on Film in the People's Republic of China.

*On Film*, 14, Spring 1985, Special Chinese Cinema Section.

# CUBA
## Cuban Cinema before the Revolution and After

DENNIS WEST

Though the present-day Cuban film industry is a product of the Revolution that came to power on 1 January, 1959, sporadic attempts had been made to establish a significant national movie industry in prerevolutionary Cuba. A leader in this effort was Manuel Alonso, who by 1950 controlled the island's film production resources. Alonso was also a director, and his well-crafted thriller *Seven Deaths by a Fixed Deadline* (*Siete muertes a plazo fijo*, 1950) is one of the most memorable feature films made in Cuba before the Revolution. Unfortunately, Alonso and other prerevolutionary Cuban filmmakers failed to create an artistically or economically viable national industry; and they produced few films of lasting interest.

In the 1950s some American movies and many Mexican-Cuban coproductions were filmed in Cuba. Mexican movie makers were attracted to the island by its "exotic" locales and by the popularity of Cuban music. Most of these Mexican-Cuban coproductions were run-of-the-mill musicals, gangster movies, or melodramas. Probably the most ambitious and best known of these coproductions was *The White Rose* (*La rosa blanca*, 1953), which was made by the famed Mexican director Emilio Fernández and his equally renowned cinematographer Gabriel Figueroa. Although *The White Rose* portrays the life of the great Cuban patriot and writer Jose Martí, this mediocre feature nevertheless suffers from the narrative and stylistic conventions characterizing typical Mexican melodramas.

Movie going was an extremely popular form of entertainment in the 1950s; on a per capita basis it was more common in Cuba than in any other country in Latin America. During this period, a modest film culture was nurtured by the activities of cultural and film societies. Two members of the Nuestro Tiempo society, Tomás Gutiérrez Alea and

Julio García Espinosa, studied filmmaking at Rome's Centro Sperimentale in the early 1950s. Both men returned to Cuba and, with other young filmmakers, made the 16 mm documentary *The Charcoal Worker* (*El mégano*, 1955), a scathing exposé of exploitation and miserable living conditions. Though the neorealist *The Charcoal Worker* is esthetically a failure, the film is nonetheless a landmark in the history of Cuban cinema because of its social theme, because it was confiscated by Batista's repressive regime, and because the filmmakers who worked on the documentary later rose to prominence in the revolutionary government's national film institute (Instituto Cubano del Arte e Industria Cinematográficos or ICAIC).

ICAIC serves as both a film production facility and as a training ground for developing filmmakers. In addition, ICAIC handles both Cuban and international distribution of its films; and the institute foments film culture via its cinematheque and its publications such as *Cuban Cinema* (*Cine cubano*), Latin America's leading film journal. ICAIC was founded in the early days of the Revolution, on 24 March, 1959, because revolutionary leaders such as Fidel Castro realized the immense political and ideological potential of the film medium. The law that established ICAIC recognized film both as an art and as a powerful medium for the expression of ideas. This law called for the "reeducation" of the taste of Cuban moviegoers, who were accustomed to Hollywood fare. Furthermore, the law identified cinema as a vehicle for "the development and enrichment of the new humanism that informs our Revolution"; and filmmakers were urged to draw their themes from Cuban history in order "to make of our cinema a fount of revolutionary inspiration, of culture, and of information."

In the early years of the Revolution, the ICAIC filmmakers faced enormous problems because of lack of training and equipment. Shortages of film stock and equipment-related problems still persist today, but now ICAIC boasts an abundance of trained filmmakers and draws on a quarter-century of experience. From 1959 through 1982 ICAIC's production included many hundreds of weekly newsreels, dozens of animated films, 722 documentaries, and eighty fiction films. ICAIC currently aims to produce twelve fiction features each year. Because the ICAIC-produced films support the Cuban Revolution, some critics oppose them on political or ideological grounds. Nevertheless, ICAIC's films now enjoy a well-deserved reputation in Cuba and internationally because of their generally high technical quality and their substantial sociopolitical or historical themes. The following survey examines the work of ICAIC's leading filmmakers.

Tomás Gutiérrez Alea, one of the founders of ICAIC, was one of the institute's first directors of feature films. Today Gutiérrez Alea is one of Cuba's best known filmmakers both in Latin America and in the developed world. When released in the United States, the director's masterful *Memories of Underdevelopment* (*Memorias del subdesarrollo*, 1968) received high praise; and Gutiérrez Alea was voted a prestigious award by the National Society of Film Critics. Gutiérrez Alea is not only a film director. In accordance with ICAIC policy, he has frequently worked in an advisory capacity with less experienced directors such as Sara Gómez and Sergio Giral. In 1982 Gutiérrez Alea published an important book of film theory, *Dialectic of the Spectator*.

One of ICAIC's earliest major productions and Gutiérrez Alea's first feature film is *Stories of the Revolution* (*Historias de la revolución*, 1960). This feature exemplifies the problems facing ICAIC's enthusiastic but inexperienced filmmakers in the early days of the institute. *Stories of the Revolution* consists of three autonomous dramatic sketches which portray the armed insurrection against Batista in three different locales. The film, much of which was shot by an Italian cinematographer in a pedestrian fashion, reveals the influence of Gutiérrez Alea's Italian neorealist training. *Stories of the Revolution* is marred, however, not only by the director's lack of familiarity with the camera's potential but also by gaps in the story line.

Gutiérrez Alea's *The Death of a Bureaucrat* (*La muerte de un burócrata*, 1966) is a satirical comedy and a minor classic of black humor. This satire of red tape in a socialist society traces the bureaucratic misadventures of a young man intent on reburying his uncle's corpse after being required to disinter it in order to recover a document. This fast-paced feature is enlivened by the director's clever use of gags, slapstick, Catch-22 dialogue, animated cartoons, and comic parodies of famous moments in the history of film. The lead role is effectively played in a dead-pan manner by Salvador Wood, one of ICAIC's well-known actors. *The Death of a Bureaucrat* is an unusual ICAIC production in that it is a thoroughgoing satire of an aspect of revolutionary Cuban society. Gutiérrez Alea continued this vein of comic satire and black humor in *The Survivors* (*Los sobrevivientes*, 1978), in which a bourgeois family attempts to live apart from the Cuban Revolution and thereby regresses to feudalism and ultimately to savagery.

In his complexly structured masterpiece *Memories of Underdevelopment*, Gutiérrez Alea himself appears as a director making a film that will be, he says, a collage. *Memories of Underdevelopment* itself is a collage—an innovative combination of different narrative strategies and film techniques woven together to portray a middle-class Cuban intellectual and would-be writer who, in the historically critical period preceding the October 1962 missile crisis, refuses to escape to the United States or to commit himself to the revolutionary cause. The film is based on Edmundo Desnoes's novel of the same name. In his search for a new film form, Gutiérrez Alea creatively uses self-reflexive and self-critical techniques: for instance, both Desnoes and Gutiérrez Alea appear in the film in order to comment on issues relating to revolution or art. Furthermore, the film incorporates documentary sequences and television footage in order to portray the protagonist against a backdrop of the momentous historical events that are leaving him behind. Part of the success of *Memories of Underdevelopment* stems from the outstanding performance of lead actor Sergio Corrieri, who creates a sensitive portrayal of the politically uncommitted Cuban intellectual deeply influenced by European and American cultural values.

In *The Last Supper* (*La última cena*, 1976) Gutiérrez Alea uses historical documentation and a chronological narrative structure to depict a black slave rebellion on a Cuban sugar plantation in the late eighteenth century. The director, who also worked as a coscriptwriter on the film, symbolically uses the Passion of Christ and the time frame of Holy Week to arrange the confrontation of two cultures—that of the oppressor, the white slave-holding class, and the oppressed, the Afro-Cuban slaves. The lengthy banquet sequence which gives the film its name is a superbly directed, penetrating examination of the planter-class ideology, which endorses both slavery and Christianity. The music for the film was composed by Leo Brouwer, one of the world's leading composers for cinema, and his score subtly contrasts Christian religious-musical motifs with Afro-Cuban musical instruments, chants, and rhythms.

Director Julio García Espinosa has been one of the mainstays of ICAIC since its founding, and he currently serves as head of the institute and vice-minister of Culture. In addition, García Espinosa is Cuba's leading film theorist; his often republished essay "For an Imperfect Cinema" (1969) profoundly influenced those Latin American filmmakers attempting to work outside commercial movie industries. García Espinosa has frequently served as an advisor and collaborator on other filmmakers' projects. For instance, he actively advised exiled Chilean filmmaker Patricio Guzmán on the montage of the latter's monumental three-part documentary *The Battle of Chile* (*La Batalla de Chile*, 1973–1979), which was edited at ICAIC.

In "For an Imperfect Cinema," García Espinosa warned Third World filmmakers to beware artistically and technically perfect mainstream cinema, which is generally reactionary. García Espinosa has been the ICAIC director most concerned with experimentation and the search for new cinematic forms. During the Vietnam War, García Espinosa was invited to North Vietnam, where he traveled four thousand kilometers through the war zone to film the feature-length documentary *Third World, Third World War* (*Tercer mundo, tercera guerra mundial*, 1970). The central theme of this film is the determined resistance and resourcefulness of the Vietnamese people in their confrontation with the powerful American enemy. This major documentary is unusual for its combination of conventional features, such as interviews, with spontaneous and innovative techniques.

Two other features directed by García Espinosa, *Adventures of Juan*

*Quinquín (Aventuras de Juan Quinquín*, 1967) and *"Son" or Not "Son"* (*Son o no son*, 1980), are high points in the filmmaker-theorist's search for new cinematic forms for politically committed film. *Adventures of Juan Quinquín* is loosely based on Samuel Feijóo's novel *Juan Quinquín in Pueblo Mocho*. In his film García Espinosa rejects the liner plot structure of the novel as well as traditional notions of narration. Instead, he freely draws on many literary and film genres—from the picaresque novel to the Western movie—in order to parody accepted genre conventions while also expressing serious social and political themes. A rich background of Cuban popular culture is present in both *Adventures of Juan Quinquín* and *"Son" or Not "Son."* In his essay "The Four Means of Communication are Three: Cinema and Television," García Espinosa recognized Cuban popular music as one of his nation's strongest and most authentic cultural expressions; and *"Son" or Not "Son"* was partially inspired by the *son*, a Cuban musical genre. This feature is a self-conscious and self-critical musical and cabaret film which incorporates elements of traditional film genres, such as the American musical comedy, in an effort to match the box-office appeal of popular genre movies while also critiquing them.

One of the most talented of the ICAIC filmmakers is Humberto Solás, who was only twenty-six when he directed his first full-length work, the masterpiece *Lucía (Lucía*, 1968). This great historical epic consists of three love stories involving women named Lucía in three different periods of Cuban history. Solás varies the camera techniques, music, narrative strategies, and the acting styles of the three episodes in order to reflect the different class backgrounds of his protagonists as well as the particular historical periods in which they lived. Because the director depicts his individual protagonists within their sociopolitical contexts, the three tales are not simply conventional love stories—they succinctly record the changing social roles and attitudes of women in Cuban society before and after the Revolution. The film benefits greatly from stellar performances by all three lead actresses (Raquel Revuelta, Eslinda Núñez, Adela Legrá) in their roles as Lucía.

No other films directed by Solás succeed in capturing both the vast historical scope and the consistent stylistic brilliance of *Lucía*; nevertheless, he has directed several other noteworthy films. In the thirty-minute documentary *Simparelé (Simparelé*, 1974), Solás creatively melds together elements of Haitian popular culture such as folk painting, dance, religious ritual, and songs in order to sketch the history of the Haitian people. The feature-length epic *Cantata of Chile (Cantata de Chile*, 1975) alternates realist and allegorical styles to trace the political struggles of the Chilean working class. The lengthy and expensive Cuban-Spanish coproduction *Cecilia (Cecilia*, 1981) is based on the famous nineteenth-century Cuban novel *Cecilia Valdés*, by Cirilo Villaverde. To make his mythic, allegorical, and melodramatic extravaganza of romance and political intrigue in Havana's nineteenth-century slave-holding society, Solás drew on the vast material resources at ICAIC and on an all-star cast headed by the accomplished Daisy Granados, who plays the title role of the beautiful mulatta seeking to improve her social status. *Amada* (*Amada*, 1983) is an atmospherically photographed melodrama about a bourgeois woman trapped in an unhappy marriage in the Havana of 1914. The lead role in the film is sensitively played by Eslinda Núñez, who had starred in part two of *Lucía*.

Manuel Octavio Gómez has been one of the most prolific of ICAIC's directors of fiction features. Gómez has experimented widely with different narrative structures and visual styles, and his films have explored a variety of subjects. Cuban popular culture has often served as a source of inspiration for Gómez's fiction features. His *The Days of Water* (*Los días del agua*, 1971), which is based on historical events, portrays a peasant "holy woman" who heals with water; the film also examines the far-reaching political ramifications of the healer's broad popular appeal. Afro-Cuban folklore provides the inspiration for many of the characters and motifs in Gómez's *Patakin* (*Patakin*, 1982), a musical comedy which features abundant social satire and Hollywood-style production numbers.

Gómez's *Mr. President* (*El señor presidente*, 1983) is an accomplished, straightforward adaptation of Guatemalan writer Miguel Angel Asturias's similarly titled novel of betrayal and political repression under a dictatorial regime. More significant, however, are Gómez's innovative experiments in film structure and style. His black-and-white fiction feature *The First Charge with the Machete* (*La primera carga al machete*, 1969) depicts the victory of machete-wielding Cuban rebels over Spanish forces in the 1868 war of independence. Gómez's approach to history is unique: while his exaggerated use of high contrast realistically suggests primitive photography and reminds viewers that they are watching a historical film, the director also establishes an anachronistic framework in which to interpret historical events. This framework is provided by the device of a modern-day film crew which, via interviews and on-the-scene coverage, investigates the background and implications of the historical events as they unfold. Gómez's fiction feature *A Woman, A Man, A City* (*Una mujer, un hombre, una ciudad*, 1978) is an exceptional experiment in narrative structure. This film interweaves three interrelated narrative threads and temporal planes in order to explore the lives of individual characters and to capture their changing social milieu. Documentary sequences—including clips from Gómez's 1969 documentary *Nuevitas* (*Nuevitas*)—are used to trace the rapid development of the port city where the characters reside. Gómez uses suspense well in this film which, like *Citizen Kane*, is structured in the form of an intriguing investigation of a character's life.

Like Gutiérrez Alea and García Espinosa, Santiago Alvarez was before the Revolution an active member of the Nuestro Tiempo cultural association. And like his aforementioned colleagues, Alvarez has been a pillar of ICAIC since its founding. Alvarez has directed one fiction feature, *The Fugitives in Dead Man's Cave* (*Los refugiados de la Cueva del Muerto*, 1983), which meshes conventional plot development with a documentary photographic style to depict the fate of rebels who in 1953 unsuccessfully attacked Batista forces in the first significant armed engagement of the Cuban Revolution. However, Alvarez is best known as ICAIC's most prolific, influential, and gifted documentary filmmaker. In fact, most film critics and historians consider Alvarez one of the leading documentarists in the world today. In addition to making documentaries, Alvarez has since 1959 headed ICAIC's Latin American Newsreel division, which produces one newsreel a week to circulate to the island's approximately five hundred motion-picture theaters.

The themes of international solidarity (especially with Vietnam), U.S. imperialism, and support for the Cuban Revolution and Fidel Castro predominate in Alvarez's documentaries, which are openly partisan in their political perspective. In his famous documentary short *Now* (*Now*, 1965), Alvarez briskly edits still photos from American magazines and clips from newsreels to the tune of singer Lena Horne's "Now" in order to condemn racial injustice in the United States. This short is typical of Alvarez's early documentaries in which a rapid editing style created montages of still photos and archival footage. Alvarez's two-hour, poetic-epic documentary *April in Vietnam in the Year of the Cat* (*Abril de Vietnam en el año del gato*, 1975) was commissioned by the Vietnamese to commemorate the founding of the Democratic Republic of Vietnam. This feature is especially notable for its unusual use of color tinting and for its sophisticated integration of music—both Vietnamese music and arrangements by Leo Brouwer. The feature-length *I Am a Son of America . . . and I Am Indebted to Her* (*De América soy hijo . . . y a ella me debo*, 1972) and *And Heaven Was Taken by Storm* ( *. . . y el cielo fue tomado por asalto*, 1973) chronicle Fidel Castro's trips to Salvador Allende's Chile and to Eastern European and African nations, while the short *My Brother Fidel* (*Mi hermano Fidel*, 1977) casts the Cuban leader in the unusual role of interviewer of an elderly man who knew the nineteenth-century patriot José Martí.

Gutiérrez Alea, García Espinosa, Solás, Gómez, and Alvarez are ICAIC's leading directors. Several other directors have also made notable films. Sara Gómez's only fiction feature, *One Way or Another* (*De cierta manera*; shot in 1974 and released in 1977), is one of ICAIC's most significant experiments because it successfully alternates documentary and fictional styles as well as conventional and experimental techniques. *One Way or Another* tells a traditional love story—young lovers attempt to surmount the obstacles (different racial and class backgrounds) to their union. While the director uses conventional narrative film strategies to advance her plot, she also prevents viewers from becoming too uncritically interested in the romance by rupturing the flow of the narrative. Devices which break the flow of the narrative include *cinéma vérité* sequences, intercalated film essays, interviews, and even a huge title asking "Who is Guillermo?" when this character initially appears. Sara Gómez shot this film in 16 mm in order to encourage spontaneity in her players, and lead actor Mario Balmaseda responded with a natural and convincing performance as the street-wise manual laborer who, given the social goals of the Revolution, is attempting to modify his old-fashioned macho code of conduct. *One Way or Another* is also important in the history of cinema because it was directed by a Third World black woman who had personally experienced the problems of racism and sexism explored in the film. Unfortunately, ICAIC lost one of its most promising directors when Sara Gómez died before postproduction of *One Way or Another* was complete.

Like many of ICAIC's features, Pastor Vega's documentary *Long Live the Republic!* (*¡Viva la república!*, 1972) is an attempt to reexamine and reinterpret Cuban history. This one-hundred-minute compilation film offers a thorough historical survey of the republican period, which ended with the advent of the Cuban Revolution. The director highlights the political, social, and economic considerations appropriate to a Marxist interpretation; U.S. influence over Cuba receives particular attention. Vega tapped the extensive ICAIC archives and the collections of the U.S. Library of Congress in order to obtain still photos and original documentary footage for his film. *Long Live the Republic!* is briskly edited in step with voice-over commentary which shapes the viewer's understanding of the actuality footage.

Pastor Vega's first fiction feature, *Portrait of Teresa* (*Retrato de Teresa*, 1979), is important not for its style or structure, but rather for the controversial and timely themes with which it deals: old-fashioned machismo, the sexual double standard, and the work-housework routine which confronts mothers employed outside the home. *Portrait of Teresa* was a box-office hit: approximately one quarter of the population of Havana viewed the film within one month of its release. The issues portrayed in the film had been widely debated by Cubans in the mid-1970s, when a controversial family code became law. In order to ground his film in the everyday social realities facing Cuban working women, coscriptwriter and director Pastor Vega drew on research conducted by a Cuban psychological institute. The film features memorable performances by the two leads: Adolfo Llauradó as the old-line macho paterfamilias and Daisy Granados as the wife who finally rejects her abusive husband.

Manuel Pérez's fiction feature *Black River* (*Río negro*, 1977) depicts counterrevolutionary activities in Cuba's Escambray mountains in the early 1960s. The film's nonchronological structure is a partially suc-

(Left)
In *Memories of Underdevelopment* (1968) an uncommitted intellectual is caught between his admiration for European and American cultural values and his understanding that the Revolution will benefit most Cuban people.

(Below)
The banquet sequence in Gutiérrez Alea's *The Last Supper* (1976) dramatizes a clash of cultures: that of the oppressed Afro-Cuban slaves and of the white, slave-owning class.

This visually striking scene reflects one period of Cuban history of the three highlighted in Humberto Solas's masterpiece, *Lucía* (1968).

In the musical comedy *Patakin* (1982), a Hollywood-style production number glorifies work in a socialist society.

cessful attempt to foster a reflective attitude in viewers without eliminating the element of intrigue from the plot. Pérez draws on typical features of the Western genre—gunbattle sequences, the theme of revenge, the importance of landscape—to trace the career of a counterrevolutionary leader and his revolutionary counterpart. Though the story line is at times facile, the film does succeed in depicting believable, evolving characters caught up in the grandeur and muddle of revolutionary change.

Like *Black River*, Octavio Cortázar's fiction feature *The Teacher* (*El brigadista*, 1977) is set in the early 1960s, when counterrevolutionary military operations threatened Cuba's newly installed revolutionary government. In *The Teacher* an inexperienced teenage literacy teacher is sent by the government to a remote community of charcoal workers during Cuba's 1961 literacy campaign. This film has two unusual features: an epic note is sounded at the beginning when, in voice-over, a village elder recalls the past; and this color film ends with a black-and-white documentary sequence of the 22 December, 1961 assembly in which Fidel Castro addressed the returning teachers in Havana's Plaza of the Revolution. This ending serves as a distancing device to shatter the film's fictional framework and to stimulate viewers to recall a specific historical moment; the protagonist's experience, then, is made to seem a part of the nation's shared collective memory.

In general, however, *The Teacher* exemplifies a type of ICAIC filmmaking which uses the conventions of Hollywood commercial cinema in order to make slick, intellectually unchallenging movies in support of the Cuban Revolution. Cinematographer Pablo Martínez's lush color photography enthralls the viewer with the spectacle of the swampy, primeval world which confronts the protagonist. Violent machismo is frequently on display, and thrills and excitement are provided in hunt sequences and in shoot-outs. A gratuitous subplot adds sex to the film's attractions. Smooth editing facilitates the flow of the linear plot, and musical motifs highligh important emotional moments. This sort of conventional commercial-style movie-making with a pro-Cuban ideological twist was popular at the box office, where *The Teacher* broke established records.

Black director Sergio Giral has made several films which explore the Afro-Cuban slave experience. His documentary short *Runaway Slave* (*Cimarrón*, 1967) features an interview with Esteban Montejo, a centenarian runaway slave, and reconstructs sections of Miguel Barnet's and Montejo's widely read *Biography of a Runaway Slave*. Giral's fiction features *Runaway Slave Hunter* (*Rancheador*, 1976) and *Maluala* (*Maluala*, 1979) are both based on historical documentation. *Runaway Slave Hunter* focuses on the fugitive slave hunter as the repressive arm of the slaveowning class, while *Maluala* depicts the armed resistance to slavery offered by remote communities of runaways. Both *Runaway*

*Slave Hunter* and *Maluala* bear the look of well-crafted mainstream commercial cinema, and both films extol slave culture as a culture of resistance. ICAIC has supported these film projects because the Afro-Cuban tradition of resistance to slavery and to the Spanish colonial administration is seen as being historically linked to the establishment of an exploitation-free revolutionary society.

*The Other Francisco* (*El otro Francisco*, 1975) is Sergio Giral's most important feature because it represents a unique experiment in using film as a medium to interpret and critique literature. *The Other Francisco* is a Marxist analysis of the liberal-bourgeois ideology informing Anselmo Suárez y Romero's *Francisco* (1839), Cuba's first antislavery novel. The film at times follows the novel's melodramatic plot while adding scenes and voice-over commentary to criticize the book's romantic aspects and to elucidate socioeconomic conditions. In many sequences, Giral examines life on a nineteenth-century plantation through a historical materialist lens which focuses on decisive economic factors and the often violent class conflict between slaves and masters. Giral's critique of *Francisco* mixes in an innovative manner elements of a fiction film—lovers in a melodramatic plot—with documentary techniques, such as an off-screen narrative voice and interviews with historical personages.

One of the successes of ICAIC has been in the field of animation. Forty-five animated cartoon shorts were produced from 1979 through 1982. The most popular of the cartoon heroes is Elpidio Valdés, an intrepid soldier in Cuba's wars of independence from Spain. The feature-length *Elpidio Valdés* (*Elpidio Valdés*, 1979), which was written and directed by Juan Padrón, was a major hit at the box office. Padrón's latest Elpidio Valdés adventure feature, *Elpidio Valdés Against Dollars and Cannon* (*Elpidio Valdés contra dólar y cañón*, 1983) was painstakingly created over a thirty-six-month period from more than ninety thousand drawings.

Another major success of ICAIC has been documentary filmmaking. The institute annually produces some forty technically accomplished documentaries on a wide range of subjects. Pedro Chaskel's shorts *A Photograph Goes Around the World* (*Una foto recorre el mundo*, 1981) and *Che Today and Always* (*Che hoy y siempre*, 1983) are homages to revolutionary leader Ernesto "Che" Guevara. Many documentaries illustrate and support government-sponsored programs. Octavio Cortázar's short *For the First Time* (*Por primera vez*, 1967) registers the wide-eyed amazement of children and adults viewing a movie for the first time—Chaplin's *Modern Times* is playing as part of ICAIC's mobile-cinema program, which takes films to rural communities. Manuel Octavio Gómez's *Story of a Battle* (*Historia de una batalla*, 1962) is a documentary record of the 1961 literacy campaign. In the feature-length *Fifty-five Brothers and Sisters* (*55 hermanos*, 1978) director-writer Jesús Díaz used a 16 mm *cinéma vérité* style to record the visit to Cuba of Cuban-born women and men who had been taken from the island as children.

Luis Felipe Bernaza has made two fine documentary shorts which are portraits of exceptional individuals. *Cayita, Legend and Feats* (*Cayita, leyenda y gesta*, 1980) features a ninety-six-year-old woman who reminisces about Cuban revolutionary history, and *Pedro Zero Percent* (*Pedro cero por ciento*, 1980) stars a dedicated dairy farmer, Pedro, who never lost a cow to illness. The world of art and entertainment is frequently recorded in documentaries. The short *Let the Guitar Raise its Hand* (*Que levante la mano la guitarra*, 1983), directed by Víctor Casaus, is a portrait of the popular singer and composer Silvio Rodríguez. Director Oscar Valdés's *Art of the People* (*Arte del pueblo*, 1974) examines the art of papier-mâché; Octavio Cortázar's *Speaking of the Cuban Punto* (*Hablando del punto cubano*, 1972) offers an appreciation and a history of the *punto*, a traditional Cuban musical form. Cuba's elusive, predaceous wild dogs are the subject of Daniel Díaz Torres's documentary short *Wild Dog* (*Jíbaro*, 1982), a remarkable example of the difficulties of filming wildlife on location. In Rolando Díaz's short *Controversy* (*Controversia*, 1981), wives and husbands in an agricultural cooperative heatedly discuss work obligations and sex roles. Director Melchor Casals is an exceptional documentarist because of the investigative approach he brings to contemporary Cuban subjects: his *Fulfillment* (*Cumplimiento*, 1980) reveals serious production problems in a sugar mill.

In 1984 ICAIC marked the twenty-fifth year of its founding. In terms of the law which founded the institute in 1959, the greatest success of ICAIC has been in producing films which present and interpret Cuban history and culture from a revolutionary perspective. However, the ICAIC filmmakers have been less successful in reeducating the taste of the movie-going public in terms of the aesthetics of film—slick Hollywood-style movie-making is still seen by some fiction filmmakers as the surest way to reach a wide audience.

According to Julio García Espinosa, current head of ICAIC, one of the institute's most important future directions will be to encourage fiction filmmakers to devote less attention to historical subjects in favor of contemporary issues. Gutiérrez Alea has recently pointed the way with his fine fiction feature *Up to a Certain Point* (*Hasta cierto punto*, 1983), a stylistically innovative exploration of the interrelations between artistic creativity and the artist's personal life. The film, which features a love story, is also a pointed critique of the ingrained machismo of certain Cuban writers, filmmakers, and intellectuals. It is films such as this which suggest that ICAIC will continue in the foreseeable future to be one of the leading film industries in Latin America.

# SELECTED BIBLIOGRAPHY

## Books

Agramonte, Arturo. *Cronología del cine cubano*. Havana, ICAIC, 1966.

Chanan, Michael, ed. *BFI Dossier number 2: Santiago Alvarez*. London, British Film Institute, 1980.

*Cine y revolución en Cuba*. Barcelona, Fontamara, 1975.

Douglas, María Eulalia, ed. *Filmografía del cine cubano (1959–1981)*. Havana, Cinemateca de Cuba, 1982.

Fanshel, Susan, ed. *A Decade of Cuban Documentary Film: 1972–1982*. New York, Young Filmakers [sic] Foundation, 1982.

García Espinosa, Julio. *Una imagen recorre el mundo*. Havana, Letras Cubanas, 1979.

Gutiérrez Alea, Tomás. *Dialéctica del espectador*. Havana, Unión de Escritores y Artistas de Cuba, 1982.

Myerson, Michael, ed. *Memories of Underdevelopment: The Revolutionary Films of Cuba*. New York, Grossman, 1973.

## Articles

Aufderheide, Pat. "Red Harvest." *American Film* 9, no. 5 (March 1984): 28–34.

Burton, Julianne. "Cuba." In Guy Hennebelle and Alfonso Gumucio-Dagron, eds. *Les cinémas de l'Amérique latine*. Paris: Cherminier, 1981, pp. 259–313.

――――. "Revolutionary Cuban Cinema, First Part: Introduction." *Jump Cut*, no. 19 (December 1978): 17–20.

Chanan, Michael. "Cuban Images: An Introduction." *Framework*, no. 10 (spring 1979): 19–22.

Hernández, Andres R. "Filmmaking and Politics: The Cuban Experience." *American Behavioral Scientist* 17, no. 3 (Jan.–Feb. 1974): 360–92.

Pick, Zuzana M. "Towards a Renewal of Cuban Revolutionary Cinema: A Discussion of Cuban Cinema Today." *Cine-Tracts* 2, nos. 3–4 (summer–fall 1979): 21–31.

# CZECHOSLOVAKIA

## JOSEF ŠKVORECKÝ

Film is the ideal art form for the semiliterate, and it is also the most expensive art. If you combine the two and think in terms of *art engagé* or, pragmatically speaking, propaganda art, it translates into the formula that whoever has the money can influence the masses via film. Lenin saw it this way, and this is the rationale for his famous pronouncement that "to us [the Bolsheviks] film, of all forms of art, is the most important."

Film, therefore, was the first industry which the Communists in Czechoslovakia forced the aging president Beneš to nationalize. He signed the decree on 11 August 1945, a mere three months after the guns of World War II had gone silent.

The only trouble was that Czech moviegoers were not semiliterate.

Only one man tried to prevent the coming of socialized cinema. He was Miloš Havel, the founder of the modern Czech film industry, who built, and owned, the Barrandov studios, before and during the war the most modern in Europe. Havel was a sort of Maecenas rather than a Louis B. Mayer, and his company, the Lucerna Film, had produced a number of remarkable movies, including the Venice Festival winner *The Guild of the Virgins of Kutná Hora* (*Cech panen kutnohorských*, 1938), by the prewar Communist Otakar Vávra. In 1945 Havel suggested that a company be established in which the state would hold at least 51 percent of shares. But during the war, the exiled government in London had arbitrarily decided on a *numerus clausus* for political parties which reduced their number from about sixteen to just four: one Communist, two socialist and one Catholic centrist. The decision also left Havel with no power base in the political establishment. Consequently, his proposal was rejected.

Nothing really remarkable happened during the short three years of semidemocracy between 1945 and 1948, when the bureaucrats in the Barrandov studios were still somewhat restricted by the existence of the competing parties. Only one film is usually mentioned in surveys, also a Venice Festival winner, *The Strike* (*Siréna*, 1947), by Karel Steklý, the story of a miners' strike in 1889. It was a traditionally made social melodrama but, in Venice, it benefitted from the then political mood among Italian intellectuals, and from the impact of the rising neorealism with its accent on proletarian themes. A much more interesting movie, *The Premonition* (*Předtucha*, 1947), by Otakar Vávra, a subtle study of puppy love, goes relatively unnoticed.

The coup of 1948 established the Communist party's monopoly of power. The bureaucrats at Barrandov received a *carte blanche*. They now had all the financial resources of the state at their disposal, and no opposition could hinder them from using that money to mold the mind of the masses. Unfortunately for them, the mind of the masses was that of an ancient, fully literate people with Western cultural traditions, and the method they used was socialist realism: a primitive, didactic formula art, divorced from reality by its ideological false consciousness. And so they freely lavished huge sums of money on the tales of the proverbial girl-tractorists and unwavering workers with the result that the masses, instead of spending their evenings at the cinema, went to the tavern.

From this period of rampant sociorealism covering roughly the years from 1948 to 1957, only three names seem worth mentioning. In 1949 Jiří Krejčík made *The Conscience* (*Svědomí*, 1949), a psychological drama about a man who kills someone in an automobile accident and then leaves the scene to keep his wife from learning about his mistress, who is with him in the car. The script had been approved before the 1948 coup, but after its release, the film was labeled existentialist (which in those days equaled reactionary) and banned, and its screenwriter, Vladimír Valenta, who years later appeared as the station master in *Closely Watched Trains*, was sent to a concentration camp for slandering Soviet cinematography. Alfréd Radok, the stage director who later conceived the Magic Lantern Theatre, had his film debut in the same year with *The Long Journey* (*Daleká cesta*, 1949), a film about Jews under Nazism, which combined a quasi-documentary method with expressionistic visions and psychological immersion. An artistically premature and politically anachronistic work, it was also immediately banned and not rereleased until the mid-sixties.

The only director who, in this era of bannings and primitivism, created a veritable *oeuvre* that, in its freshness and authenticity, fully survives, was Miloš Havel's friend Václav Krška. His is the case of a stubborn artistic vision which overcomes incredible nonartistic obstacles. Among Czech directors he is probably the first *auteur*, a film artist with a clearly defined style whose interest lay not in tractors but in the movements of the soul. He is both the culminator of the lyrical tradition of the Czech cinema, shaped by an early Venice Film Festival winner, *The River* (*Řeka*, 1933), by Josef Rovenský, and a precursor of the Czech New Wave, with its stress on intimate and individualized stories and on the *situation humaine*. Two films of his are clearly the best works of the otherwise uninteresting period. *Moon Over the River* (*Měsíc nad řekou*, 1955) is a melancholy story of a handsome, no longer young woman who, hampered by small-town prejudices, rejects her much younger admirer, and grows hopelessly into old spinsterhood. *The Silver Wind* (*Stříbrný vítr*, 1954), banned after release because of alleged homosexual overtones and rereleased in 1956, is about the sexual turmoils of adolescence. That these two movies could have been endorsed at all by the studio bosses seems a miracle. Articles on the film of that period mention that the final OK followed long periods of negotiations and came partly as a result of the director's literally begging that he be permitted to shoot his film. He had one point in his favor, though: both stories are based on works by a renowned Czech author who was politically a radical, at times almost a fellow traveler. That made objections more difficult to raise.

The money lavished on the industry had one side effect, unforeseen by the bureaucrats. Large sums were also invested in the Film Academy (FAMU), intended as a hatching ground for the future masters of socialist realism (or, as the common derogatory term had it, socrealism). But a very natural dialectics set in. The students, unlike the rest of the population (except for the prominent circles of the establishment who had private cinemas that catered to their private tastes, mostly American Westerns and musicals), were exposed to both the classical and the best contemporary Western films at weekly all-day screenings at the school. Many of them were talented young people who soon perceived the discrepancy between the reality of which they were a part and the "socrealistic" formula that was to be their mandatory method, designed to depict that reality. They saw the aesthetic abyss gaping at them from between what their professors officially presented as triumphs of socialist art and what the same professors silently screened as interesting, though bourgeois products: works of Orson Welles, of the neorealists, of the French New Wave. In a situation like that, only a blind filmmaker could make the wrong choice.

The death of Stalin in 1953 inaugurated an era of erosion of political certainties which is best labeled as the thaw. Revelations of various crimes and "mistakes" led to the collapse of belief in the Party's unerring wisdom, and, naturally, even more so in the canons of socialist realistic aesthetics. Some former Party enthusiasts among the professors, directors, dramatists, and film critics lost their blinders—or their timidity—and began to support the youngsters from the academy who never had worn blinders in the first place.

But it is hard to jump from a formula right into reality, to abandon overnight the pseudoproblems of Party life and replace them with the burning issues of the life of the people. Logically, there followed a period of the gradual breaking up of the formula, of cautiously changing the stress from unreserved optimism to reserved criticism: the years, roughly, from 1957 to 1963. The new trend, a kind of *Ur*-New Wave, probably started with Vojtěch Jasný's *September Nights* (*Zářiové noci*, 1957), a melodrama about a ruthless army officer who shows no understanding for the anguish of a private whose wife lies in childbirth and who, therefore, temporarily defects. The film barely escaped banning, only because the infuriated Stalinist commander in chief of the army was sacked a day or two after it had been screened for him. What saved the work politically, and what also stifled it dramatically, was the cautious use of a *deus ex machina* figure, a wise political officer who, in the end, smoothes everything over. The Stalinists, after the death of their leader, were in retreat, but they regularly foraged into the liberated territory. Therefore, dramaturges had to play it safe. Both this and the following decades were marked by periodical ups and downs in artistic suppression, by a kind of yoyo movement which, in Marxist-Leninist countries, replaces the natural dialectics of societal development.

A political step forward was *School for Fathers* (*Škola otců*, 1957), by Ladislav Helge, whose protagonist, a village schoolteacher, faces obstacles similar to those of the frustrated private in *September Nights*. He fights them and loses. In another film by Helge, *Great Solitude* (*Velká samota*, 1959), the Communist chairman of a collective farm alienates the workers by his efficient but ruthless methods. After a private screening for the Party censors Helge was forced to reshoot the ending and make the brute win back the affection of his subordinates—and the film critics had to take back a prize they had intended to bestow on the movie.

In 1959 the entire period ended in an orgy of bans. Krška, barely recovered from the attacks on *The Silver Wind*, became the target of wrath once again for *Hic Sunt Leones* (*Zde jsou lvi*, 1958), another variation on the theme of the losing battle of an idealist against bureaucracy; the ferociousness of the attack apparently broke the sensitive man, so that he never made any significant films afterward. Another ban affected the witty comedy *The Third Wish* (*Třetí přání*, 1958), by Ján Kadár and Elmar Klos, which, in its last shot, left the hero with the dilemma of whether to betray a friend who had fallen into disfavor or help him, and thereby endanger his own career.

All these films, the most talked about in the late fifties, had several characteristics in common. Their directors were Party members who shared the theme of Party conscience. Their stories were built around sharp conflicts not rooted in the life that most of their contemporaries lived but in the pseudolife of a tiny minority that imposed its political system upon the majority. The ordeals of an unloved Communist chairman and the sufferings of a Communist teacher fighting the ghosts in whose making he had participated were hardly felt as burning issues by the general populace at a time when almost every family had a political prisoner among its members. Neither were such problems close to the hearts of the youngsters at the Film Academy who bore no guilt for Stalinism, and for whom politics was no longer a deeply felt affair of the soul, but an interfering nuisance. Much more than appreciating Party dramas, these students enjoyed films like *Wolf Trap* (*Vlčí jáma*, 1958), by Jiří Weiss, a sensitively made movie on the classical theme of a marital triangle, set in the colorful twenties; or *Local Romance* (*Žižkovská romance*, 1957), by Zbyněk Brynych, another love story, markedly influenced by neorealism; or *Desire* (*Touha*, 1958), by Vojtěch Jasný, a lyrical meditation traditionally organized by the four seasons of the year corresponding to the four ages of man, but untraditionally filmed with stress on visual beauty and devoid of politics. But above all, the young graduates of the academy were full of the Italians and the French. Soon they were to make their debuts.

The great divide was the year 1963. It brought Jaromil Jireš's *The First Cry* (*Křik*, 1963), whose young protagonists are not concerned about Party discipline but about having a baby and finding an apartment for it; Věra Chytilová's *Something Different* (*O něčem jiném*, 1963), which paralleled two unconnected female lives, one ordinary, one prominently successful; and the first two epoch-making films by Miloš Forman, *Competition* (*Konkurs*, 1963) and *Black Peter* (*Černý Petr*, 1963). In these truly filmic works of art, the last remnants of the socialist realist formula, and the last traces of the esoteric and self-delusive world of the Communists were completely obliterated, and contemporary Czech life was given its first unbiased portraiture since before World War II. Except for Jireš, none of these directors were Party members. In the years immediately following they were joined by others, equally free from any binding ideological fetters: Jan Němec, Evald Schorm, Ivan Passer, Jiří Menzel, Pavel Juráček, Ester Krumbachová, and a host of lesser names. Together they created the phenomenon known as the Czech New Wave. Unlike the neorealists or the French New Wave, they never shared an aesthetics. The devotion to art, that is, a devotion to life, which they placed above all other loyalties, was their sole common ground.

Of them, the most important, not only because the most successful, is Miloš Forman. His Czech films show only token influences by the neorealists and by the Czech novelists of the turn of the decade; his vision is fully his own. Unlike Krška who situated his films in the pre-World War I era, Forman is firmly an artist of the present time. Moreover, his protagonists are all working-class people, not troubled by questions of Party conscience but by the unchanging problems of the human race. Thus the hero of *Black Peter*, an apprentice in a self-service grocery, suffers from the unbearably bad feeling that he is a kind of informer, a watchdog snooping on customers rather than a decent boy; and he also timidly copes with the anguish and joy of first love. The girls who dream of pop stardom in *Competition* struggle pathetically with their lack of talent. The rather plain factory girl of *Loves of a Blonde* (*Lásky jedné plavovlásky*, 1965), seduced by a dance-band pianist on a one-night gig in her home town, tries unsuccessfully to move in with the boy's family in Prague. And the uncouth working-class characters of *Firemen's Ball* (*Hoří, má panenko!*, 1967) first select what must be the world's strangest looking beauty queen, and then make an effort to cover up for one of their comrades who pilfered a ham from a charity raffle. Together, these films give a realistic portrait of contemporary Czech working-class people, not from a perspective of sneering antagonism as has sometimes been suggested, even by critics in the West, but from that of empathy based on intimate knowledge—or, simply, from the point of view of an artist who is in love with his subject matter. Naturally, such portraits tend to be ideologically unflattering, even "cruel"; they resemble life so much, and life is hardly ever perfumed and soft.

However, the political yoyo was not put to rest, not even in these years of artistic triumphs: all these films were viciously attacked by influential establishment critics, but—and this is where the situation differed from the fifties—also, sometimes, successfully defended by other critics. *Black Peter* was seen as a defamation of working-class youth and *Loves of a Blonde* as pornography; *Firemen's Ball* allegedly slandered voluntary firemen, who even threatened to quit their fire engines if the film was not banned. All of this is characteristic of works that pave a new way. In the context of Czech cinematography, Forman meant a true revolution.

Věra Chytilová, more eclectic, more formalist, and also more of a virtuoso, gained prominence with her second feature *Daisies* (*Sedmikrásky*, 1966). Stylistically, this film is a collage of influences of—and also of tributes to—the great filmmakers of the past, from the Lumiéres to Meliés to Gance to Chaplin; a veritable experiment with the possibilities of film techniques. As complex as its form is its message: apparently, it is an evocation of the youthful ennui of two girls who revolt against their drab world, but it is also a satire on the easy solutions offered for such problems by all the reformed-sinner schools of art which, of course, include socialist realism. The film's provocative fame reached the Czech parliament where an interpellation was read, asking for its ban, which duly followed.

The film is rather different from Chytilová's first feature, *Something Else*, a much less formalist probe into the intimate lives of women, and from her pioneering portrayal of young female factory workers in con-

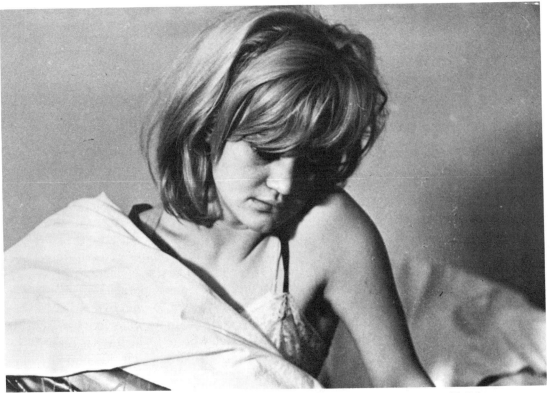

Part of Miloš Forman's neorealistic heritage was his preference for the "unrepeatable" faces of nonactors: Hana Brejchová in *Loves of a Blonde* (1965).

In this still from *Firemen's Ball* (1967) firemen jurors assess what must be the world's strangest-looking line-up of beauty contest participants.

(Above)
The most disturbing
aspect of the Slovak
fascist state—the
persecution of the Jews—
was the subject of Kadár
and Klos's Oscar-winning
*Shop on Main Street*
(1965).

(Right)
Jiří Menzel's *Closely
Watched Trains* (1966)
daringly combined themes
of adolescent sex and
guerilla warfare. Here
the apprentice Milos
pursues a young woman
conductor.

(Left)
Always an excellent
actors' director, Menzel
assembled what amounts
to a repertory company
for his films. Its most
distinguished member is
Rudolf Hrušínský, shown
with Magda Vašáryová in
*Short Cut* (1980).

(Below)
Labeled a "decadent
formalist," Vera
Chytilova revealed a
superb sense of balletic
stylization and
composition in *Daisies*
(1966).

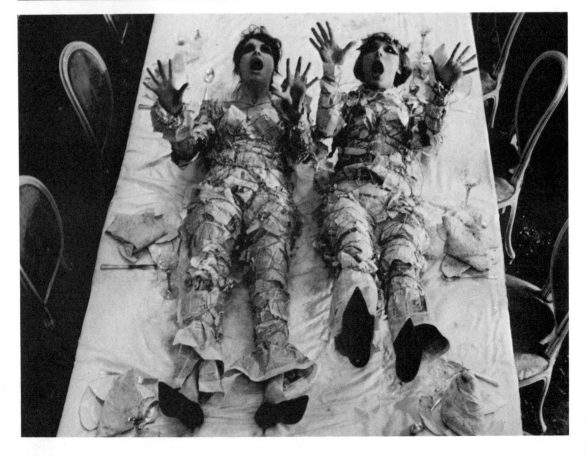

flict with the old generation *A Bag of Fleas* (*Pytel blech*, 1962), a short which may have influenced Forman. And it is very close to *The Fruit of Paradise* (*Ovoce stromů rajských jíme*, 1970), a quasi-biblical parable of women in a world dominated by men.

If Forman and Chytilová still mirror—although Chytilová rather indirectly—the objective outer world, Jan Němec shaped in his films a universe that resembles the life on our planet only in the form of a dream, often of a nightmare. The harsh *Diamonds of the Night* (*Démanty noci*, 1964) is a nightmare by its very nature: an unsuccessful attempt of two Jewish boys to escape from a death march which ends in tragedy. Dreamlike also are the three comic stories about the love affairs of the charmingly shy lovers in *Martyrs of Love* (*Mučedníci lásky*, 1967) where the tradition of Czech film lyricism is combined with surrealistic elements. Němec's magnum opus, *The Party and the Guests* (*Zpráva o slavnosti a hostech*, 1966), is a nightmarish parable: the story of a strange group of guests attending a garden party whose host wants to force happiness down everybody's throat, and sends police dogs after the only guest who left without permission because he could not stomach the enforced false bliss. Banned for two years, the film was eventually released only a short time before the arrival of the tanks in 1968.

Bans and semibans (that is, restricted showings in marginal theaters) marked also the career of Evald Schorm, the Christian philosopher of the New Wave. The hero of his first feature, *Courage for Every Day* (*Každý den odvahu*, 1964), is an idealist worker who failed to "grow up" (that is, remained a worker while his former partners were rewarded with successful bureaucratic careers); he embodies the clash between the ideological vision of society and real life. The theme of Schorm's second film *The Return of the Prodigal Son* (*Návrat ztraceného syna*, 1966) was made relevant years afterward by the publicity surrounding the misuse of psychiatry in the USSR. The protagonist, a young architect, is confined to a mental institution because his refusal to make moral compromises appears to his fellow citizens, including the psychiatrists, as madness. Schorm's third feature, *Five Girls To Deal With* (*Pět holek na krku*, 1967), in my view the most beautiful film of the New Wave, reverses the socrealist cliché: here, the good girl is the rich one, the bad ones are her proletarian school friends. However, when these envious girls forge a ridiculous love letter to her boyfriend, the angelic virgin turns into a vicious informer. The theme of this flawlessly executed black-and-white poem of a film is enhanced by a point-counterpoint between the girl's trifling world and the grandiose world of Weber's *Der Freischütz* which plays in the local opera house and whose romantic passions move also the tiny heart of the adolescent heroine.

Schorm's last pre-1968 film, *End of a Priest* (*Konec faráře*, 1968), is the only film ever made in any socialist cinematography that openly promotes Christian values—and also the only film to deal skeptically with the chances of the Communist reform movement before it was crushed by the tanks. Its story of a fake priest and a genuine village teacher reveals that the genuine one is really the priest-imposter, and the fake is the diploma-owning teacher who, without asking anybody, assumed the "leading role" in the village. Schorm's last film, *Seventh Day, Eight Night* (*Sedmý den, osmá noc*, 1970), was banned before release, and, except for finishing a feature for the exiled Jasný, Schorm has not made another film to date.

The fifth member of the leading quintet of the New Wave, Jiří Menzel, came into prominence, after two remarkable shorts, with his first feature *Closely Watched Trains* (*Ostře sledované vlaky*, 1966), which provocatively paralleled a young railway apprentice's sexual difficulties with his political involvement in wartime Czechoslovakia; due both to its intrinsic human value and to the Oscar it received in 1968, it is probably the best-known Czech movie internationally. Menzel's all-pervading theme is the vicissitudes of sex: it marks his second feature, a comedy about three aging men attracted by a pretty artiste, *Capricious Summer* (*Rozmarné léto*, 1967), and his crime-musical *Crime at the Nightclub* (*Zločin v šantánu*, 1968), where a bumbling murderer, hired by the minister of the interior to silence witnesses of the minister's frolickings, kills various innocent bystanders until a court of law, obeying the sharp-eyed minister rather than Blind Justice, sentences the dangerous witnesses to the gallows. Menzel's next film, *Larks on a String* (*Skřivánci na niti*, 1969), told in beautifully neorealistic images, is the story of the sexual yearnings of a working-class boy for female political prisoners slaving in the junkyard of his factory. It was banned before release and prevented Menzel from returning to the studios until the mid-seventies.

This period also offered other talented directors and other remarkable films. Ivan Passer, Forman's scriptwriter, made his debut with a humorous but devastating portrait of life's futility, *Intimate Lighting* (*Intimní osvětlení*, 1965); Jaromil Jireš filmed Milan Kundera's scathing satire on the absurdities of Stalinism, *The Joke* (*Žert*, 1969), sarcastically utilizing Eisenstein's "vertical montage"; Pavel Juráček made what is probably the only truly Kafkaesque Czech movie *Josef Kilian* (*Postava k podpírání*, 1963), a satire on bureaucracy in the manner of *The Castle*; and beyond many of the best films of Němec, Chytilová, Vávra, and others loomed the personality of the brilliant scriptwriter Ester Krumbachová. There were also good musical comedies like Ladislav Rychman's *The Hop Pickers* (*Starci na chmelu*, 1964), and there was František Vláčil's haunting evocation of the High Middle Ages, *Markéta Lazarová* (1967), when remnants of paganism were still infusing Christianity. In addition, there was another Oscar-winning wartime drama *Shop on Main Street* (*Obchod na korze*, 1965), by Ján Kadár and Elmar Klos. Quite a few other outstanding works would merit discussion in a longer piece.

The seeming mystery of this veritable miracle within the confines of a totalitarian state is easily explainable. The more cultured comrades who became responsible for the film industry in the sixties simply "forgot" that Lenin saw film solely as a propaganda tool, and made the "mistake" of viewing it as an art form. Retaining the organizational structure of the industry which had been designed for the production of propaganda, they used its bottomless financial resources to fund artistic probes into the situation of man on this earth. State ownership of the industry can, indeed, be ideal, as Forman once said, provided that the state, or at least its film agency, is run by philosophers. But once the bureaucrats oust them, the capitalist way is preferable, for you always have "the chance that you will find some fool who will let you have the money you need."

More came to an end with the Soviet military intervention of 1968 than just an interesting era in the history of Czech cinema. When, a year later, the regime of Gustáv Husák established itself in power, it proclaimed a summary ban on almost an entire year's output of the studios, and returned Czech cinema to its original Leninist function: to propaganda, to entertain, and to fake "art" films that address themselves to marginal problems.

Forman, Passer, Kadár, Weiss, Jasný, Němec, Radok, and a few lesser directors left the country, never to return. Some continued their filmic careers in the West: Forman with remarkable success (*Taking Off, One Flew Over The Cuckoo's Nest, Hair, Ragtime, Amadeus*); others with changing fortunes: Passer (*Born To Win, Law And Disorder, Love And Passion, Silver Bears, Cutter's Way*); the late Kadár (*Adrift, Lies My Father Told Me, Freedom Road*); and Jasný (*Ansichten eines Klauns*). Some disappeared in the shadows of Hollywood. Of those who remained at home, a number were banned from the studios (Helge, Schorm, Juráček, Krumbachová, and others); some resigned and turned into makers of conformist propaganda or entertainment (Jireš, Brynych, Rychman, Bočan, and so on). Two, Menzel and Chytilová, for a long time stubbornly resisted and eventually achieved an interesting victory.

Since the basic precondition for an emergence of modern art, the freedom of expression, is outlawed at the Barrandov studios, reality, the only source of art, has to be once again approached through an ideological sieve. In the seventies and early eighties, this produced: at worst a second generation of socialist realist atrocities; at best a few decent historical and biographical films; a number of clever comedies; and in between an occasional well-made musical and an exceptional drama about the "errors of the past." For the most part, however, the products were slick, often cumbersome, tearjerkers posing as art.

Examples in the first aforementioned category are *The Hippopotamus* (*Hroch*, 1973), by Karel Steklý, an inept satire on Dubčekism misusing Dostoevskii's story "The Crocodile," and Otakar Vávra's *The Dark Sun* (*Temné slunce*, 1980), which has about as much of the spirit of Karel Čapek's 1924 novel *Krakatit*, from which the story is borrowed, as Veit Harlan's *Jew Süss* had of the humanistic content of Lion Feuchtwanger's novel of the same name that was also based on the tragedy of the unfortunate eighteenth-century courtier. In the second category, *The Divine Emma* (*Božská Ema*, 1978) contains some great singing, and is a censorial mistake, for the refusal of the heroine, the Metropolitan Opera prima donna Ema Destinnová, to work as an informer for the Austrian secret police repeatedly provoked roaring ovations in the cinemas, which had nothing to do with *Austrian* police; the film was eventually relegated to restricted screenings, and sold to a distribution company in the United States, where audiences, presumably, will miss the relevant association. Among comedies, perhaps *Run, Waiter, Run!* (*Vrchni, prchni!*, 1980), by Ladislav Smoljak and Zdeněk Svěrák, should be mentioned. It is an intelligent throwback to the screwball comedies of the thirties with overtones of the theater of the absurd. Perhaps one should mention three efforts by Forman's second former scriptwriter Jaroslav Papoušek to carry the Forman team's (Forman, Passer, Papoušek) tradition into the seventies: *Ecce Homo Homolka* (1970), *Big Shot Homolka* (*Hogo fogo Homolka*, 1970), and *Homolka and the Wallet* (*Homolka a tobolka*, 1972). The trilogy captured the unappealing conformism of yet another group of working-class types who, in all publicity and reviews, for the sake of censorship, were constantly referred to as *petit bourgeois*, and explained much of the psychology of post-1968 "normalization," that is, of adjustment to the status quo. In spite of the enormous popularity of the series, Papoušek was not able to continue with it, and in the semiofficial survey of Czech comedy in the seventies the trilogy is not included, allegedly because "although chronologically [it] belongs to the seventies . . . Papoušek's new vision in a new social era is not apparent until his [non-Homolka] film *Television in Bublice, Bublice on Television* (*Televize v Bublicích, Bublice v televizi*, 1974)." As for the third category, there was one good musical based on a Czech version of the Robin Hood story, *Ballad for a Bandit* (*Balada pro banditu*, 1979), by Vladimír Sís, and a village drama *About Moravian Land* (*O moravské zemi*, 1977), by Antonín Kachlík, obviously aimed at export; in any case, vigorously offered to Western distributors. Making great use of the lovely Moravian landscape and heavily overstressing the material well-being of the collective farmers, the film is a story of a private farmer who, in the fifties, is forced to join the cooperative. He even becomes its chairman, but since he demands hard work he is finally expelled by the workers. What prevents the movie from becoming a true drama is the lack of the tragic element that is prevalent in such excellent versions of the same story model as Vojtěch Jasný's *All My Countrymen* (*Všichni dobří rodáci*, 1968) or Ladislav Helge's *Shame* (*Stud*, 1968), both banned in 1970. As for the third type of film in this category, kitch posing as art, a good example among many is *Solo for an Old Lady* (*Sólo pro starou dámu*, 1979), Václav Matějka's fairy tale for the Party where a cab driver, realizing that his customer is a Westerner, proudly refuses not only a tip but any payment whatsoever, and even buys the astonished West German lady a Czech wurst.

Among the rustle of bureaucratic protocols, all individual voices were thus eventually silenced, and only a feeble echo of a potentially original timbre penetrates, here and there, through the thick layers of closely watched and laboriously rewritten-to-order scripts. In the sixties Czech cinema resounded with the ideas of its best minds; in the seventies and eighties its most obedient ones whisper the slogans approved elsewhere. It's not that there would be no new talents, comparable, perhaps, to Forman and Chytilová; it's just that they have to talk—and even roar—with their master's voice.

The bright spots in this drab landscape were provided by the two aforementioned stubborn members of the New Wave. Jiří Menzel, after a pause of six years and a public recantation of sins (he did not, however, accede to the demand to return his Oscar to the "Hollywood Zionists"), after two indifferent films and one nostalgic evocation of the early days of Czech cinema *Magicians of the Silver Screen* (*Báječní muži s klikou*, 1978), came back with another delightful tribute to sex, *Short Cut* (*Postřižiny*, 1980), which exudes the spirit, and also the aesthetics, of the sixties, and in 1985 with a remarkable portrayal of the rudeness and voraciousness of the common people, *The Snowdrop Festival* (*Slavnost sněženek*, 1985), that can hardly be interpreted otherwise than as a scathing satire on "really existing socialism." Věra Chytilová, after an Open Letter to the President and after having gained the support of an *eminence grise* in the studios, directed one, and then, in quick succession, two more features that retain many of her formalist concerns and all of her caustic social criticism; in spite of her protector they were soon withdrawn from mass distribution and permitted only occasional screenings in suburban theaters. *The Apple Game* (*Hra o jablko*, 1976) is a sex comedy about irresponsible males and suffering females; *An Apartment House Story* (*Panel Story*, 1982) presents the microcosm of a tenement house as a drama of vicious jealousies among the supposedly "new" men and women of socialism; and *Calamity* (*Kalamita*, 1982), with its quotation from the archetypical film of the sixties, Menzel's *Closely Watched Trains*, is a satire, done with Formanesque cruelty, on the lack of readiness to help among the same "new" people— the Homolkas of Papoušek's trilogy who allegedly belong to a bygone era. Her 1984 film, *The Faun's Very Advanced Afternoon* (*Faunovo značně pokročilé odpoledne*), presents what is probably the most dazzling collection of pretty girls in bikinis, indicating the industry's "mild progress within the limits of the law" (Hašek), which now permits an amount of sex appeal on the screen that even in the sixties, so enraged by the modest and aestheticized nude in *Loves of a Blonde*, would have been unthinkable.

Thus these few veterans, and their friends working now in the West, save the good name of Czech cinema. Although the attacks on the New Wave continue unabatedly in the film journals even fifteen years after the Soviet intervention, although that by now historical movement is repeatedly pronounced dead, defunct and irrelevant, one can see, reading between the lines in the Party-line film monthly *Film and Times* (*Film a doba*) and elsewhere, that this is not so. In the May 1982 issue on page 274, for instance, Antonín Kachlík complains that the students of the Film Academy "under the influence of the old and *carefully preserved* legend of the golden age of the Czech cinema . . . endeavour to reintroduce dramaturgical conditions similar to those which shaped the 'successful' films of the sixties" (stress added).

*Das Spiel ist ganz und gar verloren, und dennoch wird es weitergehen,* wrote Erich Kästner once: the game is entirely and thoroughly lost, and yet it will go on. Are we, then, on the threshold of another upswing of the yoyo of Czech cultural development? We must be very cautiously optimistic. One name, that of Jaroslav Soukup, indicates that a new, more critical generation could be in the making. After *A Romance* (*Romaneto*, 1980), which subliminally suggests a parallel between the police persecution of intellectuals after the unsuccessful Czech uprising in 1848 and similar police actions after 1968, he made a film, *Wind in the Pocket* (*Vítr v kapse*, 1982), heavily influenced by Forman (it even includes scenes and bits of dialogue literally copied from *Loves of a Blonde* and *Black Peter*), albeit without Forman's innovative freshness. Its two teenage protagonists yearn for things practically unattainable in Czechoslovakia: the career of a seaman and travel to the West. The movie also contains some criticism of such characteristic phenomena of "socialist" life as unanimous voting, and so on, and ends on a note of pessimism, even desperation: one of the youths is killed in an accident and the other is drafted for two, long and utterly useless years in the army. That things like these were passed by the censor should, however, be explained by the establishment's efforts to appear "liberal," rather than by a genuine behind-the-scenes change of cultural politics.

It is too early to know what the future has in store for Czech filmmakers. The old men of Stalinism learn their lesson much better than the ever enthusiastic and therefore gullible youth.

## SELECTED BIBLIOGRAPHY

Boček, Jaroslav et al. *Modern Czechoslovak Film 1945–1965*. Prague: ARTIA, 1965.

Dewey, Langdon. *Outline of Czechoslovakian Cinema*. London: Informatics, 1971.

Hames, Peter. *The Czechoslovak New Wave*. Berkeley: University of California Press, 1985.

Hrabal, Bohumil. *Closely Watched Trains*. New York: Penguin Books, 1981.

Janoušek, Jiří, ed. *3 1/2: Chytilová, Forman, Jireš, Juráček*. Prague: Orbis, 1965.

_____. *3 1/2 podruhé: Schorm, Passer, Němec, Vachek*. Prague: Orbis, 1969.

Liehm, A. J. *Closely Watched Films*. White Plains: International Arts and Sciences Press, 1974.

_____. *The Miloš Forman Stories*. White Plains: International Arts and Sciences Press, 1975.

_____. and Mira Liehm. *The Most Important Art*. Berkeley: University of California Press, 1977.

Menzel, Jiří and Bohumil Hrabal. *Closely Watched Trains*. New York: Simon and Schuster, 1971.

Skvorecký, Josef. *All the Bright Young Men and Women*. Toronto: Peter Martin Associates, 1971.

_____. *Jiří Menzel and the History of the Closely Watched Trains*. Boulder: East European Monographs, 1982.

Stoil, Michael Jon. *Cinema Beyond the Danube*. Metuchen: The Scarecrow Press, 1974.

Whyte, Alistair. *New Cinema in Eastern Europe*. London: Studio Vista/Dutton, 1971.

# FRANCE
## Postwar French Cinema: Of Waves in the Sea

DUDLEY ANDREW

French cinema has always sought to be regarded as a prestige cinema, playing an important role in cultural definition and transcultural commerce. The French claim to have invented the medium in 1895; they point to the birth in 1909 of their Compagnie de Film d'Art, dedicated to the highest aesthetic standards then held by the bourgeoisie. With more genuine pride they note the birth of the world's first film clubs and serious journals during the twenties, institutions that fostered the recognition of cinema among the most elite artistic camps as well as its centrality to the great Paris expositions of 1925 and to the surrealist movement that followed this. Even though Hollywood utterly dominated the first decade of sound production, the French took the artistic honors: the films of Feyder, Clair, Carné, Renoir, and Duvivier won prizes in competitions around the globe. Throughout its history the French cinema has posed as the aesthetic conscience of a worldwide industry that Hollywood still controls commercially.

How seriously can one take such claims? Only about 20 percent of French output during the past four decades has been aimed at the prestige market, the rest happily drawing a return from Francophone audiences eager to be diverted on Saturday night by a light comedy or a witty mystery. Even among the prestige productions can we genuinely cite many films made in the spirit of the more noble arts? Of course not; yet this veneer of high culture which the French accord to the mission of cinema, and particularly to their mission within cinema, has had material consequences. Fostered by a tumult of critical discourse (no country has more aficionados of the art, more subscribers to serious film journals and cine-clubs, more discussion of movies on television), French cinema has been molded by critics. In reality, the French have inflated the role of cinema in culture and their own role in the cinema.

A modest industry in terms of size, French cinema commands the respect, or at least the eye, of the whole world. Not that the French are uniform in their assessment of what the cinema should be or how they have fulfilled their responsibilities toward it; but even in the wars of words that fill so many journals and "round table" discussions one hears an uncommonly fervent pitch. Cinema is crucial; France is, or must become, crucial for the cinema.

These sentiments were never more feverishly uttered than just after the liberation of Paris, when a glorious new cultural era seemed to be dawning, and when French cinema could look with pride at its past ten years, at the prewar poetic realist movement, and at the cinema under Vichy, a cinema that far outstripped the other arts within France during those years of trauma.

Closed in on themselves during four years of occupation, the French in 1945 thought first of the place cinema must take in their newly liberated culture. The industry, in its first move, proclaimed that it had been a cinema of resistance and disowned any implication that it had allied itself in any way with the occupying powers. An ignoble process called "purification" censured and even incarcerated those suspected of having profited from close relations with the Nazis. These reprisals affected few in the industry and were largely motivated by personal animosities rather than evidence of any real collaboration. Among the celebrated victims were Arletty and Sacha Guitry who were jailed, and Henri-Georges Clouzot, who was blacklisted for a two-year period.

Along with the purification came the call to reestablish the "Frenchness" of French cinema, a process begun during the occupation that served as a veiled attack against the often Jewish talent that had poured into Paris during the thirties and continued to work there, often on the sly, right through the war. The Eastern European and Russian set designers and actors had given an "international style" to films such as Anatole Litvak's *Mayerling* (1936). Some French *cinéastes* were eager to repudiate this internationalism in the hopes that the noble tradition of French culture might, after the rupture of the war, flow directly into the veins of a revitalized and purer cinema. This was the conservative line. But hopes for a renewed cinema came equally from the socialists and Communists. Even so level-headed a critic as André Bazin was carried away by the possibilities of cinema acquiring a new social and economic base, one that might transform the aesthetics and function of the art. Student and factory cine-clubs, left-wing film journals, and the availability of 8mm and 16mm formats for amateur filmmaking fueled these hopes which, by and large, called for a realist cinema of social engagement modeled on the scintillating example of Italy, and on Rossellini in particular.

While the conservatives and social radicals disagreed stridently about the kind of cinema that ought to emerge under the new Fourth

Republic (1945–1958), they linked arms against the ominous presence of Hollywood, a presence ready to dash the dreams of left and right alike under the weight of the twenty-five hundred backlogged films coming ashore with the troops of liberation. The cinema would be neither socialist nor French if American producers and distributors could have their way, and who was there capable of standing in the way?

Economic dikes were erected to stem this tide, but none proved satisfactory to the industry. Taxes on imported films were levied as always. Profits made by American companies in France were blocked, to be reinvested in France. A law requiring all theaters to screen French films a minimum of four out of every thirteen weeks was enacted, and after strikes and demonstrations in 1948, was renegotiated to five weeks. But these measures were not enough. Despite their capacity (in terms of facilities and personnel) to turn out 250 films a year, the figures for 1946 show only seventy-eight. In 1938 French films comprise 65 percent of gross domestic receipts; during the war, 85 percent; but from 1946 to 1954 only 40 percent.

Chief among those directors silenced by this drop in production was Jean Gremillon. From 1937 to 1943 he had come to be regarded as one of the leading directors in the country, and certainly its chief hope for the future. Yet his most ambitious plans after the war were never carried beyond the preproduction stage. What a waste of enormous genius! And Gremillon was only one of many important directors eager but unable to give work to the great camera operators and actors collecting unemployment checks. It was a frustrating return to the reality of an international market.

Nearly all members of the industry blamed the government for selling out the cinema to America in exchange for other favorable trade advantages. But the fact is that no legislation could right the balance of a disorganized French system against the Hollywood majors. Some, like the opinionated scenarist Henri Jeanson, preferred a laissez-faire system, claiming that government intervention only fostered sloppy productions. It was up to French producers to identify and promote a kind of film capable of outdrawing Hollywood's factory products both at home and abroad. Even those who supported government action agreed with this premise.

While their ideas about what might constitute a viable alternative to Hollywood ran in various directions, the French issued a single battle cry to rally against the American challenge: the word *quality*. Blaring from the headlines of the first issue of *Le film français*, this word was meant to recall France's prewar glory and to profess faith that no economic weakness could undermine so pure a thing as artistic value. This word, first mentioned in 1935, became a fully rhetorical term in 1945, set against Hollywood "quantity." France, it was declared, must preserve and export its talent, good taste, and enviable traditions in art and literature. On its success depended also the success of French culture and of products like perfume and haute couture, indirectly advertised in the movies. Conceived of both chauvinistically (the famous French superiority in taste) and commercially (films must compete like automobiles), the quality cinema would rapidly devolve into the formulaic. At the base of the formula was the literary adaptation (whereas the dominant prewar style, poetic realism, had been founded on original scripts). Even those postwar films that were based on original scenarios relied heavily on dialogue, in a literary fashion, meant for cultured voices. Every major postwar film obligingly filled its cast with actors from the Comédie-Française, which was an unquestionable source of quality.

This famous "good taste" is most apparent in visual design. During this period shots have a tendency to freeze into photographs, or, more aptly, storefront windows, dressed self-consciously by the latest trendsetters in fashion. Costumes were displayed as though for a fashion show. Even the leftist journal *L'écran français*, which incessantly excoriated Hollywood for its fictional whitewashing of real social issues, portrayed on the back of every issue some starlet dressed by a renowned couturier. Fashion in France was, perhaps is, a national pastime. From 1945 on it became associated with film art, affecting even the style of lighting and the camerawork in a noticeable way. All these formal niceties were meant to enclose French film's true gift to the world: intelligent messages about key moral issues. In promotional blurbs of the time it was this mature, reflective, and serious content that most completely distinguished French films from the bland, even moronic Hollywood product.

The inclusion of major writers, thinkers, and artists within the mainstream cinema has always been a trademark of the French system: recall Artaud, Cocteau, and Giono. It is a country that loves to display ideas, and one in which the avant-garde does not work disdainfully on the margins. Whereas Hollywood films were designed to appeal to popular tastes, quality products were meant to educate and uplift a populace. Hence the moralizing tone of the scripts and music in some of these films. Hence also the contradiction between a liberal, even leftist ideology, and a conservative, highly bourgeois "look." No doubt Stendhal, Maupassant, and Zola, whose books were a key source to this movement, would have laughed at this serious attempt to criticize culture in a culturally superior way.

France's greatest expectations were placed on Marcel Carné, the premier prewar director whose *Children of Paradise* (*Les enfants du paradis*, 1945) had just put such a glorious exclamation point to the liberation. His next project was as lavishly conceived as one might expect, an entire metro stop being erected in the studio. The script by Jacques Prévert for *The Gates of Night* (*Les portes de la nuit*, 1946) was full of the famous fatalism and misty poetic dialogue that had made this the world's leading writer-director team. Yet the film failed miserably. An intricate, brittle allegory about collaboration and resistance, couched in a fairy-tale love story, *The Gates of Night* spoke to an era other than the one in which it was made. Prévert would continue with this, his native style, in a few more films (most notably the delicate and clever *Lovers of Verona* [*Les amants de Verone*, 1948], which reworks the Romeo and Juliet story around characters playing those roles on stage); but the Prévert era was over and he returned to poetry. Many feel that Prévert's loss of a film audience spelt the end of Carné's career as well. It is true that after the disaster of *The Gates of Night* Carné had trouble financing the projects he wanted. But he did remain an important force with *Mary of the Port* (*La Marie du port*, 1950), the audacious "dream film" *Juliette, the Key to Dreams* (*Juliette ou le clef des songes*, 1950), and the powerful modernization of Zola's *Thérèse Raquin*, called in English *The Adultress* (1953). After this Carné is a man in search of the popularity he once commanded. Only with *The Cheaters* (*Les tricheurs*) in 1956 did he momentarily succeed.

If Carné couldn't resurrect his prewar glory, other carry-over directors fared just as badly. Jacques Feyder and Julien Duvivier both returned to France after the war and made beautifully crafted films of dark fatalism: *Panic* (*Panique*, 1946) and *Macadam* (1946). Neither found critical favor or popular success. It was really up to the new talent, talent that had developed during the occupation, to pick up the torch that the older masters were evidently no longer capable of holding. Chief among these directors were Jean Delannoy and Christian-Jaque, the most prolific filmmakers of the forties.

Critics have not been kind to Jean Delannoy, although the public certainly has, for nearly all his films have been solid box-office hits. But Delannoy, both by personal pretension and by the subject matter of his major films, demands serious attention. Just as André Cayatte is France's director of social problem films, so Delannoy may be considered its moral philosopher. *Pastoral Symphony* (*La Symphonie pastorale*, 1946) and *God Needs Man* (*Dieu a besoin des hommes*, 1949), made just after the war, brought him this reputation and remain his best known works, along with *The Chips Are Down* (*Les jeux sont faits*, 1947), made in collaboration with Sartre. But more than twenty films surround this core, few of which measure up to the ambition and values for which they stand. Evidently Gide, Queffelec, and Sartre inspired him to render great moral and philosophical issues in a dramatically rigorous way. Today these films seem overly cautious, pretty, even prettified. But in their day they garnered worldwide respect, the first winning the Grand Prize at Cannes in 1946 and the last, the Grand Prize at Venice in 1950. The cinematic ingenuity they display, particularly in the use of geography as a moral arena (a snowy alpine village, a destitute seacoast village), gives some, though not sufficient, justification for their staginess and weighty dialogue.

Delannoy attracted the arrows of young French critics because of the battle he lost to Bresson over rights to *Diary of a Country Priest* (*Journal d'un curé de compagne*, 1950) and the battle, also with Bresson, that he won over those to *The Princess of Cleves* (*La princesse de Cleves*, 1961). Accusations concerning his inauthenticity were borne out in the many hack productions he directed in the 1950s, including a superproduction of *The Hunchback of Notre Dame* (*Notre Dame de Paris*, 1956). While none of these films is without some merit (*La princesse de Cleves* actually is full of tasteful production values), his style more and more represented the most deprecated aspect of the cinema of quality.

Of all France's important filmmakers, Christian-Jaque has unquestionably been the most prolific. Director of more than fifty films in virtually all genres, his facility has been a mark against him in the eyes of most critics. Nevertheless, no one denies the lusty dynamism of his action scenes or the technical ingenuity he loves to display in even his most run-of-the-mill efforts. Until 1950 he had to be reckoned as one of the leading men in French cinema, not only at the box office where he has always had success, but in terms of the possibilities of the art of the cinema.

During the war he specialized in the very popular romantic mystery genre and in more cultured spectacles, like *Carmen* (1944). These led to his greatest successes just after the war, *A Man Returns* (*Un revenant*, 1946), in the mystery vein, and *Ball of Fat* (*Boule de suif*, 1945) and *Charterhouse of Parma* (*Le chartreuse de Parme*, 1948), adapted from Maupassant and Stendhal respectively. In the adaptations France's most ostentatious actors dress up as their favorite characters. While both films exhibit genuine moments of visual excitement and some of the brash tone of the originals, they remain at best on the surface.

Concerned with decoration, Christian-Jaque is finally a frothy director. When dealing with a star (and he married three of his leading ladies, Martine Carol being the most famous) or with a light action picture such as *Fanfan the Tulip* (*Fan-Fan la tulipe*, 1952), he is delightful, but aside from the short period surrounding World War II, little of his work merits a second look. That period, though, especially in *A Man Returns,* captures the dreamy romanticism to which much of the culture escaped in its most difficult moment.

Delannoy and Christian-Jaque stand at the head of a host of lesser directors who consecrated themselves to maintaining the prestige of French cinema via adaptations of literary classics and productions of historical spectacles directed at the audience with the full-throated bravura of a culture confident of its richness. To them, the cinema inherited the responsibility of representing national values for the instruction and edification of the French populace and of other nations.

Far more aesthetically advanced are those films that questioned French values but which nevertheless were proud to see themselves within the tradition of quality. Three directors stand out here: Claude Autant-Lara, Henri-Georges Clouzot, and Yves Allegret. All three had roots in the avant-garde movements of the early thirties, but their serious filmmaking careers began during the occupation and after.

Autant-Lara made the most controversial film of the postwar period in *Devil in the Flesh* (*Le diable au corps*, 1947). Taken from the celebrated novel by Raymond Radiguet and making international stars out of its illicit lovers, Gérard Philipe and Micheline Presle, this film scandalized the country with its sympathetic presentation of adultery and its disgust with patriotic and bourgeois values. On armistice day, 1918, during its flag waving and shabby parades, the hero rehearses in flashback the years he had just lived through and the love affair he has had with an older woman whose husband is at the front. The bitterness of growing up in a self-righteous community has seldom been so forcefully presented.

Autant-Lara was to make a career out of bitterness, but after 1946 it took a more paternalistic, often sardonic turn. His next film, for example, *Oh Amelia!* (*Occupe-toi d'Amelie*, 1949), brought back the lightness of French farce which by and large had left the country with René Clair in the thirties. Its pace and tone are masterful enough to put to rest nasty rumors about Autant-Lara's talent. His good taste is another matter, however. *The Red Inn* (*L'auberge rouge*, 1951) poked easy fun at the clergy and the church, drawing the ire not only of conservatives but of many film critics who rebuked him for its lack of nuance. But Autant-Lara has always seen it as his mission to affront received morality with all the rhetorical tools at his command. His greatest such tool has been the literary classic which he and his scriptwriters, Jean Aurenche and Pierre Bost, shamelessly use as they see fit. In 1953 came an adaptation of Colette's *Game of Love* (*Le blé en herbe*), and, the following year, of Stendhal's *The Red and the Black* (*Le rouge et le noir*, 1954). The audacity of taking on two such different styles of literature within two years helped make Autant-Lara the chief whipping boy of François Truffaut in the notorious essay "A Certain Tendency in French Cinema," published in the February 1954 issue of *Cahiers du cinéma*. Truffaut was most outraged by the way the subtle modalities of perception and expression in the literary sources were sacrificed for a boisterous polemical thrust against the church and in favor of free love. Autant-Lara fought back in print and on the screen, making one of his finest films in 1956, *Four Bags Full* (*La traversée de Paris*), with the aging stars Gabin and Bourvil. But after the ascendancy of the New Wave he was destined to be seen as the leading intellectual of a meretricious form of cinema. Autant-Lara must be perplexed to be categorized as a standard, predictable director since his life began in the atmosphere of surrealism and never varied in its commitment to personal liberty and even anarchy. But his artistic background was too refined to promote this spirit in the texture of his images. He was too well-bred, a bourgeois anarchist.

In a country like France, where good taste is so admired, Henri-Georges Clouzot has been a far more shocking director. A film critic during the age of surrealism, Clouzot was always eager to assault his audience with his style as well as his subjects. Like so many others, he found his chance to move from scriptwriting to directing during the occupation when there was a paucity of established directors in France. His second film, *The Raven* (*Le corbeau*, 1943), was the only truly shattering film made in this era. Retaining all the conventions of the thriller, Clouzot systematically exposed the physical and psychological grotesqueries of every character in the film. A grim picture of small-town mores, *The Raven* was attacked by the Nazis and the French patriots alike. When the war and his years of "purification" had ended, Clouzot resumed his career with an even more grim view of life. Both *Jenny Lamour* (*Quai des Orfevres*, 1947) and his 1948 adaptation of *Manon* emulate American *film noir* in their seamy settings. Both are extremely well acted, but ultimately small works. Clouzot's fame in the United States came in the mid-1950s when *The Wages of Fear* (*Le salaire de la peur*, 1953) and *Diabolique* (*Les diaboliques*, 1955) gave him a reputation as a French Hitchcock, interested in the mechanics of suspense. But in France these films, especially *Diabolique*, were seen as only well-made studio products. His 1960 *The Truth* (*La verité*), starring Brigitte Bardot, was designed to win him favor in the youth culture obsessed by New Wave life and movies. While the film outgrossed its New Wave competition, a cloyingly paternalistic style shows how far Clouzot is from the spontaneity of the younger directors. The cafe scenes are insincere and the inevitable indictment of society rings false. All of Clouzot's films, up to the 1968 *Woman in Chains* (*La prisonnière*), were financial successes, but early in his career he ceased being the instrumental force in the film industry he had been in 1945.

The third figure contributing to the postwar feeling of bitterness is Yves Allegret, whose reputation up to that time had been lost behind that of his flamboyant brother. After the war, when Marc Allegret could only be thought of as a dilettante and culture monger (*Lady Chatterly's Lover*, 1955) with an infallible eye for young starlets (Brigitte Bardot owes her career to this eye), it was Yves who had to be taken seriously. Nearly twenty years after he had entered the field, he finally achieved acclaim with *Dedée* (*Dedée d'Anvers*, 1947). He and his writer, Jacques Sigurd, here discovered a theme and a style that would carry them through several other successes. Their approach can be called "psychological realism," a product of script, direction, and acting alike. In comparison to prewar poetic realism, the style of these films was much more analytic just as Sigurd's scripts were far more bitter. *Dedée* is the story of small-time gangsters, in which Simone Signoret, Marcel Dalio, and Bernard Blier live lives of jealousy and distrust in the bistros and along the docks of Anvers. As their petty crimes move toward murder, a *film noir* style is invoked, except that the component of suspense is deliberately down played in favor of atmosphere and acting. *Riptide* (*Une si jolie petite plage*, 1948), undoubtedly Allegret's greatest work, likewise depicts an atmosphere of depair that drives the hero, played by Gérard Philipe, to a Gabinlike suicide. But Allegret doesn't share his hero's dreams the way Carné seemed to. Instead, he observes, almost sadistically, the debilitating effect of small-town life on a character whose past haunts him.

In *The Cheat* (*Manèges*, 1949) Sigurd and Allegret go further in taking apart the hypocritical lives of their characters. This time Simone Signoret is an undisguised cynic as she seduces a wealthy bourgeois and then robs him blind while consorting with lovers from her own lower class. The filmmakers' cynicism is as great as that of their heroine. While still wielding a powerfully evocative style in painting this atmosphere of upper-class hypocrisy and lower-class sex, Allegret's utter misanthropy begins to turn the film toward satire. With no respect for his characters and with a Darwinian view of private and social behavior, a supercilious tone results. Of his many later films, only *The Proud Ones* (*Les orgeuilleux,* 1952) compares in stature to the 1948–50 trilogy. The film was adapted from a screenplay by Sartre (called *Typhus*), and Allegret's penchant for nasty details and intolerable living conditions was perfectly suited to this existentialist (non)morality play. The script's philosophic theme encouraged Allegret to chisel away at its pathetic characters.

Yves Allegret is not a likeable director. His long career produced only four powerful films, all of which dwell excessively on human meanness. Yet his genius for making us feel this meanness and his audacious effort to make everything, including plot, serve the unveiling of human motivation make him perhaps the key filmmaker of the immediate postwar period.

If the dominant postwar style must be characterized as paternalistic, then Andre Cayatte is its most exemplary practitioner. No matter how well Cayatte may dramatize problems of euthanasia—*Justice Is Done* (*Justice est faite,* 1950)—delinquency—*Before the Flood* (*Avant le déluge,* 1953)—sexual hypocrisy—*To Die of Love* (*Mourir d'amour,* 1972)—and no matter how liberal or liberating his own point of view may be, the fact is that the films themselves are tyrannical. Their wellmade scripts constrict characters and spectators alike. Today one can see how vulnerable such a pedantic and stodgy cinema was against the vitality of Hollywood or against the immediacy of those films coming from Italy.

A few accomplished directors avoided the sclerosis of the cinema of quality by concentrating less on their relation to the audience and more on their approach to their subjects. These were the realists, Jean Gremillon, René Clément, and Jacques Becker, who brought forward a heritage from the thirties in which style is felt to be in tension with something it explores and seeks to bring out. Becker is the most solid of the three. The sureness of touch in each of his films derives from a precision some link to craftsmanship; but Becker was striving for far more than competence, veneer, or "quality." Becker seems to have gone out of his way to pose himself artistic problems. Many of his films are about groups of characters, most notably his final work *The Hole* (*Le trou*, 1960). Others are about milieux: *Antoine and Antoinette* (*Antoine et Antoinette*, 1946) captures the working class quarters of Paris; *July Reunion* (*Rendez-vous de Juillet*, 1949) may be the first film anywhere to explicitly deal with the youth culture of postwar Europe. *Paris Frills* (*Falbalas*, 1944) evokes the world of high fashion as only someone raised in such a world could know it; and, of course, *Golden Marie* (*Casque d'or*, 1952), his most famous film, makes the turn-of-the-century Parisian underworld come to life with a kind of grim romanticism. Becker claimed that his fastidious attention to milieu was the only way he could approach his characters. Bazin went further, claiming that through the exactitude of social particularity the universality of Becker's characters and their situations emerged. For Bazin, *Edward and Caroline* (*Edouard et Caroline*, 1950) is, if not his greatest film, at least his most revealing one. This brilliant farce in the style of Marivaux is virtually plotless. Becker was able to build a serious moral comedy from literally nothing via the swiftness of his decoupage and the sympathy he had for his actors. Becker has been called "the mechanic" of cinema, for he took a delight in its workings and he went about his own job with order and method. Becker was interested in what the cinema could do, just as he was interested in the ordinary things men and women do.

Like his teacher, Jean Renoir, Becker is generous in his observation of human beings. Their films have in common a respect for their subject matter, for the actors staging the story, and for the ambience which is that stage. Both are observers, sympathetic and curious onlookers who never fully weep in the tragedies they relate and never fully laugh in their comedies. Life is always bigger than the drama at hand.

René Clément exhibits, more starkly than had Becker, the productive tension between the realist and quality impulses. Clément began his career auspiciously, assisting Cocteau on *Beauty and the Beast* (*La belle et la bête*) in 1945, and with *The Battle of the Railroads* (*La bataille du rail*) in the same year. These films showed his range, for the first is a classic of fantasy while the second exhibits what can only be termed a neorealist style. Because the latter was shot on location with nonactors, and because its episodic story was drawn from the chronicle of everyday life at the end of the war, Clément was championed as France's answer to the powerful Italian school of the liberation.

For a time Clément seemed anxious to live up to this reputation. He associated himself with the progressive journal *L'écran français*, and he sought other realist topics, such as *The Damned (Les maudits*, 1946), in which he scrutinized the plight of a group of Germans and refugees aboard a submarine. Evidently he was more concerned with the technical problems of filming in small spaces than with the moral dimensions of his plot, for the film was not a great success. But with *The Walls of Malapaga (Au-delà des grilles*, 1948) Clément recovered his audience. This film, which won the Academy Award for best foreign film, was a Franco-Italian coproduction and brought together on the screen the most popular star of each country: Jean Gabin and Isa Miranda. The plot and style returned Clément to the poetic realist films of prewar France and continue to exhibit that tension of realism and abstraction that characterizes all his work.

Unquestionably, Clément was one of the most important figures in the French film industry during the 1950s. His *Forbidden Games (Jeux interdits*, 1952) remains a classic today and is notable both for the ingenuous performances of his child actors against a natural location background and for the moral incisiveness of its witty plot and dialogue, scripted by Aurenche and Bost. Clément's next feature, *Knave of Hearts (Monsieur Ripois*, 1954), starred Gerard Philipe. The film makes extensive use of subjective camera and voice-over. It was shot on location in London and is clearly an experimental project. But Clément's experiments have always been limited. Technical problems interest him, but he has never relinquished his belief that a film must be well crafted in the traditional sense of that term. This is what distinguishes him from the New Wave filmmakers. His all-knowing pessimism and his literary good taste finally put him in the camp of the "quality" directors. Nevertheless, his adaptation of Zola's *L'assommoir*, titled *Gervaise* (1956), must make one reevaluate this designation. It is an effective, well-balanced film, far above the average output of French cinema during its decade.

Clément, then, is consummately French. His technical mastery combines with his advanced political and moral ideas. He is cultured and trained. He makes excellent films both on a grand scale and on a smaller, more personal, one. But finally there is something impersonal about even these small films. Before representing himself, René Clément represents the institution of filmmaking in France. He is a good representative, perhaps the best it had after the war right up through the New Wave.

Jean Gremillon, with Becker and Clément, was considered among France's greatest hopes for a renewed and engaged cinema. In his mas-

terpieces of the thirties and early forties he had sought highly poetic locations in which to set his romantic dramas (mysterious villages in the
Alps and Normandy, or the evocative cities of Orange and Toulon). Gremillon emerged from the war the darling of the critics. He was open to
new conceptions of cinema yet he had the stature of an established master. Unfortunately, no one's stature was powerful enough to overcome
the economic woes afflicting the industry at that time. All that
he could bring to the screen were a brilliant documentary on D-Day,
*Dawn, the 6th of June* (*Le 6 Juin à l'aube*, 1945) and a moody *film noir*
*White Paws* (*Pattes blanches*, 1948) set in Brittany. In the fifties he
managed two more features, *The Strange Mme. X* (*L'etrange Mme. X*,
1951) and *The Woman and Love* (*Madame et l'amour*, 1953), both underrated, both fascinating, proto-feminist works. In the few years left to
him, Gremillon confined himself to the documentary. He remains a
most regretted genius, as every retrospective of his films confirms.

If Gremillon had trouble getting support for his realist films, imagine
the plight of lesser figures. Louis Daquin was, like his mentor Gremillon, a frequent contributor of journals, especially *L'écran français*,
where he promulgated his Stalinist views. Daquin struggled with producers year after year. His *Daybreak* (*Point du jour*, 1949), a modern
day *Germinal*, remains remarkable for the purity of its naturalism. But
Daquin's conception of realism is entirely one of subject matter whereas
in the area of style he generally subscribes to the quality ethos. This is
grotesquely evident in the 1945 historical allegory *My Country* (*Patrie*),
taken from Sardou, as well as in the 1947 *The Brothers Bouquinquant*
(*Les frères Bouquinquant*), a film whose first sequences are marvel-
ously neorealist before devolving into a conventional police film via a
flashback structure.

Jean-Paul le Chanois, like Daquin, was known for the seriousness of
his social beliefs. He had even begun his career as a surrealist. Yet by
1948 he could be found making rather sentimental hymns to society,
with only a token of realism. The use of nonactors and actual locations
in the 1948 *Passion for Life* (*L'ecole Bussonière*) is vitiated by the virtuoso performance of its one real actor, Bernard Blier, and by the tight
script that preaches its homiletic message about the dedication of
schoolteachers throughout France.

Despite the widespread flirtation with realism, only one rigorously
realist feature film was produced in postwar France, Georges Rouquier's *The Four Seasons* (*Farrebique*, 1946). An accomplished documentarist, Rouquier was able to film his natal village through the
course of a full year, connecting glorious descriptive landscapes and
small genre scenes with a meager family drama and several stunning
time-lapse montage sequences. The use of nonactors whose faces and
voices were utterly unpolished, together with a crude shooting technique, antagonized the more stolid members of the industry but thrilled

Bazin and the insurgent wing he spoke for. *The Four Seasons* is a landmark in part because it stands alone, an experiment never repeated in such a pure form. In 1983 Rouquier remade this essentially anthropological film by returning to his now modernized village. The result, called *Biquefarre*, still excited the critics who at Venice again rewarded him with a special jury prize.

The battle over *The Four Seasons* took place in cine-clubs and journals. Daquin, for example, excoriated the film for its ugliness; he also deplored the fact that the difficulty of its style excluded popular audiences. This became the line of *L'écran français,* which grew more and more Stalinist after the 1948 Marshall Plan fissured the leftist community into those ready to follow Moscow and those wanting a more independent socialism. Bazin, and a score of other young intellectuals like Chris Marker and Alain Resnais, were on the side of independence in everything. They were also on the side of style over subject matter. Realism for them was more than a social value; it was primarily a call to aesthetic renewal. At *La revue du cinéma,* destined to become *Cahiers du cinéma,* they found this renewal in the realist aesthetics of the new Italian cinema primarily, but also in the great art films of the past and the more "artsy" projects that Cocteau, Sartre, Bresson, and Alexandre Astruc were trying to create. In this journal, in the film club Objectif 48, and in the festivals at Biarritz, the cult of the *auteur* developed along with a passion for *film noir* and other genres formerly thought to be in bad taste.

By 1948 the ideal of the working-class film movement sputtered while a new ideal, a purely aesthetic one, grew up, and grew up in force. Into these clubs and festivals poured the members who would soon make up the corps of the New Wave: Rohmer, Truffaut, Chabrol, Godard. In their amateur film journals and soon in *Cahiers du cinéma,* they lashed out against the literary prettifications of French cinema and promoted all personal efforts, all attempts at expression directly through style. Sartre's interest in this movement was great; his influence was greater still. Immediately aesthetic issues became personalized; some filmmakers were excluded from serious consideration, while others were raised to angelic stature. Among the older French directors, only the great names of Renoir, Clair, Pagnol, and Ophuls survived this general assault on the past. These four men were impervious to the debates raging over realism and quality because their styles were already mature.

René Clair's return to France after an absence of more than a dozen years rendered a certain prestige to the era but did not otherwise affect it. Already an international figure whose films hardly touched the particularities of French life, Clair was looked upon as an individual of delightful intelligence, but an individual apart. Significantly his first effort, *Man About Town* (*Le silence est d'or*, 1946), declares outright what critics had always hinted, that Clair's is essentially a silent cinema, a cinema of elegant and articulate images that the burden of sound only tends to weigh down. In *The Beauty of the Devil* (*La beauté du diable*, 1949), a modern day *Faust*, Clair hoped philosophy could be made light enough to generate an operetta. The result was not to everyone's taste, but everyone respected his right and obligation to make whatever he felt he could. None of Clair's other films of the fifties, *Beauties of the Night* (*Les belles de la nuit*, 1952) or *Gates of Paris* (*La porte de Lilas*, 1957) had such impact on the industry, which was nevertheless proud to show them off around the globe.

While Clair suffered from having lost touch with his early audience, Marcel Pagnol maintained for over forty years a contract with the French public that was strict enough to constrain his style and subject matter. He remained the bard of Marseilles, adapting Daudet, Zola, and lesser known Provençal novelists, while reawakening the mythical land he had displayed for all the world first in the Marius trilogy. *Manon of the Springs* (*Manon des sources*, 1952) is pure Pagnol, but raised exponentially into the mythical, both because of its four-hour length and its subject (a nymphette of the mountains tied to the fructifying waters that bubble out of the ground around her). Pagnol followed his own path, not an idiosyncratic one (as in Clair's case) but one directed by the regional temperament he represents. Even when his scripts came fully from his imagination we feel he is but a medium for a general mythology to which he is tied.

With the industry fully reestablished by 1950, France suddenly received a major infusion, the return from Hollywood of Jean Renoir and Max Ophuls. What must they have expected of Renoir, their most far-sighted and important director, who had made a series of perplexing films in Hollywood? Now they were to be more consternated by those he began to make in their own country. Renoir, who never ceased to evolve as he moved from country to country and year to year, became in this final period something of a moralizer. His films began to flaunt the theatricality they had occasionally shown in the thirties. The long takes of *Picnic on the Grass* (*Déjeuner sur l'herbe*, 1959), are there to record the play of actors, whereas in *A Day in the Country* (*Une partie de compagne*) of 1936 they had meant to evoke a certain harmony of man and nature. That harmony still existed in Renoir, but it was now one negotiated through word and gesture alone. In his most intensely serious films of the thirties (*Grand Illusion* [*La grande illusion*, 1937], for example), Renoir as narrator had stood somewhat apart in an attitude of sympathetic understanding. Now in *The Testament of Dr. Cordelier* (*Le testament du Dr. Cordelier*, 1959) or *The Elusive Corporal* (*La caporal epinglé*, 1962) we are asked to enjoy that distance and the irony it affords rather than to involve ourselves so deeply in the plights of the characters whose capacity for good and evil has become a subject of curiosity. Not everyone had a taste for this new Renoir but the critics and the industry alike were proud to have him in their company. Perhaps they felt he had passed by them all into some realm of cinematic art that would be comprehensible only years later. In any case, Renoir's personal presence, more than his films, contributed to the ambitions of the younger generation, for he was an active, evolving, and yet legendary figure. He was constantly interviewed by the critics of *Cahiers*. He was the father of all the New Wave hoped to produce in their revolution: freedom, spontaneity, sensuality, play with actors, and cinematic solutions to cinematic problems.

Less might have been expected of Max Ophuls who had only passed through Paris in the thirties and whose stature in any case was nowhere near that of Renoir. But Ophuls had made a remarkable success of things in Hollywood and in genres the French were fond of, the police film and the melodrama. His arrival in Paris actually drew far more attention from the industry than did Renoir's and the four films he made before his death in 1956 were crucial to the health of the industry. Ophuls promised to appeal to the old and new guards alike. A European to his teeth, tasteful and elegant in his manners, he chose quality subjects taken from the lives of nineteenth-century aristocracy. All four films dressed up their immense casts of stars in the most extravagant of costumes. Indeed, the whole mise-en-scène of *La ronde* (1950), *House of Pleasure (Le plaisir*, 1951), *The Earrings of Madame de . . . (Madame de . . .*, 1953), and *Lola Montes* (1954) must be called extravagant. This was a cinema of quality if ever there was one.

But Ophuls fascinated those who condemned the industry and hated costumed adaptations. His excessive treatment of his subjects brought attention to the cinematic gesture by which he viewed them. The Ophulsian irony could be savored not only in the wry commentaries of Anton Walbrook and Peter Ustinov, but also in the cleverness of his intricate scenarios and in the camera angles which made a mockery of the sets festooned in draperies and multiplied them by a carefully calculated arrangement of mirrors. Then finally there was Ophuls's trademark, the tracking shot that wove itself throughout the action without ever quite becoming part of it. The sensuality of such movement excited considerable critical praise. The New Wave would emulate his techniques, making the moving camera a consecrated ritual. *Lola* (1961), by Jacques Demy, is only the most obvious of many New Wave films directly citing the work of this German who, even at the end, was a bit too ironic ever to give them the sort of direct encouragement or even the straight-answer interviews which they received from Renoir.

Ophuls, Renoir, Clair, and Pagnol, for very different reasons, were distant from the new spirit developing in journals and film clubs, even if they were frequently the subject of interviews and homages. Indeed, the very fame of these directors and the privilege of making films that fame brought with it, kept them from ever becoming practical models for young aspirants. As France headed blindly out of its fifties impasse, it proved better to look to struggling French directors who nevertheless had managed to risk a new approach, better to look to Bresson, Tati, Cocteau, and Melville.

Jean Cocteau's fame and social standing ought to have kept him equally distant from the younger generation, but he chose to associate with this group and to treat his involvement in cinema in the most independent, amateur fashion. While many had attributed the magic of *Beauty and the Beast* to René Clément, in retrospect the film, not just the subject, is pure Cocteau. This was confirmed in *Orpheus* (*Orphée*, 1950) which Cocteau handled completely by himself. One can see there not just the fantastic tricks of the camera (slow motions, reverse actions), but an ingenious understanding of the sound track (the messages coming across the car radio, for instance) and an astute observation of the cafe culture of postwar Paris. So notable was this film that Cocteau could, without pretension, end his career with a peculiar remake, *The Testament of Orpheus* (*Le testament d'Orphée*, 1959) in which he personally appears to comment on the myths and symbols he has created over the years. Of all Cocteau's films, however, he was proudest of *The Storm Within* (*Les parents terribles*), a 1948 adaptation of his own play. Refusing to open up the play, he locked his four characters in a struggle from which the deep focus photography never permits us to escape. Magnificent tracking shots from room to room tighten the drama to such an extent that André Bazin was led to proclaim a new era of adaptation in which the cinema might produce an experience more intense than the original. Bazin saw the film when it premiered at the meeting of the club Objectif 48 over which Cocteau presided. It was an event that gave to independent filmmaking a proud front against the industry.

Cocteau became a kind uncle to the young critics at *Cahiers*, but before that he gave other aspirants their chance as well. Jean-Pierre Melville's *The Silence of the Sea* (*Le silence de la mer*, 1947) had astounded him and he resolved to let Melville direct an adaptation of *Les enfants terribles* in 1949. While the result was less successful than either his own or Melville's previous efforts, it did for a time perpetuate the illusion that an independent cinema could exist in postwar France. Melville's case is instructive in this regard. His early shorts and his *Silence of the Sea* were financed entirely by himself. The aesthetic shortcuts which his budget required, particularly the use of an off-screen narrator giving us an interior monologue throughout the whole of *Silence of the Sea*, made him ridiculous to the establishment. But this solution to a scenario based on a novel of inner reflectiveness couldn't have been more precocious. Within two years Bresson would win praise for the same technique in *Diary of a Country Priest* and Alexandre

(Left)
Robert Bresson's *Diary of a Country Priest* (1950), an early example of the director's aesthetically demanding style.

(Below)
René Clement's classic *Forbidden Games* (1952) is notable for the ingenuous performances of its child actors against a natural location background.

Simone Signoret (center) in Henri-Georges Clouzot's suspenseful *Diabolique* (1955), which helped give him a reputation as a French Hitchcock.

Jean-Paul Belmondo and Jean Seberg in Jean-Luc Godard's first feature *Breathless* (1959), one of the first of the New Wave in France.

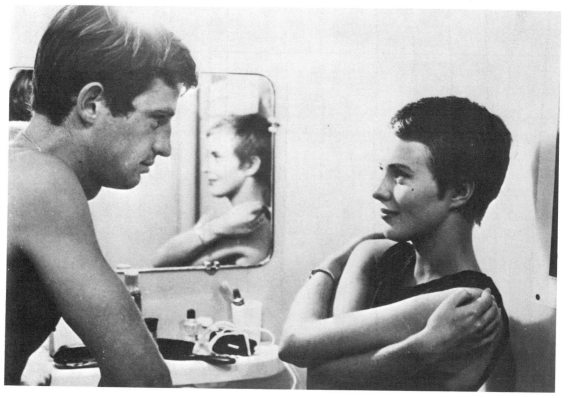

Anna Karina and Eddie Constantine in Godard's futuristic *Alphaville* (1965).

Alain Resnais and Alain Robbe-Grillet's langorous and strikingly photographed *Last Year at Marienbad* (1961).

(Right)
Truffaut's *Jules and Jim*,
New Wave cinema at its
finest.

(Left)
Jacqueline Bisset and Truffaut
in a scene from his film
about filmmaking, *Day for Night*
(*La nuit américaine*, 1973).

(Right)
Jean-Pierre Leaud in *The
400 Blows* (1959),
Truffaut's first feature
and the first in the
Antoine Doinel series.

Godard's brutal *Weekend* (1967).

The murder scene in Claude Chabrol's *Just before Nightfall* (1971).

*Claire's Knee* (1970) is one of Eric Rohmer's six moral tales treating a single theme with a single structure.

Rohmer's *The Marquise of O —* (1976), based on Kleist's celebrated German story, was an advance in the art of cinematic adaptation.

Astruc would achieve his first success with the same device in *The Crimson Curtain* (*Le rideau cramoisie*) in 1952.

Melville seldom worked in the fifties and when he did it was within traditional genres. Yet he brought to these genres, and particularly to the crime drama, an understanding of American methods that excited New Wave critics. Godard refers directly to *Bob The Gambler* (*Bob le flambeur*, 1955) in *Breathless* (*A bout de souffle*, 1959), a film for which he also recruited Melville to play the role of the intellectual whom Jean Seberg interviews. Once the New Wave had achieved success, Melville's career became one of self-parody, except for the singular case of *Leon Morin, Priest* (*Leon Morin prêtre*, 1961), a masterful dark film about a priest and a devout young woman set during the occupation. The intricate psychology which the mise-en-scène cuts through gives *Leon Morin, Priest* a strength that Melville's later, more exciting thrillers—*Doulos the Fingerman* (*Le Doulos*, 1963), *The Samurai* (*Le samourai*, 1967), *Second Breath* (*Le deuxième souffle*, 1966)—lack. He became, in short, a technical wizard and the more money he had to exploit technique, the less raw and immediate were his films.

Bresson and Tati, on the contrary, never flirted with the industry. Even when they managed to find relatively large budgets their films retained the stylistic rigor and idiosyncrasy that have made them heroes not just to the New Wave but to nearly everyone around the globe interested in the art of the cinema. Tati was especially intransigent. From 1933 to 1947 he managed to finance shorts of his mime acts by himself. When at last he put together *Festival Day* (*Jour de fête*, 1949), the industry took note since this was in fact France's first feature shot in color. That color process failed, however, and Tati found himself unable to break into any theater chain with the black-and-white version. Only a fantastic reception to a privately organized preview ensured the distribution of a film which eventually won the Prix de France. Tati's subsequent films, and there are only five of these, purify the style and themes of *Jour de fête*. *Mr. Hulot's Holiday* (*Les vacances de M. Hulot*) in 1953 won international fame, but his masterpiece, *Play Time* (*Playtime*, 1967), remains largely unknown outside film schools. *Play Time* is a film that taxes the ears through its meticulous aggregation of sounds. Few words are audible, and the camera seldom comes close enough to a character to make any one speech significant. Nevertheless, Tati's brilliant orchestration of a host of microevents in every scene is multiplied by the sound sources to produce a sensory overload. The film was shot in 70mm with stereo sound and its expense further ruined the director's chances with producers. Not even the delightful, and more accessible *Traffic* (*Trafic*, 1970) could win him backing for the films he was trying to put together right up to his death in 1982.

Robert Bresson has been equally praised and damned for his refusal to compromise, though he began his career during the occupation with two studio productions made in the quality manner. The second, *The Women of the Woods of Boulogne* (*Les dames du bois de Boulogne*), was hailed at its premiere in 1944 as an utterly befuddling work. It was praised, but critics realized that in Bresson the system had produced a new conception of the movies. By 1948 Bresson had stopped thinking of his work as belonging to the movies at all. His was an art of "cinematography" as his *Notes*, largely written in this era, are at pains to make clear.[1] His unflinching rigor won him the rights to film Bernanos's *Diary of a Country Priest* over a competing offer by Jean Delannoy. Bresson's film, financed in part by a recently created state subsidy, won the admiration of the critics. It seems he was a showpiece which the industry felt it could afford. This, together with a small but loyal international audience, permitted him to continue with *A Man Escaped* (*Un condamné à mort s'est echappé*, 1956), *Pickpocket* (1959), and seven other films, all completed without the slightest concession to any producer. His aesthetically and spiritually demanding style has resulted in one of the most personal and studied bodies of work in the history of the art. His most recent film, *Money* (*L'argent*, 1983) was still able to cause an uproar at the Cannes Film Festival even though it quite obviously follows the patterns he established thirty years earlier. Bresson's is a cinema of light and gesture, the movements of which express directly the spiritual respirations of his own soul. The very existence of sixteen films signed by Bresson is a tribute not just to him but to an industry that could tolerate him and to an international community eager to encourage him.

In his 1954 polemic Truffaut put Bresson, Tati, and Cocteau up against the cinema of quality. His essay went beyond argument; it was a declaration of all-out war. Godard, Chabrol, and Rohmer also joined battle in their critiques, while at the same time they began to find personal funds to finance 16mm shorts. In these efforts they were supported spiritually by some older renegades who gave credibility to this youth movement. Roger Leenhardt, Bazin's predecessor as dean of serious French critics, had made numerous shorts and one independent feature, *The Last Vacation* (*Les dernieres vacances*) in 1947. Alexandre Astruc, an ambitious novelist and friend of Sartre, had made several independent films and was much talked about in the industry despite his renegade tendencies. From outside France there was Orson Welles, now scavenging money in Europe, and Roberto Rossellini, virtually ostracized from Italy but preparing scripts in Paris. These men were in frequent contact with the young critics at *Cahiers* and fueled their ambitions. Nevertheless, had it not been for certain factors in the industry itself, the New Wave would never have accumulated the force it did.

By 1957 the sclerosis of the industry was of concern even to its most loyal supporters. Increasing costs were met by decreasing revenues. Audiences were turning to television and other varieties of entertainment as the old formulas, now made in color and CinemaScope and costing four times what they had in 1952, hardened into international tales about nothing. Coproductions with other countries, predominately Italy, more than doubled film budgets, but sapped from most films any contact with life. In a daring effort to revitalize the system, the Centre National du Cinéma (CNC) scuttled its policy of subsidizing producers who had earned box-office success in the past. Instead of track record, now the promise of the proposed script became the leading criterion. This method had worked wondrously for the short film ever since the inauguration of the whole system of advances in 1948. Alain Resnais, Georges Franju, and Pierre Kast, among others, had made acclaimed shorts under this system. Now CNC money would be available for features based on scripts alone.

Suddenly filmmakers appeared out of nowhere. From 1945 to 1957 very few new directors had been permitted to enter the industry. Between 1958 and 1961, with the new CNC policy in place, over one hundred directors made their maiden films. Many of these artists had been trained at the film school IDHEC (L'Institut des Hautes Études Cinématographiques), Louis Malle and Alain Resnais among them. The New Wave bubbled up in an epoch of youth frenzy. The magazine *L'express* devoted an entire issue to this phenomenon in late 1957. American jazz and automobiles were the rage. De Gaulle was pressing for a renewed conception of national character. A postwar generation wanted to forget the traditions of the past and bring into play the energies of the twentieth century.

And so there was a perfect conjunction of a new national spirit demanding new kinds of representations and regulations permitting a transfusion of new blood into what had become a moribund industry. It would be wrong to think of the New Wave as a movement planned from above, by the industry or the government or any other paternal seat of power. Only when many small film producers got behind younger talent did the revolution in the industry permit a revolution in film style. This sort of transition begins slowly before becoming a landslide. In France it began when three young assistant directors, Roger Vadim, Louis Malle, and Marcel Camus, turned their initial chances into huge international successes.

Vadim was a journalist whose friendship with Marc Allegret allowed him to enter the industry. He met Brigitte Bardot on the set of Allegret's *Starlets* (*Futures vedettes*, 1953), and they fell in love. Within three years they put together *And God Created Woman* (*Et dieu crea la femme*, 1956), whose tone was vulgar but alive. Its use of color and CinemaScope was breathtaking especially in revealing the body of the new superstar of French fashion. Vadim went on to try to maintain the scandalous reputation this first film garnered for him. He produced *Dangerous Meetings* (*Les liasons dangereuses*, 1959) with another sensation, Jeanne Moreau. The combination of a serious, though highly questionable, literary adaptation, beautiful young stars, a glimpse at the naughty new Left Bank culture (complete with an appearance by Miles Davis), made the film a sensation. Vadim's role in the New Wave was largely to show producers that there was money to be made in upbeat, sexually charged examinations of modern life. He was, in fact, quickly repudiated by the New Wave filmmakers for the stylistic opportunism of his shallow films. Still, even if Vadim's taste was bad, it was at least a taste different from the ancient cognac of quality cinema.

It is often forgotten that Marcel Camus's *Black Orpheus* (*Orfeu negro*) actually won the *Palme d'or* at the Cannes Film Festival in 1959 when Truffaut received the director's prize for *400 Blows* (*Les quatre cents coups*). Camus's bossanova recreation of the Orpheus myth in the slums of Rio de Janeiro used vibrant color and a mixture of ethnographic and hyperromantic style to win international acclaim. *Cahiers du cinéma* denounced the film for its facile style, but producers became more open to new directors and to location shooting because of Camus's success. Like Vadim, his subsequent films found favor neither with the establishment nor with the new generation.

Louis Malle presents a somewhat different case for he began as an assistant to Bresson and he has remained an important figure to this day. His first real success, and the film that helped launch the New Wave, was the *The Lovers* (*Les amants*, 1958). For its first sixty minutes it appears to be a conventional drama of manners, as Jeanne Moreau, tired of her provincial life, involves herself with a dashing Parisian playboy. Then, out of nowhere, emerges a young hitchhiker, a student whose sheer impetuosity literally sweeps Moreau off into the night. Never had the cinema witnessed such an extended visual portrayal of lovemaking. The couple dallies in the moonlit countryside, then across a lake on a boat, then, still in the moonlight, in her bedroom. All this with barely a word of dialogue and plenty of Brahms. In the morning, when they shamelessly bid adieu to husband and playboy alike, driving off to start an authentic new life, it might as well be the New Wave itself stealing the cinema away from the old guard.

The erotic excess of *The Lovers*, matched by its stylistic excess, completely overwhelmed most critics. Producers were stunned to see the lines outside the theaters and the foreign distributors bidding for rights to it. There was money to be made in taking risks, that was evident. There were also plenty of risk-takers around, particularly in the editorial offices of *Cahiers du cinéma*. These boisterous boys were finally going to get their chance. They had always claimed that films could be shot cheaply and still attract an audience. Vadim, Camus, and Malle had proved them right. With only a little luck, they could all enter an industry whose rules had changed. The story of their success is familiar. From a personal inheritance (Chabrol) and from a father-in-law

(Truffaut) came the money needed to make *Handsome Serge* (*Le beau Serge*, 1958) and *The 400 Blows*, the first of which, because of its cheap budget, made a bit of money, the other a fortune. Next, Truffaut and Chabrol fronted money to help Jacques Rivette and Philippe de Broca and they contributed to bankrolling Godard's *Breathless*. Eric Rohmer, Jacques Doniol-Valcroze, and Pierre Kast also made films. It was an avalanche, or, as they called it, a wave.

What these scores of films had in common, aside from their inexpensive means of production, is less easy to discern. All of them were concerned with style as something to be seen rather than as a smooth way of communicating a story. Hence camera movement, widescreen, editing, music, and voice-over become obtrusively visible in amplifying the sentiments of the story—*Jules and Jim* (*Jules et Jim*, 1961)—or working against the story—all of Godard might be cited here. Driven by a desire to express emotion directly through sounds and images, the themes of New Wave films are often those of adolescent romanticism. Tales of irrepressible sexual desire, of marginal loners, and of suicide abound. Indeed, nearly every New Wave hero is a young man living in contemporary Paris, allied in some way to a young woman who appears to be able to save or damn him. The influence of Sartre, or at least of a popularized version of existentialism, is profound, and "authenticity" is the catchword of the movement. Such themes and stories meshed perfectly with the production methods required of the period, for these films could be shot on location, and they could use a great many non-actors. Technical imperfections not only were overlooked; they became signs of that famous authenticity and immediacy that marked this new jazz age.

Obviously, there was in such a loose system much room for specious sentiments and sheer mawkishness. *Cahiers du cinéma* went to great lengths to keep its pedigree pure. For example, it distanced itself from the Academy Award-winning *Sundays and Cybele* (*Les dimanches de ville d'Avray*, 1963), disowning its sentimental romanticism. This popular vulgarization did serve to point to the chief vulnerability of this or any art movement making authenticity and direct expression its method and goal. There can only arise in this aesthetic a need to outdo oneself. Does this explain why so many maiden New Wave films are autobiographical, for example, those already cited by Chabrol and Truffaut? Here authenticity is easy to come by. As both of these directors moved into genre pictures (psychological thrillers for Chabrol, love stories for Truffaut), they frequently fell into the temptation of glorifying technique to assert their individuality over the genre. Less astute directors hardly recognized the problem at all and made a god of technique and its potential for arousing emotions. Jean-Gabriel Albicoco's *Girl with the Golden Eyes* (*La fille aux yeux d'or*, 1963), for example, is an absolutely hollow exercise despite its sensuous photography and magical tale. Since social issues rarely arise in these films, and when they do, are treated without subtlety, there is some truth to the charge that the New Wave was a right-wing revolution. Its heroes seek only a private salvation and are bereft of any vision beyond themselves. Their misery is never thought to have a social origin or solution. One would have to make an exception of Godard here, but even his *The Little Soldier* (*Le petit soldat*, 1961), a film about an OAS deserter in the Algerian conflict, confines itself to playing with the effect that this war has on its bewildered main character. Incredibly, this is the only New Wave film, aside from the comedy *So Long, Philippine* (*Adieu Philippine*, 1963), in which the subject of Algeria arises at all.

And yet the New Wave's true aesthetic advance, we can see today, lies in having turned the social aesthetic of the ethnographic film onto the field of fiction. Rossellini was crucial to this endeavor, but Jean Rouch was more so. The steady stream of films he had made in Africa, especially *Me, a Black* (*Moi un noir*, 1957), showed the *Cahiers* group what could be done with portable equipment. Rouch's was a cinema of the essay, a carefully thought out perspective on a given human problem. This was exactly the conception of cinema Astruc had preached in his famous 1948 article "Le Camera stylo"[2] against the omniscient perspective of standard French films. More important, the ethnological film essay presents physical reality in all its ambiguity. This had been Bazin's message for over a decade, as he ridiculed the moralizing style of quality. The New Wave hoped to put into practice Astruc's prophecy of a cinema in which every subject would be treated with a style appropriate to it alone, and Bazin's dictum that the cinema exists for exploration, not for preaching.

Truffaut and Godard went furthest in trying to touch stylistic extremes. Truffaut alternated highly personal projects like the *400 Blows* and *Jules and Jim* with exercises in genres such as *Shoot the Piano Player* (*Tirez sur le pianiste*, 1960) and *The Soft Skin* (*La peau douce*, 1964). In its abrupt changes in tone and intimate lyricism, *Jules and Jim* might be thought of as the apotheosis of the whole movement.

Godard never produced a film as satisfying as *Jules and Jim*. It would have been against his manner to have done so. More than anyone else he took the ethos of the essay seriously, turning out at least three films a year. All of them were brimming with ideas, quotations, and little cinematic experiments. In *A Woman Is a Woman* (*Une femme est une femme*, 1961) he achieved a musical comedy complete with color and CinemaScope. The next year he stripped away all accoutrements in the Rossellinian *The Riflemen* (*Les carabiniers*, 1963). Tenderness and brutal analysis alternate in *Contempt* (*Le mépris*, 1963). Godard's power comes precisely from such alternation, from the means by which he expresses the contradictions in his films and in the society from which they derive and for which they are destined. As the decade wore on, his films became more and more radical in form. *Alphaville* (1965) gave way to *Made in USA* (1966), and the brutal *Weekend* (1967), with its endless trucking shot of a lovely country road choked with automobiles and screaming humans.

Godard has always posed himself as a limit and in doing so he helps define what has been most fruitful about the movement as a whole. Never seduced by the lure of easy romanticism, Godard always saw the role of the cinema as one in which the representation of a culture and of its signs might be revolutionized. From this comes his love-hate relationship with American film genres. At times he was at pains to outdo Hollywood; more often he flaunted the rules that hold genres together. In this he is not alone. Chabrol, after his first straightforward autobiographical films, began to examine the moral weaknesses of his generation within the format of the thriller. Right up to this day, he has continued to emulate Hitchcock's psychological cruelty and grotesque humor.

Jacques Demy's genre is the musical. Even his first film *Lola* (1961) has the structure and tone of a musical that is spoken not sung. Innumerable references to film classics are woven through a wonderfully circular plot that never wants to touch ground. Still, this fantasy was shot almost entirely on location, making concrete Bazin's claim that the greatest marvels of the cinema should lift themselves from the day-to-day photographic life of the streets, transforming reality.

Jacques Rivette follows this same principle but to quite different ends. From *Paris Belongs to Us* (*Paris nous appartient*, 1960) up through the lengthy films he made in the seventies, Rivette brings a paranoid vision to a Paris that he makes us certain is controlled by powerful forces barely glimpsed in the life of the streets. A most rigorous man, Rivette has had great difficulty financing his projects. Still, his deeply felt notion of the relation of filmmaking to theater and to *cinéma vérité* has given him an immunity to aging. While none of Rivette's work has had commercial success (except for the scandalous *The Nun* [*La réligieuse*, 1966]), he, more than anyone else, has kept alive what was best about the New Wave.

In its focus on the individual and on personal artistic solutions to cinematographic situation, the New Wave effectively replaced a cinema of size and amplitude with one of the interior. Even the "musicals" of Godard and Demy, or Rivette's four-hour labyrinths, remain private manifestations which at best allude to a great public cinema of genres. This is the basis of its authenticity and of its claims to being a serious art rather than a mere spectacle. In this latter claim it is perhaps outflanked by a concurrent movement coming from the Left Bank.

Perhaps the greatest aesthetic effect the New Wave had was to make possible the films of Alain Resnais, Chris Marker, Agnes Varda, Henri Colpi, Alain Robbe-Grillet. Not linked to *Cahiers*, they were perhaps too avant-garde to maintain even a feisty relation with the industry. Once the *Cahiers* critics opened the floodgates, these filmmakers found their way into the world of the feature film. Their films are far more cerebral than those of the New Wave, though never autobiographical or romantic. They have dwelt on the nature of memory and imagination, the effects of history, and the intersection of time and desire. It is even wrong to call these "themes," for essentially the elements of time, imagination, desire, history, and space (all the basic elements of cinema) are sculptured into disturbing fictions.

Alain Resnais is certainly the most prominent member of this group. His *Hiroshima Mon Amour* was acclaimed at the Cannes festival of 1959, although out of competition. It too received a huge international distribution and permitted him to make *Last Year at Marienbad* (*L'année dernière a Marienbad*, 1961) with the "new" novelist Robbe-Grillet. Resnais has continued to stay ahead of his audience because he has had the cinematic talent and instinct to make concrete whatever thematic paradox he is obsessed with. The dreamy *Marienbad* was composed in languorous dolly shots while his next film, *Muriel* (*Muriel, ou le temps d'un rétour*, 1963), was broken into some two thousand fragments. In *My Uncle from America* (*Mon oncle d'Amerique*, 1980) he overlaid three separate biographies with the discourse of a zoologist, forcing his audience to regard his characters as rats in a maze. Naturally, he engineers their meetings and the twistings of their fates.

The stylistic precision and mentalism of these films links them to French literary traditions, especially to the philosophical *récit*, more than to any film tradition. The New Wave, by contrast, takes sustenance from popular literature and cinema, especially that of America. Doubtless this difference contributes to the spontaneity of the latter and the cold precision of the former. The Left Bank school is not one of exuberance. Its heroes are men and often women in their thirties. Frequently they are trying to make sense of a life that has been half led. These are mature characters, not the flamboyantly sincere adolescents incarnated by Jean-Claude Brialy, Jean-Pierre Leaud, Gerald Blin, and the other New Wave actors.

The complete preparation which these films exhibit, especially in their razor-sharp editing, is counterbalanced by a photographic quality that derives from documentary practice. Small pieces of the world join together to construct an abstract rhythm and a haunting mental effect. This, at least, has been the goal, though not all these films have achieved the level of Resnais's. Colpi's *The Long Absence* (*Une aussi longue absence*, 1960), for example, and many of Robbe-Grillet's efforts prove that no clever formula can by itself generate a film that is alive.

The Left Bank group essentially developed a new genre, with a distinctive tone. In the process, they found new uses for the tracking camera. They cut together images representing various levels of reality, and they revolutionized the function of music and the voice-over. In all these techniques, indeed in the genre itself, Chris Marker may be the most radical and complicated director. His travel films and situational analyses are part ethnographic, part autobiographical. Dense to the point of saturation, cinematic meditations of a most rare sort, they remain virtually undistributed.

In sum, the Left Bank school represents that aspiration which the young critics dreamt of ever since World War II, an aspiration toward art rather than artisanship, toward a cinema of "sensual ideas" rather than spectacle, toward a cinema of personal exploration through the exploration of style, and finally, toward a cinema stripped of useless accoutrements and founded on the photographic and constructive properties of the medium.

The Left Bank school looks all the more heroic today because the New Wave ethic looks today far less radical than it did in 1960 and because so many of its strident proclaimers have become absorbed into the mainstream. Truffaut and Chabrol inevitably joined forces with the industry. One might say they always had the industry's health in mind even when they screamed for its overthrow. After the first five years of the New Wave their major goal was to continue to make films as well and as often as they could. Chabrol by and large remained within one or two formulae, perfecting his surgical analysis of bourgeois marriages under the pressure of adultery and crime. Truffaut, in contrast, leaped from genre to genre, from comedy to overly serious adaptations, from nearly *cinéma vérité* episodic films to studio period pieces. But all the while he sought the approval of a large audience.

By virtue of a tenure shared at *Cahiers du cinéma* during the fifties and early sixties, Eric Rohmer is usually classed with Truffaut, Godard, Chabrol, and Rivette. Yet, except for three shorts made with Godard in the early fifties, Rohmer's films seem to share more with the traditional values of a Renoir or a Bresson or with Murnau and Griffith whom he has acknowledged as his masters, than with the youthful flamboyance of his contemporaries' iconoclasm. Rohmer has always maintained that his films are not meant for a mass audience but for that small group of viewers who appreciate the less spectacular qualities of the film medium. In 1963 Rohmer ended his association with *Cahiers du cinéma*. The journal had for some years been in the throes of a move away from the aesthetic policies of Bazin toward a more politically engaged, and thus, more leftist, variety of criticism. Seeing that this change in policy would no longer provide the forum it once had for the testing of his aesthetic hypotheses, he chose to leave the magazine and devote himself to making films. Barbet Schroeder was able to find money for a short film to be shot in 16mm. While writing the scenario for this film, Rohmer conceived the grand plan of a series of fictional films treating a single theme with a single structure. These moral tales chronicle the vacillations within the mind of a young man, who often functions as the film's narrator.[3] Rohmer recognizes the irony that resides in this use of cinema, the medium which relies on the objective, exterior image, to stage his interior moral dramas. But he feels by mastering the use of this irony it then becomes possible, when effecting minute changes in the exterior landscape, to more powerfully express subtle alterations in the tenor of his protagonist's interior drama. This explains why Rohmer pays such scrupulous attention to rendering surface detail. His obsessive attention to detail allowed him to realize an advance in the art of cinematic adaptation with his next two films, *The Marquise of O—(La marquise d'O—*, 1976) and *Perceval (Perceval le Gallois*, 1978). In the same way that Bresson in *Diary of a Country Priest* actually visualized the feeling of the novel, Rohmer, by alluding to the artwork of the respective eras, is able to visualize the feeling of Kleist's novella and Chrétien de Troyes's epic romance. In the 1980s Rohmer has embarked on a new series with such titles as *The Aviator's Wife (La femme de l'aviateur*, 1981) and *Pauline at the Beach (Pauline à la plage*, 1982). In contrast to the six moral tales, these "parables" are not played out on the interior landscape of a single character but rather engage an entire social milieu in evoking the comic ironies that attend the mating practices of contemporary Paris. Emerging from the crucible of the French New Wave, Rohmer has forged a style that draws on the best qualities of Bresson and Renoir molded to what he found distinctive in the Hollywood masters of the fifties. Although never as flamboyant as Godard or Truffaut, his appeal has proved much hardier.

By 1965 one would have difficulty separating those directors originating in the New Wave period from the more standard directors who had continued with their tried and true methods all the while. In fact, even into the 1980s, Cayatte, Autant-Lara, and Henri Verneuil have been as prolific as they were in the fifties. Their assistants in the early years who finally got an opportunity after 1958 to work on their own are likewise staples of the current cinema: Edouard Molinaro (*La cage aux folles*, 1979), Gerard Oury (*Rabbi Jacob*, 1976), Georges Lautner (nearly thirty films since 1959), and most important, Claude Sautet (*Cesar and Rosalie* [*César et Rosalie*, 1972]). Americans are familiar with the other popular directors: Philippe de Broca (*King of Hearts* [*Le roi des coeurs*, 1966]); Claude Lelouch (*A Man and a Woman* [*Un homme et une femme*, 1966]); and especially Costa-Gavras (*Z*, 1969; *State of Siege*, 1972; and *Missing*, 1982).

The last three developed as directors just after the New Wave broke through, and they represent the lucky or talented few who distinguished themselves in that chaotic era. After 1960 there have been, on the average, over thirty new directors each year. This stunning statistic testifies to the indisputable break effected by the New Wave with an old guard cinema that had not permitted thirty new directors to enter its ranks in over fifteen years. Yet the apparent openness that entered with the birth of the Fifth Republic carried with it many liabilities. Nearly all first films are shot on minuscule budgets and few of them properly display the potential of their directors. The large proportion are quickly lost in the shuffle of distribution. Knowing this, too many of the latter-day New Wavers have either sought to create ersatz films of *quality* or to shoot it all to the sky in one huge autobiographical and narcissistic skyrocket. The result shows a great flattening of the cinema after 1963 despite the constant infusion of new blood. Once again, as in the fifties, actors came to dominate the screen and the attention of the public. Fernandel, Bourvil, and Gabin went to their deaths in a flurry of production and public attention. New stars, some of them nurtured in the New Wave, grew to enormous reputations until they promoted an image more than a talent. Alain Delon and Jean-Paul Belmondo head the list of male actors. Actresses have had a more tenuous and variable stature, Brigitte Bardot and Jeanne Moreau being replaced by Catherine Deneuve and now Annie Girardot. The careers of these stars reflect the same pattern as those of the directors. Bardot, Moreau, and especially Belmondo replaced older stars on the strength of the immediacy of their presentations. Natural tics and gestures were incorporated into their scripted parts. Improvisation and sheer surprise found its place in the making of their first films. As much as anything else this enlivened New Wave products. But once the wave wore off, once these actors had worked in a dozen films under a number of directors the tics became conventionalized, the improvisations began to seem scripted. Soon little pretense was made to immediacy and these actors and actresses assumed their positions at the head of the industry like Gérard Philipe and Danielle Darrieux before them. Even those like Annie Girardot who had come into the system via the serious theater, hoping to bring a new spirit to film acting, lost their freshness within a few years even as they grew in fame and power. Today Gérard Depardieu and Nathalie Baye stand in similar positions, exploiting their métier in every possible form, trying to keep from becoming typecast and rigidified. As their public success builds even higher, their chances for contributing anything new to French cinema fall.

Between the revitalization of the acting corps and the renewal of standard genres (*policiers*, parodies, and so on), the sixties and early seventies gave French cinema a look of complacence that made it seem pale next to the emerging cinemas of other nations. Ironically, the new cinemas of Cuba, Brazil, Czechoslovakia, Hungary, and Germany all paid homage to the New Wave as the key inspiration for an authentic renewal of the art form in their lands, yet in France the wave was clearly washing back into the sea. It took the events of May 1968 to snap the industry to attention. Most evident was the scant role French cinema played in the political life of the country, especially when compared to the truly polemical films being made across the border in Italy or Germany.

Godard felt this most of all and quickly turned away from 35mm cinema altogether. Even though his films had been far and away the most politically conscious of the decade, he found himself no longer able to work within a distribution and exhibition system that was fundamentally built on middle-class notions of entertainment. For four years he worked within the rubric of the so-called Dziga Vertov group making a series of hermetic and self-conscious political essays. Since then he has reemerged into mainstream distribution with tremendous fanfare in such films as *Every Man for Himself* (*Sauve qui peut la vie*, 1980), *First Name Carmen* (*Prenom Carmen*, 1984), and *Hail Mary* (*Je vous salue Marie*, 1985). But more than ever, Godard strikes the industry with the force of the lone genius, or even the anarchist. His is not the way toward total renewal.

Along with the total radicalization of Godard was the leftward slide of *Cahiers du cinéma*. By 1969 Truffaut and Rohmer, formerly the cornerstones of this most famous of film journals, found themselves completely alienated from its positions. Truffaut ceased giving it financial support. Rohmer excoriated it in several interviews. *Cahiers*, like Godard, was committed to a Marxist position, to such an extent that it excised from its pages everything that had as its goal the reflection of cinematic pleasure. Out came photographs and reviews of popular films. Out came the interest in American cinema or in the New Wave. Soon advertising was dropped. Consistent to the end, it had to withdraw from the standard distribution companies that had seen to its popular diffusion. For four years *Cahiers* followed this ascetic policy, returning by degrees to the popular journal it once was. The results have been mixed. Its theoretical rigor utterly renewed the study of cinema in France, Great Britain, and the United States. And its team of editors, like their predecessors ten years earlier, fought their way into the margins of the cinema while striving to maintain their political purity.

Jean Eustache (*The Mother and the Whore* [*Le maman et le putaine*, 1974]), Jean-Louis Comolli (*Cecilia* [*La Cecilia*, 1975]), Andre Techiné (*Inside Memories of France* [*Souvenirs d'en France*, 1975]), and Pascal Kane (*Liberty Belle*, 1983) have to varying degrees mixed their astute theoretical conceptions of the aesthetics and sociology of the medium with the reality and tradition of making a film in France. Other critics, slightly older and from other journals, led the way in this: Robert Benayoun, Yves Boisset, Luc Moullet, and most notably Bertrand Tavernier with his *Clean Slate* (*Coup de torchon*, 1981) and *Sunday in the Country* (*Dimanche à la compagne*, 1984).

Even if 1968 brought with it less of a turn toward politics in the cinema than one might have expected, it did once again help renew the ranks of directors with these critics and with the young filmmakers they supported in their articles. René Allio and Maurice Pialat, for example, coming respectively from the theater and painting, were touted in a number of articles. Today Pialat's films such as *Lulu* (1980) carry an aura not unlike that which has always surrounded the films of Bresson. The export market to the United States has also been widened after several years when only the Emmanuelle series and the easily swallowed offerings of Lelouch seemed available. Jean-Charles Tacchella's *Cousin-Cousine* (1975), Tavernier's *Clockmaker* (*L'horloger de Saint-Paul*, 1974), Blier's misogynistic *Get Out Your Handkerchiefs* (*Préparez vos mouchoirs*, 1978), and of course Molinaro's *La cage aux folles* have once again alerted American audiences that they can expect more thematic and stylistic play in French cinema than they can possibly find in their own.

A few promising trends have appeared in French cinema since 1968. For the first time since its inception, French cinema has been sensitive to the possibilities the cinema holds for the representation of history. Since 1968 major directors like Resnais (*Stavisky*, 1974) and neophytes like Comolli (*Cecilia*) have sought to construct new codes by which to reimagine the past and, in reimagining it, to analyze the present. The historical spectacle film has been renewed in Tavernier's *Let Joy Reign Supreme* (*Que la fête commence*, 1975), but more important has been the concentration on recent history, on the fall of the Third Republic and the period of the occupation. Marcel Ophuls's *Sorrow and the Pity* (*Le chagrin et la pitié*, 1972) had an enormous impact for it proved that a four-hour inquest into the past, a film full of talk and evidence from one end to the other, could attract crowds and discussion.

Conversely, the facts and fables of history have served to complicate in a fascinating way many fiction films. Allio's *The French Calvinists* (*Les Camissards*, 1972) and his *I, Pierre Riviere . . .* (*Moi Pierre Riviere*, 1976) find new modes of address to the spectator because history permits them to highlight our alienation from the stories they tell. In the recent *Return of Martin Guerre* (*Le rétour de Martin Guerre*, 1982) we are never permitted to know, nor do the filmmakers themselves really know, what motivated the actions of this sixteenth-century event. Thus the requirements of psychological realism are suspended and other processes of representation are allowed to take over.

In this search for disturbing and productive modes of presentation, history plays a role that adaptation shares with it. Formerly the raw material stamped out into quality products, literary masterpieces today keep the cinema at bay in an exhilarating play of media differences. Jean-Marie Straub and Danielle Huillet have most radically followed out the consequences of media dialectics in their *Chronicle of Anna Magdalena Bach* (*Chronik der Anna Magdalena Bach*, 1968), *Othon* (1969), and *Moses and Aaron* (1975). Rohmer's *Perceval* and *Marquise of O* are hardly less complicated examples. In all these films the literary original is permitted its own life and difference. Undigested, it is cut into by the cinema from the side. Like history, literature serves as a pretext which absolves the director from retaining conventional codes of motivation, acting, and even set design.

Perhaps the greatest legacies coming down to the present from the New Wave period have been the backdoors through which nonprofessionals have been able to make films (shattering the homogeneous character of the industry) and the relishing of lively contradictions within films (shattering the homogeneity of the text). When a literary phenomenon like Marguerite Duras is able to make a dozen films according to her "musical" conception of visual-aural counterpoint, and when one of her most difficult works, *The Truck* (*Le camion*, 1977), not only stars France's leading actor (Depardieu) but represents the country at the Cannes festival, it is foolish to claim that the New Wave was over by 1962. In her films, in the work of Rohmer, and especially in that of Rivette, one can sense the legacy of a movement that refused to believe that cinema had been defined. The experimentation begun in 1959 goes on today not only in the use of historical and literary sources and in the interweaving of the separate lines of music, dialogue, and image that we find in Duras, but in the primary notion that the art of film takes place in the event of its being made, not in some prior text that the film relays to the audience. More than one critic has pointed to the absolute centrality of Rossellini and Rouch in turning the New Wave away from scripts and toward mise-en-scène. The improvisational acting of the New Wave has developed into the collaborative films of Rivette in which the actors literally hold themselves responsible for their lines and the thrust of whatever plot develops. In the cauldron of the filmmaking process Rivette hopes to forge an experience that is both magical, and in a powerful sense, real.

There is a major portion of French cinema that has turned away from this aesthetic. Tavernier loudly proclaims a return to the cinema of quality and has employed both Aurenche and Bost as scenarists. Nevertheless, such quality films as Truffaut's *Day for Night* (*La nuit americaine*, 1973) glorify the process of art even if this only emphasizes the limited perspective every film must take in relation to its material. On the whole, French cinema has gone beyond trying to maintain the kind of total illusion Hollywood still is capable of creating. In its place a whole range of artistic possibilities have settled.

Artistic possibilities are easier to produce than works of art. Witness the French cinema, so rich in its cinematic heritage and in the quality of personnel, yet so ordinary in its current output. Economic summaries account for much of this discrepancy. Without the Advance on Receipts policy renewed by Malraux in 1959, nearly every important artistic filmmaker in France would have had to scuttle at least one project. Without support from television, Bresson, Pialat, and other major talents would have been out of work the way Gremillon was after World War II. Yet television at the same time has stripped away half of France's audience. As a new movie channel is being installed across the country and hundreds of recent films are cheaply available, who will finance the exciting artistic possibilities which hover around French film journals, cine-clubs, and festivals? Cinema's role in France has been felt to be too important to be left entirely to an industry. The whole culture has involved itself in its problems: the government, through censorship and subsidy, the intellectuals through criticism and through backdoor entry into production. While this has made us always look to France as a country where something new and important might appear on the screen with every new film, the fact is that the very limelight in which the cinema lives has generally kept it so much a part of the culture that the complete revolution of cinema, aesthetically and socially, which has been the hope of every generation and which in the New Wave era seemed a reality, will forever be a fading mirage. Yet that mirage can still tantalize us, and it can tantalize those filmmakers capable of giving us representations of life that promise to be important, even if this promise is never utterly fulfilled. No other national cinema has lived so long under the spell and the burden of such promise.

## NOTES

1. Robert Bresson, *Notes on Cinematography* (New York: Urizen Press, 1977).
2. Alexandre Astruc, "Le Camera-stylo," in Peter Graham, *The New Wave* (Garden City, N.Y.: Doubleday, 1968), pp. 17–24.
3. The films include the Academy Award-winning *My Night at Maud's* (*Ma nuit chez Maude*, 1968) as well as *Claire's Knee* (*La genou de Claire*, 1969).

## SELECTED BIBLIOGRAPHY

Andrew, Dudley. *André Bazin*. New York: Oxford, 1978.

Armes, Roy. *French Cinema since 1946*. 2 vols. New York: Barnes, 1970.

―――. *French Film*. New York: Oxford Univ. Press, 1985.

Auriol, Jean-Georges. "Contemporary French Cinema." *Penguin Film Review* 8 (Jan. 1949): 51–70.

Bazin, André. *Le Cinéma français, 1945–1958*. Paris: Editions de l'Etoile, 1983.

Bonnell, Réné. *Le Cinéma eploité*. Paris: Seuil, 1980.

Courtade, Francis. *Les Maledictions du cinéma français: Une Histoire du cinéma français parlant (1928–1978)*. Paris: Moreau, 1978.

Clouzot, Claire. *Le Cinéma français depuis le nouvelle vague.* Paris: Alliance Francais, 1974.

Dagand, Claude. *Le Cinema . . . cette industrie.* Paris: Editions Techniques et Economiques, 1972.

Douin, Jean-Luc, Ed. *La nouvelle vague 25 ans aprés.* Paris: Cerf, 1983.

Eisner, Lotte. "Post-War Realism." *Film Culture,* May–June 1955.

Ford, Charles. *Histoire du cinéma français contemporain (1945–1977).* Paris: France-Empire, 1977.

Godard, Jean-Luc. *Godard on Godard.* Trans. and Commentary by Tom Milne, New York: Viking, 1972.

Hillier, Jim, Ed. *Cahiers du cinéma,* the 1950s. Cambridge: Harvard Univ. Press, 1985.

Jeancolas, Jean-Pierre. *Le Cinéma des françaises.* Paris: Stock, 1977.

"Le Cinéma français au présent." *Cinéma d'Aujourd'hui,* no. 12–13 (Spring, 1977).

Leprohon, Pierre. *Présence contemporaines du cinéma.* Paris: Nouvelles Editions Debresse, 1956.

Lipkin, Steven. "The Film Criticism of François Truffaut." Ph.D. Dissertation, University of Iowa, 1977. Chapter 2 provides overview of the industry.

Monaco, James. *The New Wave.* New York: Oxford, 1976.

Predal, Réné. *Le Cinéma français contemporain.* Paris: Cerf, 1984.

Sadoul, Georges. *Chroniques du cinéma français, 1939–1967*: Ecrits I. Paris: Union Générale d'Editions, 1977.

_____. *French Film.* London: Falcon, 1953. translation of *Le Cinéma français.* Paris. Flammarion, 1950, 1962.

Truffaut, François. *The Films in My Life.* New York: Simon and Schuster, 1979.

# GERMANY
## The Past that Would Not Go Away[1]

## ERIC RENTSCHLER

Postwar German film came out of the ruins, but it did not start from zero. After the unconditional surrender of a vanquished dictatorship to Allied troops in May 1945, there would be no dramatic break with the past. To look on the country's cinematic heritage prior to 1945 means gazing on the Janus face of German film history, a visage that fascinates and horrifies in equal measure. On the one hand is a significant film tradition, a legacy of formally inventive and thematically compelling productions: the expressionist frenzy and fantastic exuberance of the twenties, the seminal and universally recognized contributions of masters like Lang, Lubitsch, Murnau, Pabst, Pick, and others, not to forget the painstaking authenticity and social engagement of various street-life chronicles and proletarian dramas that came out of the later Weimar years. On the other hand, though, is the specter of a fettered cinema as an equally weighty legacy. Under the auspices of the Ministry of Propaganda and the careful guidance of Joseph Goebbels, film in the Third Reich became the instrument of cultural legitimation and mass control par excellence. It served as a crucial vehicle in the totalitarian state's endeavor to colonize the imaginations of its subjects.

A grand tradition of cinematic achievement and a diabolical heritage of film's systematic abuse: this split has made for a profound cultural schizophrenia toward the medium in postwar Germany. Inherent in the antinomy is a sharp dialectic, a sensitivity for film's creative and constructive possibilities and an attendant knowledge of the medium's powerful manipulative potential. A volatile dialectic, it has remained potent to the present, posing itself in repeated battles between image creators and image controllers, a disparity between films that open viewers to the richness of perceived and imagined worlds and ones that close minds and vitiate the heterogeneity of human experience. Indeed,

208 :

this constant tension provides the informing structure for postwar German film history.

Most accounts of postwar German film reduce this continuing drama to a simple before-and-after tale. Following a great drought during the two decades following 1945, a collection of young filmmakers crafted a New German Film, bringing succor and redemption to a depleted national cinema. This popular scenario, however, diminishes significant continuities in postwar German film history. The period before 1962 was not merely an epoch bound up by a mismanaged film industry and creative sterility. It was also a period of transition, in which films abundantly took recourse to contours well known from the Third Reich. "Grandpa's cinema" (*Opas Kino*), the expletive used to refer to a bankrupt tradition contested by the younger generation, did not disappear overnight by decree. Even if the conservative old guard, many of whom were carry-overs from the Nazi film industry, made fewer movies after the late sixties, it still maintained a dominant hold on film production, distribution, exhibition, and rating boards. With the rise of a state-subsidized cinema, the battle between ambitious and critical filmmakers and the institutional framework that circumscribes—and often stifles—image production continues well into the eighties. The apparent ease with which the Christian Democratic Union (CDU) set about restoring the film politics of the fifties after regaining power in 1982 illustrates how—to use Brecht's trope—the womb that bore the Adenauer era still remains fertile some thirty years later.

The standard treatment of postwar German film has also often obscured the question of a split nation, of two vastly different sets of conditions which have accompanied the growth of film cultures in the Federal Republic of Germany (FRG, or West Germany) and the German Democratic Republic (GDR, or East Germany). After underlining the artistic crisis and thematic insipidness of West German films of the fifties and ignoring GDR productions, most accounts of contemporary German cinema almost exclusively shift attention to the achievements of the New German Cinema. To understand the latter, though, one must grasp what came before and what still obtained long after the young directors had declared an illegitimate legacy dead.

Postwar German film seen in retrospect appears as an unceasing drama at the center of which lies the question of national identity under changed—and ever-changing—conditions. It incorporates attempts to elude the past, counterventures to rescue and gather forsaken moments and obscured traditions, the rebuilding, rediscovery, and redefinition of an occupied homeland, Germany and things German as an unceasing preoccupation. German films since 1945, even the less noteworthy ones, must be seen in their historical nexus, as the collective memory of a highly volatile experience, one framed by a burdensome past that makes for a continuingly difficult present.

## 1945–1949: No 'Nullpunkt'

With an entire nation shattered, its cities leveled, its populace fraught with a sense of existential devastation, shame, and material exigency, the Germany which Allied troops occupied presented an immense challenge. Resolute in their desire to reeducate the inhabitants still alive after six years of war and twelve years of fascism, the four powers (The United States, England, France, and the USSR) saw in film and the other media an instrument for effecting the necessary break with the Nazi legacy that had led to the cataclysm. As tensions grew between the Soviets and the Western powers, film would likewise become an extension of cold war politics.

In the Eastern zone, the occupiers immediately set about dubbing Soviet classics from the thirties into German. From the start the Soviets centralized film production, creating the government-controlled film company DEFA (Deutsche Film Aktiengesellschaft) in May 1946. Whereas over forty production companies would arise in the Western zones between 1946 and 1948, the Eastern occupiers insisted on maintaining control over the films they sponsored. Film as a mass art followed Soviet practice; its function was to be a powerful weapon against reaction and for peace and friendship between all peoples of the world. German film in the Eastern zone was from the start a *Staatsfilm*, an organ controlled by the dominant cultural politics.

American, French, and English distributors in the other zones, eager to regain a considerable market lost during the war, flooded cinemas (three thousand of the former seven thousand houses stood in 1945) with movies banned during the Third Reich, mainly light entertainment and genre films. German distributors likewise capitalized on a substantial number of German films from the thirties and forties deemed by Allied controllers to be politically innocuous. Receiving a heavy dose of escapist fare, German audiences caught up on both Hollywood productions they had missed during the Hitler years and the UFA (*Universum Film A.G.*) extravaganzas made under Goebbels, the well-crafted, technically solid films with attractive casts, lavish sets, and—for all their ideological insidiousness—no apparent relationship to the real world. Under Allied occupiers eager to foster a provincial home industry so that American productions would remain viable at German box offices, the UFA past would become the Adenauer present. American distributors dominated the German market. West Germany would likewise become a stable anticommunist base of operations in the heart of Europe, a virtual American colony whose films would reflect their economic determination and political calling in the years to come.

The first film made in Germany after World War II, Wolfgang

Staudte's *The Murderers Are Among Us* (*Die Mörder sind unter uns*, 1946) recalls another seminal work that gave shape to postwar fury at the excesses of authority, namely Robert Wiene's *The Cabinet of Dr. Caligari* (*Das Kabinett des Dr. Caligari*, 1919). Punitive fantasies directed against power figures, ones fashioned from a traumatic memory, both films also set the stage for an epoch while revisiting another: *Caligari*, as one knows well from Siegfried Kracauer's famous book,[2] points ahead to a series of films featuring demagogues and victims couched in romantic settings; *Murderers*, likewise, conjures up images of demanded retribution while rekindling memories of National Socialism. Unlike most of his filmmaking peers, Staudte had emerged from the Third Reich relatively uncompromised. His angry film was shot in the ruins of Berlin with a blend of neorealistic veracity and expressionistic shadowiness. From its very first shot, *Murderers* thematizes the relationship between past and present: the camera fixes on a grave, rising to gaze down a long lane where Mertens, the dazed physician returning from the war, staggers toward the mound and a group of playing children. Framed by the specter of war's devastation, but surrounded by youth and hopes for the future, Mertens will take flight into a bar from which honky-tonk music issues. His persistent outings into night clubs are an escape from the past and a postponement of the future, a step into a realm of excitement and gaiety where time is of little importance. Pursued by the recollection of a massacre he sought to prevent while in Poland, the physician cannot recycle the past with the ease of his ex-superior Brückner, the man responsible for the killings who has in the meanwhile settled into a smug and comfortable existence as the head of a factory where steel helmets are made into pots and pans.

Coming to grips with the past, finding one's way in the present, trying to imagine a future: these impulses inform a number of films made directly after the war. The landscape of the so-called *Trümmerfilm* ("rubble film") abounds with returning soldiers, profiteers, and innocents like Susanne (played by Hildegard Knef in a performance that made her famous) who emerges from a concentration camp. Staudte's film jolts the viewer with its shock contrasts. One image dissolves from a poster advertising *Das schöne Deutschland* ("Beautiful Germany") to the ruins of the former capital under a cloudy sky. A shot begins with the glaring headline "2,000,000 Jews gassed" before the camera pulls back to reveal that the paper is merely sandwich wrapping for Brückner who eats with oblivious gusto. In the end Mertens confronts his former tormentor, calling him to justice for his crimes, and nearly murdering him. Although the war criminal stands exposed while screaming his innocence over images of suffering which will segue into a cross and fade into the dark, demons like Brückner were not to be exorcised so easily. Staudte's recourse to similar thematics a decade later in *Roses for the State Prosecutor* (*Rosen für den Staatsanwalt*, 1959) and *Fairground* (*Kirmes*, 1960) bear this out.

*Murderers*, however impressive in its stylistic recourse to the chiaroscuro of the twenties, its evocation of the everyday in postwar Berlin, and its sincere cathartic impulse, nonetheless set a pattern which would become the rule in many German films with topical themes. Playthings in the hands of an inexorable Fate, heroes in these films suffer stoically. History is mystified, reduced to a chain of events that fetters everyone. The narrator in Helmut Käutner's *In Those Days* (*In jenen Tagen*, 1947) is a car that passes from one owner to another during the Third Reich. It comments on various victims of history: "I didn't see much of those days, no great events, no heroes, only several people's destinies. And even there only bits and pieces. But I did see several people. . . . The times were stronger than they were, but their humanity was stronger than the times."

Rather than explore the sociopolitical factors that furthered fascism in Germany, a development preceded by a long tradition of authoritarianism and militarism, one countenanced by the German masses in 1933, these films limited their perspectives to an apologetic view of martyrs, individuals who have no choice but to accede to the workings of an unfathomable fortune. "We can't do anything," says a figure in Rolf Meyer's *Migrating Birds* (*Zugvögel*, 1948), "things just simply happen to us." Guilt was displaced; a few criminals and circumstances in general became the responsible factors. Nazis on the one side, innocent bystanders on the other: this scheme conveniently overlooked the complicity of the overwhelming majority who had allowed National Socialism to rise and flourish.

Everywhere one looks, one finds helpless cogs in the wheels of "the times": the stage actor Hans Wieland and his Jewish wife, who, rather than separate, commit suicide in Kurt Maetzig's *Marriage in the Shadows* (*Ehe im Schatten*, 1947); a war exile returns from Switzerland unjustly accused of having taken the jewelry of a Jewish woman who later killed herself, in Harald Braun's *Between Yesterday and Tomorrow* (*Zwischen Gestern und Morgen*, 1947); a troubled soldier comes back to Hamburg from the Soviet front and cannot find his way through the shelled remnants of his former home in Wolfgang Liebeneiner's *Love 47* (*Liebe 47*, 1949). Gerhard Lamprecht's *Somewhere in Berlin* (*Irgendwo in Berlin*, 1946) contains striking atmospheric touches, glimpses of life in the ruins: black marketeers, rubble women, and children playing in shattered buildings. Still, these films possessed no rousing energy, no liberating impulse, no indications of political dissidence or convincing expressions of critique. This was not a new beginning, but rather a resignation to the status quo garbed in emotional rhetoric.

Even films with seemingly reflexive frameworks failed to provide an alternative. Rudolf Jugert's *Film without a Title* (*Film ohne Titel*, 1948), based on a script by Käutner, dramatizes the dilemma confronting German filmmakers in a debate between a director, writer, and actor about what sort of movie is possible after all that has happened. At the center of their deliberations is the true story of an art dealer and a country girl brought together by the war and separated by class differences. When the pair ultimately marries despite all challenges, the trio agree that no one could make a film out of this fairy tale, a conclusion belied by the film itself and further contradicted by a score of future West German productions bound up in escapist whimsy. The discursive distance in R. A. Stemmle's *Berlin Ballad* (*Berliner Ballade*, 1948), where an outer space visitor from the year 2049 takes stock of Berlin in 1949, likewise fails to convince. For all the satirical bite of the film's cabaret numbers, the ultimate conclusion reached by the alien is that egotism, hatred, and militarism are things of the past, rubble in the garbage dump of history.

## The Restoration Era: No Experiments

Hardly starting from scratch, German film replicated patterns well known from the past: deference to authority, an irrational embrace of Fate, and a transfiguration of martyrs and victims. Even films with pessimistic overtones like *Marriage in the Shadows* or unsettling endings such as *Murderers* obscured rather than revealed the dynamics of Hitler Germany. Shifting the burden of guilt, concealing tangible political facts, and resorting to an upbeat assurance that things could begin anew, many other films lacked Maetzig's incisiveness or Staudte's virulence.

The film industry, under Allied guidance, came into the hands of filmmakers who in general had been active during the Third Reich: they included directors with skeletons in their closets, like the notorious Veit Harlan, and others who had worked steadily during the Nazi years as crafters of light entertainment (Hans Deppe, Josef von Baky, Kurt Hoffmann), or of more stridently political films (Arthur Maria Rabenalt, Alfred Weidenmann, Harald Braun, Gustav Ucicky). Filmmakers like Käutner and Staudte, who had remained subdued during the war years, never delivered on the hopes raised by their first postwar efforts. Nor did the returning exiles have a greater impact, whether "inner emigrants" like Werner Hochbaum who died in 1946, or those who came back from Hollywood, like Fritz Lang, Robert Siodmak, Wilhelm Dieterle, Gottfried Reinhardt, and Frank Wisbar.

As the political tension between East and West grew, the occupation zones ceased to be merely provisional arrangements. After 1949 and the creation of two separate Germanies, one can no longer talk of a

"German" film. The split had decisive consequences. In both parts of divided Germany, filmmakers produced films reflecting their political environment. *Staatsfilm*-East or *Staatsfilm*-West, film as the educator of the incipient socialist republic or film as a means of legitimizing the status quo, productions under the beck and call of a central ministry or ones bound in a labyrinth of bank credits, state committees, and rating boards: German film of the fifties strikingly reflects the tenor of its times.

The years from 1949 to 1963 in the FRG are generally called the "Adenauer era." The commanding figure in postwar German politics, Konrad Adenauer, led a regime based on a fierce anticommunist line and a steady allegiance to American dictates. Adenauer's period in office brought the economic wonder (*Wirtschaftswunder*) hailed internationally: prosperity and relative security to a country once in shambles and composed in large part of refugees. The Adenauer era also paid a dire price: a staid atmosphere, governed by the quest for private bliss and domestic harmony accompanied by an extreme distrust of nonconformist and oppositional behavior. The Adenauer era is one of restoration: the renascence of the German economy under the aegis of capitalism, the rearming of a nation called for by NATO, the reawakening of a belief in traditional values and a trust in the state patriarchy—as well as a resurgence of intolerance toward differing viewpoints that climaxed in the banning of the Communist party in 1956.

West German film of the Adenauer era has a poor reputation. Mindless entertainments, pompous imitations of Hollywood, works devoid of formal daring or thematic incisiveness, the movies of the fifties seem to have little to recommend them; there were few memorable titles, no truly outstanding directors, and no exciting genres. Nonetheless, one can look at these films as fascinating commentaries on the FRG during its years of stabilization and growth.

The crisis of West German film in the fifties stems mainly from American hegemony over the country's film economy as well as from the media policies of the Christian Democratic party (CDU). American interests maintained a stranglehold over German film distribution (there were no quota restrictions limiting the flow of Hollywood productions into the FRG) while West German leaders fostered a strong home market and encouraged films supportive of the regime. (Alfred Braun's 1957 celebration of the famous appeasement politician, *Stresemann*, was referred to as *Stresenauer*, fitting for a work that received large Adenauer government funding.) Attempts begun in 1953 to revive the depleted UFA stock through covert and questionable transactions with major banks, which it was hoped would restore the domestic viability and international visibility of German film, ended disastrously in 1962 with the liquidation of the once mighty production and exhibition company. A second arrangement between government and capital was the so-called *Bürgschaftssystem* of government-secured bank loans to film producers established in March 1950. At first intended to spur small-scale productions, the system was amended in 1952 to favor applicants promising packages of films. This led to overproduction of throwaway fare and to a concentration of limited funds in the hands of the most powerful—and pliable—entrepreneurs.

Filmmakers thus operated in an atmosphere that did little to spur creativity or originality. Speaking in 1960 to justify the workings of the State Film Prize (*Bundesfilmprämie*), another support arrangement introduced in 1956 to replace the discontinued *Bürgschaften*, Dr. Bruno Heck of the CDU proclaimed: "Whoever asks the state—and rightly so—for help, must be aware that in doing so he must move within the existing boundaries that are given when state funds are employed. The state constitution forbids censorship and censorship could not solve the problem anyway. This remains ultimately the responsibility of the film industry itself." These and other support systems rewarded those willing to make films conforming to the official line. Scripts with unfavorable viewpoints could always be rejected for lacking artistic quality or mass appeal. Furthermore, the *Freiwillige Selbstkontrolle* (FSK or Independent Board of Control) screened every film shown in the FRG, ferreting out "negative influences"; and the *Filmbewertungsstelle* (FBW or Film Assessment Office) enabled tax breaks to films recognized for their "artistic quality." There was no overt censorship in the FRG during the fifties. There were, however, numerous instances in which East German films were not allowed or were expurgated, and films critical of the regime occasionally did not find their way into cinemas, or if they did, only in a cut version.

Perhaps no other genre carries more emotive resonance than the *Heimatfilm* ("homeland film"), the dominant and most popular form of the fifties. (Over three hundred such films appeared between 1947 and 1960, one-fifth of the entire West German output.) With droves of refugees from the East seeking sanctuary in West Germany and the population as a whole rebuilding burnt-out cities, the question of *Heimat* was a major preoccupation. Reverting to the pantheism of the blood-and-soil epics (*Blubofilme*) under Goebbels, postwar *Heimatfilme* offered comforting images of green fields untouched by devastation, mountain villages held together by tightly knit communities. Taking flight from the exigencies of reconstruction and the daily reality of occupation forces, films like Hans Deppe's *Black Forest Girl* (*Schwarzwaldmädel*, 1950) and *Green Is the Heather* (*Grün ist die Heide*, 1951) were not merely escapes from the present. These postcard panoramas provide a strikingly authentic reverse image of the period: untouched nature replaces ruined cities, church bells resound instead of ubiquitous jackhammers, quaint panel houses offer a hominess the city's ugly and quickly erected concrete edifices did not. A holiday whimsy suppresses everyday drabness and eternal verities displace more pressing topical and material concerns.

Literary adaptations (*Verfilmungen*) of works from the middle-class canon also abounded. Based on realist novels couched in a bygone era of polite civility, passionate interiority, and domestic tranquility, *Verfilmungen* were made of works by Ludwig Anzengruber, Wilhelm Busch, Gerhart Hauptmann, Erich Kästner, and Theodor Storm which featured glimpses of a culture two world wars had obliterated. The novels of Thomas Mann provided a continuing source of costume films peopled by popular stars and graced with high production values. The *Verfilmungen* clearly appealed to a sense of a lost culture. Harald Braun skillfully addressed this lack, making Mann's *His Royal Highness* (*Königliche Hoheit*, 1953) into an apologia for U.S. occupation. The film evokes a faltering grand duchy, the vestige of a feudal past. The daughter of an American millionaire brings the kingdom's leader both a renewed sense of cultural values and concern for the needs of the common folk—a curious mix of authoritarianism and democracy. Quite often the *Verfilmungen* trivialized their sources in an attempt to win a mass market. Alfred Weidenmann's two-part *Buddenbrooks* (1959) reduced Mann's sweeping epic about the fall of a class to a stuffy, chamber-room drama peopled by a well-known cast: Liselotte Pulver, Najda Tiller, Hansjörg Felmy, and Lil Dagover. Mann's ironic and complexly symbolic picaresque novel *Felix Krull* became a light comedy under Kurt Hoffmann's direction in the 1957 rendering, little more than a vehicle for Horst Buchholz, the romantic lead.

Another indication of West German film's reversion to past models remains the large number of remakes. There were reshapings of popular comedies like *The White Horse Inn* (*Im Weissen Rössl*, Carl Lamac, 1935, redone by Willi Forst in 1952 and by Werner Jacobs in 1960), popular music films (*Schlagerfilme*) starring entertainers like Caterine Valente, Connie Froboess, Peter Kraus, and Peter Alexander, movies that replicated the UFA *Revuefilme*, or warmed-over *Heimatfilme* such as *Vulture Wally* (*Die Geierwally*, 1940, by Hans Steinhoff; 1956, by Franz Cap) and *Vacation from Myself* (*Ferien vom Ich*, 1934 and 1952, both by Hans Deppe). Revisions of former glories also included attempts to imitate the golden age of Weimar cinema. None of these remakes approached the formal integrity and cinematic accomplishment of their prototypes. Employing gaudy sets, lavish costumes, and matinee idols, without any fresh impetus or novel conception, these second-hand classics were wrought by mercenary producers eager to exploit potentially lucrative properties. These works include a host of travesties such as Harold Braun's *The Last Laugh* (*Der letzte Mann*, 1955), Geza von Radvany's *Mädchen in Uniform* (1958, a star vehicle for Romy Schneider), Arthur Maria Rabenalt's *Mandrake* (*Alraune*, 1952), and Franz Antel's *The Congress Dances* (*Der Kongress tanzt*, 1955). One of the sole revisitations of Weimar films with a modicum of thematic and formal energy was *The Lost Man* (*Der Verlorene*, 1951), directed by Peter Lorre, a shadowy tale of a compulsive murderer pursued by demons and ridden with guilt. Set in the aftermath of World War II, the film recalls and recreates the mean streets of *M*.

Over 10 percent of the titles screened in West German cinemas during the fifties were war films. Although some contained a pacifist message reminding audiences of battlefield horrors, the vast majority of German war films seemed more concerned with preparing the country for rearmament. Harald Reinl's *As Long As You Live* (*Solange du lebst*, 1955) could have been made under Goebbels. In the guise of a love story, it celebrates the Legion Condor, special troops sent by Hitler to fight on Franco's side during the Spanish civil war. Paul May's popular three-part *08/15* (1954–1955) likewise helped to reinstate soldiering as an admirable calling, carefully distinguishing the noble-minded rank and file from the sinister Nazi leadership. A submarine drama like Frank Wisbar's *Sharks and Little Fish* (*Haie und kleine Fische*, 1957), an updated version of Günther Rittau's NS (National Socialist) propaganda film *Submarines West!* (*U-Boote westwärts!*, 1941), depicted war as a matter of destiny, an inevitability not to be understood or avoided, but merely endured.

Other prominent genres during the Adenauer era include the *Problemfilm*, melodramas with realistic pretensions, often based on "authentic" stories from the popular press. These schematic productions, with their stereotyped characters, staid dramaturgy, and obligatory happy endings, portrayed contradictions and conflicts as individual predicaments, eradicating all class or social determinations. Other popular escapes from the present were the many vacation films and travel documentaries in addition to numerous films with exotic settings.

In the midst of these assembly-line productions, there remained only a handful of directors of more than passing note. Helmut Käutner was the period's consummate stylist, a filmmaker known for his fluid camera, adroit handling of actors, and impressive compositions. Käutner often appeared in his films as an on-screen *metteur en scène*: as a bitter poet in *Romance in a Minor Key* (*Romanze in Moll*, 1943); a court dancing master in *The Glass of Water* (*Das Glas Wasser*, 1960); a street singer in *The Captain of Köpenick* (*Der Hauptmann von Köpenick*, 1956). A versatile talent, Käutner worked in most of the prominent genres with considerable success. Ever the champion of innocent sufferers and victims of inexorable forces, Käutner favored heroes like General Harras in *The Devil's General* (*Des Teufels General*, 1954), a *Luftwaffe* pilot who resists his diabolical superiors by plunging to suicide. *The Captain of Köpenick* features another rebellion. The cobbler and ex-convict Voigt (portrayed by Heinz Rühmann, the era's best-known incarnation of "the small man"), when unable to get a passport or a work permit, dons a Prussian officer's uniform, commandeers troops, and takes over a city hall in search of the desired papers. Yet the film's ostensible critique of German worship of authority and uniforms was so mild as to be amenable even to conservative viewers. Käutner was a skilled crafter of elegant images, who never transcended abstract categories and an overly generalized approach.

Kurt Hoffmann, another director with stylistic pretensions whose career began during the Third Reich, enjoyed a reputation for light romances like *I Often Think of Piroschka* (*Ich denke oft an Piroschka*, 1955) and historical costume extravaganzas like *The Spessart Inn* (*Das Wirtshaus im Spessart*, 1957). His most ambitious effort was *Aren't We Wonderful?* (*Wir Wunderkinder*, 1958), a film hailed internationally for its critical portrait of twentieth-century Germany and its ironic evocation of the economic miracle. The narrative traces two characters during the years 1913 to 1958. One is Bruno Tiches, the eternal opportunist, Nazi official and postwar wheeler-dealer, a voracious and greedy survivor. The other is Hans Boeckel, the introspective bourgeois, student of Schopenhauer's pessimistic philosophy, an intellectual without party allegiances, a mannered figure whose quest for domestic bliss is interrupted by a world war. Hoffmann uses two on-screen figures, a commentator and a cabaret singer, to accompany the drama, identifying Tiches with crude consumption and lasciviousness. Boeckel, the apolitical "good" German, is never satirized. On the contrary, the film explicitly applauds him. On New Year's Eve of 1932/33, dressed smartly and sipping a vintage wine, he sits alone in his room listening to Beethoven's Ninth while storm troopers get drunk and plan their takeover. *Aren't We Wonderful?*, the film of a director once decorated by the Nazis for his airforce epic *Quax, the Crack Pilot* (*Quax, der Bruchpilot*, 1941), glorifies an indifference to politics in the Adenauer era's definitive tale of a private citizen's quest to weather history in his quest for career, home, and family.

Robert Siodmak's return to West Germany in the mid-fifties awakened great hopes. The shaper of lively German crime films in the early thirties, Siodmak had gained renown in Hollywood for such exercises in *film noir* as *Phantom Lady* (1943) and *The Spiral Staircase* (1945). *The Devil Strikes at Midnight* (*Nachts, wenn der Teufel kam*, 1957) received numerous prizes. It is imbued with expressionistic contours (high contrast lighting, dank stairwells, frenzied faces, off-angle compositions) in a World War II setting. The film follows police inspector Kersten as he traces a pathological murderer through various big cities. In the end, cynical Nazi officials cover up the crimes after Kersten has hunted down the psychopath, fearing a loss of confidence and prestige. Siodmak's film excels in its scenes of greedy consumption. The movie begins at harvest time in the summer of 1944. A petty Nazi officer passes out rye and flour to school girls. Relationships are established by barter:

cigarette coupons bring Kersten and his lover together; a bottle of schnaps reinforces the liaison. The repast at a dinner party establishes a link with the postwar context: "Such delicacies—just like in peacetime." Siodmak cleverly meshed German film's most valiant formal heritage—Expressionism—with an oblique commentary on the rampant materialism of the FRG during the economic recovery. Unfortunately, Siodmak's approach all too schematically pitted corrupt Nazis against noble-minded resisters, arguing for the latter's helplessness in the midst of such imposing adversaries.

Another film consciously playing on the Weimar tradition, Lang's *The Thousand Eyes of Dr. Mabuse (Die tausend Augen des Dr. Mabuse*, 1960) at first glance looks like a B-movie, full of stock figures, cheap special effects, and broad acting. West German critics failed to see any saving graces in the tale of a criminal madman with his vast information system, his "thousand eyes." The film does have subversive charms however. In the guise of a pulp thriller, Lang created a self-reflective modernist text concerned with the dynamics of the cinematic medium, its voyeuristic penchant and insatiable desire for spectacle. Teasing the spectator with disjunctive cross-cuts, elliptical leaps from one space to another which leave out information and explanations, Lang presented a world where the police keep tabs on people every bit as rapaciously as a sinister megalomaniac. *The Thousand Eyes of Dr. Mabuse* established a link between the expressionist tours through back-street Berlin in the twenties, the critique of Nazi designs in *The Testament of Dr. Mabuse (Das Testament des Dr. Mabuse*, 1932), and offered proof that— as Fassbinder would agree some fifteen years later—"Mabuse lives" in present-day Germany.[3]

East German films of the fifties gain from any comparison with Adenauer era productions. They sought to revive the Weimar legacies of workers' films and realist cinema while incorporating Soviet traditions of montage and socialist realism. DEFA-output continued the dialogue with history broached in works like *The Murderers Are Among Us, Marriage in the Shadows*, and Erich Engel's drama about anti-Semitism in the twenties, *The Blum Affair (Die Affäre Blum*, 1948). These initial efforts had an antifascist resolve and used an antibourgeois rhetoric. As the GDR embarked on a course meant to solidify a workers' state, filmmakers were called upon to search out the origins of totalitarianism in earlier epochs. The critical reckoning with the Nazi heritage in its historical guises mingled with the "other" history of progressive resistance would amount to the crucial DEFA contribution, a continuity of focus that would persist over the years despite changes in cultural politics and party leadership.

The majority of DEFA films (whose annual production averaged fifteen to twenty features), however, had much in common with West German counterparts. East Germany, too, had its *Problemfilme*, dealing with the black market, emigrants, occupation troops, or East-West tensions. A series of "Berlin films" scripted by Wolfgang Kohlhaase focused on teenagers growing up in the divided city. They were modeled on Western dramas about juvenile delinquents, starring James Dean and Marlon Brando—as well as the West German clone, George Tressler's *The Hooligans* (*Die Halbstarken*, 1954). One reason why East German films lacked the ideological commitment urged by the *Politbüro* was apparent: the majority of DEFA-directors lived in the West before the Berlin Wall was built in August 1961. In the wake of the "New Direction" proclaimed on 9 June, 1953 after Stalin's death, the relative cultural thaw brought the East Germans a chance to make more popular films, which they managed as poorly as their neighbors in the West. The late fifties brought a series of literary adaptations, in French coproductions, none of which stand out.

The quest for working-class heroes fostered a number of historical biographies like Kurt Maetzig's two-part *Ernst Thälmann* (1953–1955) and Artur Pohl's panegyric to August Bebel and Wilhelm Liebknecht, *The Unconquerable* (*Die Unbesiegbaren*, 1953). These revisionist readings smoothly sanded off the rough edges of German history, much as their predecessors had earlier in the era. Maetzig's *Ernst Thälmann— Son of His Class* (*Ernst Thälmann—Sohn seiner Klasse*, 1954), fit the party mold, praising international worker solidarity, condemning the cowardice of the Social Democratic party (SPD), and vilifying the collusion between American capital and German heavy industry during the Third Reich, a criticism even more directly expressed in Maetzig's earlier *Council of the Gods* (*Rat der Götter*, 1949).

There were some exceptions to the schematic rule. Staudte's *Rotation* (1949) traces the developments that led to National Socialism and the public complaisance that allowed it a mass base. The film follows Hans Behnke's thoughts on the eve of his execution. The worker (in a distinguished performance by Paul Esser) is a petty bourgeois who wants to live in peace and enjoy the security of a job and the comforts of a family. Through his recollections Behnke begins to grow aware of how individuals like himself played a seminal role in the Third Reich. Staudte's film has many shock contrasts that place individual actions in a larger social framework. At one point Behnke and his family frolic on a bed. The idyll is interrupted by noise from the street: police are leading a Jewish family away. Behnke closes first his windows and then the curtains, attempting to shut out the disquieting realities. Staudte then cuts to a shot of Nazi flags and singing Hitler Youth, a shift suggesting the collusion between timid collaborators and strident marchers on the street. Behnke ultimately learns that history need not be an inalterable course of events. He takes his fate into his own hands and joins the resistance. Saved in the last minute, Behnke lives to pass on his insights to his son.

Staudte's *Rotation* challenged the fatalistic mythology of West German films. The director's most accomplished film, *The Subject* (*Der Untertan*, 1951), an adaptation of Heinrich Mann's famous portrait of the authoritarian personality, is set in the era of Kaiser Wilhelm. Coming to terms with National Socialism meant seeing it as a product of a tradition, not as a mere historical aberration or catastrophe. The film stops at crucial junctures in the life of Diederich Hessling, showing how his blind worship of authority stems from a cultural heritage full of military marches, heroic portraiture, and impassioned patriotism. The authoritarian factory owner, Hessling, worships his kaiser every bit as ardently as he expects absolute allegiance from his workers. In the film's most striking sequence, the sycophant follows his ruler to Rome. Staudte stages the confrontation between sovereign and dutiful subject in a stunning montage sequence that climaxes in Hessling's chase after the royal coach, bowing with hat in hand, screaming hurrahs, framed as a pitiful lackey between the revolving spokes of the coach wheels. A final passage updates Mann's novel of 1913 to the postwar present: the monument of Kaiser Wilhelm II that Hessling helped erect in his hometown square stands in the midst of rubble as the voice-over narrator insists that the spirit that bore Hessling lives on.

Slatan Dudow, along with Kurt Maetzig and Gustav von Wangenheim, was one of the few early DEFA directors without a Nazi past. A collaborator with Brecht on *Kuhle Wampe* (1931), Dudow sought to renew the interrupted proletarian legacy in *Our Daily Bread* (*Unser täglich Brot*, 1949). *Stronger Than the Night* (*Stärker als die Nacht*, 1954) presents a panorama of German society during the Third Reich, including Communist activists, Nazi party members, and opportunistic joiners, as well as fickle and uncertain figures. Dudow's film possesses considerable subtlety in its depiction of a spectrum of possible responses to National Socialism. He presents the battle between the German Communist Party (KPD) and the Nazis as one of conflicting systems of representation. At the beginning there are Nazi flags and a KPD sign: two different appeals, one to spectacle and emblematics, the other to the written word and the powers of rational discourse. Storm troopers march and sing; comrades prepare pamphlets. *Stronger Than the Night* contains a rhythmically spaced series of voice-overs which repeat the phrase *Deutschland*. A movie about Germany and its many possibilities, Dudow's film centers on a part of Germany obscured, a working-class movement swallowed up by another movement which for a time was more successful in capturing the imaginations of the country's inhabitants.

A younger generation of filmmakers emerged in the GDR in the late 1950s. The most important East German director of the postwar era is Konrad Wolf. Son of the famous socialist dramatist Friedrich Wolf, the filmmaker spent his formative years with his emigrant parents in the

Soviet Union. He was clearly shaped by his exposure to the exile community and the Soviet films of the thirties; his upbringing granted him immunity from certain anachronisms and sentimentality in questions of national identity. His breakthrough film was *Lissy* (1957), based on the worker's novel by F. C. Weiskopf. It, too, focused on a petty bourgeois response to National Socialism. Like Dudow, Wolf offered differentiated and complex characters, figures wavering at moments of crisis. The heroine seeks to break out of a working-class environment by marrying an ambitious careerist; her husband joins the Storm Troopers (SA), despite misgivings, to further his prospects. The final sequence shows Lissy walking away from her husband into a vague future. *Lissy* has many incisive satirical tableaux that show political go-getters who, in moments of whimsy, forsake their strident rhetoric and lapse into sentimental phrases. A film with a documentary verisimilitude, *Lissy* is the first impressive effort of a director who would remain concerned with questions of history and homeland.

## After Oberhausen: Signs of Life

West German films of the fifties engaged in a displaced dialogue with German history. Skirting the pressing issues, *Opas Kino* lacked courage and daring. (Staudte was the exception and even he quieted down for the most after moving to the West in the mid-fifties.) The Adenauer era all but stifled oppositional voices. West Germany had no authentic film culture, no academies, cinémathèques, or networks of arthouses or cine-clubs. Compared to the film cultures of other Western and Eastern European countries, German cinema seemed an arid landscape.

In 1963 a public scandal brought Adenauer's resignation. By then, even the government had recognized that the confections of *Opas Kino* were no longer appealing to a domestic market increasingly dominated by foreign productions. In recognition of how dire the situation had become, the Ministry of the Interior withheld the annual State Prize for the best film in 1961 for lack of a suitable candidate.

It is against this backdrop that the Oberhausen Manifesto appeared. This declaration by twenty-six promising young filmmakers was presented at the Eighth Annual Oberhausen Festival, a showplace for experimental and radical short films. The angry and ambitious document proclaimed: "The collapse of the conventional German film removes the economic basis for an attitude of mind towards the cinema that we reject. . . . We announce our claim to create the new German feature film. The new film needs freedom. Freedom from the conventions of the industry and from commercial interference from the establishment. We have definite intellectual, formal and economic ideas about the production of a new type of German film. We are all prepared to undertake financial risks. The old film is dead. We believe in the new one."[4]

The filmmakers did not form a united front nor did they have a shared agenda other than the desire to gain the financial means to make movies free of conventional restraints.

The Oberhausen Manifesto nonetheless served as an important catalyst. Rejecting the monotonous character of Adenauer era *Staatsfilme*, the signatories saw themselves as an alternative to the dominant cinema. Alexander Kluge, from the beginning, played a central role as Young German Film's most articulate public defender, a function he continues to fulfill. Kluge and other signatories (few of whom remain active as filmmakers today) stressed the mission of film as an exploration of reality, as a documentation of the everyday, a medium that collects and preserves things that would otherwise remain lost, incidental, or fleeting. Postwar West German cinema had been occupied—both literally and figuratively—by foreign capital and conservative administrators. Kluge and others sought to free it from its bondage.

The main task of the group was to open access to the means of film production while freeing filmmakers from the economic and dramaturgical constraints of the fifties. Kluge and Norbert Kückelmann, both lawyers, sought a source of public funding which would guarantee filmmakers' autonomy from both industry dictates and political pressures. Young German filmmakers were consciously seeking a personal cinema, an *Autorenkino*, with absolute financial and creative control. Yet by accepting funding from government institutions, they both promoted competition among themselves and created a situation in which creators relied on the very establishment they meant to call into question for their continued existence. Funded by the Ministry of the Interior and administered by film professionals, the *Kuratorium junger deutscher Film* (Board of Curators of Young German Film) was set up in February 1965. Its initial subsidy of 5 million DM financed the "knapsack" films that brought the Young German directors their first kudos.

Young German Film thus had an initial source of support. With the establishment in the mid-1960s of film academies in Ulm (the experimental Institute for Film Design under Kluge and Edgar Reitz), West Berlin, and Munich, it also secured training grounds for future generations.

Young German Film did not start from zero; it sought to restore a tradition of filmmaking forsaken or driven into exile by twelve years of National Socialism and diminished by two decades of Allied occupation. German film of the twenties was an important source for the New German Cinema, with its distinctive talents, singular genres, and a film culture that appealed to both popular and avant-garde sensibilities.

Weimar cinema had maintained a lively dialogue with its times, expressing subterranean wishes as well as overt propensities, surveying street life and the recesses of individual psyches, providing a nexus in which film history reflected upon a larger and more encompassing national history.

The young filmmakers also gazed with respect on the deconstructed narratives of Godard, films that productively put to use the subversive lessons of Brechtian aesthetics. They were suspicious of—yet perversely admired—Hollywood. West German filmmakers, like most intellectuals in the FRG, were influenced by T. W. Adorno and Max Horkheimer's critique of the culture industry. *The Dialectic of the Enlightenment* provided a primer on how the popular media—radio, film, magazines—reduce reality to ready-made schemes. The new German feature film ferreted out alternative forms and also presented new contents.

Only a handful of films had managed to merge formal experimentation and critical commentary during the fifties. Herbert Vesely's *Stop Running* (*nicht mehr flichen*, 1955) and his Böll adaptation *The Bread of the Early Years* (*Das Brot der frühen Jahre*, 1961) were ambitious attempts to mingle fragmented narratives, existentialist philosophy, and (for the time) radical politics. Ottomar Domnick's *Jonas* (1957) mixed a documentary attention to postwar urban life with a haunting voice-over narration, both inner speech and ironic discourse. The film drew heavily on German film's avant-garde tradition as well as on a grab bag of expressionistic effects. Jean-Marie Straub's and Danièle Huillet's rendering of Böll's *Bonn Diary*, the short *Machorka-Muff* (1962), amounted to a systematic antifilm, one negating point by point the usages of the dominant praxis with a radical critique of Adenauer's Germany.

The breakthrough came in 1966 when Volker Schlöndorff's *Young Törless* (*Der junge Törless*) won the International Critics Prize at Cannes, Peter Schamoni's *Closed Season on Fox Hunting* (*Schonzeit für Füchse*) gained a Silver Bear at the Berlin Festival, and Kluge's *Yesterday Girl* (*Abschied von gestern*) received a Silver Lion at Venice. These films, along with Ulrich Schamoni's *It* (*Es*, 1966), aptly gave expression to the bottled rage of German youth and anticipated the generational uprising that would ignite during the late sixties. The films center on the private rebellions of angry young people whose elders offer little help or advice. They are set in a world of stern structures and uninviting city streets; the protagonists, though eager and energetic, lack direction in a realm all but devoid of role models. The result of a fierce generational tension, works of a group now with the means to put its aspirations and disappointments on celluloid, the so-called knapsack films of the Oberhausen explorers had a documentary impulse and a critical resolve.

*Young Törless* was adapted from Robert Musil's turn-of-the-century short novel about a confused cadet who watches fellow pupils in a military academy torment a weaker classmate. *It* and *Closed Seasons* feature relationships between young couples who scorn their elders' empty lives but cannot escape these time-worn patterns. In *Yesterday Girl* a Jewish refugee from the GDR wanders through the metropolises of West Germany, treading through a labyrinth of official intransigence and bureaucratic insensitivity, trying to find a way in from an all-embracing cold. Kluge's film was the most ambitious example of Young German Film's alternative designs, with its melange of protocols, photographs, fantasy sequences, intertitles, voice-overs, nursery rhymes, hymns, and incantations. Reality as a market place of competing discourses and cinema as a site where spectators can pick, choose, and combine this wealth of stimuli into visions of their own: Kluge's approach differed greatly from the more conventional ploys of his counterparts. Schlöndorff—and the majority of Young German filmmakers who made their debuts in the mid-sixties—placed his allegory of nascent fascism in a more traditional package, drawing on a famous literary source, using familiar patterns of suspense and climax, relying on a clear-cut cinematic realism and a closed narrative structure. In the years to come the distance between the strategies paradigmatically embodied by *Yesterday Girl* and *Törless* would become even more apparent.

The initial critical success of Young German Film caused a backlash in the film establishment. *Opas Kino* managed to gain the passage of a Film Subsidy Law in 1967 based solely on economic considerations: federal subsidies favored producers whose last film had grossed more than 500 thousand DM over two years. A lower threshold of 300 thousand DM was granted to films that met standards of quality determined by the Film Assessment Office (FBW). This meant, however, that young directors were reliant on the FBW for the ratings that would insure future productions, since few of their efforts drew heavily at the box office. The result of the new financing arrangement was a new wave of overproduction, mindless schoolboy comedies, sappy melodramas, and an endless onslaught of sex films, set in the countryside with titles like *Someone's Yodeling under My Dirndl* (*Unterm Dirndl wird gejodelt*, 1973), disguised as enlightenment documentaries (Oswalt Kolle provided the model), or ridden with a forced and sadistic brand of levity (the specialty of Alois Brummer).

With the annual budget of the *Kuratorium* reduced to 750 thousand DM and the initial funds all but depleted, Young German filmmakers once more were on dangerous ground. Eager to attract larger audiences, Young German Film for a time tried its hand at popular cinema. Directors like Eckhart Schmidt, Roger Fritz, and Rob Houwer turned out films capitalizing on stylish milieux and trendy thematics. Erotic comedies such as Marran Gosov's *Engelchen or the Virgin from Bamberg* (*Engelchen oder Die Jungfrau von Bamberg*, 1967), a tale about a country bumpkin in the big city, bore much in common with the dirty-old-man sexist fantasies produced by *Opas Kino*. Young German films did have some subversive levity, nonetheless—frivolity with a cutting edge. Franz-Josef Spieker's *Wild Rider Inc.* (*Wilder Reiter, GmbH.*, 1966) incisively dramatized how a sensation-mongering opportunist manipulates the culture industry. The self-styled wild man from the woods stages a series of public scandals, finding quick fame and financial rewards. Spieker's film was an ironic view of the way the establishment turned avant-garde challenges into mainstream culture. George Moorse's *Cuckoo Years* (*Kuckucksjahre*, 1967) satirized the vapid effusions of pop-art culture. The most irreverent and accomplished comedy of the period, May Spils's *Let's Get Down to Business, Darling* (*Zur Sache, Schätzchen*, 1967) took place in a Schwabing bohemian environment. The first in a series of films Spils would make with the humorist Werner Enke, this box-office hit impressed many with its snappy script, its devil-may-care antiauthoritarianism, and the authenticity of its Munich location.

While Schlöndorff pursued wider audiences in *A Degree of Murder* (*Mord und Totschlag*, 1967), a film with a jet-set ambience, other less compromising directors like Straub/Huillet left Germany or—like Vlado Kristl—ran amok. *Film or Power* (*Film oder Macht*, 1970) was Kristl's raspberry in the face of the subsidy system, a work protesting an institution hostile to authentic image making. Kluge's *The Artists under the Big Top: Perplexed* (*Die Artisten in der Zirkuskuppel: ratlos*, 1967) encapsulated Young German Film's dilemma. The heroine, Leni Peickert, dreams of a new kind of circus, one that will open spectators to the richness of experience, one in which animals will be shown authentically. Aware that the art form's tradition stretches back to the French Revolution, Leni harbors an idealistic vision of the circus as a liberating force. Even after she gains the financial means to achieve her design, though, she fears she will betray her dream if she enacts it. She turns to more practical tasks and requites herself with the insight that "utopia gets better when we have to wait for it." The film is marked by associative montage (the opening sequence combines documentary footage from the Day of German Art in 1939 with the Beatles singing "Yesterday" in Spanish), essayistic discourse, and a Frankfurt School-influenced analysis of the culture industry. *Artists* was a metafilm that scrutinized—and embodied in its form—the gap between Young German Film's reformist aims and its lack of a public to partake of its dreams.

The late-sixties brought the arrival of a new generation of talent, just at the time when the first wave had begun to ebb. Rainer Werner Fassbinder, like Brecht's Baal (a role he would later play in Schlöndorff's

1969 TV film), emerged from the underground. Fassbinder had started with radical stage productions, deconstructive renderings of classical plays that called into question audience expectations and institutional frameworks. Fassbinder continued to work in films with his *antitheater* ensemble, with a similar intent to outrage.

Like other *Jungfilmer* who turned to the gangster film in their search for popular appeal, Fassbinder shared a fascination for the crime dramas of Raoul Walsh and Howard Hawks. But the young director— unlike his peers Roland Klick (*Deadlock*, 1970) and Rudolf Thome (*Detektive*, 1968)—did not merely attempt to imitate the pyrotechnics and glamor of the Hollywood models. *Love Is Colder Than Death* (*Liebe ist kälter als der Tod*, 1969), Fassbinder's debut feature, had characters caught between tough-guy posturing and the insecurity that motivates such self-stylizing. Staged in a petty criminal milieu reminiscent of Godard's *Bande à part*, Fassbinder's creation of low-life Munich imparted a social dimension to the borrowed genre. *Love Is Colder than Death, Gods of the Plague* (*Götter der Pest*, 1969), *The American Soldier* (*Der amerikanische Soldat*, 1970) enact—in form and content—the predicament of occupied minds harboring foreign movie-derived dreams of a more attractive life, but lacking the élan and style to carry off the pretense.

Working in a fast-and-dirty manner, Fassbinder made a virtue of low budgets and a compulsion to produce. The lack of contrast in the lighting of *Love Is Colder than Death* comments on a world where there are no corners to hide in, no places where one might escape. The long static takes of *Katzelmacher* (1969), austere compositions reminiscent of Straub/Huillet, along with the sparse background decor, underline the disenchanted confines in which the provincial drama of hostility toward foreigners unfolds. *Why Does Herr R. Run Amok? (Warum läuft Herr R. Amok?*, 1970) is a radical exercise in improvisation, a minute, documentarylike rendering of a struggling technical designer faced with career pressures and domestic responsibilities. Full of unintentional but nonetheless expressive "mistakes" (overexposed film and out-of-focus shots), the film, with all its rough edges, amateur actors, and ad-lib dialogue, painfully evokes the harsh reality that moves the protagonist to murder his family and commit suicide. *Beware of a Holy Whore (Warnung vor einer heiligen Nutte*, 1970) was a taking of stock for the quickly acclaimed and controversial director. On a movie set in Spain, Fassbinder portrayed his problematic relationship to cast and crew, appearing alternately as petty tyrant, victim, and assured stylist.

Fassbinder's early gangster films marked a return to the *film noir* heritage first crafted by the expressionist master Lang—by way of Hollywood and France (Raoul Walsh, Samuel Fuller, Godard, and Jean-Pierre Melville). Wim Wenders, graduate of the Munich Academy for TV and Film, likewise took recourse to German film history via a circuitous route. After a series of experimental shorts, Wenders completed his diploma project, *Summer in the City* (1970; original English title), a work merging the contemplative contours of Straub/Huillet with the minimalistic patterns of American B-movies. No other West German director has expressed so obsessively as Wenders—and in his own career embodied—the love-hatred of America endemic to an occupied postwar nation. This is even more apparent in his adaptation of Peter Handke's cryptic crime novel *The Goalie's Anxiety at the Penalty Kick* (*Die Angst des Tormanns beim Elfmeter*, 1971). Full of references to American cultural presence in Europe (ubiquitous juke boxes and pop music) and quotations from Hollywood films (Hawks's *Red Line 7000* plays in a Vienna suburb, Don Siegel's *Madigan* unreels in a provincial cinema), Wenders's film was a conscious effort to imitate Hollywood. *The Goalie's Anxiety* traces a few days in the life of an ex-soccer player, who, pursued by the police after he blithely murders a cinema cashier, retreats to the country. Wenders—like the intellectual Handke who blended Highsmith and Sartre—imparted a ponderousness to the galvanizing crime tale full of red herrings and loose ends. The film is full of elliptical leaps, missing transition shots, and lacking motivations. Wenders—like Fassbinder—reflected "the situation of someone who has inherited . . . the American cinema, but who doesn't have an American mind."[5]

Werner Herzog, another new arrival with a distinctive and unmistakable signature, seemed at first glance less indebted to previous models than his colleagues. Unsurveyed landscapes, subterranean recesses of the psyche, borderline situations: Herzog wanted to capture the ineffable and the undiscovered, searching out exotic terrains and examining human nature at its breaking point. A filmmaker who prides himself on his visionary powers and views his craft as a religious calling, Herzog first made an impact with a series of eccentric shorts. His debut feature, *Signs of Life* (*Lebenszeichen*, 1967), brought him a State Film Prize and considerable attention. It is about the gradual undoing of a German soldier stationed on the sleepy island of Kos during World War II. Like other titanic challengers in later Herzog films, the soldier Stroszek takes on the elements after going mad in a valley of inexorably revolving windmills—one of Herzog's breathtaking found landscapes—whose circle form essentializes the director's fatalistic vision of a trapped human condition. Herzog attracted a cult following abroad with his experimental documentary, *Fata Morgana* (1970), a science fiction invocation of the effect of modernity on a primeval desert inhabited by bizarre natives, settlers, and explorers. A filmmaker who resists traditional labels, Herzog effected an odd merger between fiction and documentary, narrative and experimental cinema.

Fassbinder, Herzog, and Wenders hoped to combine a New German art film with a wider public appeal in their merger of cinematic convention and subversive strategies meant to expand the limits of narrative film as well as to reexamine its workings. As coming years would show, their methods restored a lost tradition and a sense of their national film history. Other directors rethought German film history by revamping the homeland film, shaping it into less sentimental evocations of provincial life. Reinhard Hauff's *Mathias Kneissl* (1971) and Schlöndorff's *The Sudden Wealth of the Poor People of Kombach (Der plötzliche Reichtum der armen Leute von Kombach*, 1970) studied a past that official history had sought to repress and *Opas Kino* had resolutely falsified. These analytical *Anti-Heimatfilme* challenged the thematic and formal arsenal of the once dominant genre.

At the same time in West Berlin, other young filmmakers reawakened the obscured Weimar legacy of workers' films. (Most of these were coproductions of the German Film and TV Academy in Berlin and the public television network WDR.) Films such as Theo Gallehr's and Rolf Schübel's *Red Flags Can Be Seen Better (Rote Fahnen sieht man besser*, 1971) and the works of Christian Ziewer supplied documentary authenticity within narrative frameworks, views of wage earners and their strained relation to capital, their quest for solidarity with colleagues—matters rarely considered in mainstream films.

As Young German Film began to enjoy accolades and directors in the FRG established a working relationship with film history, activity in the GDR suffered from a return to the policies of the early fifties. Criticizing the way in which certain directors had appropriated neorealist aesthetics (an approach viewed as applicable only to the contradictions of capitalism), government officials chastised DEFA films for lacking political engagement and their all too prevalent negative emphasis. Although some filmmakers took issue with the bland sociology and schematic formulas imposed on them, the government increased ideological pressure, especially after the erection of the Berlin Wall in August 1961. As the sixties progressed, the pressure became more severe.

DEFA films of the sixties do not stand up well next to the output of other Eastern bloc countries, especially the passionate historical epics of the Polish School, the Czech New Wave that blossomed during the relaxed atmosphere of the Dubček regime, and the formal masterpieces of Miklós Jancsó in Hungary. Attempts to secure government approval led to schematic works centering on the crises of factory administrators such as Horst Seemann's *Time to Live (Zeit zu leben*, 1969) and Rolf Karsten's *Network (Netzwerk*, 1969). East German *Problemfilme* dealt with domestic conflicts, reflecting the country's high divorce rate in Frank Vogel's *The Seventh Year (Das siebente Jahr*, 1969) and the toll a career takes on one's private life in Egon Günther's *Lot's Wife (Lots Weib*, 1965). Adaptations of contemporary novels focused on the relation between individual and collective, the most successful of which were Ralf Kirsten's *Description of a Summer (Beschreibung eines*

The spector of the past: traumatic memories plague the ex-soldier Mertens (Ernst Wilhelm Borchert) in Wolfgang Staudte's *The Murderers Are Among Us* (1946).

The two Germanies face each other: Hans Boeckel (Hansjörg Falmy) and Bruno Tiches (Robert Graf) in Kurt Hoffmann's *Aren't We Wonderful?* (1958).

(Left)
The primacy of spectacle
and specularity in the
trappings of a pulp
thriller: Fritz Lang's
*The Thousand Eyes of
Dr. Mabuse* (1960).

(Right)
Anita G. (Alexandra
Kluge), a Jewish refugee
from the GDR, tries to
find her way out of the
cold in postwar Germany,
in Alexander Kluge's
*Yesterday Girl* (1966).

*I Was Nineteen* (1968) is director Konrad Wolf's own story of his return to "another Germany that today is the GDR" after service with the Red Army.

In Rainer Werner Fassbinder's *The Merchant of Four Seasons* (1971), a proletarian tragedy in the Adenauer era, the director (r.) played a cameo role.

The protagonist of Werner Herzog's *The Mystery of Kaspar Hauser* (*Jeder für sich und Gott gegen alle*, 1974), as rendered by Bruno S., before his deliverance into the world.

An arid national cinema, a film tradition at the end of its tether: combing the provinces along the German border in Wim Wenders's *Kings of the Road* (1976).

(Left)
Draining the swamp of
terrorist sympathizers:
scene from a hunt in West
Germany out of the
collective production
*Germany in Autumn*
(1978).

(Below)
Exchanging the spiritual
cold of Bavaria for the icy
scapes of Greenland:
Herbert Achternbusch
reenacts the famous pose
of Goethe in the
Campagna in *Bye Bye
Bavaria* (1977).

Two young people take flight from a humdrum existence in East
Germany in Heiner Carow's whimsical *The Legend of Paul and
Paula* (1972).

A quintessential Fassbinder composition: Franz Biberkopf (Günter Lamprecht) down and
out after the death of Mieze, in the fifteen-hour *Berlin Alexanderplatz* (1980).

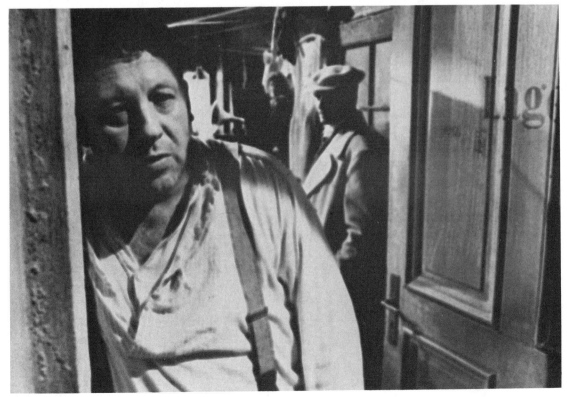

*Sommers*, 1963) and Konrad Wolf's *The Divided Heaven* (*Der geteilte Himmel*, 1964). Toward the last half of the sixties, though, many filmmakers resisted such blatantly political undertakings. They chose to film less controversial thematics such as science fiction fantasies like the international coproduction *Icaros's Signals* (*Ikaros Signale*, 1970); portrayals of teenagers on holiday like Joachim Hasler's *Hot Summer* (*Heisser Sommer*, 1967); and Westerns from the point of view of the Indians like Josef Mach's *The Sons of Great Bear* (*Die Söhne der grossen Bärin*, 1966).

Even within this subdued climate there are several outstanding exceptions. Continuing the DEFA tradition of antifascist evocations of the Third Reich, Heiner Carow's *They Called Him Amigo* (*Sie nannten ihn Amigo*, 1959) is set in the Berlin of 1939. A moving tale of a thirteen-year-old's attempt to hide an escaped political prisoner, the film portrays a Communist family surrounded by Nazi denouncers and brutal police officials. Authentic in its documentary style, only the conclusion of the film seems forced, a flashforward to the present where Amigo now serves as an officer in the People's National Army. Gerhard Klein's *The Gleiwitz Case* (*Der Fall Gleiwitz*, 1961) is a gripping reconstruction of the staged SS attack on a German radio station which would supply Hitler with a pretext for declaring war on Poland in 1939. Scripted by Günther Rücker and Wolfgang Kohlhaase (one of the GDR's best scenarists), the film is sparse and precise, recreating the action as a methodical and sinisterly impersonal event, one in which few words are spoken, characters remain faceless, and the camera dispassionately registers gestures, details, and interiors.

The national epic par excellence, Konrad Wolf's *I Was Nineteen* (*Ich war neunzehn*, 1968) tells the director's own story of his return as a member of the Red Army to his homeland in the spring of 1945. The narrative unfolds as a diary account of the protagonist's attempts to fathom the war-weary country inhabited by shell-shocked refugees, Soviet occupiers, former resistance fighters, and representatives of the new socialist order. Wolf adroitly weaves authentic material into the fictional line of action, showing newsreel footage of the approaching Red Army, and presenting nightmare images of the death camps. Never simplifying and characteristically circumventing cliches, Wolf's film evokes the state of Germany after the surrender.

Another Wolf film, his adaptation of Christa Wolf's *The Divided Heaven* (*Der geteilte Himmel*, 1964), is the most daring experimental venture during the epoch. Similar to the retrospective fragments of memory in Resnais's *Hiroshima mon amour*, the controversial film sought a visual counterpart for the protagonist Rita's confused associations. After a nervous breakdown, she reruns her life while resting in her home village, reliving her love for the chemist Manfred who will ultimately flee to the West for the sake of his career, leaving her shattered. Above all, the film's open structure with its free association and subtle patterning left the spectator to find his or her own response to a dilemma on many people's minds: taking flight to the West.

## The Seventies: Success Abroad, Troubles at Home

The seventies was the decade of New German Cinema. The works of the *Jungfilmer* gained an international following, homages in Paris, retrospectives in New York and London. While still not firmly established at home, West German filmmakers found their public abroad. Praised for their visual idiosyncrasy, personal favor, and off-beat modernity, West German directors became the most prominent *auteurs* during the decade.

The international recognition of New German Cinema was, in part, an aspect of growing world respect toward German culture: the Nobel Prizes won early in the seventies by Willi Brandt and Heinrich Böll, the flowering of the "New Wild" artists in New York galleries, and the rise of an independent pop music scene, as well as numerous translations of West German novels and stage performances of dramas. The great acclaim, especially in the United States, obscured the troubled constellations behind these provocative productions, hailing the individual creators while overlooking the background against which these works arose. New German Cinema has its other history, indeed—one of turmoil and crisis, continual challenges to the precarious support systems, institutional pressures, and infighting.

New German Film from the beginning had posed an oppositional alternative to the representations of the dominant cinema and the establishment media. The ascent of Brandt to the West German chancellorship in 1969 as the SPD (Social Democratic Party) came into power had kindled hopes among the FRG's progressive forces. In the years to come, though, it became apparent that the new government was turning against the gains of the student movement and post-1968 reforms. The left, which had hoped to transform the structural framework of the FRG, found itself increasingly marginalized. Public campaigns against radicals criminalized oppositional activity, as did a state-wide program of security checks for potential civil servants. In some professions (e.g., school teachers), those who had been active in the student movement were denied employment. Various intellectuals—notably the Frankfurt School—were branded as the theoretical harbingers of a wave of terrorism which beset the FRG during the decade. Blacklisting, state and media denunciation campaigns against suspected enemies of the state, an attendant retreat of the left into atomization and melancholy: artists in the FRG clearly were in a precarious situation.

Even while it was enjoying considerable praise at international festivals and in metropolitan arthouses, the New German Cinema faced substantial problems at home. Still unable to assert itself commercially, West German film (of which New German Cinema was only a small part) had a pauper's share of the ailing film economy. Finished films often were not exhibited at all. The production and distribution organization *Filmverlag der Autoren*, founded by young filmmakers in the early seventies as a collective to protect their interests, nearly collapsed in 1976. West Germany's most radical filmmakers had either left the country (Straub/Huillet to Rome, Klaus Wyborny to New York), stopped making films altogether (Vlado Kristl), or were dependent on other employment. Helmuth Costard made children's films for television, Werner Schroeter worked in the theater. A crusade was launched against the alleged Communist sympathies shown by the television network, WDR, the most important supporter of independent filmmakers. By the mid-seventies, the WDR no longer produced workers' films or controversial projects.

The rise of Rainer Werner Fassbinder to prominence came after the director turned away from insular provincial tales and film-buff fantasies toward more popular forms, the melodrama and the international art film. *The Merchant of Four Seasons (Der Händler der vier Jahreszeiten*, 1971) was the breakthrough work, the result of Fassbinder's exposure to Douglas Sirk's Hollywood films. From movies like *All That Heaven Allows* and *Written on the Wind*, Fassbinder learned how to recast a popular genre so as to satisfy culinary demands while simultaneously leaving a bitter aftertaste, promoting identification and estrangement at the same time. *Merchant* offered a stylized reconstruction of the Adenauer era. One feels the epoch in the clothing, the tense family circles, the severe hairstyles, kitsch paintings, and narrow kitchens. Fassbinder's portrait of a fruit vendor's humble aspirations and many disappointments—which culminate in a ritualistic suicide around a tavern table—linked the fifties with the recent past. Names like Epp and von Schirach recall those of important Nazi officials. Likewise, exteriors shot in a noticeably modern Munich updated the period piece to address the spectator's present.

Frames that circumscribe characters within tight limits, ornamental tableaux whose occupants are trapped in a web of expectations and responsibilities, disquieting conclusions that trouble and confound: Fassbinder's cinema of disenchantment was often mistakenly rejected as nihilistic. Ali, the foreign worker who marries an older cleaning woman in *Ali: Fear Eats the Soul (Angst essen Seele auf,* 1973), lies in a hospital bed in the movie's closing sequence. Victim of "guest worker's" disease, his scant hope is underlined by a final shot of a window without a view. *Effi Briest* (1974), Fassbinder's mannered rendering of the novel by Theodor Fontane, shows a young girl shackled in a marriage arranged by her father. Suffering in a lonely corner of Prussia during her priggish husband's long absences, Effi, to pass the time, has an affair, one for which she pays dearly some six years later. In crisp black-and-white photography, shot to a great extent outdoors (atypical for the Fassbinder who preferred the control of studios) with natural light, *Effi Briest* unfolds with solemn inevitability. In *Fox and His Friends* (*Faustrecht der Freiheit*, 1974), Fassbinder turned to a homosexual milieu for a tale of exploitation. Fox (played by the director) wins a lottery and is systematically taken for a ride by his lover, ultimately committing suicide in a subway station.

At the time of Fassbinder's major triumphs in the United States, the director faced his most traumatic rejections in the FRG. Attacked by the conservative press as a "leftist anti-Semite" for the drama *Garbage, the City, and Death* (*Der Müll, die Stadt und der Tod*, 1976), twice disappointed by WDR (which canceled agreed-upon major undertakings), Fassbinder contemplated emigration and even suicide. *Despair* (1977), a large-scale coproduction scripted by Tom Stoppard, starring Dirk Bogarde and Andrea Ferreol, and based on Vladimir Nabokov's novel, was financed by tax-shelter money. A conscious attempt to craft a European art film, *Despair* deals with an insecure Russian emigrant living in pre-Nazi Berlin. A film rife with leaps in perspective and narrative breaks, Fassbinder's study of a man's search for a *Doppelgänger* whom he murders to collect the life insurance marked a new internationalism in the director's career.

In an interview in 1979, Fassbinder spoke of a career project, a sweeping multifilm epic treatment of the German middle class from 1848 to the present. A crucial part of the undertaking took shape as the "FRG-Project" in three parts: *The Marriage of Maria Braun* (*Die Ehe der Maria Braun*, 1978), *Lola* (1981), and *Veronika Voss* (*Die Sehnsucht der Veronika Voss*, 1981). Set against a postwar landscape of jackhammers, American GIs, and crass entrepreneurs, and in each case using a female protagonist as a point of focus, the trilogy constitutes a psychological history of the FRG during the Adenauer era. (We see a negative photograph of the chancellor at the end of *Maria Braun* and gaze on a famous still of him leaning over a radio in *Lola*.) Each film explored new formal territory as well: *Maria Braun* was an experiment in multilayered sound editing (something perfected in Fassbinder's *The Third Generation/Die dritte Generation*, 1979), blending aural complexity with a number of equally dense deep-focus compositions. *Lola* was an experiment in the use of color, the confectionary candy shades of the Adenauer era shrouded in a highly stylized lighting characteristic of Josef von Sternberg. *Veronika Voss*, a bleak study in black and white redolent of *Sunset Boulevard*, was an acerbic recollection of the UFA melodrama.

Fassbinder ultimately became the victim of his relentless urge to work. He was found dead in a Munich apartment on the morning of 10

June, 1982 in surroundings not unlike those of his films. The inability of people to find happiness, the impossibility of love and lasting bonds with others: Fassbinder's output, for all its bitter realities and unsettling conclusions, left an irreplaceable legacy and provided a negative dialectic of hope. As the director said in 1975: "When I show people on the screen, the ways that things can go wrong, my aim is to warn them that that's the way things *will* go if they don't change their lives. Never mind if a film ends pessimistically; if it exposes certain mechanisms clearly enough to show people how exactly they work, then the ultimate effect is not pessimistic. I never try to reproduce reality in a film. My goal is to reveal such mechanisms in a way that makes people realise the necessity of changing their own reality."[6]

Werner Herzog, in contrast, maintained a more virulently fatalistic view. A director whose work recalls the dark romanticism found in various Weimar classics, Herzog stresses the power of rebellion despite insurmountable odds. Aguirre, the crazed Spanish conquistador of *Aguirre, the Wrath of God* (*Aguirre, der Zorn Gottes*, 1972), stands frozen like an heroic statue in the film's final shot, surrounded by the carnage of his crew on a boat covered with spider monkeys. As he queries, "Who is with me?" Herzog's camera solemnly does a circle salute around him.

*The Mystery of Kaspar Hauser* (*Jeder für sich und Gott gegen alle*, 1974) garnered the International Critics' Prize at Cannes in 1975. The enigmatic work is dedicated to critic and film historian Lotte Eisner and to the expatriated German film culture that fled its homeland during the Third Reich. The story of an innocent freed from his year-long dungeon and set into the world, *Kaspar Hauser* possesses the anticivilization rhetoric of Rousseau's famous discourse. On the one hand is a world of intuition, dreams, reverie; on the other, one of bureaucrats, rationalism, and categories that diminish the richness of the real. The most memorable sequences in this drama of innocence betrayed remain Kaspar's dream visions, ones harking back to the fantastic landscapes of German silent cinema.

*Stroszek* (1976) stars Bruno S., who gained notoriety as Kaspar Hauser. Moving from the tough street confines of West Berlin to the equally brutal (although more subtly so) open spaces of America, the film is a tale of displacement, of inexorable homelessness. No matter where he goes, the ex-convict Stroszek remains pursued: Berlin hoods give way to a fast-talking bank official in Wisconsin. In Germany his flat is ransacked; in America his mobile home is repossessed and auctioned off when he misses a payment. A long prison corridor with harsh vertical bars shifts to an even more poignant correlative for entrapment, Herzog's characteristic circles. In the final sequence, whirl is king: Stroszek's flaming truck twists, driverless, around a parking lot, a frantic chicken dances around a turntable, while Stroszek revolves on a ski lift. Images of madness, images of no escape: the bleakness here would be utter were it not for the rebellious music by Sonny Terry one hears while watching these disquieting sights.

Herzog continued to cultivate the image of the romantic hero-director in his next projects. *Nosferatu* (1979) involved the filmmaker in disputes with officials in the Dutch town of Delft. Like his model Murnau, Herzog shot on location. Seeking to recreate (but not remake) the 1922 version of the Dracula story, with its hallucinatory and visionary qualities, Herzog reached backward to Weimar film culture with his vampire tale, one which he believed (following Kracauer) presaged the coming of Hitler and the Nazi plague. *Fitzcarraldo* (1982), the story of an opera enthusiast's dream of bringing Caruso to the Amazon wilds, became notorious for Herzog's vicissitudes during production, ones chronicled in Les Blank's stunning portrait of an obsessed filmmaker, *The Burden of Dreams* (1982). Both the documentary of a work in progress and the finished work demonstrated frightening moments where a personal fantasy is realized despite terrifying risk.

The most introspective of the New German directors, Wim Wenders was shaped as much by romantic painting and literature as by American movies and pop music. The characters in his "Roadtrilogy" are terse and sullen, nomadic and driven, youths who seek to escape their homes and the past, but who find themselves constantly yearning for some sort of *Heimat* and in need of a sense of history. *Alice in the Cities* (*Alice in den Städten*, 1973) features a troubled journalist peregrinating through America, on assignment to write a story, but only able to collect unconnected images. Falling in with a young girl who has been separated from her mother, Philip returns with Alice to the FRG, where the unlikely pair commences a quest for a house somewhere in the Ruhr Valley. The detached gazes and idle attentions which marked Philip's behavior in the United States give way to care and sympathy— just as Wenders's filmmaking more and more moved away from imagistic studies of landscapes, cities, and found objects, concerning itself increasingly with characters and the question of communication. *Wrong Move* (*Falsche Bewegung*, 1974), scripted by Peter Handke and loosely based on Goethe's *Bildungsroman*, *The Apprenticeship of Wilhelm Meister*, follows a fledgling writer from the northern reaches of the FRG to the top of the Zugspitze (the highest German peak in the Alps). Wenders questions the German literary tradition of the young man seeking himself in showing Wilhelm's journey to be a series of false moves, for the narcissist fails to take into account anything besides his personal well-being and intellectual improvement. *Kings of the Road* (*Im Lauf der Zeit*, 1976), another mix of motion and emotion, traces a film projector repairman as he moves along the eastern border of the FRG, taking stock of the dire situation of German film in the provinces. An elderly cinema owner recalls the days of Lang's *Die Nibelungen* at the film's start; at the end an angry exhibitor swears she would rather cease business than screen the garbage sent her way. At crucial junctures in the narrative one glimpses an image of Fritz Lang, a reminder of a forsaken and exiled film tradition. Cinema is an institution where a country partakes of sounds and images that speak of itself: *Kings of the Road* invokes a rich legacy while protesting the breakdown of a once venerable film culture, its colonization by cynical merchandizers with their sickening array of "violence, action, and sex."

*The American Friend* (*Der amerikanische Freund*, 1977) brought Wenders into the spotlight. Shot in America, France, and Germany in three languages and with an international cast, the rendering of Patricia Highsmith's *Ripley's Game* both galvanized and confounded audiences. Full of references to image making (the protagonist, Jonathan Zimmermann, is an art restorer) and featuring a number of film directors in cameo performances, *The American Friend* presents an old world of substance, frames, and craft manipulated and preyed upon by mercenary U.S. interests. Ripley, the American friend strikingly portrayed by Dennis Hopper, surrounds himself with consumer items, takes endless snapshots of himself, and continually records empty utterances, signs of a life whose only substance is money making. Abrupt cuts between Hamburg, Manhattan, and Paris make the world appear as an urban inferno, one single American hell.

Wenders would go on to have trying experiences with American friends while working on *Hammett* (1982) in California. After five excruciating years, numerous scripts, and many delays, he completed the adaptation of Joe Gores's novel dealing with the detective writer's early days in San Francisco. Shot on a set (at least in the released version), with only intermittent signs of Wenders's directorial signature, the movie suffered from continued interruptions by its producer, Francis Ford Coppola. *The State of Things* (*Der Stand der Dinge*, 1982), a low-budget production made in Portugal and Los Angeles, reflects on the situation of an artist who makes images derived from observed details and felt emotions—not ready-made schemes and overworked patterns. The director Friedrich Munro (a reference to F. W. Murnau, a German *auteur* who also shipwrecked in Hollywood) runs out of money while on the set of a remake of Allan Dwan's *The Most Dangerous Man Alive*. He flies to Los Angeles, tracks down his producer, who is on the run from the Mafia, and is gunned down by hitmen in the early morning. The victim of angry creditors, Friedrich had incensed his backers because he used their money to make an unmarketable black-and-white film.

The triumvirate Fassbinder/Herzog/Wenders became synonymous with New German Cinema, whose visions of kaput worlds and a frantic nation put forward an alternative in an increasingly commercialized international film scene. More tangible box-office successes, however, were registered by Volker Schlöndorff, a director whose work blended well-known literary sources with traditional narrative structures and considerable production values. *The Lost Honor of Katharina Blum* (*Die verlorene Ehre der Katharina Blum*, codirected with Margarethe von Trotta, 1975), derived from a Heinrich Böll story, was an indictment of the collusion between government witch-hunters and a bloodthirsty yellow press. A shrill account of a young woman whose affair with a suspected terrorist makes her the target for police harassment and ugly rumors, *Katharina Blum* issued from a tense political climate. Every bit as high pitched as the boulevard press it attacked, the film replicated in its own form what it criticized in its narrative. *The Tin Drum* (*Die Blechtrommel*, 1979) brought Schlöndorff an Oscar and considerable returns at home and in foreign cinemas. With Günter Grass's novel of a dwarf's low-angle view of the Third Reich as his basis, Schlöndorff bore out what the artist Christo once said: "In the seventies the Germans began to reinvent National Socialism. The Hitler period became an extraordinary creative resource for a whole generation of filmmakers."[7] *The Tin Drum*—like Schlöndorff's next work, a rendering of Nicolas Born's novel about a foreign correspondent in war-torn Beirut, *Circle of Deceit* (*Die Fälschung*, 1981)—gained its export market appeal from its visual pyrotechnics, ensemble performances, and distinguished cinematography by Igor Luther.

Alexander Kluge's *Strongman Ferdinand* (*Der starke Ferdinand*, 1975) shared the International Critics' Prize at Cannes in 1976 but failed at the German box office. Kluge may very well be the motor force driving New German Cinema, its most cogent and thought-provoking spokesman. Nonetheless, he remains nearly unknown in America where few of his films have distributors. *Strongman Ferdinand* is his most accessible work: Ferdinand Rieche, a security expert for a large international concern, is a character who wants to systematize everything. Method is his madness; paranoia marks his lifestyle as well as the social context that produced him. "Crisis, catastrophe, general strike: the enemy," intones the off-screen narrator. "From these Rieche's work derives its meaning. Most people believe in normal situations. Rieche believes just as strongly in emergency." So too does Gabi Teichert, the school teacher heroine of Kluge's *The Patriot* (*Die Patriotin*, 1979). Her search for the meaning of German history accompanies a wish for a more positive course of events, a heritage with which she might identify. *The Patriot*—whose cast includes a talking knee, the living memory of an officer downed on the Eastern front ("Who says that the dead are dead?")—is guided by Gabi's quest to see German history in its overall context, not as an inalterable given, but as something demanding constant reflection and human intervention.

The films of Hans-Jürgen Syberberg review German history from a markedly different vantage point. His "German trilogy" provides a celebration of German mythmakers and an invocation of the forsaken powers of irrationalism and the romantic tradition. *Ludwig-Requiem for a Virgin King* (*Ludwig-Requiem für einen jungfräulichen König*, 1972) portrays Ludwig II, mad king of Bavaria, patron of Wagner and builder of fairy-tale castles. *Karl May* (1974) deals with the final twelve years in the life of the famous author of Westerns and exotic novels, cast in landscapes never seen by the writer. A figure as beleaguered as the whimsical Ludwig, Karl May defends his fantasy utopias against those who maintain the reality principle. Syberberg likewise would dramatize his own career over the years in articles and books, claiming his martyrdom and ill treatment by unimaginative critics at home. *Our Hitler* (*Hitler—ein Film aus Deutschland*, 1977), a seven-hour matrix of puppets, slide projections, quotations, long monologues, and discursive self-reflection is Syberberg's major work to date. A film split into four parts (like Wagner's *Ring* tetralogy) and shown mainly in special screenings, *Our Hitler* contains the cathartic urge to exorcise Germany of its demons precisely by appealing to that which haunts it most profoundly, the images of the Third Reich still festering within its psyche. An act of mourning, Syberberg's epic inveighs against the forces of would-be enlightenment in postwar Germany which have tried to eradicate myth and enchantment. Effecting a synthesis of Brecht and Wagner, distanciating framework and operatic pathos, the baroque effort is a dense text that found more indulgent and sympathetic viewers abroad. The conservative cultural critic Syberberg, for all his international acclaim, still has few defenders at home, a situation no doubt fostered by his frequent attacks on intellectuals as well as artists of every persuasion.

*Germany in Autumn* (*Deutschland im Herbst*, 1978) was another act of mourning, an attempt to retain memories of a traumatic time in the form of subjective momentary impressions. The abduction of the industrial leader Hanns-Martin Schleyer by a terrorist group in the fall of 1977 led to a state-wide search for the kidnappers. Suspicion ran rampant; hot lines to the police were kept busy while government crisis staffs met daily. The state maintained control over news reporting, deciding which images could be shown and what information would be released. *Germany in Autumn* sought to combat this public monopoly of sights and sounds. The production of a collective whose members included Kluge, Schlöndorff, Böll, and Fassbinder, it provided alternative images, X-ray visions of a country under siege from within, a nation at odds with itself and with its own history. Neither state nor TV funds supported the film. With its counterpoint and juxtaposition, its leaps from filmed reality to staged fiction, *Germany in Autumn* offers a wealth of variations on a central theme: *Deutschland*. The work begins and ends with funerals, the official state ceremonies for the murdered Schleyer in the opening sequence and the heavily policed burial of the Red Army Faction (RAF) inmates at the conclusion. Framing the film is a quote from a Kluge protagonist: "When cruelty reaches a certain point, it doesn't matter who's responsible; what matters is that it stop." *Germany in Autumn* with its merger of auteurist and cooperative cinema stands as the most crucial joint enterprise in New German Film since Oberhausen. A film concerned with both the frightful continuities in German history and the then-current state of emergency, it received only minor notice when released in the United States, a country otherwise receptive to this foreign cinema.

By the end of the seventies, New German Cinema had its celebrated few—and its unrecognized many. The enthusiasm of international friends of the New German Cinema drew attention to a distinctive film culture often unappreciated at home. At the same time, unfortunately, this valorization of a small circle of directors obscured the diversified and multifaceted character of the FRG's lively film output.

Among the more traditional narrative craftsmen, two directors scored significantly at American box offices. Ulrich Edel's *Christiane F.* (*Christiane F.—Wir Kinder vom Bahnhof Zoo*, 1981) was a *Problemfilm* reflecting the fate of a young girl in the Berlin hard-drug scene. A sensationalistic milieu study based on a best-seller and containing footage of David Bowie, *Christiane F.* circulated in subtitled as well as dubbed versions in showcase screenings throughout the United States. Wolfgang Petersen had long enjoyed a reputation for his technical expertise and mastery of genre cinema. *The Consequence* (*Die Konsequenz*, 1977), a story of a tragic homosexual liaison, and *Black and White Like Day and Night* (*Schwarz und weiss wie Tage und Nächte*, 1978), a TV production featuring a chess champion who comes undone, both served as small-scale previews of the director's next remarkable success. *Das Boot* (1981), a recourse to the apolitical war films of the fifties, was a smash hit, a major production that gave rise to talk of a revived German film industry able to compete with Hollywood. His even more ambitious next project, a rendering of Michael Ende's fantastic novel *The Never-Ending Story* (*Die unendliche Geschichte*, 1984), had a budget exceeding 60 million DM and contained special effects and popular appeal meant to challenge *Star Wars* and *E.T.*

Other directors have enjoyed one- or two-shot successes in the United States but have not managed to establish themselves as international presences. Reinhard Hauff's *Knife in the Head* (*Messer im Kopf*, 1978) featured a latter-day Kaspar Hauser in contemporary Munich, a victim of police violence who must learn the basic human functions from scratch. Hans W. Geissendörfer, arguably the most scintillating artisan of genre fare in the FRG, has retained a low profile outside of West Germany. His gripping rendering of Patricia Highsmith's *The Glass Cell* (*Die gläserne Zelle*, 1977) gained him a State Film Prize and an Oscar nomination, but was not distributed in the United States. Niklaus Schilling has offered several impressive works evidencing a wide knowledge of film history and considerable formal panache. However, *Der Willi-Busch-Report* (1979), a thriller set on the boundary between the two Germanies, remains the only film of Schilling's commercially screened in the United States.

Overtly political films from West Germany, a major factor in the country's production, rarely appear in America. Peter Lilienthal is the significant exception. But it is, ironically, works made outside of the FRG that have made his reputation abroad, films set in an oppressive dictatorship redolent of Chile (*Calm Prevails over the Country* [*Es herrscht Ruhe im Lande*, 1975]), an embroiled Nicaragua (*The Insurrection* [*La Insurreccion*, 1980]), or a New York suburb (*Dear Mr. Wonderful*, 1982)—besides a period piece dealing with a young Jew living underground in Nazi Germany (*David*, 1979). The studies of working-class struggles wrought by Christian Ziewer and other engaged filmmakers, usually go unmentioned in American discussions of New German Cinema. The socially minded investigations of Norbert Kückelmann (*The Experts* [*Die Sachverständigen*, 1972] and *The Last Years of Childhood* [*Die letzten Jahre der Kindheit*, 1979]) scrutinize the organizational structures that shape—and deform—public life in the FRG.

The most conspicuous signifying absence in U.S. notions about New German Cinema is Herbert Achternbusch. A frantic soul running wild, he produces small gritty works portraying his innermost fears and a harsh Bavarian environment. Another important filmmaker, Werner Schroeter, operatically mingles high art and popular culture, pathos and kitsch. He has traveled from underground ventures like *Eika Katappa* (1969) to historical epics, such as *Kingdom of Naples* (*Regno di Napoli*, 1978) and cross-cultural glimpses of foreign workers in the FRG, like *Palermo oder Wolfsburg* (1980), grand prize winner at the Berlin Festival and all but unknown in America. Rosa von Praunheim and Lothar Lambert have for years produced low-budget outrageousness, chronicles of gay life in West Germany. It was Frank Ripploh, though, with his debut *Taxi zum Klo* (1980), an autobiographical recounting of the ex-school teacher's life in the West Berlin homosexual subculture, who introduced most American viewers to this aspect of the FRG.

West Germany has a large number of women directors with a spectrum of works ranging from traditional approaches to modernistic narratives, from experimental documentaries to feminist agitprop and avant-garde explorations. Margarethe von Trotta, whose political liberalism echoes the bourgeois humanism of her husband Volker Schlöndorff, as does her conventional notion of cinematic realism, provides a token feminist presence in American considerations of New German Cinema. Her tales of solidarity among women (*The Second Awakening of Christa Klages*[*Das zweite Erwachen der Christa Klages*, 1977]) and

dramas about sisters (*Marianne and Juliane*[*Die bleierne Zeit*, 1981])
regularly grace festival and arthouse programs.

Helka Sander is the key figure in West Germany's feminist film
culture, founder of the journal *Frauen und Film* (*Women and Film*),
crafter of expressive collages and flashbacks to the early years of solidarity among women during the student movement (*The Subjective
Factor*[*Der subjektive Faktor*, 1981]). Other important female filmmakers include Helma Sanders-Brahms, Jutta Brückner, Ulrike Ottinger,
and Elfi Mikesch, exponents of a dynamic women's cinema ghettoized
within the FRG and relatively unknown abroad.

Other aspects of West German film culture relatively unknown in
the United States include the many documentary films and features
that explore German history and the Third Reich from the vantage
points of workers, resisters, and common citizens: among them, the
films of Gabriele Voss and Christoph Hübner, Klaus Wildenhahn, and
Eberhard Fechner. In a country whose critics constantly lament the
lack of an ongoing theoretical discussion about film, the most lively debate in recent years has centered around documentary redemption of
reality. A fierce controversy ensued over the relative merits of observation or intervention, one engaging a large portion of the country's film
culture. The avant-garde, also a continuing source of impetus for narrative filmmakers, has likewise been ignored in the great clamor over the
West German film wonder. As the country's filmmakers gathered in
September 1979 in Hamburg, the traditional capital of the FRG's experimental and underground talents, these independent directors found
themselves excluded from the festivities. The work of individuals like
Werner Nekes, Helmuth Costard, Klaus Wyborny, and Heinz Emig-
holz (to mention only the most prominent examples) has unfairly been
consigned to the sidelines, a fate shared in general by the rougher—
and more subversive—segments of West Germany's lively film culture.

Amidst the euphoria about the New German Cinema, new films from
East Germany rarely received notice outside of the GDR. After the barren period of the sixties, East German film underwent a renewal with a
more liberal cultural politics introduced when Erich Honecker assumed
party leadership in 1971. DEFA titles of the following decade registered
the relaxed atmosphere, unleashing a spontaneity and vivaciousness
rarely encountered in the *Staatsfilme* of the previous epoch.

In the early seventies a series of realistic contemporary films appeared, focusing on average people in working and domestic environments. Along with Rainer Simon and Roland Gräf, Lothar Warneke is
an adherent of documentary feature films. *Dr. med. Sommer II* (1970),
Warneke's debut, sketched a young physician on his first assignment in
a provincial hospital. Unlike the paternalistic authority figures found
in West German "doctor films," Warneke's unsure hero blunders at
times, even making serious mistakes. Warneke was primarily con-

cerned with recreating an atmosphere and detailing telling gestures. *The Uncorrectable Barbara* (*Die unverbesserliche Barbara*, 1976) and especially *Apprehension* (*Die Beunruhigung*, 1982) likewise avoid movie cliches in their treatment of crisis moments in the daily lives of female workers.

Egon Günther, the commanding figure of the decade, broke new thematic ground in *The Third One* (*Der Dritte*, 1971)—scenes from the life of a mathematician who has been married twice and is willing to risk a third try. *The Third One*—one of several DEFA films with feminist thematics made by male directors—contains glimpses of the woman's personal interactions, including a lesbian encounter, done with an intimacy and intensity rare in East German dealings with the private sphere. Günther merged authenticity with a free-wheeling narrative in *The Keys* (*Die Schlüssel*, 1974), his most important work to date. A young couple, an intellectual and a factory worker, go on vacation to Poland. Offered the keys to an apartment by a stranger they meet at an airport, the unmarried pair confronts questions of living together and human relations in socialist society in general and their own lives in particular. The visitors see the foreign country with new eyes and rethink the dynamics of their relationship. A long altercation demonstrates the distance between the two, the male student's feelings of superiority, and the young woman's sense of responsibility and pride as a worker. While on holiday, Klaus and Ric gain a heightened regard for their nation's history and their collective present. Shortly before her sudden death (a surprise turn in this narrative of a mutual learning process), Ric asks her lover: "Do you really know enough about our lives?"—the main question addressed by DEFA films of the seventies.

Heiner Carow collaborated with the nonconformist writer Ulrich Plenzdorf on *The Legend of Paul and Paula* (*Die Legende von Paul und Paula*, 1974), a whimsical melodrama about a spirited couple who dare to live out their fantasies. One of the most successful DEFA productions ever, the film attracted over a million viewers in the GDR and much media attention in West Germany. What was noteworthy about *Paul and Paula* were scenes that move from workaday Berlin into a projection of wishes, surrealistic extensions of characters who resist the claims on their lives made by the collective.

Literary adaptations with a topical impulse played a crucial role in East German output of the decade. Siegfried Kühn's rendering of Goethe's *The Elective Affinities* (*Die Wahlverwandtschaften*, 1974) emphasized the challenge to social codes, a frequent subject in the films of the period. Egon Günther also dealt with a discontented and rebellious individual living in a stifling society in his adaptation of Goethe's *The Sufferings of Young Werther* (*Die Leiden des jungen Werthers*, 1975). The same director's version of Thomas Mann's novel about Goethe, *Lotte in Weimar* (1974), offered a critical image of a writer who has be-

come a prima donna, an Olympian hero who rarely deigns to come out
of the clouds. More discerning viewers glimpsed in the work a political
parable, a reckoning with the socialist personality cults around Stalin
and East German leader Walter Ulbricht. Two works by the exiled
writer Leon Feuchtwanger formed the basis for further commentaries
on the cultural policies of the GDR in historical settings. Konrad Wolf's
*Goya* (1971), a large-scale coproduction with the Soviet Union shot in
wide-screen, enacted the painter's struggles with the Grand Inquisitor,
his resolve to create radical visions instead of the official court portraits
demanded of him. Egon Günther translated Feuchtwanger's trilogy
*Exil* (1982) into a West German TV production aiming to show characters skilled in the art of surviving in difficult political times. One of the
few East German works screened in the United States during the seventies, Frank Beyer's *Jacob, the Liar* (*Jakob, der Lügner*, 1975) received an Oscar nomination in 1977. Set in a Jewish ghetto in Poland
during the Nazi occupation, the film depicted one man's attempts to
fabricate news of imminent rescue, which sustains hope among his
friends and neighbors.

East German film today remains isolated from the international
mainstream despite its growing maturity. It no longer simply espouses
party mythologies. It has an impressive array of talents; it incisively
observes a worker state's growing pains and individual dilemmas
within the collective. Konrad Wolf died in 1982, leaving behind a legacy of films bound up in the GDR's national history, an epic commentary comparable in its magnitude to that of Fassbinder. *Solo Sunny*
(1980), his last feature, championed a singer who knows what she
wants but finds little she likes in the drab world around her. Existing
on the margins of socialist society, Sunny stands as East German cinema's most provocative challenge to a smug status quo and an administered collective. Another indication of a willingness to show the not always attractive side of life in the GDR is Winfried Junge's *Biographies*
(*Lebensläufe*, 1981), a four-hour documentary study of nine individuals.
A long-term project, *Biographies* provides portraits of people growing
up during the years from 1962 to 1979, tracing six-year-old pupils
through their mid-twenties, observing them as they progress through
school, choose a vocation, and settle into domestic arrangements. "People who are fully aware of their past escape fateful mistakes in the future," Konrad Wolf once said.[8] East German filmmakers—much more
so at times than their West German counterparts—have resolutely
scrutinized their history and worked toward an equally authentic examination of the GDR's present state. A national cinema that sees its
function as a running social commentary, East German production has
perhaps for this reason failed to arouse foreign interest.

In June 1983, a year after Fassbinder's death, people gathered in
Frankfurt to commemorate the director. He was a constant provoca-

tion, a filmmaker who moved freely between major productions and more modest ones. One critic called him "the heart of New German Film." German film culture recognized its immense loss. Later that month, Alexander Kluge's long-awaited *Taking of Stock: Utopia Film (Bestandsaufnahme: Utopie Film)* appeared in book stores. The thick volume reviewed the twenty-one years since Oberhausen, the path of Young and New German Film, its many crises and numerous successes. For the national cinema now, claimed Kluge, there was no time to lose, given the real challenge of the new media, the competition with commercial television, and the general status of film in the age of electronic reproduction.

With the coming of a conservative turn in 1982 as the Christian Democrats assumed power in a coalition with the Free Democrats, West German cinema faced the threat of a return to the policies of the 1950s. A relatively liberal framework of film subsidies and television coproduction fostered the personal visions of the *Jungfilmer*. With the ascent of the new government, this support network, the product of many years' lobbying and struggle, seemed seriously threatened. Born of discontent, New German Film has had a history of success—and crisis. Following a precarious course over time, West German filmmakers have nonetheless managed to create an original film culture of worldwide importance. Whether they can continue to do so, in the face of potential government intervention, is once more the issue. The further existence of the national cinema will very much depend on how effectively filmmakers are able to combat those forces which seek to administer their endeavors.

## NOTES

1. I am indebted to the Alexander von Humboldt-Stiftung, whose generous study stipend provided the means and time for me to write this article in West Germany during the summer of 1983.
2. *From Caligari to Hitler: A Psychological History of the German Film* (Princeton: Princeton University Press, 1947), pp. 61ff.
3. "A New Realism: Fassbinder Interviewed by John Hughes and Brooks Riley," *Film Comment*, November–December 1975, p. 17.
4. Felix Bucher, *Germany: An Illustrated Guide* (London: Zwemmer, 1970), p. 131.
5. Jan Dawson, *Wim Wenders*, trans. Carla Wartenberg (Toronto: Festival of Festivals, 1976), p. 9.
6. Christian Braad Thomsen, "Five Interviews with Fassbinder," in *Fassbinder*, ed. Tony Rayns (London: British Film Institute, 1979), p. 93.
7. Quoted in "The German Issue" of *Semiotexte* 4, No. 2 (1982), 227.
8. *Konrad Wolf: Sag' Dein Wort!*, ed. Hermann Herlinghaus (Postdam-Babelsberg: DEFA, 1982), p. 18.

## SELECTED BIBLIOGRAPHY

Bucher, Felix. *Germany: An Illustrated Guide.* London: Zwemmer (Screen Series), 1970.

Corrigan, Timothy. *New German Film: The Displaced Image.* Austin: University of Texas Press, 1983.

Hembus, Joe. *Der deutsche Film kann gar nicht besser sein: Ein Pamphlet von gestern. Eine Abrechnung von heute.* Munich: Rogner & Bernhard, 1981.

_____ and Christa Bandmann. *Klassiker des deutschen Tonfilms 1930– 1960.* Munich: Goldmann, 1980.

_____ and Robert Fischer. *Der neue deutsche Film 1960–1980.* Munich: Goldmann, 1981.

Hochschule für Film und Fernsehen der DDR, ed. *Film und Fernsehkunst der DDR: Traditionen, Beispiele, Tendenzen.* Berlin: Henschel, 1979.

Jansen, Peter W. and Wolfram Schütte, ed. *Film in der DDR.* Munich: Hanser, 1977.

Kluge, Alexander, ed. *Bestandsaufnahme: Utopie Film.* Frankfurt: Zweitausendeins, 1983.

Kreimeier, Klaus. *Kino und Filmindustrie in der BRD: Ideologieproduktion und Klassenwirklichkeit nach 1945:* Kronberg: Scriptor, 1973.

Liehm, Mira and Antonin J. *The Most Important Art. East European Film After 1945.* Berkeley: University of California Press, 1977.

Pflaum, Hans Günther and Hans Helmut Prinzler. *Cinema in the Federal Republic of Germany.* Trans. Timothy Nevill. Bonn: Inter Nationes, 1983.

Phillips, Klaus, ed. *New German Filmmakers: From Oberhausen through the 1970s.* New York: Frederick Ungar Publishing Co., 1984.

Pleyer, Peter. *Deutscher Nachkriegsfilm 1946–1948.* Münster: Fahle, 1965.

Rayns, Tony, ed. *Fassbinder.* 2nd rev. ed. London: British Film Institute, 1979.

Rentschler, Eric. *West German Film in the Course of Time.* Redgrave: South Salem, NY, 1984.

_____, ed. *West German Film in the 1970s.* Special issue of *Quarterly Review of Film Studies* 5, no. 2 (spring 1980).

Richter, Rolf, ed. *DEFA-Spielfilm-Regisseure und ihre Kritiker.* Berlin: Henschel, 1981.

Sandford, John. *The New German Cinema.* Totowa, NJ: Barnes & Noble, 1980.

# GREAT BRITAIN

## ANDREW SINCLAIR

The world of British cinema broke in two after 1945. The war had refined its great traditions, particularly that of the documentary film. The prewar GPO (General Post Office) Film Unit, which was taken over by the Ministry of Information and became the Crown Film Unit, used the realistic techniques pioneered by John Grierson to produce patriotic films rooted in the behavior of ordinary people—civilians and members of the armed forces—during the war. *London Can Take It* (1940), *Merchant Seamen* (1940), and *Target for Tonight* (1941), (which was seen by an audience of fifty million) set a credible unheroic style for the three major films praising the services: the navy's *In Which We Serve* (1942), the army's *The Way Ahead* (1944), and the air force's *The Way to the Stars* (1945). Following the example of the down-to-earth British documentaries, war pictures and thrillers, comedies and even romantic pictures seemed to work best when they evoked the atmosphere of the street rather than the studio. Wartime conditions were the ultimate realism. In David Lean's fourth collaboration with Noël Coward after *In Which We Serve* (1942), the film of *Brief Encounter* (1946), the ambience of seedy buffets and stations, blackouts and rationing, municipal parks and run-down lodgings make the unachieved affair between Trevor Howard and Celia Johnson the most moving of all English romances, the quintessence of understatement, so everyday that it could have happened to anyone or his friend on that beleaguered island.

The flamboyant Alexander Korda had created an opposite tradition before the war, the film of magnificence and fantasy, often based on great works of literature or the lives of royalty. While the tradition drew heavily from Hungarian dreams of East and West, as in subjects like *Rembrandt* (1937) with Charles Laughton or *The Thief of Baghdad*

(1940) with Sabu, Korda could outdo the imperialism of the British in *Sanders of the River* (1935) and *Elephant Boy* (1937) and wrap himself up in a borrowed flag and local history in *The Private Life of Henry VIII* (1932) and *The Scarlet Pimpernel* (1934). His finest and most under-rated major film, the science fiction epic written by H. G. Wells, *Things to Come* (1936), was a forerunner of the great studio pictures to be made for American film companies on the largest stages in England in El-stree and Pinewood, which took over when Korda's Denham Studios went out of business. British technicians had the skill to make epics for the world market, but Korda had disillusioned English financiers with the rewards to be had from them. At the end of the war, another Hun-garian, Gabriel Pascal, received George Bernard Shaw's permission to make a film of his *Caesar and Cleopatra*. The resultant film (*Caesar and Cleopatra*, 1945), with the largest budget ever contributed by J. Ar-thur Rank, was a fiasco that discouraged British investment in future studio spectaculars.

Korda himelf returned from America at the end of the war to set up MGM-London Films and make his presence felt again in British cin-ema. Soon he was acquiring studios and distribution outlets until he was rivaling J. Arthur Rank himself. Korda's new spectacular, *An Ideal Husband* (1947), was based on Ocscar Wilde's play of the same name, but was not a success despite a gallery of epigrams and stars. Laurence Olivier, however, made a superb version of *Henry V* (1944), certainly the finest Shakespeare film made to date and glorious in its bravura and confidence. David Lean's *Great Expectations* (1946), from Charles Dickens's novel, also showed that cinematic masterpieces could be made from classic works, although neither Olivier's subsequent *Hamlet* (1948) nor Lean's *Oliver Twist* (1948) approached their previous film versions of their chosen great writers. Generally, period pieces and historical films fared badly in the late 1940s, except for that highway-woman's jaunt, *The Wicked Lady* (1945).

A small studio at Ealing run first by Basil Dean and then by Michael Balcon turned out more successful films than those by Korda or Rank. During the war, Ealing had mainly produced working-class comedies starring Gracie Fields and George Formby and Will Hay. These had a direct and popular appeal, as did the postwar thrillers from Ealing, *Hue and Cry* (1946) and *It Always Rains on Sunday* (1947), which showed blitzed London and street life in the East End. Their realistic back-ground was retained in the series of comedies that made Ealing the best-known studio in Britain and Alec Guinness a world star. *Passport to Pimlico* (1948), *Whisky Galore!* (1948), *The Man in the White Suit* (1951), *The Lavender Hill Mob* (1950), and *The Ladykillers* (1955) were enormously popular, partially because each villainous and satirical comedy had a defined social sphere that was contemporary and recog-nizable. Only the most perverse and talented of the Ealing directors,

Robert Hamer, demonstrated in *Kind Hearts and Coronets* (1949) that a black comedy could be made out of a period setting.

Balcon was responsible for ninety-six films being made, including the acclaimed *Scott of the Antarctic* (1948), *The Cruel Sea* (1952), and that first inspiration for a close look at police working life, *The Blue Lamp* (1950). Outside Ealing, a few major directors were making some good films, particularly Carol Reed with his *Odd Man Out* (1947), which gave James Mason his most demanding role as an Irish terrorist on the run, and Michael Powell and Emeric Pressburger with *A Matter of Life and Death* (1946) and *The Red Shoes* (1948), the latter being a mythological ballet film with Moira Shearer that became a cult film in the United States. Generally, however, the products of Ealing Studios were *the* British cinema in the years after the World War II.

The secret of a successful national cinema is a large home market. In 1946 more people than ever went to the cinema in Britain. Audiences numbered more than thirty million persons a week. But television, an experiment begun in England before the war and suspended during hostilities, was started again that same year. It took as guidelines for its drama series the realism of the wartime documentaries and propaganda films and that of Ealing's small-scale postwar productions. Tight budgets provided a further incentive for filming life as it was. A determined attempt by the new Labour government to restrict the import of American films and save tens of millions of dollars yearly foundered in 1948 when Harold Wilson, a future Labour prime minister, opened the flood gates to American movies and submerged the British film industry under the glittering deluge. How could Korda or Rank cope with the resources of Hollywood or Ealing deal with Burbank? If local realism attracted audiences during the war years, the shortest way out of a restricted Britain, still on rations until 1951, was a ticket to a Hollywood extravaganza of song and dance or high living, based in that never-never land called California. The tragedy and the opportunity of the British cinema have always been the language it shares with the Americans.

The British government, however, extended a helping hand to domestic film production. The National Film Finance Corporation was set up in 1948 with a capitalization of five million pounds. Korda, who scented movie money as a pig sniffs truffles, immediately borrowed three million for his productions. He had given up spectacle for realism and induced Graham Greene to write the script of the finest film of the period, Carol Reed's version of *The Third Man* (1949), a story of racketeering in divided Vienna with Orson Welles playing the villainous Harry Lime. One of the few British films to be shot on foreign locations, it represented the virtues of the British wartime cinema: a feeling for documentary detail and social purpose. The wet, brooding labyrinths of ruined and occupied Vienna expressed the traps and ambiguities facing its people, the harsh and shifting choices forced on the survivors of the fighting.

Korda also produced another successful war story, *The Wooden Horse* (1950), the true account of a mass escape from a German prison camp. He also gave the twin Boulting brothers their chance to make a science fiction film about a mad scientist prepared to detonate an atom bomb in London. Their *Seven Days to Noon* (1950), disguised a far-fetched plot with the social detail that made the fantasy credible.

Outside Korda productions, only Powell and Pressburger continued to make distinguished films with *The Small Back Room* (1948) about a bomb disposal expert; another version of Korda's Pimpernel film, *The Elusive Pimpernel* (1950), starring David Niven; and an ambitious sequel to *The Red Shoes* (1948), called *The Tales of Hoffman* (1951), that failed to recreate the manic intensity of their original ballet film.

A Conservative victory in the general elections of 1951 and the return of Winston Churchill to power led to the closure of the Crown Film Unit, the guardian of the British documentary tradition. Britain was becoming more and more the haven of American or mid-Atlantic productions. The more distinguished films made in Britain in the early 1950s were directed by John Huston with American stars: Humphrey Bogart and Katharine Hepburn in an adventure story, *The African Queen* (1951), José Ferrer as the painter Toulouse-Lautrec in *Moulin Rouge* (1953), a whole rogues' gallery of stars in *Beat the Devil* (1953), and Gregory Peck in *Moby Dick* (1956).

Indigenous British comedies sank from the glories of Ealing to the series of "Doctor" films that followed *Doctor in the House* (1953); they displayed hospital smut and pretty nurses (including Brigitte Bardot) along with an embarrassed Dirk Bogarde. The "Carry On" series (1958– ) that succeeded the "Doctor" films plunged to a morass of puns and *double entendres* that was as triumphant at the box office as it was derisory on the screen.

Audiences during this period steadily decreased. In 1954 nearly twenty-five million people still went weekly to the cinema; by 1960 it was only ten million. It was not exclusively television that was keeping the people at home. British films were inferior in the main, while Hollywood films were little better after Senator McCarthy's attack on the industry and the purges of its major talents. The reequipment of the larger cinemas with CinemaScope, and the changing of movie palaces into bingo halls by Rank, hell-bent on diversification, led to a decline in the availability of places to see films. Seat price increases further deterred audiences, who needed strong inducements to be lured back to view the new wide screens.

The American producer Sam Spiegel provided such inducements when he hired David Lean to direct the epic *The Bridge on the River Kwai* (1957), a drama of British prisoners in a Japanese camp building a railroad through the jungle. The film won seven Academy Awards and was a huge success at the international box office, although another spectacular of the time, *Dunkirk* (1958), showed that nostalgic war heroics on a large scale did not necessarily mean money in the bank. The most promising young British director was J. Lee Thompson, whose realistic social dramas, *Yield to the Night* (1956) with Diana Dors as the condemned murderess and *Woman in a Dressing Gown* (1957), won some foreign awards in these dry years of the national cinema. Even Laurence Olivier's genius seemed to be deserting him with a film of *Richard III* (1956), as exaggerated to the point of caricature, and a meretricious comedy with Marilyn Monroe, *The Prince and the Showgirl* (1957).

Alexander Korda's death in 1956 was a fitting epitaph for British cinema at the time, which was experiencing a climacteric and a change. It was becoming best known for the horror films developed by Hammer, particularly *The Curse of Frankenstein* (1957) and *The Horror of Dracula* (1958), carefully crafted exercises in gore and thrills and historical farce. But with the debacle of British foreign policy during the Suez crisis and the rise of the Angry Young Playwrights and Filmmakers, a resurgence of the cinema of realism and social protest took place under the aegis of Woodfall Films, husbanded by the young theater director Tony Richardson. With *Look Back in Anger* (1958) and *The Entertainer* (1960), he turned John Osborne's stage triumphs into gritty films. Based upon the John Braine novel, Jack Clayton's *Room at the Top* (1959), gave the equivocal Lithuanian Laurence Harvey the chance to become one of the most upwardly mobile cads ever seen on the British screen and won leading lady Simone Signoret an Academy Award. The editor Karel Reisz directed the most moving and important film of the neorealism of the late fifties, *Saturday Night and Sunday Morning* (1960), in which Albert Finney depicted an impossible effort to rebel against the drudgery of factory work in Nottingham.

The new emphasis on proletarian life was carried on by Richard Attenborough and Bryan Forbes, both of whom had been actors. Now they became the producers of *The Angry Silence* (1959), a British version of Elia Kazan's *On the Waterfront* (1954), about a worker who is ostracized by union pressure and suffers from mob violence. Its Midlands setting helped give it its gritty flavor. Forbes followed by directing *Whistle down the Wind* (1961), a moving rural story of young farm children protecting an escaped criminal in the mistaken belief that he is Christ come again. The religious element was again brought down to earth by the credible setting. The Boulting brothers, however, decided to satirize the preoccupations of contemporary British filmmakers and created a comic star, Peter Sellers, in his performance as a shop steward in *I'm All Right, Jack* (1959), which turned industrial relations into a farce of stupidity and bad feeling.

The older directors still chose subjects far from the factory floor. Carol Reed again used Graham Greene to adapt his own novel for *Our Man in Havana* (1959), with Alec Guinness selling plans of vacuum cleaners as secret military installations and Noël Coward appearing as a suave and incompetent diplomat. Guinness also played an alcoholic Scots colonel in *Tunes of Glory* (1960), Ronald Neame's examination of military life in a bleak castle serving as a barracks. J. Lee Thompson made his most successful war film of all: although not as hard-edged as his *Ice Cold in Alex* (1960), *The Guns of Navarone* (1961) was an exercise in sustained excitement and an international hit.

Tony Richardson continued his film career with productions that seemed to become more theatrical and self-conscious, the more they were set in working-class backgrounds. Salford only seemed a backdrop in *The Taste of Honey* (1961), as Borstal did in *The Loneliness of the Long-Distance Runner* (1963), although both films were redeemed by moving performances, particularly from Rita Tushingham and Tom Courtenay. But in *Tom Jones* (1963), Richardson's flair and trickiness came to the fore in a bawdy and robust eighteenth-century romp with Albert Finney playing the lusty and naive hero in a series of escapades kept flowing by Walter Lassally's beautiful camera work. John Schlesinger first appeared as a sensitive director in *A Kind of Loving* (1962), the story of an ordinary man in Stockport trapped into a marriage he does not want, and in *Billy Liar* (1963), an English version of a daydreamer rather like Thurber's Walter Mitty.

Lindsay Anderson made his first film about professional rugby players in Wakefield, *This Sporting Life* (1963). The effect was of muddy mastodons crushing each other to death. The back streets of northern England had come to the screen with a vengeance. Except for *Tom Jones* (1963), young British filmmakers hardly ever left the kitchen sink or the workbench. London's East End provided the setting for Joan Littlewood's *Sparrows Can't Sing* (1963), a film of her theater production, recorded in Cockney accents so excruciating that it had to be subtitled when it was released briefly in the United States.

Against these low-budget films of contrived realism, the old tradition of lavish historical spectacles continued. Sam Spiegel was its godfather. Most stupendous was his production with David Lean directing of *Lawrence of Arabia* (1962), in which Peter O'Toole played his finest role as the mystic, self-torturing, charismatic leader of the desert Arabs in their war against the Turks. Spiegel and Lean followed it with an adaption of Boris Pasternak's *Doctor Zhivago* (1965); an effort to make Spain look like Russia in winter involved draping whole mountains with sheets, while even Alec Guinness failed at playing a convincing young Russian revolutionary, looking more like Mr. Polly than Trotsky. The romanticism of the film, however, heightened by the playing of Julie Christie and Omar Sharif and the score by Maurice Jarre, saved the film and made it an international success at the box office. Carol Reed also directed a rollicking version of Lionel Bart's musical of *Oliver!* (1968) and won an Academy Award for it, although it was hardly superior to David Lean's version of *Oliver Twist* (1948) made twenty years before.

Bryan Forbes became one of the more interesting directors in Britain before making on unfortunate attempt at studio management. His *The L-Shaped Room* (1962) was a gripping exegesis of squalid life in the bed-sitting rooms of Notting Hill Gate, while *Seance on a Wet Afternoon* (1964), used Richard Attenborough at his best as the mild husband of an overweening medium. *The Whisperers* (1967), too, was an admirable study of the paranoia of old age with Edith Evans hearing the imagined voices of doom and *déjà vu* in every crack and cranny of her kitchen. Forbes mistakenly accepted an appointment as managing director of the Associated British Picture Corporation and was also put in charge of running Elstree studios. He announced a program of ten films, including one of his own, *The Raging Moon* (1970), a paraplegic romance starring his wife Nanette Newman and Malcolm McDowell. The program was never completed and foundered in bad box-office returns. Forbes's talent lay on either side of the camera, not in the office.

Spy stories provided the new commercial successes, particularly adaptations of the works of Ian Fleming about his superhero, James Bond. These escapist fantasies about secret agents were redeemed by their occasional shafts of humor and the virile playing of Sean Connery, whose tongue in his cheek was his most lethal weapon against assorted villains. Michael Caine also emerged as the antihero agent, scruffy and bewildered in *The Ipcress File* (1965).

Where John Huston had led, Joseph Losey followed. Although his initial three films in Britain were far from remarkable, his direction of Harold Pinter's screenplay of *The Servant* (1963) transformed Dirk Bogarde from an uneasy *jeune première* into a sinister and complex actor, playing the corrupt and corrupting butler with menacing obsequiousness. Bogarde was again superb in Losey's next film, *King and Country* (1964), as the defending officer at the trial of a deserter from the massacre at Passchendaele, Belgium, during World War I. But he and Losey lost their touch in their next effort, a camp spoof of the Bond films, *Modesty Blaise* (1966), in which Bogarde looked even more embarrassed than he had in the "Doctor" films while trying to deliver appalling asides in ludicrous circumstances. But another screenplay by Harold Pinter, *Accident* (1967), put Losey and Bogarde back on target in a love story set in Oxford, filled with the ambiguities and melancholy of middle age.

Another expatriate to England was the redoubtable Stanley Kubrick with three remarkable films: *Lolita* (1962); *Dr. Strangelove, or, How I Learned to Stop Worrying and Love the Bomb* (1963); and *2001: A Space*

*Odyssey* (1969). Nabokov's novel and screenplay about a professor's obsession with a nymphet *Lolita* gave James Mason the chance to show the full range of his emotional charm and Peter Sellers to clown on the edge of hysteria, even making a farce out of dying. In *Dr. Strangelove* (1963), however, Sellers outdid even Alec Guinness in *Kind Hearts and Coronets* (1949) in the playing of black comedy and multiple roles. Visceral and shattering, the very excesses and hilarity of *Dr. Strangelove* made it a most powerful plea for nuclear disarmament. *2001: A Space Odyssey* was the most mammoth space production in Britain since *Things To Come* (1936) and proved the technical capabilities of the local studios. Its crafted direction and special effects made it a model for dozens of space extravaganzas to come, while suggestions of deep meanings in the future teased the minds of audiences into far speculations.

Other expatriate directors achieved magnificent films with the aid of British actors and technicians. Fred Zinnemann's *A Man for All Seasons* (1966) was a triumph of British production with Paul Scofield playing Sir Thomas More and Orson Welles playing Cardinal Wolsey. Tudor England seemed to breathe again in the designs of John Box and the camera work of Ted Moore. Moreover, a strange film by Michelangelo Antonioni, *Blow-Up* (1967), caught the new "swinging" London scene of photographers, models, insubstantiality and perverse gloss. Roman Polanski, an émigré director from Poland, brought a hallucinatory quality to his macabre study of the maddened Catherine Deneuve in *Repulsion* (1965), and a scabrous humor to the antics of a grotesque group of villains in *Cul de Sac* (1966). His work introduced a streak of perversion into the convention of the British horror or haunted house drama.

Television provided the training ground for many rising British directors who were trying to replace the older breed. The most exciting of these talents were Ken Loach and Ken Russell, who represented the opposite poles of British movie perceptions. Loach's *Poor Cow* (1967) and *Kes* (1969) achieved the believability of documentary within the structure of feature film. Loach had the power to show tragedy and feeling within a minor social ethos. Ken Russell, on the other hand, thrived on extravagance, psychiatric manifestations, and implausibility. After a shaky start with two poor feature films, his *Women in Love* (1969) was a lush recreation of the world of D. H. Lawrence. It included a naked wrestling scene between Oliver Reed and Alan Bates that set new standards of erotic behavior in British motion pictures. A wild jaunt into Tchaikovsky's supposed life in *The Music Lovers* (1970) showed the spirit of Diaghilev in Russell, while his next film, *The Devils* (1971), outraged many with its nude nuns cavorting about in mania and Oliver Reed blistering blackly as he burned at the stake. Wallowing in his own excesses, Russell demonstrated the most ravish and lascivious flair ever let loose in British cinema.

(Left)
The muted lighting and set around Celia Johnson reflect the understated tone of David Lean's deeply romantic *Brief Encounter* (1946).

(Below)
Dennis Price and Alec Guinness (in one of his eight roles) in the black comedy *Kind Hearts and Coronets* (1949).

The sinister, *noir*-like lighting around Orson Welles helps create the dark and corrupt environment of postwar Vienna in *The Third Man* (1949).

*The Horror of Dracula* (1958) was one of the successful cycle of horror films from Hammer Films.

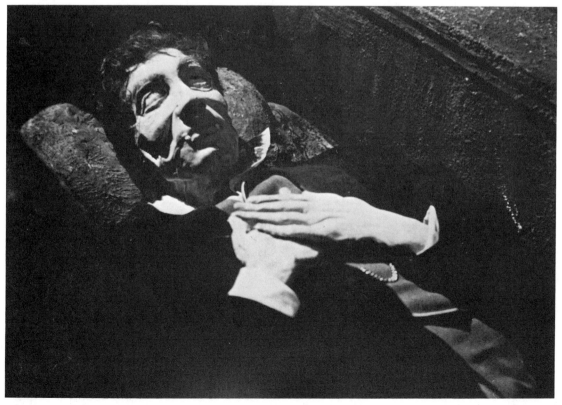

The international success of the spectacular *The Bridge on the River Kwai* (1957) gave a needed boost to the declining British film industry in the late 1950s.

Peter O'Toole in the title role of the epic *Lawrence of Arabia* (1962), which won the Academy Award for Best Picture of the year.

(Right)
Albert Finney as the
rebellious factory worker
in the neorealistic
*Saturday Night and
Sunday Morning* (1960).

(Below)
Sue Lyon and James
Mason in *Lolita* (1962),
by the American
expatriate Stanley
Kubrick.

David Hemmings as the photographer in the decadent London of Michelangelo Antonioni's *Blow-Up* (1967).

Peter Finch and Murray Head exchange a homosexual kiss in John Schlesinger's *Sunday, Bloody Sunday* (1972).

(Right)
Malcolm McDowell in
Lindsay Anderson's
anti-establishment *If . . .*
(1967).

(Below)
One image of useless
sacrifice from Richard
Attenborough's *Oh! What
a Lovely War* (1969).

The decadent milk bar in Stanley Kubrick's controversial *A Clockwork Orange* (1971).

The international success of *Chariots of Fire* (1981), which won the Oscar for Best Picture, renewed interest in the British film industry.

The older, established directors were escaping from the mean streets into magnificent epics. After a couple of forgettable films with Jeanne Moreau, Tony Richardson embarked on an antimilitaristic version of *The Charge of the Light Brigade* (1968), which foiled by his inability to create the actual death gallop of the gallant Six Hundred into the Russian guns. He followed this screen disaster with the underrated *Laughter in the Dark* (1969), derived from a Nabokov novel, only to put an end to his career as a major director with *Ned Kelly* (1970), miscasting Mick Jagger as the Australian bandit and inexplicably halting the final shoot out with the armored bushwackers to interpolate a lyrical interlude. Richardson seemed unable to sustain the mood of his films. Karel Reisz equally escaped from the factory bench into *Isadora* (1968), the story of the American dancer Isadora Duncan, but he lacked the lurid and sensual imagination of a Ken Russell or an Alexander Korda.

Lindsay Anderson, however, made the most original film of the 1960s, *If . . .* (1967), a poetic assault on the values of English public schools. Its inspiration may have owed much to Jean Vigo's *Zéro de Conduite* (1932), but its execution showed Anderson's flair for resonant realism and his memory of school sadism. Of all attacks on the established values of England, *If . . .* most hurt the establishment and turned Anderson into the leading social critic of his period. John Schlesinger's partially successful *Darling* (1965), with Julie Christie, dealt with the lack of values in the advertising world. But in *Far from the Madding Crowd* (1967), Schlesinger directed the most beautiful and faithful adaptation of Thomas Hardy's novel that did not deserve its failure at the box office. Julie Christie, Alan Bates, Peter Finch, and Terence Stamp as Sergeant Troy proved how fine British actors could be in a period drama that smacked of actual country life.

Richard Attenborough now emerged as a film director with a recreation of Joan Littlewood's theater production, *Oh! What a Lovely War* (1969). The device of staging World War I as a pier show with contemporary patriotic songs translated oddly onto the large screen. Yet the use of the British popular theater to create a new image of useless sacrifice was effective and proved Attenborough to be a director to watch, a man who could make his audiences review what they saw.

By the opening of the 1970s, British cinema was losing once more its revived realism of the sixties. Kitchen-sink dramas seemed more appropriate for television with its small screen that favored looking through a keyhole at other people's private lives. The wide screen seemed more suited to subjects that were larger than life. But American film companies were counting their losses after a succession of big-budget failures, and British film financing was difficult to get. Audiences had dropped in 1971 to 14 percent of their total in 1948. One film, John Schlesinger's *Sunday, Bloody Sunday* (1972), seemed to express the doldrums of the time, as well as a disgust with the permissiveness and violence of the late sixties. Schlesinger had only been allowed to make it because of his American success with *Midnight Cowboy* (1969) that both reveled in and condemned the Manhattan values of the time. The mood was swinging away from the outrageousness of Mick Jagger's display in the curious film *Performance* (1972), where rock-and-roll life blended with criminal fantasies as Nicholas Roeg codirected his first feature film. Even the thrillers were nasty and brutish now, Mike Hodges's *Get Carter* (1971) and Richard Burton's seedy gangster in *Villain* (1971). The times were slack and out of joint.

Sam Peckinpah came across the Atlantic to direct the most brutal film yet made in England, *Straw Dogs* (1971). It dealt with the terrorizing of Dustin Hoffman and the double rape of his wife in the film, Susan George, by a gang of yokels. Protests mounted against such films, swelling to a chorus of disapproval with the exhibition of Kubrick's masterpiece of 1971, *A Clockwork Orange*, taken from Anthony Burgess's extraordinary novel of urban decay and violence. Playing the gang leader in the mask of a perverse clown, Malcolm McDowell became the idol of his generation after his success in *If . . .* [1967]. The imagery and the aimless violence, the rebellion and the frightful aversion therapy, all seemed to prophesy a world of horror in the slums to come.

Both Ken Loach and Lindsay Anderson seemed to be losing their edge. Loach's *Family Life* (1972) was derived from the teachings of R. D. Laing and showed mental confusion reducing a girl to a mute vegetable. Anderson's *O Lucky Man!* (1972) lost any sense of structure in a succession of visual swipes and fantastic escapades against assorted bourgeois targets in England. This episodic attempt showed the influence of Jean-Luc Godard's *Pierrot le Fou* (1966), but lacked its sympathy for the main characters.

Even the sure-handed makers of the great spectacles were getting it wrong. David Lean overblew the slight story of *Ryan's Daughter* (1971) into an expensive Irish epic and lost tens of millions of dollars. He was not to direct an epic again for fourteen years, when he returned with *Passage to India* (1985), a film of E. M. Forster's novel that won a host of Academy Awards. Even Sam Spiegel believed he could repeat the success of *Doctor Zhivago* with the story of the Tsarist tragedy *Nicholas and Alexandra* (1971), but the result was a plodding bore. Spiegel was essentially a spent force in international cinema until his final two films (both with Pinter scripts), *The Last Tycoon* (1976) and *Betrayal* (1983).

The rising producer destined to revive the British cinema internationally was David Puttnam. His first successes were with the singer David Essex, *That'll Be the Day* (1974), a recreation of aimless life in the 1950s, and *Stardust* (1975), a lucid and critical look at the pop music scene. But in 1974 the film world collapsed along with the stock market, while inflation soared up, out of control. In such topsy-turvy times, only Ken Russell seemed always to be creating his special con-coctions: a failed attempt to introduce Twiggy and Busby Berkeley rou-tines into the slight musical *The Boy Friend* (1971); *Lisztamania* (1975), a film title that describes the film itself; *Mahler* (1974), produced by David Puttnam; and *Savage Messiah* (1972), the strange life of Henri Gaudier-Brzeska made even stranger. Puttnam took a great chance in using Alan Parker to direct a children's gangster film *Bugsy Malone* (1977). Its discovery was Jodie Foster, a lethal nymphet who played "Miss Tallulah" and promised everything to come.

Joseph Losey had spent some years out of England, but returned to make a nightmarish film of chase and escape, *Figures in a Landscape* (1970), and the haunting evocation of Edwardian country life, *The Go-Between* (1971), which Harold Pinter turned into a commentary of time present on time past. But the mid-seventies were lost years for most of the British film industry, and the rising producers did not have the flair or the taste to choose the right vehicles for their investments.

Lew Grade, one of three remarkable brothers, all powerful in inde-pendent television, launched into a program of making films. At first he was successful by backing sequels to Blake Edwards's *Pink Panther* films (1963–1978), starring Peter Sellers, and the first of the Muppet films (1979– ), but he fared poorly with a number of films such as *Voy-age of the Damned* (1976), *March or Die* (1977), *Movie Movie* (1978), *The Legend of the Lone Ranger* (1980), and *Raise the Titanic* (1980). Grade's pictures merely reflected the mediocrity of the British cinema. Yet his pictures were poetry compared with the average British film of the pe-riod, the Hammer horror pictures of Dracula forever rising from the grave or Frankenstein cursed and put together again and the soft-core pornography and dirty jokes extending from *Confessions of a Window Cleaner* (1974) to *Carry on Behind* (ca. 1970). EMI (formerly Electric and Musical Industries Ltd.,), which had taken over from ABC as the rival to Rank as exhibitors and producers, did make a success of an Agatha Christie thriller, *Murder on the Orient Express* (1973), but the company lost twenty-five million dollars on John Schlesinger's most unlikely disaster, *Honky-Tonk Freeway* (1981), which proved to be even worse for the British film industry than *Heaven's Gate* (1980) was for the American.

At a time when both EMI and Rank were largely withdrawing from film production, David Puttnam returned from the United States where he had made a failure, *Agatha* (1979), and a success, *Midnight Express* (1978). He helped in setting up a production company, Goldcrest, and produced the first British winner of Academy Awards since *Oliver!*— *Chariots of Fire* (1981). This brilliantly orchestrated story of two rival runners reaching the Olympics seemed to bring out the best qualities in British filmmaking—an attention to detail, understated dialogue, and acute social observation. Its director, Hugh Hudson, was to proceed to the lavish *Greystoke* (1984), an effort to recreate the original novel of Tarzan at ten times the cost of a usual Tarzan picture, and the epic *Revolution* (1985), an extraordinary attempt to stage the American Revolution in Suffolk. The losses incurred by *Revolution* brought Goldcrest down just when it seemed able to raise enough film finance to do for British films what Alexander Korda had done fifty years before. Despite the great success of *Gandhi* (1982), Richard Attenborough's admirable revival of the life of the Indian sage and nationalist, Goldcrest staggered under the big budget of *Revolution,* which cost even more than *Honky-Tonk Freeway* (1980). Just as a savior appeared for the British film industry, it was crucified by its failure to control its directors and their costs.

In fact, the preserver of the modern British film industry was also its destroyer. The new independent television Channel Four launched a program of twenty films to be made on a low budget with small independent film producers. One of them, Jerzy Skolimowski's *Moonlighting,* shared the Director's Award in 1982 at the Cannes Film Festival with Werner Herzog's *Fitzcarraldo.* Peter Greenaway's lauded rationalist and structuralist seventeenth-century thriller, *The Draughtsman's Contract* (1982), also benefited from this financing as did Richard Eyre's *The Ploughman's Lunch* (1983), a jaundiced look at contemporary Britain under Margaret Thatcher as prime minister that bid fair to be the *Room at the Top* of its age, with the nervous Jonathan Price playing the newly upwardly mobile Laurence Harvey. Neil Jordan was also backed by Channel Four in making his Irish thriller, *Angel* (1982); he then proceeded to make the most interesting fantasy film in a decade, *The Company of Wolves* (1984), based on Angela Carter's stories of pubescent sexuality and lupine fears. This imaginative seeding of new films by Channel Four suggested that there was a future for the film industry, in which the small screen coproduced features for the large screen and guaranteed them exhibition at least on television.

Small seemed best in British pictures. An interesting new director was Bill Forsyth from Glasgow, who based a tiny comedy there, *That Sinking Feeling* (1979), about a gang that literally steals kitchen sinks. Forsyth followed it with the amusing *Gregory's Girl* (1981) about a young female football player smoothing her way into male locker rooms. Puttnam used him to direct a Scots fantasy with a mermaid and a Texan oilman, *Local Hero* (1983), but this larger scale and the intrusion of Prospero in the shape of Burt Lancaster led to an uneasiness in Forsyth's vision. Recently engaged on his first epic about the Tolpuddle Trade Union martyrs, Forsyth may yet find that his films are like the poems of William Blake; little is often beautiful.

One other strange talent in England, more far-fetched than Ken Russell, promised extraordinary pictures. Derek Jarman made *Sebastiane* (1976) on a shoestring that hardly covered the naked flesh of his male actors. No Christian martyr ever enjoyed more the arrows that pricked him so delicately. Jarman followed with *Jubilee* (1978), a punk assault on every British value system with sequences intended to make the audience vomit: its shock effects made Lindsay Anderson's last release, *Britannia Hospital* (1982), look like a peevish array of squibs set in a hospice for the dying and fired off by a genius who had followed Timon of Athens into misanthropy. Jarman's *The Tempest* (1979) was far removed from its Shakespearean source, and his *Caravaggio* (1986), incredibly filmed in the docklands of London rather than in Rome or Naples, could perhaps change him from the *enfant terrible* of the British cinema to its Jean Cocteau.

One other independent company, Handmade Films, set up on some of the Beatles' money, made good comedies, and produced two zany successes, *Life of Brian* (1979), about a comic Christ and *A Private Function* (1985), in which a pig on the black market caused social disturbances and nasty smells in a northern British town at the end of the war. Handmade Films has not committed itself to large productions and seems unwilling to follow Goldcrest into another *Revolution*. It is likely to become the Ealing of the late 1980s, which did not become the society which George Orwell had predicted in his *1984*, brilliantly made into a film in that very year with Richard Burton playing his last great role as the inquisitor and John Hurt again proving that he is the best British actor presently appearing on the large screen.

To mark the forty years since the end of World War II, the Conservative government decided to end the National Film Finance Corporation (NFFC) and "privatize" finance for the medium. It was the epitaph of that tradition of state aid to a national film industry. It also recalled the decision of the Conservative government of 1951 that ended the Crown Film Unit and state aid for that jewel in Britain's movie crown, the social documentary. The National Film Finance Corporation had partly financed hundreds of films and had served as a beacon of hope for serious filmmakers in an industry always starved for investment. Before Goldcrest only Korda had seemed to possess any umbilical cord to City of London money. But the NFFC had not lost many millions of pounds, given its large turnover, and had financed many films of quality that had won awards, from Andrew Sinclair's magical *Under Milk Wood* (1973) to Peter Greenaway's *The Draughtsman's Contract* (1982). Its demise was a knell and a shame to the British cinema.

The expatriate producer Sam Spiegel also died on that New Year's Eve of 1985 on a Caribbean island, alone in a hotel. His last film, *Betrayal* (1982), based upon Harold Pinter's play, was brilliantly directed by David Jones; it has not recouped much money. But that was always the paradox of the British cinema as it was of all national cinemas. Rarely do indigenous films of quality and importance recoup their costs from the paying public. They should be partially subsidized by the state or wealthy patrons, but the maker must be left free to make the film he or she desires. That is the honorable tradition of the British cinema.

## SELECTED BIBLIOGRAPHY

Armes, Roy. *A Critical History of the British Cinema*. New York: Oxford University Press, 1978.

Barr, Charles. *Ealing Studios*. London: Cameron and Tayleur/Newton Abbot: David and Charles, 1977.

Betts, Ernest. *The Film Business: A History of British Cinema*. London: Allen and Unwin, 1973.

Butler, Ivan. *Cinema in Britain: An Illustrated Survey*. London: Tantivy Press, 1973.

Chanan, Michael. *Labour Power in the British Film Industry*. London: British Film Institute, 1976.

Curran, James and Vincent Porter, eds. *British Cinema History*. Totowa, N. J.: Barnes and Noble Press, 1983.

Durgnat, Raymond. *A Mirror for England: British Movies from Austerity to Affluence*. London: Faber and Faber, 1970.

Gifford, Denis. *British Cinema: An Illustrated Guide*. London: Zwemmer, 1968.

——. *The British Film Catalogue 1895–1970: A Guide to Entertainment Films*. Newton Abbot: David and Charles, 1973.

——. *The Illustrated Who's Who in British Films*. London: Batsford, 1978.

Low, Rachel and Roger Manvell. *The History of British Film, 1929–1939: Documentary and Educational Films of the 1930s*. London: Allen and Unwin, 1979.

——. *The History of British Film, 1929–1939: Films of Comment and Persuasion of the 1930s*. London: Allen and Unwin, 1979.

Perry, George. *Forever Ealing: A Celebration of the Great British Film Studio*. London: Pavilion/Joseph, 1981.

——. *The Great British Picture Show*. London: Hart-Davis MacGibbon, 1974.

——. *Movies from the Mansion: A History of Pinewood Studios*. London: Elm Tree Books/Hamish Hamilton, 1976.

Pirie, David. *Hammer: A Cinema Case Study*. London: British Film Institute, 1980.

Sussex, Elisabeth. *The Rise and Fall of British Documentary*. Berkeley: University of California Press, 1975.

Taylor, John Russell, ed. *Masterworks of the British Cinema*. London: Lorrimer, 1974.

Vermilye, Jerry. *The Great British Films*. Secaucus, N. J.: Citadel Press, 1978.

Walker, Alexander. *Hollywood, England: The British Film Industry in the Sixties*. London: Joseph, 1974.

——. *National Heroes: British Cinema in the Seventies and Eighties*. London: Joseph, 1985.

### Useful Periodicals

*Screen* (published by the Society for Education in Film and Television Ltd.)
*Sight and Sound* (Published by the British Film Institute)

# GREECE

## DAN GEORGAKAS

World War II had an impact on the development of Greek filmmaking quite distinct from that on other European cinemas.[1] The unique factor in Greece was that when fighting against the Nazis ended, a new conflict arose between the guerrillas of the Communist-dominated National Liberation Front in Greece proper and the governmental officials who had safely sat out the war in the Middle East. The dispute quickly led to what became a full-scale Communist insurrection. Anyone who had ever participated in the National Liberation Front was suspected of being a potential revolutionary and thousands of Greeks were held in preventive detention concentration camps located on desolate islands. The ideological fallout following the victory of the monarchy in 1949 was that for more than a decade any art work with a hint of social criticism was considered subversive and a likely candidate for censorship.

## The Occupation and Civil War (1943–1950)

With nearly continuous warfare in Greece throughout the 1940s, film production was meager, totaling five films during the occupation and a dozen more during the civil war period. The first of these was *The Voice of the Heart* (*Phone tis karthas*, 1943), starring some of Greece's finer stage actors in a melodrama about a father separated from his daughter. The film had a tremendous popular reception, but soon after its release, the filmmakers were arrested for belonging to the resistance. Although the standards attempted in *The Voice of the Heart* were not maintained, the melodrama as a form had been established as a staple of Greek popular cinema. Typical of the increasing vulgarity of the genre was *I Sinned For My Child* (*Amartisa yet tou pethi mou*, 1950) which created a national stereotype of the unwed mother. *Farsocomedies*, another genre favored in the 1940s, also outlived the decade. These comedies were based on theatrical shows and Greek vaudeville.

Few films of the era made direct reference to war. Those that did usually chose as their time frame the Albanian campaign of 1940 when a united Greek nation had won the first victories in Europe against fascism by repelling the invading forces of Benito Mussolini. More commonplace were films using the war as a background to intrigues involving military officers in the Middle East or Greece's minuscule urban middle class. Actual combat footage and other newsreel-type materials were rare, owing to the limited availability of camera equipment, trained personnel, and film stock, the direct consequences of the cinematic underdevelopment of prewar Greece.

## A Modest Rebirth (1951–1959)

Under normal political conditions, the neorealism prevalent in most postwar European cinema might have had a fruitful expression in Greece. Greek filmmakers were receptive to innovation, and tight budgets required frequent use of natural settings, nonprofessional actors, and various improvisations. But the Greek censors kept a stern lookout for any film that questioned the recently established status quo. What amounted to a bias against Greek cinema was underscored by a 6 percent tax on the domestic industry, a levy waived for the substantially higher returns from imports, mainly American films dubbed or subtitled in Greek. In spite of such obstacles among the fifteen to thirty films made in each year of the 1950s were works by filmmakers anxious to shape a national cinema of artistic merit. Some creativity was also seen in the commercial cinema which launched a new genre with *Golfo* (1955), a film featuring males wearing the traditional Greek kilt, the *foustanela*. Subsequent *foustanela* films enfused action adventure stories with strong patriotic trappings and traditional moral values.

Two of the earliest alternatives to commercial pap were Grigoris Grigoriou's *Bitter Bread* (*Picro psoume*, 1951) focusing on the privations of a working-class family, and Stelios Tatasopoulos's *Black Earth* (*Mavri yee*, 1952), featuring emery miners on Naxos. The films, unfortunately, were commercial duds, selling only 33,824 and 27,489 admission tickets respectively. Greek producers were much more inclined to invest limited funds in *farsocomedies* which could sell six to seven times as many tickets. One reaction to this economic problem involved attempts by serious filmmakers to make comedies that appeared to be frivolous but actually experimented with elements of fantasy and neorealism. An example of such a strategy was *Windfall in Athens* (*Karikatiko Xipnima*,

1954), the first film of Michael Cacoyannis, the man who would become the most celebrated Greek director of the decade.

Cacoyannis's second and third films, *Stella* (1955) and *A Girl in Black* (*To koritsi me ta mavra*, 1956) broke new thematic and formalist ground for Greek cinema. The mercurial taverna singer in *Stella* and the oppressed village maiden in *A Girl in Black* advocated themes of women's liberation amid a context offering scathing criticism of traditional Greek culture. While utilizing aspects of neorealism, the greater debt in terms of plotting, acting, and cinematography was to classic drama, a foretaste of the work Cacoyannis would later do with the Greek tragedies on stage and screen. The films were also innovative for the sophiscated manner in which they incorporated national music. In *Stella*, rather than having bouzouki numbers artificially dropped into the story, the score of Manos Hadjidakis is skillfully braided into the fabric of the plot and was most effective in introducing bouzouki to an international audience. More traditional music was used to similar effect in *A Girl in Black*. Cacoyannis would later spotlight the work of Mikis Theodorakis in *Electra* (1962) and *Zorba the Greek* (1965).

Not least of Cacoyannis's contributions during the seminal 1950s was his ability to get superlative performances from untrained or novice actors. Melina Mercouri, making her screen debut in *Stella*, was an instant international sensation. Elli Lambeti, the haunting beauty of *A Girl in Black*, felt less enthusiastic about film as a medium and chose to devote herself to what became a long and distinguished career in Greek theater. Playing against these powerful women in both films was George Foundas, cast as a repulsive if sensual Greek macho. Although his brand of sex appeal failed to translate abroad, Foundas remained a fixture on the Greek stage, screen, and, later, television. *Electra*, the fourth Cacoyannis film, would introduce Irene Papas.

Two other directors who made key contributions in the 1950s were Nikos Koundouros and George Tzavellas, both of decidedly radical political persuasion. Immediately upon Koundouros's release from the Makronisos concentration camp, the young filmmaker made two documentaries about earthquake disasters in Greece. Both films were promptly banned. Koundouros then turned to feature films, making *Magic City* (*Migiki polis*, 1954) and *Drakos* (1956). These motion pictures probed the Greek underworld and the life of the poor with some of the style of the Warner Brothers "easterns" of the Roosevelt era. George Tzavellas's *Counterfeit Coin*, (*Kalpiki lira*, 1955) managed to cross the two hundred thousand mark in domestic tickets and, along with the work of Cacoyannis, became among the few Greeks films to be honored at international film festivals.

Nearly all the major filmmakers of the 1950s received some formal training at the Stavrakos Film School in Athens. Koundouros and Grigoriou later taught at the school, a common practice of its graduates. Whether formal members of leftist organizations or not, the faculty of the Stavrakos Film School sympathized with efforts in theatrical and musical circles to break out of the cultural straitjackets imposed by the government. Bouzouki music, particularly as developed by Theodorakis, emerged as the cutting edge of cultural and political dissent and became "people's music," because of its unique blend of Greek blues forms, folk traditions, and church chorals. Directors who used such music in their films were signaling their identification with the new democratic yearnings that would soon surface as massive political movements.

## Two Steps Forward, Three Steps Back (1960–1969)

Commercial Greek cinema experienced a boom in the 1960s that reached a historic peak at the decade's end when production reached approximately one hundred films per year. The pace of filmmaking was so frantic at that time that technicians and actors worked on numerous films simultaneously. Performers often dashed about Athens changing costumes in route to new sets, often not quite sure exactly which film they were about to appear in. Given the interchangeable nature of most characters and plots, their confusion was barely noticeable. For a moment there was a seemingly insatiable national appetite for any film that was made in the Greek language and nominally about Greek subjects. Augmenting the domestic market were outlets for Greek-language films in Cyprus, "guest worker" communities in Europe, and immigrant centers in North America, Great Britain, and Australia.

Sharing the prosperity of the commercial cinema to some degree were films reflecting the new demands for increased personal and political liberty voiced most loudly by a generation coming of age a decade after the civil war. From the established directors of the 1950s came Cacoyannis's *Electra* which emphasized the democratic rather than the aristocratic aspects of the myth and Koundouros's *Young Aphrodites* (*Mikres Afrodites*, 1963), a study of eroticism in pre-Christian Greece. *The Sky* (*Ouranos*, 1962) by Takis Kanellopoulos, *Blockade* (*Bloko*, 1965), by Ado Kyrou, and *With Glittering Eyes* (*Me tin lampsi sta matia*, 1966) by Panos Glykofridis, condemned militarism with plots based on incidents from World War II. *District of Dreams* (*Sinikia to oniro*, 1961), by Alekos Alexandrakis, explored the daily life of the Athenian poor; *On the Way to the Boat* (*Mehri to plio*, 1966), by Alexis Damianos, told the tale of a mountain man about to immigrate to Australia; *Face to Face* (*Prossopo me prossopo*, 1966), by Roviros Manthoulis, used a love story to illustrate how Greek national culture had been sold out to foreign interests; and *Death of Alexandros* (*O thanatos tou Alexandrou*,

1966), by Dimitis Kollatos, touched on the meaning of life for a young man dying in a hospital.

Efforts to give some recognition to the more ambitious film projects in Greece and to upgrade the level of popular cinema were catalyzed by the creation of the Thessaloniki Film Festival in 1960. Cash prizes and the ensuing press exposure had considerable impact on the economic fate of winning films. Clashes between competing schools of cinema and between rival political tendencies as well as periodic struggles between government officials and filmmakers were to mark many festivals, particularly after the Greek government began to take a hand in funding and distribution. All of these disputes, however disruptive in any given year, served to make the festival a viable cultural institution.

The Festival also stimulated interest in the making of nonfiction films. Many of the projects undertaken early in the decade attempted to film village routines, ceremonial dances, and traditional folkways that were swiftly disappearing from the Greek scene. The resulting documentaries, usually running from fifteen minutes to half-an-hour and shot in black and white, were heralded as ethnographic studies, but many scenes were reenactments staged for the camera and most films had a voice-over sound track obviously aimed at the tourist trade. The kind of sophisticated theorizing about questions of form, content, and audience that marked discussions of fiction film would not be paralleled in the documentary. Thus, while there was a most visible French influence on fiction films, there is little on celluloid to indicate much impact of films such as *Night and Fog* (1955), *Chronicle of a Summer* (1963), or *The Sorrow and the Pity* (1969). Nor were Greek documentary filmmakers well acquainted with the *cinéma vérité* and political documentary movements that were vital components of American filmmaking in the 1960s and 1970s, movements that were far more congenial to Greek political sensibilities than the commercial cinema of Hollywood.

The major theoretical focus for Greeks in the 1960s, and in the 1970s as well, was on the film form most appropriate for a genuine national cinema. Students of film were angry, even embarrassed, by the technical quality of Greek cinema, yet they were not attracted by the standards associated with Hollywood products. The slick pacing, celebrity performers, rapid cutting, and passive audiences of the Hollywood syndrome were particularly upsetting. Greek filmmakers felt that there was considerable cultural imperialism in the most apolitical of Hollywood fare and that alternative political and cultural views were not compatible with Hollywood formats. The search for alternatives soon led to various nonnarrative and neo-Brechtian experiments popular among the French intelligentsia. The anti-Hollywood sensibility became so pronounced in Greek film culture that even the most politically radical Greek filmmakers would be relatively cool to the kind of political thrillers that Greek-born Costa-Gavras would initiate with *Z* (1969) and pursue in films such as *The Confession* (1970), *State of Siege* (1973), *Special Section* (1975), and *Missing* (1982). Greeks believed that whatever radical messages such films contained were dissipated by their pandering to forms that the popular audience immediately associated with escapist entertainment that was not meant to affect behavior in the real world.

Greek filmmakers were even more contemptuous of earlier efforts to use commercial forms, Cacoyannis's *Zorba the Greek* and Jules Dassin's *Never on Sunday* (1960). Although Dassin lived in Greece, was wed to Melina Mercouri, and utilized an all-Greek cast (his own performance excepted), *Never on Sunday* was considered a foreign production with decidedly American shortcomings. Despite its clever parody of certain aspects of *Stella*, the film was dismissed as little more than an international *farsocomedy* popularizing demeaning national stereotypes and a debased form of bouzouki.[2] Similarly, *Zorba*, which was made with foreign funds and a mainly foreign cast, was seen as exploiting rather than exploring Greek culture. Cacoyannis appeared to many former admirers to have turned his back on the development of an indigenous Greek cinema.

In truth, Greek filmmakers were finding it difficult to keep up with the volatile shifts in Greek political and cultural life. Events in the real world quickly outpaced the most daring and imaginative of scripts. The 1963 police murder of parliamentary member Gregory Lambrakis (the Z of the 1966 Vasili Vasilikos novel upon which Costa-Gavras based his film) led to the fall of the right-wing establishment. The brief democratic interlude that followed was marked by constant rumors of military and monarchist plots which finally materialized in the colonels' coup of 21 April 1967.

This period of national frenzy found expression in one of the strangest films of the decade, *The Shepherds* (*I voski*, ) (also distributed under the title *Thanos and Despina*). The film was made with French funds by Nikos Paptakis, a Greek permanently residing in Paris. Using harsh black-and-white lighting, the director explores divisive class conflicts through a myriad of unconventional film techniques, whose odd qualities are further exaggerated by amateurish production values linked to an inadequate budget. The story line revolves around the sadomasochistic attraction between a prosperous village girl and a destitute village boy. Each carries the crippling baggage of the traditional and modern conventions associated with their class, yet each is a rebel. When the youths, still not sure if they love or hate one another, flee the village to start a new urban life, the army is called out to halt their escape. The final scenes were completed after the junta came to power so that the death of the lovers and the imposition of military dictatorship are consciously equated. Although severely flawed technically and politically confusing, *The Shepherds'* bold mix of political and esthetic radicalism was a portent of the styles that would emerge in the 1970s as the New Greek Cinema.

## Greek Cinema Comes of Age (1970–1982)

The first years of the dictatorship brought all cultural life to a near standstill. The island concentration camps were reopened, and many artists were among the first imprisoned or exiled. For a time even bouzouki and some of the Greek classics were officially proscribed. The need to find some relief from the barbarous regime may have played a role in the momentary craze for Greek commercial cinema, but that economic bubble burst dramatically in the 1970s. Under the impact of newly established national television and a reawakened artistic cinema, commercial film production plummeted to below the levels of the 1950s.

An irony of the military effort to stem social change was that it spawned a film movement that proved to be far more radical, politically and culturally, than anything on the horizon in 1967. From the first years of the junta, intellectuals gathering to speak about film played the same social function for dissent that musical circles had played in the 1950s. Everything was up for debate, and in speculating on what kinds of films should be made, Greeks were really talking about what kind of nation they wanted. If it was a truism of previous generations that every Greek intellectual wanted to be a poet, in the 1970s every Greek intellectual wanted to be a filmmaker.

The first material manifestation of revitalized film culture was the remarkable *Reconstruction* (*Anapatastassi*, 1970), the debut film of Theodore Angelopoulos who would be the single most important Greek director of the decade and, in the judgment of most critics, of any decade. The murder of a returned immigrant worker by his wife and her lover is the nominal subject of the film, but in "reconstructing" the crime, the public prosecutor comes to realize that the real culprit in the killing is a social system that breeds emigration, privation, and abandonment. The viewer is sufficiently distanced from the action to be able to question if the prosecutor or the filmmaker really have the resources and evidence needed to comprehend the brutalities of contemporary Greek life.

The commitment to unsettling political speculations and esthetic experimentation that was announced in *Reconstruction* was escalated in each of Angelopoulos's subsequent films, *Days of '36* (*Meres toy*, 1972), *Traveling Players* (*Thiassos*, 1975), *The Hunters* (*I kynigi*, 1977), and *Alexander the Great* (*Megalexandros*, 1982).[3] Just as Costa-Gavras had chosen a kind of Orwellian directness for his radical films, Angelopoulos opted for the stylistic complexity of a James Joyce. His films

The first screen adaptation of a Greek tragedy by Michael Cacoyannis, *Electra* (1962), which introduced Irene Papas, stressed populist rather than aristocratic aspects.

An international success, *Zorba the Greek* featured direction by Cacoyannis, music by Mikis Theodorakis, and a stellar cast including Anthony Quinn and Alan Bates.

In the later 1960s the French-backed *Thanos and Despina* explored in surrealistic fashion the fate of two young villagers seeking a new life in the city.

Theodore Angelopoulous brought his bold experimental style to *Traveling Players* (*Thiassos*, 1975), about an acting troupe whose story reflects Greek history from 1939 to 1952.

would not permit viewers to be passive. Awareness of camera movements, the continuous shot, languid pacing, and deliberate "dead" spaces were techniques used to provide opportunities for contemplation or emotional release. Rather than close-up shots and explication of a few lives, Angelopoulos favored the long distance shot and contrived methods to keep the viewer from getting too involved with specific individuals. Poetic elements entered the films without any preparation or explanation. In *The Hunters* the warm corpse of a rebel partisan is discovered many years after the civil war by a group of ruling-class hunters. As the panicked sportsmen mount an investigation of the impossible phenomenon of an ever-warm corpse, their deliberations are punctuated by views from their hunting lodge windows of a flotilla of barges with silent passengers flying red banners as their crafts float across an adjacent lake like some lost echoes of a communist manifesto. In *Traveling Players* a troop of soldiers scattering a street demonstration in 1948 are back in 1941 when they complete their task, or a speech begun in 1937 concludes before a 1952 audience. In *Alexander the Great* Alexander as an elder and Alexander as a youth coexist in the same time and space. And at any moment during the films a protagonist is apt to turn abruptly and begin speaking directly to the camera.

A whole decade of Greek filmmaking would be influenced by the stylistic roads opened by Angelopoulos. What would soon be dubbed the New Greek Cinema exhibited a strong proclivity to experiments involving fantasy sequences, Greek vaudeville elements, painterly tableaus, and elaborations on surrealism and expressionism. Frequently the story line would depart from what seemed the main line of development in an unlikely mixture of style and behavior that defied convention and logic.

The political task of the films immediately following *Reconstruction* was to test the limits of the dictatorship. These works tended to be more sociological than political in orientation and more conservative in style than films that would be made after the fall of the junta in 1974. Alexis Damianos's *Evdokia* (1970) explored the popular opposition to a marriage between a prostitutue and an army sergeant; Pandelis Voulgaris's *The Engagement of Anna* (*To proxeno tis Annas*, 1972) depicted the exploitation of a servant girl by her middle-class employers and "protectors"; Pavlos Tassios's *Yes, But* (*Nai men alla*, 1972) looked at the consequences of repressed eroticism; Theodore Marangos's *On Your Marks* (*Lavete thesis*, 1973) lamented the decay of rural villages; and Tonia Marketaki's *John the Violent* (*Ioannis o vieos*, 1973) condemned the patriarchical roots of violent sex crimes. In *Women of Troy* (*I gynekes tis Trias*, 1973) Dimitris Mavrikios chose the familiar intellectual ploy of reworking an ancient tale to talk of contemporary events; and in *Great Love Song* (*O megalos erotikos*, 1973) Pandelis Voulgaris took advantage of patriotic pride in Greek poetry to celebrate erotic works from Sappho to modern times.

New Greek Cinema was very much one of author-directors who almost always scripted or coscripted their films and sometimes acted in them.[4] The economics of filmmaking, during and after the dictatorship, required Greek directors to assume functions which in other nations would normally be divided among several persons. This often included detailed business and organizational responsibilities usually associated with producers. Films created under this system had the advantage of carrying the definitive imprint of a single creator. Individual styles developed rapidly, and there was considerable artistic freedom. Negative aspects were that directors had few restraints against overindulging idiosyncracies and whims. In their enthusiasm for nonconventional cinema, directors sometimes shaped films that were esthetically precious and even snobbish.

The main thrust of post-Junta filmmaking was to reappraise more than forty years of Greek history, but every kind of subject was addressed in a dazzling outburst of creativity. There were Godardian investigations of reality and media: Nikos Panayiotopoulos's *Colors of Iris* (*Ta chromata tis iridos*, 1974); experiments with animated and still drawings: Thanasis Rentzis's *Bio-Graphy*, (*Vio-graphia*, 1975); expressionistic denunciations of the concentration camps of the 1950s: Pandelis Voulgaris's *Happy Day*, (*Happy Day*, 1976); feminist examinations of literary and cinematic images of the female body: Antoineta Angelidi's *Idees Fixes-Dies Israe*, (*Parallages sto idio thema*, 1977); grandiose historical epics: Nikos Koundouros's *1922*, 1978); meditations on aging and death: George Panoussopoulos's *Honeymoon*, (*To taxidi toy melitos*, 1979); new treatments of the bouzouki subculture: Pavlos Tassios's *Special Request*, (*Parangelia*, 1980); depictions of roving bandit gangs of the ninteenth century: Lakis Papastathis's *When the Greeks . . . (Ton kero ton ellinon*, 1981); and explicit rendering of homosexual passions: George Katakouzinos's *Angel*, (*Angelos*, 1982).

When successful, the new Greek films were among the best work being done anywhere at the time, but many of the films were far stronger in their parts than in their entirety, far stronger in inspiration than realization. Truly startling images, ideas, and scenes appeared in films whose production values and overall execution were disturbingly inept. This uneven development of Greek cinematic skills and sensibilities provides an example of a thesis advanced by Vasili Vasilikos that the frequent imposition of military rule has destroyed natural continuity in many of the arts.[5] Art movements often develop spasmatically, resulting in their hurtling over or rushing through esthetic periods without fully realizing the uniqueness of the particular experiences involved. Extreme intellectual reaction may set in against artistic styles that never had a true national expression.

A new set of political challenges presented themselves to Greek filmmakers with the 1981 election of socialist Andreas Papandreou as prime minister under the slogan *Allaghi* (Change). Among Papandreou's early appointments were Melina Mercouri as minister of culture and Vasili Vasilikos as director of one of the nationally administered television channels, selections in sharp contrast to the days when domestic filmmaking had been discouraged and radical views censored. Given the democratic reforms that had taken place during seven years of conservative rule and the peaceful transference of power to the duly elected socialists, the era begun with the prewar Metaxas dictatorship seemed to have finally come to its end. The traditional argument between the monarchist and republican forces had now shifted to discussions of what kind of democracy for Greece and, even, what kind of socialism.

Theodore Angelopoulos, the one Greek film director guaranteed an international audience for any of his work and the one Greek director able to raise funds relatively easily, responded to the new era with *Alexander the Great*, a film dealing with a guerrilla hero of ninteenth-century folklore. Using his most complex format up to that time, Angelopoulos placed the struggle between the classes in the background of a study of struggles within the revolutionary peasant forces. The tradition of patriarchical authoritarianism as exemplified by the militaristic Alexander is seen to literally murder the anarchocommunism achieved by a workers council on which men and women serve equally. Added complexity is achieved in scenes depicting ways in which groups within the village shift from one faction to the other or ways in which the conflicting traditions struggle for dominance within individuals. Not a few radicals were upset or confused by what they felt was a critique of the guerrillas of the 1940s by a director heretofore famed for lauding their cause. Emboldened by a cool public reception to the film, some critics began to question more loudly than before whether the slow pacing of Angelopoulos's films, their length, and their stylistic virtuosity had not degenerated into individualistic mannerisms.

The majority of Greek filmmakers also responded negatively to the direction Angelopoulos chose to pursue. Many felt that the bias against straight narrative had gone too far and the political discourse had become overly esoteric. If one of their objectives was to affect mass consciousness, they felt that they could not employ styles that mass audiences had begun to reject as tiresome and irrelevent. The drift back toward more conventional film forms was an admission of sorts that the earlier rejection of the work of Costa-Gavras had been overly hasty and unnecessarily harsh.

Resisting the dominant view was a minority of filmmakers who believed it was imperative to push forward with formal innovations however high the immediate cost in terms of audience acceptance. Thanasis Rentzis, filmmaker and editor of *Film*, reiterated his well-known view that the Greek language was incompatible with forms devised for Anglo-Saxon expression. He further argued that Greece must have a pluralistic cinema that was multiform rather than uniform.[6]

Whatever the visual and thematic traditions favored, most Greek filmmaking was still marred by structural and technical shortcomings. These usually involved conceptual flabbiness, faulty pacing, and dubious light and sound quality. Failure to achieve greater control in such areas surely risked the viability of Greek cinema abroad and probably at home as well. The major challenge for filmmakers in the 1980s was to increase their formal discipline without losing the ingenuity and boldness that had characterized a beleaguered cinema for three decades.

## NOTES

1. Some twenty films of the postwar Greek cinema were shown at the Public Theater in New York in the spring of 1983. *The New Greek Cinema*, a small pamphlet of extensive program notes, was produced by the festival organizers. Included in the pamphet were excerpts from "A Brief History of the Development of Greek Cinema," by Nikos Fenek-Mikelidis, which was useful in shaping the present essay. Another rich source was a two hour interview (unpublished) with Diamantis Leventakos, director of the Center for Independent Greek Cinema, a filmmaker, a founder of the film journal *Modern Cinema (Synchronos kinematographos)*, and a festival organizer. Not very useful and often quite inaccurate is the only booklength study of New Greek Cinema published in the United States, Mel Schuster, *The Contemporary Greek Cinema* (Metuchen, NJ: Scarecrow Press, 1979). See the review of that work by Peter Pappas, *Cinéaste* 10, no. 1 (winter 1979/80, pp. 20–24). Far more dependable are the annual reports in *International Film Guide*, edited by Peter Cowie for Tantivy Press in London, and the summaries and credits in *The Catalogue of Greek Films*, published by the Center for Independent Greek Cinema in Athens, 1983.
2. Dassin's own evaluation of *Never on Sunday* and a discussion of his Greek-oriented films can be found in "A Dream of Passion—An Interview with Jules Dassin," by Dan Georgakas and Petros Anastasopoulos, *Cinéaste* 9, no. 1 (winter 1978, pp. 20–24).
3. Andrew Horton, "Theodor Angelopoulos and the New Greek Cinema," *Film Criticism* 6, no. 1 (fall 1981), offers an excellent discussion of Angelopoulos's work.
4. Dan Georgakas and Peter Pappas, "The Greek Cinema Today: An Interview with Nikos Panayotopoulos," *Journal of the Hellenic Diaspora*, 6, no. 1 (summer 1979). A postscript by Georgakas deals with a number of economic and stylistic problems.
5. Dan Georgakas and Peter Pappas, "To Be a Writer in Greece: A Discussion with Vasili Vasilikos," *Journal of the Hellenic Diaspora*, 7, no. 3/4 (fall–winter 1980).
6. Thanasis Rentzis, "The Three Cycles of Greek Cinema," excerpted in *The New Greek Cinema*.

## SELECTED BIBLIOGRAPHY

Alexandropoulo, Soula. "Death of a Beekeeper." *The Greek American*, 17 May 1986, p. 17.

Cacoyannis, Michael. "An interview." *Films & Filming*, 6, no. 4, (January 1960), p. 13.

Cacoyannis, Michael. "Greek to Me." *Films & Filming*, 9, no. 9, (June, 1963), p. 19.

Dallas, Athena. "Michael Cacoyannis." *Film Comment*, 1, no. 6, (Fall, 1963), pp. 44–45.

Georgakas, Dan. "The Bacchae on Broadway: A conversation with Michael Cacoyannis and Irene Pappas." *Greek Accent* (October, 1980), pp. 32–35.

# HUNGARY

## JOHN MOSIER

Hungary, the smallest of the world's major film producing countries, has had an impact on world cinema out of all proportion to its size. This fact is made all the more remarkable when one considers that Hungary's language and its geography have effectively isolated it from the West and that a relatively small number of feature films have been produced there. In such a case, it becomes tempting to see a national cinema as having a unity that it does not in reality possess, and it becomes even more of a temptation to see the national art form as being dominated by one or two artists. But in the case of Hungary this is close to the truth: Hungarian cinema, although containing disparate strands of thought and many excellent artists, really can be seen as a reasonably unified national art form frequently dominated by one or two artists at key periods in its development.

Although films were exhibited in Budapest as early as 1896, and there was a reasonably accomplished industry before World War II, the events of the 1930s and 1940s were such that the film industry essentially started from scratch after 1945. The first major film of the period is the excellent and unjustly neglected *Somewhere in Europe* (*Valahol Európában,* 1947), whose subject is the lifestyle of a marauding group of children displaced by the war.[1] The film attracted international attention to Hungarian cinema. More important, it gave several of Hungary's future directors, notably Félix Máriássy and Károly Makk, a chance to work on a project during this difficult time. The noted film theoretician Béla Balász collaborated with Máriássy in writing the script. Balász died in 1949, but his contributions to the development of film criticism both in Hungary and in the world were substantial. Although best known for his pioneering attempts to see the movies as an art form, as well as for writing the first (and still one of the best) introductions to film, his major contribution to cinema in his own country was to raise the status of the screenplay as an art form.

*Somewhere in Europe* also contains most of the major tensions that would later dominate Hungarian cinema. Much of the excellence of the film is generally attributed to scriptwriters Balász and Máriássy and to cameraman Barnabas Hegyi rather than to the director, Géza Radványi, who appears to have been overpowered by the script and the cinematography. In retrospect, this dominance of script and, to a lesser extent, of cinematography, set a trend in Hungarian film. From the nationalization of the industry in 1948 well into the 1950s, the script assumed an overriding importance in the Hungarian cinema. This emphasis suited the needs of the new socialist states of Eastern Europe perfectly, and Balász was forced to lend to the idea his considerable prestige as one of the great Marxist film critics. Initially he had argued that it was the film that was the work of art, while the script was simply a script. At about the same time as the making of *Somewhere in Europe,* however, he reversed his position, arguing that the script was in and of itself a work of art. This position, which conformed to the dictates of the rigidly authoritarian governments throughout the area, became a convenient intellectual peg on which to hang a bureaucracy of censorship. So in the early 1950s filmmakers were assigned scripts, their task simply being to photograph them. The film studio, far from being a center of improvisation, was merely the place where the script was transferred onto celluloid. Beginning in 1954 both films and theoretical writings began to appear which argued for a return to the earlier position of Balász, asserting that the film in itself was an important art medium differing greatly from the script and was not merely an extension of it. This intellectual revolt shaped the ideas of the major Hungarian directors about their art, and explains both their distinctive directorial signatures, which have impressed so many critics, as well as their frequent reliance on cinematic pyrotechnics, which has attracted less favorable comment.

To a less publicized but nevertheless substantial extent the dominance of the cinematography which *Somewhere in Europe* exemplified also had a substantial impact on Hungarian movies: the general excellence of the photography in Hungarian cinema is one of its most striking features from the very first films of the postwar period to the present. At the same time, it has made it somewhat difficult for younger directors to establish distinctive directorial signatures in their work, given the inclination of cinematographers to develop their own visions of the scripts.

The story concerns a group of displaced children who live like animals. They are befriended by an adult, fight off a fascist-inspired attack, and are finally integrated into society. This brief summary is necessary to understand the third and most important area where

*Somewhere in Europe* was an important prolepsis. There is a conflict in the script between two differing sets of ideas. The film is authentically Hungarian on the one hand. Its treatment of children as a separate society mirroring the adult world, for example, reflects ideas developed by the Hungarian writer Géza Csáth before World War I. But on the other hand, the scriptwriters were deeply influenced by Soviet ideas about filmmaking, as the opening montage reveals. Much of the film also reminded enthusiastic early critics of Italian neorealism. Moreover, although the idea of a film about children was commercial, the script is a rigorously intellectual one in which the children's society both disintegrates and recombines itself according to Marxist ideas about social and political development. Such tensions—between the national and the foreign, the popular and the intellectual—when combined with conflicts between the director and the cinematographer and between the director and the scriptwriter, would have two substantial results. First, they would frequently result in movies in which these elements were poorly integrated. Second, this combination of forces would mean that over the span of a normal working career only a few artists would be able to establish themselves as decisive filmmakers, and the careers of those few would be marked by all too many unsuccessful films.

However, these tensions would have another, more fortuitous results: Hungary would produce some formidable artists whose abilities are scarcely matched by filmmakers anywhere else in the world, which is why the films of such a small and linguistically and culturally isolated country have the importance that they have today. Virtually all of these major film artists are still living and working; since the war, Hungary has supported at least three world class directors—Zoltán Fábri, Miklós Jancsó, and András Kovács—as well as at least six directors whose work solidly establishes them as substantial talents: Péter Bacsó, István Gaál, Zsolt Kézdi-Kovács, Marta Mészáros, Pál Sándor, and István Szabó.

In terms of chronology, the first of these major artists is Zoltán Fábri, whose first important film, *Fourteen Lives Saved (Életjel)*, was made in 1954. Fábri went on to make eighteen feature length films, the most recent of which is *Balint Fabian Meets God (Fábián Bálint találkozása istennel,* 1980). Virtually all of these films reveal similar preoccupations and have comparably high levels of quality. The general subject is invariably the same: the response of a group of individuals subjected to extreme stress, whether, for example, because of a natural disaster *(Fourteen Lives Saved)*, or the collapse of the traditional Hungarian society in 1918 *(Fabian Balint)*. This is not to imply that Fábri's films are all the same, only that they reveal the workings of a man who, like many thoughtful intellectuals, is concerned with the implications of one substantive idea.

Since Fábri's seminal years occurred when Hungary was under a
script dictatorship which made it quite difficult, if not impossible, for
the directorial signature to emerge, the fact that his thematic preoccupations appeared so early is significant. It was Fábri who first showed
concretely what a signature really is, and that signature comes not simply from his theme, but from his distinctive and somber view of the
world. Consider what may be his best film, *The Merry-Go-Round* (*Kö-
rhinta*, 1954), which deals with the integration of private agriculture
into the cooperative system—scarcely an enthralling subject. Although
the struggles of the characters are successful (for obvious reasons),
Fábri's view of the situation is somber, and his films show both a careful consideration of color and of framing to produce scenes which stand
as visual correlatives to this mood. Both the members of the collective
and the independent farmers are living under stress, and the film
shows us what this stress is like—without, of course, explaining why it
is there. One of Fábri's other distinctive contributions is ellipsis. In the
sobriety of his filmmaking and in the elliptical way in which he discusses social problems, Fábri sets the tone for much of the best of Hungarian cinema: a sober and thoughtful social discourse conducted so
allusively that the real subject of the film is frequently never even mentioned on screen. This useful ellipsis presents a recurrent problem in
the evaluation of Eastern European cinema by outsiders, and a simple
example will suffice. In *Fourteen Lives Saved* the lives referred to by
the title belong to miners who are trying to survive a cave-in. But in the
context of the time it is important to realize that Fábri's film is built
around a natural disaster, rather than the results of sabotage. Officially speaking, there was no such thing as a natural disaster in socialism: such things were caused by saboteurs. Essential to understanding
this film is what the director has chosen *not* to do; reliance on situations
of this sort is a distinctive feature of Fábri's work.

In the 1950s Hungary produced less than a hundred feature length
films. After Fábri, the two most important artists were Makk and Máriássy, neither of whom produced anything of substantial importance
during this period, although Makk made several polished comedies
which are still highly regarded in Hungary, for example, *Liliomfi*
(1954), and Máriássy managed to make films on "official" events such
as the liberation of Budapest in 1945 that avoided the pompous didacti-
cism characteristic of films on similar subjects produced in neighboring
countries. In 1962 Makk made *The Fanatics* (*Megszállotak*), his most
important film. The main thrust is a criticism of the official bureaucracy: two engineers conceive an ingenious plan to raise agricultural
productivity, their ideas are resisted and they are persecuted, finally
succeeding only when a member of the government backs their plan.
The film was important because its criticism was directed at contemporary society, not the society of the past. However, the works of Makk,

Mariássy, and their talented but less well-known colleagues were completely displaced by the works of successive groups of film artists who came to prominence in the next decade.

During the 1950s even the best Hungarian films were pieces of incremental social criticism, and they were technically conservative. During the 1960s this situation changed drastically. Hungarian cinema became aesthetically innovative, intellectually difficult, and socially revolutionary. The social criticism of the best films of the earlier period intensified: although somewhat more difficult to perceive, it was (and still is) the case that the more significant Hungarian films were films whose general subject was the critical analysis of Hungarian society. Although it is possible to trace this cinematic revolution to structural changes in the film industry which in turn mirrored changes in the state itself, similar transformations appeared everywhere, particularly in the socialist world. The chief difference between Hungary and its neighbors in this regard is not the fact of the revolution of the 1960s, but its longevity. Unlike any of its neighbors, the Hungarian state has both supported its artists and largely accepted their goals. This institutionalization has meant that certain areas, for example, the 1956 revolt, have historically been off limits. Artists who strayed too close to the lines found the release of their films postponed for years. At the same time, however, filmmakers have had nearly two decades of freedom that, while relative, is virtually absolute when compared to their neighbors.

The two most important filmmakers to emerge as a result of this freedom were Andras Kovács and Miklós Jancsó. Miklós Jancsó's position in Hungarian and in world cinema is such that comparing him with anyone might seem preposterous, but both men are approximately the same age (Jancśo was born in 1921, Kovács in 1925), and both had long careers in cinema before they started making feature films at almost the same time (Jancsó in 1958, Kovács in 1960). The contrast between them is also instructive: Kovács's work is firmly grounded in the documentarist's principles of close observation, and his general theme is how historical circumstances have affected the individual. His first significant film was *Difficult People* (*Nehéz emberek,* 1964), and it marks a decisive turning in Hungarian film, being a documentary about inventors who have been thwarted by the red tape of the bureaucracy. The film marks a successful shift away from the various constrictions that had crippled Hungarian cinema in the 1950s. By relying on documentary techniques Kovács avoided the twin tyrannies of set scripts and formalistic cinematography. But the subject matter is equally important: although virtually every serious Hungarian film made after the war had dealt with social problems, all of these problems had been those that faced the men and women who planned, built, and carried out the socialization of Hungary. But *Difficult People* is about brilliant and sometimes crazy individualists whose talents are being throttled by that same state.

Kovács continued this train of thought and turned toward Hungary's recent past with *Cold Days* (*Hideg napok*, 1966), which memorializes the massacre of the villagers of Ujvidek (Novi Sad; now a part of Yugoslavia) during World War II. Films about war atrocities were scarcely new in Eastern Europe, but the Novi Sad massacre was committed not by foreigners but by Hungarian fascists, the last of which we see in their cells waiting for their sentences to be handed down. Kovács not only reminded Hungarians that World War II had in certain respects been a civil war for them as well, but underscored the responsibilities of the common man for the role that he had played: significantly the soldiers in their cells are ordinary fellows, enlisted men. To a certain extent, the film supports the needs of the socialist state as a grim reminder of the realities of the fascist terror. But Kovács's common people are handled in such ways that one's realizations go far past the wretched peculiarities of fascism and toward a consideration of how easy it is for authoritarian regimes to force ordinary people into whatever mold the state has in mind. The real Hungarian revolution then, lay in the discovery of a genuine social criticism that dealt with issues on a case by case basis without regard to anything other than simple justice and humanity.

With varying degrees of success Kovács would continue along these lines in his next six films, producing in *The Stud Farm* (*A ménesgazda*, 1978) one of the two or three most important films of historical analysis to come out of Hungary. *The Stud Farm* follows two brothers who have risen to power in postwar Hungary. The older, who manages a collective farm, has his younger brother made director of a horse-breeding farm. The younger brother knows nothing about breeding horses, fails to win the confidence of the ex-army men who are the farm's specialists, takes to drink, and is finally killed by them before they attempt to escape. The older brother's problems, while less tragic, are also painful. As we follow his experiences, we see the workings of the state: the nocturnal visits by the police, the forced labor camps, the insecurities of even those who are at the higher levels of government. What Kovács captures is the peculiar mood created by the Stalinist reign of terror as it existed in Hungary.

Both Kovács and Fábri are major artists, but their international reputation has been eclipsed by Miklós Jancsó. Jancsó is one of those artists whose works, while having a profound impact, have little influence. This is because of the extremes his work represents. First, his films leave little or no room for characterizations or for acting in any conventional sense. Second, his films rely heavily, and sometimes exclusively, on diegetic music, which is to say music generated on-camera by the activities of the actors. Third, in the majority of his films editing has all but disappeared. In *The Red Psalm* (*Még kér a nép,* 1972) there are perhaps only twenty separate shots. Fourth, the photography consistently relies on one or two simple techniques, for example, long tracking shots, that work because the execution is perfect. Jancsó does not rely on obscure techniques, but in many of his films the overriding intellectual aim seems to have been to make a film that is as technically sparse as possible. Paradoxically, this minimalism has meant that most of what has been written about him as an artist has to do with his technique. He is not, however, a purely formalist artist interested only in the possibilities of the medium. His works, like those of Kovács, reveal a deep-seated attempt to force audiences to reconsider the nature of their universe. The chief difference is that Jancsó is essentially concerned with the problems of Marxism on a theoretical and philosophical level, while Kovács and Fábri are concerned with the specific effects of such problems on individuals and individuated groups.

His major interest is the history of Hungary (and to a lesser extent the West) as examined through Marxist analysis. This is not to say that his films are historical films conforming to the ideas of socialist ideology as usually understood in the socialist film producing countries, for example, films in which the interests of the workers are optimistically illustrated as triumphing over their exploiters. Jancsó uses Marxist analysis in two extremely important and unusual ways. First, his actual historical situations are stripped of all of the particulars which might individualize them. Although it may be easy to recognize that films such as *The Roundup* (*Szegénylegények,* 1966) and *Agnus Dei* (*Égi Bárány,* 1971) refer to actual historical situations in Hungary (the aftermath of the failure of the Kossuth rebellion in the first film and the failure of the Republic of the Councils in the second), one has to know Hungarian history reasonably well to identify the actual situation. Nor are the events or individuals portrayed realistically. Jancsó never illuminates the particulars of a situation as Kovács does. Rather, he provides those who know the particulars with the underlying structures that determine why what happened happened.

This stripping away of traditional realism, whether socialist or otherwise, has the same purpose as it had for Marx himself: we understand capitalism not when we see it personified by some greedy villain evicting widows and orphans and carrying off bags of money, but when we see it as a principle that causes perfectly ordinary people to do absolutely frightful things—not because they are inherently villainous, but because their class interests have been threatened. This accounts for why the opposing sides in Jancsó's films are frequently represented by equally photogenic individuals whose behavior is, if anything, thoughtful or puzzled. By stripping away the details, Jancsó is able to show us what really happens—which is what Marx was trying to do as well. Why have all of those spontaneous revolutions with high ideals re-

A perfectly composed shot from *Somewhere in Europe* (1947), the first major Hungarian film of the postwar period.

Meticulous attention to detail marks Andras Kovacs's *The Stud Farm* (1978), which captures the Stalinist excesses of earlier years.

(Right)
A characteristic pattern of Miklós Jancsó: a formally posed group backed by successive planes of figures in motion, from *Hungarian Rhapsody* (1978).

(Left)
The joke is in what is missing: no rope, no executioner. *The Witness*, a film by Péter Bacsó, was the first to deal with the postwar show trials. Completed in 1969, it was released only in 1982.

(Right)
One of the best Hungarian films of the 1980s: a typical scene from Márta Mészáros's autobiographical *Diary for My Children* (1982).

sulted in totalitarian states? *Red Psalm* explains how peaceful revolutions that are spontaneous are both taken over from within and terrorized from without. Where did Stalinism come from? For genuine Marxists this is an important question, and *Agnus Dei* is an attempt to answer it. Similarly, *The Confrontation* (*Fényes szelek,* 1969), deals with the role of intellectuals and students in shaping a socialist society, while *The Red and the White* (*Csillagosok, katonák,* 1967) adumbrates the realities of Hungarians caught up in the armed struggles for socialism. *Hungarian Rhapsody* (*Magyar repszódia, allegro barbaro,* 1978) recapitulates all of these themes as it follows the fortunes of a Hungarian family from the dissolution of the monarchy through World War II.

Jancsó's films present several problems for critics. First, since his films do not have ordinary stories and individuated characters, the only way to account for them critically is as philosophical exercises. While his innovative techniques may make the films seem merely like poetic exercises in cinema, there are substantive cinematic critiques of Marxist thought present as well. This aspect of his work is seldom addressed, even by critics in socialist countries. One reason for this lack of commentary on Jancsó's political critiques may be because his political analysis is as unusual as his style. Jancsó presents problems of interest to a Marxist but his solutions, and much of his treatment, are of a whole different order of thought. The metahistorical situations his films portray end in betrayal, slaughter, despair. Far from portraying situations that will resolve themselves beneficently, they portray closed cycles of violence in which redemption comes, if at all, only through self-sacrifice. In a strange way Jancsó's films resemble Peckinpah's with their emphasis on bonding, betrayal, and sacrificial redemption achieved by massive ritual violence.

His works, then, are admired for a variety of different and sometimes contradictory reasons, all of which take into account their technical excellence and substantial departures from the conventions of the cinema. The large doses of intellectual content that unify his works are detected subliminally: some of the films seem like puzzles, and most audiences can only surmise that there is finally some sort of unifying principle to his works. Actually, however, the form and the content go together. As a revisionist, Jancsó's rejection of characterization, montage, and the like point him back to a fundamental reconsideration of film, as though he were trying to rediscover the real principles of Marxist filmmaking before they were contaminated by, successively, Eisenstein, Balász, and the party hacks of the 1940s and fifties who gave socialist realism such a bizarrely comic twist. Taken from this point of view, Jancsó is the most important filmmaker since Eisenstein, since his works involve the rediscovery of a simpler (and cheaper) cinema whose subject is profoundly intellectual. Although he has certainly come to symbolize in the West the idea of the "Eastern European" cinema artist par excellence, and although his impact has been great inside Hungary, there are few films made there that in any shape or form reveal his influence.

For a variety of reasons, Istvan Gaál, Márta Mészáros, and Istvań Szabó are substantially better known internationally than Pál Sándor, Péter Bacsó, and Zsolt Kézdi-Kovács. Yet the two most neglected of the group are probably the most important. In the case of Péter Bacsó there is a peculiar reason. Bacsó, born in 1928, is three years younger than Kovács, and was a scriptwriter before he started directing in 1963. Like Kovács, he turned to documentarist techniques in his films. But in 1969 Bacsó directed what is probably the single most coherent analysis of postwar Hungary. *The Witness (A tanu)* was a comedy following the fortunes of a simple Communist dike keeper, Pelikan, who is put into positions of higher and higher responsibility, and also into jail, in alternating incidents which culminate in his being groomed as a "witness" for one of the "trials" that took place in Hungary after 1947. *The Witness* is the first film from anywhere in Eastern Europe to deal openly with the paranoid shams of the show trials, and to expose the absurd lengths to which postwar communist states pushed their beliefs. Some of the most absurd events the film depicts actually took place. But the satire was too accurate, the film too perceptive, for its time, so *The Witness* was not released until 1982. This has meant, among other things, that its impact has been overshadowed by later works of an equally strong critical nature such as Pál Gábor's *Angi Vera (Angi Vera,* 1978), which deals with the Party indoctrination of an impressionable young woman during the same period. Bacsó's earlier films led up to such works, and the movies he made during the 1970s, in various ways, circled about the same themes, but his reputation was to a certain extent diminished in Western eyes owing to the absence of his key film.

In 1983 Bacsó made another, even darker, comedy about the immediate postwar years in Hungary, called *Oh Bloody Life (Te rongyos elet).* Most Hungarian social criticism had been elliptical or veiled, but here Bacsó referred directly to actual historical events and to typical situations. Some of the things that Western audiences find most improbable in both films actually happened, such as Hungary's determination to conquer nature and grow oranges. Although their disconcerting brand of humor may limit their audience, the two films probably make Bacsó one of the most important directors in the group.

Another little known but key director is Pál Sándor. Only a year younger than István Szábo, he has made the same number of films. Of these the most recent, *Daniel Takes the Train (Szerencsés Daniel,* 1983), is arguably the most important, since this is the first Hungarian film to speak directly of the traumatic events of the 1956 revolt. The film follows the fortunes of two young men, one of whom was in a rebellious army unit and must flee Hungary. His friend, Daniel, wants to go to the

West because his girlfriend is going there. Neither youth finally escapes. Daniel's friend commits suicide, and he returns to Budapest. Sándor's portrayals of closed, trapped worlds which the chief characters are finally unable to escape dominate his work. Like Fábri's, his works are sober exercises in color, although the characterizations are substantially different. Sándor and Bacsó are highly individual talents of the first order whose appreciation abroad has consistently been less than is deserved.

This has not been the case with Márta Mészáros, István Szabó, and István Gaál. As a result of their work in the 1960s, they were thought to represent the future of Hungarian cinema. Szabó, in particular, represents a kind of filmmaking congenial to Western audiences. His earlier films reveal an unusual number of Western influences (mostly linked to Truffaut), and almost all of his films deal with purely personal problems. Given the overriding impulses of Hungarian cinema to deal with complex social and intellectual issues, this in itself may be no mean feat. Although his most successful film to date has been *Mephisto* (1981), which chronicles the way that a self-absorbed actor rises to fame under the aegis of National Socialism, his earlier *Confidence* (*Bizalom*, 1980) is more typical of his work at its best, and follows the growth of a romantic relationship between a man and a woman who are forced to assume an identity as husband and wife in order to hide from Fascists at the end of World War II. His most recent film, indicative of his growing international visibility and a jury prize winner at Cannes, is the Hungarian-West German-Austrian coproduction, *Colonel Redl* (*Redl Ezredes*, 1985).

If Szabó represents a personal and romantic approach to filmmaking, Márta Mészáros became important in the 1970s as one of the unfortunately very few woman directors. Her films seem more of a piece than those of any other filmmaker working in Hungary, since her interest is invariably in the difficulties women have in society. This does not prevent her from making some very shrewd judgments about what life in a socialist country is really like. At her best Mészáros gives one a vivid sense of the quality of life there. Seen from this perspective, her best film is probably *Two of Them* (*Ok ketten*, 1978). The two women referred to by the title are an older, established woman and a younger asocial woman whom she befriends. The curious and contradictory nature of their friendship—and of the motives for their behavior—is astutely delineated. Her best film, and one of the best Hungarian films of the 1980s, is an autobiographical work called *Diary for My Children* (*Napló gyermekeimnek*, 1982). Even in 1982 a film that graphically demonstrates how the postwar Hungarian state both imitated and recapitulated the excesses of Stalinism is dealing with a touchy subject. This black-and-white film skillfully blends documentary footage into the story of a young girl who returns to Budapest in 1947. The photography (by her son, Miklós Jancsó, Jr.) and the music give the film a propulsive quality her other films have not had, while the narrative deals with the events of the late 1940s in an unusually blunt fashion. After making thirteen feature-length films, Márta Mészáros is very close to being the most experienced woman director in the world, and *Diary* should establish her as one of the best.

This number makes her senior to both István Gaál and Zsolt Kézdi-Kovács, who have each made seven feature films. Gaál's *The Green Years (Zöldár,* 1966) and his recent *Quarantine (Cserepek,* 1981) are representative of his work. Both are thoughtful analyses of the ways that talented individuals (a young student in the first film, an architect in the second) react when faced with the bureaucratically induced malaise that permeates their society. The architect, for example, who has been abroad, has great difficulty reconciling the corruption and selfishness he sees at the higher levels of society with the very real needs of the people. Gaál is always concerned with the extent to which individuals in such situations can maintain their sense of internal worth and surmount the internal crisis of conscience generated within the film. However, unlike some of the other directors, Gaál's films end on a more optimistic note. The architect, for instance, regains his faith without losing his integrity.

One of the curiosities of socialist films, both in Hungary and elsewhere, is the extent to which their thematic concerns seem to lead them to focus either on typical figures in the past engaged in decisive events, or, in dealing with the present, to focus on members of the intelligentsia. In all of the films mentioned, for example, only Josef Pelikan is an authentic proletarian, and even he is somewhat atypical, since he was Communist during World War II. Even in the films of Mészáros the workers appear to represent a higher strata of the work force. One of the intriguing things about Kézdi-Kovács is that his best films deal mainly with people on the fringe. In *Forbidden Relations (Visszæsöit,* 1983), the brother and sister are distinctly on the lower edges of the social order: György has constant scrapes with the law, even before he starts sleeping with his half sister, whose life, even before she met him, is equally bleak. *Forbidden Relations* is not really a piece of social criticism: two lovers discover they are relatives and try to keep on living their lives together even though society condemns their relationship and sends them to jail. But neither is it a purely personal or romantic film, since the fates of its characters are largely a function of a given social and political system.

The major accomplishment of the Hungarian state, then, has been to make it possible for large numbers of talented individuals to work in relative freedom over the greater part of the postwar period. In return, the artists have produced films which, no matter how scathingly critical of the state they may be, are significant reinforcements of the Hungarian national consciousness. This is no small achievement in a country with a national identity that has historically been as fragile as Hungary's. Over and above such pragmatic nationalistic aims, Hungary has supported artists who have made a significant contribution to world cinema.

## NOTES

1. The release dates and both Hungarian and English language titles of Hungarian films mentioned in the text are taken from the authoritative (and anonymous) in-house manual *Hungarian Feature Films Released since 1948* (Budapest: Hungarofilm, n.d.), and frequently differ from those given in other sources. I am indebted to the following individuals for their help: Péter Bacsó, Hegi Gyula, János Huszar, András Kovács, Pál Sándor, István Szabó, and András Török.

## SELECTED BIBLIOGRAPHY

Liehm, Mira and Antonin J. *The Most Important Art: Eastern European Film After 1945*. Berkeley: University of California Press, 1974.

Nemeskurty, Istvan. *Word and Image: History of the Hungarian Cinema*. Budapest: Corvina, 1968.

Passek, Jean-Loup et al. *Le cinéma hongroise*. Paris: Centre Georges Pompidou, 1979.

Petrie, Graham. *Hungarian Cinema Today: History Must Answer to Man*. Budapest: Corvina, 1978.

Somgyi, Lia, ed. *Hungarian Film Directors, 1948–1983*. Budapest: Interpress, 1984.

Stoil, Michael Jon. *Cinema Beyond the Danube*. Metuchen, NJ: Scarecrow Press, 1974.

White, Alistair. *New Cinema in Eastern Europe*. New York: Dutton, 1971.

———. *New Cinema in Eastern Europe*. New York: Dutton, 1971.

# INDIA
## Mythologies and Modern India

ROSIE THOMAS

In a small temple in a dusty suburb of Bombay crouches a skinny *saadhu*—an orange-clad ascetic, a "world renouncer"—on his way to an important pilgrimage venue in the desert. Oblivious to the heady incense, the cacophony of bells and Sanskrit chants of the temple priests performing *puja* (ritual offerings) for the faithful, the *saadhu* sits alone and calmly turns the pages of a glossy film gossip magazine. "Of course I visit the cinema, why not? 'If the Ganges is flowing—wash your hands in it.'"

In India the film industry and its products are the focus of extraordinary fascination. Film culture forms a central core of all popular culture, a pervasive backdrop to daily life. The influence of films themselves extends well beyond the trivia of fashion and hairstyles: as recently as 1975 a devotional film *Goddess Santoshi Maa (Jai Santoshi Maa)* could elevate an obscure local goddess to the popular pantheon and convert hordes of devotees throughout rural and urban India, who began fasting on Fridays, avoiding sour foods, and building new temples—or reconsecrating old—for her worship.

However, apart from the comparatively Europeanized minority "art" cinema of Satyajit Ray and successors, little is known in the West of Indian films, bar the bald statistic that India produces more films than any other country (763 in 1983) and some hazy clichés characterizing the popular cinema as incompetently made, sub-Hollywood trash, and the industry as a chaotic jungle. In fact, not only is there a richly diverse "new" cinema movement, but mainstream films themselves deserve far better attention, with recognition that their conventions are unique and have traditional roots. Moreover, while the industry is indeed anarchic, its constraints have always been formidable: heavy taxation, lack of institutional finance, strict censorship, culturally disparate audiences and, more recently, legislative impotence in the face of rampant video piracy together with, since 1985, massive government support of television production, largely at cinema's expense.

India's cinema history is virtually as long as that of the West. The Lumière brothers reached Bombay only months after dazzling Paris with their *cinématographe* and the first completely Indian feature, Phalke's *King Harischandra* (*Raja Harischandra*), introducing a uniquely Indian genre, the mythological, was released in 1913. Sound arrived in 1931. Early fears that, because India is in fact a political grouping of numerous distinct languages and cultures, the "talkies" would hopelessly split markets, were unfounded. Originally most films were made in Hindustani (the predominant language of north India), but an emphasis on song, dance and spectacle ensured large audiences throughout the country, and regional film industries grew up slowly *alongside* the Hindi mainstream.

Nowadays the industry comprises more than a dozen filmmaking centers throughout India, working in fifteen languages, the major centers being Bombay, Madras, Calcutta, Trivandrum, Hyderabad, and Bangalore. Each region has its own revered stars who in the southern states have even infiltrated politics, with the veteran M. G. Ramachandra as chief minister of Tamil-Nadu since 1979, and N. T. Rama Rao, better known playing the god Krishna, as chief minister in Andhra Pradesh following a sensational defeat of Indira Gandhi's party in 1982.[1] Regional chauvinism has been nurtured and exploited by cinema in most states (with more or less direct political involvement), but broad differences in thematic emphases can also be discerned. Telugu and Tamil industries (today the most prolific) are particularly associated with family melodramas and mythologicals; Marathi with social satire and comedy; Malayalam with both an "artistic" naturalism and with "sexploitation"; and Bengali and Kannada with a more literary, serious, and melancholy ethos. India's "alternative" or "art" cinema (which is still little distributed within India) grew primarily through the regional language cinemas, notably in Bengal (home of Ghatak, Ray, and Sen), and drew on diverse influences—from European and Soviet cinema conventions to various Indian traditions of drama, music, representation, and myth. The bulk of regional cinema is, however, more directly influenced by mainstream Hindi cinema (and Indian performance and narrative traditions as mediated through this), whose glossy, big-budgeted, megastar extravaganzas are produced mostly in the glamour capital Bombay (and more recently also Madras).

Although Hindi films now account for less than 20 percent of national production, they alone have pan-Indian distribution and, because they make their appeal to primarily nationalist and traditionalist—rather than regionalist—sentiment and identity, have come to be known as the "all-India film." Interestingly, Hindi films also have major distribution networks throughout vast areas of the Third World and Russia, where they are frequently the dominant cinema, preferred among many non-Hindustani-speaking peoples to Hollywood, or even to indigenous cinemas.

Of course, as with any mainstream film industry, much dross is produced, but the Indian mass audience has always been ruthlessly discriminating—showing appreciation with effusive clapping, singing, throwing of coins at the screen, and repeated viewings, and boycotting what it considers bad. Even throughout the box-office bonanza of the 1970s at least 70 percent of Hindi films released regularly lost money (including many big-budgeted, megahyped productions), while a mere 10 percent actually went into profit. With the 1980s' incursions of video piracy and television, box-office success rates have plummeted still further. However, a few films have always made fortunes and, on television Hindi film reruns and film song programs still hold the top ratings. Rather than subjecting Indian cinema to inappropriate criticism (as is often done—either in terms of alien aesthetics or such unproductive notions as escapism), it seems more crucial to look at the various Indian cinemas within their own terms of reference. The article begins by broadly surveying the conventions and range of mainstream films (since 1945) and then examines the forms of opposition presented by "alternative" cinemas. Because of space limitations much important work has had to be omitted or cursorarily glossed, particularly in the regional cinemas, and the interested reader is encouraged to follow up the bibliography.

## Conventions and Genres

Mainstream filmmakers have generally agreed that they aim to make films that differ in format and content from Western films and that comparison with these, or the Indian art cinema, is irrelevant. Although conventions are always evolving, the mainstream form does remain distinctive. Even borrowings of story ideas and sometimes complete sequences from Hollywood and elsewhere must always be significantly adapted and integrated within Indian conventions for the film to work in India. No close copy of a Hollywood film has ever been a hit.

Since Indian cinema always had its own vast audiences capable of sustaining the industry, its conventions were able to develop without conforming to the expectations of international audiences. Thus traditional entertainment forms, notably village dramatizations of the mythological epics and also, more directly, the urban nineteenth- and twentieth-century Parsee theater with its adaptations of Shakespeare and Victorian melodrama, inflected this development, interacting, of course, with other factors. A mainstream film form has evolved in which the narrative is comparatively loose and fragmented, realism irrelevant, psychological characterization disregarded, elaborate dialogues prized, music essential, and both the emotional involvement of the audience and the pleasures of sheer spectacle privileged throughout the two and one-half- to three-hour duration of the entertainment. Crucially, it involves the skillful blending of various modes—song and dance, fights, comedy, melodrama, romance and more—into an integrated whole that moves its audience.

By the 1930s a number of distinctly Indian genres were well established. These included socials, mythologicals, devotionals, historicals, and stunt, costume, and fantasy films. As song and dance are a central and integral part of films of *all* genres, the term "musical" is seldom used. Although genre distinctions began to break down in the 1960s, they are still relevant, not only to an understanding of the range of films made today and in the past, but because the form of the now dominant socials has in fact integrated aspects of all earlier genres.

The social has always been the broadest and, since the 1940s, the largest category and loosely refers to any film in a contemporary setting not otherwise classified. It traditionally embraces a wide spectrum, from heavy melodrama to light-hearted comedy, from films with social purpose to love stories, from tales of family and domestic conflict to urban crime thrillers.

Historicals are predominantly epic displays of ornate grandeur, often located in Mughal court life, which peddle magnificent settings, passionate love affairs, heroism on the battlefield and grand Urdu rhetoric—invariably at the expense of any historical fact. Evolving directly out of the gaudy, spectacular Parsee theater (notably via theater-man turned filmmaker Sohrab Modi), the historicals are usually expensive, high status productions and include some very big hits.

The original Indian genre was the mythological. Indian cinema pioneers immediately recognized the potential of cinematic special effects and trick photography to portray miracles and superhuman spectacle, and thus make inroads into village story-telling and folk-theater traditions. Moreover, they banked on the familiarity, eminent respectability, and pan-Indian appeal of the Hindu religious epics, while incidentally offering fights, love affairs, melodramatic misunderstandings, gorgeous costumes, and comfortable moralizing. The mythological and its subgenre, the devotional (tales primarily about the gods' human devotees, intercut with scenes of the gods themselves) have remained a staple of Indian cinema throughout its history, fading out only in the late 1970s in Bombay, but still made in the south.

While the mythologicals were generally respected, the stunt films were unequivocally despised in "polite" circles as mindless escapist trash. Somewhat ironically, both genres were largely produced by the same studios and directors, who in fact talked of mythologicals as "nothing more than stunt films that happen to be about gods." Stunt films were adventure, action, and fighting films about *dacoits* (rural outlaws), masked bandits or musclemen, often with deliberately comic undertones.

Scarcely higher in status, and frequently exploiting similar stunts and special effects, were the costume, magic, and fantasy films. The latter looked to the Persianized exoticism of the Arabian Nights: an extravagant world of fairies and genies, with tales of revenge or of manhood tested through dangerous missions, and rewarded with beautiful heroines. While the stories were clearly part of an indigenous tradition and had been popular in Urdu Parsee theater, Hollywood was also an influence: Douglas Fairbanks's *Thief of Baghdad* was the most popular film of the 1920s in India. The Arabian ambiance appealed particularly to India's extensive Muslim population.

While some costume films were also quasi-Arabian, most, nicknamed "Raja Rani" (king and queen) films, dealt with a cloak-and-dagger Ruritanian never-never land of princes, princesses, usurped kingdoms, dank dungeons, and brave (or beautiful) commoners. Baroque medieval palaces, feudal tyranny and bows and arrows coexisted with Cadillacs, helicopters, and guns, or even—as in the 1960s Dara Singh cycle—with burly gladiators and ancient Rome. Stories were often built around conflict between good and bad brothers, or separated family members and mistaken identities (forerunners of the 1970s "lost and found" films: see page 318) and heroes frequently championed the poor, robbing the evil rich and fighting oppression. The early films in the costume, stunt, and mythological genres which dealt with usurped kingdoms or heroes (and heroines) freeing the oppressed were more subversive than they might appear, for in pre-Independence India their meaning was clearly political and anti-British.

## The Late Forties

The year 1945 found India, and its film industry, in the throes of rapid transition. World War II had had a devastating effect on the film industry. In the 1930s a studio system had been in operation, all filmmaking staff, including stars, were under contract to big extended family-type studios. War profiteering and illicit arms deals produced much black market money, which needed laundering, and this prompted an influx of wealthy independent producers who lured the major marketable asset, stars, away from the studios with enormous fees. Although at the time production seemed to be booming, consequences would be dire. By the end of the 1940s most major studios had collapsed, the star system stranglehold had begun and the fly-by-night producer had arrived: of 804 producers listed between 1946 and 1949 only eighteen were in continuous production over these four years.

Within India, World War II's importance lay largely in its implications for India's growing independence movement. The war had been officially boycotted by Indian nationalists who claimed that, "India cannot associate herself in a war said to be for democratic freedom when that very freedom is denied to her,"[2] but sympathies were mixed, so that 1945 was of major significance in giving fresh impetus to the anti-British struggle. Almost all major film producers supported the freedom movement and throughout the 1930s and 1940s had played ingenious games to subvert British censorship vigilance, producing covertly allegorical films or allowing Congress Party motifs like Gandhian spinning wheels or snatches of freedom songs to make apparently casual intrusions on screen, guaranteeing wild cheers from the audiences.

With independence in 1947, films could openly celebrate nationalism. However, much of the "radical" cinema kept its focus on criticism of the injustices of certain traditional values (e.g., widow remarriage, dowry, taboos on love outside arranged marriage and, occasionally, caste taboos) and on iniquitous landlord-peasant relations, rather than on angry, overt reprisals against the British. It appeared primarily concerned with the construction of a new "modern" Indian national identity.

Some formal exploration was in evidence at this time, notably among a small group centered around IPTA (the Communist party-affiliated Indian People's Theatre Association), whose films, although primarily melodrama, were influenced by Soviet Realism. One central figure was Chetan Anand, whose *The Lower Town* (*Neecha nagar,* 1946) won the 1946 Cannes Grand Prix. Equally notable was founder-member K.A. Abbas, whose *Children of the Earth* (*Dharti ke lal,* 1946) a gruelling saga set in the 1943 Bengal famine, began a long career of committed, quietly innovative filmmaking. While Abbas's own films gained some recognition abroad, they invariably flopped in India. Nevertheless, he had tremendous impact there as a provocative left-wing critic and writer, and as script collaborator on Raj Kapoor's legendary 1950s proletarian films (see page 308).

This pioneering refusal of Indian filmic conventions was very marginal: far more influential was the heritage of the popular 1930s radical socials of Prabhat Studios, Poona, and New Theatres, Calcutta. While New Theatres drew much from a Bengali literary heritage, Prabhat's main influence was Marathi folk and popular theater forms and their themes ranged from socially critical melodrama to mythologicals and devotionals, of which Damle and Fatehlal's *Saint Tukeram* (*Sant Tukeram,* 1936/Marathi; 1948/Hindi-dubbed) on the life of a Maharashtrian poet-saint is the most outstanding example and legendary box-office success. However, it was V. Shantaram (b. 1901), another co-founder of Prabhat, whose career has been most notable. He made (and acted in) films for almost sixty years—from the silent days until the late 1970s—and still, in the 1980s, oversees the running of the studio he first set up in Bombay in 1943. He directed many of Prabhat's most adventurously radical socials and from Bombay continued to produce eminently popular films on themes of social or cultural concern, alternating films on dowry iniquities *Dowry (Dahej,* 1950), black market corruption *Our Country (Apna desh,* 1949) or penal reform *Two Eyes, Twelve Hands (Do ankhen baarah haath,* 1957), with spectaculars on Indian classical arts—for example, a version of a classic Sanskrit play *(Shakuntala,* 1943) and an early Technicolor success about kathak dancing *The Jangle of Anklet Bells (Jhanak jhanak payal baje,* 1955). His films are crafted fully and skillfully within mainstream conventions: they are theatrical, spectacular, and finely melodramatic, although he also acknowledges other influences, notably German expressionism. Although he is often accused of populist selling-out in his post-Prabhat period, and is undeniably patriarchal in outlook, Shantaram reached very large audiences with unusually serious themes and set the agenda for much that followed.

Many socials in the 1940s were simply family melodramas, love or crime stories, with absolutely no pretensions to social or political substance, and other genres were even more popular. A letter to *Film India* in the 1940s ran: "Shantaram may be great but . . . don't bother with realism. We want color and entertainment." Prabhat had largely financed their socials with their infinitely more popular and spectacular mythological, devotional, and costume films, while other studios' big money makers were stunt and fantasy films. The Wadia brothers' Basant Studios had dominated the 1930s and 1940s with these genres and were best known for their stunt series starring an amazing blonde, whip-cracking wonder woman of Australian origin, known as "Fearless Nadia," undoubtedly Indian cinema's most remarkable cult heroine.

## The Fifties

In the 1950s the balance of genres changed somewhat. Possibly because of their Western resonances, stunt films went out of fashion after independence. There was a slight increase in patriotic historicals and mythologicals, and an enormous boom in costume films. One reason was the unexpected success of S. S. Vasan's Madras-made costume drama *Chandralekha* (1948), a big breakthrough for Madras into Hindi markets and the first of a stream of 1950s costume hits for Vasan's Gemini Studios. A story of two princes fighting over a throne and a princess, its draw was its lavish spectacle, particularly its extravagantly choreographed chorus dances (including a famous drum-top dance) and dazzling sword fights. Second, color technology was arriving and costume films were the perfect showcase. Mehboob's *Savage Princess* (*Aan*, 1952) was the first color hit—and even got bemused, if somewhat patronizing, critical acclaim at its London release in 1952. Fantasy films largely replaced stunts at Basant Studios, with a string of films drawing on Muslim/Persian legend: *Aladdin and the Wonderful Lamp* (1952), *Alibaba* (1954) and *Hatiim Tai* (1956). Together costume and fantasy films account for over 30 percent of releases in the mid-fifties. Color took over gradually throughout the decade, although until the 1960s many big films were in black-and-white—or only partly colored (i.e., with selected reels on color stock or laboriously hand colored).

However, the 1950s is primarily remembered as the heyday of the black-and-white era and popular cinema's golden age, with (so the legend goes) artistically committed filmmakers, immortal music, and semidivine stars, an age of innocence before Indian cinema was corrupted by the vulgar excesses of garish color and crass commercialism. Nostalgia apart, the actual picture is more complex, although many classics were indeed made then. Love stories were in vogue, both maudlin melodramas about thwarted love, usually with a doomed, self-destructive tragic hero (associated with star Dilip Kumar), and lighter-hearted romances with an urban, Westernized ambiance, with a new type of optimistic, happy-go-lucky hero (associated with Dev Anand). The genteel quasi-Lucknowi[3] setting of the so-called Muslim social was also popular, as were domestic melodramas—often Madras made— built around tensions and repressions in the family, and celebrating self-sacrifice with tear-sodden excess. However, the legend of the 1950s really rests on the work of a few filmmakers who managed to combine huge box-office success with serious themes and mastery of, plus innovation within, the formal conventions of Indian cinema. Despite the dangers of auteurist histories, four names must be privileged: Raj Kapoor, Bimal Roy, Guru Dutt, and Mehboob Khan.

Raj Kapoor (b. 1924), eldest son of veteran theater/film star Prithviraj Kapoor, now heads a veritable dynasty of Kapoor filmmakers and stars. As producer, director, and star, renowned for his ebullient showmanship, Raj Kapoor has always combined lavish spectacle—magnificent sets (with Art Director M. R. Achrekar), dazzling locations, and dream sequence fantasy—with powerful emotional drama, technical finesse (with cameraman Radhu Karmaker) and unusually good music. Although known for tackling social issues whether urban poverty and corruption in the early 1950s: *The Vagabond* (*Awaara*, 1951; *Shri 420*, (*Mr 420*, 1955); *Boot Polish*, 1954; *Keep Awake* (*Jagte raho*, 1957) dacoitery in the 1960s *The Country Where the Ganges Flows* (*Jis Desh main Ganga behti hai*, 1960), or widow remarriage in 1982 (*Love Sickness*, *Prem rog*), Raj Kapoor's ultimate preoccupation has always been the love story—or, more precisely, a male obsession with idealized femininity, moving from *Confluence* (*Sangam,* 1960) to *Bobby* (1972), *Truth, Power, Beauty* (*Satyam shivam sunderam,* 1978) and his 1985 film *Ram, Your Ganges Is Dirty* (*Rama teri Ganga maili*), one of his biggest box-office hits ever. Raj Kapoor's star persona ranged from handsome romantic hero (making a legendary couple with Nargis in the 1950s) to Chaplinesque tramp, but its essence has always been the (clearly populist) golden-hearted innocent at sea in a corrupt, sophisticated world. Although Raj Kapoor has produced important films in each decade, his 1950s proletarian films still stand out, particularly *Awaara.* With its captivating music, stars, and an innovative and remarkable dream sequence, *Awaara,* the story of a judge's abandoned son lured into criminality in order to survive, even became a box-office legend in Russia.

Bimal Roy (1912–66), a more unassuming idealist, combined an unusually sincere socialist commitment with crowd-pleasing properties, making films with restraint, simplicity, and, at times, radical formal innovation, yet using big stars, fine music (usually by S. D. Burman), melodrama, and confident mastery of Indian film conventions, including sensitive integration of songs within narrative, and delicate, poetic song picturization. Bimal Roy began filmmaking at New Theatres in Calcutta with the bold and unexpectedly successful *Toward the Light* (*Udayer pathey,* 1944) about trade union battles in a newspaper office, but his major intervention is usually seen to be the Italian neorealist influenced *Two Acres of Land* (*Do bigha zameen,* 1953), a film about feudal and capitalist economic oppression, in which a peasant fights to preserve his small holding from a greedy landlord and city property developers. Its innovative use of location shooting, moving camera, and naturalistic acting and dialogue made the film stand out in its Indian context and brought critical acclaim abroad (including the International Prize at Cannes in 1954). Although he usually pinned themes around a romance and a melodramatic form, Bimal Roy explored a range of subjects and styles, from *Madhumati* (1958), a lyrical mountain romance with a reincarnation theme (and intriguing screenplay by Ritwik Ghatak—see below), to *The Jew* (*Yahudi,* 1958), a costume melodrama about persecuted Jews in ancient Rome, or *Sujata* (1959), the tale of an untouchable (outcaste) girl adopted by a Brahmin family who scandalously marries the Brahmin boy chosen to be the husband of the family's real daughter. *Sujata* is one of the very few Indian films that has dared to tackle the ultrasensitive issue of caste directly.

Guru Dutt (1925–64) was a less overtly political filmmaker, more concerned with the anguish of the creative artist struggling for recognition and self-expression in a callous materialistic world—an anguish he lived out himself, dying at thirty-nine of alcohol and sleeping pills. His early films were light-hearted socials such as *Mr and Mrs 55*

(1955). However, his nostalgic following today rests largely on his three later melodramas. *Eternal Thirst* (*Pyaasa*, 1957) and *Paper Flowers* (*Kaagaz ke phool*, 1959) are both tales of the tormented creativity of self-destructive melancholy artists (in *Pyaasa* a poet, in *Kaagaz* an idealistic filmmaker); both are recognizably semiautobiographical, and star Guru Dutt himself. *Pyaasa* was his biggest hit, although the Cinemascope *Kaagaz ke phool*, which flopped disastrously and finally demoralized Dutt, is perhaps even more finely crafted. The third, *The Master's Wife and Slave* (*Sahib bibi aur ghulam*, 1962), technically directed by associate Abrar Alwi, is an evocation of turn-of-the-century Bengal presented through a portrait of a decadent and decaying *zamindari* (feudal aristocrat) household. It focuses largely around the youngest son's neglected, alcoholic wife (one of Meena Kumari's key performances), but it has wider social resonances, dealing, as it does, with the incursions of a rising, Western-educated middle-class against the backdrop of British imperialist brutalities. All three films are exemplary Hindi melodramas, combining powerfully expressive *mise-en-scène* and camerawork (by V.K. Murthy), exceptional music (many songs are perennial hits) with imaginative song picturization and appropriately placed interludes of comedy and slapstick. Indisputable classics, Dutt's films have begun to get deserved recognition abroad.

While Kapoor, Roy, and Dutt all worked in black and white in the 1950s, Mehboob Khan, who had already made a name for himself throughout the 1940s, moved successfully on to color following *Aan*'s acclaim (see page 308). Mehboob, a barely educated Gujerati village boy, had worked his way up from extra roles to directing films in the 1930s, and by the 1940s had established his own studio with a strong reputation for socially concerned, technically skilled, and very popular films, from *Woman* (*Aurat*, 1940) to *Humayan* (1945) and *Style* (*Andaaz*, 1949). His legendary status, however, rests ultimately on *Mother India* (1957), indisputedly *the* all-time classic of popular Indian cinema, a film that still guarantees full houses today. It concerns traditional rural life and oppression and shows the struggle for survival of a poor village woman (Nargis's most memorable role) who, left alone with her children, defends her self-respect and an ideal of virtuous womanhood against tremendous odds: famine, flood, a corrupt moneylender and finally her own rebellious son, turned outlaw. Combining Soviet realism, Hollywood dramatic spectacle, grand melodrama, and Hindu religious and folk imagery, it is a powerful film. Its ideological ambiguities are perhaps not so surprising in view of Mehboob's own studio emblem, which had blithely combined a Soviet hammer and sickle with an Urdu couplet meaning: "Man proposes, God disposes."

Undoubtedly crucial to *Mother India*'s enduring popularity were its appeals to Indian nationalist and traditionalist sentiment. The working through of, and attempts to build on, notions of "tradition" in the context of postcolonial India in a modern capitalist world was an underlying preoccupation of the era and surfaced in various ways in cinema. The mainstream films were (and largely still are) regularly structured around an opposition between good (ultimately the traditional often personified by the virtuous mother figure) and evil (a decadent nontraditionalism, often explicitly westernized). Its contradictions are generally mediated by the protagonist, and order is restored through the triumph of "good," although this usually incorporates some modification to negotiate—however precariously—a "modern traditionalism." The underpinnings of Hindu mythological references and narrative/dramatic strategies further fuel the traditionalist appeal.

However, the post-Independence decade also marked the emergence of a new sensibility in Indian filmmaking, equally concerned with the meaning of the traditional in contemporary India, but seeing no answer in what they regarded as the excesses and naive populism of a highly commercialized mainstream cinema. Although Satyajit Ray's *Song of the Road* (*Pather panchali,* 1955), which combined the authenticity of a Bengali realist novel about dispossessed villagers with the poetic understatement of naturalist conventions broadly borrowed from European art cinema, caused by far the biggest stir owing to its understandable acclaim by Western critics, the work of Ritwik Ghatak was in many ways more fundamentally innovative. Beginning before Ray, with *The Citizen* (*Nagarik,* 1952/3), Ghatak's films deal primarily with the alienated and uprooted of post-Independence India. He eschewed the conventions of both the Indian mainstream and of a Western bourgeois humanism and instead devoted himself to developing an epic cinema, which drew rigorously on Indian material traditions and mythic archetypes to involve, and disturb, the audience with reverberations across a number of different levels. These developments, however, were little known or noticed within India at the time, and perhaps the most significant shift of emphasis within the mainstream Hindi cinema was a move from stolid patriotism in the early 1950s to a new, youthful iconoclasm by the end of the decade, symbolized by the patently Westernized star hero Shammi Kapoor, heralding the mood of the 1960s.

## The Sixties

With the influx of a large rural population into the towns in the 1960s, and the widespread adoption of color, came a fresh, brash exuberance in mainstream cinema. Action returned, both in cheap stunt and costume films and in more respectable socials, where dacoit (rural outlaw) themes offered fights and horsemanship tempered with social concern. The key dacoit film remains *Gunga jumna* (1961), directed by New Theatres veteran, Nitin Bose (whose earlier radical filmmaking had inspired his apprentice Bimal Roy), which tells of a revenge-seeking dacoit confronting his estranged policeman brother. Heralded for its new naturalism, with authentic dialects and village color, but still exhibiting spectacular excess, together with song, dance and melodrama, it became, like *Mother India,* a perennial hit.

The epitome of the new energy was superstar rebel hero Shammi Kapoor (brother of Raj Kapoor), whose wild antics as singing-dancing-clowning-fighting playboy started a new trend in zany pop entertainment, largely instigated by producer S. Mukherjee. Scandalizing traditionalists with his wild coif and quasi-rock and roll gyrations, Shammi frolicked in the snows of fashionable mountain resorts and raced sports cars around glamorous European capitals with the new "mod" heroines (Sadhana, Asha Parekh, Saira Banu), superficially Westernized but indubitably virtuous and traditional at heart. Although invariably critically disparaged, many of these films were well-crafted, lively entertainment and undoubtedly of sociological importance, marking the encroachments of Western youth culture on modern India and constantly renegotiating the boundaries between an excitingly dangerous moral decadence and a virtuous, but hide-bound tradition.

Alongside these was a vogue for mystery, suspense, and crime thrillers. Family socials ranged from heavy Madrasi melodramas about self-sacrifice and duty to, among the more sophisticated Bombay filmmakers, a new concern with extramarital affairs, or triangles involving the reappearance of a wife's former lover—hitherto considered a very risky subject. Important filmmakers in the 1960s were: Chetan and Vijay Anand, B. R. and Yash Chopra, Nasir Hussein, Raj Khosla, H. S. Rawail, Shakti Samanta, and Mohan Segal.

If many socials became lighter and brasher in the 1960s, romance and poetry remained in the Muslim historicals and socials, and the decade is framed by two truly remarkable Muslim classics. Both were more than ten years in production and are legendary in Indian cinema history for their lavish mise-en-scène, extravagant melodrama, and richly poetic Urdu dialogues. *The Mughal Age (Mughal-e-azam,* 1960), K. Asif's magnum opus, recreates a version of the (historically unsubstantiated) legend of the passion of King Akbar's son for a court dancer, Anarkali, which almost destroyed the Moghul empire. It boasts epic battle scenes, a spectacular glass palace, compelling music and dance, exceptionally charismatic stars (Prithviraj Kapoor, Dilip Kumar, and Madhubala), and stunning photography (mostly) in black and white. The film ranks with *Mother India* and *Ganga Jamuna* as one of three perennial box-office draws. One of Asif's writers, Urdu scholar and poet Kamal Amrohi, went on to produce his own classic *Pure of Heart (Pakeezah,* 1972), an extraordinarily delicate CinemaScope extravaganza about hypocrisy and the oppressive world of the Muslim courtesans and their noblemen lovers. A haunting, sensuous, romantic fantasy, steeped in the rich imagery of Urdu mystical love poetry, *Pakeezah* is legendary within India as the swan-song of tragedy queen Meena Kumari, whose star-persona it echoes, but the film has also had considerable acclaim from Western audiences.

The 1950s and 1960s are remembered particularly for their film music; in India the music director has always been considered as important as the stars (and often more important than the director) in selling a film, and there are still extraordinarily few films without songs in Indian cinema history. In the late 1940s, Husenlal Bhagatram and C. Ramachandran, and Naushad were top music directors. In the 1950s, S. D. Burman, Roshan, and Naushad joined the ranks, and later the duos Shankar-Jaikishen and Kalyanji-Anandji. In the mid-1960s, Laxmikant-Pyarelal and R. D. Burman rose to prominence and continue to dominate the scene today, together with more Westernized newcomers such as Annu Malik and Bappi Lahiri. Playback singers, the people who actually sing the songs to which the stars only mime, are also important celebrities, most notably the phenomenal Lata Mangeshkar, who has been the top female playback singer since the late 1940s, and today holds the Guinness record for having recorded more songs than any other singer in the world. Mohammed Rafi, and more recently Kishore Kumar, have been the major male singers. Sound recordists are less celebrated but very few names dominate this field too: Minoo Katrak, Kaushik, and Sharma in the 1950s and 1960s, and more recently D.O. Bansali and S. Chatterjee.

Hindi cinema has a long tradition of megastars: Ashok Kumar became a top hero in the early 1940s, the trio Raj Kapoor, Dilip Kumar, and Dev Anand were superheroes from the late 1940s until at least the late 1960s (in fact, all four still work in the mid-1980s), and from the late 1950s onward were joined by Shammi Kapoor, Raaj Kumar, Rajendra Kumar, Shashi Kapoor, and Sunil Dutt. Among female stars, Nargis and Madhubala dominate from the 1940s, joined by Meena Kumari, Nutan, Vijayantimala, Geeta Bali, Waheeda Rehman, and others from the 1950s and 1960s.

## The Seventies

While the 1970s marked the beginning of a viable, low-budget, non-star "parallel" cinema movement, largely instigated by the success of Mrinal Sen's government-funded *Mr Shome* (*Bhuvan Shome*, 1969), together with a burgeoning of activity in the regional cinema, Hindi mainstream cinema became increasingly more extravagant and star-oriented as huge amounts of black market money, from shady business and smuggling operations, poured in to be laundered. The star system became, both conceptually and commercially, completely dominant,

Nargis as the virtuous mother left alone with her two sons, in Mehboob Khan's all-time classic *Mother India* (1957).

An eccentric taxi driver is at one with his temperamental, delapidated vehicle in *Pathetic Fallacy* (*Ajantrik*, 1958), one of Ritwik Ghatak's innovative films.

Legendary tragedienne Meena Kumari as the doomed, lovelorn courtesan in her opulent Pink Palace, from the Muslim classic *Pure of Heart* (*Pakeezah*, 1972).

The three goddesses, right, are jealous of young Satyawati's devotion to the goddess Santoshi Maa, in the immensely popular film bearing her name, *Jai Santoshi Maa* (1975).

Satyajit Ray, a towering figure in Indian cinema, was the first to achieve world-wide acclaim. Most of his many films are in Bengali, a regional language, among them *Distant Thunder* (1974), left, set in Singapore in 1942. *The Chess Players* (1977), below, was his first Hindi film and thus reached a larger audience within India.

One of Manmohan Desai's fast-paced, witty films, *Destiny* (*Naseeb*, 1981) had superstar Amitabh Bachchan as the poor waiter-cum-boxing champion hero.

The splitting of the "feminine principle" in *Vibrations* (*Tarang*, 1984), a significant film by Kumar Shahani that has achieved some success abroad but has not been released in India.

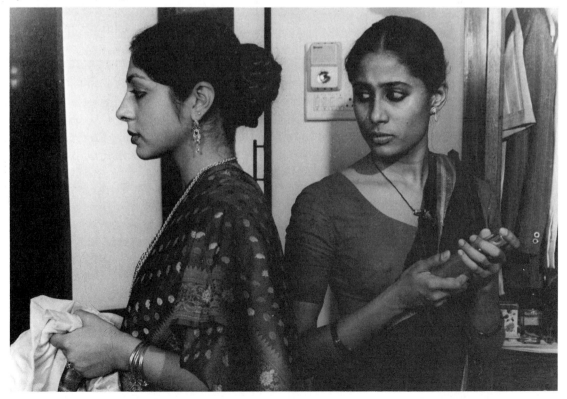

and it is hard to discuss the 1970s mainstream films without the star personae around which they were built.

The decade was ushered in with a range of light-hearted romances, from those of cocky, lover-boy-next-door Rajesh Khanna, a megastar known as "The Phenomenon," to the decade's top romantic pair: simple golden-hearted he-man Dharmendra and pristine dream girl Hema Malini, who remained top heroine throughout the 1970s.

In 1973, Prakash Mehra's *Chains (Zanjeer)*, about a tormented policeman singlehandedly avenging his parents' murder, presaged an important change. Scripted by a bright new duo, Salim and Javed, and clearly inspired by Hollywood gangster and *noir* films, it introduced the macho melodrama: slick, witty, comparatively tightly scripted and more violent than anything earlier, while retaining a traditional Indian structuring of music, mythology, and family sentiment. Crucial to this was the new superstar persona of Amitabh Bachchan as a tough, brooding "angry young man," an underdog wronged by society and out for revenge, which, combined with Hindi cinema's recurrent themes of conflict between family love and wider moral duty, was commercial dynamite. Salim-Javed's most intriguing screenplay was probably *The Wall (Deewaar, 1975)*, an undisguised adaptation of *Mother India* and *Gunga jumna*. This time one brother is a poor honest city policeman and the other a wealthy smuggling gang leader in a corrupt urban underworld, who nevertheless lives, and finally dies, for his mother's love. The film, slickly directed by Yash Chopra, is a fascinating blend of gangster motifs, sunny love songs, kung-fu fights, and excruciating family melodrama, and stands as a good example of the genre.

With Amitabh (one of the biggest star phenomena India, and possibly world cinema, has ever known; see also note 1), came the multistarrer films with, by Indian standards, enormous budgets. They were crammed with stars to increase the apparent market value, which had come to depend almost completely on star casts. Top male stars were Amitabh, Dharmendra, Jeetendra, Vinod Khanna, Shashi Kapoor, Rishi Kapoor, and Shatru; major female stars were Hema, Raakhee, Rekha, Zeenat Aman, and Parveen Babi. Although the economic basis of the film industry had become particularly anarchic, periodic attempts at regulation were invariably frustrated by the short-term self-interest of those at the top. In the long term, the multistarrer proved disastrous. As the stranglehold of the already unwieldy star system intensified, production became a nightmare of chasing and cajoling busy stars who sometimes worked in over fifty productions simultaneously, and when, in the early 1980s, these dinosaurean films began to crash at the box office, industry finance was severely depleted. The legendary multistarrer is a glossy, big-screen "curry Western" *Flames (Sholay, 1975)*, which ran for over six years in Bombay. Directed by Ramesh Sippy and written by Salim-Javed (inspired this time by Italian and Hollywood "buddy" Westerns), it remains a masterly integration of macho action with light comic relief, pathos, romance, and even a male buddy love song. Amitabh and Dharmendra starred as outlaws hired to capture a sadistic dacoit, the monstrous Gabbar Singh (played by Amjad Khan), who unexpectedly and unprecedentedly became a cult hero.

Two exponents of the multistarrer stand out: Prakash Mehra and Manmohan Desai. Mehra followed *Zanjeer* with increasingly more sentimental films, whose appeal lay primarily in skillful manipulation of Indian emotion and canny populism, together with all the other required "*masala.*"[4] His biggest hit was *Conqueror of Fate* (*Muqaddar ka sikander,* 1978). However, Manmohan Desai had the lighter, and more consistent, Midas touch, with a string of influential megahits throughout the decade. Playing gleefully with artifice and the clichés of Hindi cinema, his inimitable films are witty, fast-paced, exuberant fun, boasting spectacular showmanship and a wild surreal logic, as well as astute commercial calculation and excellent crafting in the terms of mainstream conventions. Desai invariably, and brazenly, repeats a patently preposterous "lost and found" narrative device (brothers are separated in childhood brought up in homes of different class and religion, and reunified, preferably with their real mother, after some melodramatic misunderstanding). *Amar Akbar Anthony* (1977), *Dharam veer* (1977), *Destiny,* (*Naseeb,* 1981) and *Coolie* (1983) are his most characteristic and interesting films, and bear, like most of his work, intriguing evidence of his apprenticeship in Basant's stunt/fantasy/mythological studios. Looked at in many ways, Desai's films can be called modern-day mythologicals.

Of course, smaller films were also produced. A stream of family socials promoted themselves as "good clean family entertainment," notably those of Hrishikesh Mukherjee, Basu Chatterjee, and others, who aimed predominantly at a middle-class urban audience with quiet, gently amusing, inextravagant films, well within Indian formal conventions. At the other end of the scale was the unsophisticated Madras-style family melodrama, aimed mostly at a rural or barely educated urban audience, particularly women. In this idiom was the decade's most unexpected superhit, the tiny-budgeted devotional film, *Goddess Santoshi Maa* (*Jai Santoshi Maa,* 1975), about a long-suffering Cinderella figure, cruelly abused by her in-laws, but finally bountifully rewarded for her unswerving devotion to the goddess Santoshi Maa. This apart, traditional mythological genre production virtually died out in Bombay, but continued successfully in the south, with some brilliant exponents, notably Bapu, some of whose spectacular Telugu epics were also dubbed in Hindi Bapu's *The Complete Ramayana* (*Sampoorna Ramayana,* 1973) was an all-India hit, and his *Sita's Wedding* (*Sita kalyanam,* 1976) received rave reviews in London and Chicago festivals.

## The Eighties

By the turn of the decade the beginning of a crisis was sensed in Bombay. The multistar format was clearly running out of steam, video (and, more remotely, television) loomed on the horizon, and a number of younger filmmakers were beginning to challenge the dominant Hindi film form and work toward a parallel cinema that, drawing primarily on Western "realist" filmmaking conventions, would answer the needs of the Westernized, culturally aspiring, urban middle-classes, and also of a Government preoccupied with the acclaim of international critics and a safe respectability. This new movement had been little threat to the mainstream with its mass audience and established distribution circuits in the 1970s, but as filmmakers like Shyam Benegal began to use mainstream stars (mostly eager for the status and international exposure) and even songs and comedy, and as the parallel cinema's stars began to be accepted by mainstream audiences, the possibility was emerging of a low-budget "middle cinema" that could offer not only prestige on the international film festival circuit but also a viable commercial proposition within India.

In the early 1980s the mainstream began gradual forays into smaller budgets, with a number of softer, more emotional family melodramas, a run of young love stories as numerous aging stars launched their sons into second generation stardom, and a purported concern with women's issues. These run from Raj Kapoor's *Love Sickness* (*Prem rog,* 1982) on widow remarriage, to the more overtly opportunistic small films of B.R. Chopra: *Scales of Justice* (*Insaaf ka tarazu,* 1980) on rape and *Divorce* (*Nikaah,* 1982) on Muslim divorce laws.

In the long run, the most significant development may have been a series of films that broke a long-standing censorship taboo and dealt with corruption in police and political circles—to wildly enthusiastic audience response. Indian cinema has always suffered from comparatively harsh censorship. There have been protracted battles between censors and filmmakers over apparent inconsistencies and absurdities in the system (including the relatively lenient censoring of imported Western films). Explicit sexual activity, including kissing on the mouth, is still more or less taboo in Indian cinema although, in fact, the ban on screen kisses came only with the puritanical reformist zeal after Independence that saw kissing in public as an immoral Western import. For most mainstream filmmakers this is a comparatively minor constraint: not only have they perfected the art of extravagantly suggestive eroticism in their song and dance sequences, but it appears that audiences themselves boycott what they consider crudely "immoral." Instead, the highly sensitive political censorship—which, until 1983, meant a ban on depicting the police as corrupt or even inefficient—has always been more of an issue, particularly since there were clear anomalies in the rules, with wide regional differences. The changes of 1982 arose because a vogue for Hindi remakes (in Madras) of Telugu, Kannada, and Tamil films forcefully exposed these discrepancies. Controversy broke out when *Blind Law (Andha kanoon,* 1983), a Hindi remake of a Telugu film, with Amitabh Bachchan, framed for murder, seeking revenge by exposing loopholes in a corrupt and inefficient legal apparatus, became a test case. Government authorities tried to ban the film but, since it had already passed censorship in Telugu, eventually had to relent. The film became a big hit and was followed by a stream of films on corrupt police and, subsequently, on politicians. The most significant of these was *Half Truth (Ardh satya,* 1983). Not only was this particularly hard-hitting but, since it was constructed within the low-key naturalistic conventions of the "new"/"alternative" cinema movement, its extraordinary commercial success among mainstream audiences marked an important breakthrough, and the ground for a "middle" cinema that might bridge the perceived polarization between elitist "high-brow" and populist "low-brow" appeared to have been established.

The effects of this are as yet uncertain. Certainly the bigger mainstream filmmakers continue to make films as they have always done, and Desai, Mehra and, most notably, Raj Kapoor, as well as newcomers such as Rahul Rawail, have all had big hits in the mid-1980s. However, the move towards more naturalistic conventions has been exploited in increasingly gory and "realistic" depictions of, and macho obsession with, violence that is far from the buddy ethos and predominantly fantasy violence of 1970s Amitabh films. On the other hand, while something of a "middle" cinema is becoming established, despite frequent references to it as "serious," "political," or even as "art" it has often meant little more than an eschewing of extravagant spectacle, music, and stars and a canny exploitation of a new, lucrative market.

## Art/Nonmainstream Cinema

Indian cinema is invariably described as split between two opposed and unrelated movements, "art" versus "commercial" cinema, a rigid polarization that is dangerous on several counts, not least because it masks a great heterogeneity within each broad category. However, it is undeniable that the work of Ray and Ghatak in the 1950s marked important interventions, from which a number of alternative cinemas eventually developed.

Crucially, Ray's international success embarrassed the Indian Government into setting up a Film Finance Corporation in 1960, which laid an economic infrastructure to support alternative filmmakers. However, while European art cinemas have always drawn much of their strength from being national cinemas that opposed the U.S. cultural imperialism of Hollywood,[5] the Indian art cinema opposed not Hollywood but another Indian cinema, the Hindi mainstream, which itself drew primarily on nationalist rhetoric. This meant that Indian art cinema was always more easily marginalized and somewhat ironically, the thunderous acclaim from Western audiences for Ray's debut film gave the movement its initial impetus and support.

Satyajit Ray (b. 1921) is, of course, India's most established auteur and something of a gargantuan figure in world cinema, although his films are still little seen within India. This is largely due to the dominance of a free-market commercial distribution structure but, since most of Ray's work is in Bengali, a regional language, and since his refusal of mainstream conventions is uncompromising, the films are not easily accessible to most Indian audiences. Ray came from a family of artists and intellectuals, steeped in the liberal humanism of Tagore's nineteenth-century Bengali cultural renaissance, and showed early talent as artist, musician, and writer, with an obsessional interest in films. In 1947 he co-founded the Calcutta Film Society, which offered a forum where Bengali intellectuals and cinéastes (including the young Sen and Ghatak) could see and discuss a range of world cinema otherwise not easily available in India.

Ray's original influences were Italian neorealism, Renoir, and classical Hollywood, and he has chosen to work within a realist aesthetic, concerned primarily with psychologically sensitive characterization and cinematic and poetic lyricism. While he says that "In rhythm, form and content I like to follow a simple classical structure. . . . I believe in plot"[6] his films also show complex formal organization and structuring. His filmmaking is, in fact, highly Europeanized, despite its dealing with very Indian subject matter, often drawn from Bengali literature.

Ray's reputation rests both on his exceptional mastery of cinematic form and the breadth of subject matter and style he has tackled. His work ranges from the Apu trilogy (*Pather panchali, Aparajito, The Unvanquished,* 1956, and *The World of Apu (Apur sansar,* 1959) an epic about a family that moves from traditional village poverty to modern city anomie, to films about the world of feudal aristocrats *The Music Room (Jalsagar,* 1958), the Calcutta business world *The Adversary (Pratiwandi,* 1970); *Company Limited (Seemabaddha,* 1971), the middle classes (*Kanchanjanga,* 1962), movie stars *Hero (Nayak,* 1966), and the British colonial takeover of feudal Lucknow *The Chess Players (Shantranj ke khilari,* 1977, Ray's first Hindi film). He has worked in tragedy, satire, comedy, and even fantasy *Goopy and Bagha (Goopy gyne Bagha byne,* 1969) as well as documentaries, children's films, and several adaptations of Bengali literature (notably the trilogy *Three Daughters* [*Teen kanya,* 1961], based on Tagore's stories). No adequate consideration of his exceptional body of work is feasible here, and as he is the best documented of all Indian filmmakers, interested readers are referred to the bibliography.

Ray's two contemporaries in the vanguard of alternative Indian cinema have both been politically and cinematically more radical, although their work has had considerably less attention, both outside India and within.

Ritwik Ghatak (1925–76) is only now getting long overdue recognition as probably India's most exceptional and original filmmaker, grappling to construct an "epic cinema" that could be true to its traditional and material roots, yet have universal resonances, many years before the notion of a "Third Cinema" became widely disseminated.[7] Ghatak was an uncompromising iconoclast and radical Marxist intellectual, who burned himself out after leaving only eight films. Much of his work was fired by the trauma of Partition (when his homeland became East Pakistan), and the acute pain he felt at "the splintering of every form of social and cultural values"[8] in modern India. Although his best-known work is *Pathetic Fallacy* (*Ajantrik*, 1958), about an eccentric rural taxi driver who treats his ramshackle taxi as a feeling (almost human) being, this is surpassed in intensity and scope by a trilogy on East Pakistani refugees: *The Cloud-Capped Star* (*Meghe dhaka tara*, 1960), *E Flat* (*Komal gandhar*, 1961) and *Subarnarekha* (1965). While the first is best known as his masterpiece, a story of a young woman who devotes her life to supporting her emotionally and economically dependent refugee family, in the process losing her lover to an insensitive younger sister, *Subarnarekha* is an even more complex and powerful film. It depicts a refugee brother and sister's struggle to survive in contemporary West Bengal but, as in all Ghatak's films, it reverberates across many layers of myth and meaning. Drawing on mythic archetypes (such as the goddesses Kali, Durga, Sita) it sets into play wider human and political concerns in an epic mode very similar to that championed in Europe by Brecht and his successors. Ghatak was often misunderstood and accused of melodramatic excesses, but his films' power lay precisely in their masterly combination of excruciatingly overdetermined melodrama with astonishing subtleties, both political acuity, exquisite visual images (notable for their powerful contrapuntal use of nature), and highly inventive, (and often breathtaking, soundtracks, which mix classical ragas or folk music with the most mundane of recorded sounds: frogs, boiling rice, a studio projector. After several years of teaching, writing and mostly frustrated attempts at new projects, he finally completed *Reason, Debate and a Tale* (*Jukti takko aur gappo*, 1974), about an alcoholic intellectual, played by Ghatak himself, who is torn between revolutionary ideals and armed struggle against the state and is finally killed in his confrontation with young revolutionaries. The film was starkly autobiographical and an ominous foreboding of the tragically premature death, two years later, from tuberculosis and alcohol abuse, of Ghatak himself.

Mrinal Sen (b. 1923) also began with open Marxist affiliations and has often talked of cinema as a polemical tool through which to expose poverty and exploitation. His filmmaking, however, has been much less consistent than that of Ray or Ghatak, exploring throughout his career an array of different formal strategies, as well as humor and irony. Sen mostly disowns his early films now as faltering steps toward control of the medium and considers his first important work *Mr Shome* (*Bhuvan Shome*, 1969). This critical and commercial success was crucial to the "new" cinema, since it was only after its release that the F.F.C. began funding genuinely low-budget alternative filmmakers. It is an apparently simple but rich film about a sour, desiccated railway official whose life is transformed by moving to a remote country station and meeting an uninhibited village girl. Sen followed this with a period of extravagant formal experimentation—very obviously influenced by Brecht and Godard—in the Calcutta Trilogy: (*Interview*, 1971; *Calcutta '71*, 1972; *The Guerilla Fighter* [*Patidak*, 1973]), which dealt with lingering colonial attitudes and the hegemony of multinational corporations in modern India. The formal play and distancing strategies became less gimmicky, more assured and assimilated within narrative in his next films on poverty: *The Outsiders* (*Oka oorie katha*, 1977) and *Man with the Axe* (*Parasuram*, 1978), the former being a particularly powerful and complex handling of issues of rural exploitation, individualistic resistance, and women's oppression. With *Quiet Rolls the Dawn* (*Ek din pratidin*, 1979), *The Case Is Closed* (*Kharij*, 1982) and *The Ruins* (*Khandaar*, 1983), Sen has moved on to tackle middle-class angst and hypocrisy. Although the first of these films makes cogent observations on women's oppression within the Indian family, and although Sen is now highly regarded by an international art cinema establishment, the trend of his work seems to be increasingly less innovative or explosive.

If broad differences of approach are apparent in the work of these three filmmakers, there is even greater variety among their successors, both those enabled to get into production with the help of Film Finance Corporation (later, National Film Development Corporation) grants or loans, and the boom of new regional language filmmakers encouraged by a number of states' local film-funding policies.

Kumar Shahani and Mani Kaul, both ex-students of Ghatak, stand at the forefront of the most uncompromisingly exploratory and innovative work in Indian cinema today, contributing not only as filmmakers, but also through their theoretical writings and lectures, to attempts to build a new cinema aesthetic from traditional roots. Both make reference to myth and the structurings of classical music, although their films are distinctively different. Mani Kaul focuses on the significance of gesture and the parameters of cinematic time and space, and draws overtly on both the formal structures and improvisational principle of Indian classical music to construct a film language, stylistically marked by a highly poetic use of bare, slow, sensual, and compelling shots, and subtle, often minimal, soundtracks. His early films used sparse narrative: *A Day's Bread* (*Uski roti,* 1969) centers around the fears and frustrations of a village woman dutifully awaiting her errant, bus-driver husband; *In Two Minds* (*Duvidha,* 1973) is based on a Rajasthani folk tale about a love affair between a young bride and a ghost who takes the form of her absent husband, and is a uniquely potent and compelling film. More recently Kaul has turned to a poetic, loosely documentary form as more appropriate to his structural concerns, and uses this to explore the relationships among Dhrupad classical music, Mughal architecture, and film language (*Dhrupad,* 1982), or traditional myths, the potters of central India today, and cinema, *Mind of Clay* (*Mati manas,* 1985).

Kumar Shahani, like Kaul, is interested in the breakdown of feudalism and the rupture represented by capitalism and modern technology but he has, in many respects, remained closer to Ghatak's project, working within a broadly Marxist perspective to develop an epic narrative cinema for modern urban India. *Mirror of Illusion* (*Maya darpan,* 1972) focuses on an unmarried woman trapped within the confines of her aging father's decaying ancestral home but through this, and a masterful use of rhythm, space, and color transformations, all rigorously motivated, the film also speaks of more fundamental and far-reaching social schisms. Shahani's characters are archetypal figures rather than psychologized individuals, and his second feature, *Vibrations* (*Tarang,* 1984), while taking a verse of Sanskrit mythology as its starting point, moves into the milieux of rich bourgeois industrialists and proletarian political struggle in contemporary Bombay. This story of a fiery young widow (Smita Patil) of a union activist who becomes a servant in the factory owner's household, befriends his wife, and becomes his lover, but finally rises triumphantly above the oppression and poverty of spirit that he represents, works on many levels. It is both about class conflict, and about a deeper psychic splitting of the "feminine principle" (as represented by Hindu goddesses in their various aspects), but it also sets up delicately ironic tensions by playing with formal conventions usually associated with mainstream cinema (yet also relating to older Indian artistic practices): luxuriant wide-screen, lush color, melodrama, familiar star actors, and even certain camera angles. *Tarang* is undoubtedly a crucial film in suggesting a way forward for an alternative cinema that does not avoid sensual or emotional pleasure, but also refuses to patronize or exploit its audience. Sadly, it has been largely ignored within India and since there is no effective independent or government distribution network, it is still, in 1986, unreleased there while having gained considerable praise and interest abroad.

For other new filmmakers, finding a niche in the current distribution market has been an important priority, and Shyam Benegal stands out for the commercial and popular critical impact he has had both in India and abroad. Benegal began with enormous small-budget success by keying into the potential of an urban middle-class market and has now, largely through the patronage of filmstar Shashi Kapoor as producer, moved on to bigger budgets and stars (although several of the actors he "discovered" have now become stars themselves). *The Seedling* (*Ankur*, 1974), his debut feature, financed by his erstwhile employer, an advertising company, brought immediate recognition to both Benegal and actress Shabana Azmi, as a servant girl, with a deaf-mute husband, seduced by a rich landowner's son. Directed within predominantly Western naturalistic conventions, *Ankur* was lauded for both its stylistic polish, its apparent realism, and its socio-political conscience. Rural exploitation remained the theme of his two subsequent successes *Night's End* (*Nishant,* 1975) and *The Churning* (*Manthan,* 1975). The focus changed to women's oppression with *The Role* (*Bhumika,* 1977), the biography of a 1940s Marathi film actress, Hansa Wadkar, which launched another star actress, Smita Patil, as the fast-living, desperate Hansa, struggling wildly against sexual and social stereotypes and exploitation. In an attempt to broaden and consolidate his market, Benegal has since made various attempts to introduce Indian mainstream conventions within his primarily Europeanized style, from *Possessed* (*Junoon,* 1978) about a Pathan's passion for the daughter of an English family hiding from the mutineers of 1857, to *The Machine Age* (*Kalyug,* 1981) on rival families of industrialists (a cross between the Hindu epic, the Mahabharat, and *Dallas*), or *The Market Place* (*Mandi,* 1983) on prostitution, which combines a study of hypocrisy and opportunism with lively farce and song and dance spectacle. Benegal's output has also included prestigious documentaries (on Ray and on Nehru) and, keeping abreast of the times, he is now also moving into television production.

Much of the new cinema has come from the regional industries, and Malayalam films, notably those of Ramu Kariat (1928–79), were the first to gain pan-Indian recognition. Kariat's *The Shrimp* (*Chemeen,* 1965), based on the superstitious beliefs of Keralese fisherfolk, inspired new filmmakers throughout the regions. G. Aravindan, also of Kerala, established a reputation for his original, imaginative style, which draws on folk theater, children's tales, and mythology in a series of delicate films, from *Golden Sita* (*Kanchana Sita,* 1977), which subtly subverts the Sita legend, retelling it through a group of wandering tribal actors, to *The Bogeyman* (*Kumatty,* 1979), a children's tale with wider implications. More recently, Adoor Gopalakrishnan has had considerable acclaim for films with increasing political resonances, from *Rat-Trap (Elipathayam,* 1981) about the lethargic resistance to change of the guilt-ridden, dispossessed, rural middle-classes, to *Face To Face (Mukhamukham,* 1984) on one man's struggle against the system, in the context of the disintegration of Keralese communist politics from the 1960s to today.

In Karnataka the most refreshing intervention has come from Prema Karanth, one of a handful of women who have successfully fought for access to finance and facilities in the overwhelmingly male-dominated industry that rules both regional and Hindi filmmaking. In the whole of India fewer than a dozen women have directed films. *Phaniyamma* (1982), about a teenage widow who, helped by a wise old aunt, herself a child widow victim, rebels against the prejudice and orthodoxy that attempt to control and limit her life, was an explosively successful debut. However, there had been a number of Kannada films throughout the 1970s dealing, in a docudrama style, with the hypocrisy of rigid orthodoxy in traditional village life, beginning with P. R. Reddy's *Last Rites (Samskara,* 1970) on Brahmin rituals and prejudices, and continuing with Girish Karnad and B. V. Karanth (Prema's husband), who worked both separately and together. Thus Karnad's *The Forest (Kaadu,* 1973) watches the conflict between two feuding villages through the eyes of a child; Karanth's *Chomana's Drum (Chomana dudi,* 1975) shows a Harijan family tempted with conversion to Christianity in order to get land; and *Once Upon a Time (Ondanondu kaladalli,* 1978) is a martial arts picture about medieval Karnataka.

Concern with oppression and the decadence of much that is legitimated as traditional is also a key note of other regional new cinemas, notably Gujerati and Marathi, in both of which local folk theater forms have been powerfully exploited. In Gujerat the form is *bhavai,* and Ketan Mehta's *A Folk Tale (Bhavni bhavai,* 1980) is a particular highlight. The film is based upon a folk tale about the son of a king who grows up with untouchable outcastes, becomes their militant leader and eventually has to fight his own father. It pays open tribute to Brecht and adapts the "distancing" devices and comic-strip-like stylization inherent in the *bhavai* form to talk with irreverence and humour about the still very serious problems of caste and untouchability. The *tamasha*—a bawdy comedy, song, and dance cum agit-prop entertainment form—has always inflected Marathi cinema, which has a long tradition of socially critical filmmaking (see page 306) but has produced some particularly exciting political films in recent years. Most notable is the work of Jabbar Patel, a doctor who began in amateur theater, and was strongly influenced by Brecht: his *The Throne (Simhasan,* 1981) is an unusual exposé of contemporary state power struggles; *The Threshold (Umbartha/Subaah* (Hindi), 1983) deals with a woman social worker's fight against male oppression and corruption and, with Smita Patil in the lead, was an impressive box-office success.

It was suggested earlier that *Ardh satya*'s commercial success was crucial in consolidating the arrival of a viable middle cinema. In fact, *Ardh satya* stems directly from the work of Shyam Benegal and the regional cinemas, both through its director, ex-cameraman Govind Nihalani, and its screenplay writer, Vijay Tendulkar, who not only wrote Benegal's early successes, *Nishant* and *Manthan,* but was also Jabbar Patel's writer and collaborator since his early theater days. The "middle"/alternative cinema is, in fact, dominated by a smallish group of technicians and stars who have been working together for over a decade: stars such as Smita Patil, Shabana Azmi, Om Puri, Naseeruddin Shah; camera operators such as Govind Nihalani and K.K. Mahajan; music directors such as Vanraj Bhatia.

That a space has emerged for a middle cinema—however defined and for whatever reasons—must be set against the fact that it has coincided with a moment of particular crisis for Indian cinema in general. Since 1982–83 illegal video libraries have been mushrooming in the cities, video tea shops have sprung up in the remotest towns and villages, and "video buses" snake the country spinning the latest Hindi releases. More recently Rajiv Gandhi's new policy to pump money into television production and expand the television network (in 1986, television already potentially reached 70 percent of the 900 + million population) has been a particularly rude jolt to an industry cushioned for far longer than most against the incursions of television technology. While individual blockbusters can still draw big audiences, cinema returns overall are at an all-time low, and public interest, especially in cities, has shifted to the numerous new television soap operas and a fresh breed of television star. Clearly, big changes are imminent and crucial to the form they take will be the terms in which the government defines its media policy. While it seems certain that the Ganges will continue to flow, it remains to be seen, however, whether our *saadhu* (world renouncer) will be washing his hands in bubbles of multistar *maya,*[9] homespun soap, imported effluents, or new fermentations.

## NOTES

1. Since 1985 three Hindi film stars have become members of Rajiv Gandhi's national government: Sunil Dutt, Vijayantimala, and, most notably, megastar Amitabh Bachchan.
2. Congress Party, quoted in Barnouw and Krishnaswamy, *Indian Film,* p. 125.
3. Lucknow, particularly C19th Lucknow, is popularly known as the center of Mughal high culture, etiquette, and arts.

4. Lit. spices, as used in cooking.
5. See Neale, S. "Art Cinema as Institution" in *Screen* 22 no. 1.
6. *Satyajit Ray,* ed. Das Gupta, C., 1981, p. 127.
7. See Teshome Gabriel, *Third Cinema in the Third World: the Aesthetics of Liberation.*
8. Kumar Shahani in *Ritwik Ghatak,* ed. Shampa Banerji, 1982.
9. Illusion.

## SELECTED BIBLIOGRAPHY

Banerjee, S., ed. *New Indian Cinema.* New Delhi: N.F.D.C., 1982.
————. *Ritwik Ghatak.* New Delhi: N.F.D.C., 1982.
Barnouw, E. and S. Krishnaswamy. *Indian Film.* New York/Oxford: Oxford University Press, 1963 and 1980.
Burra, R., ed. *Looking Back 1896–1960.* New Delhi: N.F.D.C., 1981.
*Cinema Vision India* 1–5 (Bombay), 1980 et sq.
Da Cunha, Uma, ed. *Indian Cinema 77/8, 78/9–.* New Delhi: N.F.D.C., 1978.
————. *The New Generation.* New Delhi: N.F.D.C., 1981.
Das Gupta, C. *The Cinema of Satyajit Ray.* New Delhi: Vikas, 1980.
————, ed. *Satyajit Ray.* New Delhi: N.F.D.C. 1981.
*Framework* Nos. 30–31. Dossier on Kumar Shahani.
Krishen, P., ed. *Indian Popular Cinema.* Indian International Centre Quarterly, 8, No. 1, 1981.
*Le avventurose storie del cinema indiano.* Marsilio Editori, Cinemasia 85/ Pesaro, 1985.
Parrain, Philippe. *Regards sur le cinéma indien.* Paris: La Cerf, 1969.
Passek J-L., ed. *Le cinéma indien.* Paris: L'Equerre, 1983.
Rajadhyaksha, A. *Ritwik Ghatak: A Return to the Epic.* Bombay: Screen Unit, 1982.
Rangoonwalla, F. *Indian Cinema Past and Present.* New Delhi: Clarion, 1983.
————. *Pictorial History of Indian Cinema.* London/New York/Sydney/Toronto: Hamlyn, 1979.
————. *Satyajit Ray's Art.* New Delhi: Clarion, 1980.
Ray, Satyajit. *Our Films, Their Films,* New Delhi: Orient Longman, 1976 and 1979.
*Screen* 26, nos. 3–4, May–August 1985. "Other Cinemas, Other Criticisms" (articles by Vijay Mishra, Ashish Rajadhyaksha, Rosie Thomas).
Sen, Mrinal. *Views on Cinema.* Calcutta: Ishan, 1977.
Seton, Marie. *Portrait of a Director: Satyajit Ray.* London: Dobson, 1971.
Willeman, P. and B. Gandhy, ed. *Indian Cinema.* London: B.F.I., 1980 and 1982.
Wood, Robin. *The Apu Trilogy.* New York: Praeger, 1971.

# ISRAEL

## ELLA SHOHAT

Israeli cinema is emerging on the world scene, struggling to forge an authentic national expression. Its recurrent themes—from the heroic nationalism of the early films to the rootless alienation of some of the later ones—reflect the tangled problems of identity characteristic of a developing nation. At the same time, the films display the complexity of a society whose history is in many respects unique.

A religious as well as a political entity, Israel is both the fulfillment of an age-old dream and the product of a secular nation-building process. A veritable palimpsest of historical influences, Israel stands at the point of convergence of many cultures, languages, and traditions. The Israeli cinema, like the society that it reflects, is inevitably marked by conflicting ideologies and political tensions. Along with the obvious conflict with the Arabs generally and the Palestinians in particular, Israel is rent as well by the internal divisions between oriental Sephardic Jews and Ashkenazi Jews of European background who, although a demographic minority, occupy the major positions of power. Other conflicts divide right from left and religious from secular Jews. This survey of film production in Israel considers both the films themselves and the historical-cultural context from which they spring.

Even before the establishment of Israel as a state in 1948, films were produced with the aid of certain national institutions such as the Jewish Agency, Qeren Hayessod, and the Histadrut. The newsreels, documentaries, and fiction films (many by the film pioneers Natan Axelrod and Baruch Agadati) tended to be strongly inflected by Zionist ideology, reflecting a commitment to Israel and to world Jewry, and were largely designed to present an overwhelmingly positive image abroad. With the establishment of the state a special department for journalism and film was instituted within the framework of the Ministry of the Interior; its function was to encourage the cinema by establishing links between the government and the film industry. At the same time, two major studios were founded: Geva, in 1950, and Herzeliyya in 1951. The production of these studios was limited mainly to documentaries and informational films, sponsored primarily by Israeli government agencies for propaganda and educational purposes. Production facilities and techniques in this period were primitive and filmmakers from the United States and elsewhere were invited to direct some of the more ambitious films.

The most notable work of this period is *Hill 24 Does Not Answer* (*Giva 24 eina ona*, 1955), directed by the British filmmaker Thorold Dickinson with the assistance of local Israeli talent. Like many films of this period—and of later years such as *The Column of Fire* (*Amud ha'esh*, 1953), *They Were Ten* (*Hem hayu asara*, 1961), *Rebels Against the Light* (*Mordei ha'or*, 1964), *Five Days in Sinai* (*Hamisha yamim bei Sinai*, 1969), and *The Great Evasion* (*Ha'pritza ha'gdola*, 1970)—*Hill 24 Does Not Answer* emphasized the heroic dimensions of the nation-building struggle. The successful construction of the Jewish state, the victories over the Arabs in 1948, 1956, and 1967 were presented as the heroic accomplishment of a country under siege, resulting in a somewhat dualistic representation of the conflict. *Hill 24 Does Not Answer*, for example, set during the 1948 war, deals with the personal stories of four fighters assigned to defend a strategic hill outside Jerusalem, and thus guarantee Israel access to the city. A heroic-nationalist film, *Hill 24 Does Not Answer* offers little analysis of a knotty political situation and its portrayal of the Arabs shows little sensitivity to their history and culture. Struggling for their very survival, Jewish quality is shown to triumph over Arab quantity. Baruch Dienar's *They Were Ten* (*Hem hayu asara*, 1961), meanwhile, deals with the valiant struggle of ten Russian Jews to found a settlement in Palestine in the late nineteenth century, focusing on their attempt to develop the land in the face of Arab resentment and Turkish obstructionism.

In the wake of the furor surrounding the Eichmann trial in 1962, the heroic-nationalist theme came to be linked with the story of the Holocaust and Nazism. Both *Judith* (1964) and *Hour of Truth* (*Shat ha'emet*, 1964) sound this theme, while *Operation Cairo* (*Mivtza Cahir*, 1965) suggests a link between the Nazis and the Arabs. This last film, by Menahem Golan, portrays the audacious kidnapping, by an Israeli agent, of the daughter of a German scientist working for the Egyptians. The heroic theme, however, became steadily less relevant, especially after the disillusionment that set in after the 1973 Yom Kippur War. In the wake of the war, Israeli society became less sure of itself and more introspective, doubting once unquestioned assumptions. Israelis began to worry about the status of the occupied territories and the question of the Palestinians began to insert itself into political discourse. With the rise of Menachem Begin's Likud party in 1977, the left opposition became restive, voicing a discontent which had been more muffled under the reign of the Labor party. Menahem Golan's *Operation Thunderbolt* (*Mivtza Entebbe*, 1977), a filmic homage to the Israeli hostage rescue at Uganda's Entebbe airport represents, in this sense, one of the last expressions of a dying genre.

During the fifties and sixties Israel came to participate in the worldwide wave of international coproductions. The coproductions filmed in Israel provided much-needed training for many young Israeli technicians and directors, a service which the native industry was not yet equipped to perform. Directors also came from local theatrical groups, from immigrants with film experience abroad, or from returning students of the film schools in the United States and Europe. Local technicians gained essential technical experience by working on such Hollywood films as Edward Dmytryk's *The Juggler* (1953), Otto Preminger's *Exodus* (1960), and Melville Shavelson's *Cast a Giant Shadow* (1966). The Knesset, meanwhile, passed the Encouragement of Israeli Film Law (1954), which provided substantial government financial aid and tax abatements to films produced locally. It was only in the sixties, however, that there was sufficient money and talent to guarantee a sizeable and regular production.

The economic prosperity which came in the wake of the 1967 war led to an increase in film production. In 1968 Israeli television was inaugurated with a single noncommercial channel and although often blamed for drawing audiences away from the movie theaters, it must also be credited with providing work for filmmakers in all sectors of the medium. A year later, the Ministry of Commerce and Industry established the Israel Film Center to foster filmmaking by both local and foreign producers. Hoping to attract investment from abroad, the center promoted Israel as an ideal locale for film production and services, and has concretely aided filmmakers by providing commercial incentives while facilitating contact with governmental agencies. The seventies brought the founding of the first film schools as well as the establishment of the Israeli Film Institute and a number of cinematheques. In 1979 the Ministry of Education and Culture created a Fund for the Encouragement of Quality Films, which has helped finance many projects such as Dan Wolman's *Hide and Seek* (*Machboim*, 1980), which otherwise would have been considered commercially nonviable. Such support was especially crucial in a context of a country suffering the economic double whammy of a small internal market and astronomical inflation.

After the first phase of enthusiastic postindependence nation-building, Israeli society settled in the sixties into discernible patterns of class division and ethnic domination. As a result, the films of the heroic-nationalist genre were joined by films exploring social and cultural tensions within Israeli life. Some of these films portrayed the Sephardic communities. Ephraim Kishon's *Sallah* (*Sallah shabatti*, 1964) and Menachem Golan's *Fortuna* (1966), for example, attempted to depict the life of oriental Jews in Israel. *Sallah*, directed by the right-wing satirist Kishon, is a comedy tinged with political and social satire. The protagonist Sallah soon becomes aware of class and ethnic discrimination, inadequate housing, bureaucratic morass, and the political corruption of the Ashkenazi-dominated parties. As a Sephardi, he is portrayed as emotional, relying on instincts rather than logic. Laughter in the film is generally provoked by the touching naiveté of the protagonist, who is treated as a kind of Jewish noble savage. The "happy ending"—a mixed marriage linking his children to the Ashkenazim of the kibbutz—implies a somewhat simplistic integrationist ideology. The film presents the central social problem of Israeli Jewish society—that is, the political, economic, and cultural powerlessness of the Sephardic majority—with condescending humor. The happy ending inherent in the classic comedy structure makes mixed marriage a solution for the financial problems of the oriental family. Sallah is portrayed as a "good Jew" but he is also patronized. Upon arriving in Israel, he sits down to play backgammon before even looking for a job, thus confirming the stereotypical explanation for Sephardic unemployment. The film shows the typical ambivalence of many stereotypes: on the one hand, Sallah is warm, honest, charming; on the other, primitive, ignorant, sexist. He is portrayed as the incarnation of the woman-oppressing Sephardi ("I don't speak to women," he tells a woman from the kibbutz) and the prolific breeder of endless children.

*Sallah* helped to further the careers of many of its participants. Chaim Topol, who played the title role, became internationally famous after playing the lead role in Norman Jewison's *Fiddler on the Roof* (1971). The producer Menahem Golan, a leading figure within the film-making milieu, subsequently produced successful local films as well as international coproductions, some of which were nominated for Academy Awards. His success allowed him to form, with Yoram Globus, one of Israel's leading film companies, Noah Limited, which has been producing roughly a half-dozen features per year and in 1976 became an international production company. (In 1979 Golan and Globus became the heads of Cannon films, an American production and distribution company.) *Sallah* also established the basic conventions of what came to be known as the *Bourekas* (a pastry made by oriental Jews) genre. Commercially successful but critically distained, these films placed tensions and contrasts between Ashkenazim and Sephardim within a stereotypical framework, geared toward comic relief. The term *Bourekas* also implies a melodramatic framework with certain fairy-tale elements and a happy ending. The Bourekas films of George Ovadia, for example, reflect melodramatic conventions common to many Mediterranean-oriental cinemas, conventions whose partial roots can be traced to the Arabic tradition of *The One Thousand and One Nights*, but which are here contextualized and updated within present-day Israel. Since the late seventies, another popular genre emerged, the "youth" genre. *Lemon Popsicle* (*Eskimo limon*, 1979), produced by Golan and directed by Boaz Davidson, is perhaps the most notable example. Transparently influenced by George Lucas's *American Graffiti*, the film features the erotic adventures of high school boys along with a sound track dominated by American and Italian pop songs of the late fifties.

In the early seventies the rising political and cultural self-awareness of oriental Jews came to exercise a subtle pressure on the arts in Israel, most notably in music and dance, but also in film. Menahem Golan's *Kazablan* (Casablan, 1973), one of the most commercially ambitious ventures ever undertaken by an Israeli filmmaker, combined local folklore with the conventions of the American musical comedy, all against the backdrop of Ashkenazi-Sephardic tension. Based on a sixties stage success, performed first as drama, then as a musical, *Kazablan* is in some respects an Israeli *West Side Story*, integrating two major themes: juvenile delinquency and the cultural gap between Ashkenazim and Sephardim. The title character, whose very name indicates his Moroccan origin (Casablanca), courts and wins an Ashkenazi woman despite the objections of her family and neighbors. The integrationist happy ending, reflecting the feelings of the song "All of Us Are Jews," consists of a celebration of the couple's marriage by the two communities. Taking its cue from the neooriental movement in music, dance, and theater, *Kazablan* is one of the first attempts to feature the "folklore" associated with the Sephardic communities. The film played a positive role in sympathizing with oriental culture, long considered "primitive" and even "barbaric" by the elite, but was marred by a somewhat naive and sentimental portrayal.

Golan's basically Hollywoodlike approach to social and cultural problems contrasted sharply with other films on the same theme. Filmmaker and critic Nissim Dayan's first feature, *Light Out of Nowhere* (*Or min ha'hefker*, 1973) constituted a quasi-neorealist attempt to portray the sociopolitical roots of crime in the Sephardic communities. Relying largely on nonprofessional actors, the film was shot on location in one of the poorest Tel Aviv neighborhoods. The narrative revolves around a conflict between a working class father and his two sons. As a result of social and economic problems, the older son goes off to a life of crime, while the younger son is unable to break the vicious circle of poverty and ultimately loses the will even to try. Produced in a period of strong social agitation marked by the stirrings of revolt by oriental Jews (who took the name Black Panthers from the American black organization) against Ashkenazi hegemony, *Light Out of Nowhere* represents one of the first serious attempts to analyze the social and cultural problems of oriental Jews. Dayan's most recent film, *The End of Milton Levy* (*Sofo shel Milton Levy*, 1981), in the same vein, reflects on the consequences of economic crises on marginal blue-collar orientals as well as on the cultural interaction between Ashkenazi "first Israel" and Sephardic "second Israel," seen largely from the point of view of the oriental protagonist.

The authentic Sephardic culture and tradition as it existed in late nineteenth-century Jerusalem is portrayed in Moshe Mizrahi's *I Love You Rosa* (*Ani ohev otach Rosa*, 1972). Structured as a flashback, the film begins with the recently widowed Rosa waiting, in accordance with Judaic law, for her husband's younger brother Nissim to attain maturity and either marry her or offer her *haliza*, the freedom to marry someone else. As Nissim enters adolescence, he begins to desire Rosa, but Rosa, who is portrayed as a strikingly independent woman, demands *haliza* even though she loves him in return. Her demand is motivated, it turns out, by a desire to be chosen not solely because of Judaic law but also by Nissim's personal choice. After telling her story to her grandson Nissim, named after her husband, Rosa expires peacefully. Mizrahi sets this love story within an authentically reconstructed Sephardic culture, suggesting the deep-rootedness of this community in the area. Both *I Love You Rosa* and Mizrahi's later *The House on Chlouch Street* (*Ha'bait be'rechov Chlouch*, 1974) suggest cultural affinities between oriental Jews and Arabs. In *I Love You Rosa*, for example, both Nissim and Rosa share intimate thoughts with Arab friends. In *The House on Chlouch Street*, an autobiographical film set around the time of the foundation of the state of Israel, Mizrahi shows the early stages of exploitative discrimination against Sephardic Jews. At the same time, he stresses cultural links between oriental Jews and Arabs by the use of Arabic music for the sound track and by having the characters occasionally speak Arabic. Mizrahi later won the Oscar for a film he directed in France with Simone Signoret *Madame Rosa* (*La vie devant soi*, 1978).

The first attempts at a more intimist and personal cinema, focusing on the psychological problems of individuals, appeared in the late sixties. These films emphasized rootlessness, alienation, and solitude. Although some filmmakers, Uri Zohar in particular, used this format as a springboard for social commentary, others virtually eliminated all specific reference to the Israeli social and political context. Uri Zohar was one of the first to explore personal themes in what came to be called in the seventies *Kayitz* cinema (Hebrew initials standing for "Young Israeli Cinema" but also "summer")—a body of often low-budget films which subverted national myths of idealism, heroism, and collectivity. Zohar began his career as a comic stage and screen entertainer, establishing himself as a kind of "national clown," and turning out a number of popular film comedies in which he at times played the lead. At the same time, he directed more experimental films such as *Hole in the Moon* (*Hor ba levana*, 1965). In *Three Days and A Child* (*Shlosha yamim ve'yelled*, 1966), based on a short story by A. B. Yehoshua, Zohar reflects on love and childhood. One of the first Israeli prizewinners abroad, the film was nominated for several awards at Cannes, and its lead (Oded Cotler) was named best actor. Zohar's most ambitious achievement is his "trilogy," consisting of *Peeping Toms* (*Metzitzim*, 1972), *Big Eyes* (*Einaim gdolot*, 1974), and *Save the Lifeguard* (*Hatzilu et ha'matzil*, 1976), together forming a poignant and humorous portrait of the "never-grown-up" instability of the restless *sabra* (the Israeli-born citizen named after the local cactus plant, prickly on the outside but sweet on the inside). Thus the films demystify the ideal sabra image whose basic features were first delineated in such early films as Natan Axelrod's *Oded the Wanderer* (*Oded hanoded*, 1933). Zohar's accomplishments were recognized in 1976 when he won the highest state award, the Israel Prize, traditionally restricted to celebrated artists and intellectuals, and never before given to a filmmaker.

Of all of Zohar's films *Peeping Tom* merits special attention as a personal film with a social orientation. Set mainly on a Tel Aviv beach, the film focuses on Israel's post-1967 war "lost generation," those sabras who lost interest in the larger struggles of their country and retreated into a life of bohemian escapism. The rootless beach bums of the film, the partial products of the economic prosperity of the period, superficially mimic the lifestyle of the American counterculture, without absorbing the political impetus of that movement. The lives of the characters, presented by the director with a kind of bemused sympathy, revolve around phallocentric sex, pop music, and a strong aversion to responsibility and family life. An old Ashkenazi man, a veteran of the pioneering idealism of another generation, scolds them: "That's the problem. You never accomplished anything, and you never will accomplish anything!" The literal voyeurism of the characters—they peek at women in the dressing rooms—acts as metaphor for the passivity and noninvolvement of the protagonists. As the title already suggests, their voyeurism is not only sexual. Uncommitted observers in relation to mainstream Israeli society, the film's marginal characters have a voyeuristic relation as well to Western counterculture.

Unlike Uri Zohar, who came to the cinema from the theater, the new wave of Israeli filmmakers—Itzhak (Zepel) Yeshurun, Yehuda (Judd) Ne'eman, Avraham Hefner, Igal Burstein, and others—came from film schools and apprentice work in the cinema. Their first films in the late sixties clearly showed the influence of the French New Wave. Films like Ne'eman's *The Dress* (*Ha'simla*, 1969) and Yeshurun's *The Woman in the Next Room* (*Isha ba'heder hasheni*, 1967) emphasized individual imagination and fantasy. Despite a certain New Wave charm, the films tend to be unrooted in Israeli reality. Micha Shagrir, one of the filmmakers, later explained the social irrelevance of these films as a flight from the "commitment" so emphasized in the literature of the fifties. As a symptom of this social identification, Yeshurun hesitates even to name the characters in *The Woman in the Next Room* so as not to associate them with real-life locales and environments. One of the three episodes in *The Dress*, entitled "The Return of Thomas," is especially reminiscent of Truffaut's *Jules and Jim* in its triangular love affair of two men and one woman. The characters, living in their private world, out of touch with ambient reality, at times seem to have souls more French than Israeli.

Dan Wolman's personal films emphasize a world of solitude with artistic restraint. In two early films, *The Dreamer* (*Ha'timhoni*, 1970) and *Floch* (1972), the theme is linked to the question of aging. In the former film a young artist working in an institution for the elderly comes to be torn between his involvement in that world and the youthful world of his girlfriend. *Floch* tells the story of an aging immigrant from Europe who, after losing his only son and his son's family in a car accident, becomes obsessed with the idea of divorcing his wife to begin a futile search for a younger woman who might provide him with a son and heir. Floch's obsession with continuity, typical of Jewish tradition, becomes especially understandable in the post-Holocaust era. Despite his absurd irascibility, Floch elicits a certain sympathy when seen within this historical context. The film was coscripted by the director with Hanoch Levine, one of Israel's most sardonic and anarchistic playwrights, known for gloomy surrealist plays in which Everyman is a hapless and lonely creature unworthy of any compassion. Levine returned to screenwriting again with *Fantasia on a Romantic Theme* (*Fantasia al nosse romanti*, 1979), directed by Vitek Tracz. This ironic and oneiric film deals with provincial "little people" who spend their days eagerly preparing for the arrival of the queen of Sweden. Adoration of the quintessentially Nordic glamor of the queen comes to symbolize the inferiority complex of a small Middle Eastern country which dreams of sharing the far-away romance of an idealized West.

Nostalgia for Europe is viewed from a different perspective in Daniel Waxman's *Transit* (1980). The film is a slow-paced portrayal of an aging European, Erich Neusbaum, who decides after twenty years in Israel to return to Germany. The film depicts one week during the winter of 1968 as Neusbaum bids farewell to his old-maid sisters (who never learned Hebrew), to his sabra ex-wife, and to their twelve-year-old son. Despite his many years in Israel, Neusbaum cannot adjust. His German cultural formation leads to contradictions with the norms of Israeli life, between his compulsively neat and modest *Yekke* (German-Jewish) mentality and the more free-wheeling conventions of an Israel heady with confidence after the six-day war. In this atmosphere he pines for his old Berlin, even while he recognizes that the Berlin of his youth no longer exists. Thus he belongs nowhere; the old has vanished (and as a Jew did he ever really belong to it?) and the new remains foreign. In this sense, the film resurrects the archetype of the wandering Jew, unable to find roots or solace, even, paradoxically, in the land of Zion. Waxman's intimist style successfully conveys the uprooted solitude of a secular European Jew.

Dan Wolman's later films, *My Michael* (*Michael sheli*, 1975) and *Hide and Seek* (*Machboim*, 1980) also deal with the question of solitude. *My Michael*, based on a novel by Amos Oz, and set in the Jerusalem of the fifties, explores the internal world of Hanna, the wife of a geology professor. Filtered through her subjectivity, the film recounts her progressive disenchantment with her reliable but unimaginative husband, evoking the claustrophobic existence and private hallucinations of the introverted protagonist. The film faithfully follows the events and atmosphere of the novel, interweaving the political symbolism of Hanna's childhood memories of two Arab friends, Twins, with the mundane realities of the Israeli sector of Jerusalem. Wolman's *Hide and Seek*, meanwhile, set in Jerusalem in 1946, focuses on the relationship between a twelve-year-old boy, his mother, and his tutor. His crisis of self-discovery is engendered by his discovery of the homosexual relationship between his admired tutor and an Arab, pointing to the sensitive issue of forbidden love between Arab and Jew. The film's subdued drama reflects the conformism of a society living in a state of crisis and siege, permeated by a kind of everyday political violence. By returning to a scene in some ways less complicated than the anguished present, *Hide and Seek*, as well as other *Kayitz* films, communicates a sense of lost possibilities on both a human and political level. Made with the collaboration of his immediate family, Wolman's film, like the Kayitz films generally, offers an alternative low-budget approach to filmmaking, one which eschews the well-made Hollywood formula film in favor of a modest strategy more in keeping with the resources available to an Israeli filmmaker, a strategy not without analogies to that adopted by certain Third World filmmakers.

Like *Hide and Seek*, other films of the late seventies and eighties explore the psychological impact of past historical moments and present political conflicts. Ilan Moshehson's *The Wooden Gun* (*Rove huliot*, 1979), for example, is set in the tense atmosphere of Tel Aviv in 1950, after Israel had become an independent state. The struggles and the anxieties of the grown-ups are reflected in the war between two rival child gangs who play "war games." Their behavior and interpretation of heroism, honor, nationalism, and friendship show the problematic aspect of values that had been taken for granted prior to the Yom Kippur War, and certainly within the majority of films throughout the sixties. Zepel Yeshurun's *Noa At Seventeen* (*Noa bat shva-esre*, 1982) is similarly set in the past (1951) and revolves around an adolescent, the seventeen-year-old Noa. A member of a socialist Zionist youth movement, Noa fights for her right to question received wisdom. With the Korean War at its peak, the Israeli Labor Movement is undergoing an ideological crisis, confronted with the dilemma of whether to follow Soviet-style socialism or the social democracy of certain Western countries. The film portrays the ideological stresses that tore families apart, splitting the kibbutz movement and even triggering outbursts of violence. This conflict is focalized through Noa as part of her process of maturation. As a rebel, Noa fights her way through a world of shattered values. The simple sets and minimal camera work of the film, meanwhile, appropriately mirror a fictional world prizing simplicity and modesty of appearance.

Many of the Young Israeli Cinema directors, actors, and cameramen participate in each others' films, thus offering an alternative production schema. Gedalia Besser, for example, who played the leading role in Waxman's, *Transit* also had an important role in Yaki Yosha's *Rockinghorse* (*Susetz*, 1977), which led to his being honored with the Oxford Film Festival's best actor award. The cameraperson for both films was Ilan Rosenberg and the filmmaker, Waxman, played the cameraperson in *Rockinghorse*. In this film Yaki Yosha portrays rootless alienation through a personal story. Based on a novel by Yoram Kaniuk (who collaborated on the script), the film deals with an unsuccessful painter who goes back to Israel after spending ten years in the United States. When he returns, however, hoping for self-revelation, he finds himself a stranger in his own country. In order to understand his roots, and to answer his many questions he tries to retrace his origins by registering his findings, feelings, and reflections on film. The film within the film, concerning the past (beginning with his parents first relations in Vienna before immigrating to Israel), is in black and white, a choice which, though originally motivated by financial necessity, nevertheless serves to emphasize the gaps between the different generations. Just as he reaches the moment of his birth, when he has traveled back to his mother's womb in order to set himself free, he burns the film. The open-ended narrative structure, shared by many films of the Young Israeli Cinema, reflects the collapse of the confident value systems so dominant during the two first decades of Israeli existence. The protagonist himself, who had fought in the early wars, is now far from any strong emotional or intellectual involvement in the activities of mainstream society. The title *Rockinghorse* (*Susetz*) is both a family name and a pun. The family name of the author of the novel, Kaniuk, means small horse or pony in Russian. By giving his hero such a striking name, Kaniuk not only hints at autobiographical elements, but also suggests the major leitmotif of both novel and film: constant movement without real change. The protagonist, despite his eternal wanderings, never finds peace or fulfillment. In *Rockinghorse*, as in his earlier work *Peace*,

The seriocomic adventures of a Sephardi faced with class and ethnic discrimination in Israel are underscored in *Sallah* (1964), with Topol in the title role.

Nissan Dayan's *Light Out of Nowhere* (1973) was a serious effort to explore the sociopolitical roots of crime in the Sephardic communities.

(Above)
Caught between nostalgia
for a lost European world
and the "foreignness" of
modern Israel, the aging
protagonist of Daniel
Waxman's *Transit* (1980)
bids good-bye to his son.

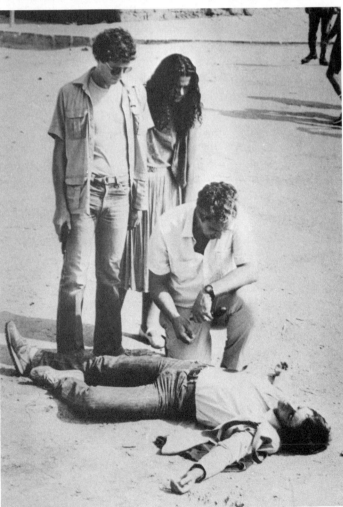

(Right)
In the thriller *Fellow
Travelers* (1983), an
ex-army officer who
supports cultural
autonomy for Arabs is
hunted down by both
Palestinian and Israeli
forces.

*a Prayer for the Road* (*Shalom, tfilat haderech*, 1973), Yosha links the concern with personal discovery with the imprisonment of his characters within the closed frame of a suffocating world.

Another reflexive film, Amos Gutman's *Drifting* (*Nagooa*, 1983), ties the isolation and alienation of its protagonist to the problems faced by homosexual men in Israel. The film begins with Robby's direct-address monologue to the camera in which he speaks of his need to make a film *Drifting*, therefore, continues the romantic tradition of laments concerning creative blocks or artistic paralysis in production. Robby also recounts the financial obstacles confronting a would-be filmmaker living on the margins of a society hostile to deviance. the antihero's alienation from Israeli mainstream society is reflected in his relationships with his family and especially with the disdainful grandmother with whom he lives. Most of the film takes place in the apartment, a visual strategy that reinforces the sense of isolation. Although Robby finds Israeli political and cultural struggles irrelevant, he is nevertheless caught up in its power structures. Certain men he brings home are on the margins not only because of homosexuality: the oriental Jew Ezri, a high school dropout who becomes a male prostitute, and two Palestinian "terrorists" who find refuge in his apartment. The film's narrative leaves ambiguous the Palestinian's rationale for having sex with Robby, but the possibility of prostitution for survival is intimated. The display of certain sympathy for the oriental Jew and the Palestinian men, however, is undermined by mesogynistic portrayal of women. At the same time, the narcissism of *Drifting* is not without self-mockery. Early in the film, for example, Robby recounts his daydream: living in Beverly Hills with his lover, Ilan, and receiving the Oscar for the first Jewish gay film. Gutman's own non-Hollywoodlike film, however, ends with Robby's voice-over explaining what the film is about: "It is about what still has to be done and the need to make this film." In *Drifting* (not unlike *8½*) Robby's failure to even begin his film ends in the realization of Gutman's film.

Women filmmakers in Israel also tend to highlight the quest for self through intimate relationships, and the quest is set, once again, in the artistic milieu. Michal Bat-Adam began her career as an actress (she played the female lead in Mizrahi's *I Love You Rosa*). Her first feature, *Moments* [U.S. title *Each Other*] (*Regaim*, 1978), an Israeli-French coproduction, revolves around a chance meeting between two young women—an Israeli writer and a French photographer on holiday—in a train from Tel Aviv to Jerusalem. Structured around a flashback to an earlier meeting between the pair, the film progressively zooms in on their relationship, so that the film becomes a review of past memories, of feelings they had but never managed to define. Bat-Adam made two more films, *The Thin Line* (*Al chevel dak*, 1980) and *First Loves* (*Ben lokeach bat*, 1982), within this same intimist psychological spirit. Another woman filmmaker, Mira Recnati, sets her *A Thousand Little Kisses* (*Elef neshikot ktanot*, 1981) in an artistic milieu as well, dissociating itself from any larger Israeli context. The visual style of the film, with its self-conscious preoccupation with painterly devices and compositional sophistication, reflects this artistic milieu. The story of Alma, the protagonist, is told through her relationship with her mother following the death of her painter-father. The discovery of her father's secret affair draws her to his ex-lover's son and she becomes torn between loyalty to her mother and her father's passionate past. Her mother, tormented by jealousy and feeling doubly betrayed, goes on a rampage of self-destruction. Despite the mother's attempts to provoke guilt, Alma fights for her independence and right to self-realization.

Films that diverge from the purely introspective mode feature artistic themes as a means to illuminate broader Israeli concerns. Based on Kaniuk's novel *The Last Jew*, Yosha's *The Vulture* (*Ha'ayt*, 1981) offers an antiheroic protagonist, Boaz (the vulture of the title), an alienated reserve officer who has lost his childhood friend Menachem in a pointless skirmish on the Egyptian front, just moments after the cease-fire that ended the 1973 war. (Strangely enough, it took almost a decade for Israeli cinema to register the after effects of that war in terms both of a certain disillusionment within Israeli society and of a sharply changed attitude toward the Arab-Israeli conflict.) In a hapless attempt to comfort the dead man's parents, Boaz informs them that Menachem (evidently something of a lout) had taken to expressing himself in poetry in his final days. Under the somewhat hysterical pressure of Menachem's school teacher father, Boaz feels obliged to actually produce some of the putative poems—which he cynically plagiarizes from a book. When the poems deeply impress the parents, Boaz becomes the reluctant "editor" of an entire memorial volume. Despite his apparent self-assurance, Boaz is a man adrift, scarred by the memories and pains of war and displaying the typical symptoms of survivor-guilt. His sexual adventures reflect his confusion, as he first sleeps with Menachem's girlfriend and then seduces a librarian employed by an organization dedicated to memorializing the young casualties of the war. For Boaz what began as a sincere attempt to console the parents of a fallen comrade soon becomes a business enterprise creating memorial booklets for other bereaved parents. Without any real effort, Boaz finds himself at the head of a small but lucrative industry devoted to the dead. The Israel IRS finally puts an end to this necrophiliac enterprise by arresting Boaz, the vulture, the bird of prey living off carrion. Not surprisingly, *The Vulture* stirred up considerable controversy in Israel and was ultimately shown only in a censored version. Probing the open war-wounds of the Israeli national psyche, the film demystifies the whole notion of military heroism that had sustained the cinema of earlier decades. The film also exposes an unforeseen side-effect of war: the felt need of many parents to idealize, through art, the sacrifice of their children, as a way of immortalizing the dead and thus coping with otherwise unbearable grief.

The social and psychological impact of constant military preparedness, along with the demystification of national heroic myths surrounding the sabra were further explored in such films as *The Paratroopers* (*Masa ha'alunkot*, 1976) and *Repeat Dive* (*Tzilala chozeret*, 1981). Unlike the idealizing attitude typical of the heroic nationalistic films of the fifties, both films undercut the myth of the brave Israeli warrior. Rather than set the films in combat situations, a more likely locus for heroism, both films emphasize the more mundane reality of military training. The disabused view of the military is especially striking in that it centers on two elite groups within the Israeli defense forces— paratroopers and frogmen. Such criticism is a sensitive issue in a country where every male Jewish citizen is obliged not only to serve three years in the armed forces, but also to spend roughly thirty years in the reserve. Military experience is an integral part of Israeli life; for many Israelis, having served as a soldier forms part of one's self-definition as a man and as a citizen. Until the war in Lebanon, the consensus was that failure to fulfill one's military duty was tantamount to being tainted. Judd's *Paratroopers* portrays the plight of Weissman, a recruit who volunteers for an elite corps of paratroopers but finds himself unable to bear the physical and mental strain involved. He tries to repress his own doubts, but his desire for self-respect prevents him from requesting a transfer. In the end, intense peer pressure and a conflict with the company commander make him break under the stress and commit suicide. Interestingly, the film does not end with his death, but rather with the cutting off, by the high command, of an investigation into its causes. Shimon Dotan's *Repeat Dive*, meanwhile, focuses on the contradictory aspects of the lives of a unit of volunteer frogmen. After the death of his diving comrade, the commando Yoav tries to console the comrade's widow Mira, and to overcome his own trauma. Unlike Weissman in *The Paratroopers*, Yoav is an efficient professional, whose bravery borders on the heroic. But the film contrasts this bravery and efficiency in battle with the ineptitude and even cowardice that characterize his private life. The challenge of combat, paradoxically, provides Yoav and his peers with a kind of refuge from the more banal, but equally real, "dangers" of everyday emotional life.

Recently the Young Israeli Cinema has become somewhat less timid about approaching explicitly political subjects, daring to deal directly with the Israeli-Arab conflict as well as with the Palestinian question. As the rise of the Likud party, the war in Lebanon, and the continued occupation of the West Bank and Gaza sparked intense debate, filmmakers such as Ne'eman and Waxman, whose earlier films were detached from such concerns, now reflected directly on political questions.

While operating within the general framework and assumptions of Zionism, they raised new questions, while remaining faithful to the genre of psychologized drama. The untranslated title of Waxman's *Hamsin* (1982), winner of the coveted Israel Prize for the Arts, refers to the hot desert wind which blows through the Middle East. Set in an old farming village in Galilee, the film focuses on the Birman family—Malka, the mother, Gedalia, her son, and Hava her daughter—who are descendants of the Jewish European immigration of the turn of the century, those pioneers who devoted themselves to *Avoda Ivrit* (the ideal of Jewish labor working Jewish land). Some of the current farm employees, ironically, are now Israeli Arabs (Palestinians). One employee, Halled (played by the Palestinian Yasin Shawap, unlike earlier films where Arab roles were generally played by Jewish Israelis), works for the Birman family. When Gedalia hears that the Israeli government plans to confiscate the Abass land, he attempts to buy it, hoping to construct a dream ranch on land conjoining his family's ancestral land with that of the Abass family. The head of the Abass family, who had been on friendly terms with Gedalia's father, is willing to sell, but he changes his mind under pressure of young Arab nationalists. For the nationalists an imposed nationalization is more honorable than the apparent "choice" of selling the land. An erotic relationship between Halled and Hava, meanwhile, breaks a taboo in the segregated society of Israel. Tensions escalate between Arabs and Jews, leading inexorably to the film's violent end in which a wild bull, impulsively set free by Gedalia, gores Halled to death.

Whereas Waxman's first feature, *Transit*, portrays rootless European immigrants, *Hamsin* examines people, both Arabs and Jews, deeply attached to ancestral land. The conflict over the land, while on one level material and economic, also takes on strong emotional and symbolic connotations within an atmosphere which is heavy and suffocating like the *hamsin* itself. By setting its drama in Galilee, which is assumed by most Jewish Israelis to form an integral part of the state, rather than on the West Bank, where the ideological lines are more clearly drawn, the film implicitly opens up sensitive issues concerning Zionism and its relation to the Palestinian question. Another film, Ne'eman's *Fellow Travellers* (*Magash hakessef*, 1983) sets political issues within the generic context of the thriller. The Hebrew title (literally in Eng., *Silver Platter*) refers to the celebrated Nathan Alterman poem whose central motif is the idea that Israel was not handed to Jews on a "silver platter." Loosely based on the case of Udi Adiv, who was jailed in Israel for his militant activities, the film tells the story of an intellectual ex-kibbutznik and army officer who wants to help Arab in Israel achieve a measure of cultural autonomy. He participates in a leftist Palestinian group, raising money in Europe to support the founding of a Palestinian university in Israel, but protests when the members of the group turn to violence. Consequently, he is hunted both by the Palestinian group and by the Israeli Security Forces, which leads to his inevitable death. Like *Hamsin*, ending the film with death suggests the pessimistic feelings generated by the ongoing Israeli-Arab conflict.

The recent explicitly political films, then, reflect the larger Israeli trajectory from self-assured idealism to a certain disillusionment. In this sense, the recurrent themes of alienation and identity crisis, typical of the *Kayitz* films, serve as a metaphor for a society constantly questioning its national and ideological identity. (That this questioning is possible at all assumes of course a kind of substratum of confidence, that the state exists and is strong.) The open-ended narrative structure of many of the *Kayitz* films, their tendency to end the narrative sentence with a question mark, forms part of this uncertainty concerning Israel's present and future destiny. Although the films still confront these issues within the framework of the individual psyche, they nevertheless show heightened critical awareness of the complexities of Israeli life. At the same time, these films offer an alternative to Menahem Golan's Hollywoodlike model, adopting a different production stance toward "Israel reality." Both trends, however, reflect the creation of an ongoing and viable film industry in the face of serious economic and political obstacles, and this must be regarded as a significant achievement.

## SELECTED BIBLIOGRAPHY

Arzooni, Ora Gloria Jacob. *The Israeli Film: Social and Cultural Influences, 1912–1973*. New York and London: Garland, 1983.

Elon, Amos. *The Israelis—Founders and Sons*. New York: Holt, Rinehart and Winston, 1971; revised ed. New York: Penguin, 1983.

Erens, Patricia. "Israeli Cinema." *Film Comment*, 18, no. 1, Jan.–Feb. 1981.

Klausner, Margot. *The Dream Industry; Memories and Facts—Twenty-Five Years for the Israeli Motion Picture Studios* [in Hebrew]. Tel Aviv: Israel Publishing Ltd., 1974.

# ITALY

## PETER BONDANELLA

Outside of Italy, little was known of Italian cinema during the fascist period (1922–43), and this ignorance created the erroneous idea abroad that the postwar Italian cinema had arisen miraculously from the ashes of the war. In retrospect, it is clear that many important contributions laying the groundwork for the creative explosion we know today as Italian neorealism must be credited to the prewar period, and the fascist regime played a major role in these contributions. The regime built one of the world's great film complexes, Cinecittà (inaugurated by Mussolini in 1937), and founded a major film school, the Centro Sperimentale Cinematografico (1935). Both of these institutions are still in operation and constitute the backbone of the present industry. Several film journals—*Bianco e nero*, the official organ of the Centro, and *Cinema* (edited at one time by Mussolini's son Vittorio)— helped to spread information about foreign theories and techniques through translations and reviews. Most of the great directors, actors, technicians, and scriptwriters of the neorealist period received their training in the fascist period, and some directors, such as Roberto Rossellini, made their first important films in the service of the fascist government. The most significant influence upon Italian cinema during the fascist era came not from Hollywood but from the French cinema of the same period. The term "neorealism" was in fact first used in an essay by Umberto Barbaro to describe the cinematic style of French directors such as Carné and Renoir.

Traditional definitions of Italian neorealism stress its emphasis on social themes (the war, the resistance, poverty, unemployment), its rejection of both traditional dramatic and cinematic conventions, its preference for on-location shooting rather than studio work, its documentary photographic style, and its use of nonprofessional actors in original

ways. In addition, the seminal essays of André Bazin popularized the
view that Italian neorealism continued the long-take, deep-focus techniques of Welles and Renoir, rejecting the ideological montage of Eisenstein and respecting, in the process, the ontological wholeness of the
reality it filmed. Film historians have unfortunately tended to speak
of neorealism as if it were an authentic movement with universally
agreed-upon stylistic or thematic principles. While the controlling fiction of the best neorealist works was that they dealt with universal human problems, contemporary stories, and believable characters from
everyday life, the best neorealist films never completely denied cinematic conventions, nor did they always totally reject Hollywood codes.
The basis for the fundamental change in cinematic history marked by
Italian neorealism was less an agreement on a single, unified cinematic
style than a common aspiration to view Italy without preconceptions
and to employ a more honest, ethical, but no less poetic cinematic language in the process.

The masterpieces of Italian neorealism are represented by Roberto
Rossellini's *Rome, Open City* (*Roma città aperta*, 1945) and *Paisan*
(*Paisà*, 1946); Vittorio De Sica's *The Bicycle Thief* (*Ladri di biciclette*,
1948); and Luchino Visconti's *The Earth Trembles* (*La terra trema*,
1948). *Rome, Open City* so completely reflected the moral and psychological atmosphere of the immediate postwar period that its international critical success alerted the world to the rebirth of Italian cinema.
With a daring combination of styles and moods, Rossellini captured the
tension and the tragedy of Italian life under German occupation and
the partisan struggle out of which the new Italian republic was subsequently born. Don Pietro, a partisan priest, joins with a leftist partisan
leader named Manfredi to combat the Nazis. Manfredi is betrayed by a
former mistress, Marina, to the diabolic Gestapo officer, Major Berg-
mann and his lesbian assistant, Ingrid. Manfredi is tortured to death
and Don Pietro is shot by the Germans, but neither reveals anything to
their captors.

The film is far from the programmatic attempt at cinematic realism
viewers believed it to be when it first appeared: characters are sharply
divided into good and evil categories by virtue of their position in the
struggle against the Germans; Rossellini skillfully manipulates the
tone of the film from moments of comic farce to instances of intense
tragedy as he concentrates upon the human emotions behind the events
leading up to the liberation of Rome. It is far from an objective, neutral
perspective typical of the realist tradition in literature, since Rossellini
aims to move our emotions rather than our intellects. After Don Pietro
is executed, Rossellini's panning camera follows the children who have
witnessed his death, setting them against the background of St. Peter's
Basilica and underlining the dominant ideology of the work—Christian humanism and a belief in the brotherhood of man.

*Paisan* reflects to a far greater extent the conventions of the newsreel documentary, tracing in six separate episodes the allied invasion of Italy and its slow process up through the boot of the peninsula. Yet, the grainy film, the awkward acting of the nonprofessional actors, the authoritative voice-over narration, and the immediacy of subject matter we associate with newsreels does not completely explain the aesthetic qualities of the work. Rossellini aims not at a merely realistic documentary of the allied invasion and Italian suffering. His subject is a deeper philosophical theme employing a bare minimum of aesthetic resources —the encounter of two alien cultures, resulting in initial incomprehension but eventual kinship and brotherhood. The title of the film, a colloquial form of the word *paesano* ("kinsman," "neighbor," "countryman," even "friend") was typically used between Italians and American soldiers as a friendly greeting, and the implications of its deeper meanings provide the basis for the work.

The opening episode in Sicily, where the Americans are cautiously suspicious of the Italians, develops into successive moments of greater understanding. In the Naples sequence, Rosellini uses the reaction of a black soldier to poverty in the city to underline the common humanity of the defeated population and the occupying army. The Roman sequence depicts a soldier's infatuation with a young Roman girl who first greets him when the city is liberated but is later forced into prostitution. The Florence episode shows the partisan struggle and the death of an Italian painter who is in love with an American nurse whom he met before the war. In northern Italy, three American chaplains visit an Italian monastery and are puzzled by the fact that the Catholic monks pray for the salvation of the souls of two of the chaplains (a Protestant and a Jew). Finally, in the concluding Po River Valley episode, Americans and Italians die together in the common struggle against the Germans.

Rossellini has provided us with the "facts" of the allied invasion in this pseudodocumentary, but the surface of reality portrayed in his simple style reveals levels of meaning that are more complex. In the beginning "Joe from Jersey" died on Sicilian soil without understanding the Italians for whom he died; at the conclusion of the film, Dale sacrifices his life willingly for his Italian comrades and becomes one of them, a *paisà* who is akin to everyone who struggles for what the Italians in *Rome, Open City* had called "springtime in Italy." Linguistic barriers thus fall in the face of moral commitment.

De Sica's *The Bicycle Thief* represents the finest example of nonprofessional acting in neorealist film. The performances of Ricci, the unemployed father who needs a bicycle in order to make a living for his son hanging posters on city walls, and Bruno, his faithful son, could hardly be surpassed by professionals. While De Sica employs nonprofessionals, on-location shooting, and social themes (unemployment, the effects of the war on the postwar economy) typical of many neorealist films, *The Bicycle Thief* is an intricate film and one that cannot be completely explained by its superficially realistic style. The mythic structure of the plot—a quest for a bicycle, ironically a *Fides* (Faith) brand, that has been stolen—suggests the film is not merely a political film denouncing a particular socioeconomic system. Social reform may change a world in which the loss of a mere bicycle spells economic disaster, but no amount of social engineering or even revolution will alter the basic facts of life—solitude, loneliness, and individual alienation. Ultimately, after Ricci has lost his bicycle and presumably his future, he only has his faithful son to carry him through his personal disaster.

Visconti's *The Earth Trembles* is a far more ambitious undertaking. An adaptation of the naturalist novel by Giovanni Verga, *The House by the Medlar Tree* (1881), it is colored by the Marxist theories of Antonio Gramsci. In many ways, this film fits the traditional definition of Italian neorealism better than other equally famous works of the period. No studio sets or sound stages were used, and the cast was selected from the Sicilian fishing village of Aci Trezza, the novel's setting. Visconti even refused to dub the film in standard Italian, preferring the more realistic effects of the Sicilian dialect and synchronized sound. Visconti retains Verga's basic plot: the story of 'Ntoni's unsuccessful attempt to better himself and his family by challenging traditional ways and borrowing money for a fishing boat, which is eventually destroyed in a storm. The film's visuals underline the cyclical, timeless quality of life in Aci Trezza. Visconti's typically slow panning shots with a stationary camera or his long, static shots of motionless objects and actors produce a formalism that bestows dignity and beauty on humble, ordinary people. In no other Italian film does the photography capture the inherent nobility of the human spirit so naturally as in *The Earth Trembles*. Of particular interest is Visconti's use of extreme depth of field in both exterior and interior shots, producing a marvelous sense of open space. Ultimately, the poet triumphs over the Marxist ideologue: Visconti captures the timeless drama of man's struggle against a hostile environment and a restrictive social structure.

These four masterpieces by Rossellini, De Sica, and Visconti are undisputably major works of art, which capture the spirit of postwar Italian culture and remain original contributions to film language. But with the exception of *Rome, Open City*, they were relatively unpopular within Italy and achieved a critical success primarily among intellectuals and foreign critics. One of the paradoxes of the realist era in Italian film history is that the ordinary people such films set out to portray were relatively uninterested in their screen self-image. In fact, of the approximately eight hundred films produced between 1945 and 1953 in Italy, only a relatively small number (about 10 percent) could be classified as neorealist, and most of these works were box-office failures. It seems that the public was more interested in Italian films that employed, however obliquely, the cinematic codes of Hollywood. A number of less important but very interesting neorealist films were able to achieve greater popular success by incorporating traditional Hollywood genres within their narratives.

Works which thus expanded the boundaries of traditional neorealism include Luigi Zampa's *To Live in Peace* (*Vivere in pace*, 1946); Alberto Lattuada's *Without Pity* (*Senza pietà*, 1948); Giuseppe De Santis's *Bitter Rice* (*Riso amaro*, 1948); and Pietro Germi's *The Path of Hope* (*Il cammino della speranza*, 1950). These four works continued the shift away from the war themes of Rossellini to the interest in postwar reconstruction typical of De Sica's best efforts, but they are even more important as an indication of how the Italian cinema moved gradually closer to conventional American themes and film genres within a superficially neorealist style.

*To Live in Peace* turns the tragic thematic material of *Paisan* and *Rome, Open City* into comic farce as two escaped American prisoners of war destroy a small village's desire to "live in peace" until the end of hostilities. When the erroneous news of the war's end reaches the town, the Americans (one of whom is a black GI who plays the trumpet) dance the boogie-woogie in the streets with the single German soldier of occupation, but in the morning when it is clear that the war is still continuing, other Germans appear and a number of the townspeople are killed. Rossellini's evil Gestapo officer is replaced by a simple German enlisted man out of the *commedia dell'arte* tradition of the braggart soldier, and Zampa abandons any attempt to achieve a sense of documentary realism in his farcical vision of a world gone mad with war.

Lattuada's *Without Pity* employs the narrative structure of the traditional American gangster film to study the effects of the American occupation on postwar Livorno, including a rather daring love affair between an Italian girl falsely accused of prostitution and a black GI. American racism is implicitly criticized, as Jerry and Angela are eventually united only in death. Lattuada's film reflects a typically neorealist message of human brotherhood that transcends not only national but also racial boundaries. Yet its generic code is distinctly American: a sinister character named Pier Luigi controls Livorno's underworld and is obviously patterned on Peter Lorre; Pier Luigi's base of operations is an American-style nightclub complete with American jazz, a symbol of the corruption brought into Italy by the black market which centered around the American naval base in the city; the film is liberally sprinkled with gunbattles, car chases, and a melodramatic prison escape.

Germi's *The Path of Hope* represents an attempt to combine Visconti's interest in the disenfranchised masses of southern Italy (*The Earth Trembles*) with the American Western, particularly narrative patterns from the classic works by John Ford. The trek of a group of exploited sulfur miners from Sicily to jobs in France now replaces the familiar Western plot of settlers in search of a better life on the frontier, and the climax of the film—a traditional Sicilian knife fight between rival lovers—replaces the expected showdown with a pistol. Germi's photography manages to achieve an epic tone and is indebted both to Visconti and to Ford.

Perhaps the most popular and most complex of these neorealist films reflecting a debt to American cinema is De Santis's *Bitter Rice*. Its melodramatic plot treats the disastrous effects of violent love on two couples. Francesca and Walter, fleeing from a jewel robbery, join a train carrying women to work in the northern rice fields; there Francesca falls in love with Marco, an Italian soldier, while Walter jilts Francesca for a star-struck riceworker named Silvana, whom he used to help him steal the rice harvest. A Marxist, De Santis began this film with the intention of providing a realistic study of the exploitation of the female rice workers and of condemning the corrupting influence of American popular culture on working-class values. The style of the film which he actually completed was quite different. It represents an uneasy compromise between his Marxist critique of America and his admiration for the American cinema, its typical genres (like the Western, the musical, *film noir*), and its classic actors (like Joan Crawford) and directors (like John Ford and King Vidor). Silvana embodies the superficial side of American culture: movie magazines, chewing gum, fast music, beauty contests—in short, everything a Marxist director would attack. But the actress De Santis chose to play the role of Silvana (Silvana Mangano) emerged from the film as the embodiment of everything De Santis professed to detest. The erotic poses struck by Silvana in a tight-fitting sweater, and not the indictment of an oppressive social system corrupted by American popular culture, made *Bitter Rice* into one of the very few commercial successes of the neorealist era. Moreover, the film's sophisticated technique implicitly rejected the neorealist contention that authentic films must be made with a poverty of economic means. While leftist critics were understandably uncomfortable with the finished product, De Santis had discovered that social protest combined with cheesecake could score at the box office, even if the work's style undermined the very values it was designed to promulgate.

Until recently, criticism of Italian neorealism consistently viewed its departures from the canons of cinematic realism, those advocated in the theoretical statements of Zavattini, as part of a so-called crisis of neorealism or even as a betrayal of the movement. Yet it is inaccurate and misleading to see the progressive rapprochement of the Italian cinema to American genres or styles as a betrayal of a movement, since no such programmatic movement even really existed. It was perhaps inevitable that the Italian cinema would move toward the archetypal commercial cinema, that of Hollywood, in the wake of its initial postwar success, precisely because Hollywood controlled the international film market. Any national cinema that set out to exploit this vast market could not, of necessity, speak in a language completely incomprehensible to its intended audience.

The American myth that had come to play such an important role in many of the best neorealist films was destined to be transported directly from Hollywood to Rome in the 1950s and 1960s. This period witnessed the dramatic increase of American filmmaking in Italy itself, what *Hollywood Reporter* columnist Sam Steinman aptly called "Hollywood on the Tiber." This development was the result of many complex factors: Hollywood itself was experiencing a financial crisis during the period it transferred some of its activities to Italy, and thus cost-saving was a primary goal. Since the studios had huge amounts of profits tied up in Italy that were unavailable to them in America due to currency restrictions, they decided to put these monies to use on the spot in Italy. They were encouraged when one of their first efforts, a B-film on the life of Cesare Borgia starring Tyrone Power—*Prince of Foxes* (1949) —made a handsome profit at the box office. Soon, a number of other, even more elaborate "colossals" were to follow, the genre encouraged by the relatively cheap labor and the extensive technical facilities at Cinecittà. In short order, works such as *Ulysses* (1954) with Kirk Douglas, *Ben Hur* (1959) with Charlton Heston, *War and Peace* (1956), *Roman Holiday* (1953) with Gregory Peck and Audrey Hepburn, and *Cleopatra* (1963) with Elizabeth Taylor and Richard Burton managed to transport much of the tinsel and glitter usually associated by Italians with Hollywood to Via Veneto and Cinecittà.

Several interesting developments emerged from this second American invasion of Italy. A number of Americans working in film fell in love with Italy, married there, or lived there off and on (e.g., Richard Basehart, Shelley Winters, Tennessee Williams, Gore Vidal, Anthony Quinn, Audrey Hepburn). Enterprising Italian producers, such as Carlo Ponti and Dino De Laurentiis, used this occasion to insert the Italian national cinema into the Hollywood-dominated market by employing casts and crews from both countries. Inevitably, such a move toward a mass market of international proportions diluted the specifically Italian content of such works; few, if any, of these projects can be said to have reached the artistic levels of the best purely Italian films of the same period. Yet many of the best-known Italian works of this era, films such as Fellini's *La Strada* (*La strada*, 1954), Antonioni's *The Outcry* (*Il grido*, 1957), and Visconti's *The Wanton Contessa* (*Senso*, 1954), did not hesitate to employ key Hollywood actors or scriptwriters. Thus, the influx of American film people in Italy assisted the Italian industry not only to open up its relatively small markets but also to choose from a broader group of actors, directors, and technicians. However, it should never be forgotten that this phenomenon of Hollywood on the Tiber was primarily the result of a crisis in the American industry. Many of the Americans who made films in Italy were on the decline in their own countries. Rarely has there been a sadder spectacle than the sight of Laurel and Hardy (Stanlio e Ollio in Italy) making their last film in Italy, the wretched *Atoll K* (*Atollo K*, 1952), because there was no work for them in their native land. Much the same experience befell Buster Keaton, whose *Enchanting Enemy* (*L'incantevole nemica*, 1953) was made in Italy toward the end of his career, and Gloria Swanson, who made *Nero's Mistress* (*Mio figlio Nerone*, 1956) with a youthful Brigitte Bardot.

In spite of the fact that Italian intellectuals and social critics preferred the implicitly political and sometimes even revolutionary messages of the neorealist classics, it had become evident that the public preferred Hollywood works or Italian films made in the Hollywood spirit. And even the great neorealist directors soon became uncomfortable with the restrictive boundaries imposed upon their subject matter or style by such well-meaning critics. In Italian cinema history this transitional phase of development is often called the "crisis" of neorealism, but in retrospect it can be more accurately described as a natural evolution of Italian film language toward a cinema concerned with psychological problems and a search for a new cinematic style.

Crucial to this historic transition are a number of early films by Michelangelo Antonioni and Federico Fellini. In *Story of a Love Affair* (*Cronaca di un amore*, 1950), Antonioni's first feature film, Antonioni employs a plot indebted to James Cain's novel *The Postman Always Rings Twice* and to American *film noir*. But his distinctive photographic signature is already evident: characteristically long shots, tracks and pans following the actors; modernist editing techniques which attempt to reflect the rhythm of daily life; and philosophical concerns with obvious links to European existentialism. The plot, a traditional story of guilty lovers and a crime of passion, is unfolded in an unconventional manner, as Antonioni refuses to divulge the information the viewer needs in a logical or systematic way. Plot thus takes second place to psychological nuances as Antonioni avoids dramatic development toward a crescendo of suspense.

Federico Fellini's early works continue this evolution from neorealist preoccupation with social problems. In *The Vitelloni* (*I vitelloni*, 1953), Fellini provides a portrait of six provincial characters which another neorealist director might have employed as an indictment of small-town Italian society. But here, Fellini, as in his later works, is more interested in creating a private poetic universe of his own than in social criticism. Moreover, the main thrust of his work concerns the clash of illusion and reality in the dreary lives of his flawed characters. This implicit symbolism looms even larger in two masterful films he made in this period which established his international reputation as an *auteur*:

*La Strada* (*La strada*, 1954) and *The Nights of Cabiria* (*Le notti di Cabiria*, 1956). In both works Fellini moves beyond mere portrayal of provincial life to reveal a new dimension, one motivated by a personal poetic vision and a particular Fellinian mythology concerned with spiritual poverty and the necessity for grace or salvation. While he is no apologist for Christianity, Fellini nevertheless employs the Christian notion of conversion as a readily understandable metaphor for the existential crises his lonely protagonists suffer.

In contrast to the characters of earlier neorealist films, whose personalities seemed fashioned primarily by economic concerns or political problems, Fellini's Gelsomina of *La Strada* and the plucky prostitute Cabiria in *The Nights of Cabiria* are more concerned with a failure of human communication and a consequent lack of human warmth. Each character is portrayed by the director's wife Giulietta Masina, and there is a clear similarity between the two figures: each functions within Fellini's poetic universe as a unique individual with the potential to receive spiritual grace. In each film Fellini substitutes for the traditional well-made narrative a relatively formless, picaresque plot. Fellini's "road" (*la strada*) represents a quest for wholeness and personal fulfillment, set within a cinematic universe of symbolic forms indebted to the surrealistic painting of Giorgio De Chirico. Fellini's vision of the possibility of human salvation offers a life-affirming vision, one which is often in sharp contrast to the more pessimistic views of Antonioni's films.

In the decade between 1958, a time when the "crisis" of neorealism had clearly been surpassed, and 1968, a year of violent social and political upheavals in Europe and Italy, which shook the country to its foundations, the Italian cinema gained a level of artistic quality, international popularity, and economic strength which it had never before achieved. Film production continued at well above two hundred films a year in Italy, while a prolonged crisis in the American industry reduced Hollywood competition within the domestic market and abroad. Not only did Italy boast a number of distinguished *auteurs*—Antonioni, Fellini, Visconti, De Sica, Rossellini—who were producing their greatest masterpieces, but the Italian cinema also witnessed the appearance of a group of younger directors who had apprenticed with their older masters—Pier Paolo Pasolini, Bernardo Bertolucci, Marco Bellocchio, Gillo Pontecorvo, Ermanno Olmi, Paolo and Vittorio Taviani, Elio Petri, Francesco Rosi, and Sergio Leone. Perhaps even more important than the many festival prizes and plaudits from critics or film historians was the Italian industry's success in gaining a large segment of the international market with film comedies (a typical product of Italy's industry) as well as with "spaghetti" Westerns, a genre usually associated with Hollywood.

The most popular films of this period (and many of the most successful works from an artistic perspective) came from two genres: the *commedia all'italiana* and the Western. Film comedy was dominated by a number of excellent commercial directors, such as Mario Monicelli, Luigi Comencini, and Dino Risi, but the greatest work of the period, and the film which best reflects the combination of comedy and social criticism typical of the *commedia all'italiana* was Pietro Germi's *Divorce, Italian Style* (*Divorzio all'italiana*, 1961). Made before Italian law admitted legal divorce, Germi's satire of Sicilian sexual mores chronicles the comic attempts of a Sicilian nobleman to force his hated wife into adultery, so that he can murder her, receive a light sentence for a crime of honor (hence the film's title), and marry his mistress. Utilizing a complex narrative juxtaposing the director's critical view of this affair with the Sicilian's biased justification of his misdeeds, Germi recreates the oppressive atmosphere of Sicilian provincial life that forces men and woman to commit violent crimes in order to obtain sexual fulfillment.

Italian film comedy was once denigrated by Italian critics as merely "commercial" cinema without artistic pretensions. This critical estimation overlooked the fact that Italian comic films often contained more trenchant social criticism than the more acceptable ideologically oriented "art" films of the period. The many excellent comic films of the decade from 1958 to 1968 provide an accurate mirror of changing Italian customs and values. They helped to force the average Italian into a greater awareness of conflicting values, by attacking age-old prejudices and questioning the inept rule of governing elites and institutions. Furthermore, they produced a wealth of great comic actors—Alberto Sordi, Vittorio Gassman, Marcello Mastroianni, Nino Manfredi, Ugo Tognazzi, Claudia Cardinale, Sophia Loren, Monica Vitti, Stefania Sandrelli—which no other national cinema outside of Hollywood could ever match.

The other remarkably successful commercial genre during this period was the Western, dominated by a single man, Sergio Leone. The Italian "spaghetti" Western owes a debt to another popular genre, the so-called neomythological or peplum film (which accounted for 10 percent of Italian production between 1957 and 1964). Set vaguely in classical times and populated by mindless musclemen and buxom damsels in distress, these works appealed to a predominantly male audience that thrived on violent action and strong, antiintellectual heros such as Steve Reeves (only one of a number of American stars who were used by the Italian industry in such works). Between 1963 and 1973, some four hundred Italian Westerns were produced, but none of them had the impact of Leone's first work, *A Fistful of Dollars* (*Un pugno di dollari*, 1964). Leone revolutionized what was at the time an almost exhausted Hollywood genre by a conscious departure from what had come to be known as the "classic" Western formula. The plot of the film was indebted both to Kurosawa's *Yojimbo* (1961) and to Carlo Goldoni's play *The Servant of Two Masters*. The Stranger, or the Man with No Name (a part which was to make Clint Eastwood an international star), is released from prison to clean up a border town infested by two rival clans—American gunrunners and Mexican bootleggers. Leone plunges us into a violent and cynical world far removed from the traditional West of John Ford or Howard Hawks. The hero is motivated by the same greed as the evil bandits, and graphic violence is accompanied by grotesque comic gags and mannered close-ups indebted to Eisenstein. A crucial artistic element is the skillful music of Ennio Moricone, whose unusual sound track composed of gunfire, ricocheting bullets, cries, trumpet solos, Sicilian folk instruments, and whistles became an international best-selling record. The classic Western gunfight becomes, in Leone's hands, a ritualistic act which concludes a narrative cycle. It employs a crescendo of music not unlike the close of an aria in a grand opera. In other important Westerns such as *For a Few Dollars More* (*Per qualche dollaro in più*, 1965), *The Good, the Bad, and the Ugly* (*Il buono, il brutto, il cattivo*, 1966), and *Once Upon a Time in the West* (*C'era una volta il west*, 1968), Leone continued to produce record-breaking profits at the box office as well as important contributions to the stylistic evolution of the Western genre. Eventually, in a number of interesting but lesser works, the Italian Western began to parody its own hybrid style as in Tonino Valerii's *My Name is Nobody* (*Il mio nome è nessuno*, 1973), or to incorporate radical political themes as in Damiano Damiani's *A Bullet for the General* (*Quien sabe?*, 1966) and Marco Ferreri's *Don't Touch the White Woman* (*Non toccare la donna bianca*, 1975).

If film comedy and Western pictures produced the industry's profits, so-called art films by major *auteurs* proved, during this decade, to be almost equally good investments. In fact, one of the remarkable features of this period in Italian film history was its ability to produce great art that also turned a handsome profit. Works such as Fellini's *La Dolce Vita* (*La dolce vita*, 1959), Visconti's *The Leopard* (*Il gattopardo*, 1962), or Antonioni's *Blow-up* (1966) were not only major films with important artistic pretensions; they were also highly marketable products on a world scale. Fellini, Antonioni, and Visconti dominated the decade with a remarkable series of major works. *Rocco and His Brothers* (*Rocco e i suoi fratelli*, 1960); *The Damned* (*La caduta degli dei*, 1969), and the somewhat later *Death in Venice* (*Morte a Venezia*, 1971) represent the best work by Visconti. Antonioni contributed many important films, including his highly acclaimed trilogy of *L'Avventura* (1960), *La Notte* (1961), and *The Eclipse* (*L'eclisse*, 1962) in black and white, and such major color films as *Red Desert* (*Il deserto rosso*, 1964). Fellini's best work includes *La Dolce Vita* (1959), his masterpiece *8½* (*Otto e mezzo*, 1962), *Juliet of the Spirits* (*Giulietta degli spiriti*, 1965); and *Fellini Satyricon* (1969).

*8½, Red Desert,* and *The Damned* are reflections of the highly complex stylistic shifts which had occurred in the work of these three dominant directors, each of whom had his origins in the Italian neorealist era. Visconti usually aimed at establishing a link between his films and a broader historical context. In the case of *The Damned,* it was the rise of the Nazis in Weimar Germany, as the film examines the tragedy of National Socialism through its disastrous effects upon an aristocratic family which controls a gigantic steel works. Its plot is highly baroque, and the family is a collection of misfits, power seekers, and sexual perverts. Influenced by the works of Wilhelm Reich, Visconti draws a parallel between homosexuality and the rise of National Socialism in the character of Martin von Essenbeck, who embraces Hitler's ideology and hands over control of the family's industries to the Nazi party in return for a sense of belonging made necessary by his guilt over his sexual escapades. The work is thus a powerful visual metaphor for the infernal nature of German moral degradation, a pathological case history underlined by the violent and hellish colors which dominate the film's visuals.

With Antonioni's *Red Desert* color photography preempts the central function of traditional plot and character. It is the story of a woman, Giulia, married to an electronics engineer who has experienced a nervous breakdown but who is now out of the hospital. The central event in the picture is her brief affair with her husband's friend Ugo. Antonioni concentrates upon the relationship of the characters to their environment, represented by the machinery and contemporary technology of a modern oil refinery. In his view, modernity's technological capabilities have outstripped its moral values. The woman's alienation is not caused by the industrial world around her but, paradoxically, by her failure to adapt to it. Antonioni's color photography is superb and thoroughly modern (only a single scene, a dream of a desert island, is shot in what we have come to consider as "natural" color). Its hues come from the industrial world of plastics, chemicals, and artificial fabrics. In some cases, the director changes the colors of objects to reflect the psychological states of his alienated characters. And he frames his shots as if he were a contemporary abstract painter, asking us to consider objects from the world of technology primarily as art forms and only later as objects with a utilitarian function. Even industrial debris and slag heaps have a peculiar beauty for Antonioni's modernist photography.

In spite of the fact that the American invasion of Rome and of the Italian cinema attracted much media attention, it failed to make a major change in the Italian film industry. Of course both languages were enriched by the new word *paparazzi,* and vulgar gossip photographers who roamed Via Veneto in search of lurid pictures and suggestive poses focused upon the superficial glamor of the resident American community. But we remember the era of Hollywood on the Tiber not so much because of its impact upon American cinema, but, rather, because of its importance in the creation of an undeniable masterpiece, Federico Fellini's *La Dolce Vita* (1959). In fact, the word *paparazzo* derives from the name of the photographer in Fellini's bittersweet portrait of the shotgun marriage of Via Veneto and Hollywood, and it is in Fellini's film that the myth of the American cinema achieves artistic expression as the era it chronicled was drawing to a close.

In *La Dolce Vita*, Fellini transforms the tinsel world of Via Veneto and the lifestyle imported from Hollywood to Rome into a metaphor for an entire civilization. It is set against the backdrop of the magnificant ruins of other eras (classical Rome, Christian Rome, baroque Rome), a notion brilliantly synthesized by the memorable image of the helicopter carrying Marcello, the public relations man, over the aqueduct of Claudius with a statue of Christ. Fellini's film (once tentatively entitled *2000 Years After Jesus Christ*) shows us a culture based upon meaningless intellectual debates, sterile love affairs, and public relations stunts, a popular culture permeated with Hollywood values and Hollywood characters. Yet unlike De Santis's Marxist denunciation of Hollywood earlier in *Bitter Rice*, Fellini's view is more forgiving; rather than the attitude of the indignant moral reformer viewing Rome as the traditional whore of Babylon, Fellini's attitude in *La Dolce Vita* is "not a trial seen by a judge but rather by an accomplice," as the director himself aptly put it. Sylvia, the sensual Hollywood actress in Rome for a film, seems to embody the kind of healthy energy and enthusiasm typical of America that jaded Italians like Marcello no longer possessed. Thus the celebrated Trevi Fountain sequence in the film, preceded by the mad dancing of Sylvia and her American friends at the Baths of Caracalla (now transformed into a fashionable nightclub) may be interpreted as Fellini's own symbolic rendition of the confrontations of these two cultures and their cinematic counterparts. Predictably, as Marcello wades into the fountain to embrace Sylvia, the water nymph who is the very essence of spontaneous and innocent sensuality, the water mysteriously ceases to flow (an obvious reflection of his spiritual poverty and that of his culture). Later, when Sylvia's boyfriend knocks Marcello to the ground, we recognize him not only as an American actor playing the role of an American working for Hollywood on the Tiber but also as the physical embodiment of another familiar Hollywood myth, for he is Lex Barker, the Tarzan of the movies.

Fellini's *8½* is the reflection of the director's belief that the cinema exists primarily for the purpose of individual self-expression: fantasy, rather than reality, is its proper domain, because only fantasy falls under the director's complete artistic control. Since cinema entails expression, not the communication of information, its essence is imagery and light. *8½* also makes an important statement about the nature of film art itself. The harried protagonist of the film, the director Guido, possesses many of Fellini's own traits. The narrative employed by Fellini in this work moves rapidly and disconcertingly between Guido's "reality," his fantasies, and flashbacks to the past of dreams—a discontinuous story line with little logical or chronological unity. The influence of pyschoanalysis is obvious in the view Fellini presents of sexuality in the film, as personal problems prevent the director from achieving artistic fulfillment. Just as the film seems to end in a psychological impasse, Guido experiences the magic moment of artistic creativity. The various characters in his life or his fantasies assemble, now purified by Guido's acceptance of them, and the film concludes with a magnificent portrayal of the sources of artistic inspiration and a moving dramatization of the moment of creativity itself. In no other film by Fellini has there been such a perfect synthesis of personality, style, and cinematic bravura.

If Visconti, Antonioni, and Fellini dominated the cinema of the period, their international prestige coincided with the rise of an extremely talented group of younger men whose first works were indebted to neorealism but characterized by more ideological intentions. The best examples of such works are Pier Paolo Pasolini's *The Gospel According to Matthew* (*Il vangelo secondo Matteo*, 1964); Gillo Pontecorvo's *The Battle of Algiers* (*La battaglia di Algeri*, 1966); Bernardo Bertolucci's *Before the Revolution* (*Prima della rivoluzione*, 1964); Marco Bellocchio's *China Is Near* (*La Cina è vicina*, 1967); Francesco Rosi's *Salvatore Giuliano* (1962); and Ermanno Olmi's *The Sound of Trumpets* (*Il posto*, 1961).

Olmi's touching examination of the loneliness of a young office worker named Domenico seems closest to the tone of Christian humanism that neorealist films frequently espouse. In its use of nonprofessional actors, its emphasis upon expressive deep-focus shots in office interiors, and its concentration upon moments of crisis in the protagonist's life where film time coincides with elapsed narrative time, *The Sound of Trumpets* is indebted to the neorealist style of Vittorio De Sica. Francesco Rosi moves beyond neorealist presentation of facts, however, to what he terms a "documented" method of making films. *Salvatore Giuliano* is less a work of fiction than an investigation (*inchiesta*) into the ambiguous historical circumstances surrounding a Sicilian bandit whose career, under the director's close scrutiny, reflects the machinations of the Christian Democratic party as well as the Mafia. Rosi combines a documentary style with a series of ingenious flashbacks to present a legal brief against Italian political institutions. It is the first of many so-called political films with an antiestablishment tone that would appear during the next two decades.

Like Rosi, Pontecorvo employs a documentary style in *The Battle of Algiers*, with a narrative structure that uses flashbacks and flashforwards to provide critical commentary on the "facts" the film presents. His careful recreation of a case history of Third World revolution owes an important debt to the style of Rossellini in his early war films. With a variety of techniques—highly mobile, hand-held cameras employing fast film stock; telephoto lenses common in television news reporting; duplicating the negative of the film in the lab to reproduce the grainy, documentary texture of *Paisan*—Pontecorvo is able to produce a hybrid style indebted not only to Rossellini's photography but also to Eisenstein's special form of ideological montage.

Bertolucci, Bellocchio, and Pasolini exhibit a far more ambiguous relationship to the heritage of Italian neorealism. Pasolini accepted many of the characteristics of neorealism—nonprofessional actors, on-location shooting, contemporary themes, natural lighting—but rejected any attempt to employ cinema to present a naturalistic view of life. He describes his love for reality as "philosophical and reverential," not naturalistic. For Pasolini reality includes mythology and dream. The style he developed in *The Gospel According to Matthew*, a biblical film made by a Marxist atheist, can be described as pastiche, mixing the most disparate cultural and thematic materials. Nothing is more striking about this highly original work than its editing and sense of rhythm, for it is with a continuous process of rapid cuts and the juxtaposition of often jarring images that Pasolini forces us to experience the life of Christ through a new perspective. Pasolini's Christ is a man who comes to bring not peace but a sword. He is a revolutionary, but the Marxist director remains remarkably faithful to the biblical text as he strips away from the sacred narrative the layers of pious cliches that the Hollywood versions of Christ's life have left in the viewers' minds.

Bertolucci and Bellocchio present a fresh view of Italian politics in their youthful works. With *Before the Revolution* Bertolucci adapts Stendhal's *The Charterhouse of Parma* in a poetic and highly lyrical study of a young bourgeois intellectual from Parma who toys with Marxism and eventually prefers a safe, middle-class marriage to revolution or an incestuous love affair with his aunt. Fabrizio, the protagonist of the film, is clearly a reflection of many of Bertolucci's own personal concerns, and like Bertolucci, he suffers from the "nostalgia for the present." He lives in an era *before* the revolution and is doomed, like so many of Bertolucci's characters, to embrace the coming workers' victory but never to take an active role in it. Bertolucci attacks the way of life which is so much a part of the class to which he belongs (like Visconti), but his most lyrical moments capture not the decadence of this bourgeois existence but its bittersweet charm.

Bellocchio's artistic perspective is angry and provocative rather than lyrical and elegiac. While Bertolucci's Fabrizio retreats into the protective womb of the Italian family, Bellocchio's film attacks the very institution of the family itself. In *China is Near* the director portrays a thoroughly dislikable middle-class family in a satire of Italian political corruption. A proletarian couple manage to insinuate themselves into the beds and thus the family structure of this group, but in the process their political ideals are corrupted and they become worse than the opportunistic family. The result is a political allegory attacking the historic compromise between the right and the left in Italy, viewed from the microcosm of a small, provincial family.

Since the upheavals in Italian society that took place in 1968 and immediately afterward, a number of major critical trends can be traced in the evolution of Italian film. Politics and ideology dominate the period, even in many of the best film comedies of the era, and even nonideological directors such as Fellini, who ordinarily remain aloof from the polemical political squabbles typical of Italian political life, are affected. Political films, and ideologically motivated film comedies, seem to represent the major trend of the period. Excellent examples of this emphasis upon political themes (hardly an exhaustive list) include: *Medea* (1969) and *The Decameron* (*Il Decameron*, 1971) by Pasolini; *The Conformist* (*Il conformista*, 1970) by Bertolucci; Fellini's *Amarcord* (1976); Elio Petri's *Investigation of a Citizen Above Suspicion* (*Indagine su un cittadino al di sopra di ogni sospetto*, 1969); *Padre Padrone* (1977) and *The Night of the Shooting Stars* (*La notte di San Lorenzo*, 1982) by Paolo and Vittorio Taviani; and *The Tree of the Wooden Clogs* (*L'albero degli zoccoli*, 1978) by Ermanno Olmi. The fact that this list is only a sampling of the many excellent and critically acclaimed Italian political films of the post-1968 period is a testimony to the great diversity and artistic richness of the industry during this era.

With *Medea* Pasolini employs the classic text of Euripides' play to explore the confrontation of Western, industrialized society with the preindustrial cultures of the Third World. Jason's theft of the golden fleece, assisted by a Medea played superbly by Maria Callas, is an analogy to the process by which underdeveloped societies lose their identity, their mythical consciousness, and their sense of purpose in a technological civilization. For Pasolini alienation derives not merely from an economic system (that of capitalism) but also from any culture which does not recognize a sense of harmony with nature and myth. In *The Decameron* Pasolini transforms Boccaccio's panoramic portrait of the rise of middle-class, mercantile culture in an age dominated by the city of Florence into an amusing portrayal of the subproletariat of Naples and its sexual adventures. His adaptation of Boccaccio's masterpiece performs an important ideological task. It underlines not only the class-oriented nature of the original text but it also proposes liberated sexuality as a characteristic of nonindustrialized cultures and uses this innocent sense of sexuality as a critique of modern values.

Bertolucci's *The Conformist* and Fellini's *Amarcord* are two very different interpretations of Italy's Fascist heritage. In Bertolucci we witness a complicated plot with frequent flashbacks and reliance upon psychoanalytic theories indebted to Wilhelm Reich on the link between homosexuality and fascism. Yet Bertolucci's adaptation of Alberto Moravia's novel also reflects his definitive break with Godard and anticommercial cinema and is itself indebted to the poetic style of Sternberg, Ophuls, and Welles. The protagonist of the film, Marcello Clerici, is a part of the decadent middle-class which supported the Fascist regime, and his search for conformity leads him to complicity in the murder not only of his former professor but also of his mistress. Bertolucci's mature grasp of his craft is evident in the famous tango scene between the wife and the mistress, with its quickly shifting camera angles, positions, graceful motions, and skillful editing.

Fellini's portrait of a provincial town during the Fascist era in *Amarcord* is much less stridently ideological but is no less a condemnation of Mussolini's attack upon the freedom of the individual. If Bertolucci agrees with Reich that Fascist worship of authority represents a repressed homosexual tendency, Fellini believes (more reasonably) that fascism in Italy displayed the nation's arrested development, its paralysis in adolescence, and the average Italian's wish for a delegation of moral responsibility to others. Every collective event that takes place in the town is an occasion of total stupidity, part of a gigantic leveling process which buries individuality in mass conformity before absurd symbols of power. This is clearest in the imaginary Fascist wedding before an enormous bust of Mussolini made from pink and white flowers: the entire population is turned into a collective, unthinking entity under Il Duce's benevolent gaze. And viewers of every culture can recognize themselves in the townspeople, who are not only unquestionably Italian but are also typical of every contemporary society.

Two directors became identified almost exclusively with trenchant critiques of Italian political life in this period: Elio Petri and Francesco Rosi. Petri's works, blending his ideological message with suspense and slick commercial presentation, have always been popular abroad. *Investigation of a Citizen Above Suspicion* is his best work and succeeds because it presents contemporary Italian politics in an abstract, almost philosophical manner, not unlike one of Kafka's parables, and his message is applicable not only to power in Italy but everywhere. The film employs a masterful plot concerning a police inspector who murders his mistress, then defies the police to arrest him now that he has been promoted to head of the political section. For Petri power reduces all of us to an infantile state, and in the flashbacks picturing the inspector and his mistress, we witness the policeman playing a role as her surrogate father. Part of the policeman's motivation for his crime is his wish to experience the cathartic experience of confession available to the average

Anna Magnani as Pina, trying to reach her arrested lover in Rossellini's celebrated neorealist classic *Rome, Open City* (1945).

In Rossellini's pseudo-documentary *Paisan* (1946), a drunken GI named Joe confuses illusion and reality in a Neapolitan puppet show.

Vittorio De Sica made brilliant use of nonprofessional actors in *The Bicycle Thief* (1948), with its overtones of an almost mythic quest.

The stately formalism of the camera work in Luchino Visconti's *The Earth Trembles* (1948) captures the statuesque dignity of fishermen's wives awaiting their husbands' return.

In Federico Fellini's *The Nights of Cabiria* (1956), the prostitute Cabiria (Giulietta Masina) is once again frustrated in her search for love and human compassion.

In Pietro Germi's satirical *Divorce, Italian Style* (1961), a Sicilian nobleman (Marcello Mastroianni), left, tries to lure his wife into adultery so that he can dispose of her in a "crime of passion."

Harmonica (Charles Bronson) confronts three gunmen sent to kill him in Sergio Leone's *hommage* to *High Noon*, the 1968 film *Once Upon a Time in the West*.

Color was central in Michelangelo Antonioni's *Red Desert* (1964). Here he arranges his actors (Carlo Chionetti, Monica Vitti, Richard Harris) within a frame emphasizing the abstract use of color in modernist paintings.

In the finale of Fellini's masterpiece, *8 1/2* (1962), his alter ego Guido (Marcello Mastroianni) forms the magic circle that symbolizes perfect artistic creation.

Bernardo Bertolucci's *The Conformist* (1970) explores the psychology of a middle-class Fascist. Marcello (Jean-Louis Trintignant) watches impassively as his anti-Fascist mistress (Dominique Sanda) is murdered by Fascist agents.

The debt to the grotesque *commedia dell'arte* is vivid
in the portrayal of the Nazi concentration camp
commandant (Shirley Stoller) in Lina Wertmüller's
*Seven Beauties* (*Pasqualino settebellezze*, 1975).

A child's fantasy of the liberation of Tuscany colors a battle between partisans and Fascists
in Vittorio and Paolo Taviani's masterful *The Night of the Shooting Stars* (*La notte di San
Lorenzo*, 1982).

citizen, but his wish is impossible, for he cannot be held accountable for his misdeeds since he represents the ultimate power of the state. Petri leaves us with a puzzle: who will guard the guardians?

Francesco Rosi's many interesting political films are less comprehensible abroad, since they have a more specific connection to actual events in Italian daily life. He continued the richly documented briefs against the political system he began with *Salvatore Giuliano* in a series of excellent works: *Lucky Luciano* (1973), a probing look into the link between American politicians and the rise of the Mafia in Sicily; *Excellent Cadavers (Cadaveri eccellenti*, 1975), a chilling parable of the connection between political power and corruption in Italy, adapted from a novel by Leonardo Sciascia, where the image of the Mafia is transformed into a universally comprehensive metaphor for corrupt, absolute power everywhere in the world. Perhaps his best recent work is *Three Brothers (Tre fratelli*, 1981), a view of contemporary Italian life seen through the lives of three brothers who return to southern Italy for the funeral of their mother. These three men embody the political and social problems of the last decade: one is a Roman judge leading an antiterrorist squad; another teaches delinquent children in an overcrowded correctional institution; the third is a factory worker in Turin who supports an autonomous workers' group that espouses the very urban terrorism his older brother combats. The three men are displaced peasants, now part of a culture that is totally different from the society of their childhood. Each of the brothers feels a nostalgia for the past he has left behind and is shown as being rootless in a world he hardly understands. In a flashback to the American invasion of Sicily, one of the brothers encounters Italo-American soldiers, who jump from their tanks and kiss the soil from which their ancestors sprang. Rosi thus juxtaposes the Italo-Americans, who have returned to their origins, to contemporary Italians, who have lost their cultural roots and therefore their personal identities in the modern world.

The last decade has witnessed the maturation of the Taviani brothers and Ermanno Olmi. These three men have emerged as major figures whose works frequently contend for prizes at international festivals and who have made important contributions to the evolution of the Italian cinema. Olmi's most important recent work, *The Tree of the Wooden Clogs*, is one of many examples of a successful work financed originally by the Italian state-controlled television system (the RAI), an increasingly important source of funding for major Italian works or for co-productions with other national cinemas. Olmi's film is a patient recreation of peasant life on a farm near Bergamo at the turn of the nineteenth century. Its style recalls the conventions of neorealism, employing nonprofessional peasants from the area who speak their local dialect. The three-hour length of the film allows Olmi to recreate the slow rhythms of life in a preindustrial peasant culture. The central event of the film occurs when a peasant's son breaks his wooden clogs on the way home from school; intent upon safeguarding his son's education (and a possible economic improvement in his future), the father (having no other wood) cuts down one of the master's trees to fashion another pair of clogs. When his deed is discovered, the entire family is driven from the land. Here, in one seemingly insignificant event, Olmi tells the viewer more about the exploitation of a cruel and inhuman economic system in the past century than all of the richly orchestrated revolutionary rhetoric of Bernardo Bertolucci's *1900* (*Novecento*, 1976). Olmi's film contains a political message, yet its implicit denunciation of man's inhumanity to man is combined with its reverence for the simple Christian brotherhood reflected in the peasant community.

Equally eloquent political statements are contained in the best recent works by Vittorio and Paolo Taviani: *Padre Padrone* and *The Night of the Shooting Stars*. The first work is based upon an autobiographical account of how an illiterate Sardinian shepherd struggled to become a professor of linguistics. The acquisition of standard Italian thus becomes a metaphor for the acquisition of full citizenship in modern Italian society. The directors draw a chilling portrait of the authoritarian relationship between fathers and sons in the stern, archaic Sardinian culture which they use as a metaphor for the even more repressive relationship between the individual and the state. In the process, the Tavianis play with the conventions of cinematic realism (both the actor who plays the linguist Gavino Ledda and Ledda himself appear in the film).

*The Night of the Shooting Stars* is an even more masterful work, creating a world of fantasy and imagination in the midst of the horrible events surrounding the liberation of Tuscany in August 1944. For the villagers of San Martino, the feast of San Lorenzo is a time when wishes come true. The essentially true account of the flight of a group of villagers from San Martino to meet the advancing American army is told from the viewpoint of an adult woman, who lived through the event years earlier. As she recounts the story to her daughter on another night of San Lorenzo, the shooting stars return and the villagers make their traditional wishes. We thus see the horror of the war through the eyes of a child and as if it were told as a simple bedtime tale for children. The result is a compelling mixture of fantasy and lyric poetry rarely achieved by the cinema. One young girl encounters some soldiers and sees them as American soldiers come to rescue her (in fact, they are Germans who murder her). Villagers hear the strains of "The Battle Hymn of the Republic" and rush to greet their liberators, only to discover that the music emanates from a mysteriously abandoned record player. The death of one of the Fascists is portrayed as a struggle between good and evil, as partisans and Fascists fight for survival in the richly golden wheat fields surrounding the village. The resulting combination of tragedy and poetry in the work is ample evidence that the Italian cinema continues to produce directors of genius.

While politically oriented films have tended to dominate film production after 1968, traditional film comedies continue to provide the backbone for the Italian industry and are consistently the most popular works in the peninsula. The comedies of the current period are, however, far more concerned with important social issues than were similar works produced before the upheavals of 1968. Taken as a group, these works embody a black, grotesque vision of contemporary Italian society, and the laughter in these works is bittersweet. Perhaps the best example of this kind of modified *commedia all'italiana* is Franco Brusati's *Bread and Chocolate (Pane e cioccolata*, 1973), an indictment of the conditions experienced by Italian "guest workers" in Switzerland. Nino Manfredi's performance as Giovanni Garofoli, a southern Italian worker pathetically out of step with the cleanliness and tidiness of Swiss culture, is one of the best of the era. The film cruelly juxtaposes a Swiss vision of Germanic racial purity to the more exuberant and humane (if more tragic) southern Italian mentality. Garofoli is condemned to live in a sterile culture he detests in order to eke out a meager living. Perhaps the most disturbing scene in the film is a surrealistic vision of a group of illegal Italian immigrants who work and live in a chicken coop, killing chickens for their Swiss employer. Housed in a building which forces them to stoop when they work, they turn into grotesque parodies of the animals they kill to survive, even speaking in henlike clucks. No film of the recent past does more to destroy the superficial image of Italy as a land of happy peasants playing the mandolin than *Bread and Chocolate*. Instead of the sunny Italy we see in tourist brochures, Brusati offers us a very unflattering portrait of a nation forced to send its sons abroad to survive.

The best comedies produced in recent years have been directed by Ettore Scola and Lina Wertmüller. Ettore Scola began working in the cinema as a scriptwriter on dozens of comic films produced in the 1950s and the early 1960s. His recent works are indebted to earlier comedies. In a number of important films—*We All Loved Each Other Very Much (C'eravamo tanto amati*, 1974), *Dirty, Mean and Nasty (Brutti, sporchi e cattivi*, 1976), and *The Terrace (La terrazza*, 1980)—Scola employs a metacinematic narrative to treat the history of Italian cinema itself, examining not only the heritage of neorealism (especially his model Vittorio De Sica) but also the assumptions of *commedia all'italiana. We All Loved Each Other Very Much* is the most complex of these films, combining a consideration of the many social and political changes Italy has undergone since the fall of the Fascist regime with an equally comprehensive survey of major developments in the history of postwar Italian film. It opens in color in the present. Three friends who once fought together in the Resistance—a wealthy lawyer, an intellectual, and a worker—provide Scola with a cross-section of Italian life. The personal histories of these three individuals are presented in flashbacks shot in the various cinematic styles of different historical periods. A flashback to the partisan days is shot in black and white in a documentary style typical of Rossellini's *Paisan*. Aldo Fabrizi, the actor who achieved international fame with his role as Rossellini's partisan priest in *Rome, Open City*, is used by Scola to symbolize the degeneration of the ideals of the Resistance in the postwar era. He is now a disgustingly obese gangster whose daughter marries the lawyer—once the most idealistic of the three friends, but now a man who trades away his principles for wealth and social position in a consumer-oriented society. In scenes devoted to the 1950s and the 1960s, Scola combines a treatment of the so-called Italian economic miracle with a style reminiscent of Antonioni's *Eclipse*. He also recreates the shooting of Fellini's *La Dolce Vita*. Each of the three friends falls in love with the same woman, although only the worker manages to win her affection. Scola's work can thus be read on a number of levels. It is, of course, an excellent résumé of Italian cinematic history from neorealism to the present. But it is also a political allegory: the three friends represent different social groups (middle class, intelligentsia, proletariat), with the woman they love symbolizing Italy herself; their relationships reflect the shifting social and political interchange among Italy's major social groups in the postwar era.

*Dirty, Mean, and Nasty* is a humorous remake of De Sica's proletarian fairy tale, *Miracle in Milan* (*Miracolo a Milano*, 1950). However, Scola completely alters De Sica's fanciful utopian shantytown and his happy poor; in Scola's contemporary shantytown every positive characteristic of the poor in De Sica's classic work is reversed. Instead of patient, long-suffering, and downtrodden people, Scola shows us vicious, brutish, mean, and nasty individuals without any redeeming moral values who have become what they are because of a desperate economic system. In *The Terrace* Scola examines the genre so crucial to his own career as a director and scriptwriter, the *commedia all'italiana*. He continues his metacinematic examination of Italian film history in this work with a narrative that addresses the very possibility of making film comedies. The structure of the film is episodic: vignettes of different characters are presented around one of Rome's open-air terraces. All of the characters are connected to the cinema—an intellectual, a scriptwriter, a journalist, a film producer. All of the episodes are repetitious, beginning and ending nowhere, underlining the emptiness and lack of creativity Scola sees in the industry. The presence of Italy's greatest comic actors, Gassman, Mastroianni, Tognazzi, makes this lack of creativity even more troubling, for they represent comic types who are no longer capable of making us laugh. Yet *The Terrace* is a very successful work; like Fellini's *8½*, it is comedy that treats the impossibility of making comedy, a bittersweet vision of a society in which we no longer can employ laughter as a corrective.

One of the most interesting developments in Italian cinema in recent years is the rise of two front-ranking women directors, Lina Wertmüller and Liliana Cavani. While all of their films may be classified as politically oriented, Wertmüller's works reflect traditional Italian comic conventions (with a special debt to Federico Fellini), while Cavani may be considered closer in spirit to the late films of Luchino Visconti in theme and style. Cavani began her work in documentaries for the RAI after graduating from the Centro Sperimentale. From brief films on Nazi Germany, Stalin, Pétain, and women in the Italian Resistance, she passed to her first feature-length work for television, *Francis of Assisi* (*Francesco d'Assisi*, 1966). She avoids the traditionally pious interpretation of this religious reformer and concentrates on Francis's concern for the poor and his rejection of the hierarchy of the Catholic Church. Equally interesting is her next coproduction for Italian television, *Galileo* (1968), a didactic but interesting study of the great Florentine scientist and his conflict with the church.

Cavani's most controversial and most important film to date is *The Night Porter* (*Il portiere di notte*, 1974), a work savagely reviewed in the United States but one which was highly regarded in Europe. A chance encounter in Vienna in 1957 between Max, a former SS officer in a concentration camp and Lucia, a former inmate there with whom he carried on a sadomasochistic love affair, leads both characters to revert to their relationship of twelve years earlier. Cavani's interpretation of the Holocaust is one of the most disturbing in recent memory. Her thesis is that the most horrifying aspect of life in the concentration camps was that it revealed the depths of evil *every* human being is capable of; victims were not innocents but had learned from the Nazis how to practice evil as well as how to experience it. What disturbs most critics in this film (and in works by Lina Wertmüller) is that eroticism is employed as a vehicle for discussing the Holocaust and the moral dilemmas it poses. In a more recent work, *The Skin* (*La pelle*, 1981), Cavani provides a novel interpretation of Italian life under the American occupation that revises the optimistic view espoused in many neorealist works. During the liberation of Rome, an American military parade is interrupted by a symbolic accident, as one of the Italians trying to grasp a chocolate bar from a passing vehicle is squashed under its treads. Human history, Cavani reminds us, is made at the expense of sacrifice, literally from our hides.

While Cavani's style, inspired in part by Visconti's lush historical recreations, has never gained much popularity in the United States, few Italian directors in recent memory have created such a positive critical reception as Lina Wertmüller. In a series of excellent films—*The Seduction of Mimi* (*Mimi metallurgico ferito nell'onore*, 1971); *Love and*

*Anarchy (Film d'amore e d'anarchia,* 1972); *Swept Away (Travolti da un insolito destino nell'azzurro mare d'agosto,* 1974); and her master-piece, *Seven Beauties (Pasqualino Settebellezze,* 1975)—Wertmüller combines an exuberant imagery indebted to Fellini with a concern for topical political issues, all set within the conventions of traditional Italian comedy, with its vulgarity, stock characters, and frontal attack upon society's values. The comic vehicle of her films guarantees her works a wider audience than Cavani, but her films are no less polemical and political in tone.

*Seven Beauties* treats the Holocaust in a manner almost as controversial as *The Night Porter.* In flashbacks the plot moves from wartime Nazi Germany to prewar Fascist Italy (Naples): the main character is a Neapolitan dandy who lives by his wits but whose nefarious deeds eventually cause him to be sent to the eastern front and ultimately to a concentration camp. There, in order to survive, he desperately seduces the obese commandant of the camp, who then forces him to murder his best friend in order to save his own life. Wertmüller's film thus portrays a man whose sole reason for living is to survive, even at the expense of neglecting all moral values. Her combination of comic tragic moods in depicting the Holocaust offended many critics, but this debt to the traditional Italian grotesque *commedia dell'arte* is an absolutely essential characteristic of her style.

Forty years after the appearance of Rossellini's *Rome, Open City,* the direction of Italian cinema seems somewhat uncertain. With the passage of time, of course, many of its greatest talents have disappeared; Rossellini, De Sica, Petri, Pasolini, Visconti, Germi, and a number of distinguished scriptwriters and actors have all died. Antonioni and Fellini are still working, and a majority of the second generation of directors are still productive (Rosi, the Taviani brothers, Scola, Wertmüller, Cavani, Bertolucci). The weakness of the Italian industry has never been a result of lack of talent. Instead, it has been caused by its unstable economic structure and its inferior production, distribution, and financial system in competition with the giant Hollywood companies that control even the internal market in Italy. However, the Italian cinema has of late received important assistance from the state television network (RAI) with major coproductions that have produced some of the best works of the past decade (*Padre Padrone, The Tree of the Wooden Clogs,* Fellini's *Clowns* [*I clowns,* 1970], Bertolucci's *The Spider's Stratagem* [*La stratagia del ragno,* 1969]). Furthermore, a number of major Italian productions have received international screening on world television with very profitable results: Franco Zeffirelli's *Jesus of Nazareth (Gesú di Nazareth,* 1977) and Giuliano Montaldo's *Marco Polo* (1982). Italian producers have recently begun work on mini-series for television to rival such popular American imports as *Dallas* and *Dynasty.* Whether the Italian industry can meet the stiff American competition in the growing market for television films (not to mention the expanding video market) remains to be seen, but the industry shows signs of recognizing this serious economic challenge and responding to it with imagination and determination.

Perhaps the most encouraging news in the last several years has been the emergence of what must be termed a third generation of Italian directors, younger artists whose performance at the box office has of late far outdistanced even their more illustrious older colleagues, such as Fellini and Antonioni. Their names are not yet familiar to American audiences: Maurizio Nichetti, Nanni Moretti, Carlo Verdone, Massimo Troisi, Peter Del Monte, Pupi Avati. But their achievements at the box office in Italy and at various European film festivals have already demonstrated their precocious talents. Some of the new faces—Nichetti, Moretti, Verdone, Troisi—work in the comic genre but have brought important modifications to the traditional conventions of the *commedia all'italiana*. Nichetti's *Ratataplan* (1979; the title is the Italian onomatopoeic equivalent for a drum roll) looks back to the classic American silent comedy and is entirely done in pantomine. This hilarious tale of a waiter's misadventures in Milan stole the show at the 1979 Venice Film Festival from older directors such as Bertolucci, Pontecorvo, and the Taviani brothers. Moretti's second feature film, *Golden Dreams* (*Sogni d'oro*, 1981)—a work indebted not only to the classics of American film comedy (the Marx brothers, Laurel and Hardy, Buster Keaton, Chaplin), as well as to recent films by Mel Brooks and Woody Allen—is a metacinematic and playful treatment of filmmaking in which Moretti plays a young director producing a film entitled *Freud's Mama*. It is a contemporary version of Fellini's *8½* and was awarded a Golden Lion at the Venice Festival of 1981.

Other directors have returned to dialect comedies, employing not standard Italian but the patois of Naples or Rome. Carlo Verdone's *Life is Beautiful* (*Un sacco bello*, 1980) stars the director himself in a number of different roles in the same film. Verdone's model is obviously Peter Sellers, but his humor is strictly Roman in flavor. Even more successful at the box office was Troisi's first feature, *I'm Starting from Three* (*Ricomincio da tre*, 1981), a version of an American road picture, which came close to breaking box-office records in Italy at a cost of only $450 thousand. Works such as these encounter a major obstacle in foreign markets, however, since so much of their humor depends upon comprehension of the dialects so integral to their appeal.

Mention should also be made of Peter Del Monte, a younger director whose *Sweet Pea* (*Piso pisello*, 1981) was a commercial success in Italy and whose other recent films have attracted favorable critical notice at festivals and even foreign capital for future works. Del Monte's personal background reflects the hybrid nature of contemporary Italian filmmaking itself: born in the United States to an Italian father and a

German mother, Del Monte emigrated to Italy at the age of ten. As one might expect, the dominant theme in his films is the search for identity that is accompanied by the search for a personal style. His work is often compared to that of Wim Wenders in Germany, for whose films he feels a particular affinity.

While musicals are traditionally linked to Hollywood, one of the most original Italian films of the past decade is a musical by Pupi Avati, *Help Me to Dream* (*Aiutami a sognare*, 1981). Its title inspired by the Fats Waller song, this film is a bittersweet interpretation of Italy's love affair with America and American culture, set in a northern Italian town where a group of upper-class Italians are awaiting the arrival of American troops in 1943. There, a star-struck Italian girl meets a downed American airman, falls in love with him (while playing old American jazz records and, from time to time, breaking out into hilarious production numbers taken from Hollywood musicals). With the end of the war, the airman leaves, and the Italian girl waits for his return— an event that never occurs. *Help Me to Dream* represents a final goodbye to the myth of America that has been so integral a part of Italian cinema since the advent of neorealism. The Italians are ultimately betrayed not so much by America itself (which promised nothing) as by the myth of the American cinema, which is revealed by Avati to have been a projection of their own illusions and dreams.

Perhaps no other national cinema since the war has so consistently provided such an honest, entertaining, and important vision of a national culture as has Italy's postwar cinema. This brief essay can only hope to suggest the variety of its production and the richness of its artistic contributions to the evolution of cinematic language in the last four decades. While its industry has continuously been plagued by economic instability and stiff competition from Hollywood, its filmmakers have continued to show an originality and a perennial response to pressing artistic and social issues of the postwar period that augurs well for its future in the last years of this century.

## SELECTED BIBLIOGRAPHY*

Aprà, Adriano and Patrizia Pistagnesi, eds. *The Fabulous Thirties: Italian Cinema 1929–1944*. Milan: Electra International, 1979.

Armes, Roy. *Patterns of Realism: A Study of Italian Neo-Realism*. Cranbury: A. S. Barnes, 1971.

Bazin, André. *What Is Cinema? II*. Berkeley: University of California Press, 1971.

*A fuller bibliography on the Italian cinema can be found in the author's *Italian Cinema: From Neorealism to the Present*. (Ungar, 1983), including works in languages other than English, interviews, filmscripts, and catalogues of yearly film production.

Betti, Liliana. *Fellini: An Intimate Portrait.* Boston: Little, Brown, 1979.

Bettetini, Gianfranco. *The Language and Technique of the Film.* The Hague: Mouton, 1973.

Bondanella, Peter. "America and the Italian Cinema." *Rivista di Studi Italiani* 2 (1984): 106–25.

———. "Course File: Italian Cinema from Neorealism to the Present." *American Film Institute Education Newsletter* 6 (March–April 1983): 4–10.

———, ed. *Federico Fellini: Essays in Criticism.* New York: Oxford University Press, 1978.

———. "The Historiography of the Italian Cinema." *Film Studies: Proceedings of the Purdue University Sixth Annual Conference on Film.* W. Lafayette: Purdue University Press, 1982, pp. 120–25.

———. *Italian Cinema: From Neorealism to the Present.* New York: Frederick Ungar Publishing Co., 1983.

Brunetta, Gian Piero. "The Conversion of the Italian Cinema to Fascism in the 1920's." *The Journal of Italian History* 1 (1978): 432–54.

Burke, Frank. *Federico Fellini.* Boston: Twayne, 1984.

Cameron, Ian and Robin Wood. *Antonioni.* London: Studio Vista, 1968.

Cannella, Mario. "Ideology and Aesthetic Hypotheses in the Criticism of Neo-Realism." *Screen* 14 (1973–74): 5–60.

Carroll, Kent E., ed. *Closeup: Last Tango in Paris.* New York: Grove Press, 1973.

Chatman, Seymour. *Antonioni; or, The Surface of the World.* Berkeley: University of California Press, 1985.

Costello, Donald. *Fellini's Road.* Notre Dame: University of Notre Dame, 1983.

de Lauretis, Teresa. "The Case of *The Night Porter*: A Woman's Film?" *Film Quarterly* 30 (1976–77): 35–38.

Fellini, Federico. *Fellini on Fellini.* London: Eyre Methuen, 1976.

Ferlita, Ernest and John R. May. *The Parables of Lina Wertmüller.* New York: Paulist Press, 1977.

Frayling, Christopher. *Spaghetti Westerns: Cowboys and Europeans from Karl May to Sergio Leone.* London: Routledge and Kegan Paul, 1981.

Guarner, José Luis. *Roberto Rossellini.* New York: Praeger, 1970.

Hay, James W. *Popular Film Culture in Fascist Italy.* Bloomington: Indiana University Press, 1986.

Horton, Andrew and Joan Magretta, eds. *Modern European Filmmakers and The Art of Adaptation.* New York: Frederick Ungar Publishing Co., 1981.

Huss, Roy, ed. *Focus on Blow-Up.* Englewood Cliffs, NJ: Prentice-Hall, 1971.

Kolker, Robert P. *The Altering Eye: Contemporary International Cinema.* New York: Oxford University Press, 1983.

———. *Bernardo Bertolucci.* New York: Oxford University Press, 1985.

Lawton, Ben. "Boccaccio and Pasolini: A Contemporary Reinterpretation of *The Decameron*." In Mark Musa and Peter Bondanella, trans. and eds. *The Decameron: A Norton Critical Edition* (New York: Norton, 1977), pp. 306–22.

———. "Italian Neorealism: A Mirror Construction of Reality." *Film Criticism* 3 (1979): 8–23.

Leprohon, Pierre. *Michelangelo Antonioni.* New York: Simon and Schuster, 1963.

_____. *The Italian Cinema*. London: Secker & Warburg, 1972.

Liehm, Mira. *Passion and Defiance: Film in Italy from 1942 to the Present.* Berkeley: University of California Press, 1984.

Mellen, Joan. *Film Guide to The Battle of Algiers*. Bloomington: Indiana University Press, 1973.

Nowell-Smith, Geoffrey. *Visconti*. New York: Viking, 1973.

Overby, David, ed. *Springtime in Italy: A Reader on Neo-Realism*. Hamden: The Shoe String Press, 1978.

Perry, Ted. *Filmguide to 8½*. Bloomington: Indiana University Press, 1975.

Prats, Armando J. *The Autonomous Image: Cinematic Narration & Humanism*. Lexington: University of Kentucky Press, 1981.

Rosenthal, Stuart. *The Cinema of Federico Fellini*. New York: A. S. Barnes, 1976.

Rossi, Patrizio. *Roberto Rossellini: A Guide to References and Resources*. Boston: G. K. Hall, forthcoming.

Roud, Richard, ed. *Cinema: A Critical Dictionary*. 2 vols. New York: Viking, 1980.

Siciliano, Enzo. *Pasolini: A Biography*. New York: Random House, 1982.

Snyder, Stephen. *Pier Paolo Pasolini*. Boston: Twayne, 1980.

Stack, Oswald, ed. *Pasolini on Pasolini*. Bloomington: Indiana University Press, 1970.

Stirling, Monica. *A Screen of Time: A Study of Luchino Visconti*. New York: Harcourt Brace Jovanovich, 1979.

Stubbs, John C. *Federico Fellini: A Guide to References and Resources*. Boston: G. K. Hall, 1978.

_____, ed. and trans. *Federico Fellini: "Moraldo in the City" and "A Journal With Anita."* Urbana: University of Illinois Press, 1983.

Tonetti, Claretta. *Luchino Visconti*. Boston: Twaye, 1983.

Willemen, Paul, ed. *Pier Paolo Pasolini*. London: British Film Institute, 1977.

Witcombe, R. T. *The New Italian Cinema: Studies in Dance and Despair*. London: Secker and Warburg, 1982.

Yakir, Dan and Stephen Harvey. "The Italians." *Film Comment* 19 (1983): 31–49.

# JAPAN

## KYOKO HIRANO

When Japan surrendered to the Allies in August 1945, its film industry, as all spheres of its national life, was severely damaged. American occupation forces landed in Japan in September and immediately abolished the wartime laws restricting ideological and political freedom; they also dismantled the totalitarian administration of the film industry itself.

## Under the American Occupation: 1945–1952

Ironically, the Americans promptly implemented their own censorship to promote the "democratization" of Japan. This pre- and postproduction censorship continued from January 1946 to June 1949. Postproduction censorship continued until the end of the occupation in April, 1952. They condemned such themes as wartime militarism, fascism, and *zaibatsu* (economic and political conglomerate families), and encouraged dramatizations of those who fought for political freedom in the past as well as contemporary figures endeavoring to reconstruct Japan. Furthermore, they prohibited such subjects as nationalism, revenge, sympathetic suicide, the degradation of women, and racial discrimination. Simultaneously, they banned 236 prewar and wartime films as "ultranationalistic," "militaristic," and "propagating feudalism."[1] Under such conditions period films were easily labeled "feudalis-

*Acknowledgments:* The author thanks the following gentlemen for their generous assistance: Kazuto Ōhira of Tōhō International; Hiroshi Yamauchi and Hidenori Ōhyana of Tōei Film, Inc.; Fran and Kaz Kuzui; Peter Grilli, David Owens and Bill Thompson of New York City; Nagisa Oshima, Masahiro Shinoda, Masaru Konuma, Mitsuo Yanagimachi, Yoshishige Yoshida, Shinsuke Ogawa, Toru Ogawa, Norio Nishijima and Ms. Katsue Tomiyama; Kawakita Memorial Film Institute and the National Film Center of Toyko.

tic," and it became difficult to make any period swordplay films, a popular genre in Japan before the war.

The Japanese film industry reacted quickly to the drastic ideological shift and new political apparatus directed by the occupation. The studios began to impose the ideas suggested by the CIE (Civil Information and Education section) of the SCAP (Supreme Commander for Allied Powers) on their producers and directors; compliance was sometimes voluntarily, sometimes under pressure. Tadashi Imai's first postwar film, *An Enemy of the People* (*Minshū no teki*, 1946), which attacked the corruption of the wartime *zaibatsu*, was regarded as typical of the "postwar democratic enlightenment film" and received critical awards that year. Keisuke Kinoshita's *A Morning with the Osone Family* (*Ōsone-ke no asa*, 1946) was also harshly critical of wartime militarism, and as its title suggests, an attempt to initiate a completely new start in postwar Japan.

Akira Kurosawa's *No Regret for Our Youth* (*Waga seishun ni kuinashi*, 1946), deals with the famous case of Professor Takigawa's persecution in 1933 for his liberalism under the military government. One of the characters is a student of Takigawa, modeled on Hotsumi Ozaki, who was arrested and executed in 1944 as an enemy spy. Kurosawa created an unusually strong character in the professor's daughter (Setsuko Hara), who becomes a lover of this student and after his death goes to live and work with his parents in a poor farming village. Her idealism had a great impact on the audience of this period, but it also provoked negative criticism as extreme and unnatural. Noteworthy also is Teinosuke Kinugasa's *Lord for a Night* (*Aruyo no tonosama*, 1946), a light comedy that criticizes feudalism through a story set in a newly built inn during the Meiji Era (1868–1912). Partly due to its stars (Isuzu Yamada, Kazuo Hasegawa, and Hideko Takamine), this film became a great commercial success.

Kenji Mizoguchi's *Victory of Women* (*Josei no shōri*, 1946), *Love of Actress Sumako* (*Joyū Sumako no koi*, 1947) and *My Love Has Been Burning* (*Waga koi wa moenu*, 1949) are considered his "women's democratization films." They are regarded as critical failures, evidence of Mizoguchi's apparent confusion about the aims of the sudden postwar democratization. Until he finally found his creative energy rekindled with works such as *Women of the Night* (*Yoru no onnatachi*, 1948), a study of the hard lives of prostitutes in barren postwar Osaka, Mizoguchi was among many other directors who merely followed the guidance of the authorities. Almost all the major directors made war propaganda films during the war and then made a swift, 180-degree turn after the surrender to follow the guidelines of the American-imposed democratization.

Due to the energetic encouragement of the early SCAP (Supreme Commander for the Allied Powers), the unions grew quickly in the film industry. The labor union of the biggest company, Tōhō, struck three times between March 1946 and August 1948, winning first a salary hike, then union participation in the decision-making process. During the second strike (October to December 1946), Tōhō's ten top stars and some directors who were against the strikes left for Shin-Tōhō "new" Tōhō). The third and final strike came when Tōhō, balking at the union's demand for participation in the company management, fired twelve hundred employees, mostly active unionists and Communists in April 1948.

SCAP had already begun to regret their early liberal policies, which they felt nourished communism. General MacArthur responded to this by banning the first nationwide general strike, which was set for 1 February 1947, on the grounds that the nation's economic stability would be endangered. Four months after the strikers occupied the Tōhō studio in Tokyo, the company removed them with the aid of the police and an occupation task force in August 1948. As a result, expelled leftist directors such as Satsuo Yamamoto, Fumio Kamei, and Imai began their own independent productions to pursue their ideals.

Films were most ardently welcomed in the postwar period, a time when the country was poor, and there were not many other forms of entertainment. Physically and mentally exhausted, people sought spiritual fulfillment; films by Kurosawa, Kinoshita, and Imai, among others, powerfully affected the immediate postwar Japanese audience.

Kurosawa's films, one after another, attained high critical acclaim as well as popular success. With startlingly authentic images of the postwar Japanese confusion of black markets and slum gangsters, Kurosawa established his dramaturgy of contrasting dynamism and stasis, emotional explosion and stabilizing morality. *One Wonderful Sunday* (*Subarashiki nichiyōbi*, 1947) responded to Italian neorealism (although the first postwar Italian film was shown in Japan only in 1949); a young couple without money wanders around the miserable streets of Tokyo, finally finding spiritual contentment when the hero conducts an imaginary orchestra for his lover (which we hear on the sound track). *Drunken Angel* (*Yoidore tenshi*, 1948) features an alcoholic doctor's friendship with a gangster suffering from tuberculosis. Both Takashi Shimura and Toshiro Mifune, as the doctor and the gangster respectively, gave exceptional performances, and thus began their long collaboration with Kurosawa. *The Quiet Duel* (*Shizuka naru kettō*, 1949) represents Kurosawa's moral concern in its depiction of an ascetic doctor (Mifune) who was contaminated by VD at a wartime field hospital and rejects his fiancee without telling her why.

*Stray Dog* (*Norainu*, 1949) depicts the struggle of two detectives (Mifune and Shimura) to recover a stolen pistol. Asaichi Nakai's photography reveals the vivid atmosphere of the crowded black markets and desolate back streets where they tirelessly search under the burning sun. The relationship of the two detectives is most impressively developed: touched by his senior's character, the younger one grows as a human being. *Scandal* (*Sukyandaru*, 1950) expresses Kurosawa's moral anger toward irresponsible yellow journalism through the story of a victimized artist couple (Mifune and Yoshiko Yamaguchi).

*Rashōmon* (1950) became the most popular Japanese film in the world through its success at international film festivals. With a script by Shinobu Hashimoto, based on Ryūnosuke Akutagawa's short story, the film illustrates four different versions of a murder case of the twelfth century. A bandit (Mifune) attacks an aristocrat couple and rapes the wife (Machiko Kyō) but the bandit, the wife, and the dead husband (Masayuki Mori), through a medium, each tell the story differently. Finally, the woodcutter (Shimura) who witnessed the murder gives another account. The film's philosophy, skeptical of absolute "truth," had a more enthusiastic response abroad than at home. The scenes of the woodcutter walking through the wood in flickering sunlight, the work of master photographer Kazuo Miyakawa, remain legendary, as does Fumio Hayasaka's soundtrack. The following year, Kurosawa worked on a Dostoevskii adaptation, *The Idiot* (*Hakuchi*), but this film suffered tremendously when the Shōchiku studio ordered the director to shorten his four-and-a-half hour version down to 160 minutes.

Kinoshita was regarded as Kurosawa's rival, because of his highly developed talent in many genres and his strong popular appeal. His films include lyrical and romantic melodramas, such as the popular *The Girl I Loved* (*Waga koiseshi otome*, 1946), political critiques such as *Apostasy* (*Hakai*, 1948) and *The Good Fairy* (*Zemma*, 1951), and satirical family comedy, such as *Broken Drum* (*Yabure daiko*, 1940).

Kinoshita could also make light comedy, as *A Toast to the Young Miss* (*Ojōsan ni kanpai*, 1949) about a romance between a man from the rising capitalist class (Sūji Sano) and a declining aristocratic lady (Hara). He also made the first color film in Japan, *Carmen Comes Home* (*Karumen kokyō ni kaeru*, 1951), a satirical comedy about a half-witted but good-natured stripper creating problems when she returns to her small mountain town after success in Tokyo. With Hideko Takamine's splendid acting, this film became very popular and led to a sequel, *Carmen's Pure Love* (*Karumen Junjōsu*, 1952).

Imai's two-part *Green Mountains* (*Aoi sanmayku*, 1949), came to symbolize postwar democratization. It is based on an extremely popular newspaper serial novel, about a young, small town high school couple's fight against the feudalistic school system and corrupt city politics. A great commercial hit, this light comedy's jubilant mood reflects the spirit of this age of reconstruction. The film's theme song was heard everywhere in Japan, and the film itself was later remade several times. It was also one of the first films featuring Tōhō's newly recruited actors and actresses after the strike drove away its big stars. *Until the Day We Meet Again* (*Mata au hi made*, 1950), another of Imai's great critical and commercial successes, is an appealing romantic and tragic love story set during the war; the scene of the young lovers (Yoshiko Kuga and Eiji Okada) kissing through a window pane became legendary.

After Imai left Tōhō, he made *And Yet We Live* (*Dokkoi ikiteiru*, 1951), a portrayal of day laborers' hardships, shot on location with the collaboration of the leftist theater troupe, Zenshin-za. His next film *Echo School* (*Yamabiko gakkō*, 1952) depicts the movement to democratize education at a junior high school in a small, poor, mountain village.

Ozu's first postwar film, *The Record of a Tenement Gentleman* (*Nagaya shinshi-roku*, 1947), was his last film in the *shomingeki* (lower-middle-class life) genre. Its main focus is on the subtle emotional changes among the inhabitants of a working class tenement when an orphan is brought there. His next film *A Hen in the Wind* (*Kaze no naka no mendori*, 1948) deals with the relationship between a woman who was forced to resort to prostitution to survive during the war and her repatriated husband, who is enraged when he finds out. It is a subtle depiction of the emotional development leading to the couple's reconciliation.

Beginning with *Late Spring* (*Banshun*, 1949), Ozu only concerned himself with bourgeois families' domestic problems in an atmosphere of serenity. With this film, writer Kōgo Noda, photographer Yūharu Atsuta, and actor Chishū Ryū began to collaborate regularly. *Early Summer* (*Bakushū*, 1951) and *Munakata Sisters* (*Munakata shimai*, 1950) explore similar themes of family drama between and within generations.

Other important films of the immediate postwar period include films directing people's attention to the social problems of handicapped children and war orphans. Hiroshi Inagaki, the master director of swordplay films, surprised his audience with his sensitive depiction of mentally handicapped children in *Children Hand in Hand* (*Te o tsunagu kora*, 1948) and *Forgotten Children* (*Wasurerareta kora*, 1949). Hiroshi Shimizu, already regarded as an expert in this genre, experimented in *Children of the Beehive* (*Hachi no su no kodomotachi*, 1948); by using actual street orphans and shooting only on location, he succeeded in transmitting the children's delicate and naïve feelings onto the screen.

The Tōei studio (which started as Tōyoko Film in 1947, became Tōkyō Eiga in 1949 and then Tōei in 1951) emphasized action films such as a series starring former swordplay actor Chiezō Kataoka and directed by Teiji Matsuda. Due to the occupation's prohibition of period films, these were made in the contemporary detective, gangster, and police genres. Toei began to make period films around 1950 as the occupation censorship policy on period films became more relaxed, and soon the swordplay genre prospered again using prewar stars such as Kataoka and Utaemon Ichikawa.

During this period Toho mostly produced democratization films, while the Shōchiku studio was concentrating on melodramas and family dramas aimed at the women's audience. The Daiei studio's period genre films were initiated by the international success of Kōzaburō Yoshimura's *Tale of Genji* (*Genji monogatari*, 1951), an adaptation of the eleventh-century court novel, and Kurosawa's *Rashōmon*.

As a result of the Americanization of Japan, "kissing films" appeared. Kissing scenes had been strictly censored by the Japanese prewar and wartime authorities, who considered them Western and anti-Japanese. Now, under the American occupation, kissing scenes were allowed to be shown. They were sometimes even justified as a symbol of democratization. The first kissing scenes, although rather suggestive and awkward, appeared on the Japanese screen in May 1946 in two competing films: Daiei's *A Certain Night Kiss* (*Aruyo no seppun*) by Yasuki Chiba and Shōchiku's *Twenty-Year-Old Youth* (*Hatachi no seishun*) by Yasushi Sasaki. In the next year Chiba made two prizewinning films: *Blossoming Family* (*Hanasaku kazoku*, 1947), a critical postwar view of the relationship between a woman and her mother-in-law; and *Invitation to Happiness* (*Kōfuku e no shōtai*, 1947), a humanistic study of women's lives in postwar society. Sasaki's reputation was established in the "popular song" film series: his *Breeze* (*Soyokaze*, 1945) included the phenomenally popular postwar song, "The Apple's Song." Between 1948 and 1950 Sasaki made a number of other popular musicals with scores by Tadashi Manjōme and featuring singer-actress Mieko Takamine.

## The Peak of the Film Industry: the 1950s

Corresponding to the McCarthy movement in the United States in the late 1940s and early 1950s, the American occupation forces in Japan changed the course of Japan's reconstruction to a conservative reorganization of Japan based on the cold war mentality. The conservatives who took over the occupation forces regarded the early policies as too radical. The birth of the People's Republic of China in 1949 and the beginning of the Korean War in 1950 brought the threat of communism to the Far East. Americans began to focus on a hasty recovery of the Japanese economy so that Japan would serve as a faithful ally. Due in large measure to the Korean War (1950–1953), the Japanese economy boomed.

The film industry grew with the larger economy during the 1950s. At its peak in 1959 the number of theaters had increased nearly tenfold since 1945, from 845 to 7,400. Audience attendance reached 1,127,452,000 in 1958, up nearly 50 percent from 1946. The distribution income from Japanese films amounted to ¥.30,602,830,000 ($85 million) in 1959, ten times the 1946 figure. The industry was producing from 208 (1950) to 514 (1956) films every year during the 1950s, compared to 21 in 1945.

However, the economic growth of the late 1950s stimulated the growth of television even more. In 1959 the marriage of the Japanese prince to a commoner led almost every Japanese household to buy a TV set so that they could view this big event. This certainly affected theater attendance. For the first time, audience attendance decreased dramatically (by 39,300,000) in 1959, and since then, the decrease has continued.[2]

At the same time, the international recognition of Japanese films as they began to collect awards at film festivals abroad gave confidence not only to the film industry but also to the nation. Their artistic achievements confirmed the Japanese's faith in their identity as the material abundance of life increased.

The first Japanese films to win international prizes were Daiei's period films, including Mizoguchi's *Life of Oharu* (*Saikaku ichidai onna*, 1952), *Ugetsu* (*Ugetsu monogatari*, 1953), and Kinugasa's *Gate of Hell* (*Jigoku-mon*, 1954). Mizoguchi is actually believed to have regained his creative capability with his two films. Based on the seventeenth-century novel by Saikaku Ihara, the first is a powerful depiction of the life of a woman at the mercy of men in feudal Japan. *Ugetsu* is a medieval ghost story, magnificently photographed by Miyagawa. Both films express Mizoguchi's critical view of the exploitation of women by men, of the feudal system and of war. They also show his image of the ideal woman, represented as a benevolent savior of men in roles played by Kiniyo Tanaka.

Mizoguchi continued to explore his obsession with woman's fate until his death in 1956. Among his films most highly regarded for his successful infusion of aesthetic expressionism with a feminist message are: *Sansho the Bailiff* (*Sanshō dayū*, 1954), a thorough, historical recreation showing the director's condemnation of slavery in medieval Japan; *A Story from Chikamatsu/Crucified Lovers* (*Chikamatsu monogatari*, 1954), an adaptation of Monzaemon Chikamatsu's eighteenth-century puppet play, the story of a torrid cross-class love affair challenging the feudal system. His last film, *Red Light District/Street of Shame* (*Akasen chitai*, 1956), is a strong and scathing depiction of contemporary prostitutes' lives, made at the time of a great national debate over the abolition of public red-light districts. This film also caused controversy over Toshiro Mayuzumi's experimental use of electronic music.

Kinugasa's *Gate of Hell* was the first Japanese film to use Eastmancolor stock after the Daiei studio sent their photographers to study in America. This twelfth-century melodrama impressed foreign audiences with its beautiful color and exotic settings. Kinugasa, more prolific than master directors like Mizoguchi, Ozu, and Kurosawa, continued to make two or three films a year during the 1950s, mainly period melodramas and swordplay films. The more privileged masters were allowed to pursue more artistic directions, making only one film a year on average, supported by the prosperity of the film studio (Mizoguchi at Daiei, Ozu at Shōchiku, and Kurosawa at Tōhō) in the 1950s.

During this period Ozu often dealt with similar subjects and characters, in fact, remaking his old films, using the same actors (such as Ryū, Shin Saburi, Keiji Sata) and actresses (such as Hara, Haruko Sugimura, Ineko Arima). *The Flavor of Green Tea Over Rice* (*Ochazuki no aji*, 1952) is a remake of his 1937 comedy *What Did the Lady Forget?* (*Shukujo wa nani o wasuretaka*): it focuses on a wife who does not appreciate her husband's true worth. *Tokyo Story* (*Tōkyō monogatari*, 1953) became a landmark film for its superb development of family problems. Each character, and each familial relationship, is delicately portrayed, yet Ozu manages to avoid sentimentalism in this story about an old couple ill-treated by their children, who finally find true affection in their widowed daughter-in-law. *Early Spring* (*Sōshun*, 1956) is a light film about adultery. *Equinox Flower* (*Higanbana*, 1958), Ozu's first color film, humorously contrasts the old and young generations' concepts of marriage. Ozu succeeded in drawing out exceptional performances from the all-star cast (Fujiko Yamamoto, Ineko Arima, Kinuyo Tanaka, Chieko Naniwa).

*Ohayo* (1959), similar to Ozu's 1932 film *I Was Born, But...* (*Umaretewa mitakeredo*), and much loved abroad, is a humorous study of children's rebellion against their parents. *Floating Weed* (*Ukikusa*, 1959) is a remake of his 1934 film *A Story of Floating Weeds* (*Ukikusa monogatari*). With the help of photographer Miyagawa, the film attained a beautiful visualization of a story about a father, son, and a shared mistress. *Late Autumn* (*Akibiyori*, 1960) deals with a story of a daughter's marriage and is very similar to *Late Spring*.

Kurosawa continued to fill the screen during this period with his dynamic images. *Ikiru* (1952) features Shimura's moving performance as a city clerk with terminal cancer who tries to find a meaning in life by working for the construction of a children's park, fighting endless bureaucracy. In this film the screen writer Hideo Oguni began to work with Kurosawa. *Seven Samurai* (*Shichinin no samurai*, 1954) is another internationally acclaimed masterpiece, renowned not only for its dramatic action scenes showing the struggle between hired samurais and bandits but also for Kurosawa's moralistic assertion of the importance of human dignity as incarnated in the old samurai (Shimura).

*Record of A Living Being/ I Live in Fear* (*Ikimoni no kiroku*, 1955) is the director's somber epistle against nuclear weapons, depicting an old man who loses his sanity out of fear of the atomic bomb. In *Throne of Blood* (*Kumonosu-jō*, 1957) Kurosawa adapted Shakespeare's *Macbeth* to a stylized Japanese medieval setting. *The Lower Depth* (*Donzoko*, 1957) is another adaptation, a Maxim Gorky story placed in late feudal Japan. Set in a poor tenement, the film affirms human vitality despite miserable surroundings. *The Hidden Fortress* (*Kakushi-toride no san-akunin*, 1958), Kurosawa's first CinemaScope film, is a dynamic, entertaining period work, centering on the struggle between two clans. During this period Kurosawa began to collaborate with screenwriters Oguni, Hashimoto, and Ryūzō Kikushima.

During the 1950s Kinoshita kept making two films a year on the average, repeatedly winning great commercial success as well as critical acclaim for his experimentation within the framework of the Shōchiku studio family melodrama. The mother (Yūko Nochizuki) in *A Japanese Tragedy* (*Nihon no higeki*, 1953), unappreciated by her children despite her endeavors, is driven to commit suicide. This film became one of the most successful "mother" films which began to appear in the late 1940s. A favorite theme of these films was the tragedy of mothers whose sons were killed during the war and whose efforts at home are not appreciated by the family members.

*Twenty-four Eyes* (*Nijushi no hitomi*, 1954) has been one of the most popular films in Japanese history. Based on a best-seller by Sakae Tsuboi, it is about the effect of the war on a woman teacher (Hideko Takamine) and her twelve pupils on a small island. Kinoshita's skillful narrative technique enlivens this otherwise sentimental film. In *You Were Like a Wild Chrysanthemum* (*Nogiku no gotoku kiminariki*, 1955), based on the lyrical love story by Sachio Itō about a pastoral youth, Kinoshita heightens the romantic mood by framing flashback shots in an oval-shaped white fog. *Time for Joy and Sorrow/The Lighthouse* (*Yorokobi mo kanashimi mo ikutoshitsuki*, 1957) is a sentimental chronicle of a couple (Hideko Takamine and Keiji Sata) working at an isolated lighthouse through several decades. It is a typical melodrama of the struggles of good-natured people's daily life.

*Ballad of Narayama* (*Narayamabushi-kō*, 1958) is adapted from Shichirō Fukasawa's folkloric novel on a village tradition of sons abandoning their aged parents in the mountains. By using artificial stagelike sets and colors, and employing Kabuki style and technique, Kinoshita created fablelike images for this human drama. Kinoshita established the postwar archetype of the Shōchiku humanist melodrama, continuing the studio's long tradition of family dramas, yet responding to the postwar social and political consciousness. His skillful cinematic technique is infused with sentimentality. Although extremely successful at home, his films were never introduced to foreign audiences.[3]

The 1950s was also the decade in which Mikio Naruse impressed his audience almost every year with contemplative studies of women and the subtle nuances of their relations with men, in the *shomingeki*. Naruse's strong-willed heroines were frequently played by Hideko Takamine. *Lightning (Inazuma,* 1952) is about the struggle of daughters trying to break out of their mother's indulgent lifestyle. The world of aged geishas is studied in *The Late Chrysanthemum (Bangiku,* 1954). *Floating Clouds (Ukigumo,* 1955) is a milestone of the postwar Japanese cinema; Hideko Takamine powerfully portrays a woman endlessly betrayed and exploited by a man whom she cannot escape until her death. Their doomed love begins in a wartime Japanese colony in Southeast Asia and moves into the confusion of postwar Japan. *Floating (Nagareru,* 1956) is another study of the geisha world, this time through the eyes of a housemaid (Tanaka).

Literary adaptations of this period include Imai's highly acclaimed masterpiece *Muddy Waters (Nigorie,* 1953) from three short stories by Ichiyō Higuchi. This film exemplifies the consistent excellence of his independent production, as does *Here Is A Spring (Koko ni izumi ari,* 1955), based on a true story about a city people's effort to enjoy music as a collective social activity.

Imai's political and social consciousness is lucidly demonstrated in a number of prizewinning films which boldly protested authority and social evils, but in a lyrical and popular style. Tōei produced *Tower of Lilies (Himeyuri no tō,* 1953), a film about the Okinawa girls' desperate attempts to defend themselves against the Americans. This tragedy of school girls, victimized by both Japanese and American forces, became a record-breaking commercial success, and greatly helped Tōei's financial situation. *Darkness at Noon (Mahiru no ankoku,* 1956) condemns the unjust judicial authority, dealing with a true case in which the procedures of the police and the court were proved wrong. The success of this film stimulated the production of other films criticizing the judicial system. *Rice (Kome,* 1957) portrays the poverty of a farming village, set against idyllic village scenery. *Story of Pure Love (Jun 'ai monogatari,* 1957) is a sentimental but refreshing story of love between a war orphan and a girl doomed by the effects of the atomic bomb. *Kiku and Isamu (Kiku to Isamu,* 1959) affectionately presents the problem of mixed-blood children in a rural area.

Other films of this period included vivid work by Heinosuke Gosho in the *shomingeki* genre which combined pathos and humor, for example, *Where Chimneys Are Seen (Entotsu no mieru basho,* 1953) and *An Inn at Osaka (Ōsaka no yado,* 1954); and Shirō Toyoda's excellent literary adaptations such as *Wild Geese (Gan,* 1953) which portrays a subtle love story between a kept woman (Hideko Takamine) and a university student (Hiroshi Akutagawa) in the Meiji era. Toyoda also made lively comedies such as *Married Relations (Meoto zenzai,* 1956) and *Cat, Shozo* and Women (*Neko to Shōzō to onnatachi*, 1956), both of which starred Hisaya Morishige as a weak-willed, lazy Osaka husband.

Minoru Shibuya made a series of satirical comedies on postwar Japanese society. *The Moderns* (*Gendaijin*, 1952) portrays a new type of postwar youth (Ryō Ikebe) who bribes a lower governmental official. *Medal* (*Kunsho*, 1955) is a scathing criticism of anachronistic ex-military personnel.

In addition to Imai, leftist independent production companies made many politically and socially oriented films that could not be supported by the conventional capitalist studios. After leaving Shōchiku, Kōzaburo Yoshimura and Kaneto Shindō established the Kindai Eiga Kyōkai (Modern Film Society) in 1950. Their first project, *Clothes of Deception* (*Itsuwareru seisō*, 1951), directed by Yoshimura and written by Shindō, criticizes the Kyoto geisha world as a symbol of the struggle for money and lust. Shindō made his debut as a director with his autobiographical *Story of My Loving Wife* (*Aisai monogatari*, 1951).

Being from Hiroshima, Shindō's next passion was to show the aftermath of the atomic bomb in *Children of the Atomic Bomb* (*Genbaku no ko*, 1952). Based on Hiroshima children's compositions and helped by the leftist theater group Mingei and labor unions, this film's subject could only have been treated after the American occupation had ended. Shindō continued to pursue this subject in *The Number Five Blessing Dragon Boat* (*Daigo fukuryūmaru*, 1959), a dramatization of the true story of a fishing boat covered with residue from an American atomic test in the South Pacific. Shindō also created striking images of strong-willed women in the face of exploitation in *Epitome* (*Shukuzu*, 1953) and *Gutter* (*Dobu*, 1954). In this sense, Shindō followed his teacher Mizoguchi.

Satsuo Yamamoto harshly condemned military authority in films made by Communist-backed independent production companies. *Vacuum Zone* (*Shinkū chitai*, 1952) is a devastating critique of wartime military corruption based on a best-selling novel. *Floating Weed Diary* (*Ukikusa nikki*, 1955) portrays a traveling theater troupe aided by a coalmining unionist. *Typhoon Turmoil* (*Taifū sōdō-ki*, 1956) is a satirical comedy on the corruption of local politics. These films demonstrate Yamamoto's unique ability to combine comedy and politics. *Human Wall* (*Ningen no kabe*, 1959) is a more somber account of the government's suppression of a teacher's union.

Hideo Sekikawa became well known for his successful adaptation of the essays of drafted wartime students, in *Listen to the Roar of the Ocean* (*Kike wakatsumi no koe*, 1950). Most of his work, dealing with such topics as Hiroshima and the problems of children fathered by American soldiers, follows the Communist ideological line. His most highly received film was *Bombing Noises and the Earth* (*Bakuon to daichi*, 1957), a social drama in a semidocumentary style, set around an

American military base. Masaki Kobayashi's three-part, overwhelming war epic, *Human Condition* (*Ningen no jōken*, 1959–61), was made with independent backing from the Ninjin Club. It is about a conscientious Japanese youth tormented by the militarist cruelty in Manchuria during and after the war and became one of the most successful antiwar films in Japan.

As for the large studios, Tōhō boasted the internationally acclaimed swordplay films by master director Hiroshi Inagaki, such as the *Musashi Miyamoto* (*Miyamoto musashi*, 1954–56) series. Ishirō Honda began a monster film series with *Godzilla* (*Gojira*, 1954), and this spectacular series soon became a domestic and international box-office attraction. *Godzilla* had an antinuclear message, for this monster was supposed to have been awakened by undersea atomic testing. Its successors, however, lost such sympathetic attributes.

Several entertaining contemporary comedy series were also started by Tōhō in the early 1950s. The "salaried-man" series (directed by Chiba, Toshio Sugie, Kunio Watanabe, Kajirō Yamamoto, Shūei Matsubayashi, and so on, starring Keiju Kobayashi, Morishige and Daisuke Katō, written by Ryuzō Kasahara and produced by Naozone Fujimoto) shows the humorous as well as the hard side of the rigidly hierarchical relationships in trading companies. They symbolize Japanese economic growth abroad and provide a convenient rationale for using exotic foreign settings. This series was sometimes criticized, however, for ignoring the existence of company unions. There was also a successful series of comedies set in inns across from railway stations (started by Toyoda in 1958, and directed by Sugie, Seiji Hisamatsu, and others). These films reflect the nation's active mobility on business or on vacation, and were inspired by the country's new-found economic stability.

Shōchiku emphasized melodrama, such as Hideo Ōhba's enormously successful *What Is Your Name?* (*Kimi no na wa*, 1953). Modeled after the phenomenally popular radio series, the film attracted a huge cult following. The tragic story deals with a young couple's constant struggle to reunite after a single fateful encounter. Keiko Kishi starred as the heroine, whose way of wearing her scarf quickly became a nationwide fashion. Yoshitarō Nomura made a fine detective film, *Stakeout* (*Harikomi*, 1958), adapted from Seichō Matsumoto's novel, which initiated the socially oriented suspense film genre at Shōchiku.

Aside from making period films, Daiei soon began to exploit the *Taiyō-zoku* (upper-class juvenile delinquency) phenomenon, as did Nikkatsu (which re-opened its studio in 1954). Kon Ichikawa's *Room of Punishment* (*Shokei no heya*, 1956), along with Takumi Furukawa's *Season of the Sun* (*Taiyō no kisetsu*, 1956) and Ko Nakahira's *Crazy Fruit* (*Kurruta kajitsu*, 1956), is based on Shintaro Ishihara's sensational novels. These films provoked nationwide protests from PTAs, and women's and educational groups over the depiction of violent and self-indulgent hooligan students. Consequently, more people went to see the films, which led to the reorganization of the Film Ethic Administration Society (established with studio participation in 1949).

Nikkatsu also produced fine literary adaptations of war experiences such as Kon Ichikawa's *Burmese Harp* (*Biruma no tategoto*, 1956), whose humanistic approach won both commercial and critical success. Ichikawa made another successful film in this genre for Daiei, *Fire on the Plains* (*Nobi*, 1959), whose stark battlefield realism simultaneously appealed to and shocked its audience. The best comic achievement at Nikkatsu is considered to be Yūzō Kawashima's *The Story of the Sun at the End of the Edo Era* (*Bakumatsu taiyō-den*, 1957), which accompanied classic comedy narrations with contemporary popular songs.

Tōei prospered from its period films. Stars such as Ichikawa and Kataoka became swordplay idols of the young audience. Through the efforts of its expert period film directors such as Matsuda, Sasaki, Watanabe, Tadashi Sawamura, Masahiro Makino and writers such as Fuji Yahiro and Yoshitake Hisa, Tōei continued to make a great number of period films—103 in 1954 alone. In 1957 Tōei made the first Japanese CinemaScope film, *The Bride of Ontori Castle* (*Ōntori-jō no hanayome*), directed by Matsuda. The success of this period action film soon inspired other studios to exploit this new technology. In 1957 a total of seventy-nine films were made in CinemaScope (including forty-five by Tōei). This growing outfit superseded Shōchiku in 1956 to become the leading film company in Japan.

## The Decline of the Studios and the Rise of the Independents

In their late twenties, Nagaisa Ōshima, Yoshishige Yoshida, and Masahiro Shinoda began directing at Shōchiku despite the traditional requirements of long apprenticeship as assistant director. The studio was trying to appeal to a young audience, and these rebellious youths responded. Their ideological and stylistic approaches were refreshingly new: they did not believe in utilizing the Shōchiku melodrama and traditional humanism to solve social and individual problems. A striking illustration is Ōshima's *The Cruel Story of Youth* (*Seishun zankoku monogatari*, 1959) which depicts the anger and self-destruction of an uncompromising young couple (Miyuki Kuwano and Yusuke Kawazu). Written by Ōshima, this film started Ōshima's collaboration with photographer Kō Kawamata, editor Keiichi Uraoka and his future cowriter Yoshirō Ishidō. Journalism began to label this new trend of filmmaking the Shochiku *Nouvelle Vague* or Japanese *Nouvelle Vague* corresponding to the French movement. The commercial success of this film encouraged Shōchiku to support Ōshima's next productions.

The year 1960 brought unprecedented political uproar at the national level. Upon the renewal of the Japan-U.S. security treaty, those who feared Japan's involvement in international military operations demonstrated on an enormous scale. They included not only Communists and socialists, as the conservative government claimed, but a rather wide spectrum of Japanese society. The treaty was reissued in June, however, and the failure and disillusionment of the left keenly questioned and passionately dramatized by Ōshima in his fourth film *Night and Fog in Japan* (*Nihon no yoru to kiri*, 1960). Set at a wedding, this film depicts the arguments between two generations of political leftists. Flashbacks to a previous wedding and other events justify the scathing criticism of the opportunistic Stalinist wing of the Communist party. The style of the film was as revolutionary as its ideological concerns: the whole 107 minute film consists of only forty-seven shots, the long crawling tracking camera illustrating the characters' emotions, sometimes using spotlighting. The film was withdrawn from the theaters four days after its release in October for what Shōchiku claimed were commercial reasons. Speculation arose, however, that the company was afraid of provoking political unrest because of the recent assassination of the Socialist party chairman. In protest, Ōshima left Shōchiku with his actress wife Akiko Koyama, who had appeared in the film.

After making an independent production, *The Catch* (*Shiiku*, 1961), about a wartime village that captures and keeps an injured black American airman, and a Tōei film, *Shiro Amakusa* (*Amakusa shirō tokisada*, 1962), depicting a Christian revolt during the Edo period (1603–1868), Ōshima established his own company, Sōzō-sha (or Creative Company), which made a series of politically provocative films. *Violence at Noon* (*Hakuchū no tōrima*, 1966) portrays a youth who, disillusioned with a local young collective movement, becomes a rapist. The film used an elaborate editing style that consists of only extremely short shots. *The Treatise on Japanese Pornographic Songs* (*Nihon shunka-kō*, 1967) is a study of the Japanese obsession with sexuality, centered around a group of high school students fantasizing about raping a girl. *Death by Hanging* (*Kōshi-kei*, 1968) is a stylistically innovative film in which Ōshima presents the problems of discrimination against Koreans in Japan and capital punishment. *Diary of a Shinjuku Thief* (*Shinjuku dorobō nikki*, 1969) intertwines the story of a shoplifter with actors' discussions about sex, a sexologist's lectures, and documentary footage of Juro Kara's popular experimental theater and scenes of street life in Tokyo's busy Shinjuku district.[4] *Boy* (*Shonen*, 1969) is an extremely sensitive depiction of a boy whose family travels all over Japan and forces the child into fake car accidents to blackmail innocent motorists. Often using factual stories as well as experimental forms of narrative, editing, and sound, Ōshima constantly questioned the Japanese political and social situation.

In 1967 Ōshima entered into partnership with the ATG (Art Theater Guild), inspiring other ambitious directors to leave their studios and make low-budget films (starting at ¥.10 million [$28 thousand] then) for which the ATG would provide half the budget. It would also show the completed films at its theaters. These directors included Shinoda and Yoshida.

Shinoda impressed his audience from the beginning with his modernist aesthetic sensibility. Using the decadent lives of cheap entertainers and petty hooligans, he showed the frustration and disillusionment of youth in a number of films made during the early sixties. *Pale Flower* (*Kawaita hana*, 1963) is a highlight of this genre. Its middle-aged gangster hero (Ikebe) meets a mysterious, rich and beautiful girl (Mariko Kaga) while gambling. His stoic attitude toward the barren gangster world is vividly portrayed. *Assassination* (*Ansatsu*, 1964) is a powerful historical film about a talented assassin whose life was wasted in the chaotic end of the Edo period.

After leaving Shōchiku, Shinoda began to express more of his political concerns, most importantly his critical view of authority. His independent company, Hyōgen-sha (or Express Company), produced *Double Suicide* (*Shinjū ten no amijima*, 1969), an ambitious stylization of Chikamatsu's puppet play about a doomed couple under the feudal system, which received high critical acclaim. *The Scandalous Adventure of Buraikan* (*Buraikan*, 1970) is a colorful adaptation of a Kabuki story of a group of outlaws challenging authority. The collaboration among Shinoda's actress wife Shima Iwashita, experimental music composer Tōru Takemitsu, and coscenario writer Taeko Tomioka has long continued.

Yoshida's early films about alienation, frustration, and detachment through the depictions of outlaws, proletarian youth, and cut-throat businessmen did not please Shōchiku, and he left the studio in 1964. His independent production, *The Story Written by Water* (*Mizu de kakareta monogatari*, 1965), delicately depicts the incestuous relationship of a son and his beautiful mother. After establishing his own company, Gendai-Eiga-Sha (or Modern Film Company), Yoshida began to explore the restless emotions of women through stark visual images—frequently created by overexposed shots—in *Lake of Women* (*Onna no mizuumi*, 1966), *Flaming* (*Jōen*, 1967), *Flame and Women* (*Honoo to onna*, 1968), and *Affairs in Ice* (*Juhyō no yoromeki*, 1968). Yoshida created a striking eroticism in his juxtapositions of women with fluid images of water.

*Eros plus Massacre* (*Erosu purasu gyakusatsu*, 1970) portrays Taisho era (1912–1925) socialist-anarchist Sakae Ōsugi and his pursuit of free love. This historic story used overexposed black-and-white shots constructed in multilayered flashbacks. A legal protest, raised by a socialist female politician after whom one of the film's characters was modeled, attracted many people to this "difficult art film," which normally would be more appealing to critics than to the general public.

Imamura was already famous for his energetic and grotesque comedies at Nikkatsu. His *Pigs and Battleship* (*Buta to gunkan*, 1961) shows the life of a petty gangster around an American base and presents a representative example of his brand of black comedy (Imamura called it "grave comedy"). All of Imamura's subsequent works had a great impact on the Japanese cinema. *The Insect Woman* (*Nippon konchū-ki*, 1963) is a harshly realistic portrayal of the life of a prostitute (Sachiko Hidari) surviving in a world of lust and money. *Intentions of Murder* (*Akai satsui*, 1964) deals with an oppressed housewife (Masumi Harukawa) who transforms herself into a strong woman, finally dominating both her petty husband and her rapist. The first film produced by Imamura himself was *The Pornographer* (*Jinruigaku nyūmon*, 1966), which affectionately depicts a man who sells sexual toys out of a sense of dedication to the world. *A Man Vanishes* (*Ningen jōhatsu*, 1967) begins as a documentary of a woman's search for her fiancé who has suddenly disappeared. Imamura develops and cruelly exposes the emotions of the heroine, using an actor who traveled with her on her search and including shots taken without the woman's knowledge. The film deals with the ambiguity of the boundary between reality and fiction. *The Profound Desire of the Gods* (*Kamigami no fukaki yokubō*, 1968), set in a mythologically primitive southern Japanese island invaded by mainland industrialization, explores Japanese concepts of sexuality.

These new directors were among the few graduates of elite universities chosen by Shōchiku out of several thousand applicants in the early 1950s. As newly recruited assistant directors, they demonstrated the ability to write excellent scenarios, and Ōshima, Yoshida, Tamura, and others began to publish a scenario magazine. When the studio acknowledged their talents they grabbed the opportunity to direct. Their strong ideological concerns were typical of intellectuals in the 1960s.

Susumu Hani was among the other important young independent directors who emerged in this period. Having started as a documentary film director in the 1950s, his first feature film, *Delinquent Boys* (*Furyō shōnen*, 1961), employed a documentary style to depict a boys' reform school. Using only nonprofessionals and boys who were actually delinquent, Hani worked these boys' opinions into his script and created scenes spontaneously. The result was an unprecedentedly fresh film. Hani made another film with the same educational film company (Iwanami), *He and She* (*Kare to Kanojo*, 1963), about the spiritual awakening of a housewife. *Buana Toshi's Song* (*Buana Toshi no uta*, 1966) depicts a Japanese engineer encountering and gradually learning to respect the native culture in Africa. In a similar vein, *The Bride of the Andes* (*Andes no hanayome*, 1966) is about a Japanese woman gradually adjusting to her new environment. This was the first film by Hani Production, coproduced by Tokyo-Eiga, an associate of Tōhō. *The Inferno of First Love* (*Hatsukoi jigoku-hen*, 1969) is another sensitive depiction of youth, in this case an alienated young couple living in the city.

Hiroshi Teshigawara also started as a documentary film director in the field of fine arts. After working on Kamei's leftist social documentary films, he established Teshigawara Production and began to adapt Kōbō Abe's existentialist novels for the screen. Abe wrote the scripts, and all of their collaborations are highly regarded for their imaginative treatment of the complex situation in which modern human beings are caught, evoked through highly stylized surrealist images. These striking black-and-white films include *The Hole* (*Otoshiana*, 1962), *Woman in the Dune* (*Suna no onna*, 1964), *Face of Another* (*Tanin no kao*, 1966), and *The Ruined Map* (*Moetsukita chizu*, 1968).

Satsuo Yamamoto continued to make protest films with leftist independent production companies. His impressive drama *Struggle Without Weapons* (*Bukinaki tatakai*, 1961) is a biography of an academic socialist who was assassinated by a right-wing terrorist for his antifascist activity. *The Matsukawa Case* (*Matsukawa jiken*, 1961) pleads the case of unionists convicted in a mysterious railroad sabotage, but who were later proved innocent, and *Girls Who Embrace the Breast* (*Nyubō o idaku musumetachi*, 1962) depicts an attempt to collectivize poor farmers. These films were financially supported by labor unions, teacher's unions, and farmer's organizations. Similarly, *The Witness Box* (*Shōnin no isu*, 1965) elucidates the danger of false testimony that drives innocent human life into tragedy.

Working for Daiei again, Yamamoto made *Band of Spies* (*Shinobi no mono*, 1962) and *Band of Spies: Sequel*, (*Zoku shinobi no mono*, 1963) set in the civil war period. The excellent performances by Raizo Ichikawa in these films won public acclaim. *Japanese Thief Story* (*Nippon Dorobō monogatari*, 1965), a satirical comedy, deals again with the Matsukawa case, here seen through the eyes of a thief whose morality is gradually awakened, inspiring him to help the convicted workers. *The Big White Tower* (*Shiroi kyotō*, 1966), based on a best-selling novel about an ambitious young doctor at a corrupt medical school, became critically and commercially successful.

Kobayashi made a powerful drama, *Harakiri* (*Seppuku*, 1962), about an individual's attempt to challenge the inhuman feudal system. He then made *Kwaidan* (*Kaidan*, 1964), an elaborate adaptation of ghost stories, produced independently. Painstaking direction with inspired, off-beat art direction by Jūshō Toda, made this film a masterpiece, but a commercial disaster. Kobayashi thus had to wait until 1967 to make his next film for Tōhō/Mifune Production, *Rebellion/Samurai's Rebellion* (*Jōiuchi*). Again written by Hashimoto, it is another strong criticism of the feudal system, with dramatic fight scenes.

Kurosawa established Kurosawa Production and, with Tōhō, he kept making powerful and successful films. *The Bad Sleep Well* (*Warui yatsu hodo yoku nemuru*, 1960) is a suspenseful drama of a young man (Mifune) who attempts to avenge his father's death by attacking big business and government corruption. *Yōjimbō* (1961) features Mifune as a wandering samurai who single-handedly destroys two competing gangs in a village. This extraordinarily dynamic film humorously depicts the Mifune character in counterpoint with the intense fight scenes. Due to its enormous success, Kurosawa made its sequel, *Sanjuro* (*Tsubaki sanjurō*, 1962).

*High and Low* (*Tengoku to jigoku*, 1963) is an exciting crime film. Not content with a breathtakingly skillful development of the crime, Kurosawa shows the class differences motivating it, and depicts the moral dilemma of a father (Mifune) in saving his chauffeur's son who is kidnapped by mistake instead of his own son. Many kidnapping attempts were in fact modeled after the one in this film, and it became a social problem. *Red Beard* (*Akahige*, 1965) portrays the emotional growth of a young doctor (Yūzō Kayama) under the influence of an older doctor (Mifune) dedicated to helping poor people during the Edo period. Laboriously directed, it was to be the last achievement of the most active part of Kurosawa's career.

Naruse and Toyoda continued to make carefully directed women's films. Many of Toyoda's films were literary adaptations. Scenario writer Zenzō Matsuyama directed his first film, *Nameless, Poor and Beautiful* (*Na mo naku, mazushiku utsukushiku*, 1961), a touching story, employing sign language and subtitles, of a deaf couple's struggle and love. Following his mentor Kinoshita, he continued to specialize in human interest films, depicting the sincere efforts of people of goodwill to find their own happiness.

Tōhō began to produce fine action films in the late 1950s, such as Eiichi Sugawa's hard-boiled crime film *The Beast Must Die* (*Yajū shisubeshi*, 1959), starring Tatsuya Nakadai as a cool assassin, and Kihachi Okamoto's *Scarface* (*Ankokugai no kaoyaku*, 1959), which began a successful gangster series. Okamoto also started a unique war-action comedy series with *Independent Hooligans* (*Dokuritsu gurentai*, 1959) and its sequels.

A war genre, with Tōhō's special effects by Tsuburaya, began as a series of large-scale, semidocumentary style films on the Pacific war, highlighted by Okamoto's powerful *Japan's Longest Day* (*Nippon no ichiban nagai hi*, 1967). With an all-star cast, it recreated the last day

Akira Kurosawa's *Rashomon* (1950), with its many-sided views of a twelfth-century rape and murder, was a milestone in the international popularity of Japanese cinema.

Kurosawa is known for his skillful handling of complex crowd scenes, as in this still from *Seven Samurai* (1954).

(Right)
The legendary scene of
two lovers kissing
through a window pane,
from Tadashi Imai's *Until
We Meet Again* (1950), a
lyrical romance with an
antiwar theme.

(Below)
*Carmen Goes Home*
(1951), Keisuke
Kinoshita's satirical light
comedy, was the first
Japanese film in color.

In Yasujiro Ozu's landmark *Tokyo Story* (1953), the parents, ignored by their own children, are treated affectionately by their daughter-in-law.

(Left)
A woman cannot escape her love for a selfish man, in Mikio Naruse's masterful study of lower middle-class emotional life, *Floating Clouds* (1955).

(Above)
Masaki Kobayashi's
three-part antiwar epic,
*Human Condition*
(1959–61), which ran
over nine hours, had a
powerful impact in Japan.

(Right)
Revolutionary in style
and in its criticism of
left-wing opportunism,
*Night and Fog in Japan*
(1960) was the work of a
young "new-wave"
director, Nagisa Ōshima.

Since 1969 Yōji Yamada has entertained the Japanese audience twice yearly with his comedy series *Tora the Tramp*, about a Tokyo working-class community.

Kinji Fukasaku's *Fight Without Code* (1973) initiated the docu-drama studies of the *yakuza* gangster world in postwar Hiroshima.

In *Farewell to the Earth* (1982), the young, independent filmmaker Mitsuo Yanagimachi looks at the effects of new industrialization on family life.

Shōhei Imamura's *Ballad of Narayama* (1983), a realistic study of a poor mountain village, won the Grand Prix at the Cannes Film Festival.

of the Pacific war. After this critical and popular success, several similar films—dubbed "8-15s" (August 15, the day of the Japanese surrender by the Japanese calendar)—made their appearance.

Tōhō also began a youth genre in the early 1960s. One of the most popular and longest series of this type is the "Young Boss" (Wakadaishō) series, recounting the loves and adventures of a student (Kayama). Beginning in 1961, seventeen films were made, amply demonstrating Kayama's versatile talents as a singer, an invincible sportsman, a romantic lover, and a kind son. Much of the great success of this series is attributed to a comic character (Kunie Tanaka) playing the hero's rival. Other films featuring young potential or established stars in upper-middle-class settings became the norm for Tōhō's youth films. The comic "Irresponsible Man" (Musekinin-Otoko) series started in 1962, starring Hitoshi Ueki as an opportunistic salaried man using everyone for his own advantage.

At Shōchiku, Ozu kept recreating his world of tranquility, transcending the young directors' criticism of the studio's conventionalism. *The End of Summer* (*Kohayagawa-ke no aki*, 1961) was made for Takarazuka Film, an associate of Tōhō. Humorously as always, Ozu portrays a sake-brewer's family whose grandfather (Ganjirō Nakamura) hangs around the house of his old mistress (Naniwa). Ozu's last film, *Autumn Afternoon* (*Samma no aji*, 1962), depicts a traditional story of a widower (Ryū) trying to get his beautiful daughter (Iwashita) to marry, despite his own loneliness that will result. Ozu's last image of the father returning home from her wedding left his public with a quintessential image of the loneliness of human life.

Kinoshita chronicled successive generations of a poor family involved in civil war in sixteenth century Japan in *The River Fuefuki* (*Fuefuki-gawa*, 1960), in which he experimented with color tinting. His next film, *Immortal Love/The Bittersweet Spirit* (*Eien no hito*, 1961) portrays a woman's deep-rooted feeling for her lover who was killed at war, and her hatred of the man who raped her and became her husband. Both films achieved critical success, as did *The Scent of Incense* (*Kōge*, 1964), a powerful drama of mother and daughter. Uncompromising in his standards like Kurosawa, Kinoshita gradually became inactive after the mid-1960s, as the industry floundered with economic difficulties. Kinoshita successfully shifted his energies into television.

Nomura made a critical comedy, *Dear Your Highness Emperor* (*Haikei tennō Heika*, 1964), offering the viewpoint of a lower-class soldier (Kiyoshi Atsumi). His period film *Five-Petals' Camellia* (*Goben no tsubaki*, 1964) is a suspenseful piece about a woman's revenge. Nomura's work, ranging from conventional melodramas, gangster films, literary adaptations, and comedies to socially oriented crime films, is always presented from ordinary people's points of view.

Young directors who remained at Shōchiku showed their talent for comedy in the studio's tradition of making "light and enjoyable films." Yoji Yamada began a monumentally successful comedy series *Tora the Tramp* (*Otoko wa tsuraiyo*) in 1969. It stars Atsumi as Tora, a traveling street merchant who occasionally returns home to downtown Tokyo, where the feeling of the old community is preserved, along with the twin concepts of *giri* and *ninjō* (that is, the sense of obligation to return favors and the natural human feelings with which that sense often conflicts). Every film in the series repeats the same narrative pattern. Without fail, Tora falls in love with a beautiful woman out of his reach, and failing in love, leaves to wander again. Despite this sameness, audience attention is sustained by the different actresses playing the object of Tora's affections, as well as the ever-changing settings. A Communist director, Yamada always shows the labors of the oppressed, although this perspective is tempered by Shōchiku's traditional philosophy that those who live sincerely eventually find their own little happiness. The Japanese audience never seems to tire of the lovable character Tora; for more than a decade, two new Tora movies have come out every year.

At Daiei, Kon Ichikawa continued his successful career with the collaboration of his scenario writer and wife, Natto Wada. *Her Brother* (*Otōto*, 1961), a literary adaptation, affectionately depicts the loving family relationship between sister and brother. It is beautifully visualized through Ichikawa's ingenious sense of composition and color. *I Am Two/Being Two Isn't Easy* (*Watashi wa nisai*, 1962) is a humorous criticism of modern life as seen through the eyes of a baby. *The Outcast/Broken Commandment* (*Hakai*, 1962), a remake of Kinoshita's 1948 film, portrays the agony of a young teacher (Raizō Ichikawa) over class discrimination.

In 1965 Ichikawa was commissioned by the Tokyo Olympic Film Committee to direct *Tokyo Olympiad* (*Tōkyō Olympikku*). Using many telephoto close-ups and slow motion, Ichikawa captured the personal and poetic moments of the competition. The film irritated one committee member who had expected a more conventional and official record of the national event, saying that the film might be artistic but is questionable as a record. However, the Japanese responded to this film as enthusiastically as they had to the Olympic Games themselves. By this time, constantly declining film attendance had dropped to 370 million a year, and out of this, 20 million went to see *Tokyo Olympiad*. The Olympiad itself was symbolic, coming at the peak of Japanese economic growth and regaining of national confidence on the international scene. The period preceeding the 1970 World Exposition in Osaka showed the greatest postwar increases in consumption and leisure time.

Although film audiences were generally shrinking, the changing dynamics in Japanese society gave rise to popular genre films, such as Daiei's action series. The *Zatōichi* series, which started in 1962, features Shintaro Katsu as a blind masseur and gambler, incredibly skillful in swordplay, who wanders around Japan of the Edo period, helping the oppressed. He is molested by local gangsters until the final moments when he shows his magnificent skill with the sword and kills countless men. The dynamic swordplay scenes and Zatōichi's humorous characterization attracted not only domestic but also international fans. *The Bad Guy* (*Akumyō*) series directed by Tokuto Tanaka, which started in 1961, portrays the adventures of a tough hoodlum, also played by Katsu. These two series became exceptional commercial hits in the early sixties. Daiei also produced the first Japanese 70mm film, the historic epic *Buddha* (*Shaka*, 1961), followed by several grand-scale period films in 70mm.

The most prosperous films from Nikkatsu in the 1960s were also action films starring young idols and often including pop songs sung by the films' heroes. Suzuki was a particularly popular cult director for his stylization and surrealistic use of bright colors. Representative works of his include *The Youth of Beast* (*Yajū no seishun*, 1963), *Kawachi Carmen* (*Kawachi Karumen*, 1966), *Tokyo Wanderer* (*Tōkyō nagaremono*, 1966), and *Elegy to Violence* (*Kenka erejii*, 1966). When a cine-club planned a Suzuki retrospective and asked Nikkatsu to rent the prints in 1968, Nikkatsu refused and, moreover, fired Suzuki, complaining that he had been making incomprehensible films. This was followed by a surprisingly large-scale protest movement, including street demonstrations. Suzuki brought the case to court and eventually won a handsome settlement. Another important case involved the popular actress Fujiko Yamamoto, who wanted to break her contract with Daiei in 1963. When she finally did leave, she was blacklisted by the other studios. This case exposed the retrogressive character of the Japanese film industry and as a result the "Five Studios Contract" disintegrated in the 1970s.

At Tōei in the early 1960s, Daisuke Itō and Tomu Uchida continued to make dynamic period films. Gradually the "group swordplay" films took over, represented by Eiichi Kudō's dynamic *Thirteen Assassins* (*Jūsan-nin no shikyaku*, 1963) and *Big Swordplay* (*Dai-tate*, 1966) This series' popularity indicated the increased attraction of group protagonists, as opposed to individual heroes.

As the film industry began to decline, film companies expanded their investments in bowling alleys, restaurants, recreation centers, and real estate to respond to different tastes in mass entertainment. At the same time, Tōei found another way to combat the situation. In 1965 contemporary gangster films such as the *Abahiri Prison* (*Abashiri bangaichi*) series and *yakuza* (old-style gangster) films became popular. The *yakuza* films followed very similar narrative and stylistic patterns. The story is set in either the Meiji (1868–1912), the Taishō (1912–25) or the early Shōwa (1925–) period. The hero is generally very moralistic and respects the old *yakuza* rules. Gradually he gets involved with a new generation of evil bosses who are frequently supported by corrupt authorities and big business. Traditional gambling scenes and the *yakuza* boss meetings are often shot from an extremely low angle. The hero decides to help the sincere and oppressed *yakuza* group. Most likely, a romance develops between the hero and the daughter of his boss, although the stoic hero's love is only platonic. Only after being ill treated, deceived, betrayed, and after his boss and his men are cruelly killed by the enemy does he silently rise up to kill the enemy by himself or with the aid of a few others. Surrounded by countless enemies, he kills them in bloody choreographed sequences in which many paper doors are broken and knocked over. He finally kills the big bosses.

The stoic *yakuza* heroes developed a fanatical following among students and young workers. In 1966 Tōei began "all night" theater operations in big cities, showing several films from Saturday night to Sunday morning, and most of the films shown were *yakuza* films. The dedication of this audience reflected the strong feeling against the "my-home" culture, whose petty-bourgeois and conformist values prevailed then in Japan.

This was also a time of turmoil, when students in the major universities protested the corrupt education system. The streets were filled with citizen activists, armed with Molotov cocktails (bottle bombs) and rocks, confronted by the riot police. Many of the protesters probably patterned themselves to some extent on the *yakuza* film heroes, although the group aspect of the demonstrations did not reflect the re-emerging individualism of their role-models.

Outside the major companies, Tetsuji Takechi and Kōji Wakamatsu emerged as brave pioneers of sexual expression. Takechi, an innovative theorist of Kabuki, came onto the film scene in 1963. With Dai-san Production he made *White Day Dream* (*Hakujitsumu*, 1964), *Red Bed Dream* (*Kōkeimu*, 1964), and *Black Snow* (*Kuroi yuki*, 1965). He shocked Japan with his radical exploration of sexual consciousness in these films; in the mid-1960s, they were criticized as obscene. The police took *Black Snow* to court in the first obscenity trial in Japan and lost.

Kōji Wakamatsu is the master of the "pink film" (low-budget sex film, normally made for ¥.2 million ($5,555) in several days. His scandalous films began to appear in 1963, and were greatly admired by some critics, students, and the urban working class, as an expression of oppressed sexuality and anger against the establishment. *Red Crime* (*Akai hankō*, 1964), for example, depicts a man who rapes the wife of the prosecutor of his court case, in which he was actually innocent. The legendary black comedy *Violated White Clothes* (*Okasareta Hakui*, 1967) cast an avant-garde theater director-actor, Jūrō Kara, as a thief who breaks into a dormitory of nurses and shoots everybody.

Wakamatsu supported the talent of many directors such as Atsushi Yamatoya, Chūsei Sone, Masao Adachi, and Shinya Yamamoto by using them as screenwriters or by producing their films. During the turmoil of the nationwide student movement (1968–69), Wakamatsu's films, along with Tōei's *yakuza* films, were most popular among the students and most frequently shown on campuses occupied by students.

## The Age of Search: 1970–1986

The political and social turmoil of the late 1960s suddenly dissolved in 1970. Perhaps in its stead, the new Osaka World Exposition attracted huge crowds. Both phenomena might be explained as examples of Japanese monomania, or fanatic curiosity over something new. Ideologically the year 1970 was a total failure for the leftists, as almost no protest over the renewal of the U.S.-Japan security treaty developed. Many intellectuals who had supported the antitreaty movement ten years before had become conservative by 1970, and the conservative national government was able to distract the people into focusing on a nationalistic event such as the World Exposition.

The opportunities of master filmmakers were further lessened. Kurosawa made his first color film, *Dodeskaden* (1970), a fantastic story of the dreams and realities of a slum neighborhood. The title refers to the sound of an imaginary train that a half-witted boy operates. His next film was *Dersu Uzala* (1975), entirely shot in the USSR, using only Russian actors. Taking place in an awesome Siberian setting, it is a story of friendship between a Russian captain and a Mongolian guide. Kurosawa's next chance to make a film only came when Twentieth Century-Fox, persuaded by his admirers Francis Ford Coppola and George Lucas, agreed to finance it. They also became producers of *Kagemusha/Shadow Warrior* (1980). It is a grand-scale period action film, and many of the fight scenes used a number of horses far beyond the modest budgets of the Japanese film industry. Also unusual was the casting, as all but the title roles were cast after an open call, with no consideration given to prior acting experience. The film established a new box-office record in Japan (¥.2.7 billion/$10 million) and won international critical and commercial success. The domestic critical response, however, was mixed. Despite this success, it was clear that for an uncompromising master like Kurosawa, who demanded technical and artistic perfection that only unprecedented sums of money could guarantee, it had become almost impossible to make a film in Japan.

Kurosawa's next film, *Ran* (1985, the title roughly translates as "chaos") was made only with the participation of French producer Serge Silberman. Setting Shakespeare's *King Lear* against the period of Japanese civil war, it is again a grand-scale period film. This time Kurosawa questions why human beings cannot escape the absurdities of greed, jealousy, and revenge. Including dazzling battle scenes, lavish costumes, and exquisite sets, *Ran* had a better reception abroad than at home.

Another example of a master making films outside of Japan after the mid-seventies is Ōshima. He presented a postwar history of Japanese war consciousness through the ceremonies (for example, weddings and funerals) of a family involved in complicated psychological and sexual relationships in *The Ceremony* (*Gishiki*, 1971). His next film was *Dear Summer Sister* (*Natsu no imōto*, 1972), dealing with the question of the consciousness and political position of Okinawa—an island officially returned to Japan by the United States in this year through the romances between an Okinawan boy and two Japanese girls. This refreshing film may be considered together with other politically oriented films such as *Three Resurrected Drunkards* (*Kaettekita yopparai*, 1968) and *The Man Who Left His Will on Film* (*Tokyo sensō sengo hiwa*, 1970). The former, in a highly experimental narrative style, inquires into the problem of identity using the story of three youths who are mistaken for illegal Korean immigrants. The other film, also experimental, explores the filmmaking method and ideology of a high school student group. *Dear Summer Sister* became the last film of the seven coproductions of Ōshima's Sōzō-sha and ATG.

After disbanding Sozo-sha in 1973, Ōshima established Oshima Production in 1975 and made the first hard-core pornographic film officially directed by a Japanese. Since Japanese censorship prohibits any exposure of sexual organs and sexual acts, Ōshima shot *In the Realm of the Senses* (*Ai no koriida*) in a closed Japanese studio, sent the raw film stock to France, and developed and edited the film there. The complete version was only shown in countries without censorship, and when the film came to Japan, many scenes were chemically processed to blur the prohibited images, as is normally done to foreign films with such scenes. Based on an actual 1936 story of a woman named Sada Abe (Eiko Matsuda) who chopped off her lover's sexual organ after several days of extreme forms of love-making and ecstasy, it caused a major challenge to Japanese censorship. The police brought the case to court in 1977 (not relating to the revised film itself but to its scripts and photo-story book published upon the film's release in Japan), and Ōshima eventually won the case in 1982.

After the international success of *In the Realm of the Senses*, its French producer, Anatole Dauman, and Ōshima made another film again based on a real story, with the popular actor Tatsuya Fuji playing against veterans Kazuko Yoshiyuki and Takahiro Tamura. This film, *Empire of Passion* (*Ai no bōrei*, 1978), is another powerful expression of human passion: two lovers are haunted by the ghost of the man they murdered. The film is magnificently photographed by the veteran leftist cinematographer Yoshio Miyajima who had created such master-pieces as *Human Condition* and *Kwaidan*.

Ōshima's next film was produced by an Englishman, Jeremy Thomas, and shot on a South Pacific island and New Zealand. The film, *Merry Christmas, Mr. Lawrence* (*Senjō no Merii Kurisumasu*, 1983), based on a novel by a South African, Laurens van der Post, is about the relationship of Japanese and British officers at a Japanese prisoner-of-war camp during World War II. The casting of two extremely popular rock singers, the British David Bowie and the Japanese Ryūichi Saka-moto (who wrote the music), in addition to a very popular Japanese TV comedian named Takeshi, contributed to the film's international and domestic commercial success. Also important were the artistic contri-butions of cinematographer Tōichiro Narushima and art director Shi-gemasa Toda, who helped create the atmosphere for the psychological struggle of love and hate between individuals from different cultures at war.

The fact that Japanese master directors were tending to make films abroad was a sign of the desperate situation of the Japanese film indus-try. Attendance at film theaters dropped until it finally fell below 200 million in 1972. In 1959 the average Japanese saw around twelve films a year, while twenty years later he was seeing only 1.5. By the end of the 1970s, the Japanese Society of Film Directors (established in 1936) listed twice as many of its 280 members as TV directors than as film di-rectors. According to the society's 1978 research, only some sixty mem-bers made more than one film for theaters in the previous year. (A total of 337 Japanese films were made in 1977, of which 199 were independ-ently produced.) In the same year, 222 foreign films were shown.[5]

Why did the Japanese stop going to see films at the theater? In addi-tion to the obvious factor of television, the major studios could not pro-duce films interesting or entertaining enough to lure people back into the theaters.

By the mid-1970s, foreign films, predominantly American Hollywood productions, began to attract more viewers than did domestic produc-tions. This precipitated a crisis within the Japanese industry, but in a few years domestic productions regained their former primacy. When such immensely popular Hollywood films as *Star Wars* and *Jaws* first appeared in Japan, with great success, the Japanese studios (mostly Tōhō) immediately imitated them with their own "disaster" and "outer-space" films. But because these Japanese-produced films were cheaply made and lacked originality, they could not compete with the originals. The peculiar structure of the industry was also an issue. The major stu-dios control distribution and theaters, severely restricting the distribu-tion of independent productions. Even if an independent production achieves commercial success, it will not make much profit, after paying for distribution. Surprisingly, the film companies' largest expense is preserving the now unnecessary jobs of thousands of employees from the industry's golden age of the 1950s. Normally, only one-fourth or one-fifth of the companies' total budget goes to the shooting of new films.

Considering such difficult conditions, many Japanese directors have shown remarkable achievements. At Tōei, after the *yakuza* series declined, a new "docudrama" (Jitsuroku) series appeared. This trend was represented by Kinji Fukasaku's *Fight Without Code* (*Jingi naki tatakai*, 1973–76) series that became critically and commercially successful. The struggles of a young and ambitious hero (played by Bunta Sugawara) start in the confusion of the immediate postwar Hiroshima, and are closely patterned on real Hiroshima *yakuza* struggles. To expand their territories, the local *yakuza* organizations wage bloody fights with each other. Fukasaku created dynamic fight scenes with an ever-swaying hand-held camera and punctuating titles to give the stories the air of documentary presentation. The realistic portrayal of these gangsters as slaves to their grotesque drive to power, with no compunctions about betraying their allies to achieve their goals, sharply contrasts with the heroic and idealized images of the *yakuza* in the films of the 1960s. The hero of this series not only expresses the anger of those left out of society but cooly criticizes the ugly side of the gangster world. He gradually wins the power he seeks, knowing its implicit contradictions.

Variations on this docudrama trend were made by Fukasaku and Sadao Nakajima, two particularly talented action directors. Especially memorable were Fukasaku's two films: *The Tomb of the Code* (*Jingi no hakaba*, 1975), a ruthless depiction of the short life of a fanatic *yakuza* youth (Tetsuya Watari) who refuses to compromise with anything, and *Prefecture Police vs. Organized Crime* (*Kenkei tai soshiki bōryoku*, 1975), an exploration of the roots of violence and a critique of the structure of police and gangster organizations. Nakajima is a Tōei director who attracted a cult following with emotional gangster films. His *Crazy Beast* (*Kurruta yaju*, 1975) is an excellent example of suspenseful and ironic drama. Its sloppy protagonists fail in robbing a bank and hijack a local bus containing a group of greedy and aggressive passengers who eventually overwhelm the hijackers.

Tōei produced a very popular comedy series, *Truck Drivers* (*Torraku yarō*, 1975–79), with action film director Noribumi Suzuki. A rival to Shōchiku's successful *Tora the Tramp* series, this Tōei comedy features a rough truck driver Momotarō (Sugawara) and his married colleague Janathan the Widower (Kinya Aikawa) traveling all over Japan in their glittering painted truck. Junyō Satō's *Great Bombing of the Bullet Train* (*Shinkansen daibakuha*, 1975), starring Ken Takakura and Sony Chiba, is an exciting and well-made suspense film, whose success inspired Tōei's all-star, absurd period action film, Fukasaku's *Shogun's*

*Samurai* (*Yagyū ichizoku no imbō*, 1978). Tōei also specialized in sophisticated animated adaptations of Japanese, Chinese, and European fairy tales, which were consistent commercial successes at home and abroad.

In 1971 Daiei went bankrupt. In 1975 the company was reorganized by its labor union and began operations again, with the help of Yasuyoshi Tokuma, the president of a book, record, and entertainment business, and a former union activist. One of Daiei's most monumental achievements since this time is the first Chinese-Japanese coproduction *The Go Master* (*Mikan no Taikyoku*, 1983), directed by Satō and Dua Ji-shun, which portrays the friendship of Japanese and Chinese *go* (chess) masters through the war period.

In 1971 the near-bankrupt Nikkatsu stopped operations, reemerging several months later with a new policy of producing only soft-core pornographic films, called "Roman Porno" (romantic porno). The many talented Nikkatsu directors were free to pursue their artistic and ideological concerns, so long as they met the company's demand for quickly produced, low-budget films that included indirect sex scenes. Because Japanese censorship does not allow direct sexual expression, Nikkatsu Roman Porno created a unique eroticism of hidden and suggested sexual expression, rooted in traditional Japanese forms of erotic art and literature. The camera work was exquisite, the scenarios well conceived and witty; and the female stars soon began to appear in nonpornographic films and on television after their success at Nikkatsu. These sophisticated, artistic films displayed social and human insight portrayed through sexuality, not at all comparable to most cheap pornography. Because of the censorship, many Nikkatsu pornographic films resort to voyeurism, fetishism, and sadomasochism (S and M), to compensate for the absence of explicitly shown sexual organs.

Pornographic films normally cater to male fantasies of subjugating women, and, indeed, Nikkatsu's heroines are often socially oppressed as strippers, prostitutes, and barmaids, or sexually oppressed as housewives, teachers, and office workers. However, a number of Nikkatsu productions could be interpreted as feminist films because of their depiction of strong women who spiritually dominate men. In this sense, the Nikkatsu Roman Porno remained in the tradition of Japanese feminist film (for example, Mizoguchi, Shindō, Imamura, and Ōshima) whose heroines are often stronger than their men. Supported by an audience of students, intellectuals, and workers, at least one or two Roman Pornos have been chosen every year since 1971 as among the ten best films of the year by Japanese critics.

Several directors are responsible for the most representative achievements of Nikkatsu. One of the most important is Tatsumi Kumashiro, whose radically innovative narrative style and use of music and sound has attracted many followers. *Sayuri Ichijo: The Wet Desire* (*Ichijō Say-*

*uri: Nureta yokujō*, 1972) explores the world of striptease, showing a popular real-life stripper (Sayuri Ichijo) seen through the eyes of her young colleague (Hiroko Isayama), exposing their love-hate relationship. *The Lovers Get Wet* (*Koibitotachi wa Nureta*, 1973) portrays a disillusioned small-town boy who delivers film reels to theaters, continually denying his identity when he is recognized. With Kumashiro's marvelous interpolations of popular songs, this film created an intriguing mood.

*The Back Paper of the Sliding Door of A Four-and-Half Tatami Mat Room* (*Yojōhan fusuma no urabari*, 1973) cleverly intertwines four stories developing around a Taisho era brothel in Tokyo. It is an erotic film infused with political references—in the form of newspaper clips and photos about rice riots, the Japanese army being sent to Siberia to interfere in the Russian Revolution, and Korean nationalist resistance under the Japanese colonial government. *The Black Rose Goes to Heaven* (*Kurobara shōten*, 1975) is a comedy about a cheap erotic film production company determined to oppose all authority.

Other Roman Porno directors include Toshiya Fujita who specializes in depicting the sensibility of urban youth with a light and fresh touch, and Noboru Tanaka, who adapted the same story that Ōshima used in *In the Realm of the Senses* in his *Document of Sada Abe* (*Jitsuroku: Abe Sada*, 1975). This film, set almost entirely in a small room of an inn, with flashbacks to the past, brought to life the passion of this legendary woman (played by Junko Miyashita). Tanaka effectively uses popular songs and subtitles that not only explain the situations in the film but accentuate the characters' feelings. Set in the Taisho era, *Stroller in the Attic* (*Yaneura no Sampo-sha*, 1976) is about a relationship based on voyeurism and fetishism between a nihilistic youth who spies on people from his attic and a high society woman (Miyashita). Tanaka's surrealistic sensibility is superbly realized, particularly in his early works, by his striking use of bright colors and artificial designs.

Masaru Konuma created an even more fantastically colorful and artificial world as the setting for his keenly perceptive, realistic depiction of sensuality. Konuma's aesthetic and exquisite sensuality is frequently based on voyeurism and fetishism, represented by *Old Capital Mandala* (*Koto mandara*, 1973). *Violated* (*Okasareru*, 1976) is a Hitchcockian suspense drama of a couple involved in diamond smuggling. Konuma also adapted popular S and M stories by Kiroku Dan, which radically and ironically depict not only the pleasure of S and M but also scatology, beginning with Konuma's comic *Flower and Serpent* (*Hana to hebi*, 1974), followed by *Madame Sacrifice* (*Ikenie fujin*, 1974). Beneath the apparent seriousness of these shameless films, there is an unyielding spirit of detached mockery of sexual fantasies.

Chūsei Sone made a successful comedy series: *Ah! Flowery Cheer Leaders* (*Ah! Hana no ōendan*, 1976) and its sequels. These films portray rough male cheerleaders, based on popular cartoon characters. Sone's masterpiece of adolescent comedy is *Hakataite's Pure Love* (*Hakatakko junjō*, 1978), made for Shōchiku. In it he depicted the world of local junior high school boys during an annual summer festival, through their fights and naive love affairs. *My Sex Document: Degree of Zenith* (*Watashi no sekkusu hakusho: zecchōdo*, 1976) is Sone's unique exploration of the sexuality of a gangster, a nurse, and other women. *Angel's Belly: The Red Classroom* (*Tenshi no harawata: akai kyōshitsu*, 1978) is based on a popular and explicit adult sex cartoon series. Sone created a pathetic love story about a beautiful ex-teacher (Yūki Mizuhara), who was raped and then made a film about it for an underground sex film network, and a middle-aged man (Keiji Kanie) shamefully engaged in the sex photo business. The dark passion of the heroine is memorably depicted.

Tōru Murakawa impressed critics with his first film at Nikkatsu, *Ecstasy of White Fingers* (*Shiroi yubi no tawamure*, 1972), a study of the eroticism of young pickpockets, and again with a Tōei production, *The Most Dangerous Game* (*Mottomo kikenna yūgi*, 1978), an action film about a young assassin challenging the police.

The police seized two Nikkatsu pornographic films by Seiichirō Yamaguchi and Katsuhiko Fujii in 1972 and took them to court. As in the Ōshima case, many film and anticensorship people supported the Nikkatsu defendants, and they were found innocent both in 1976 and in 1980. Meanwhile, the management of Nikkatsu was taken over by its labor union in the mid-seventies. Although Fujii continued to make films after 1972, Yamaguchi was practically forced to stop filmmaking at Nikkatsu.

These excellent Nikkatsu directors developed their own aesthetics and sensibility while their common mentor Seijun Suzuki had not made any films since his highly publicized legal dispute with Nikkatsu. After ten years' absence, Suzuki made *A Sad Love Story* (*Hishū monogatari*, 1977) for Shōchiku. The film's experimental approach to the story of a woman golfer did not win it popular success but attracted some enthusiastic critical response. However, his next film, *Ziguenerweisen* (*Chigoineruwaizen*, 1979), became an amazing commercial and critical success. Independently produced, the film also employed a new method of distribution. Shown in a big movable tent called "Cinema Placette," easily set up in a park or on a department-store's roof, the film traveled all over Japan. The enigmatic Taisho era story, full of remarkable erratic images and fantasies, evolves around two middle-aged couples who go back and forth between this world and that of death. Suzuki made another enigmatic film, *The Troupe of Heat Haze* (*Kagerō-za*, 1980), in which the characters transcend time and space. This did not become as popular as his previous film.

At the beginning of the 1980s, the Nikkatsu studio promoted approximately ten assistant directors (mostly in their late twenties) to director, a decision welcomed by film audiences and critics as a sign of the revitalization of the Japanese film industry. Compared with the Nikkatsu films of the 1970s, this new generation of directors makes lighter and less ideological films, probably reflecting the changed values of the period. A typical example of this new trend is Yoshimitsu Morita, who began his career making experimental 8mm films before working for Nikkatsu for a period. His *Family Game* (*Kazoku geimu*, 1983), an ingenious comedy about contemporary urban family life and education, was hailed abroad as enthusiastically as at home.

In the field of pink films, Shinya Yamamoto's works in the 1970s were remarkable. An extremely prolific director, he was critical of current political and social issues such as government corruption and loan sharking; he also parodied well-known films. For instance, *Close Encounter with Horny Men* (*Chikan tono sōgū*, 1979) was not only a parody of Steven Spielberg's spectacular film but also a remake of Billy Wilder's *Apartment*, transformed into the sad yet funny situation of a Japanese employee dominated by his bosses. One of his most popular series is the comical *Widow's Lodging* (*Mibōjin geshuku*) series, which began in 1974, starring Shinji Kubo as an aggressive and frustrated student.

At Shōchiku, while Yamada's successful *Tora the Tramp* series financially supported the studio, Yōichi Maeda specialized in more nonsensical comedies. His iconoclastic views of bourgeois values were presented in his thoroughly absurd, jesting style. His slapstic comedies are represented by *Ah! Military Song* (*Ah! Gunka*, 1970) and *Catch the 300 million Yen* (*Sanoku-en o tsukamaero*, 1975).

Toshiyuki Yamane was known as an excellent director of youth films. Compared with Tōhō's upper-middle-class settings, Shōchiku youth films focus on young workers and students from the countryside living in big cities, those from a social class between that of the protagonists of Tōhō and Nikkatsu films. First, Yamane was assigned to adapt a popular cartoon series about a young couple living together, *The Age of Living Together* (*Dōsei jidai*, 1973). With its sequels, this film first attracted attention to the director. However, his real talent was shown in *Farewell to Summer Light* (*Saraba natsu no hikari yo*, 1976) and *Permanent Blue: The Love of Mid-Summer* (*Paamanento bruu: manatsu no koi*, 1976), in which Yamane depicted the sensibility of current youth in delicate images of light and shadow.

Ex-cameraman Kōichi Saitō presented a series of visually striking and sensuous films, *The Weight of Trip* (*Tabi no omosa*, 1972) for Shōchiku, *Promise* (*Yakusoku*, 1971) for Saito Production and Shōchiku, and finally the most successful, *Jongara-bushi of Tsugaru* (*Tsugaru Jongara-bushi*, 1973) with ATG.

Shōchiku allowed the young medical student and amateur filmmaker, Kazuki Ōmori to direct his first 35mm feature film, *Orange*

*Road Express (Orenji roodo ekusupuresu*, 1977) when his scenario received a prize at a prestigious competition commemorating the late Shōchiku studio head Shirō Kido. Ōmori was already popular among young people for his 16mm independent films (often parodies of filmmaking itself), the most famous of which was *We Cannot Wait Until Dark (Kurakunaru-made matenai*, 1975). Ōmori's essential talent was recognized in his next film, *Hippocrates (Hipokuratesu-tachi*, 1980), about medical students.

At Tōhō, Kei Kumai made *Sandakan Brothel #8 (Sandakan hachiban-shōkan*, 1974), about the hardships of young prostitutes sent to the front for the Japanese Imperial Army during the war. The film, as well as the original story written by feminist writer Tomoko Yamazaki, became successful, reflecting the rising Japanese feminist movement.

Shinoda coproduced several films with Tōhō. *Silence (Chinmoku*, 1971) studied the struggle in Japan between indigenous and foreign cultures, as shown through the persecution of Christians by the Edo government. The mood of *Sapporo Olympic Games (Sappro Orinpikku*, 1972) contrasted strongly with the optimism of Ichikawa's Olympiad film, as it anticipated various social contradictions in modern Japan. *Himiko* (1974), coproduced with ATG, is an exploration of ancient (third century A.D.) Japanese society through the political struggles around the legendary queen Himiko. This film introduced the interesting avant-garde dancers, Takumi Hijikata and his Ankoku-buto dan group. Again with Tōhō, *Under the Cherry Blossoms (Sakura no mori no mankai no shita*, 1975) presents a mysterious obsession symbolized by cherry blossoms. *Banished Orin (Hanaregoze orin*, 1977) depicts the tragic love between a blind wandering player of the *samisen* (traditional banjo-like instrument) and an army deserter, set against beautiful but often harsh landscapes.

Shinoda's Shōchiku coproduced *Demon Pond (Yashagaike*, 1979), an elaborate mythological story using popular Kabuki actor Tamasaburō Bandō in a double role as a modest housewife and the princess of the Demon Pond. *MacArthur's Children (Setouchi Shōnen Yakyūdan*, 1984) is a popular independent film on the changing period of the American occupation observed through the eyes of the children of a small inland-sea island. Shinoda's 1985 film, *Gonza, the Spearman (Yari no Gonza*), is based on Chikamatsu's Edo period adultery story, powerfully played by Iwashita and Hiromi Go (who were also stars of the previous film), and exquisitely shot by veteran cameraman Miyakawa.

Imai's lyrical *Elder Brother and Young Sister (Ani imōto*, 1975) is a modern story adapted from a literary classic which became the source of many films. He remade his earlier film *Tower of Lillies* in 1982, using the same script written by Yoko Mizuki thirty years before. This time, he featured young actresses and location shots in Okinawa which were not previously allowed.

Tōhō distributed Satsuo Yamamoto's *Elaborate Family* (*Karei naru ichizoku*, 1974) with an all-star cast, about a powerful conglomerate family, as well as *Sterile Area* (*Fumó chitai*, 1978), modeled on the Lockheed scandal. Curiously, while Tōhō was allowing leftist filmmakers to work, they, along with Tōei, also began to be criticized in the early 1980s for making a series of militaristic films. These war films included Toshio Masuda's *203 Heights* (*203 kōchi*, 1981), *Great Imperial Japan* (*Dai Nippon teikoku*, 1982), and Sōei Matsubayashi's *United Fleet* (*Rengō kantai*, 1982), all of which glorify the history of the imperial army and navy, and the war criminals who were their heroes.

Coproduction with ATG became something of a euphemism for an artistically ambitious independent filmmaker aiming at critical success. These productions included Akio Jissōji's *Ephemerality* (*Mujō*, 1970), which explores the root of Japanese eroticism through incest, Kazuo Kuroki's *Assassination of Ryoma* (*Ryōma ansatsu*, 1974), and *Preparation for Festival* (*Matsuri no jumbi*, 1975). Kuroki portrays a famous revolutionary, Ryoma, in the confusion of the end of the Edo period; the latter is an autobiographical story about a local youth trying to be a scenario writer, and the people around him.

Veteran Teshigawara presented the problems of the Vietnam War, depicting the organization in Japan that helped American deserters, in his *Summer Soldier* (*Samā sorujā*, 1972). Avant-garde theater director and poet Shūji Terayama, after making a number of short experimental films, moved into feature filmmaking with the experimental *Abandon Books, Go to the Street* (*Sho o suteyo machi ni deyo*, 1971), and then the colorful *Pastoral Hide and Seek* (*Denen ni shisu*, 1975), full of erratic, poetic, and ingenious images originating from his northern home country.

Yōichi Takabayashi had also started as an amateur experimental filmmaker in the early 1960s with Nobuhiko Ōbayashi, Taka Iimura, and others. In the mid-seventies he began to make feature films such as *The Murder Case of Honjin* (*Honjin satsujin jiken*, 1975) and *The Golden Pavilion* (*Kinkaku-ji*, 1976). Both films evidence his unique aestheticism, which became more striking than the plots (a mystery in the former case; in the other, an adaptation of Yukio Mishima's famous novel of a stuttering temple apprentice setting fire to a beautiful golden pavilion). Takabayashi is considered an expert in an exquisite expressionistic style, evident in his Daiei-produced *Irezumi* (*Sekka tomurai-zashi*, 1982) about a master tattooer who creates his art on the back of a beautiful woman.

Imamura's few films all starring Ken Ogata, consistently won critical acclaim. *Vengeance Is Mine* (*Fukushū suruwa wareni ari*, 1979), a coproduction with Shōchiku, is a portrayal of an imposter-murderer traveling through Japan. Based on a novel about an actual criminal in the 1960s, Imamura presents his analysis of the criminal in relation to his Catholic father and to his incestuous wife. His next film, *Eijanaika* (*Eejanaika*, 1980), became the most expensive film in Shōchiku's history. It is an epic about the mass energy at the end of the Edo period, shown through the wild activities of a group of young people (Shigeru Izumiya, Kaori Momoi, Masao Kusakari, and so on). Imamura's remake of Kinoshita's *Ballade of Narayama* (*Narayamabushi-kō*, 1982) for Tōei is a more realistic portrayal of a poor mountain village. In it, he analyzes the villagers' seemingly cruel customs in light of their aggressiveness and tough will to survive in the face of poverty, by relating a story of patricide from a novel of Fukasawa.

In independent production, veterans as well as newcomers created remarkable films under difficult conditions. Shindō's *Naked Nineteen Year-Old* (*Hadaka no jūkyū-sai*, 1970) is a sensitive exploration of the character of a mass murderer whose actions had shocked Japan in the previous year. This boy, after reading classics and philosophy in prison, began to claim that poverty had made him a criminal and that the authorities were therefore not entitled to judge him. In *The Life of a Film Director* (*Aru eiga kantoky no shōgai*, 1975), Shindō interviewed actors, actresses, producers, writers, and others who worked for Mizoguchi. Inserting clips from Mizoguchi's masterpieces, Shindō elucidates the great achievements and intriguing personality of his mentor, successfully depicting their shared passion for film.

Among young independent filmmakers, Mitsuo Yanagimachi attracted critical attention with his enthusiasm, political concerns, and sympathy for youth. After making a documentary on motorcycle gangs, he picked out one gang member to star in his first feature film, *The Map of a Nineteen-Year-Old Boy* (*Jūkyū-sai no chizu*, 1979). Adapted from a successful novel by Kenji Nakagami, the film depicts a frustrated boy (Yūji Homma) preparing for the university entrance exam while delivering newspapers to earn money. Yanagimachi concentrates upon the boy's feeling of anger toward society and his intimate relationship with an unsuccessful middle-aged man (Kanie). *Farewell to the Earth* (*Saraba itoshiki daichi*, 1982) examines the family relationships of a newly industrialized area, showing the harmful social and economic effects of modernization.

Yanagimachi was chosen by a department store named Seibu for their first attempt to finance the production of a Japanese film. Seibu had extended their cultural affairs activities—art exhibitions, book publishing, and record production—into the film business by opening several new specialty theaters in and around Tokyo over several years. Yanagimachi chose Nakagami to write the screenplay of "Fire Festival" (*Himatsuri*, 1985). The film explores the haunting power of Japanese animistic pantheism over the protagonist (Kinji Kitaōji), who resists the threat of industrialization and chooses to kill his family and himself. This ambitious film has been very successful abroad.

Kōhei Oguri attracted domestic and international success with his first film, *Muddy River* (*Doro no kawa*, 1981), financed by Motoyasu Kimura, an iron factory owner. Oguri returned to a conventional 1950s filmmaking style, with black-and white images on a standard-size screen, firm control of the film's pace, and detailed depiction of the characters' emotions. The story deals with the friendship between two boys and a girl of lower-class Osaka in the 1950s, and it affectionately relates the children's world to that of the adults around them.

Oguri's next film, *For Kayako* (*Kayako no tameni*, 1984) was financed by a children's theater company. Based on an autobiographical novel by Li Kai-sei, a Korean writer in Japan, this steady-paced color film adapts the love story of a Korean boy and a Japanese girl into a detailed study of the characters' emotions.

Another milestone of the Japanese cinema of this period is the series of political documentaries by independent filmmakers Shinsuke Ogawa and Noriaki Tsuchimoto. In his *Sanrizuka* series (1968–73) Ogawa captured the struggle of farmers, aided by leftist students and workers, against the government's construction of a new international airport in a fertile farming area. Tsuchimoto made his *Minamata* series (1971–76) on the effects of mercury pollution on the fishing village of Minamata, and the victims' struggle with the company responsible for this unprecedented crime. Both directors have been highly acclaimed for their tireless efforts, including living among the victims to help expose modern Japanese social and political problems. Ogawa moved to an agricultural village in northern Japan to make a series of documentary films on the farmers' lives, while himself farming as well. His first endeavor, *Japanese Village* (*Nippon furuyashiki-mura*, 1983), a four-hour-long film on the geology, history, and life of the village, was enthusiastically received by the domestic audience after the film achieved international acclaim. Tsuchimoto has been focusing on the problems caused by nuclear plants in Japan.

Other important young talents include Sōgo Ishii, who made his debut at the age of 19 with an 8mm film on a high school revolt, which was remade two years later by Nikkatsu and codirected with a veteran Yukihiro Sawada as *High School Great Panic* (*Kōkō dai panniku*, 1978). Ishii followed this with several successful films, including *Crazy Family* (*Gyakufunsha kazoku*, 1984), an explosive black comedy about a "crazy" family suffering from various extreme social pressures. Shinji Sōmai made popular adolescent films such as *Flying Couple* (*Tonderu kappurru*, 1980) and *Sailor Uniform and Her Machine-gun* (*Seiraafuku to kikanjū*, 1981).

Thanks to the presence of pop star Hiroko Yakushimaru, the latter film was the best attended domestic film of the year. Sōmai began to attract attention as one of the most "auteur" directors of his generation, due to his extremely longtake style. A 1985 film, *Typhoon Club* (*Taifū kurabu*), could not find a distributor until it received the prestigeous "Young Cinema" one-and-a-half-million dollar grand prize at the first Tokyo International Film Festival that year.

Yoshitarō Negishi won acclaim for his youth films, particularly *Distant Lightning* (*Enrai*, 1981), about a youth in a changing farming village. Banmei Takahashi, after making pink films, made the ambitious *There Is Tattoo* (*'Tattoo' Ari*, 1982), a psychological study of a true-life criminal who robbed a bank and took bankers and customers as hostages for three days, allegedly indulging himself in scandalous behavior modeled on a Pasolini film. Ironically, the film ends at the point when he attacks the bank. In 1982 Ishii, Sōmai, Negishi and Takahashi, along with four other young directors (Kazuhiko Hasegawa, Kazuo Izutsu, Toshiharu Ikeda, and Kiyoshi Kurosawa) established the Director's Company, to produce each other's individual projects. From that point on their films (previously mentioned) were produced only by this company.

In 1976 the young and aggressive publisher Haruki Kadokawa began to produce films, adapting popular books that his company had already published. He promoted his films with TV spot commercials as much as possible, and as a result, the advertising expenses outweighed the production budget. Thanks to this large-scale advertising, his films have been commercially successful; however, many critics deride them as superficial. Good or bad, it is true that Kadokawa has had a great impact on the Japanese film industry. He has produced twenty-six films to date, including one which he directed. Kadokawa is practical enough to use and even develop many young, attractive stars idolized by youth. The first of his films was Ichikawa's visually stunning detective story *The Inugami Family* (*Inugami-ke no ichizoku*, 1976), followed by big-budget, all-star films such as Sato's mystery melodrama *Proof of Men* (*Ningen no shōmei*, 1977) and large-scale action films such as Sato's *Proof of Wildness* (*Yasei no shōmei*, 1978), Mitsumasa Saito's *Civil War Defense Army* (*Sengoku jieitai*, 1979), and Fukasaku's *Day of Resurgence* (*Fukkatsu no hi*, 1980). Kadokawa has begun to use young talented directors such as Ōbayashi, Sōmai, and Negishi, as well as veterans Shinoda, Fujita, and Murakawa, and the artistic reputation of his works seems to be rising. Seibu, the department store investor, chose Yoshishige Yoshida for its second director. *Human Promises* (*Ningen no yakusoku*, 1986) was the director's first film after a twelve-year hiatus, a suspense film also involving the problems caused by senility. (The problem of aged people has been a serious social matter in Japan for the past several years.)

In 1984 two outsiders made remarkable debuts as directors. Juzo

Itami, a successful actor and essayist, wrote and directed *The Funeral* (*Osōshiki*, 1984), which dominated the major film awards of the year. Based on his own experience of having to perform the ceremony for his dead father-in-law, Itami created a clever comedy on the ritual and human behavior involved in a funeral. Makoto Wada, a popular cartoonist and fanatic film fan, made *The Wandering Record of Mahjong* (*Mājan hōrō-ki*, 1984). Set against the immediate postwar confusion, it is about the ambitions and conflicts of professional mahjong players. In black-and-white, Wada's fluid yet intense style in conveying the characters' emotions was highly acclaimed.

It is in some ways shameful that the Japanese film industry could not itself generate such active producers as Kadokawa, Kimura, and Seibu. On the other hand, the fresh energy these newcomers bring to filmmaking may help restore the traditionally high artistic and commercial standards that the world has come to expect from Japanese cinema.

## NOTES

1. This number varies according to sources. The American Occupation document entitled *Memorandum Concerning the Elimination of Undemocratic Motion Pictures*, issued 16 November 1945, claims that 236 were banned.
2. These statistics are cited in *Kinema jumpō sekai eiga sakuhin kiroku zenshū* (Kinema Jumpō's World Film Encyclopedia, (Tokyo: Kinema Jumpō-sha, 1977.
3. The Kinoshita retrospective at Locarno International Film Festival in 1986 is the first comprehensive introduction of this director abroad.
4. It may be easy to regard Oshima's ideological and formal concerns as parallel to those of European directors such as Jean-Luc Godard and Dušan Makavejev. However, it is inaccurate to assume that Oshima was influenced by these directors. Indeed, Oshima once claimed that his innovations preceded those of Godard by several years.
5. Cited in Yoshio Shirai's "Nihon no eiga-kantokutochi wa ima?" (What Are the Japanese Film Directors Doing Now?), in *Bungei Shunjū*, April 1979, pp. 212–28; *Kinema Jumpō Sekai Eiga Sakuhin Kiroku Zenshū*, pp. 264–65; and Japan Association of Film Producers, cited in *Cine-Front* (March, 1983), pp. 32–33.

## SELECTED BIBLIOGRAPHY

### Japanese

*Kinema jumpō sekai eiga jiken jimbutsu jiten* (Kinema Jumpō's World Film Encyclopedia of Events and People). Tokyo, 1970. Kinema Jumpō-sha.

*Kinema jumpō nihon eiga kantoku zenshū* (Kinema Jumpō's Japan Film Director's Encyclopedia). Tokyo, 1976. Kinema Jumpō-sha.

*Kinema jumpō sekai eiga sakuhin dai jiten* (Kinema Jumpō's World Film Great Encyclopedia). Tokyo, 1970. Kinema Jumpō-sha.

*Kinema jumpō sekai eiga sakuhin kiroku zenshū* (Kinema Jumpō's World Film Encyclopedia). Tokyo, 1977. Kinema Jumpō-sha.

*Purojusā Jinsei: Fujimoto Naozane Eiga ni Kakeru* (A Producer's Life: Naozane Fujimoto's Challenges to Film). Ed. Hideki Ozaki. Tokyo: Tōhō Company, 1981.

*Sekai no eiga sakka* (The World Film Makers) series. #3 Akira Kurosawa, 1970; #6 Nagisa Ōshima, 1970; #10 Masahiro Shinoda and Yoshishige Yoshida, 1971; Tokyo: Kinema Jumpō-sha.

*Tōei eiga 30-nen* (Tōei Film's 30 years). Tokyo: Tōei Company, 1981.

*Tōhō 50-nen-shi* (Tōhō's 50-year-history). Tokyo: Tōhō Company, 1982.

Articles

Masaharu Saito. "Sei no ikagawashisa to ikagawashii Sei" (Sexual Indecency and Indecent Sexuality). in *Gengai no Me* (Tokyo), March 1979, pp. 82–91.

Tōru Ogawa. "Pink eiga to sei hyōgen no genkai" (The Pink Films and the Limit of Sexual Expression). *Gendai no Me* (Tokyo), March 1979, pp. 76–81.

Yoshio Shirai. "Nihon no eiga-kantokutachi wa ima?" (What Are the Japanese Film Directors Doing Now?). *Bungei Shunjū* (Tokyo), April 1979, pp. 212–28.

Periodicals

*Cine-Front*, Tokyo.

*Cinéma Gras*, Tokyo.

*Eiga geijutsu* (Film Art), Tokyo.

*Image Forum*, Tokyo.

*Kinema Jumpō*, Tokyo.

English

Anderson, Joseph L. and Donald Richie. *The Japanese Film: Art and Industry* (expanded edition). Princeton: Princeton University Press, 1982.

Bock, Audie. *Japanese Film Directors*. Tokyo: Kodansha International, 1978.

Burch, Noel. *To the Distant Observer: Form and Meaning in the Japanese Cinema*. Berkeley: University of California Press, 1979.

Kurosawa, Akira. *Something Like An Autobiography*. Trans. Audie Bock. New York: Alfred A. Knopf, 1982.

McDonald, Keiko I. *Cinema East: A Critical Study of Major Japanese Films*. East Brunswick: Associated University Presses, 1983.

Mellen, Joan. *Voices from the Japanese Cinema*. New York: Liveright, 1975.

Mellen, Joan. *The Waves at Genji's Door: Japan through Its Cinema*. New York: Pantheon, 1976.

Richie, Donald *The Japanese Movie: An Illustrated History.* Tokyo: Kodansha International, 1966.

_____. *The Japanese Cinema: Film Style and National Character.* New York: Doubleday and Co., 1971.

_____. *The Film of Akira Kurosawa.* Berkeley: University of California Press, 1965.

_____. *Ozu: His Life and Films.* Berkeley: University of California Press, 1974.

Sato, Tadao. *Currents in Japanese Cinema.* Trans. Gregory Barett. Tokyo: Kodansha, 1982.

Schrader, Paul. *Transcendental Style in Film: Ozu, Bresson, Dreyer.* Berkeley: University of California Press, 1972.

Svensson, Arn. *Japan.* London, Tantivy and New York: A. S. Barnes, 1971.

Tucker, Richard N. *Japan: Film Image.* London: Studio Vista, 1973.

# LATIN AMERICA
## On the Periphery of the Periphery

JULIANNE BURTON

In many of his writings, Argentine author Jorge Luis Borges equated the universe with the towering family library of his childhood memories. For subsequent generations of Latin Americans, particularly those who came of age in the 1930s and 1940s, it was films rather than books that offered initiation into seemingly limitless realms of imagination and vicarious experience. Despite their geographical dispersion, novelists like the Mexican Carlos Fuentes, the Argentine Manuel Puig, Colombian Nobel laureate Gabriel García Márquez, and Cuban-born Guillermo Cabrera Infante draw upon a common set of cultural references because, in the words of the latter, "we are in an orbit which revolves around the movies." That orbit incorporated not only the intellectuals but large strata of the urban populations throughout Latin America and significant portions of more rural populations as well.

Given Hollywood's increasing incorporation into the war effort, the years between 1939 and 1945 constituted a boon to film-producing nations in Latin America, which had been losing ground to their North American competitor since the introduction of the (for many) prohibitively expensive sound technologies. Though the curtailment of raw film stock from U.S. suppliers (neighboring Mexico was the fortunate exception) constituted a formidable obstacle to film production, the vacuum left by the reduction in Hollywood exports—and the suspension of film imports from Europe—provided an incentive to national producers. Many among the smaller film-producing countries of Latin America—Uruguay, Bolivia, Peru, Chile, Colombia, Venezuela, and various Central American nations—produced their first important features of the sound era and introduced their first protectionist legislation for domestic film production during and immediately after this period of diminished U.S. presence.

At the end of the war, Hollywood hoped to reassert hegemony over worldwide film production, distribution, and exhibition, as evidenced in 1945 by the creation of the Motion Picture Export Association (MPEA), the international arm of the government-sanctioned cartel the Motion Picture Association of America (MPAA). This drive to reestablish and consolidate its worldwide hegemony met with new-found resistance in those European countries with long-standing national cinema traditions, as well as in those peripheral nations where reduced competition from Hollywood had sparked the growth of domestic filmmaking.

One European national film movement that evolved during and after World War II posed a direct challenge to the growing U.S. film empire and offered an example to incipient national cinemas. Italian neorealism challenged the studio system, the star system, and the very concept of the Hollywood product as the norm against which all movie-making must be measured. The neorealists were commited to location shooting, nonprofessional actors, documentary-style techniques, and loosely scripted stories of the downtrodden and dispossessed. The neorealist example was echoed in a dozen Latin American countries, inspiring a New Cinema movement throughout the region which, for all its eventual formal and thematic diversity, continues to acknowledge its shared debt to that first concerted alternative to the hegemony of the Hollywood system and the Hollywood style.

For those Latin Americans who came of age in the 1950s and 1960s, cinema retained the "universalizing" cultural importance which it had held for the previous generation while now also claiming considerable local political significance as well. This postwar generation recognized that film's utility as a vehicle for the exploration and expression of national experience was not limited to the metropolitan countries of North America and Europe, but was also within the reach of dependent, peripheral nations which were not bound to the replication and imitation of metropolitan prototypes. The officially encouraged climate of modernization and developmentalism, as well as the more critical and often militant tendency to reject forms of economic and cultural dependency, rekindled nationalist and regionalist fires. Film was the medium designated to fan the flames. The impulse toward a New Latin American Cinema, simultaneously national and continental in scope, sought both to transform existing film genres and institutions and to replace established approaches with alternative forms, contents, and modes of production.

The impulse to bring previously ignored aspects of "national reality" —indigenous communities, marginal urban populations, economically and culturally isolated groups of all kinds—to the screen for the first time in films that asserted their conceptual, formal, ideological, and technical independence from Hollywood models was registered in unprecedented efforts throughout South America in the 1950s: Jorge

Ruiz's and Augusto Roca's *Come Back, Sebastiana* (*Vuelve, Sebastiana,* Bolivia, 1953), a meditation on the imperiled survival of an ancient Andean Indian community; Ruiz's subsequent *The Watershed* (*La vertiente,* Bolivia, 1958), made in collaboration with screenwriter Oscar Soria, Bolivia's first feature-length sound film, also set and shot among the indigenous peoples of the Andes; Nelson Pereira dos Santos's neorealist feature *Rio, Forty Degrees Centigrade* (*Rio, 40 graus,* Brazil, 1955); *The Charcoal Worker* (*El mégano*), Cuba's first neorealist effort made the same year; Manuel Chambi's ethnographic documentaries *Carnival in Kanas* and *Snow Star* (*Carnaval de Kanas* and *Lucero de nieve,* Peru, both 1957); Linduarte Noronha's regionalist documentary *Aruanda* (Brazil, 1959); Venezuelan Margot Benacerraf's *Araya* (1958), a feature-length documentary on a remote fishing village; Alberto Miller's understated documentary view of the Montevideo shantytowns called *Cantegriles* (Uruguay, 1958); and finally, Fernando Birri's *Toss Me a Dime* (*Tire dié,* Argentina, 1958–1960), the first product of his Documentary Film School of Sante Fe, established in 1956. If a number of these films turned out to be isolated efforts, without sequel, others heralded the inception of sustained national film movements. The examples and activities of Nelson Pereira dos Santos in Brazil and Fernando Birri in Argentina established those countries initially as the sites of the most concerted activity. Production in Uruguay, Bolivia, Peru, and Chile was more sporadic.

The late 1960s and early 1970s marked the highpoint of the New Latin American Cinema movement and its maximum recognition throughout the world. Between 1971 and 1976, first Bolivia, then Uruguay, Chile, and finally Argentina fell to brutally repressive military takeovers, sending literally hundreds of filmmakers into exile. Peru, under "progressive" military rule since 1968, moved sharply to the right in 1975. The mid-to-late seventies brought a compensatory increase in filmmaking activity in the Central American countries as well as in Colombia and Venezuela. Growing opposition to and/or the successful ouster of military regimes in Bolivia, Argentina, Brazil, Chile, and Uruguay marked the first half of the 1980s as a period of "redemocratization" in the very area where the New Cinema movement received its initial impetus twenty-five years earlier.[1] Yet the resurgence of filmmaking activity in these countries does not disguise the fact that the medium is in crisis throughout the continent—and beyond. Film is a luxury in countries with massive unemployment, runaway inflation, and ballooning foreign debts. In recent years television has asserted itself as the more potent and pliable mass medium, relegating film to a secondary place in both economic priority and popular consciousness.

## Uruguayan Crossroads

The leading role played by Uruguay in the evolution and diffusion of the New Latin American Cinema stands in inverse proportion to the tiny size of the country (three million inhabitants in 1970) and its persistent inability, given its minuscule internal market, to generate sustained film production. Film societies and archives, specialized magazines, a number of serious and talented critics writing both in film journals and in the popular press, the early stimulus to amateur filmmaking activity, and an impressive number and variety of film festivals both stimulated and were the product of a high level of cineliteracy on the part of the Uruguayan public, who in 1953 saw an astounding yearly average of nineteen films per capita.

Film festivals, principally the biannual event sponsored by SODRE, (a state-run radio station which eventually became a kind of "substitute national ministry of culture"), were Uruguay's earliest and most important contributions to the incipient New Latin American Cinema movement. As early as 1958, this International Festival of Documentary and Experimental Films provided a meeting ground for independent and socially conscious filmmakers from the southern part of the continent.

The first attempt to organize a pan-Latin American film producers' association grew out of the 1958 SODRE festival and the concurrent First Congress of Independent Latin American Filmmakers. The founding membership of PRIDAL (Independent Producers and Directors of Latin America) included Brazil's Nelson Pereira dos Santos, Peru's Manual Chambi, Chile's Patricio Kaulen, Bolivia's Jorge Ruiz, as well as Leopoldo Torre Nilsson and Simon Feldman from Argentina. The goal of the organization, according to its founder, Uruguayan Danilo Trelles, was to provide an industrial base for the development of independent filmmaking in Latin America through facilitating access to equipment, raw film stock, specialized technicians, laboratories, and so on, as well as general financial backing including, for example, coproduction arrangements with European countries. The fact that PRIDAL subsequently evaporated, leaving very little of substance to show for the effort, does not diminish the pioneering nature of the initiative.

Despite enormous technical and financial obstacles to film production, the mid-sixties in Uruguay saw an apparently sudden burst of activity in production and diffusion which was to sustain itself until the military coup d'etat of June 1973, leaving a lasting imprint on filmmaking activity throughout the hemisphere. A small but dedicated group of documentarists focused on pressing issues of national life (the marginal population, the electoral process, student militancy, labor problems in the meat-packing industry), positing an artisan's model of often bitingly ironic political documentary which was to spark similar efforts in countries as distant as Colombia, Panama, Venezuela and Mexico. Ugo Ulive's satiric short *There's No Place Like Uruguay* (*Como el Uruguay no hay*, 1960) combines archival material and primitive animation techniques with original footage. Mario Handler's *Carlos: Film-Portrait of a Vagabond* (*Carlos: cine-retrato de un caminante*, 1965) is among the earliest and most important Latin American adaptations of *cinéma vérité*. The two documentarists collaborated on *Elections* (*Elecciones*, 1966), a formally audacious satire of a national political campaign. When the film was barred from one of the national festivals, Ulive left the country for permanent exile in Venezuela. Handler would follow a few years later, when the 1973 coup dispersed all their colleagues. Before leaving his homeland, Handler would make his primitive and powerful *I Like Students* (*Me gustan los estudiantes*, 1968), one of the most widely circulated of all the New Latin American documentaries, and two other shorts.

Uruguay was the site of an early effort to create alternative structures of commercial distribution and exhibition. Walter Achugar sought to create a financial base for Uruguayan film production—to "use movies to make movies." His Renacimiento Films distributed works by Chaplin, Hitchcock, and Jacques Tati, and later imported a number of now classic examples of Brazil's Cinema Novo, as well as the Bolivian feature *Blood of the Condor* (*Yawar mallku*, 1969), *The Jackal of Nahueltoro* (*El chacal de Nahueltoro*, 1969) from Chile, and several Cuban titles. Uruguayan audiences thus had access to a broader range of regional cinema than viewers in any other country in Latin America (except Cuba). Recognizing the insufficiency of "parallel circuits" and New Cinema's need to have its own commercial outlets, Achugar leased a major theater in 1967. He helped found another vanguard institution in Montevideo, the Third World Cinematheque, in 1969. The inaugural program presented a retrospective of work by the Dutch documentarist Joris Ivens, who was present to acknowledge the homage. At its peak, the Cinematheque had an archive of one hundred prints from Latin America, Europe, the United States, and Vietnam, which circulated throughout the country. It sponsored courses in 16mm and Super-8 film production and published a magazine, *Cine del Tercer Mundo* (Third World Cinema). As the political situation in the country grew more tense, the organization became a target for governmental repression. In May 1972 Achugar was arrested. An international protest campaign on his behalf secured his release after two months in prison. The animated short *In the Jungle There's A Lot to Do* (*En la sleva hay mucho por hacer*, 1976), an allegory of popular resistance to political repression in the guise of a children's story, was the last effort of this group of Uruguayan *cinéastes*, subsequently dispersed to Peru, Argentina, Venezuela, and Europe by the 1973 military takeover.

## Following the Festival Route

In 1965 the Cine Club del Uruguay sponsored the Festival of Independent Film from the "southern cone" in recognition of incipient activity in Argentina, Uruguay, Brazil, and Chile. Unlike the SODRE Festival, which was held every other year from the late forties through the early sixties, this festival was not repeated. But two years later, a society of amateur filmmakers on the Chilean coast organized the Fifth Annual Viña del Mar Amateur Film Festival and simultaneously hosted the first Encounter of Latin American Filmmakers, still regarded as the most important Latin American Film event ever held.

The more than twenty-five *cinéastes* in attendance from countries other than Chile included such key figures as producer Edgardo Pallero and directors Gerardo Vallejo, Jorge Cedrón, and Rodolfo Kuhn from Argentina; Carlos Diegues, Sergio Muniz, and Geraldo Sarno from Brazil; Mario Handler and Walter Achugar from Uruguay, and most significantly, given the hard-line stance against the Castro government maintained for half a decade by the United States and the OAS, Saúl Yelin and Alfredo Guevara, leaders of the Cuban Film Institute (ICAIC). Films premiered included *Now!* (1965) and *Manuela* (1966) by Cubans Santiago Alvarez and Humberto Solás; Mario Handler's *Carlos* (1965) from Uruguay; *Revolution* (*Revolucion*, 1963) by Bolivian Jorge Sanjinés; no less than seventeen documentaries from Brazil; and a revival of Argentine Fernando Birri's *Toss Me a Dime* (*Tire dié*, 1958–1960).

Viña 1967 stands as a watershed in the history of the New Latin American Cinema. A few months later, largely as a result of the Viña encounter, the tenth annual *Marcha* Film Festival, sponsored by the prominent Uruguayan newsweekly of the same name, was reoriented to reflect the growing interest in *cine de combate* from Latin America and around the world. The following year, the newly founded Documentary Film Center at the University of Los Andes in Merida, Venezuela, hosted the first Latin American Documentary Exhibition. Among the sixty films shown, several now-classic documentaries had their premieres, foremost among them: Fernando Solanas and Octavio Getino's *The Hour of the Furnaces* (*La hora de los hornos*), Mario Handler's *I Like Students* (*Me gustan los estudiantes*), Colombians Marta Rodríguez's and Jorge Silva's *Brickmakers* (*Chircales*), *Assault* (*Asalto*), by Carlos Alvarez, also from Colombia; and Cuban Octavio Cortázar's *For the First Time* (*Por primera vez*)—all made in 1968. The following year the Viña del Mar group hosted the Second Encounter of Latin American Filmmakers, premiering a number of significant documentaries and a remarkable crop of feature films. Among the latter were: *Blood of the Condor* (Bolivia, Jorge Sanjinés); *Antonio das Mortes* (Brazil, Glauber Rocha); three Chilean offerings, *The Jackal of Nahueltoro, Three Sad Tigers* (*Tres tristes tigres*), and *Valparaiso, My Love* (*Valparaíso mi amor*), by Miguel Littín, Raul Ruiz, and Aldo Francia—all made in 1969; and an equal number of now-classic Cuban films, *Lucia* (1969), *Memories of Underdevelopment* (*Memorias del subdesarrollo,* 1968), and *The First Charge of the Machete* (*La primera carga al machete,* 1969), by Humberto Solás, Tomas Gutiérrez Alea, and Manuel Octavio Gómez.

The route of these festivals—from Uruguay to Chile to Venezuela—recapitulates the northward migration of concentrated filmmaking activity from the mid-sixties to the mid-seventies. No event of rival importance would take place until 1979 with the inauguration of the annual International Festival of the New Latin American Cinema in Havana. In the 1980s major pan-Latin American festivals were organized in Brazil and in Mexico.

## The Andean Countries: Bolivia, Peru, Chile

Due to a unique configuration of national and international circumstances, at the end of the 1960s there emerged in each of these countries one or more feature filmmakers whose work was greeted with unprecedented national and international acclaim. In Bolivia Jorge Sanjinés and the Grupo Ukamau made *Blood of the Condor* (*Yawar mallku,* 1969). When the government tried to "postpone" the première, spontaneous popular demonstrations forced the release of this powerful exploration of the social cleavages between the indigenous peoples of the Andean plateau and the urbanized mestizos and whites of La Paz. The film's denunciation of sterilization without consent and the insidious role of the U.S.-sponsored "Progress Corps" won it a wide audience. It was shown in several Latin American countries as well as in Europe and the United States, where it was one of the first offerings of the New Latin American Cinema to receive extensive 16mm distribution.

Chilean filmmaker Miguel Littín made his feature debut with a desensationalized recreation of a sensational mass murder which had occurred in southern Chile a few years before. *The Jackal of Nahueltoro* (*El chacal de Nahueltoro,* 1969) retraces the course of a landless peasant called the Jackal—childhood poverty and abandonment, chronic exploitation and flight, drunkenness, murder, imprisonment, social regeneration, and eventual execution. Like *Blood of the Condor,* this film, released in 1970, was seen by more Chileans than any previous movie, domestic or foreign, in the country's history. *Condor* is believed to have been a significant factor in the Peace Corps' decision to leave Bolivia; *Jackal* provoked a national debate on class discrimination within the Chilean judicial system.

In Peru Armando Robles Godoy released his third and most successful feature, *The Green Wall* (*La muralla verde,* 1970). This tale of the travails of a young city couple who decide to homestead in the Amazon region is told with Robles's characteristic technical and stylistic virtuosity. The film drew a large audience at home and won a number of prizes abroad. Robles, who shot most of his films in color and had them processed in Venezuelan laboratories, insisted that Latin American films did not need to eschew the higher production values maintained by Hollywood and European products. Though he organized and led Peru's first training course for filmmakers, he saw himself as an individual *auteur* rather than as part of a national or pan-national movement. From the mid-seventies he dedicated himself to the production of *telenovelas* (soap operas).

What preceded this sudden flowering in these three countries and to what degree were these successful films evidence of more sustained and generalized activity? Parallels are overshadowed by differences from one country to the next. Peru's Armando Robles Godoy was the most *sui generis*. In contrast to the brief flourishing of feature films prior to and during World War II when President Manuel Prado imposed a ten-cent surcharge on movie tickets "to encourage national filmmaking," the 1950s offered a bleak horizon dominated by *actualidades* (commercial or officially sponsored newsreels). The single exception was to be found not in Lima but high in the Andes. In 1955, in the ancient Incan city of Cuzco, local architect Manuel Chambi and his brother Víctor founded the Cuzco Film Society (Cine-Club de Cuzco) and began shooting amateur ethnographic records of regional festivals. Two years later, two Italian filmmakers, Enrico Gras and Mario Craveri, shot *The Empire of the Sun* (*El imperio del sol,* 1957). The film received wide international circulation and, more importantly for the members of the Cuzco Film Society, it provided them with a practical apprenticeship which would form the basis of what French film historian Georges Sadoul would recognize as "the Cuzco School." That same year Manuel Chambi shot *Carnival in Kanas* (*Carnaval de Kanas,* 1957), an ethnographic short which was shown at a number of festivals in Latin America and Europe. *Kukili* (1960), an ethnographic feature made by Eulogio Nishiyama, Luis Figueroa, and César Villanueva, represented the apogee of the Cuzco School. The commercial and critical failure of its sequel, *Jarawi* (1965), testified to the decline of the group.

The subsequent decade brought a gradual renewal of activity in Lima: the founding of a number of short-lived film societies as well as two more lasting institutions, Miguel Reynal's University Film Archive and the magazine *Hablemos de cine* (both 1965). Later in the decade several groups of documentarists, a number of them trained by Robles, began producing their first work. Extreme difficulties in financing and recuperating investments led these groups to unite in their effort to lobby for government legislation in favor of national film production. Law #19377 was finally passed in 1972, and the subsequent years saw a burst of documentary activity—commercial as well as independent—since this was the area most favored by the legislation. Prominent Peruvian independent documentarists include Nora de Izcue, Nelson García, Mario Jacob, and Mario Tejada. The first Semana de Cine National (National Film Festival Week) was held in 1977. In 1983 some twenty-five independent production companies produced seventy documentaries. The late 1970s and early 1980s also brought forth a significant crop of feature films by directors like Francisco Lombardi, whose *Death at Dawn (Muerte al amanecer,* 1977) has been the only recent feature to recoup its investment within the domestic market, and Federico García, whose films consistently deal with indigenous themes.

Unlikely as it may be for one of the most underpopulated and underdeveloped nations in South America, Bolivia can lay claim to one of the most important pioneers of an autochthonous national cinema, Jorge Ruiz. In 1947 Ruiz and Augusto Roca founded Bolivia Films with the assistance of an American physician and film buff, Kenneth B. Wasson. The company survived for more than three decades (a remarkable lifespan in a continent where few such enterprises last more than five years) and produced over one hundred shorts and features. Later in his career Ruiz worked on commission for such organizations as the United States Information Agency, the Agency for International Development, and the Alliance for Progress, as well as a number of international corporations, on contracts which sometimes took him to Ecuador, Peru, and Guatemala. In historical and artistic terms his most important works are the early independent features *Come Back, Sebastiana (Vuelve, Sebastiana,* 1953) and *The Watershed (La vertiente,* 1958), both of which deal with indigenous communities' struggle for survival.

In 1952, after a national uprising brought the popularly supported MNR (National Revolutionary Movement) to power, a film department was created as part of the Ministry of Press and Information. The department was the forerunner of the Bolivian Film Institute (ICB), which came into being the following year. Between 1953 and 1956 the organization made 150 newsreels and documentaries in support of the programs of the MNR. Ruiz became technical director of ICB in 1956.

In 1960 a young man who would eventually surpass Ruiz in his importance as a filmmaker returned from Chile where he had been an official student of philosophy and an unofficial student of filmmaking at the Catholic University in Santiago. Jorge Sanjinés teamed up with scriptwriter Oscar Soria (*La vertiente*) to found three short-lived projects: a film magazine, a film society, and a film school. In 1961 the pair made a short film for the national lottery, and then a second commissioned fictional documentary short for the MNR two years later in collaboration with Ricardo Rada. *Revolution (Revolución,* 1963), a ten-minute silent montage on the social conditions that sparked the 1952 revolution that brought the MNR to power, is the group's first important film. The following year a military takeover ousted the MNR, and the new president, General René Barrientos, offered the technical directorship of the ICB to Sanjinés. *That's the Way It Is (Ukamau,* 1965) was the first feature-length film shot in the Aymara language. Sanjinés, Soria, and Rada eliminated the voice-over narration they had often used in the past in an attempt to let the Indian peasants tell their story from their own perspective. Though officially compelled to praise the film because it was made under their aegis, the government promptly closed down the ICB. In commemoration of the experience, the Sanjinés group assumed the name *Grupo Ukamau.*

*Blood of the Condor* (1969), discussed above, was their next film. Footage for a subsequent project, *The Roads of Death (Los caminos de la muerte),* was destroyed in an Argentine laboratory. In 1971 Radiotelevisione Italiana offered to coproduce a film with the group. *The Courage of the People (El coraje del pueblo,* 1971) marked a change in direction for Sanjinés. Dissatisfied with the fictional overlay of *Blood of the Condor,* he began to experiment with collaborative, on-site historical reconstruction using entire communities as his cast. *The Courage of the People* recreates the events preceeding, during, and subsequent to the infamous St. John's Eve massacre of miners and their families in Bolivia's Siglo XX (Twentieth-Century) tin mines in June 1967. The opening montage of names and faces of Bolivian officials responsible for the attack was ostensibly one of the reasons that the film's European and American release was delayed for several years.

A right-wing military coup in Bolivia while Sanjinés and Rada were doing postproduction on the film in Rome effectively split the Ukamau Group in two. Cameraman Antonio Eguino and scriptwriter Oscar Soria decided to remain in Bolivia. Sanjinés and Rada, unwelcome in their home country, began to explore opportunities in other Andean nations, working semiclandestinely among the indigenous communities. They made *The Principal Enemy (El enemigo principal,* 1973) in Peru, *Get Out of Here! (¡Fuera de aquí!,* 1976) in Ecuador, and *That's Enough! (¡Basta ya!,* 1979) in Colombia and Venezuela, before a change of government allowed them to return to Bolivia in 1979.

In the meantime the other Ukamau Group had made two successful features within Bolivia: *Small Town (Pueblo chico,* 1974) and *Chuquiago* (1977). The second film, a four-part exploration of the social topography of the capital city, La Paz,—from the Indians who barely subsist on its rim to the sheltered lives of the superrich in the valley of this urban crater—was the biggest box-office success in the nation's history. After successful premieres in New York and Europe, it was rereleased in Bolivia in early 1979, playing again to sell-out crowds.

The return to democratic government followed a shaky course in Bolivia in the 1980s, under the dual threat of national bankruptcy and military takeover. Before the brutal military coup of 1980 considerable headway had been made in establishing Super-8 workshops in a number of peasant and worker organizations throughout the country, due in large part to the efforts and example of French filmmaker Alain Labrousse and the Bolivian filmmaker, historian, and critic Alfonso Gumucio Dagrón who had trained in Paris in the 1970s. Return to democratic government provided the conditions for the resumption of this work, with its impulse toward a representative popular cinema of, for, and *by* the majority of Bolivian citizens—the working class and the indigenous peasantry.

The directorial debut of Miguel Littín in Chile in 1969 was part of a much broader cultural and political movement. That same year a number of other directors who would soon assume pivotal roles also released their first features: Raúl Ruiz's *Three Sad Tigers* (*Tres tristes tigres*), Helvio Soto's *Blood-stained Nitrate* (*Caliche sangriente*), and Aldo Francia's *Valparaíso, My Love* (*Valparaíso, mi amor*). These films heralded a period of remarkable creative energy which would last through and extend beyond the years of the Allende government (1970–1973). Though the Viña del Mar festival two years before had provided the immediate impetus, a history of Chilean filmmaking reveals a number of institutional and individual antecedents. During the whole of Chile's cinematic history, from the turn of the century to 1960, barely 160 features were produced—fully half of them during the silent period (1916–1931) and half of those in turn between 1925 and 1927, the fleeting "golden years" of the national film industry. The introduction of sound in the late 1920s put a brake on this activity, with but one additional brief period of productivity at the end of the following decade, under the Popular Front government which came to power in 1938. The Popular Front government also created a national film production company, Chile Films, with financing shared between the private sector and a national development agency. Chile Films released its first feature in 1944 and suspended production five years later, having been unable to sustain the Hollywood-inspired studio model it had sought to imitate. In 1950, in reaction to the influx of Argentine directors, many of whom had been imported by Chile Films, Chilean filmmakers formed their own association, DIPROCINÉ. Despite this initiative, feature production during the subsequent decade remained sporadic, seldom exceeding one per year.

Despite its erratic rate of feature film production, Chile was more fortunate than its neighbors in having early and relatively effective governmental support, and in the establishment—from the mid-fifties to the mid-sixties—of a number of university-based centers for film study and production. Among the most important were the Film Institute of the Catholic University, founded by Rafael Sánchez in 1955, which became, in 1970, part of the School of Communication Arts (and then, in 1978 reverted to the Film Institute, still under Sánchez's direction); the Film Society of the University of Chile, also founded in 1955, which created its own Experimental Film Center two years later, with Sergio Bravo as its first director (this became the audiovisual department of the University of Chile until the military coup of 1973 closed it down); the University Cinematheque, founded in 1962 under Pedro Chaskel's direction, also at the national university; the Viña del Mar Film Society, founded and directed by Aldo Francia in 1962, which promoted amateur activities in 8mm and 16mm and in 1967 sponsored the first Festival of the New Latin American Cinema; and finally, the Film Degree Program (Carrera de Cine) at the University of Chile at Valparaiso, which functioned between 1968 and 1973.

For forty years, beginning in the early 1930s, government agencies and private companies produced a series of national newsreels like *Chile on the March* (*Chile en marcha*). During this period the majority of Chilean documentarists were independent filmmakers who did work for hire through their own private production companies, occasionally producing an unsponsored film on a topic of their own choosing. This group, among whom Patricio Kaulen is perhaps the most representative, constituted an intermediary generation between the pioneers of the 1930s and the university-trained generation which would emerge after the mid-sixties. Sergio Bravo's career unites the two dominant tendencies in Chilean documentary: the exploration of specific regional and national cultural traditions, and the explicitly political documentary. His early films—*Wicker* (*Mimbre,* 1957), *Threshing* (*Trilla,* 1958), *Scenes from Almahue* (*Láminas de Almahue,* 1961)—belong to the first tendency. In 1962 the Dutch documentarist Joris Ivens was invited to Chile to attend a retrospective of his work at the national university's cinematheque. Over the next two years Ivens returned several times, making two films in collaboration with Sergio Bravo and the Center for Experimental Films. Two of Bravo's most famous documentaries— *Coal March* (*La marcha al carbón,* 1963), about a coal miners' strike, and *The People's Banners* (*Las banderas del pueblo,* 1964), made in support of Salvador Allende's electoral campaign of that same year—date from that period and signal a new level of political engagement. There was no direct link between Bravo and the politically involved generation which immediately followed him, however, since the first of this pair of documentaries was lost and the second was banned by the censors. Bravo left the university and his filmmaking activity declined. He later resumed teaching at the University of Valparaiso. Few members

Young Andean peasants in a contemplative moment from Jorge Sanjinés's *Blood of the Condor* (*Yawar mallka*, 1969, Bolivia).

Here Sanjinés strives to retain a collective context for the indigenous communities he examines. This long shot is from *Get Out of Here!* (1976, Ecuador).

The police, with the media, return an accused man to the scene of his crime. Miguel Littín's *The Jackal of Nahueltoro* (1969, Chile) indicted the Chilean justice system.

*Popular Power* (1979, Chile), the third and final part of *The Battle of Chile*, tried with limited success to get beyond the anonymous masses to a more personalized vision of social change.

In *Brickmakers* (1968, Colombia), the documentary team of Jorge Silva and Marta Rodríguez links primitive working conditions to forms of social and cultural alienation.

(Left)
The great success of *Portable Country* (1978, Venezuela), based on a novel of the same name, confirmed the existence of a large domestic market for national films.

of the generation of "Popular Unity" filmmakers who burst on the scene in 1970, with the election to the presidency of socialist coalition candidate Salvador Allende, were fully aware of their debt to Bravo.

The Popular Unity government had not yet completed its third year in power when it was overthrown by the bloodiest military coup in Latin American history. A fully articulated cultural policy was never developed during that brief period. Miguel Littín, named by Allende in 1970 to head Chile Films, resigned before the year was out in frustration at the lack of resources and the impossibility of reconciling the different political affiliations which the national film production company had by law to encompass. Despite these and related difficulties, this period was the richest in the history of Chilean filmmaking. Scores of new filmmakers emerged, particularly in the field of documentary, where the annual rate of production had reached fifty by 1973. Among the most important were: in 1970, *We Shall Win* (*Venceremos*), by Pedro Chaskel and Héctor Ríos, *Houses or Shit* (*Casa o mierda*), by Carlos Flores and Guillermo Cahn, *My Little Daughter* (*Mijita*), by Sergio and Patricio Castilla, *The Ramona Parra Brigade* (*Brigada Ramona Parra*), by Alvaro Ramírez, Samuel Carvajal, and Leonardo Céspedes; in 1971, Miguel Littín's *Compañero Presidente*, Claudio Sapiaín's *Santa María de Iquique*, *No Time for Tears* (*No es hora de llorar*), by Pedro Chaskel and Luis Alberto Sanz, Angelina Vázquez's *Nitrate Chronicle* (*Crónica del salitre*), and Patricio Guzmán's *The First Year* (*El primer año*); in 1972, Patricio Guzman's and El Equipo Primer Año's *The Answer to October* (*La respuesta de octubre*), Hector Ríos's *To Drink or Not to Drink* (*Entre ponerle y no ponerle*); and in 1973, *The Insolent and Disheveled* (*Descomedidos y chascones*), by Carlos Flores, Raúl Ruiz's *Stocking Up* (*Abastecimiento*), Douglas Hubner's *Popular Songbook* (*Cancionero popular*). Of the feature films made under the Allende period, the most outstanding are Miguel Littín's *The Promised Land* (*La tierra prometida*, 1973, never released in Chile), Raúl Ruiz's *No One Said a Thing* (*Nadie dijo nada*, 1971), Helvio Soto's *The Vote and the Gun* (*Voto + fusil*, 1970) and *Metamorphosis of a Political Police Chief* (*Metamorfósis de un jefe de la policía política*, 1973), and Aldo Francia's *Praying Is No Longer Enough* (*Ya no basta con rezar*, 1971).

After the coup d'etat Aldo Francia and Carlos Flores were among those who opted to remain in Chile, but all the other feature filmmakers and most of the documentarists left the country. Miguel Littín went to Mexico, Raúl Ruiz and Helvio Soto to France, Patricio Guzmán and his group first to France and later to Cuba, where between 1975 and 1979 they edited their magnificent three-part documentary on the last year of the Allende government: *The Battle of Chile* (*La batalla de Chile*); *The Insurrection of the Bourgeoisie* (*La insurrección de la burguesía*, 1975); *The Coup d'état* (*El golpe de estado*, 1977) and *Popular Power* (*El poder popular*, 1979). Cuba opened its doors to a number of Chilean *cinéasts,* including Pedro Chaskel, Sergio and Patricio Castilla, and leading actor and actress Nelson Villagra and Shenda Román. Germany, Finland, Canada, and a dozen other countries became home to a number of other Chilean filmmakers. Some of these filmmakers have managed to establish themselves as recognized members of the local avant-garde—Raúl Ruiz's Parisian success is the foremost example. Miguel Littín preferred to work on Latin American soil, and after Mexican state funding was restricted, had to establish elaborate coproduction and cooperative financing schemes in order to produce films like *Viva el Presidente* (*El recurso del método,* 1978), *Montiel's Widow* (*La viuda de Montiel,* 1980), and *Alsino and the Condor* (*Alsino y el condor,* 1983).

Early in the 1980s a number of Chilean filmmakers began receiving permission to return to their country. Despite the bleak economic prospects and continued political tension, many have chosen to do so. All centers of independent film production were early targets of the military regime. The last training center, part of the Catholic University's School of Theater, Film, and Television, was closed down in 1978. Government policy discouraged all film production outside of the publicity sphere. Only a handful of significant films have been produced in Chile since the coup: the anonymous *Message from Chile* (*Recado de Chile,* 1980), containing clandestine interviews with female relatives of "disappeared" persons; a few serious documentaries on cultural topics by Carlos Flores, including one on Chilean novelist *Pepe Donoso* (1977), and a single feature, Silvio Caiozzi's period piece on the coming of age of a landowner's son, *Julio Begins in July* (*Julio comienza en julio,* 1979). Because of their portability, flexibility, and economy, there is growing interest in Super-8 and particularly video formats. Returning filmmakers bring with them a wealth of technical knowledge and practical experience acquired in countries throughout Europe and the Americas —a creative capital potentially capable of reinitiating an impressive national cinema movement so brutally disrupted.

## Cinema and the State: Colombia and Venezuela

Patterns of film production have historically been markedly different in Colombia and Venezuela. The war years saw the founding of a number of feature production companies in Colombia (most of them short-lived), as well as the introduction of protective legislation, while neighboring Venezuela, despite encouragement from Rómulo Gallegos, president of the country and its most famous novelist, experienced no similar flurry of activity. In the following decade, however, Venezuela could boast the pioneering work of Margot Benacerraf, whose two documentaries (*Reverón,* 1952, and *Araya,* 1958) won international recognition. Struggling independent documentary movements surfaced in both countries in the late 1960s. In Colombia these included Jorge Silva and Marta Rodríguez, makers of *Brickmakers* (*Chircales*, 1968), Carlos Alvarez's *Assault* (*Asalto*, 1968), Julia Alvarez's *One Day I Asked* (*Un día yo pregunté*, 1970), and Carlos Mayolo's *Bolivar's Country House* (*La quinta de Bolívar*, 1969). Among Venezuelan documentarists active during this period were Jesús Enrique Guedes (*The City Which Sees Us* [*La ciudad que nos ve*, 1967]), Carlos Rebolledo (*Dead Well* [*Pozo muerto*, 1967]), and Alfredo Anzola (*Santa Teresa*, 1969). Cine Urgente, a particularly interesting group experiment in documenting specific social problems of, for and with, particular marginal groups as a means of mass education and mobilization, lasted from 1968 to 1973. Because of the nature of the project, only the last film of the cycle (Josefina Jordán's and Franca Danda's *María de la Cruz*, 1973) was designed for and received more generalized distribution.

The cases of Venezuela and Colombia are similar to the extent that in the 1970s the governments of both countries recognized the political, economic, and cultural importance of the film medium and decided to participate in its financing and promotion. In 1971 the Colombian government passed a law decreeing obligatory exhibition of Colombian shorts at first-run theaters, raising admission prices, establishing a system of rebates to producers and distributors, and setting up a government-appointed Film Quality Advisory Board to determine which films qualify for exhibition and rebates. Though the statistics are impressive (by 1975 annual production of short films—fictional and documentary—had soared to nearly one hundred), debate has often flared up over both the uneven quality of this "surcharge cinema" and the conservative political bias of selection criteria. In 1978 the government set up FOCINE (Film Development Company), a state-owned commercial enterprise tied to the Ministry of Communications and funded through the Film Development Fund, to implement state policy in the film sector.

Several Colombian documentarists most closely associated with the New Latin American Cinema movement were either unable to get their films admitted to the surcharge circuit or were opposed to trying. Other young filmmakers attempted to beat the government at its own game, devising fictional shorts which concealed subversive messages beneath ingratiatingly comic or melodramatic wrappers. Carlos Mayolo's and Luis Ospina's *Without Curtain* (*Sin telón*), *Asunción*, and *The Hammock* (*La hamaca*)—all 1975—are early examples of this approach. In 1983, on the heels of legislation defining and promoting "feature films which highlight national values," these two young filmmakers were responsible for two of the eight projects then underway.

In Venezuela state entry into the film sphere, which dates to the government's 1973 resolution in support of national cinema, eventually resulted in an outstanding harvest of features films—outstanding in both critical acclaim and audience interest. Intermediate steps, implemented from 1975, included state subsidies to finance film production; attempts to regulate the import, distribution, and exhibition of foreign films; legislation requiring that a minimal number of prints of foreign films be processed in national laboratories; exhibition quotas for national films; and imposition of a ceiling on the percentage of box-office receipts demanded by distributors. Between 1975 and 1980 credits granted by the state partially financed twenty-nine feature films. Foremost among these are Mauricio Wallerstein's *Sacred and Obscene* (*Sagrado y obsceno*, 1975) and *The Company Excuses a Moment of Insanity* (*La empresa perdona un momento de locura*, 1978) Román Chalbaud's *The Fish That Smokes* (*El pez que fuma*, 1977), Carlos Rebolledo's *Alias the Joropo King* (*Alias, el rey del Joropo*, 1978), and Iván Feo's and Antonio Llerandi's *Portable Country* (*País portátil*, 1978).

In 1980, when *Variety* magazine deemed Venezuela the fastest growing national film industry in Latin America, internal rivalries and reversals were already converting boom to bust. Funding allocations, which had increased markedly from 1975 to 1977, began to decline in 1977 and were in effect "frozen" until 1980. Delayed release of many films gave the appearance that the boom was continuing despite the freeze on allocations, but many filmmakers had to suspend projects or seek private funding. Jurisdictional struggles accounted in large part for this paralysis, as the National Film Board under the Ministry of Development fought usurpation by the Ministry of Information and Tourism. Filmmakers attempted to unite to lobby the outgoing government of Carlos Andrés Pérez and the incoming (1980) regime of Luis H. Campins for a coherent National Film Law—long debated but still unimplemented, but factional splits divided and weakened their efforts.

Despite many reversals, unfulfilled promises, conflicts and frustrations, prolonged discussion on the issue of national film legislation has had the virtue of stimulating widespread dialogue on the issue of national culture in a country that once seemed quite content to simply import its culture, like its whiskey and its stereos, direct from Miami. An active independent documentary movement in Venezuela, with a significant proportion of training provided by the film department of the University of the Andes in Merida, has made the national culture issue a central focus. In 1981 three such documentaries enjoyed the unusual distinction of being blown up to 35mm for joint theatrical release: *Listen, Caracas* (*Yo hablo a Caracas*), in which an Amazonian tribal chief denounces the deculturation of his people by North American missionaries; *El Afinque de Marín,* on the multiethnic influences of urban music; and *Our Miami* (*Miyami nuestro*), a satiric meditation on the Venezuelan consumer "takeover" of that Florida city. The commercial success of this unlikely grouping, like that of the feature films listed above (which often enjoyed more box-office success than their foreign competition) proves that there is an internal market for national cinema in Venezuela. Whether the momentum of the mid-seventies will be regained hinges on the government's willingness to recreate the conditions of its own remarkable but controversial success.

## Central America: Political Economies of Scale

Nicaragua is the largest and least populous of the six Central American republics; El Salvador is the most densely populated and the smallest. The history of film production in both countries is scant indeed. The Somoza dynasty, during its five decades in power in Nicaragua, tolerated no oppositional media. Progressive film culture was limited to a few struggling film societies in Managua. El Salvador was somewhat more fortunate. Pioneer Alfredo Mussi made the first Salvadorean feature in 1924. In the 1960s Alejandro Cotto received some international recognition before he abruptly terminated his career after his second film. Baltazar Polió made a number of shorts in the late 1970s. In 1980 El Taller de los Vagos (Loafers' Workshop), a theater collective, made an experimental documentary about the victims of violent repression. One of the members of this group, French-trained Guillermo Escalón, also works in Super-8.

Neither the Sandinistas nor the opposition in El Salvador can produce more than a handful of films per year. Equipment is often primitive and always in short supply. (In 1980 the Nicaraguan Film Institute's (INCINE) entire arsenal of cameras numbered only six, including one Super-8 sound camera and a vintage 35mm Mitchell.) Trained personnel are also few in number. (Among INCINE's staff of fifty-five are six cinematographers, three editors, one sound person, and one scriptwriter.) Both countries depend heavily on international donations of equipment and film stock. Despite these acute limitations, the political struggle waged in these two countries since the late 1970s has made them a focal point of worldwide media attention and the site of some of the most important developments in Latin American film and media history.

Nicaragua's limited size, population, and resources stand in stark contrast to the enormity of the tasks which it has undertaken and of the internal and external obstacles to their realization. Exactly twenty years after the overthrow of Batista in Cuba, Nicaragua became the second Latin American country to depose a U.S.-supported dictator through prolonged guerrilla warfare and massive insurrection. It is one of only three countries during the same period (after Cuba and Chile) to undertake reorganization of the national political economy and a parallel redefinition of the bases of national cultural production. Since coming to power in 1979, the Sandinista government has founded several media organizations: the National Film Institute (INCINE); Sistema Sandinista de Televisión (SST); Taller de Cine Super-8 (Super-8 Film Workshop), a joint project of the United Nations and the Union of Sandinista Workers; and the video arm of the National Agrarian Reform agency (MIDINRA).

The largest of these, INCINE, is divided into two sectors, production and distribution. Its primary emphasis has been the production of periodic 35mm black-and-white newsreels for theatrical distribution. These *noticieros,* averaging eight per year, include #1: *The History of Sandinismo,* #5: *The Literacy Campaign,* #11: *The Atlantic Coast,* #26: *The Penal System.* Ramiro Lacayo, Frank Pineda, and María José Alvarez have collaborated on a large number of these, with Rafael Ruiz as cinematographer. INCINE has also made a number of color "feature documentaries." The first of these, *Education Was Not Interrupted (La educación no se interrumpió,* 1979) was produced in video pending access to 16mm equipment and trained personnel. Subsequent films include *Gold's Other Face (La otra cara del oro,* 1981), by Rafael Vargas and Emilio Rodríguez Vazquez, and *Story of a Committed Cinema (Historia del cine comprometido,* 1983), also by Rodríguez. INCINE's third function involves "special projects"—collaborations with other government agencies and coproduction or liaison with foreign filmmakers. Documentarists from throughout the Americas and Europe have come to film in Nicaragua and, directly or indirectly, to train Nicaraguan filmmakers. These include a number of North Americans, Mexicans, Cubans, Chileans, Argentines, Bolivians, as well as the Brazilian-American director Helena Solberg (*Nicaragua: From the Ashes,* 1981), the German Peter Lilienthal (*The Insurrection,* 1980, a feature film), the Finnish documentarist Victoria Schultz (*Women in Arms,* 1980). The most ambitious of these special projects was the coproduction of the allegorical feature, *Alsino and the Condor,* (1983, directed by Chilean Miguel Littín). Jackie Reiter and Wolf Tirado, German and Chilean filmmakers, have formed the Tercer Cine Collective, which has produced both 16mm and video films primarily for international audiences. Committed to transferring their skills to Nicaraguans, they founded Taller Popular de Video in 1981 and Videonic in 1984 for that purpose.

The situation in El Salvador has been even more fragile and beleaguered. With the continuing guerrilla war, media activists and organizations like the Instituto Cinematográfico de El Salvador, Radio Venceremos (which includes a film and video unit), the Underground Film and Cero a la Izquierda (Zero to the Left) Collectives, and others have been forced to function clandestinely. Like Nicaragua, El Salvador has also been the locus of "solidarity cinema": films made by non-Salvadoreans in support of the rebel cause. Cero a la Izquierda's *Decision to Win*

(*La decisión de vencer*, 1981) was the first film about the revolutionary campaign to be made with an exclusively Salvadorean crew.

Now known as Sistema Radio Venceremos Film and Television Collective, this group produced the remarkable *A Time of Daring* (*Tiempo de audacia*) in 1983, a disarmingly close and candid look behind the lines of both government troops and guerrilla forces, edited with subtlety, wit, and a brilliant sense of the visual.

The proliferation of media groups has borne testimony to the heightened importance of image culture—not just as a means of providing counterinformation on the war effort and national political situation in order to challenge hegemonic international news sources, but also as a tool of sociopolitical consolidation in zones where the military offensives have been supplanted by campaigns for popular education. The experience of the Radio Venceremos film group is particularly noteworthy in this context. In the liberated zone of Morazan, where Radio Venceremos has been based, the focus is civilian rather than military: making didactic films for practical education, recording meetings and seminars for purposes of political education, and providing a medium through which people can offer testimony of their own experiences. Most of this group's work has been done in video because it has the unmatched advantage of being instantly viewable (whereas 16mm and even Super-8 footage has to be smuggled outside the country for processing). In addition, video can be reviewed an indefinite number of times and then eventually recycled. Clandestine distribution and exhibition becomes much more feasible when tapes can be easily duplicated, carried in a pocket, and screened on an increasingly common home appliance.

In terms of the proliferation, conceptualization, and utilization of the visual media, El Salvador and particularly Nicaragua have developed more rapidly and on more simultaneous fronts than any other countries in Latin American history. Many factors help to account for the key role being accorded the visual media in this region: the confluence of media makers from throughout the developed world, the heightened awareness of the role played by the media first in prolonging and eventually in terminating U.S. military involvement in Vietnam and of the parallels between the Southeast Asian and Central American conflicts, the growing awareness of the twenty-five-year history of politically committed film movements throughout Latin America. The eclectic mixture of media—16mm, Super-8, video, black and white, color, odds and ends of film stock—which has given Central American documentaries their particular "look" is both the result of an accommodation to practical limitations *and* a creative media synthesis which reflects evolving modes of distribution and exhibition, as well as production, and undertakes to meet the multiple challenges implicit in the crisis of national film production in contemporary Latin America.

## NOTE

1. Cuba's exclusion from this geo-chronology and the pages that follow derives from the fact that its status as the only socialist regime in Latin America has made the evolution of its national cinema, however much it both inspired and responded to developments on the mainland, a case apart. See separate article on Cuba.

## SELECTED BIBLIOGRAPHY

Burton, Julianne, ed. *Cinema and Social Change in Latin America: Conversations with Filmmakers*. Austin: University of Texas Press, 1986. Twenty interviews covering the past three decades.

Chanan, Michael, ed. *Twenty-five Years of the New Latin American Cinema*. London: British Film Institute and Channel Four Television, 1983. Translations of six key theoretical essays by Birri, Rocha, Solanas and Getino, García Espinosa and Sanjinés.

Hennebelle, Guy, and Alfonso Gumucio Dagron, eds. *Les Cinémas de l'Amérique Latine*. Paris: Textimages, 1981. Country-by-country histories.

Mattelart, Armand, Xavier Delcourt, and Michele Mattelart. *International Image Markets: In Search of an Alternative Perspective*. Translated from the French by David Buxton. London: Comedia, 1984. Overview of the international political economy of visual media with strategies for challenging existing power imbalances.

Schnitman, Jorge. *Film Industries in Latin America: Dependency and Development*. Norwood, NJ: Ablex, 1984. Contrasts the development of the larger national industries (Brazil, Argentina, Mexico) with the experience of smaller countries (Chile, Bolivia).

# MEXICO
## From the Golden Age to the Present

DENNIS WEST

By 1945 the Mexican motion-picture industry had entered its so-called golden age. A financial base for the industry had been created in 1942 with the establishment of a centralized, government-supported credit agency (the Banco Cinematográfico), which extended financing to private producers. World War II stimulated many of the country's economic activities, including movie production. Because Mexico supported the Allies, its movie industry received film stock and economic and technical aid from the United States. During the war the Mexican film industry captured an increased share of the Latin American market because Hollywood had ended its own production of Spanish-language films, and had retreated from this market. Mexico's motion-picture industry produced a record eighty-two films in 1945 while the competing Argentine and Spanish industries together turned out only fifty-six. In the Mexican industry in 1945 major studios were being consolidated, and a star system was emerging. Some of the luminaries, such as the comic Cantinflas (Mario Moreno), had large international followings. Mexico even boasted a director who was soon to be acclaimed in Europe: Emilio Fernández.

Emilio "El Indio" Fernández was the greatest directorial presence in Mexico in the 1940s. In 1943 he made two of his most famous (and also most typical) films: *Wild Flower* (*Flor silvestre*) and *María Candelaria* (*María Candelaria*). One-third domestic melodrama, one-third ranch comedy, and one-third revolutionary adventure, *Wild Flower* is the story of a young rural couple who marry in spite of class differences and who eventually are swept up in the violence of the revolution of 1910. *María Candelaria* is a poignant tale about the tragic love and suffering of an Indian peasant couple in Xochimilco, a picturesque area on the southern edge of Mexico City famous for its canals and gardens. *María*

*Candelaria* won prizes at the Cannes (1946) and Locarno (1947) film festivals and was the first Mexican film to become widely known in Europe. These two films are particularly important in the history of Mexican cinema because they launched the successful Mexican career of the strikingly beautiful Dolores del Río, who had previously appeared in many Hollywood pictures; more importantly, these movies marked the beginning of Fernández's collaboration with the talented cinematographer Gabriel Figueroa. Figueroa and Fernández collaborated on many films, and they generally used the characteristic visual style that they had established in *Wild Flower* and *María Candelaria*.

The Fernández-Figueroa style is exemplified in *Hidden River* (*Río escondido,* 1947), one of their finest films. It stars María Félix as the sickly schoolmarm sent personally by Mexico's president to bring literacy to a remote village ruled by a brutal *cacique* (local boss). This patriotic story is filmed in an epic and poetic style apparently influenced by Eisenstein's unfinished *¡Que viva México!* and Zinnemann's and Strand's *The Wave (Redes,* 1934). Fernández and Figueroa favor carefully composed, stationary-camera long shots to capture the beauty of the vast Mexican landscape and man's place in that landscape. Low-angle long shots admire the boundless sky and stress the diminutiveness of the human figure, which is often positioned next to a "typical" Mexican plant such as the maguey or the prickly pear cactus. In many long shots the actions of the characters are beautifully framed by the limbs of a dead tree, the weathered boards of a fence, the branches of a prickly pear, and so forth. In closer shots the camera has two favorite subjects: typically Indian faces, or María Félix's face, which is sometimes set off by a rebozo or bathed in a halo of light, as when she makes a speech in the school.

The team of Emilio Fernández and Gabriel Figueroa did not limit themselves to rural themes and settings; they made other types of movies, such as the cabaret melodramas *Mexico Dance Hall* (*Salón México,* 1948) and *Victims of Sin* (*Víctimas del pecado,* 1950), which portray the violently emotional lives of prostitutes and other habitués of dance halls. For decades Fernández acted in Mexican and American films (he played the bandit leader Mapache in Peckinpah's *The Wild Bunch*), and he continued directing movies in Mexico into the late 1970s. Unfortunately, Fernández's later movies, such as the blatantly commercial *Red-Light District* (*Zona roja,* 1975), show little artistry. Although the Fernández-Figueroa pictures of the 1940s and 1950s established a visual style recognized as "typically Mexican" by many international critics, current critical opinion underscores the serious flaws of many of these films: the Mexican landscape frequently becomes a film's principal character, and the all-too-beautiful picture-postcard photography lapses into mere formula. Many of the characters are flagrant stereotypes, such as the idealized, pure and good Indians of *María Cande-*

*laria,* and some of these films are informed by facile ideologies, such as the naive and demagogic nationalism of *Hidden River.* The cabaret movies are governed by the tired conventions of melodrama and never explore prostitution as a real social problem.

Another leading director of the late 1940s and early 1950s was Alejandro Galindo, who had learned filmmaking in the United States. This leftist director was not an innovator in the aesthetics of cinema, but his finest films—whose scripts he himself wrote—evidence a serious concern with social issues, a sharp eye for the details of daily life and typical customs, and a keen understanding of the psychology of his characters.

In three of Galindo's best films, actor David Silva plays a macho working-class character struggling against his own personality for success or just for survival. *Champion Without a Crown (Campeón sin corona,* 1945) features David Silva as the street fighter who, when he finally hits boxing's big time, squanders everything. This film takes up a common theme of Mexican intellectual life—the national inferiority complex in which Mexico considers its Anglo neighbors superior. In one fight scene boxer Joe Ronda psychologically whips the protagonist simply by taunting him in English. *Champion Without a Crown* marked a new departure in Mexican cinema—an authentic portrayal of poor urban neighborhoods and the types of people who live there. Even their street-wise language is faithfully rendered. *Corner, Getting Off!* (*¡Esquina, bajan!,* 1948) and *There's Room for Two (Hay lugar para dos,* 1948) also convincingly portray urban working-class characters and their environment; David Silva plays a self-destructive bus driver in these films.

Three other films scripted and directed by Galindo also star David Silva and examine significant socioeconomic problems. *A Family Like So Many Others (Una familia de tantas,* 1948) is a well-crafted domestic melodrama notable for its sensitive depiction of the clash of old and new values in a traditional middle-class household strictly governed by an old-fashioned authoritarian father. Though the low-budget *Wetbacks (Espaldas mojadas,* 1953) suffers from poor production values, it is extremely important thematically as a rare, in-depth treatment of one of Mexico's most pressing social problems: undocumented workers who illegally cross the border to work in the United States. Like *Champion Without a Crown, The Fernandezes of Peralvillo (Los Fernández de Peralvillo,* 1953) traces the rise and fall of a man of humble origin.

Galindo was one of Mexico's most prolific directors; he made nearly seventy films from the late 1930s to the early 1980s. His interest in serious social issues reappeared in later films such as *The Trial of Martín Cortés (El juicio de Martín Cortés,* 1973). This film is particularly noteworthy for its unusual structure (the restaging of a play in which a murder was committed) and its seldom treated theme (the historical roots of racial prejudice in Mexico). Unfortunately, because of the demands of the movie industry, Galindo also made dozens of unimaginative and uninspired pictures which aimed unabashedly at the box office.

The greatest box-office hit in the history of Mexican cinema was the populist *We Poor Folks* (*Nosotros los pobres*, 1947), directed by Ismael Rodríguez. This fast-paced urban melodrama alternates scenes of brutal violence with comic moments and musical numbers. Set in a slum neighborhood of Mexico City, *We Poor Folks* follows Galindo's lead in capturing the popular language of the streets. This film has been criticized for sentimentalizing the poor and their poverty and for depicting complacent and unorganized workers unable to escape their subordinate status. Nevertheless, *We Poor Folks* captured a vast popular audience and inspired a successful sequel featuring the same principal characters: *You Rich Folks* (*Ustedes los ricos*) was directed by Rodríguez in 1948.

Ismael Rodríguez also directed notable rural melodramas such as *The Black Sheep* (*La oveja negra*, 1949) and *You Will Not Desire Your Son's Wife* (*No desearás la mujer de tu hijo*, 1949). Both of these films star the famous singing idol Pedro Infante as the macho son who obeys his father and adores his long-suffering mother. *The Black Sheep* and *You Will Not Desire Your Son's Wife* are unusual rural melodramas in that they question traditional values. Both films depict a crisis of paternal authority and portray a paterfamilias whose abusive authoritarian nature and vice-ridden lifestyle threaten his family.

Like Galindo, Ismael Rodríguez continued directing films—many of them undistinguished—into the early 1980s. Ismael Rodríguez was instrumental in the development of Pedro Infante's career, and Rodríguez's *We Poor Folks* and *The Black Sheep* helped to establish Infante's immense popularity. Many movie fans still revere Pedro Infante as the prototypical macho hero of Mexican cinema.

In the 1940s and early 1950s Mexican cinema boasted a galaxy of talented movie stars. Many of the movies of this period were unoriginal formula pictures plagued by predictable plots, the timeworn conventions of genre movies, and mediocre production values. Nevertheless, audiences flocked to these films in order to see their favorite stars; and many of these movies were merely vehicles for famous actors and actresses.

Mexican actor Mario Moreno (alias Cantinflas) is the most famous comic in the Spanish-speaking world. This comic's best-known screen type is the poor Mexico City street bum (*peladito*) who wins out over persons of authority and other well-educated or important people. Cantinflas's success against these adversaries is due to the inimitable barrage of incoherent language that the comic unleashes—a rapid-fire mishmash of innuendos, mispronounced or made-up words, and double-talk, which has now become known in Spanish as *cantinflismos*. Much of Cantinflas's charm stems from his ability as a pantomimist and from his countenance and manner of dress: a small, impish face with a tiny moustache at the ends of the upper lip; baggy trousers barely held up by a piece of rope; a long-sleeved undershirt; and a battered hat. Cantinflas also comically portrayed men in occupations ranging from policeman, *The Unknown Policeman* (*El gendarme desconocido*, 1941), to bullfighter, *Neither Blood nor Sand* (*Ni sangre ni arena*, 1941). Many critics claim that after the 1940s Cantinflas lost his spontaneity and originality—the comic situations and characteristic linguistic humor were merely repeated in film after film into the 1970s. Nevertheless, for decades Cantinflas maintained a remarkable rapport with poor and unsophisticated moviegoers who identified with this fast-talking hero who, though ignorant and ridiculous, bested his opponents with humor.

Cantinflas's principal rival was Germán Valdés, "Tin Tan." Like Cantinflas, Tin Tan had worked as a music-hall comic before appearing in motion pictures. As a music-hall comic, Tin Tan was known for his portrayal of a pachuco (Mexican-American of Los Angeles) who wore a zoot-suit and spoke a macaronic Spanish influenced by English. Though Tin Tan played a pachuco in his first film, *Summer Hotel* (*Hotel de verano*, 1943), he later developed other personas. Tin Tan's best comedies were directed by Gilberto Martínez Solares and written by Martínez Solares and Juan García. One of the finest is *The King of the Neighborhood* (*El rey del barrio*, 1949) in which Tin Tan plays a confidence trickster and leader of thieves. This role allowed Tin Tan creative outlets for his spontaneous and often frantic humor, since the gang leader must do outlandish impersonations in order to enter the homes of the rich. Tin Tan's phony accents, gags, and wisecracks allowed him to deflate high society much as the Marx Brothers did. Tin Tan also relied on slapstick and his ability as a song-and-dance man.

Many other male stars were well known to moviegoers during the golden age of Mexican cinema. The wide-eyed comic Adalberto Martínez, "Resortes," was a talented, acrobatic dancer who in 1946 launched a prolific movie career after having appeared in popular tent shows. Famed singer Jorge Negrete played the boastful, fearless, and very macho romantic lead in ranch comedies such as *Over There on the Big Ranch* (*Allá en el Rancho Grande*, 1948), veteran director Fernando de Fuentes's remake of his classic of the same name. Though Negrete had a finer voice than Pedro Infante, the latter's popularity eventually became greater.

Among the leading female stars was María Félix, best known for her portrayals of beautiful, domineering, and unscrupulous vamps who heartlessly exploit and discard suitors in films such as *The Devourer* (*La devoradora*, 1946), directed by Fernando de Fuentes. Cuban rumba dancer Ninón Sevilla's defiantly vulgar eroticism was thoroughly exploited in cabaret melodramas such as the outstanding *Adventuress* (*Aventurera,* 1949) and *Sensuality* (*Sensualidad,* 1950), both of which were written by Álvaro Custodio and directed by Alberto Gout. In countless melodramas Sara García played a supposedly archetypal Mexican mother: self-sacrificing, sentimental, overly protective of her children, venerated by her sons. Sara García is enshrined as the "Mother of Mexico" in popular iconography.

The ranch comedy (*comedia ranchera*) was one of the most prevalent genres of the golden age, enjoying substantial popularity throughout Spanish America. These authentically Mexican comedies generally focus on a dashing, two-fisted macho, who is not rebelling against society but rather is integrated into its middle or upper classes; his problems, then, are personal ones relating to honor, love, revenge, family feuds, and so on. The local cantina is a common setting for the action; and cock fights, tavern brawls, serenades, and horse races are typical pastimes. The ranch comedy endorsed traditional conservative values and projected a simplistic and nostalgic vision of an idyllic past. In this mythical past a benign paternalism held sway on semifeudal haciendas untouched by serious socioeconomic problems. The exalted regionalism of the ranch comedies was at times evident in titles such as *Oh How Pretty Puebla Is!* (*¡Ay, que rechulo es Puebla!,* 1945); and typical customs, songs, and costumes provided a backdrop of regional folklore. One of the most interesting of the ranch comedies was Ismael Rodríguez's *Two Kinds of Care* (*Dos tipos de cuidado,* 1952), because it successfully played the genre's two greatest singing idols and star personalities—Jorge Negrete and Pedro Infante—against each other. The genre began to decline by the early 1950s.

A popular genre during the administration of President Miguel Alemán (1946–1952) was the cabaret melodrama. The rise of this genre has been linked by film historians to the changing moral codes and values of an increasingly materialistic, urban-industrial society during Alemán's administration—a boom period when new power brokers (technocrats, builders and other businessmen, bureaucrats) rose to national prominence. The cabaret melodramas reflected the challenges to traditional conservative values posed by an urban society in flux. These films portrayed unfortunate B-girls and prostitutes who had been driven to work in cabarets because of economic necessity. The era's fascination with Afro-Cuban music is reflected in the rumbas and other suggestive dances punctuating these melodramas.

The greatest filmmaker ever to work in the Mexican movie industry was Spanish-born Luis Buñuel, who acquired Mexican citizenship in 1949. Buñuel directed twenty films in Mexico from 1946 to 1964, and he frequently succeeded in using and adapting the traditions of Mexican commercial cinema in order to express his own iconoclastic vision of the world. Because of the movie industry's powerful studio system, Buñuel often had to direct actors and actresses he did not choose; nevertheless, he became a fast-working and efficient director able to finish low-budget films on schedule. *The Young and the Damned (Los olvidados,* 1950), one of Buñuel's masterpieces, was made in only twenty-one days.

*The Young and the Damned* won the Cannes Film Festival prize for best direction in 1951 and thereby reestablished Buñuel's international reputation. In a generally realist style, the film depicts the brutal world of a gang of Mexico City slum children whose lives are shaped by poverty, criminal violence, and a lack of love and understanding at home. Buñuel, a coscriptwriter on the film, personally researched the lives of slum dwellers before filming. *The Young and the Damned* shares many of the aesthetic and ideological principles of Italian neorealism: a documentary look fostered in part by low-budget, on-location shooting in slum districts; an episodic plot which portrays workaday people; and social criticism which reveals serious problems but proposes no socioeconomic or political solutions. However, Buñuel's early formation as a surrealist caused him to reject a purely neorealist approach to his subject matter, and he used suggestive surrealist dream sequences and visions to symbolically reflect the inner lives of his characters.

The producer of *The Young and the Damned* prevented Buñuel from using several bizarre surrealist images in his film. In *The Exterminating Angel (El ángel exterminador,* 1962), however, Buñuel was given a freer rein, and he created a masterful surrealist comedy of manners. *The Young and the Damned* and *The Exterminating Angel* were scripted by the team of Buñuel and Luis Alcoriza; both films present a fiercely critical vision of society.

*The Exterminating Angel* is a social satire in which a group of elegant upper-class guests are, for no clear reason, unable to leave a formal dinner party in a mansion. Their entrapment suggests the *haute bourgeoisie*'s conformity and paralyzing lack of willpower. As fear and hunger besiege the marooned group, their hypocritical facades crumble; polite conversation, gentlemanly conduct, and other social conventions give way to cowardice, sadism, lust, degradation, and fanaticism. To attack the bourgeoisie's moral and religious hypocrisy, Buñuel uses the surrealist's weapons of surprise, dream imagery, bizarre gags, comic horror, and unexpected assaults on logic and order. Gabriel Figueroa's restrained camera style simply records unforgettably surreal scenes such as the bourgeois guests' slaughter of a lamb in an elegant drawing room.

Several of Buñuel's most significant Mexican films center around an exceptional individual. Two of these films portray psychopaths. *The Criminal Life of Archibaldo de la Cruz (Ensayo de un crimen,* 1955) is a surrealist horror comedy in which chance repeatedly intervenes to kill off the protagonist's intended female victims before he himself can murder them. Unlike most of Buñuel's psychologically disturbed characters, this one finally liberates himself from his obsession—he discards the object which since childhood had linked sexual pleasure with murder in his subconscious.

Luis Alcoriza and Buñuel scripted, and the latter directed, *This Strange Passion* (*Él,* 1952), a study of a psychopath in the throes of a self-destructive mania. The well-to-do protagonist, Francisco, is an exemplary bourgeois, a respected member of his church, and a virgin in his forties when he succumbs to *l'amour fou.* Although love and possession are esteemed bourgeois values, Francisco's jealous possessiveness of his spouse leads to paranoiac behavior which ultimately reaches a frenzied hallucinatory phase. Buñuel does not merely trace his protagonist's mania; the director also explores and criticizes the aspects of Francisco's Catholic-bourgeois milieu that prevent his sustaining a mature and balanced relationship with a woman. Though the director draws on certain conventions of the Mexican melodrama, the uniquely Buñuelian touch is especially evident in several striking images and actions: the fetishistic protagonist's erotic urge is first ignited during a foot-washing ceremony in a church when he glimpses a pair of feminine feet in high-heeled shoes; the jealous husband rams a long pin through a keyhole to blind a Peeping Tom; at midnight Francisco steals to his wife's bedroom with scissors, rope, a razor blade, and needle and thread in order to subject her to an unspecified sadistic rite.

Two of Buñuel's Mexican films, *Nazarín* (*Nazarín,* 1958) and *Simón of the Desert* (*Simón del desierto,* 1964), are remarkable depictions of the ascetic personality. *Simón of the Desert* is a forty-three minute surrealist piece inspired by the life of St. Simeon Stylites, a hermit who in the fifth century lived on top of a pillar in the Syrian desert. The film's short length and abrupt ending were caused by unexpected financial problems during production; Buñuel was forced to omit half the material he had shot. Though Buñuel's film is a humorous farce, it is also a serious condemnation of Christian asceticism as practiced atop a column. Buñuel's stylite withdraws from the world and lives an absurd, self-centered existence of barren contemplation, battles with the demands of the flesh, self-mortification, and absentmindedness.

Buñuel's *Nazarín* is based on the novel by Spanish realist author Benito Pérez Galdós. Under Buñuel's direction, cinematographer Gabriel Figueroa photographed this film in a straightforward realist style which avoided the carefully composed and overly beautiful outdoor shots typical of the Fernández-Figueroa visual style. Buñuel's Nazarín is both Quixotic and Christlike: a self-sacrificing, humble, and idealistic Catholic priest, he attempts to live simply, according to the teachings of Christ. His single-minded devotion to his Christian mission distances him from ordinary people and their problems and plunges him into confrontations with both civil and Church authorities. The protagonist finally comes to question his priestly calling as he is emotionally torn by the conflict between the human and the divine. Pro-Christian and anti-Christian interpretations of this subtle, complex, and controversial film have been widely debated.

In addition to the films discussed above, Buñuel's Mexican work includes a musical, *Great Casino (Gran casino,* 1946), which stars Jorge Negrete and the renowned Argentine singer and actress Libertad Lamarque. Buñuel also made melodramas, such as *Daughter of Deceit (La hija del engaño,* 1951), and two political films (Mexican-French coproductions) which intertwine romantic and moral themes: *Death in This Garden (La Mort en ce jardin,* 1956) and *Fever Mounts on El Pao (La Fièvre monte à El Pao,* 1959). Two famous novels were adapted by Buñuel. The U.S.-Mexican coproduction *Robinson Crusoe (Robinson Crusoe,* 1952) was the director's first color film; his *Wuthering Heights (Abismos de pasión,* 1953) is a surrealist adaptation of Emily Brontë's novel. *Mexican Busride (Subida al cielo,* 1951) and *Illusion Travels by Streetcar (La ilusión viaja en tranvía,* 1953) are delightful populist comedies which trace the adventures of ordinary rural folks and urban workers while also presenting a gallery of social types. *The River and Death (El río y la muerte,* 1954) examines men caught up in the vindictive and violent code of machismo which for generations has held sway in a Mexican town. Buñuel's best Mexican films illustrate the many ways in which a great director's personal vision may be expressed within the restrictive financial framework and short production schedules imposed by a tightly structured commercial moviemaking industry. Unfortunately, Buñuel's example had little impact on the Mexican filmmaking scene.

By the late 1950s and the early 1960s the golden age of Mexican cinema had ended. Two of the greatest stars, Negrete and Infante, had died; and the talent and popularity of others had declined. The leading directors of the golden age (except Buñuel) were generally unable to revitalize their work, and there was little development of new directing talent because of the closed-door policy of the directors' guild of the powerful Cinematographic Production Workers Union (Sindicato de Trabajadores de la Producción Cinematográfica or STPC).

Annual film production dropped from a record high of 136 movies in 1958 to a low of seventy-one films in 1961. At this time, crass and unimaginative commercialism gripped the industry, and the aesthetic quality of these movies was almost uniformly poor. The same conventional narrative and stylistic formulas were repeatedly used to churn out popular genre pictures: melodramas; musical comedies capitalizing on current dance or music crazes such as the twist; Westerns; ranch comedies; movies starring masked superwrestlers such as El Santo; horror flicks; and routine vehicles for well-known comics like Piporro (Eulalio González) and Clavillazo (Antonio Espino).

However, a few significant features—in addition to Buñuel's—were

Luis Buñuel's hard-hitting realism in depicting the culture of poverty in Mexico City made *The Young and the Damned* (*Los Olvidados*, 1950) a memorable film.

The good Christian, an idealistic priest, is confronted by the imperfections of human society in Buñuel's controversial *Nazarín* (1958).

In Buñuel's satirical *The Exterminating Angel* (1962) guests at an elegant dinner party, trapped by their own fears, find their polite social façades crumbling.

In one of two adaptations of famous novels, Buñuel used Emily Brontë's work for his surrealist *Wuthering Heights* (*Abismos de pasión*, 1953).

116

Paul Leduc's *Reed: Insurgent Mexico* (1971) covers journalist John Reed's career during the Mexican revolution up to his active involvement in the cause.

Miguel Littín, a Chilean exile, powerfully depicts, in his *Letters from Marusia* (*Actas de Marusia*, 1975), the savage repression of a miners' strike by the Chilean army.

made during the late fifties and early sixties. In *Bullfighter* (*Torero*, 1956) director Carlos Velo skillfully blended documentary and newsreel footage with realistically recreated sequences to produce a psychologically penetrating film biography of famed Mexican bullfighter Luis Procuna. Luis Alcoriza scripted and Rogelio A. González directed *Mrs. Morales' Skeleton* (*El esqueleto de la señora Morales*, 1959), a satirical comedy unusual in Mexican cinema because of its black humor. Veteran director Roberto Gavaldón's *Macario* (*Macario*, 1959) was an ambitious attempt to produce a major film on a national theme; unfortunately, this allegorical tale of a poor peasant's struggles with hunger and death depicts the indigenous world in a fanciful and overly picturesque manner. Another veteran director, Julio Bracho, made the polemical *The Shadow of the Caudillo* (*La sombra del caudillo*, 1960), which was banned in Mexico for its unsavory depiction of that nation's military. This film, which is based on Martín Luis Guzmán's famous novel of the same name, explores the role of violence and assassination in Mexican politics during the late 1920s. The Western *The Del Hierro Brothers* (*Los hermanos del Hierro*, 1961) is one of Ismael Rodríguez's best films. Director Jomí García Ascot's fine *On the Empty Balcony* (*En el balcón vacío*, 1961) is a haunting exploration of the memories of a Spanish civil war refugee; the film, shot in 16mm, was made on a minuscule budget outside the mainstream movie industry.

One of the few to begin a director's career in the movie industry in the late 1950s and early 1960s was Luis Alcoriza, the Spanish-born friend and collaborator of Luis Buñuel. Before taking up directing, Alcoriza had worked in the Mexican movie industry as an actor and scriptwriter. Though as a director he did not become an outstanding stylist, Alcoriza generally scripted the films he directed, and his willingness to treat timely themes of social significance made him an exceptional figure in a talent-starved industry geared to routine formula pictures. His first feature, *The Young Ones* (*Los jóvenes*, 1960), portrays middle-class adolescents in the "rebel-without-a-cause" tradition; Alcoriza's film is notable for its finely written, slangy, and realistic dialogue. In his second film, *Tlayucan* (*Tlayucan*, 1961), Alcoriza spices his ironic satire of small town life with Buñuelian motifs. The comic *National Mechanics* (*Mecánica nacional*, 1971), a major box-office success, ferociously satirizes the vulgarity and consumerism of the urban middle classes.

Alcoriza's two finest films may be *Shark Fishermen* (*Tiburoneros*, 1962) and *Tarahumara* (*Tarahumara*, 1964). The former is an insightful portrait of a city dweller who has changed his lifestyle to become a shark fisherman. The film deals sensitively with the themes of family life, work, friendship, love, and urban vs. rural life. *Tarahumara* is one of the few features in the history of Mexican cinema to explore profoundly the social world of an indigenous people, the Tarahumaras.

Alcoriza rejects the superficial exoticism and mystery pervading many cinematic depictions of indigenous groups and offers an in-depth fictional-ethnological treatment of the Tarahumaras and their relations with the dominant white society. Filmed on location in the remote, mountainous region where the Tarahumaras live, the film successfully combines fictional and documentary elements.

The Mexican movie industry continued in the doldrums in the middle and late 1960s. However, in August 1964 the STPC moved to counter its own unemployment problems and the widespread stagnation in the industry by announcing the First Contest of Experimental Cinema. The contest was designed to attract independent and aspiring filmmakers who had been excluded from the movie industry. The first-place winner, Rubén Gámez's *The Secret Formula* (*La fórmula secreta*, 1965), is a forty-five minute film-poem which rejects a narrative line in favor of a rhythmic montage of images—realist, surrealist, satirical, pop— which powerfully depict the myths, contradictions, and obsessions of the Mexican character. Alberto Isaac's *There's No Thieves in This Town* (*En este pueblo no hay ladrones*, 1964), winner of second prize, uses a spare, realist style to capture the tedium of everyday life in a small town. *There's No Thieves in This Town* is adapted from the short story of the same name by Colombian author Gabriel García Márquez. Alberto Isaac and several other filmmakers who entered the First Contest of Experimental Cinema later succeeded in working within the movie industry.

In Mexico the term "independent cinema" refers to films produced without recourse to the facilities and other resources of the movie industry (for example, studios and financing). The independent cinema movement blossomed in the 1960s, and its importance continues today. The movement was stimulated in 1963 with the establishment of Mexico's first film school, the University Center for Cinema Studies (Centro Universitario de Estudios Cinematográficos or CUEC).

CUEC has trained numerous leading independent filmmakers and produced some of their films. When a growing student movement openly challenged the repressive regime of President Gustavo Díaz Ordaz on the eve of the 1968 Summer Olympics, CUEC students took to the streets to film the fast-paced events. This footage was molded by Leobardo López Aretche into *The Shout* (*El grito*, 1968), one of the few Mexican documentaries to record a popular political movement.

López Aretche's assistant director on *The Shout* was Alfredo Joskowitz. These two filmmakers scripted the fiction feature *The Change* (*El cambio*, 1971), which was directed by Joskowicz and produced by CUEC. One of the themes of *The Change*, ecological disaster caused by private industry, was unusual in the Mexican cinema of the time. Joskowicz also scripted and directed *Constellations* (*Constelaciones*, 1978), an exploration of the society in which Sor Juana Inés de la Cruz (a famous seventeenth-century Mexican poet) lived. Because its mono-logue-meditation structure rejects traditional narrative, temporal, and spatial continuities, Joskowicz's *Constellations* is a most unusual cine-matic experiment.

CUEC produced director Federico Weingartshofer's first film *Maybe I Will Die After All* (*Quizá siempre sí me muera*, 1971), a complex tale of a middle-class youth's search for the meaning of his life. In the independ-ently produced *Walking on . . . Walking* (*Caminando pasos . . . cami-nando*, 1976), Weingartshofer focuses on the problems confronting a newly arrived schoolteacher in a rural community. In spite of its occa-sionally obscure narrative line, the film represents an intriguing rever-sal of the story of *Hidden River:* in *Walking on . . . Walking* the rural folk teach the teacher—first words in their language and then the na-ture of the exploitative socioeconomic system which governs their lives.

Independent cinema production has encompassed a wide range of styles and subjects; the following are, along with the above mentioned titles, some of the most notable films. Though the cinematography and acting of Marcela Fernández Violante's fiction feature *The General's Daughter* (*De todos modos Juan te llamas*, 1975) are mediocre, the film is nevertheless exceptional because it questions the conduct of Mexican military personnel. Alexandro Jodorowsky adapted the Western genre to Zen Buddhism and added bizarre sexual, religious, and surrealist im-agery, outrageous social satire, and an exhibitionistic attitude to por-tray his hero's visionary quest for spiritual enlightenment and saint-hood in *El Topo* (*El Topo*, 1970). Eduardo Maldonado's documentaries *Atencingo* (*Atencingo*, 1973) and *Time After Time* (*Una y otra vez*, 1975) deal with labor issues. The poor technical quality of Óscar Menéndez's *1968* (*1968*, 1970) reminds viewers that much of the footage they are seeing was filmed clandestinely at great personal risk: Super-8 footage shot by political prisoners inside the infamous Lecumberri prison as well as footage of the government-ordered Tlatelolco massacre, which savagely repressed the 1968 student movement.

Perhaps the most talented of the independent filmmakers is Paul Leduc. His technically proficient *Reed: Insurgent Mexico* (*Reed: México insurgente*, 1971), which was photographed in 16mm and in sepia, traces American journalist John Reed's career during the Mexican revolution—from his strictly professional coverage of the conflict to his active commitment to the revolutionary cause. Leduc's feature-length examination of Otomi culture, *Ethnocide: Notes on the Mezquital* (*Etno-cidio: Notas sobre el Mezquital*, 1976), one of the most important docu-mentaries in the history of Mexican cinema, is a fine example of docu-mentary film as denunciation. The film graphically records the death throes of an indigenous culture and succeeds in revealing the causes of that demise.

The 1971 to 1976 period saw a dramatic resurgence of the motion-picture industry under President Luis Echeverría Álvarez, who considered himself a pro-left spokesman for the Third World. Echeverría recognized the ideological and artistic potential of his nation's movie industry, and he challenged filmmakers to upgrade the quality of their films and to reach a wider audience. The president formally invited filmmakers to join with the state to produce films of social criticism and films on the great themes of the Mexican revolution. Furthermore, Echeverría provided filmmakers the wherewithal to make such movies: state-operated production houses were established; and the powerful, state-owned Banco Cinematográfico, which was headed by the president's brother Rodolfo, favored quality film projects rather than run-of-the-mill formula pictures. Under Luis Echeverría, the movie industry became virtually nationalized, and state control of film production led to the emergence of new directors, an upgrading of production values, and the appearance of controversial subjects seldom treated by previous filmmakers.

Human sexuality, the roles and conduct of women, and other timely social and political issues and problems were the new subjects explored by filmmakers during the Echeverría period. Political corruption, the Chicano movement, and homosexuality also appeared on screen. The traditional cinematic treatment of machismo was challenged in films such as Jorge Fons's *The Cubs* (*Los cachorros*, 1971). This film, adapted from the novel of the same name by Peruvian author Mario Vargas Llosa, deals with male sexual impotence and female response to this phenomenon. In the complexly structured *The Bricklayers* (*Los albañiles*, 1976), Fons uses the device of a police investigation to expose police brutality and the many layers of corruption underlying a construction project. Felipe Cazals's *Solitary Confinement* (*El apando*, 1975), based on the novel by leftist author and political prisoner José Revueltas, is an exposé of the brutality and corruption of the penal system as exemplified by Lecumberri prison. *Solitary Confinement* also presents an unusual portrait of Mexican women as determined fighters willing to struggle against a corrupt and repressive social institution.

Brutal governmental repression was another new topic taken up by filmmakers during the Echeverría era. The well-known director Miguel Littín, a Chilean exile, develops this theme in his fine *Letters From Marusia* (*Actas de Marusia*, 1975), which depicts the Chilean army's savage repression of a miners' strike against a foreign-owned company. Littín's costly, state-produced blockbuster supported the Echeverría administration by reflecting the antiimperialist, pro-Third World ideological bent of the president's foreign policy.

Arturo Ripstein, Felipe Cazals, and Jaime Humberto Hermosillo were three of the most talented young directors working during the Echeverría years. These *auteurs* sought increased directorial control over their films, and they attempted to deal with significant Mexican themes in a meaningful manner. All three have continued to direct in the post-Echeverría period; and, though they lack the artistic genius of a Buñuel, they are arguably the brightest lights in contemporary Mexican filmmaking.

Arturo Ripstein has developed into a mature film director possessing a firm control over the medium and a sensitive touch with his players. One of his overriding thematic concerns has been intolerance, which is explored in two of his finest films: *Castle of Purity* (*El castillo de la pureza,* 1972) and *The Place Without Limits* (*El lugar sin límites,* 1977). *Castle of Purity,* which is scripted by Ripstein and poet-author José Emilio Pacheco, takes up a theme from *A Family Like So Many Others:* paternal authoritarianism which demands the absolute submission of wife and children. In Ripstein's treatment of this theme, the unbalanced paterfamilias exercises total control over his spouse and children by keeping them literally locked up in the deteriorating colonial mansion that is their home. *The Place Without Limits* questions traditional notions of machismo and examines the status of the homosexual in Mexican society. Another fine Ripstein film is *In For Life* (*Cadena perpetua,* 1978), an in-depth treatment of police corruption.

Felipe Cazals's work has been uneven; he is at his best dealing with the exploitation and brutality of the sociopolitical system in *Solitary Confinement, Canoa* (*Canoa,* 1975), and *The Poquianchis* (*Las Poquianchis,* 1976). The latter film, which is inspired by a historical incident, reveals the brutal exploitation and outright violence underpinning a prostitution ring. Based on a historical occurrence of mob violence, *Canoa* draws its strength from its quasi-documentary style, which realistically captures the tense atmosphere of political unrest prevalent at the height of the 1968 student movement.

In the post-Echeverría period, both Ripstein and Cazals have at times found it necessary to accept pedestrian directing assignments of little interest to them. In contrast, Jaime Humberto Hermosillo, who generally scripts his own films, has been more successful in concentrating his considerable talents on worthwhile projects within or outside the industry. His outstanding independent film *My Dearest María* (*María de mi corazón,* 1979), shot in 16mm, was produced on a shoestring by the University of Veracruz. Hermosillo is an astute observer of the values and myths of his nation's middle class, and he has been particularly successful in his examination of middle-class sexual mores. *The Passion According to Berenice* (*La pasión según Berenice,* 1975), for instance, portrays the routine, drab existence of a sexually frustrated, middle-class widow who reacts to her stifling social milieu by initiating a love affair and, after her lover rejects her, by murdering her avaricious godmother. Thus Hermosillo challenges the usual female stereotypes which for decades have plagued Mexican cinema.

President José López Portillo (1976–1982) named his sister, Margarita López Portillo, to oversee the movie industry, and she initiated a vast reorganization of the industry in 1977. Her policies returned filmmaking to the private sector; the Banco Cinematográfico disappeared, and the state withdrew from production. As a result, production values and the overall artistry of films plummeted as profit-oriented private producers churned out routine commercial pictures. Many talented filmmakers who had worked in the industry during the Echeverría period found no outlets for their creativity. On 24 March 1982 Mexico's Cineteca Nacional, Latin America's most important national cinematheque, burned. Critics of Margarita López Portillo's policies saw the conflagration as a metaphor for her destruction of a high-quality, state-controlled movie industry. Though the Mexican motion-picture industry has for decades been afflicted by periodic crises, the economic and artistic crisis of the early 1980s may prove to be the most serious.

## SELECTED BIBLIOGRAPHY

### Books

Aranda, Francisco. *Luis Buñuel: A Critical Biography*. New York, Da Capo, 1976.

Ayala Blanco, Jorge. *Aventura del cine mexicano*. Mexico City, Era, 1968.

————. *La búsqueda del cine mexicano: (1968–1972)*. 2 vols. Mexico City, Universidad Nacional Autónoma de Mexico, 1974.

Buñuel, Luis. *My Last Sigh*. New York, Alfred A. Knopf, 1983.

Cesarman, Fernando C. *El ojo de Buñuel: Psicoanálisis desde una butaca*. Barcelona, Anagrama, 1976.

Durgnat, Raymond. *Luis Buñuel*. Berkeley, Los Angeles, and London, University of California Press, 1977.

García Riera, Emilio. *Historia documental del cine mexicano: Época sonora*. 9 vols. to date. Mexico City, Era, 1969–.

Higginbotham, Virginia. *Luis Buñuel*. Boston, Twayne, 1979.

Mora, Carl J. *Mexican Cinema: Reflections of a Society 1896–1980*. Berkeley, Los Angeles, and London, University of California Press, 1982.

Reyes Nevares, Beatriz. *The Mexican Cinema: Interviews with Thirteen Directors*. Albuquerque, University of New Mexico Press, 1976.

Ruy Sánchez, Alberto. *Mitología de un cine en crisis*. Mexico City, Premia, 1981.

### Articles

García Riera, Emilio. "Las desventuras del cine mexicano actual según Emilio García Riera." *Hablemos de cine 19 (February 1983):36–40*.

_____. *"Mexique."* In *Guy Hennebelle and Alfonso Gumucio-Dagron,* eds. *Les Cinémas de l'Amérique latine.* Paris, Cherminier 1981, pp. 361–403.

Ramón, David. "Lectura de las imágenes propuestas por el cine mexicano de los años treinta a la fecha." In Aurelio de los Reyes, David Ramón, María Luisa Amador, and Rodolfo Rivera, *Ochenta años de cine en México.* Mexico City, Filmoteca de la Universidad Nacional Autónoma de Mexico, 1977, pp. 93–120.

Treviño, Jesús Salvador. "The New Mexican Cinema." *Film Quarterly* 32 (spring 1979):26–37.

West, Dennis. "Mexican Cinema in 1977: A Commentary on the Mexican Film Festival Presently Touring the U.S." *The American Hispanist* 2 (May 1977):6–7, 13–14.

# THE NETHERLANDS

## ELAINE MANCINI

Filmmaking in the Netherlands has centered around the work and fame of a particular documentarian: Joris Ivens. Like Henri Storck in Belgium, Ivens founded an early film society (Filmliga, in 1926) and established his reputation long before World War II (with *The Bridge,* 1928; *Rain [La pluie,* 1929]; and the silent and sound versions of *Zuiderzee,* 1930 and 1934). With Storck, he made *Borinage,* a film about a strike, in 1933. Ivens is not, however, solely a Dutch filmmaker; in fact, throughout his long career, he has spent little time in Holland. Instead, he has traveled to and lived in areas where he saw a need for his filmmaking, a tendency that became evident early in his life and which Ivens views as the only productive method for a documentarian. He filmed *The Four Hundred Million* (1939) and *The Letter of China* (1949) in China, *Power and the Land* (1940) in the United States and *Spanish Earth* (1937) in Spain. For Italian television he filmed *Italy Is Not a Poor Country* (*L'Italia non è un paese povero,* 1959); in Mali he made *Tomorrow at Nanguila* (*Demain a Nanguila,* 1960); in Chile *The Smallest Circus in the World* (*El circo mas pequeno del mundo,* 1963); and in France *The Wind* (*Le mistral,* 1964). Engagement in social realities and personal commitment are very strong qualities of Ivens. After making *Indonesia Calling* (1946) when he was film commissioner of the Dutch East Indies, he left the post because he thought his own government "wanted to go back into Indonesia again as a colonial power, and it was not my opinion to do so after the war."[1] His *Song of the Rivers* (1954–55) depicted the struggles of the international working class. He filmed the antiimperialist *17th Parallel* (1967) in North Vietnam and *The People and their Weapons* (*Le peuple et ses fusils,* 1969) in Laos. Returning to China in 1973–75, he directed *How Yukong Moved the Mountains*

466 :

(*Comment Yukong depleca les montagnes*) on the impact of the cultural revolution.

Besides this strong personal commitment, Ivens's works display an affinity between man and the environment, a pervasive aspect of Dutch cinema. Ivens has stated: "I work very much with the natural effects of nature, which are all visual, because my art is very visual. And through these big important things that everybody knows also, everybody can identify himself, because everybody in his life has to have some relation to earth, some relation to the sky, some relation to the land, the sun, to the wind, even."[2] Ivens's pictorialism is not an uncommon trait in a country with a strong tradition in the plastic arts, especially landscape painting. A communion with nature and a Calvinist faith in life have given Holland its outstanding cinematic qualities.

Bert Haanstra emerged as the major figure of postwar Dutch documentary. Like Ivens, he exhibits a strong pictorial sense developed in the company of his father and two brothers who are painters and in his own work in poster and portrait making. Ivens's other legacy, a communion with nature, was evident in Haanstra's tremendously successful film *Mirror of Holland* (*Spiegel van Holland*, 1951) which was awarded the Grand Prix for Shorts at Cannes. Without any commentary it relates the life of the Netherlands as reflected in the canals that weave through the country, a theme that became a staple of the Dutch documentary. Water as a life source played a significant role in his 1951 cinepoem *Panta rhei*, his 1952 *The Dike Builders* (*Dijkbouw*), his 1956 *And There Was No More Sea* (*En de zee was niet meer*) on the IJssel Meer being closed by a massive dike, and his 1965 and 1966 *The Voice of the Water* (*De stem van het water*). Haanstra also made several important art films, including *Medieval Dutch Sculpture* (*Nederlandse beeldhou wkunst tijdens de late middel eeuwen*, 1951) and *Rembrandt, Painter of Men* (1956), the latter made for the 350 anniversary of the artist's birth in which Haanstra relates the events in Rembrandt's life to his work through a series of close-ups of sixty paintings. He made an impressive science film in color, *The Rival World* (1954), about man's battle with the insects, that had been commissioned by the Shell Film Unit. *Fanfare* (1958), his first feature, was a comic view of provincial factional disputes which enjoyed commercial success. *Glass* (*Glas*, 1958), on the other hand, was a straightforward documentary. This humorous film won an Academy Award in 1960 and, within four years, one thousand prints were in circulation. The "ambassador of the Dutch short"[3] then devoted himself to the candid camera technique, first with *Zoo* (1962), which compares the human visitors with the animals, and *The Human Dutch* (*Alleman*, 1963), a humorous yet respectful view of his countrymen. The latter's success enabled Haanstra to set up his own studio. There he worked for years on *Ape and Super-Ape*, (*Bij de beesten af*, 1973), a feature-length documentary studying animals on six continents. Despite a few films such as his 1975 *When the Poppies Bloom Again* (*Doctor Pulder zaait papavers*) about a doctor visited by an old university classmate, a morphine addict who later dies and whose mistress commits suicide, Haanstra's name will always be linked to the documentary in its various forms: scientific, artistic, humorous, instructional, and institutional.

The second major Dutch filmmaker of the postwar generation, Herman van der Horst, was a much more private individual than Haanstra. Van der Horst lived in a small village where he could conceive his films in peace and devote much time to studying every aspect of them. This perfectionist never saw films as a child, unlike Haanstra, but in his zeal to make films would splice together odds and ends of film he bought from a druggist. Unlike Haanstra's ethnographic and eclectic cinema, Van der Horst specialized in nature photography, evident from the start in his debut film *Metamorphosis* (*Metamorphose*, 1945) on the transition from caterpillar to butterfly. He had a brief career, due to his early death and the long gestation periods of his projects. As befits the best of Dutch documentary, Van der Horst paid much attention to problems of the land and the life of the sea. Sea films included *Lekker* (*Vieren maar*, 1954) on the trawler's routine at sea and his well-known *Shoot the Nets* (*Het schot is te boord*, 1952), which won the Palme D'or at Cannes. In this last-mentioned work on herring fishermen in the North Sea, Van der Horst matched the rhythm of the camera to that of the sea. His final film *Toccata* (1968) orchestrated various sounds from diverse sources.

Another documentarist of the postwar period is John Ferno. When only fourteen, he acted as Ivens's assistant on *Breakers* (1932). The son of a famous painter, he displays the national characteristic of pictorialism but, like Ivens, has spent much of his adult life living outside the Netherlands. Ferno has worked in the United States, and also in Israel, making *The Tree of Life* (1971). His first efforts, like those of Max de Haas with *LO-LKP* (1947) and H. M. Josephson with *Six Years* (*Zes jaren*, 1946), were inspired by the war, resistance, and rehabilitation. He filmed *Fortress of Peace* (1965), a documentary on the Swiss army, in 70mm and his 1967 *Sky over Holland*, again in 70mm with six-channel sound and aerial photography, won him the Grand Prix at Cannes.

An interesting figure in the post-war period is Charles Huguenot van der Linden; he exemplifies the versatility necessary for a Dutch filmmaker's success. He served as publicity director of Paramount News in Paris and is credited with the discovery of Audrey Hepburn. With his wife Martina as producer, he directed the well-known *Interlude by Candelight* (*Tussenspel bij kaarslicht*, 1959) on Harry van Tusschenbroek's puppets, films on industrial training, oil drilling, and flood damage, and a feature called *The Seven Ages of Man*. He is known for his simple, direct, acerbic wit, perhaps best exemplified in *The Morning*

*Star* (*De morgenster,* 1957), the story of a bag lady and her optimistic attitude in the face of all her troubles.

There are two categories of films in which the Dutch documentary are very strong: psychological studies and art films. Theo van Haren Noman, a free-lance director and producer, made *The Injured Man* (*De gewonde,* 1966), a psychological portrait of a man's journey to death through delirium after an accident. Fons Grasveld's *Do I Really Want to Die?* (*Wil ik wel dood?,* 1974) studies the suicidal impulse while Rene Van Nie's *Anna, Child of the Daffodils* (*Kind van de zon,* 1975) studies schizophrenia in a nonlinear style. The cinema of Louis A. Van Gasteren also deals with psychological states: *The House* (*De huis,* 1962), inspired by Resnais's *Hiroshima mon amour,* is a fictional short described by Peter Cowie as an "attempt to split up a fragment of thought in time, flashing back and forth throughout the history of an old house that is in the process of being demolished."[4] One of the few women directors in the Netherlands, Nouchka van Brakel, focuses on emotional and sociological issues. *Sabotage* (1967), *Baby in the Tree* (1969), and *The Debut* (1977) all center on children and their relationships to adulthood and responsibility. Her film *Ouder worden* (1975) turns to the opposite side of human experience in its analysis of aging.

Art films comprise a significant portion of Holland's reputation in documentary. *Vincent Van Gogh* (1952), by Dr. Jan Hulsker, set the standard in this genre for historical accuracy, psychological and aesthetic analysis, and the use of details from paintings. Remembering Holland's great painting tradition from Rembrandt to Breughel to Mondriaan, Frans Dupont made *Portrait of Frans Hals* (1963) two years after *Promise of Heaven,* a documentary on stained glass.

The 1970s saw a renewed interest in the genre. Nico Crama began the period with *Photo Portrait* (1979), a history of the photographic portrait. This was quickly followed by the study *Daumier, Eyewitness of an Epoch* (1971) and *Piet Mondriaan* (1973). Hans von Gelder filmed *Adventures in Perception* (1970) on Maurits Escher's optical designs, and Jonne Severijn offered *A Pause in Time* (1974), an examination of Giovanni Boldini's work incorporating dialogues with his widow. Jos Stelling's *Rembrandt fecit 1669* traces the artist's life year by year, displaying a laudable rigorousness and attention to detail.

Fons Rademakers is the exception to the rule concerning feature filmmaking in the Netherlands. Cowie notes that "only one man in Holland since the war has managed to build a career in feature films spanning more than twenty years, and for many audiences the work of Fons Rademakers remains the only glimpse they have caught of Dutch cinema."[5] As a youth, he traveled widely, served as assistant to Vittorio DeSica, David Lean, and Jacques Becker, and acted on stage. His first feature *Village on the River* (*Dorp aan de rivier,* 1958) brought the services of Hugo Claus to Dutch cinema, initiating a working relationship

Joris Ivens, the famous Dutch documentary maker, made politically committed films in many countries. *The Spanish Earth* was made in Spain in 1937.

Wim Verstappen saw his *The Unhappy Return of Joszef Katus to Rembrandt's Country* (1967, filmed in English) as an escape from the ivory tower of Dutch art films.

Paul Verhoeven's *Spetters* (1980), about teen-agers and their dreams, achieved a rare distinction: a Dutch-made film that was the top box-office hit in The Netherlands.

Verhoeven's *The Fourth Man* (1983), a stylish sex comedy, won the International Film Critics' Award at Toronto for that year.

that made Holland an adopted country for the Belgian novelist. Claus collaborated again with Rademakers on *The Dance of the Heron* (1966), an analysis of male menopause, which was adapted from Claus's play. Belgium coproduced *Mira* (1971), a huge success for Rademakers in which he himself plays a pompous functionary who justifies the building of a bridge. *That Joyous Eve* (1969), a comedy set during St. Nicholas festivities, won Rademakers the Silver Bear in Berlin. *Max Havelaar* (1976) was six months in preproduction, sixteen weeks in shooting and ten days in editing. It is based on an autobiography of 1859 about Dutch colonial corruption in Java. Cowie calls it the most important film ever produced in the Netherlands because it is not about Dutch corruption, or Indonesian corruption, but human corruption. Through his skill and grasp of culture, Rademakers was able to break the provincialism of the bulk of Dutch filmmaking.

Production financing and international marketing have proved elusive for Dutch filmmakers. They have tried to combat the prevailing notion expressed by Paul Rotha that "since the Liberation, Dutch film activity has been limited to a group of documentaries and some interesting educational films for children."[6]

In 1956 the Ministry of Cultural Affairs, Recreation, and Social Welfare began a Production Fund with all subsidies in the form of loans covering up to two-thirds of a film's budget. These monies, however, have been hopelessly inadequate to spur national production (in 1975, for example, roughly $750 thousand was available—enough for only twenty shorts). Various alternative practices have therefore been adopted. One instance was *Melancholic Stories,* produced by Matthys van Heyningen. Taking a cue from the Italian practice of episode films, van Heyningen took four stories by Heere Heeresma and asked for separate subsidies for four episodes directed by four different directors. The resulting feature-length program did much better at the box office than four shorts could have managed on their own and van Heyningen quadrupled his funding allotment.

A recognition of the sorry state of affairs led to the foundation of the Netherlands Film Academy (NFA) in 1958. Several NFA graduates started the popular and influential film magazine *Skoop* in 1964, which waged war against the lack of support—monetary and critical—for feature production. Even so, the Dutch audience still had to be convinced that national films were as worthwhile as imported ones. Jan Vrijman blames the audience's unwillingness and the filmmakers' ineptness on the fact that Holland lacks a tradition of spectacle due to Calvinism,[7] while Rob du Mie insists that the Dutch people's big error was in underestimating Hollywood due to latent anti-Americanism. Frans Weisz, now a maker of television commercials, exasperated by the doldrums in which he found Dutch filmmaking, stated, "We young filmmakers can only cling in desperation to one another's mediocrity."[8]

NFA graduates tried different approaches to Dutch feature filmmaking. The first is the most obvious—low budgets. For example, Nikolai van der Heyde's first feature *A Morning of Six Weeks* (*Een ochtend van zes weken,* 1966) cost only $35 thousand. A second alternative, emigration to Hollywood—with Rene Daalder as a prime example, set no historical precedent for a small European industry. Jan Vrijman had another idea; he set up his own production company, Cineproductie, in 1963. He directed several films such as *Identity—Confessions of an Ad Addict* (1971), and financed others such as Hugo Claus's *The Enemies* (1967) and Frans Weisz's *The Gangster Girl,* but his hope of succeeding with what he considered nonvulgar products was not realized and he was forced to return to shorts. He did introduce, however, the potential of shooting with English dialogue which gave the films a trump card for exportation.

Other alternatives have been chosen: the avant-garde and political documentaries. The first category, best represented by Johan van der Keuken who makes avant-garde documentaries and by Frans Zwartjes who has made films on sex and perversion for the past fifteen years, is not meant for a wide audience. The second, supported by the radical magazine *Skrien* and by film clubs such as Film International in Rotterdam and Fugitive Cinema in Amsterdam, are also geared to a specific audience: those already politically committed.

Two pairs of producers have nonetheless been successful. Paul Verhoeven and Rob Houwer joined forces in 1971; their early formula for success was sex comedy. *Business Is Business* (*Wat zien ik,* 1971) was a burlesque on prostitution in Amsterdam while *Turkish Delight* (*Turks fruit,* 1972) portrayed the sexual misadventure of a sculptor and a young girl. Verhoeven's *The Fourth Man* won the International Film Critics' Award at Toronto in 1983. It continues the filmmaker's concern with sexual comedy as it follows a famous homosexual writer through a complicated and comic bisexual affair. The other pair of producers, Pim de la Parra and Wim Verstappen, wanted Dutch cinema to escape from its ivory tower of respectful art films and respected documentaries and thus established their own company, Scorpio Films, in 1965, alternating directorial and producer credit. Of their 16mm *The Unhappy Return of Joszef Katus to Rembrandt's Country* (*Le retour malencontreux de Joszef Katus au pays de Rembrandt,* 1967) directed by Verstappen and shown at Cannes, they said "finally a Dutch film that is *not* a masterpiece."[9] Devoted to "quickies," they produced the unprecedented (for the Netherlands) amount of fifteen features in twelve years. Like Vrijman, they filmed in English. Their first films, made before they had completely mastered their craft, dealt with eroticism and grotesquerie: *Obsessions* (1968), *Blue Movie* (1970), *My Nights with Susan, Olga, Albert, Julie, Bill and Sandra,* (1975) and *VD* (1982) proved that they could be successful while being sloppy. They broke as a producing team in 1976.

Progress has been made and the efforts of the Dutch feature filmmakers have not been in vain. In 1980, at least, the top box-office hit was Dutch (*Spetters*), although the next nineteen were foreign productions with twelve American titles and the rest divided among British, Italian, French, and German. There is still a long way to go before the Dutch public and foreign markets totally accept the Dutch feature. The strongest hope at this time for Dutch visibility lies in the talents of an actor: Rutger Hauer. Now an international star, he served an apprenticeship in Holland in the 1970s; he played a conservative businessman faced with the changing needs of women in a modern society in Herbert Curiel's *Year of the Cancer* (*Het jaar van de Kruft,* 1975) and a member of an impoverished emigrant family living in nineteenth century Amsterdam in Paul Verhoeven's *Cathy Tippel* (*Keetje Tippel,* 1975). His strong screen presence and control were evident in his portrayal of Albert Speer in a television dramatization of the Third Reich and most especially as the "replicant" fighting for an identity in Ridley Scott's *Blade Runner.*

## NOTES

1. Gordon Hitchins, "Joris Ivens Interviewed by Gordon Hitchins, November 20, 1968, American Documentaries," *Film Culture* nos. 53–55 (Spring 1972): 214.
2. Ibid., p. 217.
3. B. J. Bertina, "Les grand documentaristes: Bert Haanstra," *Cinéma international* (Vaud, Switzerland), no. 13 (January–February 1967): 548.
4. Peter Cowie, *Dutch Cinema: An Illustrated History* (Cranbury, NJ: A. S. Barnes and Co., Inc., 1979), p. 15.
5. Ibid., p. 73.
6. Paul Rotha, *The Film Till Now* (London: Spring Books, 1967), p. 614.
7. *Cinéma international* (January-February 1967): 561.
8. Cowie, p. 89.
9. *Cinéma international* (January-February 1967): 563.

## SELECTED BIBLIOGRAPHY

*Cinéma international* (Vaud, Switzerland), no. 13 (January–February 1967). Entire issue.

Cowie, Peter. *Dutch Cinema: An Illustrated History.* Cranbury, NJ: A. S. Barnes and Company, Inc., 1979.

*Dutch Film.* Annual catalogues issued by the Ministry of Cultural Affairs, Recreation, and Social Welfare.

Hitchens, Gordon. "Joris Ivens Interviewed by Gordon Hitchins, November 20, 1968, American Documentaries." *Film Culture,* nos. 53–55 (spring 1972): 190–228.

Ivens, Joris. *The Camera and I.* New York: International Publishers, 1969.

Netherlands Information Service brochures.

Rotha, Paul. *The Film Till Now.* London: Spring Books, 1967.

*Skoop.* Film journal, Amsterdam.

*Skrien.* Film journal, Amsterdam.

# POLAND

## JOHN MOSIER

In the middle third of this century Poland, which should have been the largest and wealthiest country in Eastern Europe, was virtually destroyed by a succession of national calamities. In 1939 the country was overrun by Nazi Germany, which promptly began exterminating the vast majority of Polish Jews and intellectuals, and finished by destroying Warsaw itself during the two uprisings against the occupation. Although Hitler certainly could have accomplished the destruction of Poland on his own, he had a formidable ally as a result of his treaty with Stalin. Regardless of what the Russians thought of the Germans, they shared a common set of ideas about Poland. While German troops overran the country from three sides, Russian troops partitioned the country from the fourth. While Hitler exterminated the Jews, Stalin shot all of the officers. While the Home Army and the Warsaw Jews fought against the Germans, the Russian army sat patiently by and waited for the Germans to finish them off and destroy Warsaw. After the war Soviet policies added the finishing touches: noncommunist antifascists were exiled or imprisoned, and Poland, although liberated from Germany, became an example of socialism at its most impoverished. These successive and interlocking catastrophes, for which both National Socialist Germany and Soviet Russia are responsible, made the Poland of the 1950s the poorest state in developed Europe; even now it is a substantially poorer country than either Hungary or Czechoslovakia. Ironically, Poland is one of the richest states in Europe in intellectual and cultural terms, and its filmmakers have created a national art form that has been at the center of Polish national consciousness.

Although Poland is the largest and most populous of the countries of Eastern Europe, its film industry is known internationally for the work of only a few directors. Of these the first is unquestionably Andrzej

Wajda, whose reputation emerged as the result of three formidable films which form an informal trilogy defining the shape of postwar Poland. The first postwar films in Poland, like those in the other countries of Eastern Europe, gradually diverged from the canons of Stalinist socialist realism in small steps. The Polish film usually cited as the first major postwar work, Aleksandr Ford's *Five Boys from Barska Street* (*Piatka z ulicy Barskiej*, 1953) certainly illustrates this trend.[1] But *Generation* (*Pokolenie*, 1954), Wajda's first feature film, represented an entirely new approach to filmmaking. The script, in which certain scenes were eliminated by the censors, appears to have a conventional story line: a group of young men and women join up with the resistance forces and the film follows their ultimately tragic fate. But what Wajda and Jerzy Lipman (the cinematographer) had done was to make a film whose images conveyed a set of meanings entirely different from what was in the script. The heroes and heroines of *Generation* attracted sympathy because they were young people first and Communists second. Wajda emphasized their growth and their sacrifices. The correctness of their political views was of vastly diminished importance.

Most of the armed resistance to the Germans came from noncommunist groups known collectively as the Home Army. The state, however, discouraged or suppressed all references to the Home Army and downplayed the role of all noncommunist resistance heroes. But in *Kanal* (1957) the people whose fates we watch are from the Home Army rather than from the communist Peoples Army of the Lublin Committee. For the sake of historical accuracy, it could scarcely be otherwise, but by recording history objectively Wajda contradicted the official line, in which only politically correct protagonists were allowed. The last film of the three is the masterpiece. *Ashes and Diamonds* (*Popiól i diament*, 1958) is significant for two main reasons. First, with it Wajda found a cinematic style that was distinctly his own. Although Wajda was accused of being too much under the influence of Italian neorealism, his handling of the opening and closing murder scenes is completely different from anything that had been seen in Italy. These scenes are brutally violent, but the violence has been harnessed for symbolic purposes, as when the innocent victim's lifeless body is forced through the door of the church by the force of the bullets penetrating him, only to fall prone before the altar in a posture that recalls a prostrate supplicant. This symbolism was reinforced by the dawn sequence at the end of the film in which the characters sleepwalk into the sunlight to the accompaniment of an incredibly bungled polonaise. The use of symbolic structures with such overtly and specifically political applications was new. Where the Italian directors had evoked sympathy or pathos, Wajda used symbols to evoke defiance and rejection of the system.

The second major reason for the significance of *Ashes and Diamonds* is that it firmly marks Wajda's political status of opposition to the party line: he took a novel whose politics were exemplary of the orthodox Polish communism of the period, and stood it on its head. The novel is a panorama of society in May 1945, but the film concentrates on a few characters, the two most important being the assassin Chelmicki and the barmaid Cristina. They are probably the least important of the many characters in the novel, where the Communist Podgorski and the ex-kapo Kossecki are followed in a much more systematic fashion. While the novel followed all of its characters, the events of the film are seen mostly from Chelmicki's point of view, and, to a lesser extent, from that of Szczuka, the Communist veteran whom Chelmicki is supposed to kill. Finally, the novel has a fairly unequivocal message: in Poland in 1945 it was impossible, on the balance, not to support the efforts of the Polish Communist party which, backed by the Red Army, was trying to construct a new state. Those who opposed this order are shown to be numerous and blindly selfish, and their behavior is presented as though it is virtually hereditary. The film has a dramatically different message: the tragedy of Poland is that Chelmicki and Szczuka (who is old enough to be his father) are on opposite sides, that they perish, and that they are survived by despicable people.

The best Polish films, then, follow an unusual course. Instead of the struggles to build socialism, they analyze successive struggles for national independence or honor. The protagonists, far from being Communists or socialists, are primarily Polish nationalists. In the case of Wajda's three films, the protagonists are in actuality members of the three groups thought politically suspect by the official regime—workers who were purely (or merely) antifascist, members of the Home Army, and Polish nationalists. From the 1950s on it is nearly impossible to find a major Polish film whose protagonist is a Communist intellectual, and even in the 1970s there are very few films which address the issue of communism, much less its failures, as was the case in Hungary. The difference is partly because the Polish government never allowed the degree of social criticism that was tolerated in Hungary, and partly because of the drastically differing histories of the two nations in this century. But in retrospect it also seems true that the better Polish film artists, after being exposed to the internal contradictions of the Polish communist state, rejected its claims more thoroughly and completely than did artists elsewhere. Polish film is an expression of Poland rather than of Polish socialism, which explains the continuous tensions between the filmmakers and the state. Even though political events in Poland paralleled those in Hungary—an apparent relaxation of governmental controls throughout the early 1960s followed by a convulsive reaction after 1968 and a gradual recovery during the 1970s—the response of Polish filmmakers was quite different.

One of the most important filmmakers of the 1950s was Andzej

Munk, whose career was tragically ended by a fatal accident in 1961. His second feature film, *Man on the Track* (*Czlowiek na torze*, 1957), dealt with the consequences of a world in which issues of political unreliability and reliability were constantly intruding into everyday life. When an elderly railroad engineer is killed in an accident, his heroism is ignored during an investigation that is more concerned with his alleged political unreliability: for a government where accidents are seen as acts of sabotage, it is inevitably the case that someone must have been the saboteur. The conveniently dead engineer is a perfect candidate. His heroism is ignored as the investigation tries to discredit his political reliability. In Munk's other films he also investigated the ramifications of heroism and the extent to which heroic self-sacrifice is a national characteristic. This was very much the case in *Eroica* (1957), which portrays officers of the prewar army during World War II. Munk's masterpiece, however, is unfinished, since he died before he could complete *The Passenger* (*Pasażerka*, 1963; it was completed using still photographs by Witold Lesiewicz). *The Passenger* is about the experiences of a Polish woman in a concentration camp, although it takes the point of view of a German woman who was a guard there—a startling and unexpected shift of perspective. Even in its present form it contains the most moving, and macabre, scenes of concentration camps ever filmed.

In addition to Wajda and Munk, two other major directors emerged during the 1950s. Both Jerzy Kawalerowicz and Kasimirz Kutz differed substantially from Wajda and Munk: Kawalerowicz was interested in the significance of history, and Kutz in the working classes of his native Silesian Poland. The restricted nature of the subjects has made their films less well known than they should be. Kawalerowicz's first important work was a two-part analysis of Poland between the wars, *Night of Remembrance* (*Celuloza*, 1954) and *Under the Phrygian Star* (*Pod gwiazdą Frygijską*, 1954). The director's concern appears to have been to portray the dynamics of Poland during this period, something that he would return to in his later *Death of a President* (*Smierz prezydenta*, 1978), which is a scrupulously documentarylike fiction about the election and assassination of Poland's first democratic president, Gabriel Narutowicz, in 1922. Kawalerowicz's most famous film, however, is on a theme that is, at first glance, unrelated. *Mother Joan of the Angels* (*Matka Joanna od Aniolów*, 1961) is a case study of religious possession in the seventeenth century. What ties all of his films together, however disparate their subjects may seem, is a concern with the psychology of group behavior, and particularly the extent to which fanaticism, whether religious or political, can decisively influence major events.

If Wajda is concerned with personalized symbolic histories of his country, Kawalerowicz is more concerned with the actual workings out of Polish history. It is this preoccupation that gives his films their documentary aura and also accounts for the distance between director and subject. In this sense he represents a real alternative to Wajda's intense and personal style of filmmaking. In general, Polish films fall relatively neatly into two groups: films which are detached and objective analyses of situations, and those which are deeply subjective and involved portraits of individuals.

Even bearing this in mind, any meaningful description of the works of the most significant Polish filmmakers invariably makes them seem like historians or social scientists rather than artists. To some extent this is true: directors like Wajda are not merely accomplished artists, they are forceful thinkers whose thoughts are presented on film. As a result, the works of such men focus either on the actions of those few individuals whose behavior is historically significant, or on individuals whose lives have significance by virtue of the parable that the director is constructing in his film. And, to shift the perspectives slightly, when such artists turn to contemporary society, they portray intellectuals and professionals. The working class, the peasants, the poor, the common man, all are seen from a distance—sometimes with great compassion, understanding, or incisiveness, but invariably from a long way off looking down. The less talented director follows the dictates of socialist realism more closely, and his films portray that same class, but only in cartoon fashion. This gives rise to the central paradox of socialist film: the best socialist films are by, for, and about intellectuals, while the ordinary films are made by the state for no one.

The films of Kasimierz Kutz stand in strong contrast, then, both to the best of Wajda and of Kawalerowicz, as well as to the mediocrities of the state hacks. Although Kutz is like Wajda in his interest in the personal dimension and in his passionate convictions about his characters, he is unique in that he is an accomplished artist whose subject is the lives of the ordinary workers of Silesian Poland, and whose attitude toward them is one of acceptance, understanding, and admiration. Although his subjects come from ordinary life, he composes each frame with such care that frequently the effect is of a fine still photograph. Again, although his films are like Wajda's films of the same period in their constant and conscious manipulation of cinematic components, Kutz emphasizes different aspects of the medium. While Wajda's images are quickly perceivable as attractive symbolic constructs, Kutz's images generally stand as objects in themselves: their significance lies only in their unusual clarity and grace. Kutz's first film, *Cross of Valor* (*Krzyz walecznych*, 1959), is a triptych of stories about Polish soldiers, none of whom really do anything. As is the case with most soldiers anywhere, their chief concerns are survival. Kutz's films are permeated with an ironic peasant humor that frequently undercuts or modifies the ideas. In *Cross of Valor* the ironic tone of the third story, in which the widow of a deified army officer tries to make her way amidst the relics of her husband's life which are assiduously cultivated by his men, produces a work that says much more about the reconstruction of Poland than the plot suggests. Similarly, *Salt of the Earth* (*Sol ziemi czarnej*, 1970), which recounts an uprising of the Silesians against the Junkers, is more a complex set of folktales, rather than an excursus into the Marxification of Polish history.

If Munk was fascinated with the idea of heroic sacrifice, Kutz concerns himself with the natural state of the working classes, which he consistently interprets as being fundamentally anarchist, and scarcely an incubator for Communist revolutionaries. This is most clearly revealed in his two later films, *Pearls in the Crown* (*Pela w koronie*, 1971) and *The Beads of One Rosary* (*Paciorki jednego rózánca*, 1980), both of which offer instances of successful small revolts on the part of individual miners against the bureaucracy. In the first the revolt is a group action against the prewar establishment, but in the later film the revolt is in the present: one old man refuses to vacate his house and move to an apartment complex.

Ironically, although Wajda and to a lesser extent Kutz were the filmmakers responsible for establishing Poland's position in global film in the late 1950s, their best works were not to come until the 1970s. In fact the political situation in Poland during the 1960s was so difficult that very few films of any quality were produced until the very end, even though talented directors such as Jerzy Skolimowski, Wojciech Has, and Tadeusz Konwicki had emerged. Konwicki, older than Wajda, had already established himself as a distinguished novelist and had been working in the Polish film industry where, as a literary director, he decided on the literary qualities of the scripts being submitted. In addition, he was an accomplished scriptwriter who did, among other things, the script for Kawalerowicz's *Mother Joan of the Angels.* By 1965 he had directed only three films, but the third, *Salto*, was in certain respects the best Polish film of the decade, particularly in its grim humor and in its emphasis on the grotesque.[2] *Salto* continues to develop some of the more baroque tendencies of the photography of *Ashes and Diamonds,* which sometimes obscures the ways in which the film offers a revisionist view of Polish character. The hero claims to have done all sorts of things during the war; the villagers heroize and then reject him, but it is never exactly clear where the truth lies.

Wojiech Has had started off primarily as a documentarist after his graduation from Cracow in 1946, but his feature film career started in 1958 with *The Noose* (*Pętla*). His second film, *Farewells* (*Pożegnania*, 1958), was an unusually nostalgic look at prewar Poland. *The Saragossa Manuscript* (*Rękopis znaleziony w Saragossie*, 1965) was a complex historical film, which, although based on a work of Polish literature, ended up as an almost surrealistic merging of various historical periods. In 1973 Has made *Sandglass* (*Sanatorium pod klepsydrą*),

Kasimierz Kutz's carefully composed group shots are unique in Polish film, as seen in this still from *Pearls in the Crown* (1971).

Typical of Krzysztof Zanussi's directorial style is a reliance on small groups of characters engaged in intense interchanges, as in *The Constant Factor* (1980).

A more casual, intimate, and even cluttered approach is typical of the younger directors, in this case Agnieszka Holland's *Provincial Actors* (1978).

One of Europe's leading directors, Andrzej Wajda is noted for his careful attention to faces and gestures, as in *Without Anesthesia* (1978), the chronicle of a man's destruction.

based on the novel by Bruno Schultz, beautifully photographed, and stuffed with symbolic images.

During this period it was Skolimowski, however, whose works were openly skeptical essays on life in Poland. *Identification Marks—None* (*Rysopsis*, 1964), which was his diploma film, dealt with a peculiar sort of emergence: the protagonist learns that he is coming of age in a world where everything is decided for him, and where he is unable to effect any changes in the course of his life. Although in *The Barrier* (*Bariera*, 1966) Skolimowski's rebellious hero ended up by imitating what he had initially affected to despise, Skolimowki's films clearly stand as the cinematic articulation of rejectionism. In 1967 Skolimowski made *Hands Up!* (*Ręce do góry*), a surrealistic parable about the behavior of the orthodox young and their relationship with Stalinism. Although the subject matter and certain techniques make it a difficult film, it would have been an important one if it had been released in 1967. This was not to be the case however, and Skolimowski left for the West.

Unfortunately for serious filmgoers in Poland, Skolimowski was neither the first nor the most famous director to leave. Walerian Borowczyk left Poland to work in France in 1959, returning to make *History of a Sin* (*Dzieje grzechu*, 1975). Increasingly he turned to fantastic stories that emphasize the grotesqueries of human nature, although this tendency is probably a function of his early training in animation and in experimental films in Poland. Probably the most important member of this informal group of exiles is Roman Polanski, who left Poland in the early 1960s after making his first feature film, *Knife in the Water* (*Nóż w wodzie*, 1962). Although the extent to which one can classify any of the three as a "Polish" filmmaker is a matter for discussion, the fact is that all three were trained there, and they stand as an impressive testimonial to the excellence of the industry as well as reminders of the precariousness of the position of the artist in the socialist state, something emphasized by the departure of Aleksander Ford. Essentially a prewar director, Ford had been instrumental in helping to create a national cinema with a solid base, although he made several successful films. His departure after 1968 was a significant moral defeat, while the success of Polanski as an artist working outside of Poland has been as serious a loss to Polish cinema as was the death of Munk.

For most of the 1960s Wajda did not work in Poland. His only film was made in Yugoslavia. *The Siberian Lady Macbeth* (*Sibirska ledi Makbet*, 1962), which relies equally on the Leskov novelle and on the Shostakovich opera, signals Wajda's interest in making films that have many of the components of the live theater, an interest he has returned to since then, notably with *Wedding* (*Wesele*, 1973), and *Danton* (1982). Shostakovich's opera quickly got the composer into trouble with the Soviet authorities in 1934 and was not performed in the Soviet Union even in its cut form for nearly thirty years. Wajda's choice of sources, then, had substantive political overtones. At the end of the decade, however, Wajda made two important films in Poland: *Everything for Sale* (*Wszystko na sprzedaz*, 1969) and *Landscape After Battle* (*Krajobraz po bitwie*, 1970). The first of these is usually seen as an intensely personal film and is often compared to *8 ½*. Formally speaking, the film is an elegy on actor Zbigniew Cybulski, whose death in 1967 affected Wajda personally. But the quest for Cybulski and the impact that this quest had on the director is also an attempt to reconstruct, to rethink, contemporary Polish life and the artist's place in it. *Landscape After Battle* is the result of that process of self-examination. Historically the film returns to the same period of *Ashes and Diamonds,* but the treatment is completely different. The hero is not the swashbuckling Cybulski, but a poet who was incarcerated in a concentration camp. There is an equivalent shift in the implications of the film. *Ashes and Diamonds* is a classical tragedy with clearly defined choices whose protagonists are cognizant of the implications of their decisions; *Landscape After Battle* is a film in which there are no real moral choices available, and the film signals the ending of one sort of filmmaking, whose assumptions about society were ultimately optimistic, and the beginning of a different, more complex and pessimistic art.

Difficult politics and emigration did not, however, prevent newer directors from emerging. The chief of these is Krzysztof Zanussi, whose first feature film was *Structure of a Crystal* (*Struktura krysztalu*, 1968). The title suggests, appropriately, the presence of a scientific mind. Zanussi was trained as a physicist, and there is in all of his films a penchant for the mathematical and the objective. He thus both follows and intensifies the approach of Kawalerowicz toward the subject matters of film, although Zanussi differs from Kawalerowicz dramatically in that Zanussi's works reveal a concern with the discovery of underlying principles. More than any other filmmaker, Zanussi is a cinematic moralist. His earlier films are organized around the principles of confrontational meetings between two characters. For example, *Structure of a Crystal* is organized around an encounter between two men who were students together; one has become famous, the other has stayed in a small village. Zanussi's principles led him into an abstract cinema that was increasingly static and which relied to a great extent upon dialogue. Initially, then, his achievement was twofold: an elevation of the level of discourse in Polish cinema, and an attempt to deal with the actual present. Both Polanski and Skolimowski had made abortive attempts to do this in the 1960s. Had they been successful, Polish film would have taken a vastly different turn. But in Poland as elsewhere in the East, it was unacceptable for the filmmaker to turn his critical gaze on the socialist state of the immediate present: even the most critical Hungarian films of the very late 1970s confined themselves to events of twenty years ago, and the events were carefully selected. From this perspective Zanussi's success in this area—the ability to conduct discourse about the here and now—was a considerable one.

In the 1970s, Zanussi's films became more overtly concerned with the ethics of behavior under socialism, and this is the concern which underlies *Camouflage (Barwy ochronne, 1976), Spiral (Spirale, 1980)*, and *The Constant Factor (Constans, 1980)*. Each title derives from some scientific concept, and each film illustrates how this principle is, or can be, applied to human behavior. The young hero of *The Constant Factor*, for example, refuses to change his values in order to survive in a corrupt society; instead of becoming a dependent variable, like the people around him, or even an independent one, he is a constant. Zanussi makes films that are inaccessible to many people; only an educated audience can understand the scientific and mathematical concepts that represent the controlling ideas, and even an educated Western audience may have trouble in grasping just why these particular ideas are so important to the artist. The hero of *The Constant Factor* is important because in a society where every possibility exists only through corruption, for example, variation, he refuses to change. However, Zanussi's criticisms go substantially beyond sociocultural concerns, because the implication in his films is that socialist societies can be understood by objective, universal concepts that have nothing to do with Marxism. Although this idea is of decisive importance for the Marxist educated filmmaker, it is, as is usually the case with Zanussi, simply an assumption: the intellectual point of his films seems to be an explication of socialist life using such principles, the validity of which is amply confirmed by the realism of the work itself.

These austere concepts are necessary because socialist life has fundamentally shifted the grounds for human behavior; it has dehumanized individuals to the extent that only by using abstruse scientific principles can we understand their behavior. For example, people change states in order to camouflage themselves and escape detection by the state, and these individuals are not subversives or dissidents. Far from it, they are the intelligentsia whose behavior in *Camouflage* seems pointless at first. But just as one can soon realize there is a reason why chameleons change colors as their backgrounds change, so can one understand the reasons why the characters of *Camouflage* change states. By *Spiral* the confrontations of Zanussi's films have become inverted: engineer Piatek confronts people merely to remind them of their mortality; his real aim is his own destruction, which he finally accomplishes. His death is a sort of redemption for the fallen society in which he moves. This theme is amplified in *The Constant Factor (Constans)*, where the necessity to live a moral life, and the material failures that ensue, become the subject of the film. Zanussi's socialist eccentrics, in other words, begin to look remarkably like early Christians in their steadfastness, their refusal to compromise, and their eventual self sacrifice.

This later trio of films made Zanussi's reputation as a director while signaling the emergence of a talented group of younger directors. The situation of Poland in 1982 abbreviated or curtailed their artistic possibilities; consequently, it is difficult to judge their prospects as full fledged filmmakers. Krzysztof Kieslowski is often spoken of as the "third" major Polish director, largely as a result of *Camera Buff* (*Amator*, 1979) which tracks the fortunes of an ordinary worker who is given a camera and whose life changes drastically as a result. By 1982 he had made four feature films, as had Feliks Falk, whose *Chance* (*Szansa*, 1979) deals with the impact of a fanatical athletic coach at a provincial high school.[3] Kieslowski and Falk, who are the most prominent of a group of younger directors who were born during or shortly after World War II, are significant in two ways. First, trained at the film school at Łódź, they were products of a purely Polish film curriculum. Second, their skeptical social criticism is in no way derived from the works of the older or emigré artists. Their films are talky, enmeshed in what to the Westerner looks suspiciously like a student or bohemian point of view, and cinematographically they are more conventional. What binds them to the older generation is a shared view of Polish cinema as the central vehicle in the education of Polish national consciousness. That this has been an overriding concern is best demonstrated by Agnieszka Holland, an equally talented artist who studied at FAMU, the Czech film school in Prague, rather than at Łódź. Her *Provincial Actors* (*Aktorzy prowincjonalni*, 1978), is an incisive analysis of human relations in contemporary Poland. All of these younger artists embarked on careers of great promise in the 1970s. Unfortunately, there is a strong possibility that, as a group, their creativity will never come to the maturation it deserves.

The deserved attention given to the younger Polish directors initially seems to have obscured Wajda, who, in four masterful films established himself as one of Europe's most important directors: *Wedding* (*Wesele*, 1973), *Man of Marble* (*Czlowiek z marmuru*, 1976), *Without Anesthesia* (*Bez znieczulenia*, 1978), and *Man of Iron* (*Czlowiek z zelaza*, 1981). *Wedding* is based on Stanislaw Wyspiánski's famous play. Wajda's version is the most successful of his film adaptations, but it is the most underrated film of the four, probably because he relied heavily on the actual rhymed speech of the play for the film's dialogue. It is also true that the film is a deeply historical and national work that makes it difficult for audiences outside of Poland.

Stylistically it marks the end of Wajda's tendency toward baroque cinematography. *Without Anesthesia*, from a script by Agnieszka Holland, for instance, is cinematographically more conventional. What is not conventional at all is the subject matter, which is the incremental humiliations dosed out to a famous Polish journalist on his return to Poland after a trip abroad. Bit by bit his prerogatives are taken away, his wife leaves him, and his life goes down the drain, all in mysterious fashion. There is never any real explanation for the whys of all of this, although the film is full of hints. *Without Anesthesia* is a remarkable chronicle of a man's total destruction which may stand as Wajda's final word on the complex relationship between the intellectuals and the socialist state.

*Man of Iron* and *Man of Marble* form a rich and complex saga about Polish workers. Wajda invents a typical worker hero, Mathias Birkut, whom he pictures as a sincere Communist proletarian whose image as a hero of labor was created by the media in the 1950s. The true story about Birkut is ferreted out by a young woman filmmaker. In the process of searching, for the truth about Birkut, whose idealism made him a nuisance to the authorities, she herself begins to encounter difficulties; no one wants the truth to be told in 1976 either. She finds Birkut's son and learns from him that his father was killed during the 1970 riots in Gdansk. Birkut's filmic demise was cut by the censors in Poland, but is essential to an understanding of *Man of Iron,* which takes up the story of Birkut's son Tomczyk, who is involved in the student riots of 1968 and in the formation of Solidarity. Both films use a meticulous documentarist approach in which the real and the fictional are skillfully blended.

Wajda's career thus falls into two distinct phases. In the 1950s his works announced the beginning of a new Polish cinema which broke decisively with the traditions of both prewar and Stalinist filmmaking. Then in the 1970s Wajda again took the lead in Eastern European film as he began to chronicle the real history of Poland after World War II. His achievements and his remarkable endurance in the face of adversity make him the preeminent living director of all Eastern Europe as well as of Poland. At the same time, despite emigrations and inexplicable furloughs, newer generations of artists emerged, of which Zanussi is rightfully regarded as the most talented. Unfortunately, the Polish state has not supported its artists to anything like the extent that Hungary has. Consequently, Poland remains a country where the majority of the more talented filmmakers are artists whose reputations are based on a handful of films, and whose careers are all too often marked by ellipses and withdrawals.

## NOTES

1. The release dates and both the English and Polish language titles of Polish films mentioned in the text are taken from Jacek Fuksiewicz's *Film and*

*Television in Poland* (Warsaw: Interpress, 1976), with corrections supplied by Fuksiewicz. I am indebted to the following individuals for their help: Jacek Fuksiewicz, Ron Holloway, Boleslaw Michalek, Jerzy Kawalerowicz, and Krzysztof Zanussi.

2.  The title does not refer to a traditional Polish dance, despite the claims made in Mira and Antonin Liehm's *The Most Important Art: Eastern European Film After 1945* (Berkeley: University of California Press, 1974), p. 373. The word *salto* means somersault, and the dance sequence in the film is a parody, both of the famous polonaise in *Ashes and Diamonds* in particular and of village traditions in general.

3.  There has been some confusion about the exact number of feature films made by various directors. In some cases the films made for television have not been counted. Technically speaking, by 1982 Falk had made three theatrical feature flms and two television feature films. Of the five, only two had been released in Poland.

## SELECTED BIBLIOGRAPHY

Fuksiewicz, Jacek. *Film and Television in Poland.* Warsaw: Interpress, 1976.

Liehm, Mira and Antonin J. *The Most Important Art: Eastern European Film After 1945.* Berkeley: University of California Press, 1974.

Loup-Passek, Jean. *L'avant scène cinéma: special cinéma polonais.* Paris: Centre Georges Pompidou, 1983.

Stoil, Michael Jon. *Cinema Beyond the Danube.* Metuchen, NJ: Scarecrow Press, 1974.

White, Alistair. *New Cinema in Eastern Europe.* New York: Dutton, 1971.

———. *New Cinema in Eastern Europe.* New York: Dutton, 1971.

# PORTUGAL
## Redeeming the Past

JOÃO LUIZ VIEIRA AND ROBERT STAM

Portuguese cinema traces its existence back to the early years of this century. Following on the work of such pioneers as Aurélio Reis and Manuel Maria da Costa Veiga, filmmaker João Correia directed the first fiction film, a staged reconstruction of a sensational crime, entitled *The Crimes of Diogo Alves* (*Os crimes de Diogo Alves*) in 1911. Along with melodramas such as *Fatal Love* (*Amor fatal*) and Chaplin-style comedies, the predominant formula of the silent period consisted in adaptations of celebrated Portuguese novels: two such are *Doomed Love* (*Amor de perdição,* 1921), from the novel of Camilo Castelo Branco and *Cousin Basílio* (*O primo Basílio,* 1922) from that of Eça de Queiroz. With the advent of sound, Portuguese audiences rushed to the movie theaters for the chance to hear dialogue in their own language. *The Severe Woman* (*A severa,* 1931), by João Leitão de Barros, was the first Portuguese sound film, although the sound had to be dubbed in the French Epinay studios. The first sound film entirely produced in Portugal was the same diretor's *Song from Lisbon* (*A canção de Lisboa,* 1933). The Portuguese sound cinema sought commercial viability and national authenticity by drawing on the native musical tradition of fado, in a manner analogous to the use of samba in Brazil and the tango in Argentina. But the Portuguese cinema lacked important advantages enjoyed by the Brazilian and Argentinian industries, namely, the lack of a strong internal market and the absence of an industrial infrastructure. Portugal, dominated by foreign distributors, also offered no state protection for its cinema. Despite these disadvantages, however, films such as *The Severe Woman* and *Song of Lisbon* show considerable aesthetic and technical merit for a cinema with such limited tradition and financial means.

With the installation of fascist rule in the mid-thirties, the Portuguese film industry finally received state support, but unfortunately from an oppressive regime. In exchange for subventions to the cinema, initiated by the Ministry of national Propaganda in 1935, Portuguese filmmakers had to consent to rigid censorship, leading to the prohibition against certain themes and to self-censorship on the part of the directors. In 1937 the fascist New State of Salazar produced *The May Revolution* (*A revolução de maio*), directed by António Lopes Ribeiro, a film which contrasts the subversive activities of foreign agitators with the "sweet" submissive spirit of the Portuguese. Other films, such as *Imperial Spell* (*Feitiço do império*, 1940), glorify the then still extensive Portuguese colonial empire.

Not all of the films from this period were profascist, however. Jorge Brum do Canto's *Song of the Earth* (*A canção da terra*, 1936) concerns peasant revolt against the unjust distribution of water during a drought. Manoel de Oliveira, meanwhile, who had begun making his highly personal and sensitive films in the early thirties, made *Aniki-Bobo* (1942), in which the conflicts of a group of children, through references to social strife and world war, become a metaphor for the plight of a society, in a style which simultaneously looks back to French poetic realism and forward to certain procedures of Italian neorealism. The conflicts presented in Antonio Lopes Ribeiro's *The Tyrannical Father* (*O pai tirano*, 1941), meanwhile, form part of a reflexive film which revolves around the tension between a young girl enamored of the cinema and a young boy in love with the theater.

The immediate postwar period was a relatively fecund one for Portuguese cinema. Among the popular genres treated in this period were costume dramas like the Spanish-Portuguese collaboration *Inês de Castro* (1945); historical reconstructions like Lopes Ribeiro's *The Neighbor Woman* (*A vizinha do lado*, 1945), evoking the Lisbon of 1913; comedies such as Arthur Duarte's *The Lion from Estrela* (*O leão da Estrela*, 1947); Jorge Brum do Canto's *Help Wanted-Thief* (*Ladrão precisa-se*, 1946); and bucolic evocations of peasant life such as Henrique Campos's *The Man from Ribatejo* (*O homem do Ribatejo*, 1946). Another common genre, the historical-literary biography, reached its apogee with Leitão de Barros's ambitious *Camões* (1946), a tribute to Portugal's most famous poet, the epic sixteenth-century writer Camões. The film pleased the Salazarist authorities by incarnating their idea of classical Portuguese culture and national dignity. In 1948, conforming to a general European movement toward commercial self-protection, the Portuguese government passed protectionist legislation for the film industry and offered modest financial support. Unfortunately, the legislation failed to take into account the serious problem of distribution in a country which had only 250 movie theaters. Despite the modest grants, there was no coherent policy toward the industry. The decline of production in the mid-fifties (reaching zero production in 1955) coincided with the inauguration of Portuguese television in 1956, a factor which contributed to the further decline of the industry.

The films of the fifties were not remarkable for their cinematic or thematic daring. There were some timid social consciousness films, such as Perdigão Queiroga's *Dreaming is Easy* (*Sonhar é fácil*, 1951), about a man trying to create a cooperative in Lisbon, but the cautious socialism of the film is generally drowned in a sea of sentiment. In 1953 Manoel Ribeiro made *Heroic Plains* (*Planície heróica*), a melodrama about a priest torn between divine and human love. Henrique Campos filmed established dramas such as *When the Sea Covered the Earth* (*Quando o mar galgou a terra*, 1954) and *The Light Comes from Above* (*A luz vem do alto*, 1959). At the same time, Portuguese filmmakers made comic films, partially inspired by the commercial success of the Brazilian *chanchada* (light musical comedy), such as Fernando Garcia's *And Now What do We Do?* (*E agora é que são elas*, 1954), featuring most of the popular musical stars of the period. A new kind of romantic film appeared, weaving musical numbers by radio and recording stars around a sentimental theme, such as Henrique Campos's *Song of the Street* (*Canção da rua*, 1950), featuring fado singers Alberto Ribeiro and Deolinda Rodrigues. Also forming part of this genre was Manoel Guimarães's *The Seamstress from Sé* (*A costureirinha da Sé*, 1958), the first Portuguese film in CinemaScope. The historical-literary film also maintained its prestige in this period. Fernando Garcia adapted Eça de Queiroz's novel with *The Hanging Hill* (*O cerro dos enforcados*, 1954), and António Lopes Ribeiro did still another adaptation of *Cousin Basílio* (*O primo Basílio*, 1959).

The real origins of the contemporary renaissance of Portuguese cinema can be traced back to the final years of the fifties, specifically to 1959. In that year the Portuguese government began to provide scholarships for aspiring filmmakers such as Fernando Lopes, António da Cunha Teles, and Paulo Rocha, who subsequently became major directors. At the same time, the cine-clubs were becoming hotbeds of cultural agitation and antigovernment feeling. New film journals like *Visão, Imagem, Filme,* and *Boletim Cinematográfico* also emerged to contribute to the general debate, along with a number of book-length studies of Portuguese cinema. Film retrospectives introduced potential filmmakers to film art from around the world. The film milieu became especially aware of the precedent of Italian neorealism, a movement with special resonance for the Portuguese as they too were striving to emerge from fascism. At the same time, Portugal had always had close cultural ties with France, and Portuguese intellectuals were aware of the cultural effervescence surrounding the cine-club movement and such critics as Bazin, on the one hand, and the filmmakers of the New Wave on the other.

With an average yearly production of five films, Portuguese filmmakers began to experiment with new forms. Preeminent among them was Manoel de Oliveira, a veteran who had been kept from realizing his numerous film projects for over a decade. *Spring Mystery Play (O acto da primavera,* 1963) was inspired by the traditional passion plays common in the rural regions of Portugal. The religious symbolism of the play becomes completely intertwined with the daily life of the peasants, and Christ's resurrection comes to symbolize a general social renewal. In this cosmic and visionary, yet highly political film, Oliveira foregrounds the popular *mise-en-scène* of the mystery in a provocative melange of documentary and fiction. Images of war and the atomic bomb, associating the drama of Calvary with the possibility of humanity's self-annihilation, disturb the spectator, as does the inscription of the cinematic apparatus within the image. The same director's short fiction film *The Hunt (A caça,* 1963) recounts a hunt in which two boys become trapped in a swamp. This minimal story becomes a pretext in the film for a discussion of the issue of selfishness versus solidarity, in which the spectator is made to feel responsible for taking a position concerning the events depicted.

In the same period, a new generation of filmmakers, partially formed in film schools abroad, brought a new atmosphere to Portuguese cinema. Fernando Lopes, after having studied filmmaking in London, made his first feature, *Belarmino* (1964). The film follows a declining boxer around the poor neighborhoods of Lisbon, in a style clearly inflected by *cinéma vérité* and television reportage. Paulo Rocha, who studied at the film school IDHEC in Paris, meanwhile, contributed films bearing clear traces of the influence of the French New Wave. His first feature, *The Green Years (Os anos verdes,* 1963), concerns a banal crime of passion of the kind commonly reported in the sensational press. More interesting, however, is the style in which the story is presented. Rocha deploys hand-held camera and stark cinematography to expose a demystified Lisbon far from the idealized postcard image typical of earlier films. Rocha's second film, *Changing One's Life (Mudar de vida,* 1966), recounts a passionate and conflict-ridden triangle against the backdrop of a fishing village, in a style marked by calculated ruptures within an almost musical construction. The producer of *Changing One's Life,* António da Cunha Telles, also graduated from IDHEC. His film *Surrounded (O cerco,* 1970) perhaps best encapsulates the thematic concerns and cinematic strategies of the post-1959 generation. The film's protagonist Marta (Maria Cabral) is a young bourgeois woman who leaves the security of middle-class marriage in search of a more authentic life. In her trajectory toward a more and more explicit prostitution, she encounters a gallery of low-life characters: a young photographer, advertising agents, whiskey dealers, smugglers, all avatars of contemporary alienation. *Surrounded* portrays a suffocating atmosphere of dead-end corruption characterized by a pervasive am-

biance of loneliness and impotence, emblematic of a social system showing signs of imminent collapse. The style throughout is impassive, neutral, with minimal camera movement and lighting effects. In contrast
to the alienated selfishness of the characters in the film, the production
itself was marked by the spirit of generous collaboration of a small but
highly integrated and collaborative crew.

If *Surrounded* summed up the gains of the cinema of the sixties,
Manoel de Oliveira's *The Past and the Present* (*O passado e o presente*,
1971) anticipated the achievements of the seventies. This caustically
humorous film centers on the amorous hesitations of the recently widowed Wanda who becomes successively disenchanted with a series of
new attachments. Through a process of retroactive idealization, Wanda
always seems to prefer former to present lovers. In this sense, her attitudes are symptomatic, perhaps, of the attitudes of a society deeply imbued with nostalgia and a fear of the new. *The Past and the Present* was
one of the first films to profit from the financial aid offered by the Gul-
benkian Foundation in support of Portuguese cinema.

The overthrow of the Salazarist dictatorship on 25 April 1974 led not
only to liberal democracy but also to a general resurgence in the arts.
Censorship was lifted, and the Portuguese Film Institute was created
and charged with responsibility for the domestic and international distribution of Portuguese films. The interim military government also began to enforce a 1971 decree which sought to rechannel part of the profits from ticket sales back into the film industry. At the same time, the
film industry was nationalized and the Portuguese Film Institute became the major producer of Portuguese films.

One of the first by-products of the April revolution was the emergence of a militant documentary cinema. The collectively produced
*Arms and the People* (*As armas e o povo*, 1975) combines an analysis of
the historical origins of Salazarism with an account of the popular resistance that led to its demise, culminating in the powerful mass May
Day demonstration of 1974. Rui Simões's *God, Country, Authority*
(*Deus, pátria, autoridade*, 1975) also scrutinizes fascist ideology
through a didactic montage of superb archival footage. *Trás-os-Montes*,
(1976), by Margarida Cordeiro and António Reis, is a film-poem dedicated to the resilient people of a provincial Portuguese village. *Law of
the Earth* (*A lei da terra*, 1977), a collective film by the Grupo Zero,
treats the subject of class struggle in the Alentejo region and the peasant occupations (later institutionalized through agrarian reform laws)
which led to new social and human relations in the area. Leonel Brito's
*Colony and Villains* (*Colónia e vilões*, 1977) exposes the reactionary
role of the church in maintaining the colonial status of Madeira. The
film is most interesting, perhaps, for its insistence on the progressive
role of women, often aged, abandoned, and illiterate, in the political liberation of the island. The most cinematically audacious of this harvest

The celebration of the patriarch as an anti-Salazar allegory: Alberto Seixas Santos's *Gentle Customs* was released in 1975, although it was made before the overthrow of the dictatorship in 1974.

In *Francisca* (1981) veteran director Manoel de Oliveira demonstrates symmetry of *mise-en-scène* and frontality of camera address in a story of frustrated love.

of April documentaries is Rui Simões's *Good Portuguese People* (*Bom povo português,* 1980). A multileveled meditation on the chaotic politicization that took over Portugal in the eight months following 25 April, the film covers myriad topics—political alignments, demonstrations, agrarian reform, factory occupations, emigration—all unified by a poetic voice-over commentary which is at once political, literary, and anthropological. The text and images weave multiple themes—Plato's cave as metaphor for Portuguese reemergence into the political light, the sea and the seasons as perennial witnesses to Portuguese history, the cultural role of the myth of Portuguese passivity—all underlined through the ironic superimposition of musical motifs and sound and image disjunction.

Some filmmakers adopted intermediate forms mingling documentary and fiction techniques. Alberto Seixas Santos's *Gentle Customs* (*Brandos costumes*), although filmed before the revolution, was actually released only in 1975. The film manipulates three distinct kinds of material—staged fiction, musical review songs, and archival footage —in order to construct an allegorical parallel between patriarchal authoritarianism as it is manifested in the family and in the state. Alberto Seixas Santos further developed this provocative collage strategy in his *Gestures and Fragments* (*Gestos e Fragmentos,* 1982), a three-part essay in which he weaves together three interviews, with a Portuguese leftist military man, an academic, and a fictional American journalist, in order to expose the contradictions of the Portuguese military.

In the realm of the fiction film, contemporary Portuguese cinema, even if limited to an average yearly production of five or six features, has been dominated by the work of specific *auteurs,* each with a specific constellation of thematic and stylistic concerns. The common thread that links them all, from the veteran Manoel de Oliveira to newcomer João Botelho, is a passionate interest in the history and cultural heritage of Portugal. Many of the films draw their inspiration from Portuguese literature. Manoel de Oliveira's *Doomed Love* (*Amor de perdição,* 1978) offers a briliant adaptation of the classic romantic novel by Camilo Castelo Braco concerning the impossible *l'amour fou* of two children from antagonistic noble families. Over four hours long, filmed in 16mm and with a preponderance of amateur actors, the film preserves most of the original novelistic text, whether in the form of voice-over narration or staged synchronized dialogue. The transparent artifice of the decors, the studio atmosphere, and the frequent direct address to the spectator all foster a critical attitude on the spectator's part, in a disconcerting melange of literal, even obsessive fidelity to the text, on the one hand, and relentless distanciation on the other. The literary interest takes a quite different, more biographical form in João Botelho's *The Other One* (*Conversa acabada,* 1981). The film stages the friendship and the texts of two modernist Portuguese poets, Fernando Pessoa and Mário de Sá-Carneiro, through the pretext of their extensive real-life correspondence. A narrator didactically provides biographical and historical information and introduces sequences in which the actors represent the writers' discourse in front of Syberberg-style back projections.

João Cesar Monteiro's *Silvestre* (1981) reaches farther back into Portugal's literary past, adapting two medieval Portuguese tales. In this story about feminine victimization and vengeance, Monteiro deploys heterogenous decors, ranging from strict naturalism to the extreme stylization of painterly theatrical backdrops, along with a highly metaphoric and aphoristic poetic discourse utilizing the elaborate rhyme scheme and style typical of the oral narratives of the period. Paulo Rocha's *The Island of Loves* (*A Ilha dos Amores*, 1982), meanwhile, is the result of fourteen years of work, including shooting in Lisbon, Macao, Tokyo, and Tokushimi. The film's epic production well suits the film's narrative—nineteenth-century poet Wenceslau de Moraes's attempt to follow the Far Eastern itinerary of Portuguese epic poet Luis de Camões. In an excruciatingly deliberate style, inflected by Asiatic modes of poetry and painting, Rocha recounts the progressive disillusionment and disintegration of his protagonist, as a metaphor, perhaps, of the parallel dissolution and decadence of a far-flung empire.

António-Pedro Vasconcelos's *Oxalá* (1980) also treats the subject of disillusionment, this time the contemporary disillusionment of many Portuguese intellectuals in the wake of the April revolution. The film's protagonist is José, a Portuguese exile living in Paris who returns to Portugal to see the results of the revolution. Witnessing the events at first hand, he finds himself divided between his patriotic commitment and his realization that he no longer has a place in Portugal. He opts, finally, to return to Paris and become a writer. Manoel de Oliveira returned to the subject of frustrated love in his *Francisca* (1981), this time taking as his point of departure actual events drawn from the youth of Camilo Castelo Branco, author of *Doomed Love,* an episode subsequently recounted in a novel by Agustina Bessa Luís called *Fanny Owen.* Dealing with the complex and alienated entanglements of two young Portuguese men and an Englishwoman, the film explores questions of desire and alienation, possession, frustration, and sexual ambiguity in a style which weds rigorous structuring of sequential blocks (each associated with a specific decor) with painstaking visual composition and subtle understated acting.

Given decreased government funding and a worsening economic situation, the Portuguese cinema of the eighties has retreated somewhat from the intense productivity of the late seventies (which reached a high point of over twenty features in 1977). Portuguese cinema has achieved a distinct national style rooted in a long cultural tradition and based on a preference for a highly literary and theatrical style. Unlike most national cinemas, Portuguese cinema, for a number of reasons, was never totally dominated by the Hollywood aesthetic. Portuguese filmmakers have found a source of inspiration and a means of achieving a specifically national authenticity by drawing on deeply rooted cultural traditions: fado, Medieval poems, Renaissance "Autos," Camões epics, the classic novels of Eça de Queiroz and Camilo Castelo Branco. While the only forte of the Portuguese present seems to be documentaries and docu-dramas, the past has provided a substantial group of talented Portuguese filmmakers with a springboard for the creation of one of the most innovative and aesthetically fecund cinemas of the last few decades.

## SELECTED BIBLIOGRAPHY

Coelho, Eduardo Prado. *20 anos de cinema portugues*. Lisbon, 1984.

Geado, Eduardo. *O imperialismo e o cinema*.

Passek, Jean-Loup. *Le cinéma portugais*. Paris: Centre Georges Pompidou/ L'Equerre, 1982.

Pena, Richard. "Notes on the Portuguese Cinema." *Journal of the University Film and Video Association*. Vol. XXV, 3 (Summer, 1985).

See also the frequent interviews with major Portuguese filmmakers in French film journals such as *Cahiers du Cinéma* and *Positif*.

# SPAIN
## Spanish Film Under Franco: Do Not Disturb

### VIRGINIA HIGGINBOTHAM

"Spain is different" reads a Spanish travel slogan, and indeed it has been. After Hitler and Mussolini were defeated at the end of World War II, fascism lived on in Spain. Francisco Franco came to power in 1936 and established a dictatorship that lasted until his death in 1975. For thirty-nine years Spain lay in a state of cultural paralysis from which it is only now emerging.

Franco's repressive regime took merciless reprisals against the losing side of the Spanish civil war. It also established rigid film censorship that choked the development of a viable film industry. Taking lessons from Mussolini, who refused to allow any film in a foreign language to enter Italy, Franco, too, made obligatory the dubbing into Spanish of foreign films. Only documentaries produced by No-Do (Noticiarios-Documentales), the state newsreel company, could be seen in Spanish cinemas. Prohibited in feature films were topics such as divorce (illegal in Spain until 1978), suicide, abortion, and leftist politics. Many works of Italian neorealism were simply banned. Releases of other foreign films, such as *Gone With the Wind* and Chaplin's *The Great Dictator*, were delayed a decade or more. Spaniards had to wait until Franco's death to see films by Fellini or Bertolucci.

Censorship at times reached ludicrous heights. Films already authorized and advertised were often withdrawn suddenly. The weekend population of border towns such as Perpignan exploded as Spaniards flocked to see uncut versions of their own and foreign films on French screens. Among the most heavily censored subjects was that of Spain's own civil war. Just as the state selected only the most trivial events to include in newsreels, only Franco's version of the Spanish civil war was permitted to be seen in fiction film. The standard film of the Spanish war, *The Cause* (*Raza*, 1941), was written by Franco himself.

Franco designated Jose Luis Saenz de Heredia, nephew of the last Spanish dictator, Primo de Rivera, to direct *The Cause*. The film focuses upon a military family whose second son becomes a hero in the Spanish civil war. Like Franco, the hero marries his sweetheart after marching through Madrid in a victory parade celebrating "the greatness of the Cause." Twenty-two years later the same director remade *The Cause* and rereleased it as *That Man, Franco (Franco, ese hombre*, 1964). Thus a nationalistic film rhetoric was perpetuated in which good triumphs absolutely over evil in a holy war against the enemy, the Spanish Republicans, referred to in the film as "puppets of Free Masonry," and "reds."

Another key film of the Spanish postwar era is *Siege of the Alcázar (Sin novedad en el alcázar*, 1940). Although directed by an Italian, Augusto Genina, the film was shot in Spain and became a prototype for the Spanish civil war epic. It is based on the celebrated incident in which General Moscardó refused to surrender the Toledo military academy, with its small band of hostages, to the Republicans and thus sacrificed the life of his own son, Luis.

Genina conceived of *Alacázar* in grandiose terms, describing it as "the *Potemkin* of the constructive revolution."[1] With its operatic music evoking both exuberance and terror, its final shot of triumphant troops with arms raised in the fascist salute, *Alcazar* suggests the notion, reinforced in *The Cause*, of the Spanish conflict as a twentieth-century crusade against infidels.

If these war epics upheld fascist values by exalting Franco's recent victory, variations on the same themes were filmed in costume to glorify conquests of the past. Since imperial attitudes of sacrifice, heroism, and honor coincided with those of fascism, the historical epic became one of the major film genres of the postwar era, differing from modern counterparts primarily by period costumes and sets. These films bore such titles as *Inez de Castro* (1944), which recounts a fourteenth-century civil war; *Holy Queen (Reina santa*, 1946), about the life of Queen Isabella; and *El capitán de Loyola*, exalting St. Ignatius's life of sacrifice. The New World conquest was celebrated in *Dawn of America (Alba de America*, 1951), while *Agustina de Aragón* (1950), relives the 1118 siege of Zaragoza. The most successful was *Love's Madness (Locura de amor*, 1948). With its star-studded cast, including Aurora Bautista and Fernando Rey playing the roles of the mad Queen Juana and her consort Phillip of Burgundy, *Love's Madness* earned the film company Cifesa millions throughout Spain and Latin America.

Franco's regime hoped to lull the middle class with images of royal cloaks and swords. For the rest, there were endless folkloric films of flamenco songs and dances. Unchanged since before the civil war, they continued to be commercially viable because they offered unsophisticated viewers almost total escape from reality in Spain. By rewarding nostalgia and war epics through subsidies and wide distribution, the Spanish state succeeded in creating a film industry unaware of new developments in cinema abroad, and incapable of reflecting its own national reality.

Fourteen years after the civil war, one film, *Furrows* (*Surcos*, 1951), attempted to deal with a current national problem, that of rural migration to the cities. Although directed by a loyal Franco supporter, *Furrows* was altered by censors to soften its views of Spanish life. In the concluding frames, a young girl accompanying her family on their return to their village decides to jump off the train. Her apparent preference, city deprivation rather than rural starvation, was considered intolerable.

*Furrows* was submerged in a cult of nostalgia and evasion which culminated in *The Last Couplet* (*El ultimo cuplé*, 1957). A sentimental melodrama starring Sarita Montiel as Maria, who marries an impresario and becomes a famous singer, but who remains unfulfilled in love, *The Last Couplet* had a first run in Madrid lasting almost a year. It offered the passions and gallantry of the past, with Maria's love for a bullfighter, a pistol duel, and a final death scene in which Maria collapses before the thunderous applause of her adoring audience. *The Last Couplet* remains one of the greatest commercial successes of Hispanic film.

## Berlanga, Bardem, and Buñuel

By mid-century Europe was beginning to recover from a war more recent than Spain's, while postwar conditions still prevailed south of the Pyrenees. Slow recovery of the Spanish economy was compounded by political insult when the European democracies voted in 1946 to bar Franco's intransigent regime from membership in the United Nations. Franco's real motive for change came when Marshall Plan funds flowed past Spain into Europe and he realized that his country's future was at stake. To convince the United States that Spain, too, should be eligible for economic relief, slow changes, often accompanied by subsequent reversals and retrenchment, emerged in Spain from 1950 to 1960.

Official censorship controlled Spain's public movie houses, but private screens were less accessible to censors. When, in 1952, a copy of Rossellini's *Open City* crossed the Spanish border in a diplomatic pouch and was seen by a group of film aficionados, new ideas filtered into Spanish cinema in much the same way that the prohibited thoughts of the Enlightenment managed to slip into the hands of a few Spanish intellectuals in the eighteenth century.

Also in 1952 the Institute of Italian Culture held an Italian Film Week. Students of the IIEC (Instituto de Investigaciones y Estudios

Cinematográficos) were invited to screen films by Antonioni, De Sica, and Rossellini. No other event in the past fifteen years breathed life into Spanish cinema as did these two events. The impact of Italian neorealism on Spanish directors was decisive. It provided them a cinematic language with which they could articulate images of their own national experience more authentic than those yet visible in Spain.

Among the most irrepressible of the young Spanish directors of the fifties was Luis García Berlanga (b. Valencia, 1921), who was to become the master of Spanish film farce. Ebullient and populist, Berlanga grasped intuitively that, under the pall of censorship, the only form of social criticism possible was humor. In his later career Berlanga's wit became so outrageous and grotesque that he had to make some of his movies, notably *Life Style* (*Tamaño natural*, 1972), out of the country. But he began as a gentle satirist who made his countrymen laugh at their naive approach to economic realities, in *Welcome Mr. Marshall* (*Bienvenido, Mr. Marshall*, 1952). Written in collaboration with Juan Antonio Bardem and the famous comic dramatist Miguel Mihura, *Mr. Marshall* challenges the conventions of Spanish cinema of the 1950s. It was shot on location and its protagonist is neither heroic warrior nor patriotic individual, but the Spanish populace.

*The Executioner* (*El verdugo*, 1963) is Berlanga's masterpiece. As the tale of an unwilling executioner, it is rich in gallows humor deriving from the conflict between personal liberty and responsibility. The young protagonist, José Luis, carries on his father-in-law's profession of executioner in order to be eligible to live in the only decent housing available, a government-provided apartment. After executing his first prisoner, the young man mutters to his wife and father-in-law, "Never again." The father-in-law comforts him and recalls, "I said that too, the first time."[2] Thus José Luis and his newborn son are heirs to a family tradition of death dealing that passes through generations of Spanish culture. *The Executioner* appeared, coincidentally, shortly after the garroting in August 1963 of two militant Spanish anarchists. In spite of winning the critics' prize at the Venice Film Festival, *The Executioner* was protested by the Spanish ambassador, soon to become director of the state's Department of Theater and Film.

Berlanga's colleague, with whom he began his career in the first class at IIEC and collaborated on the script of *Mr. Marshall*, is Juan Antonio Bardem. Unlike Berlanga, Bardem is not at home in comedy, but he has forced his countrymen to raise their level of social awareness through serious and searching films. Twice jailed by the Franco regime, the politically committed Bardem persisted in criticism of a complacent middle class in *Death of a Cyclist* (*Muerte de un ciclista*, 1955). *Nothing Ever Happens* (*Nunca pasa nada*, 1963) is another sober attempt to hold a mirror to the rigid social attitudes which helped maintain a totalitarian government in power longer than anywhere in Europe. If Berlanga comes closer to creating a national cinema, it is Bardem who modernizes Spanish postwar film by raising its level of social consciousness to international standards.

In 1961 Bardem headed a Spanish film production company, Uninci. Deciding to take advantage of the Franco regime's new self-proclaimed flexibility, Bardem invited the legendary Luis Buñuel to make a film with Uninci. Spanish film devotees were ecstatic; few if any of Buñuel's films had ever been seen in Spain. For the first time in over thirty years he returned to his homeland, where he made one of his best films, *Viridiana* (1961). Buñuel changed the final scene at the censors' suggestion and awaited *Viridiana's* reception at the Cannes Film Festival, where it was Spain's official entry.

The title character of *Viridiana* is a young woman about to take religious vows. She visits her aging uncle who drugs her, dresses her in his dead wife's bridal gown, and stops barely short of intercourse with her inert body. Viridiana, horrified the next morning to learn of the night's events from the maid, receives another jolt when her uncle, mortified by shame, hangs himself with a child's jump rope. The thoroughly disoriented novice now encounters her uncle's handsome illegitimate son who moves into and begins renovating his father's estate.

This film, with its many jarring moments—for example, the famous freeze shot of inebriated beggars grouped at a banquet table to echo Da Vinci's "The Last Supper," and the near rape of Viridiana by the beggars whom she had befriended—won for Spain its first Gold Medal at Cannes. The award was accepted personally by the general director of theater and film, José Muñoz Fontán. The next day, however, the Catholic newspaper, *L'Osservatore romano*, pronounced the film anti-Christian and blasphemous. The Franco government, unwilling to risk church ire, quickly recoiled. All copies of the film were confiscated, the minister of information was removed from his post, and Spain suddenly became the only Western nation where public viewing or even discussion of the Cannes Gold Medal winner was officially prohibited. We know this film today only because Buñuel, with long experience in his country, carried a copy in his bag as he left Spain for Paris. (Sixteen years later in April of 1977, two years after Franco's death, *Viridiana* was at last released to the Spanish public.) The *Viridiana* affair brought an abrupt end rather than, as had been hoped, a new beginning to the film industry in Spain. Uninci was closed and all projects were canceled.

*Viridiana* was still prohibited in Spain when Buñuel, in 1969, was again invited to his homeland, this time to film *Tristana*. Based on a novel by Spain's foremost nineteenth-century realist, Pérez Galdós, *Tristana* narrates the fortunes of a young woman whose dying mother has left her in the care of don Lope, a respectable citizen and aging don Juan. The old man, whose attitude toward women is expressed in the

Spanish refrain *La mujer honrada, pierna quebrada, y en casa* ("If you want an honest woman, break her leg so she stays home"), does not hesitate to make the young Tristana his mistress. Tristana, as if bound by this destiny, loses a leg and becomes, in her prime, dependent upon don Lope. Buñuel has made of this film a compendium of social and moral attitudes that define the Spanish character no less now than in 1892 when the novel was written. Buñuel achieves in Spanish film what many Spanish filmmakers would themselves have liked to, that is, to express their national reality in a mode strong enough to catch the world's imagination. For, in Buñuel's films, the world becomes Spanish. Tristana is every young woman who desires independence, while don Lope lives on in the heart of every male supervisor who secretly hopes to dominate his female employee.

Further, Buñuel's Spain is authentic. The donkey carcasses of *Un chien andalou* could be observed rotting in boneyards on the outskirts of Madrid in the 1920s. The husband in *He* (*El*, 1953), who appears to be ready to sew up his wife as she sleeps, can be traced back to the murderous husbands of Calderon's honor tragedies. The legend of St. James in *The Milky Way* (*La vía láctea*, 1969) is just as Buñuel tells it: that the saint's bones have been lost long ago does not keep pilgrims from trekking to Santiago de Compostela. The troup of beggars in *Viridiana* was selected from the beggar population of Toledo and Madrid. Nazarín, the outcast, is a typical anarchistic clergyman, many of whom were murdered as communist sympathizers during the Spanish civil war.

For Basilio Martín Patino, Buñuel is his country's only *homo cinematographicus*.[3] Buñuel's films are a visual heritage roughly the equivalent of Goya's paintings. From his works flows a rich imagery and language Spanish filmmakers, silenced by Franco, recognize as their own. Little wonder that young Spanish directors see Buñuel as a point of departure. And nowhere is Buñuel's influence more visible than in the films of Carlos Saura, Spain's best postwar director.

## Carlos Saura (b. Huesca, 1932)

Because he devised a film language that confused the censors, Carlos Saura is the only filmmaker who expressed the losers' view of the civil war and was allowed to go on working. Saura's neorealist goal was one of filming authentic testimony to postwar misery and manipulations. Censorship prevented this story from being told directly, so Saura drew upon Buñuel's legacy of the surreal documentary (*Land Without Bread*, for example) to convey meaning indirectly. With surrealist techniques learned from Buñuel, Saura refined the ironic style with which Berlanga and Bardem avoided censors into a highly metaphorical, sharply critical art.

Saura's first success, and one of his best films, is *The Hunt* (*La caza*, 1965), a war allegory structured so that tension rises relentlessly toward its violent outcome. The hunting party is composed of three businessmen—Paco, José, and Luis—the winners of the civil war, and the young Enrique. As in Jean Renoir's *Rules of the Game*, rabbits dart helplessly in front of the advancing hunters now intent upon slaughter. The cleaning of guns and male camaraderie strongly suggest analogies to the civil war. Hostile arguments and rivalries soon sour the mood of the hunt, and the men turn on each other. The climate of warfare signified by hunting and quarreling leads to mutual slaughter; the film captures the barely concealed ferocity and terror of life in the Franco era.

From war allegory, Saura launched a series of family portraits in which he analyzed the impact of the civil war on the lives of the individuals who survived it. In *Garden of Delights* (*El jardín de las delicias*, 1970) Antonio, head of his family's cement factory, has lost his memory in an automobile accident. Like Spain throughout half the twentieth century, Antonio has no voice and is paralyzed. He is at the mercy of his greedy family who, like the fascist bureaucracy during the Franco period, tried to profit from an ailing economy. The "delights" of the title are a series of tableaux, as in Bosch's painting of the same name, in which family members enact psychodramas which they hope will cause Antonio to recall the number of his Swiss bank account.

Family members find that they cannot restore the unrestorable by trauma. In the final tableaux the camera closes in on two wrecked cars crashed head-on in the garden of the family estate. Bloody bodies lie about while Antonio, in this reenactment of his near-fatal crash, mutters from the wreckage, "Do what you want with my body, but don't touch my head." He realizes that without his mind, of which memory is a vital part, his body is useless. Like Spain, Antonio is an amnesia victim unable to understand himself because he is unable to recall his own history.

Saura's next family portrait, *Cousin Angélica* (*La prima Angélica*, 1973), created a national uproar and opened public dialogue on the very topic Franco hoped Spaniards would soon forget—the civil war. In this Proustian recall of the past, Luis, an editor in Barcelona, visits his boyhood home and encounters old relatives and his childhood sweetheart, Angélica. She is now a disillusioned housewife married to Anselmo, who strongly resembles Angélica's authoritarian, fascist father. (Indeed, the same actor plays both roles.)

Taking his cues from Buñuel, who stressed the force of dreams by photographing them on the same level of perception as daily reality, Saura emphasized the power of the past by juxtaposing scenes from Luis's boyhood with those of his present life without distinguishing between them. An example of this is the scene in which Luis and Angélica spend a few moments poring over their old school notebooks in the attic.

Captivated by renewed friendship, the two climb out on the roof and sit together reminiscing. But when Luis turns and kisses Angélica's hair, the thunderous voice of his uncle Anselmo booms out angrily, demanding that Luis come down. The voice calls again for Angélica, but when the uncle/father enters the attic, it is Angélica's young daughter who climbs back through the window, thus defining, without flashbacks, the present as an uninterrupted continuation of the past.

The boy's humiliation by his uncle, compounded by loss of the civil war, saps the adult's confidence so that when Angélica, sad and lonely, approaches him for comfort one day, Luis remains passive and plans his departure. His aunt Pilar bids him farewell and starts to send love to his father, a Republican during the civil war. But she stops, still alienated by the family division of forty years ago.

During *Cousin Angélica*, Anselmo mutters a Spanish refrain, "Raise ravens and they'll pluck out your eyes" (*Cría cuervos y te sacarán los ojos*.) Saura's *Cría* (*Cría cuervos* ["Raise ravens"], 1975), perhaps the best in his album of family portraits, takes this bitter proverb as its point of departure. In the first sequence of *Cría*, Ana, at age nine, discovers her father lifeless in bed, apparently dead of a heart attack after making love with his best friend's wife, Amelia. Another authoritarian named Anselmo, Ana's father was a volunteer in Spain's famous Blue Division which defended the Nazis against Soviet troops in 1941. Ana's mother, played by Geraldine Chaplin, chose her family over her career as a professional pianist. The generational confusion with which Ana as child and adult is presented leaves uncertain their precise relationship. Ana-as-adult relates that the child in the film is herself at age nine, but she also enacts the role of her own mother. Such merging of generations suggests that women's lives have not changed and all reflect pain, sacrifice, and marital disaster.

Ana, played by the amazing child acress Ana Torrent, is orphaned and left with only Rosa, the earth-motherly maid, to comfort her, but the dominating aunt Paulina sees that Rosa keeps her place. With a child's intuitive understanding, Ana silently resists her patriarchal family. Not only does she refuse to kiss her father's dead face and accept her aunt as step-mother, she also tries to control her small world with the two items bequeathed to her by her parents: her mother's box of sodium bicarbonate and her father's service revolver. Ana's mother assured her that the white powder was fatal, so she tries to poison her father, whom she blames for her mother's demise. She also attempts to do in Paulina. As a special favor, she offers to put her grandmother, mute and confined to a wheelchair, out of her misery.

In the final frames, bells toll the reopening of parochial school as schoolgirls file into an old building. This reference to Spanish education suggests that by the time she finishes school, Ana and her sisters will be like the generations of women before them including her paralyzed grandmother and her mother who sacrificed her own career to her husband's. *Cría*, made the year of Franco's death, reminds its audience that social codes and institutions outlast individuals, both supporters of and rebels against the dominant ideology.

## Other Directors

Spain's effort to seek economic prosperity through membership in the European Common Market in 1962 began a five-year period known as the *apertura* or crack in the fascist facade. Liberalized policies led to bureaucratic reorganization, reinstalling the moderate José María García Escudero as director of the State Department of Theater and Film. For the first time, censorship criteria were codified so that the film industry at last had a published document rather than official caprice to guide it through the intricacies of censorship. García Escudero was able to open the film industry to young directors with fresh ideas. Loosely referred to as the New Spanish Cinema, these young talents wasted no time in expressing their views of Spanish social problems. Angelino Fons adapted Pío Baroja's bleak 1904 novel of the same name into a chilling description of Spain's petrified economy, *The Search* (*La busca*. 1966). A young rural immigrant's arrival by train in Madrid is preceded by a brilliant documentary prologue of Spain in the late nineteenth century, with footage of bread lines, aging factories, and Valencian rice paddies. Views of train loads of rural migrants are interspersed with shots of sumptuous banquets in celebration of the coronation of Alfonso XIII. Problems of unemployment also preoccupy Jaime Camino in his *Tomorrow's Another Day* (*Mañana será otro día*, 1966), in which a young couple discovers that the best jobs in their country go to foreigners who are better educated and more at home in the contemporary world than most of their fellow Spaniards.

More dismal is Basilio Martin Patino's *Nine Letters to Berta* (*Nueve cartas a Berta*, 1965), in which Lorenzo, a young provincial student, confides his thoughts to his friend Berta, whom he met on a trip to London. Her father, a post-civil war exile, is a successful member of the international community while Lorenzo settles for a stultifying future in the Spanish provinces.

Especially courageous is Miguel Picazo's *Tía Tula* (1964), a rare portrait of that almost unknown species in Spain, a well-adjusted young woman who chooses to remain independent and single. Traditionally offered only two life-choices as either wives or nuns, Spanish women are often doomed to alienation, if not dementia. But Picazo portrays Tula's choice as resulting naturally from narrow, male-defined female roles.

In spite of the rigidity that engulfed *apertura* in the early 1970s,

Luis Buñuel blends reality with dream in the famous sleepwalking scene from *Viridiana* (1961).

Luis's (Jose Maria Prada) examination of his German luger in Carlos Saura's *The Hunt* (1965) underlines Saura's analogy of hunting with the Spanish Civil War.

Saura's unique merging of generations is suggested in this portrait of Ana (Ana Torrent) and her mother (Geraldine Chaplin) from *Cria* (*Cria cuervos*, 1975).

In *Spirit of the Beehive* (1973), Victor Erice captures the isolation of Franco Spain in this shot of Ana and her sister waiting for a train, their only link to the outside world.

young directors continued to dissect the Spanish character and attitudes. Like Berlanga, Manuel Summers gently ridiculed Spanish
avoidance of sex education in *Goodbye Stork* (*Adios, ciqüeña*, 1971) and
*Now I'm a Woman* (*Ya soy mujer*, 1975). Ricardo Franco and José Luis
Borau, however, do not smile at the almost medieval cruelty of the postwar era. Shotgun murders and death by garroting haunt Ricardo
Franco's *Pascual Duarte* (1975), based on Camilo José Cela's landmark
novel. One of Europe's finest character actresses, Lola Gaos (of *Tristana*
and *Viridiana*), gives a spellbinding performance in Borau's *Poachers*
(*Furtivos*, 1975) as the cunning, incestuous, yet sympathetic mother of
the vengeful Angel, who slaughters wild animals for a living.

While Borau and Ricardo Franco elaborate the barbarity of their
time with images of matricide and strangulation, Victor Erice evokes
the postwar period with techniques of horror films in *Spirit of the Beehive* (*El espíritu de la colmena*, 1974), featuring the young Ana Torrent.
When James Whale's *Frankenstein* comes to their remote village, Ana
is six-years-old and her sister Isabel, nine; both are entranced by the
movie. Isabel, who knows such things, informs Ana that Frankenstein
is a friendly spirit who talks to those who seek him. So Ana sets out
looking for Frankenstein. And she finds him, or the *maquis*, who, because of his wounds, she takes for Frankenstein. The child befriends the
unrepatriated Republican soldier still hiding from certain imprisonment by fascists, and when she discovers him missing, she is determined to find him. Unaware that he has been killed by local police, Ana
combs the woods at night. A vision of the monster appears to her as in
the movie, handing a flower to a little girl.

No mention is made of the civil war, but grass-covered mounds are silent testimonials to the recent fratricidal violence. Ana's parents have
retreated into their own silence. Her mother writes letters to an unknown person, while her father raises bees. The gifted cinematographer, Luis Cuadrado, emphasizes the beehive metaphor by use of a yellow filter which extends the honeyed, monotonous atmosphere to Ana's
home. It is another cell in the cultural beehive occupied by efficient
drones who go about their lives never questioning authority.

The film ends as Ana gets out of bed and goes to her balcony to stare
at the full moon. In a silent attempt to communicate, she recalls Isabel's advice on how to reach Frankenstein. "I'm Ana," she whispers to
the character from the horror film who, composed of the fragments of
his creator's victims, signifies the memory of the civil war created and
manipulated by Franco for his own sinister purposes.

## Films of Transition: 1975–1982

Franco's death in November 1975 brought hope that Spain would join
its European neighbors after thirty-nine years and again become a de-

mocracy. Elections were held in June 1977. In November of that year censorship laws were revoked. Spaniards could now see films never released in their country. Some, such as *Battleship Potemkin* and *October*, dated back to the 1920s. Others included Chaplin's *The Great Dictator* (1940), Buñuel's *Viridiana* (1961), and Joseph Losey's *Assassination of Trotsky* (1972). Also having their premiere in Spain were foreign films of the Spanish conflict, such as Malraux's *Sierra de Teruel* (1938–39), Frederic Rossif's *To Die in Madrid* (1962), and Alain Resnais's *La guerre est finie* (1966).

Among previously prohibited releases was Basilio Martin Patino's *Postwar Songs* (*Canciones para después de una guerra*, 1971). This is a rambling memoir of the postwar period unified by a sound track of popular songs of the era. Scenes of the bread lines, war rubble, and orphaned children of the 1940s are accompanied by the lilting voice of Imperio Argentina, a popular singer. Spanish dances and bullfight music introduce the photograph of the first atom bomb explosion, suggesting Spain's separation from the industrial and technological West.

Before the dictator's death Patino had also completed a bitter portrait entitled *Caudillo* (general term for "military leader"). Like *Songs*, *Caudillo* is an ironic juxtaposition of images compiled from newsreel footage. It attempts to explain Franco's success by analogy with the rise of dictators in other countries (Germany and Italy) as well as that of Spain's own Primo de Rivera. Support of fascism in Spain echoes in the appalling slogans *Viva la muerte* ("Long live death"), repeated by one of Franco's generals, and *Viva la Guardia Civil* ("Long live the Civil Guard"), shouted by the rural poor who hailed the dictator's advance. These cries recall the *Vivan las cadenas* ("Long live our chains") with which the Spanish populace greeted Napoleon's invaders in the nineteenth century and which resound in opening and closing scenes of Buñuel's *Phantom of Liberty* (1974).

Another harsh portrait of the dictator is *Raza, Spirit of Franco* (*Raza, el espíritu de Franco*, 1977). Director Gonzalo Herralde makes no effort to analyze Franco's career. His primary interest is to reveal how the dictator manipulated Spanish history both in his novel, *The Cause (Raza)*, and in the film based on it. This model for postwar fascist film was actually Franco's own autobiography, by which he hoped to legitimize his role as Spain's savior. Herralde intersperses excerpts from *Raza* with interviews with the dictator's sister, Pilar. By confirming that events narrated in the novel also happened in her brother's life, she unwittingly provides evidence that the early novel and film were biographical, thus confirming Franco's design to use the popular medium of film to propagate his own version of Spanish history.

These attempts to demystify Franco are the first achievements of transition cinema. They are not film history, but ironic compilations of newsreel footage and interviews taken by directors in lieu of documentary footage not yet accessible to the public. Other historical chronicles of the civil war, such as Eduard Manzanos's *Spain Should Know (España debe saber)* are still incomplete or not released. Pilar Miró's *The Crime in Cuenca (El crimen en Cuenca,* 1979) was withheld by censors for two years because of military protest of scenes of torture inflicted by Civil Guards. Although censorship laws were revoked, sensitive topics, such as the monarchy and the military, still remain untouchable.

The predominant film style of the post-Franco transition continues to be the political metaphor developed by Saura and others as a necessary subversion of censorship. Saura's *Mama Turns 100 (Mama cumple 100 años,* 1979), a pessimistic farce, ridicules Spanish society as being immune to change. Manuel Gutiérrez Aragón's bitter *Black Brood (Camada negra,* 1977) studies the emergence of the fascist personality from within a decadent and violent family. Berlanga's trilogy of national vices, *National Shotgun (Escopeta nacional,* 1978), *Patrimonio nacional* (1980), and *Nacional 3* (1982) are burlesques of a penniless aristocracy hoping to come back as a privileged minority in the present ruling monarchy.

Will Spanish film attempt to probe the collective memory in more thorough analyses of the civil war? "It will be difficult to go back to that era so long past,"[4] Basilio Martin Patino remarked to this writer in May 1982. Another young director, José Luis García Sánchez, thinks that "to talk today of *franquismo* is clearly reactionary . . . Franco was not the only problem; he has never been the only problem."[5] Film scholar and critic Roman Gubern reports that films dealing with the civil war, the democratic resistance, or the historical memory are now rejected by producers as being unprofitable and unpopular.[6]

Films made since Franco's death make clear that neither careful analyses nor balanced documentaries of the civil war have yet been made in Spain. Questions of political heritage raised by the civil war are now compounded by new ones of democracy—the role of women in society, freedom of expression, the coming to terms with Spanish attitudes and institutions.

Is Spain calling, as Ana from her balcony, in a whisper so low that film directors cannot hear? Or are Spanish producers, like Frankensteins, merely composites of economic expediency and reluctance to open the past? Until Spain's history is dealt with in its national cinema, Spain's past will remain unexorcised.

## NOTES

1. *Primer plano* 1, no. 3 (3 November 1940):3.
2. All quotations of film dialogue in the text are from the sound track.
3. Introduction to *Nueve cartas a Berta* (Madrid: Ciencia nueva, 1968), p. 9.

4. This remark was delivered at the conclusion of a round table discussion of Rossif's *To Die in Madrid*.
5. *Cinema 2002* 39 (May 1978):58–59.
6. *España sin ir más lejos* (Barcelona: Laia, 1982), p. 154.

## SELECTED BIBLIOGRAPHY

Aranda, Francisco. *Luis Buñuel: A Critical Biography*. New York: Da Capo Press, 1976.

Caparrós Lera, José María. *El cine político*. Madrid: Dopesa, 1978.

Carr, Raymond and Juan Pablo Aizpura, Fuzi. *Spain: Dictatorship to Democracy*. London: Allen and Unwin, 1979.

*Cine español: cine de subgéneros*. Ed. Fernando Torres. Valencia, 1974.

Durgnat, Raymond. *Luis Buñuel*. Berkeley: University of California Press, 1977.

Fernández Cuenca, Carlos. *La guerra de España y el cine*. Madrid: Editorial Nacional, 1972.

Gubern, Roman. *Carlos Saura*. Huelva: Festival de Cine Iberoamericano, 1979.

———. *Comunicación y cultura de masas*. Barcelona: Editorial Peninsula, 1977.

———. and Domenec Font. *Un cine para el cadalso*. Barcelona: Editorial Euros, 1975.

Higginbotham, Virginia. *Luis Buñuel*. Boston: Twayne, 1979.

Kinder, Marsha. "Carlos Saura: The Political Development of Individual Consciousness." *Film Quarterly*, 32 (spring 1979): 14–26.

Marti-Rom, J-R, and Jacqueline Lajeunesse. "Le cinéma espagnol après Franco: de la politisation au désenchantement." *La revue du cinéma* 361 (May 1981):79–97.

Mellen, Joan. *"Fascism in the Contemporary Film." Film Quarterly* 24 (summer 1971):2–19.

Molina-Foix, Vicente. *New Cinema in Spain*. London: British Film Institute, 1977.

Oms, Marcel. *Juan Antonio Bardem. Premier plan* 21 (February 1962). 94p.

———. *Carlos Saura*. Paris: Edilig, 1981.

Valleau, Marjorie A. *The Spanish Civil War in American and European Films*. Ann Arbor, MI: UMI Research Press, 1981.

*The World of Luis Buñuel*. Ed. Joan Mellen. New York: Oxford University Press, 1978.

# SWEDEN
## Past and Present

FREDERICK J. MARKER and
LISE-LONE MARKER

Although Swedish cinema often seems to be regarded as synonymous with Ingmar Bergman, its history and traditions reach back to the very birth of filmmaking. Certainly no other country of comparable population has matched Sweden's contribution to the artistic growth of world cinema. "We are such a huge country," Bergman once remarked in an interview, "yet we are so few, so thinly scattered across it. The people here spend their lives isolated on their farms—and isolated from one another in their homes. It's terribly difficult for them, even when they come to the cities and live close to other people; it's so hard, really. They don't know how to get in touch, to communicate."[1] This provocative observation suggests, of course, a theme encountered in many a Swedish film, but it also reminds us of the real nature of the film industry's heritage in Sweden.

At the beginning of the century Charles Magnusson, a self-taught newsreel cinematographer, was quick to recognize the new medium as a potential source of social reform and cultural unification. In 1912, as production manager of the company that was to become Svensk Filmindustrc, Magnusson gave contracts to Victor Sjöström and the Finnish-born Mauritz Stiller, two of the pioneering directors of the silent era. During the course of the next ten years or so, these two men created a steady stream of films that soon placed Sweden in the vanguard of the new art form. While little remains of Sjöström's earliest films, a later work like *The Phantom Carriage* (*Körkarlen*, 1921) gives evidence of his technical influence on Bergman, both in its complex intercutting of past and present and in its undeviating emphasis on the human being and the human face as the point of focus. By 1923, however, Sjöström had let himself be lured to Hollywood; Stiller, Greta Garbo, Lars Hanson, and others soon followed his example. A serious artistic decline ensued and during the years that led up to World War II, the film industry in Sweden, utterly demoralized, was at its lowest ebb.

Bergman was just twenty-six when he made his debut in the cinema with the screenplay for *Torment* (*Hets*, 1944), a somber film that reflects the darkness of the period in which it was made. Caligula, the nickname of the Latin teacher who delights in tormenting his charges, embodies the incipient fascism that Bergman had seen infect his own family and his teachers in Uppsala. *Torment* is an exception in the Bergman canon, in that it was directed not by him but by Alf Sjöberg, the renowned stage director whose best-known film is his screen version of Strindberg's play, *Miss Julie* (*Fröken Julie*; winner of the Palme d'Or at Cannes, in 1950). In *Torment* Sjöberg's tightly compressed pictorial style, shut in by ominous, brooding shadows, contributed powerfully to the topical, anti-Nazi appeal exerted by the film at the time. Bergman's concept reaches beyond this limited view, however, and bears the unmistakable stamp of his future work. Caligula is more and other than merely a sadistic schoolteacher with Nazi leanings; he manifests a condition, a state of "virulent evil" in the world that has never ceased to preoccupy Bergman. Jan-Erik, the student who is Caligula's special prey, confronts the presence of pure malevolence in our existence. But for him—unlike the student in *The Ghost Sonata* (Bergman's favorite Strindberg play, which he first directed in 1941)—there is no escape from what Strindberg calls "this penal colony, madhouse and morgue of a world," and no affirmative acceptance of it either. Instead, Jan-Erik is left at the end in isolation, the outsider, marked for life by his ordeal.

With the release of *Torment*, the Swedish cinema had reached the threshold of a new era. New companies, notably Sandrews and Nordisk Tonefilm, had now begun production. In 1942 Svensk Filmindustri had at last found a worthy successor to Magnusson in Carl-Anders Dymling, for many years Bergman's producer and a man "crazy enough" (as Bergman writes with affection in the introduction to his *Four Screenplays*) "to place more faith in the sense of responsibility of a creative artist than in calculations of profit and loss." Bergman's conspicuous success as a staunch individualist provided a sharp and reassuring contrast to the destructive commercial flirtation with Hollywood practiced by Sjöström and others of his generation. It was a contrast that taught the Swedish film industry its most valuable lesson in survival.

The early films that followed *Crisis* (*Kris*, 1946), the first feature Bergman directed, are marked by a tone, a visual rhythm, and a placement of actors in relation to the camera that unmistakably foreshadow his mature work. The key title among Bergman's films from the 1940s, however, is unquestionably *Prison* (*Fängelse*, 1949; also called *The Devil's Wanton*), his ninth motion picture but the first based on his own screenplay. Set against a stark midwinter background that is a graphic visual correlative of the bleak inner landscape of the film, *Prison* is the first sustained attempt on Bergman's part to express a theme that was to preoccupy him in the years to come. "Why do we stand so foolishly powerless against evil? . . . Why must a person sooner or later arrive at a point where he for a moment awakes to a painful and unendurable knowledge of himself and his situation, and why is there, in that moment, no help to summon?" demands a program note distributed by the director at the opening of *Prison* in March 1949.

Invariably more concerned with posing questions than with furnishing answers to them, Bergman provides neither explanations nor rational solutions in his depiction of human anguish in *Prison*. A series of stories within a framing action, intercut with sequences of silent film and dream, it creates a deliberately open, expressive pattern that prefigures this director's later use of a nonsequential, free-associational film logic. In this early experiment, the conclusion reached is one of pessimistic closure and inescapable entrapment. Birgitta Carolina, the young prostitute whose story gives the film its focus and its remorselessly dark tone, is the victim of a life riddled with suffering, brutality, and that deep-seated cruelty that human beings are uniquely capable of inflicting upon one another. The relief from this intolerable existence that Birgitta Carolina finds with Tomas, a journalist who befriends her, is brief; their interlude of happiness and fellowship (they take refuge in an attic room where they watch an old silent movie) is cut painfully short. In the end, the young girl's only means of escape from her prison world of violence and ugliness is suicide.

Rarely has Bergman's perception of the human condition seemed as unrelievedly dark as we find it in *Prison*. Its nearest companion piece now seems to be *The Serpent's Egg* (*Das Schlangenei*), the brutal, Fritz Lang-style chronicle of pre-Nazi Berlin that he filmed in Germany in 1977. In general, however, the Bergman canon spans a wide and profound register of moods and emotions. Although a sense of spiritual unrest and impending crisis is never entirely absent even in the most idyllic of his films, Bergman's artistic perspective has undergone significant changes during the course of his career. Notably in the summer films of the early 1950s, a new and deeply lyrical note was introduced into his work that sets these films apart from what had gone before. *Summer Interlude* (*Sommarlek*, 1951) and *Summer with Monika* (*Sommaren med Monika*, 1953) are memory films. They reveal moments of happiness, tranquility, and sensual pleasure that are recorded by Bergman and his cameraman, Gunnar Fischer, with a bewitching visual poetry not found in the earlier films. Fraught with a sense of nostalgia, these summer glimpses of brightness and serenity are filled with an awareness of painful brevity. This awareness deepens in the later films in which summer continues to function as a symbol of fleeting happiness—*The Seventh Seal* (*Det sjunde inseglet*, 1957) *Wild Strawberries* (*Smultronstället*, 1957) and *The Virgin Spring* (*Jungfrukällan*, 1960), to name but three.

In *Summer with Monika*, the first of Bergman's films to draw upon the eroticism of Harriet Andersson, the familiar tension in his work between escape and entrapment provides the mainspring of the action. On the remote island to which she flees with her lover, the rebellious Monika blossoms into life; but the coming of autumn signals her return to the ugliness and emotional suffocation of her grimy city existence. (Andersson's innocent, bucolic nudity in *Monika* caused the film to be banned in Nice and Los Angeles, to run a year in Montevideo, and to enjoy a wide circulation in pirated underground prints.) In the earlier and more complex *Summer Interlude* (titled *Illicit Interlude* in the United States), a different balance of forces and a different outcome prevail. Like most of Bergman's films, this work focuses on the conflict of divergent attitudes toward life. For Marie (Maj-Britt Nilsson), the ballerina who struggles with the memory of an island summer of happiness and subsequent tragedy, the present—as she contemplates her image in the mirror of her theater dressing room—is filled with shadows and bitterness. Ultimately, only her spiritual journey back in time to that idyllic summer of long ago can release her from her bondage to the past and enable her to face the future with a new determination.

Bergman's films return often to the world of theater in its many different manifestations—ballet, opera, drama, circus. In *The Naked Night* (*Gycklarnas afton*, 1953; also titled *Sawdust and Tinsel*), which was released in the same year as *Monika*, the milieu is that of an itinerant country circus at the beginning of the century—a period that holds an abiding fascination for Bergman. Humiliation is the governing theme of this early masterpiece. This familiar Bergman subject, inextricably bound up with the place and plight of the artist in society, grows and develops out of a crucial introductory episode that remains, both in technical and dramatic terms, one of the most celebrated visual sequences in Bergman's entire *oeuvre*. In a flashback, deliberately overexposed to attain a blurred, bleached intensity, Albert, the owner of the scruffy little circus, recalls a humiliating incident that occurred in the past life of Frost, his clown. In this dreamlike vision the awkward and pathetic Frost (Anders Ek) wades into the water in his clown costume to retrieve his naked wife from an exhibitionistic swim she has undertaken in front of a regiment of leering, mocking soldiers. Greasepaint running in grotesque streams down the furrows of his face, Frost hauls his wayward mate ashore, across a pebbled beach, and up a Calvary-like hill, trying desperately all the while to conceal her shame, and his own. Huge closeups of laughing, shouting mouths fill the screen. At last the clown-martyr stumbles and collapses with his burden. This excruciating nightmare of humiliation becomes the central, controlling image of *The Naked Night*, out of which the film's subsequent incidents develop as a series of variations on a theme. In turn, this film initiated a whole succession of Bergman pictures that contributed to an ongoing discourse, as it were, on the suffering and humiliation of the artist, for which no adequate recompense exists.

*Smiles of a Summer Night* (*Sommarnattens leende*, 1955), set in the same period as *The Naked Night* and likewise a work in which the intermingling of theater and life is a ruling idea, uses the metaphor of theater in a quite different manner. Here, theatricality is artifice. The ability to don a mask and play a role is the prerequisite for success in the game of love and chance that this sparkling, Marivaux-inspired comedy of manners depicts. The erotic intrigues carried on among the four couples in the film are managed with all the composed artifice of an elegant quadrille. Each finds his or her true partner when the dance is done. Yet despite the idyllic, conciliatory note on which it ends, *Smiles* is an ambiguous comedy, filled with echoes from the earlier summer films that reinforce a sense that nothing lasts and that, in the game of love, there are ultimately no real winners.

By this time, of course, Bergman had already become Bergman. Full international recognition came when *Smiles* was awarded a Special Prize at the Cannes Film Festival in 1956. By then as well, he had already begun to gather and train an ensemble of performing artists—among them Bibi Andersson, Harriet Andersson, Gertrud Fridh, Ingrid Thulin, Gunnel Lindblom, Naima Wifstrand, Anders Ek, Gunnar Björnstrand, Max von Sydow, and others were to appear with regularity both in his stage productions and in his major films. Especially during his six-year tenure as artistic director at the Malmö City Theater during the mid-1950s, the interaction between his work in theater and in cinema was intense and influenced his artistic development decisively, both in style and theme. *The Seventh Seal*, for example, was based on a short play, *Painting on Wood*, which Bergman had written for his acting students at Malmö. Completed in an astonishing thirty-five days of shooting during the summer of 1956, this film and its imagery grew directly out of his involvement with theater—as he himself admits.[2] Moreover, the principal actors in such a work bear the unmistakable stamp of classical theater training. The young Max von Sydow, who plays Antonius Block, the knight whose running game of chess with Death is the film's governing thematic image, could, for instance, be seen that same year in the leading roles in Bergman's triumphant productions of Ibsen's *Peer Gynt* and Molière's *The Misanthrope*.

"I want knowledge, not faith, not superstitions, but knowledge. I want God to stretch out his hand toward me, reveal Himself and speak to me," Block cries out in despair. "But God remains silent," replies

Death, his listener. Although the Gothic medievalism of such works as *The Seventh Seal* and *The Virgin Spring* was quickly abandoned by Bergman, the anguished religious doubt of the knight continued to reverberate through the trilogy of films he released at the beginning of the 1960s. In these films, however, the focus was on concrete human manifestations of metaphysical loss. In *Through a Glass Darkly* (*Såsom i en spegel*, 1961), Karin (Harriet Andersson), dislocated from her surroundings and trapped in the private world of the schizophrenic, takes refuge in a hallucinatory religious ecstasy that leads only to her horrified confrontation with a parody of God—a frightening spider deity with cold, calm eyes and "a terrible, evil face." In *Winter Light* (*Nattvardsgästerna*, 1963) it is Tomas (Gunnar Björnstrand), a doubting priest, who is afflicted by the crisis of faith. Compelled to administer the comforts of religion to his fellow doubters and sufferers, he finds himself in the end preaching a desperate, passionate sermon to an empty church. In *The Silence* (*Tystnaden*, 1963), the last and most enigmatic part of the trilogy, God's silence is reaffirmed in a harsh, powerfully sensory image of human isolation and loneliness. Two sisters and the son of the younger woman pause on a journey in a hostile country. They cannot speak the strange, guttural language of the place, but Ester (Ingrid Thulin), the elder, dying sister, tries—in what is the film's single positive action—to teach some fragments of it to the young boy. Ester's barren intellectualism and the desperate, violent carnality of Anna (Gunnel Lindblom), her younger sister, are two aspects of the same private hell of human solitude and misery to which both women are condemned. The streets of the oppressive city of Timoka, empty save for a lone, menacing tank, become the external sign of this inner state of spiritual and emotional claustrophobia.

The quest for knowledge and existential verification, so arduously pursued by the knight in *The Seventh Seal*, is understandable but cannot always be satisfied. Resolution of the questions of faith, doubt, and the existence of God is as distant in this trilogy as in Viktor's and Anders's seriocomic quarrel over such matters in *Wild Strawberries*. And with the completion of *The Silence*, Bergman himself seemed prepared to put these metaphysical problems behind him.

In purely formal terms, meanwhile, the trilogy represents a major advance into new territory—an advance foreshadowed, to some degree, by the experiments in style found in *Wild Strawberries*. The films of the trilogy and *Persona*, the related "sonata for two" that followed in 1966, are described by Bergman as chamber plays: "They are chamber music. That is, the pure cultivation of a certain number of themes for a strictly limited number of voices and figures. Backgrounds are abstracted. They are veiled in a kind of mist. One makes a distillation."[3] In these films, this laying bare of an inner reality is linked to the use of long, incisive close-ups that seem completely at odds with the language of film with which Bergman grew up. Like the chamber plays of Strindberg's final period, these stark, oneiric distillations of an inner truth are cleansed of distracting effects and ostentatious backgrounds, in an effort to achieve a compressed and fluid form that is, in itself, a function and image of the theme.

These revolutionary cinematic experiments of Bergman's coincided, in time if not in spirit, with a much broader upheaval that moved the European cinema as a whole. Especially in Sweden, where the new wave of directors was particularly strong, an explosive confrontation between old and new was inevitable.

Ideology and economics played crucial roles in the revolution that swept the Swedish film industry in 1962—a revolution that reflected many of the influences already at work elsewhere in Europe and in the United States. Bergman, then at the height of his powers and prestige after winning his second Academy Award (for *Through a Glass Darkly*), conveniently provided the mythos on which the new wave of Swedish filmmakers could focus their opposition and frustration. ("Symbolical patricide" is the colorful phrase used by one Swedish critic to describe this familiar process of self-assertion.[4]) Bergman's films were dismissed as "vertical cinema" devoid of social consciousness, confined to a private, metaphysical view of man in relationship to God, in terms of which man is either exalted or humbled. Bo Widerberg, who spearheaded this attack and in the process supplied the new movement with its rhetoric, fervently denounced Bergman for having embraced "the coarsest myths about us and ours," thereby perpetuating "the false notions which foreigners love to have confirmed."[5] Worst of all, Bergman's outlook clearly lacked the proper ideological commitment to social democracy.

Widerberg, a former novelist and film critic, was already in the midst of directing his first feature film, *The Baby-Carriage* (*Barnvagnen*, 1963), when he issued his polemical and highly influential manifesto, *Visionen i svensk film* (Vision in Swedish Film), published by Bonniers in Stockholm in 1962. Determined to provoke a decisive break with what he regarded as the commercial complacency and escapism of the older film tradition in Sweden, Widerberg called for a new, engaged cinema that would concern itself with the true reality of social and economic factors in everyday life. Perhaps Keve, the moody, self-questioning film director who is one of the main characters and, in some ways, Widerberg's alter ego in his *Love 65* (*Kärlek 65*, 1965) expresses his creator's intentions best when he declares: "I should like to be more simple without lying. I should like to make a film that was as real and as concrete as something you say across the breakfast table."

The desire for renewal expressed in the early 1960s coincided with a long-awaited reform of the basic economic conditions governing the film industry in Sweden. Threatened by television and foreign films and staggering beneath a 25 percent entertainment tax levied on gross box-office receipts, film production in Sweden had fallen into a state of drastic decline, both in quality and quantity. Despite the remarkable individual accomplishments of a Bergman or a Sjöberg, the 1950s had in general been a period of disappointing artistic stagnation. By 1962 the number of films being made in Sweden had dwindled to a mere fourteen new features a year.

A dramatic change occurred when Harry Schein, a prominent industrialist and cultural activist, proposed the replacement of the heavy entertainment tax with a 10 percent levy on box-office receipts, to be paid into a fund administered by a new cultural foundation, the Swedish Film Institute. When Schein's Institute officially came into being on 1 July 1963, it brought to Sweden a system of creative public funding virtually unknown elsewhere. A pluralistic subsidy arrangement continues to provide grants to defray the production costs of commercial films, to subsidize quality films and underwrite their losses, and to support the production of films made by the institute itself (by now the largest film producer in northern Europe). Predictably, the economic reform of 1963 had an immediate and dynamic effect. As had happened in France with the *nouvelle vague*, young enthusiasts and intellectuals now found themselves given an opportunity to make feature films without a long apprenticeship. As a result, during the years between 1963 and 1970 no fewer than seventy-five new directors made their debut in Sweden. By 1969 the number of new films being made annually had climbed to a record high of thirty-four.

Widerberg, doyen of the new movement, found his models in young French directors such as François Truffaut, and in films of British and American social realism such as Karel Reisz's *Saturday Night and Sunday Morning* (1960), the Paddy Chayefsky dramas filmed by Delbert Mann during the 1950s, and, in particular, John Cassavetes's *Shadows* (1960). Films of this kind, Widerberg observes, tackle "the issues of human dignity and responsibility in their proper human environment," by showing "not only the conflicts of their characters but also their material conditions, how they live, what they eat, and where they work."[6]

The Widerberg style emerged in his first major picture, *The Baby-Carriage*. The "proper human environment" to which this director attaches so much importance is, in this case, the scruffy, working-class district of Malmö where he himself grew up, shot in an unadorned, natural light. In Widerberg's work the contours of reality are rarely smooth; its flow is deliberately fractured in *The Baby-Carriage* by unexpected actions, entrances, or gestures. Characters are sometimes cut off in the middle of a sentence or a reaction. Widerberg constantly seeks to provoke our curiosity and participation by means of fragmented scenes or images. He allows Keve, the ruminating director whose creative crisis is the focus of *Love 65*, to express the attitude he holds toward the place of discontinuity in modern cinema: "The old film was a lie in its very form. . . . It told of a world which was whole and unbroken and could be interpreted in one way only. Where is that world today?"

For Widerberg the frequent use of constrictive, lower-class environments in his early films by no means implies an adherence to the naturalistic idea of determinism—the irrevocable entrapment of characters in a milieu. On the contrary, his films are often paeans to the theme of personal liberation and individual freedom. Britt, the central character in *The Baby-Carriage*, is a cynical young woman, weary of the dull jobs to which she is confined by her shoddy education, caught in the dreary home life of her working-class family, without a language in which to express her inner feelings. Her encounters with men are as random as everything else in her existence; rather haphazardly she is made pregnant by Robban, a free-spirited young musician who soon disappears. For all its apparent "naturalism," however, the film is concerned not with determinism and entrapment, but rather with the gradual, liberating process of Britt's development. By her simple, affirmative decision to keep the baby and care for it herself, she acquires a newfound responsibility that will (we are asked to believe) impart purpose and direction to her formerly aimless life. In the final sequence, she is seen pushing the baby carriage along bright, optimistically sunlit streets.

In *Raven's End* (*Kvarteret korpen*, 1963), one of Widerberg's most highly regarded films, the theme of growth and emancipation finds far more coherent and convincing expression than in his first picture. The unusual power and freshness of the film derives, in large measure, from its scrupulously truthful and hence weighty recreation of Raven's End itself—the bleak, working-class tenement in Malmö as it was in 1936. Seen against this expressive background, the painful departure of Anders, the young would-be writer, acquires a double perspective. His decision to leave is both a rejection of the life that has eroded his parents' spirit and a positive act of strength that manifests his determination to find a fresh alternative, uncorrupted by either his mother's ritualized self-sacrifices or his father's alcoholic escapism. Even Elsie, the girl he has made pregnant, must be ruthlessly left behind, along with a life of capitulation with her in a flat across the yard.

The authentic, even documentary texture of the reality portrayed in Widerberg's films owes much to this director's collectivist, argumentative method of working with actors. No one, he insists, must "get up and try to outdo the other and create a character profile all on his own."[7] His whole principle of acting, he adds, "amounts to letting the actors use one another." In the interest of spontaneity, he cast an amateur—a former photographic model named Inger Taube—in the principal role of Britt in *The Baby-Carriage*. In *Love 65*, his complex, Felliniesque exploration of the creative and emotional dilemma of the artist, Widerberg allowed his actors to retain their own names and play, as it were, themselves. Evidently as a tribute to Cassavetes's *Shadows*, he included Ben Carruthers, an actor from that picture, in *Love 65*. Improvisation, another of Widerberg's favored devices for achieving a feeling of immediacy, is used extensively in this work. Long, rambling conversations that take place between Keve's wife (Ann-Marie Gyllenspertz) and Carruthers are obviously unprepared and spontaneous. Out of their halting questions and answers, the tentative, fragile outlines of a relationship begin to emerge, only to disappear again.

On the surface, these improvisational techniques would hardly seem to apply to Widerberg's popular commercial success, *Elvira Madigan* (1967). In fact, however, *Elvira Madigan* had very little scripted dialogue and the little that existed was largely unrehearsed. There is, indeed, a spontaneous emotional flow that one associates with this film—a flow cleverly propelled by the insistent strains of Mozart's Piano Concerto No. 21 (which, for a time, enjoyed the odd distinction of being known universally as "The Elvira Madigan Theme"). The subject matter is the stuff of pure historical romance—the story of a young Swedish army deserter (Thommy Berggren) who, caught in the rigidly stratified society of the late nineteenth century, sacrifices both his honor and his career in a vain attempt to escape with his beloved Elvira, a Danish circus dancer (Pia Degermark). Yet, although the rich and rhapsodic Eastmancolor images of *Elvira Madigan* present the sharpest possible contrast to the everyday environments of this director's earlier films, the main characters themselves are familiar Widerberg figures. They are rebels at odds with the rigid values of society. For Elvira and Sixten, rebellion is hopeless. Death is their only means of attaining their freedom.

In the films Widerberg made after *Elvira Madigan*, the theme of man's relationship to his social reality has been explored within a variety of contexts. In *The Ådalen Riots* (*Ådalen 31*, 1969) the massacre of five striking sawmill workers during a demonstration in a small Swedish town in 1931 is taken up and viewed—to the dismay of Widerberg's more orthodox Marxist contemporaries—from a purely personal and subjective viewpoint supplied by the family of one of the slain strikers. In *Joe Hill* (1971) the portrayal of the itinerant Swedish folk singer and socialist agitator who was executed in Salt Lake City in 1915, reveals another rebel-romantic who must struggle in vain to promote values that the established society of his time fears and suppresses. In *The Man on the Roof* (*Mannen på taket*, 1976) Widerberg turned to the intellectual murder mystery as his vehicle for the exploration of society and the rationality of social response.

It was, however, mainly during the 1960s that Bo Widerberg's influence on the Swedish cinema was keenly felt. A whole generation of new filmmakers sprang up in the wake of Widerberg's pioneering example, encouraged by the greatly improved economic conditions. Some, such as the Finnish-born writer and film critic Jörn Donner, brought to film-making the same concern with concrete social reality and causality that Widerberg himself advocated. In *A Sunday in September* (*En söndag i september*, 1963), the first in a series of films that Donner created around Harriet Andersson, his pessimistic study of the swift deterioration of a marriage is (unlike, say, Bergman's approach to such material) resolutely anchored in a contemporary Swedish social context. Others among the new directors took a very different view of the cinema's purpose, however. "What I least of all want to make are films recording the reality we can see, I mean a sort of documentary reality," asserts Kjell Grede, a film-poet whose *Harry Munter* (1969) and *Klara Lust* (1971) are freely structured, visionary works that seek to expose, in an elliptical and inferential way, the inner emotional life of their young alienated protagonists. For Grede, the true challenge of filmmaking is to put into visual terms "what we really long for, what we really dream of." The cinema can continue being a dream factory, he adds—"but it must fabricate true dreams and not false ones. Useful dreams."[8]

Although the two directors are quite unlike in style and in subject matter, the films of Jonas Cornell partake of Grede's attitude toward the depiction of an imaginatively heightened reality on the screen. Cornell, who made three major pictures in quick succession during the late 1960s before turning to stage and television directing, defends the social purpose of the fiction film as a means of laying bare the dreams and the mentality engendered by bourgeois society. In *Hugs and Kisses* (*Puss och kram*, 1967) Cornell's first feature film, Eva and Max, a married and superficially happy couple, offer hospitality to an impoverished friend, who gratefully takes up residence as butler, domestic companion, and surrogate child. The catalytic presence in the household of friend John quickly sets off a (predictable) extravaganza of marital war games, role playing and swapping, and purposeful make-believe intended to show Cornell's audiences who and what they truly are.

*Like Night and Day* (*Som natt och dag*, 1968) develops in a less comic key the same Cornell theme of characters caught in a mesh of social patterns and poses. Here, the ostensibly poised and intelligent Susanne (played by Cornell's wife Agneta Ekmanner) discovers that her materialistic decision to discard her young lover in favor of an imperious professor with wealth and prestige, brings only grief and regret. A deft bit of landscape imagery reminiscent of Resnais's use of Schloss Nymphenburg in *Last Year at Marienbad* (1960) helps Cornell to make his point. In the closing frames the camera picks out Susanne wandering aimlessly amidst the rigidly symmetrical pattern of paths and fountains in the formal gardens of the palace at Drottningholm. As the camera continues to climb high above the scene, it gives us a final glimpse of

Susanne: a solitary, disconsolate figure lost in the maze of perfect, artificial symmetry.

A subjectively told social allegory of this kind finds its marked antithesis in the "cinema of fact" that found favor in Sweden (as elsewhere) during the turbulent 1960s. A tide of documentary or semi-documentary films, unconcerned with formal sophistication and often collectively made, took up concrete social issues ranging from juvenile delinquency and corrupt urban planning practices to the precarious existences led by American deserters and foreign workers in Sweden. Protest, implied or explicit, was the syntax of these problem films. In a tone of studied and ultimately oppressive detachment, Jan Halldoff's *Life Is Just Great* (*Livet är stenkul*, 1966) records the random antisocial actions of an urban teenage gang. In *The Corridor* (*Korridoren*, 1968), Halldoff trains his lens on the working conditions and authoritarianism of the medical profession, while in *A Dream of Freedom* (*En dröm om frihet*, 1969) this prolific but uneven filmmaker traces with case-history exactitude the doomed flight and inevitable recapture of two youthful (misunderstood) offenders wanted for bank robbery and the killing of a policeman. The not unusual motif of a repressive society's revenge against a social deviant it fears found even more direct and vehement expression in *The Assault* (*Misshandlingen*, 1969). A highly regarded work directed by Lasse Forsberg, it was created collectively by the actors in it, who contributed their own dialogue and arguments to the debate of issues. At the center is an intelligent and voluble dissenter who loudly deplores the false values he perceives in society, and at last hits out in frustration at a complacent businessman who refuses to listen to his protests. Society swiftly silences its dangerous opponent with the mind-control drugs, violence, and physical confinement that are the hospital psychiatrist's stock in trade for personality reform.

The more radical, agitprop cinema that arose in the wake of the student uprisings of the late 1960s tried to find a new political form and language for film. It was determined to subordinate the notion of a film as primarily a work of art, emphasizing instead its usefulness as a vehicle for social and political change. In such works as *Made in Sweden* (1968) and *A Baltic Tragedy* (*Baltutlämningen*, 1969), for example, Johan Bergenståhle sought a new cinematic idiom with which to focus attention on sociopolitical issues of the broadest scope. In the first instance, Bergenståhle's subject is the poverty and suffering of Third World countries and the direct role played by (Swedish) capitalistic society in that misery. In his second feature he takes up the controversial deportation to Soviet Russia in 1946 of 167 Baltic soldiers who had fled to Sweden as political refugees after Germany's collapse. In both cases, this director attempts to fuse fictional scenes with factual documentary material. Thus in *Made in Sweden* newsreel pictures of appalling suf-

In Ingmar Bergman's early success *Wild Strawberries* (1957) memories mingle with reality as the aged Isak Borg travels back through time to self-discovery.

Sven Nykvist's deep-focus photography in Bergman's *The Silence* (1963) expresses the isolation to which both Anne and her dying elder sister Ester (Ingrid Thulin, foreground) are condemned.

*Persona* (1966) was Bergman's visually striking study of the interlocking inner worlds of two women, an actress suddenly become silent (Liv Ullman, r.) and her nurse (Bibi Andersson).

In Mai Zetterling's first feature, *Loving Couples* (1964), three women relive in flashbacks their inevitable disappointment in men and marriage.

The lush, idyllic images of the historical romance *Elvira Madigan* (1967) are in sharp contrast to the sordid environments of Bo Widerberg's earlier films.

The hilarious dream sequence from Vilgot Sjöman's *I Am Curious Yellow* (1967) in which the rebellious Lena ties men to a tree to show her contempt for male opportunism.

Alexander and his sister Fanny on the threshold of their ordeal with a new stepfather, the cruel Bishop Vergerus, in Bergman's late masterpiece *Fanny and Alexander* (1982).

Jan Troell's *The New Land* (1971) presented a panoramic vision of determined Swedish pioneers' search for a new life in the American West.

fering and starvation in Thailand and India are placed in incendiary juxtaposition with idyllic images of the welfare garden of Swedish social democracy. In *A Baltic Tragedy* the physical and mental anguish of the refugees is counterpointed by newsreel footage, diagrams, maps, statistics, and the cool, detached voice of a commentator—devices all designed to impart an air of objective investigative reporting to this portrait of human misery.

In that explosive year of 1968 Bergman's *Shame* (*Skammen*, 1968) became the focus of some of the most violently hostile criticism in the history of Swedish cultural debate. Although most critics consider the film a masterpiece, Bergman found himself attacked in his own country for an alleged refusal to take sides, which the far left perceived to be an endorsement of American involvement in Vietnam. Jan (Max von Sydow) and Eva (Liv Ullmann), a pair of musicians who have taken refuge on a remote Baltic island, find themselves caught in the maelstrom of war. They refuse to side with either faction, and they fail even to recognize the difference between the two clashing armies. Yet this desperate neutrality of theirs by no means extends to the filmmaker himself. Bergman is a staunch partisan, courageously on the side of what he refers to as the misery of the third party—those weak and terrified people who make up no political party, but are experiencing the approach of darkness. *Shame* is a shaken and compassionate response to their destiny—to that condition of evil of which the war in the film is only a single manifestation. Yet this response is also a protest, filled with human feeling, that continues to live long after a great many of the social and political parables and paradocumentaries of the period have been forgotten.

Three of the most resilient and, in retrospect, most significant voices in the "new" Swedish cinema engendered by Bo Widerberg in the 1960s found, in one way or another, their points of departure in more traditional views or methods of making films. Vilgot Sjöman, apart from Widerberg the most influential figure in the new wave, had his first and most important teacher in Bergman himself, whose shooting of *Winter Light* Sjöman has documented in a remarkable production diary.[9] Mai Zetterling, a celebrated actress in the cinema of the 1940s, brought to directing a woman's point of view. The youngest of these three, Jan Troell, found in the history and culture of the Swedish people an epic subject matter from which he has quarried an international reputation unmatched today by any other Swedish filmmaker except Bergman.

Troell, a director-cinematographer whose work is marked by a strong emphasis on visual means of emotional expression, started his professional film career as the cameraman for Widerberg's *The Baby-Carriage*. His own subjects are, however, very different from the contemporary social realities of Widerberg. Troell's most successful motion pictures have been expansively pictorial illustrations of the Swedish past, seen through the perspective of its literature. In Eyvind Johnson's autobiographical tetralogy, *The Novel About Olof* (*Romanen om Olof*), Troell found the inspiration for his first feature, *Here is Your Life* (*Här har du ditt liv*, 1966). A nostalgic chronicle of a young man's journey in search of self-identity and insight, set in the poverty-stricken lumbering country of northern Sweden early in this century, it is redolent of the rich folk-epic atmosphere of Alexander Dovzhenko's Gorky trilogy. *The Emigrants* (*Utvandrarna*, 1969-70) and its sequel *The New Land* (*Nybyggarna*, 1970–71), which brought Troell international acclaim, likewise constitute a panoramic illustration of a cherished literary model—in this case Vilhelm Moberg's great cycle of novels about the hardships and courage of the Swedish farmers who abandoned their unyielding pastures in Småland to seek a new existence in the American West a century ago. With a total running time of 395 minutes, this mammoth two-film project was (until Bergman's *Fanny and Alexander* broke all spending records) the Swedish film industry's most costly undertaking—and also its biggest commercial success.

The broad appeal Troell's popular folk epics have exerted (not least in the United States) is also directly related to his shrewd selection of actors, a number of them recruited from the ranks of Bergman's well-known "company." In *Here Is Your Life* a good many old Bergman hands appear, including Gunnar Björnstrand, Allan Edwall, and Max von Sydow. By casting von Sydow (a Troell mainstay) as Karl-Oskar, the inarticulate but robust and determined pioneer at the center of *The Emigrants* and *The New Land*, the director established a direct contrast to the von Sydow of Bergman's "island" trilogy of the late 1960s: the irresolute, vulnerable, fugitive figure whose name is Johan Borg, the painter destroyed by his tormentors (and his own inner demons) in *Hour of the Wolf* (*Vargtimmen*, 1968), Jan in *Shame*, and Andreas Winkelmann, the island recluse who cannot escape being corroded by the physical and psychic forces of violence that engulf him in *The Passion of Anna* (*En passion*, 1969).

No such character complexities encumber Troell's elaborate method of telling simple stories. Like von Sydow, Liv Ullmann found an alternative image in such roles as Kristina, the winsome and patient pioneer wife in the *Emigrant* films, and Hanna, the spunky mail-order spouse in *Zandy's Bride* (produced by Warner Brothers, 1974). These Troell heroines from a simpler era afford a piquant contrast to that gallery of more complicated (and more intelligent) Bergman-Ullmann women that originated with the Norwegian star's portrayal of Elisabet Vogler, the enigmatic mistress of silence in *Persona* (1966).

Mai Zetterling's heroines, on the other hand, are above all a woman's women: defiant and frequently lonely figures drawn from a women's point of view, filled with anger and despair by the roles fastened on them by a society ruled by men (and boorish, weak, and stupid men at that). Zetterling's move from in front of to behind the camera is plainly the result of her determination to give cinematic expression to her vision of women in society. An engagingly idiosyncratic filmmaker, her assorted shorts and feature films defy reduction to a single method or style. Yet there is a strong personal sensibility that colors all of them deeply. "Men always let you down," a leitmotif of her work, is a phrase repeated often, in tones ranging from outrage to irony, in *Loving Couples* (*Älskande par*, 1964), Zetterling's first feature. The film is set in that *belle epoque* of deceit and hypocrisy that preceded World War I. Its main characters are a trio of women in a maternity ward who relive in flashbacks the intertwined events that led to their pregnancies. "Marriage," reflects Angela, the most determined and self-aware of the three, "—it's like falling asleep for the rest of your life."

In *The Girls* (*Flickorna*, 1968), that life-sleep is at last broken and the longed-for revolution is accomplished—at least in the fantasies of the three actresses (played by Bibi Andersson, Harriet Andersson, and Gunnel Lindblom) who are touring the Swedish countryside in *Lysistrata*, Aristophanes's satirical comedy about female revolt. As the women become steadily more immersed in their stage roles, they also confront truths about the unhappiness and longing for freedom in their own lives. As the line between fantasy and reality blurs in the film, they enjoy the overthrow and humiliation of their selfish male oppressors in a succession of sketchlike visions and dreams. Bibi Andersson's Liz (Lysistrata) finally incites the other women in the theater group to join her in an angry, militant striptease and flings her own bra, like a gauntlet, in the face of her uncomprehending husband. At the end, on stage in *Lysistrata*, Liz literally throws her male antagonists to the floor in a final, fantastical gesture of defiance—a gesture that provides a suitably emphatic punctuation sign for Zetterling's most vehement feminist protest.

In the wake of Zetterling's example, and undoubtedly encouraged by it, a notable number of new women directors have become active in recent years. *Near and Far Away* (*Långt borta och nära*, 1976), Marianne Ahrne's graphic study of love and mental obsession, and *Paradise Place* (*Paradistorg*, 1976), Gunnel Lindblom's intricate and intelligent film of the Ulla Isaksson novel about the lifestyles and conflicts of four generations of a Swedish family, are two of the best examples of the rising influence of women directors in Swedish film. *Broken Sky* (*Brustenhimmel*, 1982), Ingrid Thulin's impressive debut film about the experiences of a young girl growing up in the bleak north of Sweden during the 1940s, and Suzanne Osten's poignant memoir *Our Life is Now* (*Mamma*, 1982) are more recent manifestations of this same trend.

Vilgot Sjöman, the oldest and also the most prolific of the major "young" directors who emerged during the 1960s in Sweden, created one film in particular that stands apart from discernible schools and trends. *I am Curious Yellow* (*Jag är nyfiken—gul*, 1967) and *I am Curious Blue* (*Jag är nyfiken—blå*, 1968) were originally planned and shot as a single long film. They are mirror comedies that reflect one another. At the core of both is the odyssey of the inquisitive and exceedingly libidinous Lena, who searches for answers to her questions about her society and herself.

At one level, the *Curious* films aspire—as most of Sjöman's cinematic works do—to a political dimension. Armed with her tape-recorder and microphone, Lena Nyman (the actors generally retain their own names) sallies forth to conduct a sociological fact-finding mission aimed at exposing the attitudes and prejudices underlying the ostensibly frictionless Swedish social democracy. In this respect Sjöman's aim may seem pretentious—but Lena's saucy progress through her drowsy and hypocritical society is not. With a forthright impertinence she interrogates everyone from factory-workers and felons to Olof Palme, the prime minister of Sweden. The end result of these spontaneous, candid-camera interviews is not, however, an objective documentary of Swedish society. Sjöman's editing patterns are highly unconventional, and his presence is always keenly felt (often on camera), resulting in a consciously provocative political cartoon of a bloated society under attack by a new, inquisitive generation.

On another and more basic level, however, the odyssey depicted in *Yellow* and *Blue* is a personal one, illustrating a precocious young woman's search for an identity. Lena, who lives with her shiftless wreck of a father, devotes part of her quest to looking for a lost mother who walked out on them when Lena was still a child. Mostly, however, Lena's personal research centers on sex—and her encyclopedic erotic achievements are carefully recorded in her card index along with the data she gathers about Swedish society. By the time she meets Börje (Börje Ahlstedt), her energetic sexual partner in both films, she has already had twenty-three lovers. This new boyfriend, too, is ultimately disappointing; her disillusionment with his bourgeois masculine opportunism is expressed in a fantasy sequence in which the indomitable rebel Lena, breasts flung forward and rifle cocked, imagines herself tying a group of football players to a tree and then castrating the hapless Börje.

Sjöman claims that the explicit sexuality of his films is a means of striking down the barriers of puritanism in human relations, both social or emotional. "Undress people and they're all alike," as one of Lena's interview subjects remarks. "Put their clothes back on, and there you have a class society." Nudity and striptease are an essential part of the syntax of Sjöman's iconoclastic method. The graphic eroticism that made *I am Curious Yellow* and its blue companion two of the most controversial films of their day finds expression in his other films as well. In *Troll* (1971), a zany sex farce that revolves around a young couple's irrational fear that copulation is lethal, the events touch a peak of absurdity when a group of opera singers indulge in an athletic four-way orgy as they perform *Bella figlia dell'amore*, from Verdi's *Rigoletto*. At the opposite end of the spectrum from this exuberant voluptuousness is *491* (1964), an ugly homily about incorrigible juvenile offenders and the blundering efforts of society to rehabilitate them. The gang's viciousness and perversity culminate in their abduction of Steva (also played by Lena Nyman), who is forced to undergo every conceivable variant of sexual assault, including intercourse with an Alsatian wolf-hound. No matter how savage or abrasive the erotic imagery of Sjöman's films becomes at times, it is invariably endowed with a genuine artistic purpose (in contrast to the flood of forgettable skin flicks that comprise the pornographic subculture of postwar Swedish cinema). Art, for Sjöman, "is born at the frontiers of taboo."[10] If we accept his proposition that the conventional cinema is the medium of reactionary and moribund values (as he maintains in *I was Curious: Diary of the Making of a Film*, 1969), then only the intrepid invasion of previously closed territory can bring about the cinema's renewal.

In *The Mistress* (*Älskarinnan*, 1962) Sjöman's traditionally crafted debut film about four crucial days in the life of a young woman (Bibi Andersson) who becomes infatuated with an older man (Max von Sydow), there is scarcely a hint of the innovative anarchist of *Curious* fame. Nor, for all its sensationalism, was the *nouvelle vague* realism of *491* so radically new, especially once the censors had curtailed the activities of the performing dog. But *My Sister, My Love* (*Syskonbädd 1782*, 1966), Sjöman's fourth and in many ways his most integrated feature, struck a new chord. This film's subject—the incestuous love affair between a brother and sister—serves as a metaphor for the rebellion of a free spirit who defies her repressive and superstitious society. The year is 1782, but the great Gustavian era of enlightenment and culture is, for Sjöman, a dark, sinister age of moral hypocrisy and hidden corruption (the inspiration for the film was John Ford's Jacobean tragedy *'Tis Pity She's a Whore*). Charlotte (Bibi Andersson) hides behind a mask of purity that conceals her incestuous passion for her brother Jacob; later it disguises her fear of exposure and punishment as his child grows within her. Yet, despite her "crime," Charlotte remains a solitary figure of innocence surrounded on all sides by the lewdness and vulgarity of her environment. When she is mortally wounded by a rival in the final portion of the film, the baby that is delivered by Caesarian section turns out to be a healthy, undeformed child—living proof of the vitality and validity of a love that transcends society's rigid codes and taboos.

Charlotte is thus the first in a gallery of related Sjöman heroines. Like the inquisitive Lena and also like Hjördis, the housemaid who gives her opportunistic employer a lesson in love and social revolt in *A*

*Handful of Love* (*En handfull kärlek*, 1974), she is youth and openness challenging the resistance of an inhibited class-bound society.

Although most of the major new directors who emerged during the sixties and early seventies have continued to make films, the once-relevant subjects and images of the socially conscious cinema have hardened into clichés and no decisive second wave has developed to sustain creative momentum. One basic cause of this seeming stagnation is the mounting economic pressure that has come to threaten the very existence of a domestic film industry in a small country. Competition from mass-market American imports, the ravages of television, and the phenomenal growth of a home video market (cassettes can be borrowed from public libraries in Scandinavia) have conspired to undermine Swedish cinema. During the 1970s, Swedish features actually accounted for a mere 7 percent of the new films shown in the country. Reflected in this statistic is a steady decline in production. The desire to preserve a film heritage that is authentically Swedish in character remains strong, but it is counterbalanced by a feeling that, especially in view of the ascendancy of Danish and Finnish filmmaking in recent years, perhaps only a cooperative system of pan-Scandinavian film production can succeed in stimulating new creative growth and redistributing the heavy financial risks.

Even Bergman has found his work affected by the difficult conditions that arose in the early 1970s. *Cries and Whispers* (*Viskningar och rop*, 1973), his intense, oneiric vision of the agonizing process of dying and the longed-for release that is death, seemed a daring experiment. Unable to find adequate financial backing, Bergman was obliged to fall back on the faith of his cinematographer Sven Nykvist and his principal players—Liv Ullmann, Ingrid Thulin, and Harriet Andersson—all of whom agreed to forgo their salaries until the film was sold. Although the film was a resounding critical and popular success in the United States, the precarious venture convinced Bergman that he would never again risk the salaries of his colleagues. His solution was television (a medium in which he has worked at regular intervals since 1957). Each of the major films he has made in Sweden since *Cries and Whispers* has been initially conceived for small-screen distribution.

On the surface, the simple domestic realism of *Scenes from a Marriage* (*Scener ur ett äktenskap*, 1973)—first telecast in Scandinavia in six episodes and then edited for cinema distribution—might seem atypical of his other work. Yet his surgically precise dissection of the bruising marital confrontations and painful reconciliation of Johan (Erland Josephson) and Marianne (Liv Ullmann) merely transposes the familiar Bergman concern with human suffering and anguish to a new (and, in some ways, more accessible) key. Beneath the surface of the couple's brave talk at the end of the film lurks an existential anxiety that is manifested in Marianne's terrifying nightmare of sinking in soft sand, without hands, unable to reach those dearest to her. It is an anxiety bred of the nagging suspicion that utter confusion may, after all, be the inescapable condition of all human existence. Those demons of doubt and despair that lurk at the periphery of *Scenes*, in the figures of Peter and Katarina Egerman, burst once again into the foreground of Bergman's cinematic vision in *From the Life of the Marionettes* (*Aus dem Leben der Marionetten*, 1980), the deeply pessimistic companion piece that he made for German television during the years of his self-imposed exile in Munich.

Before his traumatic clash with the tax authorities led Bergman to desert Sweden in anger and disgust in 1976, he made two other significant films that illustrate the diversity of his use of the television medium. His sparkling "theater film" of Mozart's *The Magic Flute* (*Trollflöjten*), televised to celebrate the fiftieth anniversary of the Swedish Broadcasting Company in 1975, provided an unexpected and unusually serene example of the essentially Strindbergian character of his cinematic vision; that is, a vision governed by a perception of the dreamlike quality of reality that is, at the same time, always conjoined with the insistent reality of the dream. In Mozart's opera "we experience the strange quality of the dream and the fairy tale. . . . The tenderness of the dream, but also the dream's pain and longing. These small individuals chase and are chased through a dream and a reality that might just as well have been created by their own imagination."[11]

An entirely different tone and style characterize *Face to Face* (*Ansikte mot ansikte*, 1976). First seen in Sweden as a four-part television serial before it was unveiled as a motion picture at the Cannes Film Festival, the film again centered on the concept of the dream as a superreal "extension of reality." This hallucinatory study of madness and attempted suicide belongs to Bergman's darker mood—the mood that prevailed throughout the making of his "exile" films: *The Serpent's Egg*, *Autumn Sonata* (*Höstsonat*, 1978), and *From the Life of the Marionettes*. The painful psychological struggle of Jenny Isaksson (Liv Ullmann), the psychiatrist who loses her sanity in *Face to Face*, carries echoes of the more complex inner suffering and vulnerability of Elisabet Vogler (also played by Ullmann), the actress who has lost the power of speech in *Persona*. Jenny's suicidal struggle also prefigures the more desperate mental anguish of Peter Egerman, the murderer of the prostitute in *Marionettes*.

"O, endless night, when will you vanish? When will the light reach my eyes?" cries Tamino in profound despondency, as he stands in the dark courtyard of the Temple of Wisdom in *The Magic Flute*. "Soon, youth, soon, or never," answers the shadowy chorus of priests. Encountering this moment of despair in Mozart's opera, Bergman found himself closer to "the deepest secret of spiritual intuition" than ever before:

"He asks his question in darkness and from the darkness he answers himself—or does he get an answer?"[12] Bergman's own question touches the innermost core of his art—and Mozart's. In *Hour of the Wolf* it is this very scene from the opera that Lindhorst, the sinister "keeper of archives," produces as a puppet performance with miniature living puppets at the ghostly dinner party given by Johan Borg's tormentors. In that film, said by some critics to be an ironic paraphrase of *The Magic Flute*, the answer that Borg, the humiliated and stricken artist, receives is "never." He is a grotesque inversion of Tamino, condemned to journey downward into the darkness of eternal night. In Bergman's magnificent film of *The Magic Flute* itself, however, the darkness is at last dispelled; the images of evil and despair vanish like dreams; and the finale is an exuberantly theatrical celebration of love and fruitfulness. And, for one last time, this magical process is repeated in *Fanny and Alexander* (*Fanny och Alexander*, 1982), intended by Bergman as his farewell gesture as a filmmaker.

Described by him in various interviews as both "a celebration of love for life" and as "the sum total of my life as a filmmaker," Bergman's forty-third feature as writer-director was released first as a long cinema film (with a running time, unprecedented for Bergman, of three hours and fifteen minutes) and then subsequently as a four-part television serial (aired first in Denmark at the end of 1983). In both versions *Fanny and Alexander* emerges as a fairy-tale tapestry crowded with memorable images and filled with familiar faces from the Bergman past. Its unusual scope, its lavishness, and even its title all seem to set this work apart as an exception in the Bergman canon. Yet his unmistakable voice and vision pervade every corner of his rich chronicle of the "little world" of the Ekdahl family and the theater that is their cherished heritage. "A small room of orderliness, routine, conscientiousness, and love," is how Oscar Ekdahl (Allan Edwall), Alexander's father and the manager of the local theater, describes his playhouse in the first of the two crucial speeches that frame the film's complicated action. "Outside is the big world, and sometimes the little world succeeds for a moment in reflecting the big world, so that we understand it better." Probably in no other film by Bergman has the idea of a constant, suggestive interplay between the macrocosm of external human reality and the inner world of imagination, dreams, and make-believe been more effectively dramatized.

Set in a seemingly idyllic "Swedish cathedral town" (read Uppsala, Bergman's birthplace) in 1907, *Fanny and Alexander* brings its audiences back to Bergman's favorite epoch, the period from the turn of the century to World War I: "It's the beginning, the start of a new age. It's a time that's so double and so cruel and so filled with deceit."[13] To be sure, the life-denying forces of hatred and darkness threaten, as they have so often before in Bergman's "artist" films. They are embodied here in the chilling household of Alexander's cruel stepfather, Bishop Edvard Vergerus (Jan Malmsjö), the pitiless enemy of the theater (and hence of life) in this little society. But this time evil is not allowed to prevail. Vergerus is destroyed when his body is turned into a blazing pillar of flames; and in a mysterious way it is Alexander (Bertil Guve), the young conqueror, who brings about this fiery and satisfying exorcism, simply by imagining it.

The second of the two framing speeches—placed by Bergman in the mouth of Gustav Adolf Ekdahl (Jarl Kulle), the rambunctious womanizer and amiable numbskull of the family—restores to the film a concluding sense of harmony and tranquility previously experienced only in momentary, fleeting images in Bergman's cinema: in Isak Borg's last, tranquil moments of dreaming in *Wild Strawberries*; in the repast of wild strawberries and milk that Mia serves on the hillside in *The Seventh Seal*; in Agnes's idyllic memory of her stroll in the sunlit park with her sisters in *Cries and Whispers*. And, of course, in *The Magic Flute*, to which the climactic, flower-bedecked ceremony of joyous reconciliation and fruitfulness in *Fanny and Alexander* seems so directly related. "Our little world has closed around us in security, wisdom, and order after a time of horror and confusion," declares "Gusten" with robust, comic effusiveness. "The shadows of death have been routed, winter has been put to flight and joy has returned to our hearts."

The point of this speech and of the film in general is neither sentimental nor fatuously optimistic, however. Evil exists, that we do know; the ghost of the cruel Vergerus palpably dogs Alexander's footsteps as *Fanny and Alexander* draws to a close. "The world is a den of thieves and night is falling," Gusten goes on to remind his listeners. "Soon it will be the hour for robbers and murderers. Evil is breaking its chains and goes through the world like a mad dog. The poisoning affects us all, without exception, us Ekdahls and everyone else." Yet precisely because this is so, his speech is a plea that we in our "little worlds" should take our pleasures without shame. "Therefore let us be happy while we are happy."

The closing moments belong, however, not to the ebullient Gustav Adolf but to Alexander, the young dreamer of dreams (the artist as a young man?) through whose child's eyes the magical and mystical occurences in this film are perceived and ultimately understood. In the closing frames, lying with his head in his grandmother's lap, the boy listens as she reads aloud. The passage is from a "new" play by August Strindberg (appropriately titled *A Dream Play*) that the Ekdahls intend to present at their brave little theater: "Anything can happen, anything is possible and likely. Time and space do not exist. On a fleeting ground of reality, imagination spins out and weaves new patterns." As the last line of dialogue in Bergman's final film, this familiar quotation from Strindberg acquires special significance, as a testimony to the nature of a remarkable artistic kinship. *Fanny and Alexander* is a dreamplay as surely as Strindberg's great, elusive masterpiece is one, held together by a fragile logic of emotion and association that circumvents the conscious intellect and reaches the beholder directly through the senses.

This attitude toward art is much more clearly enunciated by Bergman in *After the Rehearsal* (*Efter repetitionen*, 1984), his exquisitely simple, introspective television drama about an aging theater director who sits alone on an empty stage pondering the curious interrelationship between his life and his art. (The play that the director, Henrik Vogler, is rehearsing is, of course, Strindberg's *A Dream Play*.) Although this three-character, seventy-two-minute chamber film followed close on the heels of *Fanny and Alexander* (its Swedish telecast was timed to coincide with the 1984 Academy Award ceremonies, at which *Fanny* swept four Oscars), it represents a new departure rather than an anticlimax in Bergman's long career. Created specifically for television, it exploits the technical and compositional demands of that medium to achieve a maximum sense of intimacy and intensity. Accordingly, when Bergman discovered that *After the Rehearsal* had been blown up to 35mm for large-screen distribution in the United States, he objected vehemently and only reluctantly agreed to let the work be shown in movie theaters, billed as "a TV film."

Whatever fresh surprises Ingmar Bergman may yet have in store for his audiences, the era of Swedish cinema that had been dominated by his achievements can be said to have been crowned by *Fanny and Alexander* and the attendant reflections and reminiscences of Bergman's alter ego, Henrik Vogler, in *After the Rehearsal*. For its future survival, it is to new voices and new impulses that the Swedish cinema now looks. Nor have such innovations been lacking. Throughout the Bergman years, Sweden continued to foster new films and filmmakers of the first order, sometimes unjustly overlooked by international critics. Today, although Sweden accounts for fewer than twenty new features a year, the best of these continue to supply its film industry, created by Charles Magnusson more than three-quarters of a century ago, with its conspicuous vitality.[14]

## NOTES

1. Interview in *Playboy* (June 1964), quoted in Peter Cowie, *Swedish Cinema* (London and New York, 1966), p. 10.
2. Cf. Marianne Höök, *Ingmar Bergman* (Stockholm, 1962), pp. 120–21.
3. *Bergman om Bergman*, eds. Stig Björkman, Torsten Manns, and Jonas Sima (Stockholm, 1970 & Copenhagen, 1971), p. 152. Translation by the authors.

4. Nils Petter Sundgren, *The New Swedish Cinema* (Stockholm, 1970), p. 8.
5. In Cowie, *Swedish Cinema*, p. 183.
6. In Stig Björkman, *Film in Sweden: The New Directors* (London & South Brunswick, NJ, 1977), p. 11.
7. In ibid., p. 18.
8. From an interview quoted in Sundgren, *The New Swedish Cinema*, p. 45.
9. Vilgot Sjöman, *L136: Diary with Ingmar Bergman*, trans. Alan Blair (Ann Arbor: Karoma, 1978).
10. Quoted in Björkman, *The New Directors*, p. 27.
11. From an interview quoted in Lise-Lone Marker and Frederick J. Marker, *Ingmar Bergman: Four Decades in the Theater* (London & New York, 1982), p. 113.
12. In Peter Cowie, *Ingmar Bergman: A Critical Biography* (London, 1982), p. 299.
13. Lise-Lone Marker and Frederick J. Marker, "The Making of *Fanny and Alexander*: A Conversation with Ingmar Bergman," *Films and Filming* 341 (February 1983): 9.
14. This article is taken from a larger study by the authors, and was adapted for this volume.

## SELECTED BIBLIOGRAPHY

### General Works

Björkman, Stig. *Film in Sweden: The New Directors*. London: Tantivy Press; South Brunswick, NJ: A. S. Barnes, 1977.
Cowie, Peter. *Film in Sweden: Stars and Players*. London: Tantivy Press; South Brunswick, NJ: A. S. Barnes, 1977.
———. *Sweden 2*. London: Zwemmer, 1970.
———. *Swedish Cinema*. London: Zwemmer; New York: A. S. Barnes, 1966.
Kauffmann, Stanley, ed. *A World on Film* (Part II, pp. 270ff., Sweden). New York: Harper and Row, 1966.
Löthwall, Lars-Olof, ed. *Vilgot Sjöman (New Swedish Cinema* I) Stockholm: Swedish Film Institute, 1974.
Sjöman, Vilgot. *L136: Diary with Ingmar Bergman*, trans. Alan Blair. Ann Arbor: Karoma, 1978.
Sundgren, Nils Petter. *The New Swedish Cinema*. Stockholm, The Swedish Institute, 1970.
Waldekranz, Rune. *Modern Swedish Film*. Stockholm: The Swedish Institute, 1961.
———. *Swedish Cinema*. Stockholm: The Swedish Institute, 1959.

### Books on Bergman

*Bergman on Bergman*, eds. Stig Björkman, Torsten Manns, and Jonas Sima, trans. Paul Britten Austin. New York: Simon and Schuster, 1973.

Bergom-Larsson, Maria. *Film in Sweden: Ingmar Bergman and Society*. London: Tantivy Press; South Brunswick, NJ: A. S. Barnes, 1978.

Cowie, Peter. *Ingmar Bergman: A Critical Biography*. London: Secker and Warburg, 1982.

Donner, Jörn. *The Films of Ingmar Bergman*. New York: Dover, 1972.

Höök, Marianne. *Ingmar Bergman*. Stockholm: Wahlström och Widstrand, 1962.

Kaminsky, Stuart, ed. *Ingmar Bergman: Essays in Criticism*. New York: Oxford University Press, 1975.

Livingston, Paisley. *Ingmar Bergman and the Rituals of Art*. Ithaca: Cornell University Press, 1982.

Marker, Lise-Lone and Frederick J. Marker. *Ingmar Bergman: Four Decades in the Theater*. London and New York: Cambridge University Press, 1982.

Simon, John. *Ingmar Bergman Directs*. New York: Harcourt Brace Jovanovich, 1972.

Steene, Birgitta. *A Reference Guide to Ingmar Bergman*. Boston: G. K. Hall, 1982.

Wood, Robin. *Ingmar Bergman*. New York: Praeger, 1969.

Young, Vernon. *Cinema Borealis: Ingmar Bergman and the Swedish Ethos*. New York: Avon, 1972.

# SWITZERLAND

## ELAINE MANCINI

For two decades following the end of the war, Switzerland, like Belgium and the Netherlands, produced few films, received little critical attention, and found limited distribution for its productions. In 1945 ten films appeared; that output quickly dropped to one or two a year despite the organization of the Swiss Film Library in Lausanne in 1948. Ten years later the situation had improved only slightly: annual Swiss production comprised three or four features. In this country composed of German-Swiss (the largest part of the population, over 4 million), French-Swiss (1½ million), and Italians (400 thousand), only 2 percent of the population went to the cinema in 1958. Likewise, of the 610 films released in Switzerland in 1958, 35.8 percent were American, 24 percent were French, 21.5 percent were German and 1.1 percent were Swiss. Swiss producers limited themselves to one kind of filmmaking—the folkloric—represented by such titles as *Heidi* (1952), *The Search* (1948) and *Heidi and Peter* (1954) produced by Lazar Wechsler. These were made by Praesens Film in Zurich, the largest of the four studios making German-language films, and were distributed almost entirely in Austria and Germany even though they had to be dubbed from *Schwyzer Dutsch* to *Hoch deutsch* (proper German), the former being unintelligible outside of Switzerland. The German-Swiss *The Cheese Factory in the Hamlet* (*Die Kaeserei in der Vehfreude*, 1959), based on a popular peasant novel, and the dialect comedy *The Model Husband* (*Der Mustergatte*, 1959) had long runs in German-speaking towns but were rarely booked in French Switzerland. Even these could not compete with films made in Germany. Basically, if you wanted to be a filmmaker, you left Switzerland, as did Jean-Luc Godard and Bernhard Wicki.

At the beginning of the 1960s a few official changes began to alter the situation. Admission age to the cinemas was lowered from eighteen to sixteen, and programming was extended another thirty hours per week. But the biggest change was unofficial, caused by individuals who made films against all odds and who battled the provincialism of the beautiful folkloric approach and the myth of the contented, secure citizenry. One example was Henri Brandt's realistic *When We Were Children* (*Quand nous etions petits enfants*, 1964). Another, Dr. Alexander Seiler's 1964 *We, the Italians* (*Siamo italiani*) caused a minor revolution. Even though this documentary cost little to make, it brought Seiler's Gnant Film Production Company to financial ruin because of the strong official hostility to the film's acknowledgement of a marginalized minority culture. But regardless of official response to it, and the fate of its production company, it received many awards, provided an example that rejuvenated Swiss production, and began a series of politically minded films. Some of these continued to give voice to the Italian-Swiss workers, such as Peter Ammann's documentary *Workers Yes, Humans No* (*Braccia si, uomini no*, 1971) that reacted to a government attempt to deport migrant workers, and Alvaro Bizzarri's *The Seasonal Worker* (*Lo stagionale*, 1972). Robert Boner also devoted a mid-'70s documentary to Italian immigrants with *Worker's Marriage* (*Arbeiterehe*).

The German-Swiss, most of whom came from a background in television or film documentary, showed a marked propensity for political subjects. Jurg Hassler's 1970 film *Krawall* covered a youth revolt in Zurich that was squashed by the police. Although it won a government prize, official reaction here took the form of "nonencouragement" for future work by this director. Rolf Lyssy's 1976 *Confrontations* analyzed Nazism in Switzerland through the reactions of a Yugoslav Jew. Alexander Seiler traced the activities of the workers' movement in Switzerland from 1914 to 1974 in *The Fruits of Labor* (*Die Fruchte der Arbeit*, 1974). Villi Herman's *San Gottardo* compared the class struggle involved in the construction of a railroad tunnel in 1872 to the building of a superhighway nearly a hundred years later where that class conflict was still very much in evidence. Peter von Gunten displayed a stark realism in *The Extradition* (1973) while Thomas Koerfer told an absurdist political fable in *The Death of the Flea Circus Director or Ottocare Weiss Reforms His Firm* (1973).

Daniel Schmid has emerged as an important German-Swiss director, serving his apprenticeship with Fassbinder and Peter Lilienthal. His baroque tendencies revealed themselves in *Tonight or Never* (*Heute Nacht oder Nic*, 1972), filmed in color and 16mm, blown up to 35mm for commercial release. Made on the minuscule budget of $20 thousand, it stages a bizarre annual dinner during which servants and masters change places, only to firmly retrench themselves in their original positions come midnight. This was followed by the highly acclaimed *La paloma* (1974), which received a measly government subsidy of $10 thousand. Schmid has said that the film could be a dream, as its love story works as a liberation of the imagination, an essence without logic and without rationality.

The phenomenon that put this small country on the cinematic map was Group Five, formed in the late sixties in Geneva, an unofficial band of mutually supportive directors. The films of Michel Soutter, Yves Yersin, Jean-Louis Roy, and especially Claude Goretta and Alain Tanner burst the bubble of Swiss isolationism. They had been *cinéastes* involved in film societies and the Swiss Film Today, a series of weekend-long forums where young filmmakers showed their films to audiences composed of dilettantes, critics, officials and colleagues. Yersin has shown equal adeptness in shorts such as *Angele* (1968) and features such as *Little Experiences (Kleine Erfahrungen)* and documentaries such as *The Last Home Lacemakers (Die letzten Heimposamenter,* 1973). His *Little Escapes (Les petites fugues,* 1979) played for over ninety weeks in five key cities. Jean-Louis Roy made his debut in 1967 with *The Unknown of Shandigor (L'inconnu de Shandigor)* and received major critical attention with *Black-Out* in 1970. Based on a true incident reported in the newspapers, it tells the story of an old couple who become overwhelmed with fear and anxiety. Having lost touch with reality and seeing phantom images of their dead son, they barricade themselves in their home and plan their suicide. Their state of mind is perfectly reflected by Roy's style, which emphasizes enclosed areas, ambiguous images, and lack of spatial perspective.

Michel Soutter chose a very different vein of filmmaking. He began as an assistant to Goretta and Jean-Jacques Legrange, an original member of Group Five. Soutter's low-budget, 16mm film, *The Moon With Teeth (La lune avec les dents),* was made for Swiss television and cost under $5,000; it displays a comic world in which characters rely on chance encounters in order to make decisions. Each of his films— *Escapade (L'escapade,* 1973), *The Surveyors (Les arpenteurs,* 1972), and *James or Not (James ou pas)* tells a simple anecdotal story that relies on witty dialogue and ironic situations involving people who interact even though they have nothing in common.

The two of Group Five who have succeeded in transcending national boundaries of all kinds are Claude Goretta and Alain Tanner. They had similar experiences before directing features in Switzerland: both of them had studied at the University of Geneva and cofounded the film club there. Then they worked for the British Film Institute, collaborating on the short *Nice Time* (1957), an impressive debut film about young people enjoying Saturday night festivities in provincial England. Goretta and Tanner later returned to Switzerland to work for television; many of their features have been made for that medium. Goretta's *To Live Here (Vivre ici),* a television film, won a major prize in 1969.

*The Crazy One* (*Le fou*, 1970) proved to be even more convincing and polished. Francois Simon plays a *petit bourgeois* who, as Goretta put it, "lives in hope of liberation and when he sees nothing coming, finds an individual solution that leads him to madness."[1] Goretta adapted a Chekhov story in *Memory of Lost Lives* (*Le memoire des vies perdues*, 1964) and Maupassant in *Wedding Day* (*Le jour de noce*, 1970), also for television, a film that has been favorably compared to Jean Renoir's *A Day in the Country* (*Partie de campagne*, filmed 1936, released 1946). Goretta is best known outside Switzerland for *The Wonderful Crook* (*Pas si mechant que ca*, 1974), starring Gerard Depardieu and Marlene Jobert, and *The Invitation* (*L'invitation*, 1973), which earned him an Oscar nomination and a jury prize at Cannes. About the power of eros over reality, *The Invitation* portrays a group of office workers who are invited to a summer lawn party. The group gets involved in myriad activities that they would normally shun, including drunkenness, hysteria, and striptease. This microcosm of society has received an invitation to its own disintegration. Goretta later moved to Paris where he directed a remarkable film, *The Roads of Exile* (1978). Starring Francoise Simon in an unforgettable performance as Jean-Jacques Rousseau, the film is one of the few totally successful attempts at combining biography and philosophy. Its images are incredibly rich, its balance of awe and criticism toward a figure as monumental as Rousseau remarkable, and its rhythm, composed largely of static images, is maintained throughout its 169 minutes.

Alain Tanner has achieved what no one in Switzerland before him has: international distribution, prolific output (although always on a small budget), a loose repertory company of performers, critical acclaim, and box-office rewards. His films constitute an ongoing dialogue with his audience, always centered on one major issue: the individual's place in society. The title character in *Charles Dead or Alive* (*Charles mort ou vif*, 1969), again starring Francois Simon, questions bourgeois society by renouncing it and wandering on his own journey to self-discovery. *The Salamander* (*La salamandre*, 1971), distributed by Filmpool, an organization set up in 1973 for Swiss films not acquired by commercial distributors, was a major success. In the film two filmmakers in search of a script latch onto Rosamunda who, nevertheless, defies their attempts to pigeonhole her into a certain type of character. She is both a unique individual and a product of her society. Like Soutter's characters, Tanner's do not act predictably; each character is clearly in the midst of evolving and he or she intersects with others at various points in their evolutions.

Considered by many to be Tanner's masterpiece, *The Middle of the World* (*Le milieu du monde*, 1974), like the best of Swiss films in the past twenty years, breaks through the Swiss sense of comfortable isolationism. (It received a small government subsidy of $20 thousand.) In it

Alain Tanner's films have garnered international praise. In *The Salamander* (1971) two filmmakers meet Rosamunda, who both delights and baffles them.

Tanner's masterpiece, *The Middle of the World* (1974), explores the isolation of modern-day Europe through the story of two individuals.

Tanner's bittersweet political comedy *Jonah Who Will Be 25 in the Year 2000* (1976) offered an ironic and sympathetic portrait of post-1960s disappointment and alternative lifestyles.

Adriana, an Italian waitress, is aware of being a foreigner in Switzerland, and Paul, a Swiss engineer, also has moments when he feels like a foreigner in his own land. Adriana is the critical presence, the objective observor of the "other"; Paul has an official facade behind which is a man divided against himself. Tanner remarked that there are three Pauls: the official, the dreamer, the ridiculous boy. After this came *Jonah Who Will Be 25 in the Year 2000* (*Jonas qui aura vingt-cinq ans en an 2000*, 1976) a bittersweet political comedy about eight people who have all tried different ways to resolve their conflicts with society. They grapple alternately with hope for change and with cynicism over existing conditions. None seems successful in his or her own mind. One, for example, is a supermarket cashier who is arrested for charging customers only what she thinks they can afford. Coscripted with John Berger on the basis of conversations over a ten-day period, Tanner lovingly portrays these refugees from 1968 in a nonnarrative style with elliptical dialogue. It was awarded the critics' prize at Locarno.

Tanner's individual style allowed him to be critical of Swiss customs, without being either provincial or imitative of Hollywood. In order to continue, however, he had to follow a path necessary for Swiss productions due to the lack of government subsidy—coproductions. Federal funding was cut in half between 1975 and 1978 due to inflation, at a time when American films accounted for 52 percent and Swiss films only 2½ percent of the market. One-third of the funding came from the government; the rest depended upon regional funding from sources such as small television stations or even supermarket chains. In 1980 only half the amount of the decreased federal funding went toward production; the other half going to clubs, or used for prizes and scholarships. Coproduction with France covered 50 percent to 80 percent of production, including Tanner's 1980 *Light Years Away*. Starring Trevor Howard as the proprietor of a defunct garage and shot on location in Ireland, Tanner filmed it in English because, he said, it all sounded better in English. It could also be that, as the Dutch discovered, English-language film is more easily marketed. The coproduction system has also brought Godard back to his native country for the making of his ironic *Every Man for Himself* (*Sauve qui peut/La vie*, 1980), his film about a crew trying to make a film, *Passion* (1982), with a truly international cast including Isabelle Huppert, Hanna Schygulla, and Jerzy Radziwilowicz, and his highly controversial *Hail Mary* (*Je vous salue Marie*, 1984). Bresson's stylistically rigorous *Money* (*L'argent*, 1983), has continued the French-Swiss cinematic alliance.

The remainder of the productions rely on a coproduction accord with countries other than France. Tanner's latest film, *In the White City* (*Dans la ville blanche*, 1982) was a joint effort with Portugal and stars Bruno Ganz as a Swiss engineer who becomes captivated with Lisbon. It exhibits a change of style for Tanner: there is a stronger sense of alienation and cynicism and there is very little dialogue. Switzerland and Turkey teamed up for the impressive *Yol* (1983), directed by Yilmaz Güney (recently deceased). Partially directed by Güney from his prison cell in Turkey, it won the Palme D'or at Cannes for its scathing treatment of backwardness and repression in Turkish society. The enormous obstacles Güney faced in completing the film and his undying insistence on the right of self-expression apply figuratively to the entire situation Swiss filmmakers have struggled in for the past thirty years. *Yol* is but an extreme example of the hardships any of the filmmakers discussed in this chapter undergo in order to find funding and distribution for a film project.

## NOTE

1. Gerard Langlois, "Entretrien avec Claude Goretta," *Cinéma 73* (Paris), no. 175, p. 33.

## SELECTED BIBLIOGRAPHY

Barron, Fred. "Letter from Switzerland." *Take One* (Montreal) 4, no. 11 (May–June 1974): 36–37.

*Il cinema svizzero*. Bologna: Cineteca Comunale, 1974.

Forbes, Jill. "Interview with Alain Tanner." *Films and Filming*, no. 329 (February 1982): 20–22.

Langlois, Gerard. "Entretien avec Claude Goretta." *Cinéma 73* (Paris), no. 175 (1973): 33–34.

Laurendeau, Francine, "Jean-Luc Bideau, comedien suisse." *Cinéma Québec* 3, no. 4 (December 1973–January 1974): 42–44.

Schenk, Rolf. "Is There a Swiss Film Industry?" Trans. Harriet R. Poit. *Film Society Review* (October 1967): 36–37.

Rubinstein, Lenny. "Keeping Hope for Radical Change Alive—An Interview with Alain Tanner." *Cinéaste* 7, no. 4 (winter 1976/77): 24–25.

Volontiero, Guglielmo. "Un cinema povero in un paese ricco," in *Viaggio sul Reno: identità del cinema europeo*. Leonardo Quaresima and Sandro Toni, eds. Mostra Internazionale del Cinema Libero di Porretta Terme, 1981.

Wollenberg, H. H. "The Scene in Switzerland." *Sight and Sound* 16, no. 64 (autumn 1948): 144–149.

# TURKEY

## AYSE FRANKO

From its beginnings in 1914 up to the 1950s Turkish cinema was a "cinema of theater," in the hands of stage actors and stage directors like Muhsin Ertuğrul, who used cinema to film plays, using theatrical settings and camera angles. The post-World War II period saw both the advent of Turkish pluralist democracy and the rise of an authentic cinematography in Turkish cinema.

The year 1945 also marks the beginning of the end of the importation of Egyptian films, which reached its height between 1939 and 1944, owing to the unavailability of European films. In time, Egyptian films were banned, first in a few cities, then gradually throughout the country. Their absence created a need for domestic production. Aside from encouragement from municipalities, businessmen began to see cinema as a profitable enterprise and an investment; thus the bases of Yeşilçam (Turkish Hollywood) were laid. The number of production companies went up from two in 1939 to eight in 1948 and to twenty in 1959. Along with this, the number of films produced went up from three in 1939 to sixteen in 1949, twenty-three in 1959 and fifty in 1952. During the years from 1952 to 1958 a variety of films were produced. Some placed documentary footage about the Korean war within a fictional story, some featured popular singers, and some focused largely on violence. There were cheap melodramas and impossible love stories between people of different classes. Despite the profusion of such films, a few filmmakers tried to form a language of cinema and showed a concern with socioeconomic problems in their choice of subject matter. Even though many of their films were bad imitations of Hollywood products, their attempts showed that they had broken the grip of the "cinema of theater" on Turkish film. The most important of these filmmakers are Lütfi Akad, followed by Metin Erksan, Atıf Yılmaz, Muh-

harrem Gürses, Memduh Ün, Halit Refiğ, Ertem Göreç, Duygu Sarıoğlu, and Orhan Elmas.

Lütfi Akad's *In the Name of Law* (*Kanun Namına*, 1952) started a
new period in Turkish cinema. Camera movements and editing techniques were revolutionary. The story is based on a newspaper story of a
murder. The wife of a lathe operator leaves her jealous husband and returns to her parents' home, refusing to reconcile. One day the furious
husband takes a gun and goes to his in-laws. When he can't find his
wife, he shoots his in-laws as well as a watchman who comes to help,
and finally commits suicide. The film is important not only for its technical innovations but also for being the first Turkish film to deal with
the problems of a big city like Istanbul, as presented through the life of
ordinary people in their own surroundings.

Other films of this period show the development of social concern in
Turkish cinema. *Murder In Ipsala* (*Ipsala cinayeti*, 1953), directed by
Lütfi Akad, is a social study of the period. It depicts the move from village to city, the increase of slums, the conflict between villager and
urbanite, and the consequent increase in crime. *Murdering City* (*Öl-
düren şehir*, 1954), directed by Lütfi Akad, is another social study of the
problem of life in the slums. It deals with conflict between urban and
rural life. *The Desire of the Bride* (*Gelinin Muradı*, 1957), directed by
Atıf Yılmaz, concentrates on class differences in a small town, the conflict between two rural landlords (aghas) and other townspeople. *Three
Friends* (*Üç Arkadaş*, 1958), directed by Memduh Ün, is about friendship, love, and support in an environment of danger, difficulties, and
meanness. Ün's social concern and film technique make *Three Friends*
one of the most important films in the development of a film language
in Turkey.

These first cinematographic films were the seeds of Young Turkish
Cinema, which advanced further in the congenial atmosphere of the
sixties. The 1961 constitution, prepared after the revolution of May
1960, brought political freedom, including the right of worker unions to
strike, freedom of speech and thought, and the right to have gatherings and marches. As political pressure lifted and censorship became
lighter, the kind of films to be produced became more defined. Akad's
films were taken as models, and there were more and more films of social significance, rather than cheap melodramas. These films were to
form the National Cinema or the Young Turkish Cinema. Some of the
major films: *The Awakening in the Dark* (*Karanlıkta uyananlar*, 1964),
directed by Ertem Göreç, which deals with employer-employee relations. Production of this film was only possible because of the political
freedom that the revolution of May 1960 brought. *The Dry Summer*
(*Susuz yaz*, 1965), directed by Metin Erksan, focuses on village problems such as the ownership of water and land. The film was smuggled
out of Turkey and shown at the Berlin Film Festival, where it won the

Golden Bear award. This not only attracted the attention of intellectuals and critics in Turkey; it also inspired an organization within Yeşilçam that was to be the first step in the formation of a National Cinema. *The Endless Road* (*Bitmeyen yol*, 1965), directed by Duygu Sarıoğlu, was only shown in 1967 because of problems with the censorship commission. (A commission accepts or rejects all films in Turkey and decides how much of a film or what film can be shown.) About the migration of six villagers to Istanbul and their struggles to live, it is considered the most important film in the formation of Young Turkish Cinema. *The Law of the Border* (*Hudutların kanunu*, 1967), directed by Lütfi Akad, was shot in southeast Anatolia, and deals with the smuggling problem characteristic of the area.

The development of a film language and interest in social problems since the '50s can be considered as preparation, a preliminary study, for the birth of Young Turkish Filmmakers/The National Cinema. The interest of those filmmakers in social problems received the support of the people as well as intellectuals who were indifferent toward the medium until then. Thus, in the seventies, the Turkish cinema unknown to the rest of the world gained recognition thanks to subject matter and technique characteristic of Turkey.

The rise of Young Turkish Cinema owes much to Yılmaz Güney. Güney's extremely internalized acting style and roughhewn look (he was nicknamed the "Ugly King") made him Turkey's most popular film actor in the mid-sixties. During that time, he starred in more than twenty films a year, most of which were the commercial melodramas that constituted far and away the biggest segment of the Turkish industry (turning out about three hundred features a year then). By 1968 Güney rejected the traps of stardom and demanded total independence. He set up a production company and made a series of films on his own. His career was one long crisis and struggle, reflected in the titles of his films: *Hope* (*Umut*, 1971), *Elegy* (*Ağıt*, 1971), *Anxiety* (Endişe, 1974), *Sufferers* (*Zavallılar*). That career was interrupted three times by imprisonment, for what he learned were political reasons, but Güney continued filmmaking from prison by a kind of remote control. Of all his films *Hope* was a milestone for Güney as well as for Turkish cinema. It analyzes social problems with a realism and a rage for which there was no precedent, and has become a prototype for all such films to be made in the future—though not by Güney, who died in 1985.

The title *Hope*, as Güney put it, stands for a general characteristic of the Turkish people—hope and waiting. Thus hope is the symbol of social disorder. In the film Güney plays Cabbar, the illiterate coachman in Adana, whose only hope is to win a lottery. One day his coach is hit by a car and one of the horses is killed. Cabbar is found guilty even though he is blameless, and the tribunal refuses him any sort of compensation for damages. Helpless, he sells everything he owns, aside from a revolver, and his creditors come and take away his coach and only horse. Cabbar then joins a march organized by coachmen against a decision to ban coaches. As things get tougher, he sinks into petty crime and becomes physically violent, taking out his frustrations on his wife and children. Cabbar and a friend then join forces with a crippled holy man and the three of them go off in search of treasure hidden somewhere in the desert. After a month of digging in suffocating heat, Cabbar goes mad and covers his eyes. The film ends with Cabbar walking round and round without stopping. In short, it is the story of a man and a trade both destined to become victims of industrial development. (The Turkish Government banned this film and forbade its entry in the Cannes Film Festival. A print was smuggled out anyway and shown during the 1971 directors' fortnight.)

*Elegy* is a harsh story of smugglers in an isolated mountain region; *Anxiety* deals with cotton pickers in the area around Güney's hometown, Adana. Completed by Şerif Göen because of Güney's imprisonment, *Friend* (*Arkadaş*, 1974) is based on the story of an ex-convict visiting his childhood friend and his undermining effect on a rich man's household. It is a film about the individual's achieving awareness; in this case, the corrupted bourgeoisie becomes aware of its origins. *The Herd* (*Sürü*, 1980) was written by Güney in prison and directed by Zeki Ökten. Shown in the Berlin, Locarno, and London film festivals, and at the 1981 Filmex in Los Angeles, its leading actor was Tarık Akan. It is a powerful story of a peasant family's odyssey from a country village to the city, where the film brings out the problems of the nomadic tribes in Turkey. It portrays their struggle for existence in a society that has no place for them. *Yol* (*Yol*, 1983) was written by Güney in Toptaşı prison and directed by Şerif Göen. *Yol* (literally, "the way") charts the incredible journey of a handful of prison parolees who are given a one-week leave. The characters traverse Turkey from west to east. One convict who only longs to see his child bride is incarcerated again when he cannot find his papers at a checkpoint. Another travels in the hope of reconciling himself with his wife and children, even though his in-laws are very much against this reunion. One travels to his home just across from the Syrian border, an area of extensive smuggling and consequently violence. One travels all the way to an isolated village farm where his wife, having shamed the family, must be punished by his own hand. And the fifth goes to meet his fiancée, under the very watchful eyes of her family and chaperons.

Güney's films are so powerful because he believed in his people's cause. His cinema, one of observation, is full of visual details. The settings in which the story takes place are carefully detailed. The characters in his films constitute a gallery of portraits that display different

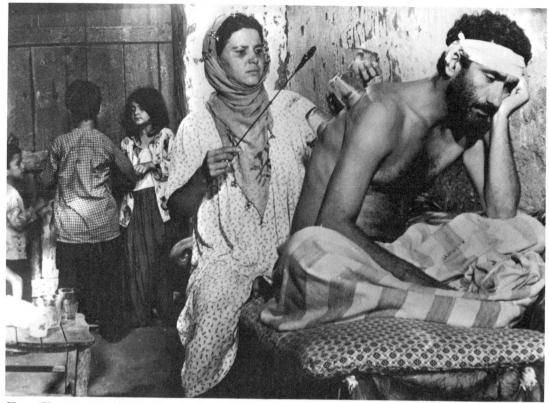

*Hope* (*Umut*, 1971) was a milestone in Turkish cinema and in the career of actor-director Yilmaz Güney, analyzing social problems with unprecedented realism.

Nomadic tribes in a society that has no place for them are the subject of *The Herd* (*Sürü*, 1980), written in prison by Güney and directed by Zeki Okten.

*Yol* (1983), also written by Güney while imprisoned and directed by Serif Goren, follows five prisoners given a week's leave and what happens to each.

segments of the society. The films detail Turkish culture and folklore to the point of being accurate ethnographic documents. This is especially so with *The Herd*, which is about a dying section of the society.

This does not mean to suggest that Yılmaz Güney was the one and only filmmaker of Turkish cinema in the seventies. During this period the postwar cinematographers continued filmmaking and at the same time trained new directors. Many of the new generation of filmmakers express their gratitude to masters like Akad and Güney. Yavuz Özkan, Korhan Yurtsever, Şerif Gören, Ali Özgentürk, Ömer Kavur, Erden Kıral, and Sinan Çetin are some of the directors referred to as the Young Turkish filmmakers. They have basically one thing in common: they criticize the present socioeconomic situation from a political standpoint. Thus, with cinema they drew the attention of the people to socioeconomic problems.

The criticism that they bring is based on Turkey's continuing transition from dying feudalism to capitalism. All other side themes are consequences of this difficult birth. These side themes include: the exploitation of poor villages by the agha (rural landlord), with the most exploited, the most underdeveloped section of the society being described; a rapid, unhealthy urbanization of the country; portrayal of the millions of people who leave their homes in the countryside and seek fortune in the cities; the traumatic clash between country and city life; social inequalities which permit the lowest classes to be swallowed up by the hardship of the city; a social democracy that develops under the sponsorship of city dwellers (this is also displayed in a comic, slightly sardonic manner that attracts a big audience and constitutes a major aspect of commercial Turkish film production); government corruption and vices; the oppression of women in family and social life; and lately the life of Turkish "guest workers" in Europe, especially in Germany as well as their life on their return "home."

A look at some of the films made in this period shows some of the themes mentioned above.

*Yusuf and Kenan* (*Yusuf ile Kenan*, 1980), directed by Ömer Kavur, deals with the experiences of two young boys who come from the countryside to find their uncle in Istanbul. *Over the Fertile Lands* (*Bereketli topraklar uzerinde*), directed by Erden Kıral and based on a novel by Yaşar Kemal, is the story of day laborers who go to southern Turkey yearly, working at different fields as cotton pickers. *Hazal* (*Hazal*, 1982), directed by Ali Ozgentürk, stars Türkan Şoray, Turkey's most famous actress, who has also directed films. The film is about the unlucky bride, Hazal, who is "bought" for the son of the village head man. When the groom-to-be dies, she is married to his ten-year-old brother, as is required by tradition. Hazal runs away with her lover and at last both are killed in order to "cleanse" the honor of the village. This film was praised at Cannes, Montreal, San Sabastian, and Mannheim. *The*

*Horse (At*, 1982), directed by Ali Özgentüurk, concerns a father whose only dream is to save his son from illiteracy and who comes to the city in order to educate him. But he dies and his son is lucky enough to be accepted in an orphanage!

Some of these films met a rather sorry fate in Turkey, not only because of censorship but also because of the oversupply of the market with commercial films, such as musicals, sex films, and melodramas, as well as the competition of television and video. In spite of all the difficulties—an absence of raw stock, problems with distribution, censorship—Turkish cinema has taken giant steps in the last decade. The world is now aware of its existence.

## SELECTED BIBLIOGRAPHY

Nijat, Özön. *Türk Sineması Tarihi* [History of Turkish Cinema]. Istanbul: Artist Publishing Company, 1977.

Oğuz, Makal. "Genç Türk Sinemacıları" [Young Turkish Filmmakers]. Master's thesis, Aegean University, 1981.

*Postif*, no. 227 (February 1980) Presentation by Adrian Turner, no. 256 Juin 1982.

Salih, Gökmen. *Bügünkü Türk Sineması* [Turkish Cinema Today]. Istanbul: Fetih Publishing Company.

*Village Voice* (23 November 1982).

"Yılmaz Güney, His Cinema, His Work, Himself." *Cinema 80*, no. 262 (October 1980).

# UNION OF SOVIET SOCIALIST REPUBLICS

## LEO HECHT

Literature, including drama, has always had a much more important political and social role in the lives of Russians than in most countries in the West. This statement may certainly also be applied to the performing arts, particularly film, which Lenin designated as "the most important art form" in its political impact.

## 1945 to the Death of Stalin

When World War II began, Stalin was facing severe internal political and economic problems. He had just completed a major purge which caused unrest and fears that threatened a united front against the Germans. Against his better judgment he was forced to moderate his intransigence against potential enemies, including the intellectual segment of the population. Although the tenets of "socialist realism," that is, the requirements that all art reflect national spirit, Party spirit, and an ideological base, were not abandoned, Stalin agreed to extend some small degree of artistic leeway to writers, composers, and filmmakers. For this reason films began to concentrate on the personal patriotism of the Soviet citizen rather than on collective Party loyalty. During the war years, Stalin himself was seldom portrayed or glorified, and an uneasy truce was established even with the church, causing the cessation of antireligious propaganda.

One of the best examples of the films of this period was *She Defends Her Homeland* (*Ona zashchishchaet rodinu*, 1943), directed by F. Ermler. A happy family is disrupted when invading Nazis murder a young woman's husband and baby. She undergoes a radical transformation and becomes a ruthless partisan leader. Despite the obvious themes of patriotism and self-sacrifice, this film was attacked by the censors soon after the war for having stressed personal feelings and desires for revenge rather than the good of the collective and the aims of communism. However, in May 1983 this film was selected for showing on national television to open the All-Union Film Festival in Leningrad. The TV program stressed only the positive qualities of the film in its commentary, and even conducted a lengthy interview with the star, Vera Maretskaia.

Although the vast majority of World War II films concerned themselves with the Nazi invasion and the ultimate defeat of the Germans, several historical films of rather high quality were also produced, among them *Ivan the Terrible*—Part 1 (*Ivan Groznyi*, 1944), directed by Sergei Eisenstein; and *Kutuzov* (1944), directed by V. Petrov. There were even some light musicals in late 1944 and early 1945 reflecting the optimism that pervaded the population. This spirit was reflected in the literature and drama of the final war days and was carried over to the time immediately following the capitulation of Germany. The handwriting was on the wall, however. Stalin considered the temporary reprieve he had extended to the arts to be over as soon as the war ended. The process began with the appearance of articles mildly attacking selected writers, composers, theater directors, and filmmakers such as Aleksandr Zarkhi and Iosif Heifits. On 9 February 1946 Stalin delivered a policy speech in which he stated unequivocally that the laxity of Party supervision during the war would be replaced by tightened Party lines and the imposition of complete control necessary for the nation to recuperate from the economic havoc and physical destruction caused by the Germans. The death knell for artistic freedom came later the same year.

On 14 August 1946 the two most beloved Soviet literary figures, the short story writer Mikhail Zoshchenko and the poet Anna Akhmatova, were sharply denounced in "Resolutions Concerning the Journals *Zvezda* and *Leningrad*." On August 28 another resolution, "Concerning the Repertoire of the Dramatic Theaters and the Measures to Be Taken to Improve Them," was published. Finally, on September 4 a resolution on the cinema entitled "Concerning the Film *A Great Life*" was promulgated. These resolutions originated in the Central Committee and were devised by Andrei Zhdanov with Stalin's complete approval. *A Great Life*—Part 2 (*Bolshaia zhizn*, 1946), directed by Leonid Lukov, was attacked for creating a false picture of the Soviet people. It showed some of them as immoral, corrupt, lazy, insensitive, and generally unattractive. In reality, the film was a rather mild sequel to Part 1 (1939). The 1946 film portrays the harsh conditions of the life of coalminers in the Donets Basin as they struggle to rebuild the mines which had been destroyed by the Germans. The film was attacked simply to impress upon the industry that radical changes were imminent. Stalin's socialist realism had to be reimposed. The world could no longer be portrayed as it is, but *as it should and will be* in accordance with Party doctrine. This general ruling was to apply to all works of art, even those which were not overtly offensive. This thinking certainly applied when another film was withheld from public distribution, namely, the second part of *Ivan the Terrible* (*Ivan Groznyi*, 1946). The first part had shown a rather strong-minded monarch who was surrounded by plotting and intrigue emanating from the nobility at court. Although Ivan was shown as ruthless, there was nevertheless a sense of majesty about him which made him worthy of the title of Tsar. He enlarged and protected the empire, as any ruler should. Part 2, however, depicted Ivan as ruthless for the sake of ruthlessness and on the borderline of insanity. The similarities between Ivan and Stalin became obvious when the censored version of the film was finally released in 1958.

Eisenstein, who died in 1948, was not the only one of the elder greats to be silenced. The same fate befell Aleksandr Dovzhenko whose only postwar film, and the first Soviet color film *Life in Bloom* (*Zhizn v tsvetu*, 1946), about the biologist Ivan Michurin appeared in horribly decimated form in 1949. Dovzhenko, disillusioned and ill, died in November 1956 without having made another film. Vsevolod Pudovkin, the third member of the great triumvirate, fared no better. In 1946 he was accused of "cosmopolitanism," i.e., lack of commitment to the Russian heritage, in *Admiral Nakhimov* (1946). Pudovkin decided on the path of least resistance, revised the film, and produced two others which were politically acceptable to the censors. The plot of *The Return of Vassili Bortnikov* (*Vozvrashchenie Vasilia Bortnikova*, 1953) seemed to show some promise in the opening reels but was resolved through the wisdom of the ever-present Party functionary. Pudovkin died the same year.

The subject matter during the years from 1946 to 1953 was extremely limited. There were, of course, a number of World War II films in which the Soviets were always victorious, the soldiers and civilian population showed the heights of morality and culture, and there was no mention of allied involvement or lend-lease programs. This was also a favorite subject for documentaries which often featured Stalin himself; while the fiction films often had him portrayed by leading actors. Some examples are: *The Great Turning Point* (*Velikii perelom*, 1946), directed by Fridrikh Ermler, which was filmed in the ruins of Leningrad and focuses on the decision making and psychological strain on the officers at the top command level; *The Story of a Real Man* (*Povest o nastoiashchem cheloveke*, 1948), directed by Aleksandr Stolper, which brings the war down to the level of the individual soldier, a fighter pilot whose legs were crushed in combat but who crawled back to the Soviet lines in eighteen days; *The Young Guard* (*Molodaia gvardia*, 1948), directed by Sergei Gerasimov, about the struggle of Komsomol members against the Nazis, a film somewhat reminiscent of *Marite* (1947), directed by Vera Stroeva, about a heroic Lithuanian girl who is tortured and killed by the Germans; *The Battle of Stalingrad* in two parts (*Stalingradskaia bitva*, 1949), directed by Vladimir Petrov, which glorifies Stalin's role in planning and commanding the campaign and thereby denigrates the regular officer corps; and *The Fall of Berlin*, in two parts (*Padenie Berlina*, 1950), directed by Mikhail Chiaureli, with music by Shostakovich, which contrasted the calm leadership of Stalin with the hysterics of Hitler and the negative personality of Churchill, and was singled out by Nikita Khrushchev in 1956 as a vivid example of Stalin's "cult of personality."

Another popular subject was anti-American propaganda, since this period saw the initiation of the cold war. The first such film was *The Russian Question* (*Russkii vopros*, 1947), directed by Mikhail Romm, based on Simonov's novel of the same title. Harry Smith, an American reporter, is sent to Moscow to gather information on Soviet preparations for war against the United States. He has a change of heart, returns home in order to expose the real villains, and is destroyed for his honesty. The much touted *Meeting on the Elbe* (*Vstrecha na Elbe*, 1949), directed by Grigorii Aleksandrov, is technically excellent. It concerns itself with a divided town in Germany that is occupied by American and Soviet forces. The Americans loot their half and put Nazis back into power while the Soviets help to rebuild their half and work with democratic Germans. *They Have a Native Land* (*U nikh svoia rodina*, 1950), directed by Aleksandr Fainstsimmer, presents an emotional discussion of the dastardly American intent to prevent forcibly expatriated Soviet children from returning to the Soviet Union. Of course there is no mention of the fact that adults who voluntarily agreed to be repatriated to the USSR were either interned in Soviet labor camps or exiled to remote areas. One of the last films of the Stalin period was *Silver Dust* (*Serebristaia pyl*, 1953), directed by Abram Room. It depicts a black Communist and five other freedom fighters who are jailed on trumped-up charges in an American town. They are to be used as guinea pigs in chemical warfare experiments but are rescued by friends. Additionally, there were several films depicting U.S. espionage in the USSR, both with and without the aid of the Vatican.

The lives and activities of important Russians of the past were the subjects preferred by the Party to instill patriotic pride, and also by writers and directors who felt that this was a relatively safe political area. The rash of biographical films included: *Glinka* (1946), directed by Lev Arnshtam, about the composer's youth; *Lenin* (1948), directed by Vasilii Belaev and Mikhail Romm, a documentary; *Academician Ivan Pavlov* (*Akademik Ivan Pavlov*, 1949), directed by Grigorii Roshal; and *Mussorgskii* (1950), directed by Grigorii Roshal, about the great composer. Among other figures who inspired films were Zhukovskii, a pioneer in aviation, Aleksandr Popov, the alleged inventor of the radio, poets Taras Shevchenko and Dzhambul, literary critic Belinskii, explorer Przhevalskii, and an eighteenth-century naval commander.

A few additional words must be said about the Georgian Mikhail Chiaureli, a talented director who became Stalin's personal protege. His mission was to rewrite Stalin's historical function for the screen. Among the long string of such films was the two-part *Fall of Berlin* (1950) which has already been discussed. The series actually started in 1938 with the release of *The Great Glow* (*velikoe zarevo*) in which Lenin and Stalin are depicted as equal collaborators—a clear distortion of fact. *The Vow* (*Kliatva*, 1946), which concerns itself with Stalin's solemn vow, at Lenin's bier, to carry on in the footsteps of the great leader, was a similar attempt at mythmaking. The final film of the series, *The Unforgettable Year 1919* (*Nezabyvaemyi 1919 god*, 1951), was a highly elaborate and costly production in which Stalin is given sole credit for the suppression of the anti-Bolshevik uprising in Petrograd. All these films were later strongly attacked by Khrushchev.

The last years before Stalin's death in March 1953 saw a steady decline of both the quantity and quality of feature films. In 1952 only five were produced. The more able filmmakers were terribly discouraged by the censorship that forced them to eliminate all elements of psychological controversy from their films. The 1951 edict that the production of black-and-white films, the forte of Russian filmmaking, was to be curtailed and that a large percentage of films be produced in color added to the decline. Agfacolor (called Sovcolor in the USSR) was of low quality, and there was little technical expertise on how to use it most effectively. Color was used primarily to film theater performances on the principal Moscow stages to be shown in more remote areas. By early 1953 approximately thirty such films had been made and enjoyed considerable success due to the Russian's love of theatre. A number of film historians have claimed that the year preceding Stalin's death was one of moderation since an increase of feature films was being encouraged by the Party. This is highly doubtful since there is proof that Stalin, up to the day of his death, was working on a plan for a series of new purges directed against intellectuals and the artistic community.

## From the Thaw Through the Sixties

At Stalin's death, the initial attitude of the Soviet cultural community was one of wait and see. The upheavals within the Party leadership and the accompanying internal purges created a feeling of insecurity and doubt. Everyone was wondering who among the leaders, Beria, Molotov, Malenkov, would emerge victorious, and what direct effect it would have on cultural development. For this reason, very little worthwhile was accompanied during this first year. No one was going to commit himself before some indication of policy was released by the Kremlin. The signal did not come until 1954 when Ilia Erenburg published his symbolic novel *The Thaw*, which became the codeword of Soviet culture for the next several years. What occurred was a veritable explosion of literature and art. All writers who had been "writing for the drawer" for years suddenly produced finished manuscripts—*Doctor Zhivago* was certainly the best example. All artists who had been "painting for the closet" were permitted to exhibit thousands of fine paintings. The Congress of Writers met for the first time in twenty years. Many artists, writers, playwrights and, composers who had been silenced for years now reappeared and participated in all artistic functions.

In the cinema a new generation of directors appeared, while several of the older generation started to do what they had wanted to do for years. This was a period of measured and careful innovation and experimentation by all artists who tried to feel out how far they could go. The limits were set in an erratic manner. Throughout the period it was not unusual for a highly controversial piece of literature or art to be deemed acceptable, while works that seemed to be utterly harmless were soundly condemned and their creators persecuted.

For the cinema the period was ushered in by a number of changes. Foremost was a return to the black-and-white medium with which directors felt most comfortable. In addition, more and more legitimate stage directors and artists swelled the ranks of filmmakers. Many of the best products were created outside Great Russia, predominantly by Georgians. Russian classical literature became one of the central themes of films. In 1956 the first films for television were made, as were a large number of full-length cartoon features and children's films. Younger stage directors started to make films alongside their elders, a number of whom had changed their political tune after Stalin's death. The main change, however, was in the treatment of human relationships which now transcended political considerations. Some of the better early examples of this genre included: *Unfinished Story* (*Neokonchennaia povest*, 1955), directed by Fridrikh Ermler, a poignant apolitical love story between a woman doctor and her crippled patient; *The House I Live In* (*Dom v kotorom ia zhivu*, 1957), directed by Lev Kulidzhanov and Iakov Segel, a low-keyed, understated, neorealist film that follows the lives and aspirations of the inhabitants of a house in a Moscow suburb during and after World War II; *Soldiers* (*Soldaty*, 1957), directed by Aleksandr Ivanov, a depiction of the psychological metamorphosis within a soldier as he fights, kills and sees his comrades dying; *Seriozha* (1960), directed by Georgii Danelia and Igor Talankin, a tender story with subtle humor as the world of adults is viewed through the eyes of a child; *Nine Days of One Year* (*Deviat dnei odnogo goda*, 1961), directed by Mikhail Romm, which courageously discusses the personal and social problems and the internal conflicts within several atomic scientists, questioning a human being's responsibilities to fellow human beings and to future generations; *Ivan's Childhood* (*Ivanovo detstvo*, 1962), directed by Andrei Tarkovskii, a somewhat surrealistic film that poignantly shows how a child is robbed of childhood by war. Possibly the best film of this genre, and the one which was most successful in the West, was *Ballad of a Soldier* (*Ballada o soldate*, 1958), directed by Grigorii Chukhrai, which covers a six-day leave with which a young soldier is rewarded for heroism in the front lines. He goes home to see his mother, interacts with many people who make demands on his sparse time, falls in love, and then returns to the front to kill and be killed. The film is simple, poetic, and contains excellent photography.

Another area warranting careful consideration are the films that thrived on controversy and even attacked facets of the political system. This was a grave departure from the Stalinist doctrine of the elimination of conflict and the caveat against social and political criticism. *Alien Relatives* (*Chuzhaia rodnia*, 1955), directed by Mosei Shveitser, takes place on a Kolkhoz and concerns itself with the conflict between the individual and the commune; *The Immortal Garrison* (*Bessmertnyi garnizon*, 1956), directed by Zakhar Agranenko and Eduard Tisse, adapted from a novel by Konstantin Simonov, portrays the fall of the Brest-Litovsk garrison to the Germans in 1941 and hints at the lack of preparedness of the Soviet army. This battle had never been publicly discussed before, since defeats were always unmentionable. *Clear Sky* (*Chistoe nebo*, 1961), directed by Grigorii Chukhrai, touches upon a subject previously taboo—the return of Soviets from Germany after the war. A Soviet pilot is shot down and interned by the Nazis. When he is finally repatriated from an internment camp, he is faced with distrust, becomes a social outcast, and is expelled from the Party after a frame-up. A clear indictment of Stalin, *The Chairman* (*Predsedatel*, 1964), directed by Aleksei Saltykov, was a big box-office success. It concerns itself with the hardships, red tape, and underhanded illogical requirements levied on a Kolkhoz chairman by Stalin's administrative machine of the forties. *The Falling Leaves* (*Padaiushchie listia*, 1968), directed by Otar Ioseliani, satirizes industrial inefficiency in a Georgian wine-producing plant. National differences are brought out when the Georgians make certain that only the poor grades of wine are served to the Russians. *Three Days of Viktor Chernyshev* (*Tri dnia Viktora Chernysheva*, 1968), directed by Mark Ozepian, examines society's responsibility and obligations to the individual, rather than the reverse. Another taboo, juvenile delinquency, is also one of the main themes of this film.

Two additional films of this genre deserve a special place. They are certainly among the very best films ever produced in the Soviet Union, and enjoyed great success abroad. *The Cranes Are Flying (Letiat zhuravli*, 1957), directed by Mikhail Kalatozov, was an adaptation of Viktor Rozov's play *Alive Forever*. The black-and-white photography is reminiscent of the work of Eisenstein, Pudovkin, and Vertov. Many hailed it as a renaissance of the old tradition. It is a nonpolitical World War II story concerned with human relationships, emotions, and ethics. As a critique of war, treachery, dishonesty, cowardice, and guilt, it is a clear reversal of the numerous war propaganda films. *Andrei Rublev*, directed by Andrei Tarkovskii, was completed in 1967 but released in an altered state in 1969. It is a lengthy two-part film describing the adult life of the most important Russian iconographer in the early fifteenth century. Although it captures the spirit of the times and is historically accurate, its primary intent is not to be a biographical-historical epic, but rather a strong affirmation of the role of the artist in a hostile sociopolitical environment. Rublev discovers that governments, politics, wars, cruelty, inhumanity come and go, while the beauty and importance of art transcends and outlasts all, an idea that caused Tarkovskii severe problems with the censors.

One type of film which has traditionally been considered more important than it is, and to which unwarranted political significance has been attributed, is the satire, which started with the onset of the thaw as a pressure valve. The hunger for sophisticated humor was appeased, but it was carefully orchestrated by the Party. It was no crime, during the anti-Stalin campaigns of the fifties and sixties, to satirize officialdom of the Stalin era, and there were some contemporary targets which were fair game, such as the incompetence and dishonesty of selected officials, and red tape which, according to Party media, was to be exterminated. It was therefore quite in keeping with policy to poke fun at them as long as safe parameters were observed. One of the first such films was *True Friends (Vernye druzia*, 1954), directed by Mikhail Kalatozov, which satirically describes the activities of three friends who band together to combat the frustrations created by an inept bureaucracy. The film was very well done, quite humorous, and a box-office success. *The Girl Without an Address (Devushka bez adresa* 1957), directed by Eldar Riazanov, was a very funny social satire about a young woman struggling through the maze of officialdom. The Georgian director Leonid Gaidai turned out a number of similar satirical comedies during the following decade, the most successful of which were *The Bridegroom from the Other World (Zhenikh inogo sveta*, 1958), *The Businessmen (Biznesmeny*, 1963), and *The Caucasian Prisoner (Kavkazskii plennik*, 1967).

There was a distinct difference between the Stalin era's films about Lenin and those which appeared in the sixties. *On the Same Planet (Na tom zhe planete*, 1965), directed by Ilia Olshvanger, was a highly controversial detente film that depicted Lenin in his final years, not as the physical wreck he really was, but full of energy and even vigor. Stalin is portrayed as a brooding, negative figure. The most interesting sections of the film deal with Lenin's conviction that the United States could be trusted and that a closer relationship should be established. *Lenin in Poland* (*Lenin v Polshe*, 1965), directed by Sergei Iutkevich, was a Soviet-Polish coproduction. It showed Lenin as a down-to-earth human being rather than as a semideity. *Stories About Lenin* (*Rassazy o Lenine*, 1957), directed by Sergei Iutkevich, and *The Ulianov Family* (*Semia Ulianovykh* (1957), directed by Valentin Nevzorov, were much in the same vein. *Lenin in Switzerland* (*Lenin v Shveitsarii*, 1966), directed by Grigorii Aleksandrov, also portrays Lenin as an infinitely humane leader among a group of Russian exiles. Mark Donskoi directed two Lenin films both of which approach the leader through his relationship with his mother, in a nearly lyrically poetic manner: *A Mother's Heart* (*Serdtse materi*, 1966) and *A Mother's Devotion* (*Vernost materi*, 1967).

Several directors tried their hand at multipartite epics based on Soviet literature. The most successful of these was *The Road to Calvary* (*Khozhdenie po mukam*), adapted from Aleksei Tolstoi's novel and divided into three parts all of which were directed by Grigorii Roshal: *The Sisters* (*Sestry*, 1957), *The Eighteenth Year* (*Vosemnadtsatyi god*, 1958), and *Gloomy Morning* (*Khmurnoe utro*, 1959). *Pavel Korchagin* (1957), directed by Aleksandr Alov and Vladimir Naumov, was a well done epic interpretation of Nikolai Ostrovskii's novel *How the Steel was Tempered*. There were many other films based on Russian literature, adapting the work of Gorkii, Dostoevskii, Maiakovskii, Sholokov, Gogol, Chekhov, and many others. The most lavish of these productions was of Leo Tolstoi's *War and Peace* (*Voina i mir*, 1964), directed by Sergei Bondarchuk, in four parts running eight hours, a 70mm color film that took five years and $40 million to make.

A number of Shakespeare's plays were also adapted for the screen at this time. Russians have always been convinced that Shakespeare was a Russian at heart and that only they know how to stage him correctly. The first such film was *Othello* (1955), directed by Sergei Iutkevich, who had unsuccessfully attempted to make this film under Stalin. Grigorii Kozintsev's outstanding *Hamlet* took several years to create and was finally released in 1964. Kozintsev had also made the highly successful adaptation of *Don Quixote* in 1957. Screen adaptations of other Western literary masterpieces were virtually nonexistent. There were, however, a small handful of biographical films on non-Soviets, the best of which were probably *Skanderbek* (*Velikii voin Albanii Skanderbek*, 1954), directed by Sergei Iutkevich, about the Albanian leader who fought the Turks; and *Charles Darwin* (1960), directed by Vladimir Shneiderov, which could now be shown since Stalin's personal, ludicrous geneticist Trofim Lysenko was no longer in power.

Another innovation was the filming of operas and ballets. These included Mussorgskii's *Boris Godunov* (1954); Chaikovskii's *Romeo and Juliet* (1955), directed by Lev Arnshtam; Mussorgskii's *Khovanshchina* (1958), directed by Vera Stroeva; Chaikovskii's *Swan Lake* (1957), directed by Z. Tulubeva; Chaikovskii's *Iolanthe* (1963) and *Sleeping Beauty* (1964) directed by Vladimir Gorikker and Kornstantin Sergeev respectively; and a plethora of full-length concert features. Most of these features are in wide-screen color and feature the Bolshoi and Kirov theater troupes.

The Soviets also tried their hand at a multitude of new cinematic genres such as science fiction, which captured the imagination of a number of Soviet writers since it allowed them to make sociopolitical statements without endangering themselves. There were only a handful of these films made, mainly in the late 1950s, without much commercial success. *The Heavens Call* (*Nebesa zovut*, 1960), directed by Aleksandr Kosir, was a technically flawed space adventure of the twenty-first century. There were also some light musicals which did better in rural areas where the audience was less demanding. *Carvinal Night* (*Karnavalskaia noch*, 1957), directed by Eldar Riazanov, was the most successful of these. Several films indicated some new problems the Soviets now had to face, for example, *By the Lake* (*U ozera*, 1969), directed by Sergei Gerasimov, deals with the conflict between engineers who want to construct a factory at Lake Baikal and biologists who warn of the ecological dangers of such a plan. There were also some good comedies that had no political overtones and did not contain satire, the best of which skyrocketed a multitalented young director to fame overnight. Vasilii Shukshin's *There Lives Such a Fellow* (*Zhivet takoi paren*, 1964) concerned itself with a Russian "good Samaritan" type who always tries to be of help, always has a joke or positive comment for everyone, but who hides his own troubles. There were also some cameramen's films, visual delights with artificial plots. Although these films were often excellent, they did poorly at the box office. The best of these, *The Letter That Wasn't Sent* (*Neotpravlennoe pismo*, 1959), directed by Mikhail Kalatozov, concerns a group of geologists who are trying to escape a major brushfire in the Siberian taiga.

The fifties and sixties also witnessed the appearance of numerous non-Russian and non-Ukrainian films made at the studios of the other thirteen republics. The Georgian influence on direction and other creative areas of filmmaking was immense, second only to the Great Russians. There were, however, examples from other nationalities, of which the following is only a small sampling (those titles which do not have a standard Russian translation are listed only under their English titles): *Magdana's Donkey* (*Lurdzha Magdany*, 1955), directed by Tengis Abuladze and Revas Chkheidze, is a warm and tender story set in a small Georgian village at the turn of the century. A little donkey foundling becomes a family's center of hope and love until its owner shows up. *Zumrad* (1962), directed by A. Rakhimov and A. Davidson, portrays the backwardness of Tadzhikistan and concerns itself with the struggle of a woman to assert her social rights against her husband who still clings to the traditional view of male supremacy. *The Story of a Mother* (1963), directed by A. Karpov, is set in 1941 and very successfully portrays the metamorphosis of a simple, illiterate Kazakh woman as she is faced with bitter tragedy of war. *The Icebreaker* (1963), directed by K. Kiisk, concerns itself with the resistance against the Nazi occupation by fishermen on a small Estonian island. *Grandma, Iliko, Ilarion and Me* (*Ia, babushka, Iliko i Ilarion*, 1963), directed by Tengis Abuladze, is the story of a Georgian boy and his family, filled with humor and tragedy, with the message that love and compassion for others gives one's life meaning. *Father of a Soldier* (*Otets soldata*, 1964), directed by Revas Chkheidze, a nearly grotesque tragicomedy about a Georgian peasant who follows his son to the front lines during World War II, was extremely successful. *Hello, It's Me* (1965), directed by Frunze Dovlatian, traces the lives of a group of Armenian physicists during the war and after. *Bakai's Pasture* (1966), directed by Tolomush Okeev, is a lyrically poetic Kirgizian film about rural life in Central Asian highlands. *The 26 Baku Commissars* (1966), directed by A. Ibragimov, tells the story of the execution of twenty-six Azerbaidzhani Communist leaders by the British in 1918. Some of these non-Russian directors, particularly the Georgians, who excelled on their home territory, were offered lucrative positions with Mosfilm and Lenfilm and ended up directing only Russian-language films.

## Into the Seventies

In many respects the early 1970s were a continuation of the late sixties. There were political ups and downs. Khrushchev had been quite permissive at times, but just as restrictive as Stalin at other times. After his departure there was a short interlude of uncertainty, but Leonid Brezhnev ushered in a period of relative stability which was to last until the early eighties. The period of detente made cultural communication and cross-fertilization between the USSR and the West a great deal easier than during previous and subsequent years. Nevertheless, we must not forget that even during the most liberal years many artists were gagged and severely persecuted, not only by the official censors but also by all Party echelons. The most appropriate illustration of this fact is the case of a man who many critics believe is the finest director in the Soviet Union, Sergo Paradzhanov.

Paradzhanov is an Armenian whose real name is Sarkis Paradzhanian and who was born and had his family roots in Tbilisi, Georgia. He started as a director at the Aleksandr Dovzhenko Studio in Kiev where he developed a strong affinity for folk legends and traditions. His first film, which he codirected with A. Bazelian, was *Andriesh* (1954), a Ukrainian fable. *The First Lad* (1958) and *Ukrainian Rhapsody* (1961) were similar in subject matter. He burst upon the international scene with the superb *Shadows of Forgotten Ancestors* (*Teni zabytykh predkov*, 1964), which won sixteen international prizes. Set in a district of Western Ukraine which was then Ruthenia—a part of partitioned Poland occupied by Austria—this nonpolitical film depicts the life of the Huzul population around 1800. It is a study in human emotions, of love and lust, of hatred and murder, of religion and pagan superstition, and is full of pathos and bathos—certainly one of the most memorable films ever made. It is shot in strong, vivid color, a medium Paradzhanov particularly enjoyed and used for great effect. For example, when a hatchet murder takes place the entire screen is filled with red. The green countryside, the mountains, and even the sky turns into a red haze. Yet, despite its foreign successes, the distribution of the film within the USSR was curtailed. Possibly this was due to the removal of Khrushchev, a Ukrainian, the same year. Nevertheless, Paradzhanov was permitted to direct another film, his last, *The Color of the Pomegranate* (*Tsvet granata*, 1969), which he made in Armenia. It is about Sayat Nova, an eighteenth-century Armenian poet and troubadour famous for his lyric love songs, who became the court minstrel of Irakli II of Georgia. He later entered a monastery where he lived for twenty-five years until he was martyred by the Persian invaders in 1795. The film is full of visual imagery. In one scene Sayat is digging a grave for his archbishop in the cathedral when a flock of sheep surges in through the main doors and surrounds him while the choir sings "The Lord is My Shepherd." Sayat dies rather than give up his faith. He is a monk but also an artist who insists on his right to express himself freely in his poetry and to turn away from the secular world—messages which the Party did not care to see propagated on the screen. Paradzhanov was never allowed to direct again. In 1973 he was arrested and sentenced to five years at hard labor. In 1982 he was again arrested on unspecified charges. There are conflicting reports on his present whereabouts.

The fate of another superb talent may further illustrate that film, like all the arts, functions only according to the political whims of the censor. Vasili Shukshin's popular comedy of 1964 has already been discussed. In 1974 he directed, wrote the screenplay for, and starred in *The Red Snowball Tree* (*Kalina krasnaia*). It quickly became a cult movie for young people although a number of scenes had been cut by the censor and distribution was limited. Even the cut version had obvious elements that contradicted Party policy. The story, about an ex-convict who had spent years in prison for armed felonies, involves pimps, prostitutes, and armed thugs, something never portrayed on the screen before. It also shows an alcoholic Kolkhoz chairman, the boredom of peas-

(Left)
A two-part epic directed by Vladimir Petrov, *The Battle of Stalingrad* (1949), falsely glorified Stalin's role in the campaign.

Highly successful at home and abroad, Grigorii Chukrai's *Ballad of a Soldier* (1958) is the best Soviet film about the war.

*Ivan's Childhood* (1962), the first film by Andrei Tarkovskii, was a surrealistic account of a young boy caught up in the war.

Considered the finest film of the decade, Tarkovskii's lengthy two-part *Andrei Rublev* (1967) was released in a cut version in 1969.

Chekhov's plays were the most frequently filmed of literary works. *Uncle Vanya* (1971) was the best film version of that classic.

Chekhov's novella *The Shooting Party* was made into an outstanding film in 1977 with a superb musical score.

The classic Soviet picaresque novel by Ilf and Petrov reappeared as the popular film *The Twelve Chairs* (1971).

Nikita Mikhalkov's *An Unfinished Piece for a Player Piano* (1977) was a superb spoof of all of Chekhov's major plays.

Set in a remote Siberian village, *Siberiada* (1978), directed by Andrei Mikhalkov-Konchalovskii, is an epic film spanning sixty years.

Vladimir Menshov's *Moscow Does Not Believe in Tears* (1980), about three women over a span of 25 years, won the 1981 Academy Award for Best Foreign Film.

Director Aleksandr Zarkhi was able to make his *26 Days in the Life of Dostoevskii* (1981) only after the recent rehabilitation of that writer.

ants forced to attend political meetings, and the hardship of old people who have to live on a pittance after a lifetime of hard work. It also advocates the cleansing quality of the soil, the important of religion, the simplicity and honesty of rural life, and the ingenuous quality of love between a man and a woman. The film clearly states that Russia cannot be saved without the moral force of the peasantry ranged against the cultural disintergration and immorality caused by accelerated urbanization. Shukshin was severely chastized and warned that he would not be able to make another film; he died later the same year (1974).

The examples of Paradzhanov and Shukshin show that great and strongly controversial films can be made in the Soviet Union, but that the cost can be quite high. In the meantime, work in the film industry continued as it had before. Classics continued to be filmed, as did films about historical figures, including foreigners. New genres took on major proportions, such as films for young people, cartoon features, and segmented television films. An ever-increasing number of non-Russian films were distributed in major Russian cities and were very well received. It appears that censors in the other republics were not as narrow-minded as the Russians. In fact, the market was so saturated with such films that, by this time, it is no longer meaningful to separate Russian from non-Russian films in this listing.

Any discussion of controversial films of this period must include *Solaris* (1971), superbly directed by Andrei Tarkovskii, a 70mm color spectacle which many call the Russian *Space Odyssey*. This innovative symbolic, metaphysical work questions whether man should attempt to venture into space before cleaning up the mess he has made on earth. The film had a very short run at only selected theaters. *Bow to Fire* (*Poklonis ogniu*) was made in 1971 but not released until two years later. The Kirkizian director, Tolomush Okeev, took a hard negative look at Stalin's forced collectivization program of 1929 to 1932. *That Sweet Word Liberty* (*Eto sladkoe slovo—svoboda*, 1973), directed by Vytautas Zalakevicius, started out as a pure propaganda film based on a real event in Venezuela, but there is more to it. It is about Communist revolutionaries in Latin America and was made in Chile under Allende. The leaders of a revolutionary group are captured by the rightists. The horde of revolutionaries becomes totally ineffectual without them. The only solution was to try to free the leaders. The film points out the paralysis of such organizations without Party leadership, and the distaste for personal initiative among the followers. *Old Walls* (*Starye steny*, 1974), directed by Viktor Tregubovich, was one of the many films in the "lathe and tractor" category. This one, however, portrays the generation gap and the extreme conflict between the older workers and the fresh, young minds in a textile factory. Even more significant is *The Hottest Month* (*Goriacheishii mesiats*, 1974), directed by Iulii Karasik, which describes the conflict between labor and management in a steel plant on the subject of production targets vs. quality control. Also highly controversial, *Agony (Agonia,* 1975), directed by Elem Klimov, is about the monk Rasputin, somewhat innovative, and with strong Brechtian overtones. For example, supposed historical facts are in black and white, while embellishments are in color. Neither the subject nor the form were acceptable to the censors.

A more important genre of the period was the "personal" film which attempted to eliminate political elements as much as possible and to focus on the life of the individual rather than on the collective. *The Lanfiere Colony* (1970), a Soviet-Czech coproduction directed by Jan Schmidt, discusses the false values and pressures of civilization which drive man to seek solitude and noninvolvement on a desert island. *The Debut (Nachalo,* 1971), directed by Gleb Panfilov, is an interesting film about a bit actress who is suddenly given the starring role in *Joan of Arc.* Both she and the figure she is portraying are heroic in that they accept their fate with personal bravery and dedication. *Anthracite (Antrasit,* 1972), directed by Aleksandr Surin, is a simple story about a coalminer who works hard during the day and tries to cope with overwhelming personal problems when he goes home. *Shine On, Shine On, My Star (Gori, gori moia zvezda,* 1972), directed by Aleksandr Mitta, is a poetic tragicomedy about the attempts of an artist to survive and cope with life during the Russian Revolution. *Melodies of the Veri Quarter (Melodii Veriiskogo kvartala,* 1973), directed by Georgii Shengelaia, is a Georgian musical with a decriptively simple story about a laundress who gives her all so that the children of her lover may attend ballet school. *Mothers and Daughters (Materi i docheri,* 1974), directed by Sergei Gerasimov, is about a young woman searching for the mother who abandoned her as a child. She finds another family by mistake, but learns life from them. *No Return (Vozvrata net,* 1974), directed by Aleksei Saltykov, points out that there is a distinct relationship between the destiny of an individual, in this case the chairwoman of a collective farm, and the destiny of the nation. *The Lovers (Roman o vliublennykh,* 1974), directed by Andrei Mikhalkov-Konchalovskii, is a trite but well-done love story. He goes to sea and is reported lost. She marries. He returns and is heartbroken. He marries another girl whom he doesn't love. Eventually, after she has his child, he falls in love with her. The beginning of the film, when everything is beautiful, is in color. The despair of the middle section is in black and white. The end is again in color. *To Dream and to Live (Mechtat i zhit,* 1974), directed by Iurii Ilienko, is a highly personal film wherein an artist attempts to formulate criteria whereby he can be fulfilled as a human being. *Afonia* (1975), directed by Georgii Danelia, about a simple plumber who has no family or friends and who finds his work unrewarding, is the story of a personal crisis. *The Summer in the County (Leto v derevne,* 1976), directed by Otar Ioseliani, is a philosophical film which centers on ontological questions and on the values of the past imposed upon the present.

As a counterbalance there were all too many unsubtle political propaganda feature films. *The Nineteenth Committee* (*Komitet deviatnadtsatyi*, 1972), directed by Savva Kulish, warned of the dangers of chemical and bacteriological warfare planned by the West. There were also a great number of espionage films in which CIA operatives were always eliminated. *For the Love of Mankind* (*Liubit cheloveka*, 1973), directed by Sergei Gerasimov, is the story of architects and engineers who sacrifice personal comfort for further construction in the far north. The love story of the main characters indicates that individual love is just a part of the love for the collective. Some films appeared to be critical of corruption and therefore controversial, but they were not. The best example was *The Bonus* (*Premia*, 1974), directed by Sergei Mikaelian, which was about a real, well-publicized case of mismanagement and dishonesty against the national economy. The film was, however, the trial balloon for an official Party mini-purge. *Meetings and Partings* (*Vstrechi i proshchania*, 1974), directed by Elior Ishmukhamedov, depicts unintegrated Soviet expatriates in West Germany who become terribly homesick and cannot find peace of mind; happiness in a consumer society is at best illusory and unstable. This film was aimed at the plethora of applications for emigration during this period. In another vein, *When a Woman Saddles a Horse* (1974), directed by Khodzhakuli Narliev, takes place in the twenties. A Turkmen woman runs away from home, becomes educated and liberated, and returns home as the all-powerful local Party secretary. The new has triumphed over the sterile old. *Soldiers of Freedom* (*Soldaty svobody*, 1976), directed by Iurii Ozerov, coproduced with Poland, Hungary, Czechoslovakia, Rumania, Bulgaria, and the German Democratic Republic, was a masterpiece of mythmaking. It depicts the international Communists who led the struggle to liberate their homelands.

World War II films were prevalent during the seventies, a decade which belonged to a new generation of Soviets who had to be indoctrinated into a war they were too young to have experienced. Most of these films were outright propaganda. Others let a bit of personal humanity creep in. The following are the most successful films on this subject: *Liberation* (*Osvobozhdenie*, directed by Iurii Ozerov, is a five-part historical epic on the role of the USSR in the war, and is visually quite impressive. *Salut, Maria!* (*Saliut, Maria!*, 1970), directed by Iosif Heifits, depicts the trials and tribulations of a Spanish revolutionary who flees to the USSR and contributes to the war effort. *The Dawns Are Quiet Here* (*A zori zdes tikhie . . .*, 1972), directed by Stanislav Rostotskii, was probably the best of the war films of this period. It describes the personal conflicts and emotional turmoil of the members of an all-female antiaircraft unit which is completely wiped out by the Germans. *Re-*

*member Your Name* (1974), directed by Sergei Kolosov, was a Polish-Soviet coproduction intending to express eternal friendship between the two nations. A Russian mother and son are separated in a Nazi labor camp. The son is eventually raised by a Polish woman and, many years later, is reunited with his real mother. *Under a Sky of Stone* (1974), directed by Knut Anderssen and Igor Maslennikov, a Norwegian-Soviet coproduction, depicts a Soviet operation into Norway in 1944 to help Norwegians hiding in a mine to escape deportation to Germany. *Dangerous Games (Opasnye igry*, 1974), directed by Velie Kiasper, describes the resistance movement in Nazi-occupied Estonia —another myth. *They Fought for Their Motherland (Oni srazhalis za rodinu*, 1974), directed by Sergei Bondarchuk, in 70mm color, was one of the most popular films of the period. It is a psychological study of 117 soldiers who are ordered to hold a hill against superior German forces. Their mood slowly changes from abject pessimism to optimism. *Flames (Plamena*, 1975), directed by Vitalii Chetvertikov, in consonance with similar attempts by non-Russion nationalities to show their contributions to the war effort, portrays the Belorussian partisan movement. *Brief Encounters in a Long War* (1975), directed by Abdusalem Rakhimov and Stanislav Chaplin, furnishes a war background for a love triangle. *The Only Road* (1975), directed by Vladimir Pavlovic, a Yugoslav-Soviet coproduction, shows the experiences of Tito partisans during a raid. *Blockade (Blokada*, 1975), directed by Mikhail Ershov, is a multisegment 70mm epic about the siege of Leningrad. *Soldier of the Motherland (Soldat rodiny*, 1975), directed by Iurii Chulukin, describes the ordeals of General Dmitrii Karbyshev during his captivity in Germany.

In the same vein quite a number of historical films were made, most of them also depicting armed conflict in previous wars. *Waterloo* (1970), directed by Sergei Bondarchuk, was an Italian-Soviet coproduction, a historical spectacle on a grand scale with an international cast headed by Rod Steiger. *The Last Relic* (1971), directed by Grigorii Kromanov, shows the struggle of the Estonian peasantry against the Germans and Swedes in the fifteenth and sixteenth centuries. *Breakup (Razval*, 1971), directed by Aleksei Saltykov, describes the crew of the cruiser Aurora on the eve of the revolution. One of the nonmilitary historical films was *With You and Without You (S toboi i bez tebia*, 1973), directed by Rodion Nakhapetov, a historical view of the social struggles during Stalin's collectivization period.

Not only famous events but also biographies of famous persons continued to be a popular subject for films. The lives of painters Pirosmanishvili and Goya, the poet Esenin, the physicist Francis Skorina, the singer Chaliapin, the Oriental scholar Abu Raihan Bruni, composers Franz Liszt and Chaikovskii, and of course Lenin were all filmed during the early seventies. *Choice of a Goal (Vybor tseli*, 1975), directed by Igor Talankin, is an interesting study of the Soviet physicist Igor Kurchatov after Hiroshima. He starts to work on the atom bomb with conflicting feelings about his personal responsibility for the future of mankind.

The literary classics also continued to be quite popular. The nearly total rehabilitation of Dostoevskii stimulated the filming of a number of his works including *Crime and Punishment* (*Prestuplenie i nakazanie*, 1970), directed by Lev Kulidzhanov; and *The Gambler* (*Igrok*, 1972), directed by Andrei Batalov. Chekhov's works were the most frequently filmed, including *The Seagull* (*Chaika*, 1971), directed by Iulii Karasik; *Uncle Vanya* (*Diadia Vania*, 1971), directed by Andrei Mikhalkov-Konchalovskii; *The Shooting Party* (*Drama na okhote*, 1977), directed by Emil Lotianu; and *The Steppe* (*Step*, 1977), directed by Sergei Bondarchuk. *Asia* (1977), from Turgenev's short story, was directed by Iosif Heifits. *Father Sergius* (*Otets Sergii*, 1978), from Leo Tolstoi's story, was directed by Sergei Bondarchuk. *The Bedbug* (*Klop*, 1975), directed by Sergei Iutkevich from the controversial play by Maiakovskii, was extremely successful. Gorkii's novella *Makar Chudra* was filmed as *Into the Sunset* (*V zakhod*, 1976), by Emil Lotianu. *The Flight* (*Beg*, 1973), directed by Aleksandr Alov and Vladimir Naumov, created a sensation as the film of a play whose author, Mikhail Bulgakov, had been on the forbidden list for more than a generation. Similarly, the filming of *It Can't Be* (*Ne mozhet byt*, 1975), directed by Leonid Gaidai, after several stories by Zoshchenko, signaled the complete rehabilitation of that writer, also. More recent Soviet writers Konstantin Simonov and Chengiz Aitmatov, who have become legends in their lifetime, also saw their work put on film during this period.

Foreign masterpieces which were filmed included *Hopelessly Lost* (*Sovsem propavshii*, 1973), directed by Georgii Danelia, after Mark Twain's *Huckleberry Finn; Til Eulenspiegel* (1976), directed by Aleksandr Alov and Vladimir Naumov, after Charles de Coster's legend; and Grigorii Kozintsev's superb version of Shakespeare's *King Lear*. The filming of operas and ballets also continued with the work of Prokofiev, Igor Borodin, and Khachaturian.

But there were also humor and comedy. As before, this genre was nearly exclusively non-Russian or, at least, under the direction of non-Russians. *Don't Grieve* (*Ne ogorchai*, 1970), directed by Georgii Danelia, a Georgian comedy, expresses the view that humor and sadness augment each other and that we must be cheerful although life has its sorrows. *Old Brigands* (*Starye razboiniki*, 1971), directed by Eldar Riazanov, is about two old codgers who plot to steal a Rembrandt. The film was severely criticized since it did not set a good example for Soviet senior citizens. *The Twelve Chairs* (*Dvenadtsat stulev*, 1971), directed by Leonid Gaidai, is an adaptation of an extremely popular picaresque novel of the twenties. *Commotion* (1971), directed by Iurii Erzinkian, is a comedy of errors adapted from an Armenian classic. *Ivan Vasilievich Changes His Profession* (*Ivan Vasilievich meniaet svoiu professiu*, 1973), directed by Leonid Gaidai, is a light comedy about a time-machine traveler who arrives at the court of Ivan the Terrible. *The Telegram* (*Telegramma*, 1973), directed by Rolan Bykov, tells the story of two youngsters who find a World War II telegram and decide to play pranks on their elders. *The Tale of How Tsar Peter I Married Off His Moor* (*Rasskaz o tom, kak Tsar Peter I zhenil svoego arapa*, 1976), directed by Aleksandr Mitta, is the story, partly historical and partly from Pushkin, of Peter the Great's favorite, the Ethiopian Ibrahim, who had a problem finding a bride. Ibrahim was portrayed by Vladimir Vysotskii, a very important Russian cult figure who died in 1980.

There is a special category of films for children and youths, which covers a great deal of material from simple cartoons to classics of music and literature. All of them, however, contain a didactic element ranging from imperceptibly subtle to overt political indoctrination. *Adventures of a Yellow Suitcase* (*Perezhivaniia zheltogo chemodana*, 1970), directed by Ilia Frez, traces the experiences of a boy's suitcase that contains pills for bravery. The suitcase is misplaced and the boy finds that he can be brave without it. *The Crown of the Russian Empire* (*Venets russkoi Imperii*, 1971), directed by Edmond Keosaian, tells the story of four Armenian youngsters and their adventures during the civil war after the Revolution. *We Are Waiting for You, Lad* (*Zhdem tebia, paren*, 1972), directed by Ravil Batyrov, portrays the inner conflicts of Uzbek youths as they stand on the threshold of adulthood. *Oh, That Nastia* (*Okh, uzh eta Nastia*, 1972), directed by Georgii Pobedonoscev, is about the misbehavior of a tomboy and her maturation. *The Ferocious One* (*Liutyi*, 1973), directed by Tolomush Okeev, describes how a Kazakh boy raises a wolf cub. Despite the love he has received, the cub grows into a ferocious wolf, and so the film asks, Can cruelty be overcome? Is nature cruel? *Shon and Sher* (1974), directed by Kanimbek Kasimbekov, impresses upon youth that they are a changing, new generation and the future of the nation. *Well, Wait a Moment* (*Nu pogodi*, 1969–74), directed by V. Kotenochkin, was an extremely popular cartoon series composed of eight segments about the adventures of a (very Aesopian) wolf and hare.

This was also a period during which television became a national pastime. The TV divisions of major film studios started producing feature films specifically for television on an irregular basis. These films were either full-length features, or mini-series. *The Whole Truth About Columbus* (*Vsia pravda o Kolumbe*, 1971), directed by Vytautas Zalakevicius, is historical mythmaking in the Brechtian style. It is set in Latin America shortly after the death of Columbus. *Seventeen Flashes of Spring* (*Semnadtsat mgnovenii vesny*, 1972), directed by N. Lioznova, was a twelve-part series, an extremely popular mock-documentary with top performers, about a Soviet spy who became a top official in Nazi intelligence. *The Accident* (*Sluchai*, 1974), directed by Vytautas Zalakevicius, was based on Duerrenmatt's play about the careerism, cynicism, egoism, and moral cowardice of a traveling salesman. *The Red and the Black* (*Krasnoe i chernoe*, 1976), directed by Sergei Gerasimov, was a five-part adaptation of Stendhal's classic. The most successful TV film, later distributed to motion picture theaters nationwide, was *The Irony of Fate—or May Your Steam Be Light* (*Ironiia liubvi—ili, s legkim parom*, 1976), directed by Eldar Riazanov, a relatively simple comedy with excellent dialogue. A Moscow doctor, drunk on the eve of his wedding, is put on a plane to Lenigrad by his friends. When he gets off he gives a taxi driver his Moscow home address, which is identical to one in Leningrad, and his key fits the apartment inhabited by a young woman. The rest is obvious, and both humorous and touching. The background is poetry, set to music, written by outstanding Russian poets who were on the forbidden list before, such as Tvetaeva, Pasternak and Akhmadulina.

## The Most Recent Period

While the trivial contemporary Soviet films unfortunately far outnumber the great ones, some things have, nevertheless, improved. The major dramatic productions of classics such as Shakespeare and Dostoevskii are still filmed only in black and white but most other films are now in color since the Soviets have learned at last how to use it relatively well. The studios have been able to acquire more land, buildings and props to make their product more professional and to increase production. There is a tendency to divide major studios into areas of concentration and to assign entire smaller studios to specific specialties to make them economically more viable. It must be kept in mind that only the very best Soviet products are distributed in the West. The vast majority of Soviet films never leave the country. These are mainly propaganda films (including documentaries); abominably poor spy, detective, and science fiction films, extremely inept historical extravaganzas, and feebleminded comedies.

The "Film Festival—Soviet Cinema Today," shown in a number of major U.S. cities in 1982 and 1983 introduced Americans to films such as: *Easy Money* (*Legkie dengi*, 1981), directed by Evgenii Matveev, a Victorian comedy in which a provincial businessman is tricked into a marriage with a city beauty who proceeds to spend all his money until he puts his foot down; and *The Take Off* (*Vzlet*, 1981), directed by Savva Kulish, in which the life of the space explorer Tziolkovskii, terribly ineptly portrayed by the poet E. Evtushenko, realizes his dreams despite persecution. *The Bodyguard* (1981), directed by Ali Khamraev, in the Kazakh language, is reminiscent of Kurosawa's *Yojimbo*. It is a Central Asian action adventure replete with shootouts and chases, collapsing suspension bridges and narrow escapes, set against a background of Red Army units and political prisoners. *A Woman for Gavrilov* (*Ozhidaia Gavrilova*, 1981), directed by Piotr Todorovski, is about an attractive thirty-eight-year-old bride whose husband-to-be doesn't show up for the wedding. The background is the fasinating city of Odessa and a variety of people whom the woman encounters and whose lives she changes. *A Slap in the Face* (1981), directed by Henrykh Malyan, in the Armenian language, is about an adopted boy who finds that his saddle making profession is not attractive to girls. He finally finds a prostitute and decides to rescue her. *Carnival* (*Karnaval*, 1981), directed by T. Lioznova, is the longest and worst musical ever devised by man. *Vassilii and Vassilisa* (1981), directed by Irina Poplavskaia, is an adaptation of a novel by Valentin Rasputin, the controversial village writer. It is a highly descriptive folk parable that traces the fate of a peasant couple from childhood to old age. *26 Days in the Life of Dostoevskii* (*26 dnei v zhizni Dostoevskogo*, 1981), directed by Aleksandr Zarkhi, is a relatively honest film about the writer's work on the novel *The Gambler* and his relationship with his second wife-to-be. *Moscow Doesn't Believe in Tears* (*Moskva slezam ne verit*, 1980), directed by Vladimir Menshov, was probably the most successfully and widely distributed Soviet film of the past two decades. It won the 1981 Academy Award for the best foreign film. Tracing the life of three women for the last twenty-five years, it was certainly not as good as critics acclaimed it to be, although it did portray life in Moscow as the Soviets would like the West to believe it exists.

Other recent films include *Siberiada* (*Sibiriada*, 1978 but not internationally released until 1982), directed by Andrei Mikhalkov-Konchalovskii. An excellent film set in a remote hamlet in the Siberian tundra, it spans sixty years of civil and scientific disruption. The film is broken into four parts, each focusing on one individual. Possibly the best film of the last decade was *Autumn Marathon* (*Osennii marafon*, 1979–80), directed by Georgii Danelia. It portrays the life of a Leningrad professor-translator, who has an unsatisfying affair with a young woman although he lives with his wife. He is taken advantage of by his co-workers, his neighbors, and his supposed friends, and there is no way out for him. *An Unfinished Piece for a Player Piano* (*Nedokonchennaia pesa na mekhanicheskom pianino*, 1977), directed by Nikita Mikhalkov, is an excellent spoof of all of Chekhov's plays. *Red Bells* (*Krasnye kolokola*, 1981–83), is a three-part eight-hour film using a large international cast and several directors and is based on the life of John Reed. It is soon to be released internationally, most probably as an eight-hour TV film.

Other recent films which have not been released for foreign consumption include: *The Insubordinate Woman* (*Nepokornaia*, 1982), directed by Anatolii Kabulov, an Uzbek film. In 1925 a young woman marries a man who not only adheres to the old principles of male dominance but who belongs to a gang of brigands. She leaves him. *The Strong Guy* (*Krepysh*, 1982), directed by Vadim Alisov, is about a champion trotter of the early twentieth century and the training and racing of horses. *Soul* (*Dusha*, 1982), directed by Aleksandr Stefanovich and Vladimir Klimov, is a biography of the pop singer Viktoria Svobodina. *The Girl and Grand* (*Devushka i Grand*, 1982), directed by Viktor Sadovskii, is a pale reflection of *National Velvet*. A young girl dreams of becoming a competitive rider and has a close relationship with her horse (Grand). *One Hundred Joys, or The Book of Great Discoveries* (*Sto radostei, ili kniga velikikh otkrytii*, 1982), directed by Iaroslav Lupii, is an adaptation of Vitalii Bianki's short stories, which are primarily directed toward a young audience. *Iaroslav the Wise* (*Iaroslav Mudryi*, 1982), directed by Grigorii Kokhan, is about the life, wars, and personal conflicts of the Grand Prince of Russian in the twelfth century. Although it received a number of Soviet prizes, it is one of the worst historical films ever produced despite its considerable budget. *The Fall of the Condor* (*Padenie Kondora*, 1982), directed by Sebastian Alarcon, a Cuban who had directed *Night over Chile* and *Santa Esperansa*. This film, with a Russian cast of the Moscow studios, is about Manuel, a peasant who becomes a soldier and a member of the dictator's personal bodyguard and commits all sorts of atrocities against his own people. *The Expectations of Colonel Shalygin* (*Ozhidanie polkovnika Shalygina*, 1982), directed by Timur Zoloev, is about World War II at the German front. A group of reconnaisance soldiers are able to complete their mission behind enemy lines and return to the Soviet side despite heavy odds.

The years after Brezhnev were marked by instability and pessimism. The rapid change of rules did not allow for the establishment of specific policies concerning the performing arts, except for periodic mentions of the need to observe the doctrine of "Socialist Realism." The conformists among the filmmakers turned out numerous films on "safe" subjects such as World War II, exemplified by films like *Marshal Zhukov* (1984), directed and written by M. Babak, or ancient Russian history, the best example of which was *The Legend of Princess Olga* (*Legenda o kniagine Olge*, 1984), directed by the Ilienko brothers. Numerous fatuous musical comedies were also produced.

More courageous and dedicated directors tested the waters by making films on dangerous subjects. Certainly the most significant of these was *The Blonde Around the Corner* (*Blondinka za uglom*, 1984), by Vladimir Bortko. It deals with "blat," the underground world of black marketeering, influence peddling, and bribery. It was approved by Andropov and released under Chernenko. Another interesting film was *Kindergarten* (*Detskii sad*, made in 1984 and released in 1985), written and directed by the major poet Evgenii Evtushenko. It is an autobiographical film that is courageous because of its avant-garde images and its controversial contents. It deals with the evacuation of children to Siberia during World War II and their conflicts and tribulations.

The XXVII Party Congress took place in February/March, 1986. Most filmmakers expected some kind of policy decisions to be verbalized by Gorbachev during his five and one-half hour introductory speech, but they were disappointed. It appeared that the concerns of the arts would have to take a back seat to economic policy matters for some time to come. Simultaneously, however, a number of theater and film directors spoke out, both orally and in written form, about censorship, funding policies, and other hindrances. On March 17, 1986, a highly important film, *Begin at the Beginning (Nachat s nachala)*, directed by Aleksandr Stefanovich, was released to sell-out audiences. It featured the songs of Vladimit Vysotskii and raises the question of whether his successors, poets and balladeers, will also have to perform in secret and distribute their work on homemade cassettes as before. Specifically, it concerns itself with dissident musician Andrei Makarevich, whose top rock group "Time Machine" is still prohibited from performing in Moscow.

Despite some hopeful signs such as these, it is still too early to speak of a "thaw" under Gorbachev. Most filmmakers have adopted a wait-and-see attitude. The more committed ones are preparing to "probe" the body of the Party to determine how far they can go without antagonizing the system.

As of 1986 there were thirty-nine major film studios in the USSR. Each of the fifteen Union Republics has at least one in its capital. The more important republics have more than one—for example, the RSFSR has five and the Ukraine three. Approximately 150 new feature films are released annually. Additionally, about 100 films for television and 1,450 short films, documentaries, and popular science films and cartoons are also released every year. Daily attendance in motion picture theaters is twelve million. There are 153,000 such theaters in the USSR, of which 16,500 are in urban and 126,500 in rural areas. The average cost of a normal-length film is 600,000 rubles; a double-length film costs about a million rubles. Films are expected to earn a profit, a percentage of which is divided among the director, composer, and writer. Salaries for actors range from 100 rubles to a maximum of 3,500 rubles per film. Bonuses for artistic achievement at home and abroad are distributed separately.

## SELECTED BIBLIOGRAPHY

Works in English

Babitsky, Paul and John Rimberg. *The Soviet Film Industry*. New York: Praeger, 1955.

Birkos, Alexander S. *Soviet Cinema: Directors and Films*. Hamden, CT: Archon Books, 1976.

Cohen, Louis H. *The Cultural-Political Traditions and Developments of the Soviet Cinema 1917–1972*. New York: Arno, 1974.

Dickinson, Thorold and Catherine De la Roche. *Soviet Cinema*. New York: Arno and New York Times, 1972.

Dolmatovskaya, Galina and Irina Shilova. *Who's Who in the Soviet Cinema*. Moscow: Progress, 1979.

*Fifty Years of Soviet Cinema: 1917–1967*. London: British Film Institute, 1967.

Hecht, Leo, ed. *NEWSNOTES on Soviet and East European Drama and Theatre*, periodical, Fairfax, VA: George Mason University.

Hibbin, Nina. *Eastern Europe: An Illustrated Guide*. Screen Series. New York: A. S. Barnes, 1969.

Leyda, Jay. *Kino: A History of Russian and Soviet Film*. New York: Collier Books, 1973.

Liehm, Mira and Antonin. *The Most Important Art: Soviet and East European Film After 1945*. Berkeley: University of California Press, 1977.

Rimberg, John. *The Motion Picture in the Soviet Union, 1918–1952*. New York: Arno, 1974.

Schnitzer, Luda, et. al., eds. *Cinema in Revolution: The Heroic Era of the Soviet Film*. New York: Hill and Wang, 1973.

*Soviet Cinematography*. Bombay: People's Publishing House, Ltd., 1950.

Stoil, Michael Jon. *Cinema Beyond the Danube: The Camera and Politics*. Metuchen, NJ: Scarecrow Press, 1974.

Vorontsov, Yuri and Igor Rachuk. *The Phenomenon of the Soviet Cinema*. Moscow: Progress, 1980.

Vronskaya, Jeanne. *Young Soviet Film Makers*. London: Allen and Unwin, 1972.

Two major distributors of Soviet films in the United States were good enough to supply the stills used in this article:

The International Film Exchange, Ltd., 201 West 52nd Street, New York, NY 10019, distributes a great many of the latest Soviet films to motion theaters throughout this country.

Corinth Films, 410 East 62nd Street, New York, NY 10021, whose most recent catalog lists over 150 Soviet films from the silents of Eisenstein and Pudovkin to the present.

Their films are available for purchase or rental.

# UNITED STATES

## BRUCE KAWIN

Any great period in film history resists generalization, and one that runs from *The House on 92nd Street* to *Return of the Jedi* and includes *Vertigo, Singin' in the Rain, Red River, Days of Heaven,* and at least six installments of *Friday the 13th* is bound to seem intractable. The years from 1945 to the mid-1980s stretched from the end of a world war to a confrontation with *1984* and included shooting wars in Korea and Vietnam, propaganda wars with Communism and the Hollywood Ten, and the election of a conservative B-movie actor to the presidency. This period saw the rise of television and a 3-D widescreen stereophonic Dolby counterattack that was itself overwhelmed by cable television and the demand for TV movies. It saw the rise of film schools, film quarterlies, film commenting, and—with the advent of the video recorder—the home film library. It gave us Orson Welles guest hosting the *Tonight* show and Johnny Carson hosting the Academy Awards.

It was also a period that saw the rise, fall, and return of *film noir*; that gave us the greatest color musicals; that responded to neorealism and the New Wave; that completed the extraordinary careers of Fritz Lang, Alfred Hitchcock, Jean Renoir, Howard Hawks, Douglas Sirk, Raoul Walsh, John Ford, Henry King, Orson Welles, Michael Curtiz, Henry Hathaway, Preston Sturges, and George Cukor; in which D. W. Griffith, Charles Chaplin, and Henry Fonda died and in which Steven Spielberg and George Lucas were born. In 1945 a dollar or so bought a newsreel, one or two cartoons, a short subject, a double feature, and a game of Keno; in the 1980s it cost four or five dollars to see one feature, augmented at best by coming attractions and at worst by advertisements. In 1945 ten million dollars was an unheard-of budget for a major film; in 1982 it was Sylvester Stallone's personal salary for *Rocky III*. If one emblem will serve for the entire period, it may be the intersection of Las Palmas and Hollywood boulevards: on the north side, Musso and Frank's Restaurant continues to serve hot dogs and chef salads to agents and filmmakers and climbers, as it has since the 1920s; on the south side, Larry Edmunds Cinema Bookshop caters to writers, film scholars, and collectors, while the Pussycat Theater is in its eighth year of showing *Deep Throat* and *The Devil in Miss Jones*. Another emblem might be taken from 1983's *The Big Chill*, where a group of friends who were born in the mid-1940s and came of age in the 1960s try to make sense of their lives while watching *It Came from Beneath the Sea* and interviewing each other with the aid of a video camera.

The end of World War II gave nearly every national cinema a similar opportunity and responsibility: to take stock of what the war had meant and to suggest the terms for peace. Whereas Italy met this challenge with diminished financial resources and an amalgam of rage, sadness, and moral fervor, producing such masterpieces as *Rome—Open City* and *The Bicycle Thief*, America found itself at the peak of its box-office demand and production capacity. The studio system was intact, international markets were assured, and the soldiers were coming home.

During the war many women had found work outside the home, particularly in heavy industry, and—as documented in the 1980 film *The Life and Times of Rosie the Riveter*—it became an immediate social priority to convince women that they ought to embrace more conventional sex roles and leave men's work to the men. This was, however regrettably, one of the "terms for peace," and it fell to Hollywood to generate much of the propaganda. Yet for all the shorts and features that presented women as wives and sweethearts celebrating the return of their husbands and lovers, sacrificing themselves for their children, or fixating on glamor and romance, there were many films with strong independent women as the focus of dramatic action. In the *films noir* of the immediate postwar years this ambivalence was dominant, as many female characters struggled for autonomy and damnation in similar terms. The struggle was begun in 1944, when Barbara Stanwyck portrayed the definitive *femme fatale* in *Double Indemnity*—a woman whose lust, ambition, cleverness, and dishonesty bring death to her husband, her lover, and herself—and when Ginger Rogers, in *Lady in the Dark*, was convinced by her male psychiatrist that she would find happiness only when she abandoned her tailored suit and compulsive work habits in favor of femininity and *her man's* loving domination. Joan Crawford, in the 1945 *Mildred Pierce*, expressed the pessimism of *film noir* and the sacrificing mother role (of the type that had reached its peak in Barbara Stanwyck's 1937 *Stella Dallas*) in one dark package, and although one of that film's messages was that the mother found her own *femme fatale* in her spoiled, murderous daughter, another was that her self-sacrifice had tragic dignity, and the last was that her business career both led to her freedom and contributed to her doom. Although women went on being both magnetic and murderous well into the 1950s, they had counterparts throughout the period who, like the narrator of *Kiss of Death* (1947), welcomed her man home from jail as if he had been a GI, believed in him no matter what, and brought him home at last to a well-earned domestic tranquility. From this period until the late 1950s there was a spectrum of female roles that had, at one end, figures like the Katharine Hepburn of *Adam's Rib* (1949) or *The African Queen* (1951), who were creatively self-determining; at the other end, figures like the Marilyn Monroe of *Niagara* (1952) and the Kim Novak of *Vertigo* (1958), who were unable to keep their roles from destroying them; and in the center, figures like the Doris Day of *Love Me or Leave Me* (1955), or *The Pajama Game* (1957), who succeeded or failed at working out a compromise between independence and dependence.

In addition to the project of splitting Rosie the Riveter into the *femme fatale* and *Blondie* (a Penny Singleton series that did good business from 1938 to 1951), Hollywood had the returning GI to deal with, and the war to evaluate. Both *Since You Went Away* (John Cromwell, 1944) and *The Best Years of Our Lives* (William Wyler, 1946) were nominated for Best Picture Oscars, and that indicates the popular endorsement of their respective treatments of the soldiers' homecoming: the former, romantic and teary, still involved in the wartime propaganda mill; the latter, both romantic and confrontational, probing the issues of mutilation, of acceptance, of *how* to start over. John Ford's *They Were Expendable* (1945) left the gung ho attitude behind and achieved a heroic portrait of wartime bitterness and loss. One of the best films to celebrate the soldier and the U.S. effort while refusing to enjoy war was Allan Dwan's *The Sands of Iwo Jima* (1949), an attitude that found its very best expression in Sam Fuller's much later *The Big Red One* (1980).

There were escapist films about the war, too, in which the war was considered an interesting comic or dramatic setting; these ranged from the innocuous *Anchors Aweigh* (George Sidney, 1945), a musical that included a wonderful sequence in which Gene Kelly danced with an animated mouse, to the high-class melodrama *From Here to Eternity* (Fred Zinnemann, 1953), in which the attack on Pearl Harbor intensified a series of powerful romantic and professional antagonisms. A film like Mark Robson's *Home of the Brave* (1949), the story of a black veteran and his postwar mental problems, critiqued racism on the front and was thus both a picture about some previously unacknowledged aspects of the war and an attempt to confront immediate social problems using the war as a setting; it also indicated the seriousness with which Hollywood was beginning to treat psychoanalysis. Both it and Fred Zinnemann's *The Men* (1950), in which Marlon Brando and Jack Webb dramatized the emotional and practical stresses of the postwar paraplegic, were produced by Stanley Kramer, a programmatically well-intentioned liberal who dominated the 1950s "problem picture," a cycle of melodramas that set out to deal with major social and ethical issues. Although some of Kramer's films were ponderous and their debates shallow (as in *Judgment at Nuremberg*, 1961), and although like David Lean he has come under attack for his sometime lack of experimental cinematic energy, Kramer must be given credit for the good taste and daring evidenced by such "problem pictures" as *High Noon* (1952), *The Wild One* (1953), *The Defiant Ones* (1958), *On the Beach* (1959), *Ship of Fools* (1965), and *Guess Who's Coming to Dinner?* (1967).

One of the most typical and enjoyable films of 1945 was Allan Dwan's *Brewster's Millions*, and it may serve as a summary example of the ways Hollywood both acknowledged the GI and cranked up the terms of the postwar economy, which was moving in the direction of inflation and into the arms of what Eisenhower later identified as the military-industrial complex. The story concerns Brewster, a young man who returns from the war to discover that he has been left a legacy of one million dollars; if he can spend every cent of it within a matter of months, he will inherit another seven million, but he has the option to take the million and be content. The project is to teach him the value of a dollar; the problem is that every bizarre investment he makes turns to gold, and although he enjoys the moral support of his faithful sweetheart and wartime buddies, he is barred from telling them what is really going on and cannot give away but must *spend* every dollar. The suspense and comedy are marvelous, and he does of course succeed in every respect —becoming, by the end, a happily married penny pincher whose friends still like him. Besides being a pleasant, upbeat welcome home picture, *Brewster's Millions*—now utterly forgotten except on the Late Late Show—preached both boom and economizing, while hinting at a community of interest between the average man and the interests and priorities of big business. Other films of 1945 that have not been so regrettably forgotten include: *The Story of G.I. Joe* (directed by William Wellman); *A Tree Grows In Brooklyn* (directed by Elia Kazan); *The Bells of St. Mary's* (directed by Leo McCarey); *National Velvet* (directed by Clarence Brown and starring the young Elizabeth Taylor, a classic children's picture, released in December, 1944); *The Lost Weekend* (directed by Billy Wilder and starring Ray Milland as an alcoholic, a "problem picture" that won the Oscar for Best Picture); *Spellbound* (in which Ingrid Bergman and Gregory Peck, under the guidance of director Alfred Hitchcock and dream-sequence-designer Salvador Dali, turned Freud into the material of romantic melodrama); *The Southerner* (Jean Renoir's greatest American film, with some help on the screenplay from William Faulkner); *Love Letters* (directed by William Dieterle, with a script by Ayn Rand, starring Jennifer Jones and Joseph Cotten, in which psychoanalysis and the war contribute to an overdone but affecting revision of *Cyrano de Bergerac*); *The House on*

*92nd Street* (directed by Henry Hathaway on location in New York, the first and one of the best of a series of pseudodocumentary melodramas that were the closest America came to a cycle of postwar neorealism); *Leave Her to Heaven* (John Stahl's slick Technicolor thriller, starring Gene Tierney as a murderously possessive *femme fatale*); *The House I Live In* (a short directed by Mervyn LeRoy in which Frank Sinatra sings about tolerance); and of course *Mildred Pierce*, which brings us around again to the brilliant cycle of melodramas known—since French critics invented the term—as *film noir*.

Although many of these films were made in black and white, with emphasis on the black (*noir* in French), the term was meant to parallel one from low-cost French publishing (the *Série Noire*), which refers to a line of violent mystery/melodramas published with black paper covers. It would make no sense to exclude a film like *Leave Her to Heaven* from this category on grounds of color. *Film noir* is defined both by its visual style and by its vision of the world, an attitude whose extreme negativity is occasionally counterbalanced by its gestures toward endings that, if not conventionally "happy," involve a version of poetic justice. Although the villains are usually dead by the end of the film, so are a number of "good" characters, and the central figure is often an ambitious or insightful man destroyed by those qualities that, in a better world, might have led to his success. It is the morally ambiguous situation in which he finds himself, an urbanized notion of Fate, that charges the visual landscape and sets up his downfall. In a *film noir* like *The Blue Dahlia* (1946), the returning GI comes home to a world that is almost all wrong and has to confront murder, adultery, psychosis, and above all a duplicitous irony, against which he struggles to establish a private space in which the values of love and friendship can survive.

These films often involve deep anxieties, feelings of alienation, entrapment, and paranoia that can escalate into obsession. The hero of *D.O.A.* (1949), for example, discovers that he has been poisoned and has one day to avenge his own murder; the detective in *Laura* (1944) becomes obsessed with the portrait of a woman whom the villain, in his own parallel way, sought to turn into an image under his own absolute control; the hero of *Gun Crazy* (1950), fascinated with firearms but unwilling to kill, falls in love with a psychopathic killer, turns outlaw with her, and in the end is forced to shoot her—to stop her from killing his friends—before he himself is gunned down. These obsessions often turn on questions of sexuality and control, whose focus may be the stock figure of the *femme fatale*, as in *Double Indemnity*; as the hero may be driven by a desire for justice, revenge, or dignified survival, the villain may be driven by a fetish for power, money, and sexual gratification. The definitive portrait of the psychopathic villain was given by Richard Widmark as Tommy Udo in *Kiss of Death*, a giggling, sneering, crafty, sadistic murderer who pushes a mother confined to a wheelchair down a flight of stairs to her death, both to convince her son not to talk and to punish the woman for lying to him. Widmark also created the archetypal doomed *noir* hero in Jules Dassin's *Night and the City* (1950), the entrepreneur Harry Fabian who is teased by the prospect of success in the midst of a lifelong run of tragic bad luck and comes to realize, just before his death, that what he had been told was true: "You've got it all, but you're a dead man."

Visually, *film noir* shares much with German Expressionism, not only in its extensive use of low-key lighting to convey psychological states and to charge the landscape—whether urban or interior—with a sense of danger and oppressiveness, but also in its fluid use of the moving camera. Much of the immediate influence here is Orson Welles and Gregg Toland's work in *Citizen Kane* (1941), rich in chiaroscuro, in high and low camera angles, and in an oppressive yet revisionist mythology of frames and framing; but these techniques were also directly connected with the German practice, in that Toland was influenced by the great German cinematographer Karl Freund, with whom he worked on *Mad Love*, a 1935 horror film. All these practices converge in *Scarlet Street* (1945), Fritz Lang's *noir* remake of Jean Renoir's black comedy *La Chienne* (1931): at the end of *La Chienne* Renoir's hero finds a kind of happiness in his new life as a bum who is not recognized as a great painter but who also gets away with murder; at the end of *Scarlet Street* Lang's hero is hounded by the ghosts of his victims, who taunt him even after death with their utter betrayal of him and all he held valuable. He becomes a penniless bum wandering the dark street of his ruined imagination. To describe the Expressionism, the Lang signature, or the *noir* ambience of *Scarlet Street*, one would use much the same set of terms. Although there is some disagreement whether *film noir* ought to be considered a "cycle" or a genre, most people know a *film noir* when they see it, and most would agree that a list of the greatest ought to include (in addition to those previously mentioned): *This Gun for Hire* (1942), *Journey into Fear* (1943), *Murder, My Sweet* (1944), *Detour* (1945), *The Woman in the Window* (1945), *The Dark Corner* (1946), *The Big Sleep* (1946), *Gilda* (1946), *Body and Soul* (1947), *Brute Force* (1947), *Dead Reckoning* (1947), *Nightmare Alley* (1947), *Out of the Past* (1947), *The Lady from Shanghai* (1948), *Raw Deal* (1948), *The Set-Up* (1949), *White Heat* (1949), *The Asphalt Jungle* (1950), *Caged* (1950), *In a Lonely Place* (1950), *Strangers on a Train* (1951), *The Big Heat* (1953), *Pickup on South Street* (1953), *Human Desire* (1954), *Kiss Me Deadly* (1955), and *Touch of Evil* (1958).

Beginning in the mid-1970s, there were attempts to revive some of the visual elements and in some cases even the ironic voice-over narration of *film noir* in several films that appear overwhelmed by the failures and corruption of American life. The urban melodrama *Chinatown*

(1974), the Vietnam epic *Apocalypse Now* (1979), and the futuristic *Blade Runner* (1982) all made good use of the *noir* sensibility, but each was in its own way too expensive and self-conscious to succeed in the hard-bitten and efficient terms of the films being rendered a *hommage*. This is not to say that those later films did not succeed on their own terms—although all of the three had problems with unmotivated endings (*Blade Runner*'s too innocent, *Apocalypse Now*'s ponderously confused, and *Chinatown*'s a cheap paranoid flourish improvised by director Roman Polanski in place of screenwriter Robert Towne's more careful conclusion)—but it does suggest that one of the virtues of *film noir* was the immediacy of its integrity, the brooding efficiency of its response to its own time. Another was the absolute authority of its motivated endings.

The heritage of German Expressionism was also evident in the work of Alfred Hitchcock, and in the genre of the horror film, for which its ability to exteriorize states of mind and evoke threatening atmosphere had long been appropriate. The acknowledged master of the horror film in the 1940s was RKO producer Val Lewton, who had carried forward the Expressionism of *Frankenstein* (1931) and *Vampyr* (1932), modified by his own gentle touch of poetic realism and suggestive understatement, in *Cat People* (1942), *I Walked with a Zombie* (1943), and *The Curse of the Cat People* (1944). The best of his postwar films were *The Body Snatcher* (1945), *Isle of the Dead* (1945), and *Bedlam* (1946), and it is arguable that the American horror film never again attained the complex humanism and subtle brilliance to which Lewton brought the genre before his early death in 1951. The only horror film of the period that can bear comparison with his was Robert Florey's *The Beast with Five Fingers* (1946), which makes up in Expressionist lighting and psychological pyrotechnics what it lacks in tenderness and profundity.

Hitchcock, who had been trained at the UFA studio in Germany and had already demonstrated his mastery in the English film industry, had been brought to America by producer David O. Selznick to direct *Rebecca* (1940) and had made at least one great film during the war, *Shadow of a Doubt* (1943). Although his skill in the genre of the psychological thriller is beyond question, it is difficult to know whether to classify his interest in psychoanalytic theory as mundane, deficient, or cleverly ironic, for he seems to have used classical Freudian material as the basis for many of his stories on the one hand (in *Marnie*, for example), and to have parodied such structures with great wit on the other (as in the shot that concludes *North by Northwest*, when a train goes into a tunnel). Whereas some of his greatest films, notably *Vertigo*, depend on the Freudian model of a reexperienced trauma, it would be hard to credit the psychologist's overneat wrap-up of the case in *Psycho* with similar claims to profundity. Comparing such films of the late 1940s as *Spellbound* (1945) and *Notorious* (1946), it seems that Hitchcock was at his best when he investigated the psychological states of his characters without the apparatus of Freudian theory, for while *Notorious* is a thoroughly masterful exercise in character and suspense, the heavily Freudian *Spellbound* appears both simplistic and programmatic. Hitchcock's last Selznick film, *The Paradine Case* (1947), was a restrained study of the ramifications of guilt and professionalism. His next film, *Rope* (1948), was a unique experiment in the illusion of seamless visual continuity—a series of ten-minute takes that, with the exception of a few deliberate reverse-angle shots, gave one the impression that the film was almost one long take. In the first shot, outside a closed window, the strangling of the victim can be heard; from there the camera goes inside the apartment and exposes, by virtue of its own long continuity, the "rope" on which the overconfident murderers metaphorically hang themselves. Yet for all its visual daring, *Rope* feels paradoxically stage bound, not only because it was based on a play but also because of its turgid acting and nonstop dialogue. The following film, *Under Capricorn* (1949), set in Australia, had a far richer color scheme than *Rope* and returned, as if with relief, to a dynamic interplay of montage and mise-en-scène; it was in this underrated film and the great *Strangers on a Train* that Hitchcock perfected the classical, brooding, ironic style that charged his great works of the 1950s, a style that was announced in *Notorious* but that was not adequately developed in his work of the late 1940s. What gives *Strangers on a Train* its special relevance is its exploration of the *Doppelgänger*, the shadow figure who acts out the forbidden desires of the hero who prefers to see himself as innocent. While its story of a lily-white tennis player, which is relentlessly paralleled with that of a psychotic killer, belongs generically to the entrapment phase of *film noir*, and shares much with such mistaken-identity melodramas as *The Wrong Man* (1956) and *Frenzy* (1972), it looks forward to Hitchcock's most brilliant analyses of voyeurism and culpability, *Rear Window* (1954) and *Vertigo* (1958), the latter being not only his masterpiece but one of the greatest films ever made.

On the strength of the work of John Ford and Howard Hawks, the Western can be said to have entered an authentically epic phase in the late 1940s. A Western like *Duel in the Sun* (1947)—torn by producer Selznick's ambition to make another *Gone with the Wind*, director King Vidor's *noir*-like vision of sexual obsession and doom, and the lush overscoring of composer Dimitri Tiomkin—had epic pretensions but lacked the ethical focus and urgent narrative economy that characterize the genuine epic. This was a genre and a stance of which John Ford was master. Working with such stars as Henry Fonda and John Wayne, Ford undertook a complex exploration of the ethics of heroism, community, and power in such films as *My Darling Clementine* (1946), *Fort Apache* (1948), *She Wore a Yellow Ribbon* (1949), *Wagonmaster* (1950), and *Rio Grande* (1950). Many of his major characters are caught between the demands of their roles and their own more tender personal impulses, and if, like the Fonda character in *Fort Apache*, they accomplish their own destruction through an inflexible attention to duty, they may yet find vindication in the eyes of the survivor who, like the Wayne character in that same film, respects and validates the complexities of integrity. If Ford was at times sentimental, and if his macho-conservative patriotism was occasionally too uncritical, he was also a bitter romantic, a sharp-eyed ironist, a concerned humanist, and a consummate observer of character. In the range of his narrative tones and the ambition of his moral scrutiny, he was the legitimate heir of D. W. Griffith. The greatest of his later Westerns, *The Searchers* (1956) and *The Man Who Shot Liberty Valance* (1962), bear out these observations and with his Irish masterpiece, *The Quiet Man* (1952), rank among the most thought-provoking and emotionally profound studies of the nature of violence, love, and honor in the history of film.

Although it is arguable that Howard Hawks did his greatest work in the comedies and melodramas of the 1930s and early 1940s, that is not to suggest that his postwar work was in any way negligible. If *Monkey Business* (1952) is inferior to *Bringing Up Baby* (1938), it is not by much, and in the comedy *I Was a Male War Bride* (1949), the musical *Gentlemen Prefer Blondes* (1953), and the adventure film *Hatari!* (1962) he demonstrated not only a continuing mastery of the medium but a developing moral perspective. In the Western trilogy of *Rio Bravo* (1959), *El Dorado* (1967), and *Rio Lobo* (1970, his last film), Hawks explored one situation from three increasingly complex vantage points and brought to a culmination his lifelong interest in the aesthetics of repetition; in those films and in particular in *Hatari!* he also explored the experience of coming to old age and evaluated, in his characteristically understated way, the value of values and the challenges of endurance. It was also in this period that he made one of his most brilliant films and one of the two or three greatest Westerns, *Red River* (1948). This is a film that both summarizes and critiques the mythology of the Western and the moral history of the Western world, focusing on both of these in the story of a cattleman (John Wayne) and his adopted son (Montgomery Clift), in which the inflexible code of the father is enlarged by the humanistic vision of the son, and what begins as a conflict between two concepts of professionalism ends in a synthesis of authentic love. No other American film has ever caught so brilliantly the dilemma of power at the heart of patriarchy, the moral complexity of capitalism, and the subtleties of male bonding; yet for all that, *Red River* also includes two strong female characters and suggests, through its own nexus of repetition and renewal, a heightened vision of male/female bonding that is capable of sustaining both the family and the culture.

When the Western determined, in the 1950s, to discuss major issues (the so-called "adult Western"), it sacrificed profundity for preaching and began a terrible decline. If *High Noon* has value, it is not as a Western. Although Henry King's *The Gunfighter* (1950) and George Stevens's *Shane* (1953) are serious and well-made films, and although the Westerns that Budd Boetticher made with Randolph Scott, such as *Ride Lonesome* (1959), have considerable generic integrity, nothing but *The Searchers* measures up to the standard set by Hawks and Ford in the 1940s until Sam Peckinpah's *Ride the High Country* (1962), and a number of the best Westerns since then have been concerned with the death of the West—from *Lonely Are the Brave* (1962) and *The Wild Bunch* (1969) to the financially disastrous and critically underrated *Heaven's Gate* (1980).

In terms of attendance figures, box-office receipts, and what was perceived as the overall health of the industry, Hollywood had its best year in 1946. The tremendous grosses in the early 1980s of individual films such as *E.T.* reflect higher ticket prices and a consumer pattern of going only to certain highly publicized films, most of which would not have the same impact if seen on television; what has disappeared is the regular habit of moviegoing, and with it the rich corpus of diverse, interesting, and relatively low-budget films. Nineteen forty-six alone saw the release and success of *The Big Sleep, The Postman Always Rings Twice, The Killers, The Yearling, The Dark Mirror, Cluny Brown, Ziegfield Follies, The Razor's Edge, The Road to Utopia, The Stranger, Bedlam, Notorious, Gilda, My Darling Clementine, Diary of a Chambermaid,* and *It's A Wonderful Life,* as well as such highly praised British imports as *Dead of Night, Stairway to Heaven, Henry V,* and *Brief Encounter.* This was also the year of a labor dispute that led both to an increase in production costs and to the beginnings of a blacklist, since a number of "agitators" were, not at all coincidentally, among those targeted for investigation by the 1947 "Hearings regarding the Communist Infiltration of the Motion-Picture-Industry Activities in the United States" conducted by the House Committee on Un-American Activities (pejoratively known as the HUAC), hearings that were again pursued in 1951–52.

Nineteen forty-eight was the year that confirmed the technical and commercial success of television, which, together with the postwar "baby boom," created new patterns of seeking entertainment and structuring time in the home, and it was also the year of a Supreme Court decision that ordered the major studios to "divest" themselves of their chains of theaters, an antitrust decision that cut deeply into the industry's expectations of revenue, patterns of release, and diversity of production. An equally significant Supreme Court decision had been handed down in 1947; in the course of considering the charges of monopolistic practices and restriction of trade that had been brought against Paramount Pictures, the Court noted that motion pictures were "included in the press whose freedom is guaranteed by the First Amendment." (In the 1952 *Miracle* case this protection was tested and reaffirmed.) This complex of challenges, opportunities, and reversals made the years from 1947 to 1948 the most critical in American film history, in comparison to which the debacle over the conversion to sound (1927–29) was virtually an in-house dispute, for it was in this later period that film was legally recognized as a medium for the expression of ideas and convictions, that it began to lose its regular audience, and that it chose, more often than not, the path of political conservatism and a "try anything" attitude geared toward commercial rather than artistic experimentation.

Not only in its *noir* melodramas but even in its comedies, America of the late 1940s began to seem a darker place. Although *Miracle on 34th Street* (1947) affirmed the existence of Santa Claus in a world that both wanted to believe in its fairy tales and had little patience for foolishness, that film had less resonance and less staying power than Frank Capra's *It's a Wonderful Life*, a heartfelt masterpiece that set the Christmas spirit, in its largest sense, against the fully realized forces of selfishness, despair, and big capitalism. Chaplin's comedy of this period, *Monsieur Verdoux* (1947), was his blackest, and it seemed, like Joseph Losey's *The Boy with Green Hair* (1947), to force the question of the cinema's claim to the expression of unconventional ideas; by the early 1950s, both Chaplin and Losey were working in Europe, branded by public opinion as Communist sympathizers.

Between 1948 and 1951, when the HUAC returned to have its say over Hollywood and an entirely different period began, a host of films in a healthy variety of genres achieved greatness along with high entertainment value and technical polish. Humphrey Bogart, Tim Holt, and Walter Huston did the best work of their careers in John Huston's *The Treasure of the Sierra Madre* (1948), a brilliant study of values adapted from the popular novel by B. Traven. Arthur Freed produced a superb string of lavish, playful, high-key color musicals at MGM, including Vincente Minnelli's *The Pirate* (1948) and *An American in Paris* (1951). Max Ophuls directed two of his best American films, *Letter from an Unknown Woman* (1948) and *Caught* (1949). Orson Welles directed Rita Hayworth and Everett Sloane in *The Lady from Shanghai* (1948), the best film he had made since *The Magnificent Ambersons* (1942) and a dazzling study of corruption, betrayal, and the nature of appearances. George Cukor made two of his best comedies, *Adam's Rib* (1949) with Katharine Hepburn and Spencer Tracy, and *Born Yesterday* (1950) with Judy Holliday. Nicholas Ray began his volatile career with *They Live by Night* (1949) and went on to make *In a Lonely Place* (1950), films that rank with *Johnny Guitar* (1954) and *Rebel Without a Cause* (1955) in their sentimental, parodistic, and anguished send-up of American values. Robert Rossen's *All the King's Men*, adapted from the novel by Robert Penn Warren, was a serious if moralistic treatment of the career of Huey Long and won the Oscar for Best Picture of 1949. Henry King's *Twelve O'Clock High* (1950) was an excellent study of combat stress. In *Sunset Boulevard* (1950), Billy Wilder directed Gloria Swanson, Erich von Stroheim, William Holden, and—in bit roles—Buster Keaton and Cecil B. DeMille in a dark tragicomedy about the death of the old Hollywood and the bankruptcy of the new, a great film that might well be considered the flip side of *Singin' in the Rain*. Joseph L. Mankiewicz's *All Above Eve*, which won the Best Picture Oscar for 1950, deserved it; it has proved to be one of the cinema's most enduring and witty comedies of manners. One of Sam Fuller's best films, *The Steel Helmet* (1951), was also the best film to come out of the Korean War. *The Sin of Harold Diddlebock* (1950), a different version of *Mad Wednesday* (1947), was the last great comedy from Preston Sturges, an underrated but hilarious treatment of how the Harold Lloyd of *The Freshman* might have fared in the world of sound. Nineteen fifty-one also saw three distinguished adaptations: George Stevens's *A Place in the Sun*, from Theodore Dreiser's *An American Tragedy*; Elia Kazan's *A Streetcar Named Desire*, from the play by Tennessee Williams, notable for the performances of Marlon Brando and Vivien Leigh; and *The African Queen*, from the novel by C. S. Forester, directed by John Huston from a screenplay by the great novelist and critic James Agee, and starring Humphrey Bogart and Katharine Hepburn.

The tensions of the cold war with the Soviets and of the battle with the HUAC for the integrity of the American Constitution were plainly evident in four representative films released early in the 1950s: *The Day the Earth Stood Still* (Robert Wise, 1951), *The Thing* (Christian Nyby, 1951), *High Noon* (Fred Zinnemann, 1952), and *My Son John* (Leo McCarey, 1952). Although these were also the years of *Ivanhoe*, *Singin' in the Rain*, and *The Quiet Man*—and of Chaplin's masterful farewell to America, *Limelight*—it would be misleading to celebrate them for their masterpieces without considering the terrible problems they raised and which many of their best films were at pains either to address or to mask.

The HUAC was not simply—despite the claims of its defenders—bent on rooting out Communist sympathizers in an industry that was perceived to have a great potential for manufacturing and distributing propaganda. It was also complicit with a backlash of anti-Semitism, as the sympathy for the victims of Hitler's genocidal campaigns was displaced by the fear of Soviet aggression, the distrust of Americans with Russian origins (many of whom were Jews, as were many powerful figures in Hollywood), and an outright fear of ideas. The fact that Senator Joseph McCarthy was able to reach and hold a national audience with his shameless and paranoid grandstanding, and that the career of Richard Nixon rose while that of Helen Gahagan (Douglas) declined, reflected a social crisis without parallel since the days of the Civil War, and many of the Hollywood professionals who were called before the HUAC saw themselves as defending the essence of the Bill of Rights— while relying, with numbing and horrific repetition, on the Fifth Amendment. Defending their rights to freedom of thought and of association, and resisting the government's violations of those rights (which were bolstered and obscured by such arguments as that a person who was not a communist would have no reason not to say so), they found themselves accused of preaching Communism and of "hiding behind the Bill of Rights." Some, like a group known as the Hollywood Ten, suffered more than blacklisting, while others told the HUAC whatever it wanted to know. From this period forward, many Americans were split between the desire to reaffirm their country as the haven of freedom and the "good life" (an attitude simplistically held to characterize the Eisenhower 1950s) and the nagging suspicion that the U.S. government could no longer be trusted. But it was only much later, under the glare of full media attention to the Vietnam war, the 1968 Chicago Democratic Convention, and finally the Watergate scandal, that the mass of Americans came to recognize how seriously and for how long the government had been failing to uphold the principles it was charged to uphold.

Those who continued to work in the industry in the 1950s made, on the whole, three kinds of films: some, like *Roman Holiday* (1953) or *Shane* (1953), were carefully devoid of political commentary; some, like *High Noon*, offered covert critiques of McCarthyism in terms that were ultimately ambiguous (since the sheriff in that film, while he is clearly a lone crusader, could be interpreted with equal justice as a blacklisted screenwriter or as an isolated anti-Communist—and there are complementary contradictions in the treatment of his wife, who is praised for violating her principles as he is for upholding his own); and some, like *Pickup on South Street*, were overtly pro-American and anti-Communist. A film like Leo McCarey's *My Son John* was intended to demonstrate to Washington and to the country at large that Hollywood had no Communist sympathizers left on the payroll and that any propagandistic tendencies in the medium were not to be exploited for any but "American" purposes. Although Christian Nyby's *The Thing from Another World* (1951) deserves credit for inaugurating an excellent cycle of horror films, and although Robert Wise's *The Day the Earth Stood Still* (1951) is one of the best science fiction films ever to come out of Hollywood, it is clear that both, however deeply embedded in their respective genres, were primarily concerned with the problems of the cold war, specifically with the question of whether to trust the military (who are presented as reflexively hostile to "invaders") or the scientists (who are presented as open-minded, if not internationalist). In *The Thing* the military is right and the principal scientist is a dangerous fool; in *The*

*Day the Earth Stood Still* this perspective is reversed, and the threat of nuclear destruction is presented as more significant than any political disagreement. One of the great moments in the history of the blacklist came in 1956, when Dalton Trumbo, one of the Hollywood Ten, won the Oscar for the screenplay of *The Brave One*, but under a pseudonym (there is still some dispute over whether the Academy members knew for whom they were voting, but the legend has it that they were well informed). When Trumbo received screen credit for two films in 1960, first for Otto Preminger's *Exodus* and then for Stanley Kubrick's *Spartacus*, the blacklist was finished. (Preminger, a stylish authoritarian who consistently rebelled against authority, also successfully challenged the Production Code with his 1953 *The Moon is Blue*, in which the taboo word *virgin* was spoken aloud, and with his graphic treatment of drug addiction in his 1955 *The Man with the Golden Arm*.) But it was only in the 1970s that the blacklist itself was considered safe material for open treatment, first in Sydney Pollack's *The Way We Were* (1973) and then in Martin Ritt's *The Front* (1976).

Throughout the 1950s the industry was embattled with television, with the government, with declining audiences, and with drastically rising budgets. Nevertheless, this was one of its great periods, a time when directors like Hitchcock and Ford were at the peak of their form; when actors like Marlon Brando and James Stewart, and actresses like Grace Kelly and Marilyn Monroe, were genuine stars; when genres as diverse as the musical and the science fiction film seemed never to run out of new material; and when the widespread conversion to color photography and large-screen formats stimulated experimentation.

Although the front-office intentions in developing and marketing such widescreen formats as Cinerama (*This is Cinerama*, 1952), CinemaScope (*The Robe*, 1953), VistaVision (*White Christmas*, 1954), and 70mm/Todd-AO (*Oklahoma!*, 1955 and *Around the World in 80 Days*, 1956) had more to do with tearing the audience away from the free entertainment provided by television's small black and white fishbowl than with expanding cinematic expression; and although the same motive was at work in the exploitation of Eastmancolor (developed in 1952 and used in the majority of Hollywood feature films by 1955) and magnetic-track stereophonic sound, one has only to look at *Vertigo* to see how brilliantly the opportunity to work in color and VistaVision suited an artist who was ready for it, or at *Dial M for Murder* (Hitchcock, 1954) or *Kiss Me Kate* (George Sidney, 1953) to see how the maligned 3-D process could enhance dramatic content as well as playfulness. The 3-D effect, developed during the silent period and resurrected to little effect early in the 1980s, did good business in 1952 (*Bwana Devil*) and 1953 (*House of Wax*), but succumbed to consumer resistance against headaches and cardboard glasses, as well as to critics who complained about the finally boring device of hurtling objects at the camera and about the planographic shortcomings of the image (so that in many cases the field appeared to consist of a series of two-dimensional objects separated in depth); but before it died, 3-D made a lot of children happy and gave a director like Jack Arnold (in *IT Came from Outer Space*, 1953, and *Creature from the Black Lagoon*, 1954) the opportunity to expand his talents and create wonderful image fields. Although *Kiss Me Kate* and *Dial M for Murder* were generally released "flat," the surviving 3-D prints are well worth seeing—*Kate* for its 3-D choreography, to which Bob Fosse contributed, and *Dial M* for its restrained use of the toward-the-camera effect (used only when Grace Kelly reaches behind her for the scissors and when the latchkey is presented at the climax) as well as for the enhanced claustrophobia of the living-room space. Even run of the mill genre pictures like *I, the Jury* (1953) and *Gog* (1954) were better for being in 3-D, but it was undeniable that the widescreen processes created a more natural impression of depth and required no glasses, and so widescreen was the innovation that survived. The shortest-lived of all these experiments was the "olfactory film," the *reductio ad absurdum* of this aspect of the period; for the documentary *Behind the Great Wall* (AromaRama, 1959), perfumes were circulated through the air-conditioning system of the theater, and for *Scent of Mystery* (Smell-O-Vision, 1960), they were shot directly into the audience's faces via copper tubing installed behind and between every few seats. Remembering the moment when Peter Lorre, in *Scent of Mystery*, stood in the middle of a crowded marketplace— doubtless a rich, if not redolent, olfactory site—and bit into a peach, and with a ubiquitous hiss a mist of sickeningly rich peach perfume filled the theater, it is hard not to lament the demise of that particular avenue of film expression.

The color musical came into its own in the 1950s, particularly in the MGM cycle produced by Arthur Freed, who had already been responsible for *Cabin in the Sky* (1943), *Meet Me in St. Louis* (1944), *Easter Parade* (1948), and *On the Town* (1949) in the 1940s and who went on to produce *An American in Paris, Singin' in the Rain, The Band Wagon* (1953), *It's Always Fair Weather* (1955), *Silk Stockings* (1957), *Gigi* (1958), and *Bells Are Ringing* (1960) in the 1950s. Fred Astaire, Gene Kelly, Leslie Caron, Ann Miller, Cyd Charisse, and others did major work in the popular, innovative, and expensively produced musicals of this period, as did a number of important directors, notably Stanley Donen and Vincente Minnelli. Donen and Kelly, who codirected *On the Town, Singin' in the Rain*, and *It's Always Fair Weather*, were a genuinely creative team, even though the work Donen did on his own— *Seven Brides for Seven Brothers* (1954), *Funny Face* (1957), and, outside the musical genre, *Two for the Road* and *Bedazzled* (both 1967)— stands up better than the work Kelly did on his own, his best being *Invitation to the Dance* (1956) and his worst *Hello Dolly!* (1969). Although

Minnelli did fine work outside the genre in such films as *Lust for Life* (1956), *Some Came Running* (1959), and *Home from the Hill* (1960), his work for Freed on *The Band Wagon, Gigi,* and *Bells Are Ringing* touched a different excellence. Several major directors tried their hand at the genre, including Rouben Mamoulian (*Silk Stockings*), George Cukor (*A Star Is Born,* 1954), Joseph L. Mankiewicz (*Guys and Dolls,* 1955), and Howard Hawks (*Gentlemen Prefer Blondes,* 1953). There was a run on adaptations of the work of Rodgers and Hart (*Pal Joey,* 1957), Rodgers and Hammerstein (*Oklahoma!,* 1955, *The King and I,* 1956, and *South Pacific,* 1958), and Lerner and Loewe (*Brigadoon,* 1954). The movement crested with Jerome Robbins and Robert Wise's *West Side Story* in 1961, a film that was as carefully choreographed for the moving camera and the wide 70mm format as *A Star Is Born* and *Silk Stockings* were designed for scope. Not much of interest followed in the 1960s, when most of the musicals were dull and overproduced, swamped by big numbers and weak scripts; even some of the better ones, like Cukor's *My Fair Lady* (1964) and Wise's *The Sound of Music* (1965), have these problems. It was Bob Fosse, in *Cabaret* (1972) and later in *All That Jazz* (1979), who picked up the cold trail and made dynamic editing, intelligent camera work, and energetic art direction once again central to the form, along with adult scripts and sharp acting. To varied extents, these have characterized the best musicals of the past ten years: Milos Forman's *Hair* (1979), Alan Parker's *Fame* (1980), Luis Valdez's *Zoot Suit* (1981), and Herbert Ross's *Pennies from Heaven* (1981).

"Movies are better than ever!" the admen of the 1950s argued; "Get more out of life—go to a movie!" Drive-ins sprouted like mushrooms in the dark. Experiments were made in subliminal advertising, where messages were flashed for fractions of a second—"Buy popcorn," for instance, and people bought popcorn—but such practices were quickly outlawed. Westerns made good use of color and the wide screen, from the medium-budget *The Last Wagon* (1956) to the high-budget *The Big Country* (1958). If a Western was made in black and white, like *High Noon* or *3:10 to Yuma* (1957), it was plainly intended to be serious. The most systematic use of the big glossy formula was made by the spectacles, for which higher admission prices were sometimes charged and which were often favored at Oscar time, from De Mille's last, bombastic film *The Ten Commandments* (1956) to such relatively superior films as *Giant* (1956), *War and Peace* (1956), *The Bridge on the River Kwai* (1957), and *Ben-Hur* (1959). Douglas Sirk made a series of romantic melodramas whose use of color and high production values was intentionally ironic; in *Magnificent Obsession* (1954), *All that Heaven Allows* (1956), and *Written on the Wind* (1957) he not only created three of Hollywood's best "weepies" but also parodied the genre with an almost tragic sense of humor, teasing his characters and his audiences with a relentless imagery of frames that, like the expensive and well-lit sets, trapped his characters in their worlds and offered them the rarely embraced opportunity to understand the limits of their roles. On the less self-conscious side, there were wonderful comedies and "costume" and adventure melodramas that were meant for "the whole family": Deborah Kerr and Stewart Granger in *King Solomon's Mines* (1950), Robert Taylor and Elizabeth Taylor in *Ivanhoe* (1952), Burt Lancaster in *The Crimson Pirate* (1952), Lon Chaney, Jr., in *Battles of Chief Pontiac* (1952), Robert Newton in *Long John Silver* (1954), Danny Kaye in *The Court Jester* (1956), Dean Martin and Jerry Lewis in *Hollywood or Bust* (1956), Kirk Douglas and Tony Curtis in *The Vikings* (1958), and for a slightly less diverse audience, Elvis Presley in *Jailhouse Rock* (1957). The Disney studios continued to release full-length animated films such as *Peter Pan* (1953) and *Sleeping Beauty* (1959); followed *Seal Island* (1949) with an award-winning series of documentaries including *The Living Desert* (1953); and made a number of excellent live-action features including *Treasure Island* (1950), *The Adventures of Robin Hood* (1952), *The Sword and the Rose* (1953), and *20,000 Leagues Under the Sea* (1954). With the rise of Disneyland, both as a TV show and as a WASP-ish exercise in Realtorland, the aesthetic value of the Disney films declined—only *Mary Poppins* (1964) can stand as an exception—until a change of management in the 1980s produced *TRON* (1982), an ambitious experiment in computer-augmented animation and live action that set a thinly disguised Passion play in the world of video games. The best animation was widely recognized as being done elsewhere: at UPA, at the Hubley Studio, and particularly at Warner Brothers.

Among the best films of the 1950s, the following deserve special mention. *Rancho Notorious* (1952) starred Marlene Dietrich in a *noir* color Western, a relentless revenge melodrama by Fritz Lang, who told a similar story in *The Big Heat* in 1953. *Limelight* (1952) was Chaplin's last American production, a slow-paced and extremely moving treatment of youth, age, and art that climaxed with a brilliant routine between Chaplin and Buster Keaton that is itself the best piece of criticism in any medium on the complementarity and difference between the two masters. Billy Wilder mixed black comedy and high seriousness in his story of the Nazi prisoner-of-war camps, *Stalag 17* (1953). Marlon Brando did good work in *The Wild One* (1953) and great work in *On the Waterfront* (1954). Henry Hathaway's *Niagara* (1953) cast Joseph Cotten and Marilyn Monroe in a powerful story of sexual obsession and murder. Fred Zinnemann's *From Here to Eternity* (1953), from James Jones's novel of Pearl Harbor, featured superb ensemble acting by Burt Lancaster, Deborah Kerr, Montgomery Clift, Donna Reed, Frank Sinatra, and Ernest Borgnine. Ida Lupino proved a distinguished director in *The Hitch-Hiker* and *The Bigamist* (both 1953). James Stewart,

Grace Kelly, Thelma Ritter, and Raymond Burr all did superior work in *Rear Window* (1954), Hitchcock's brilliant critique of the filmgoer as voyeur and the problem of passive involvement. Nicholas Ray's bizarre color Western, *Johnny Guitar* (1954), became famous for its climactic shootout between Joan Crawford and Mercedes McCambridge. George Cukor's *A Star is Born* (1954), the second film released in CinemaScope, with brilliant performances by Judy Garland and James Mason, arguably improved on the 1937 version that had starred Janet Gaynor and Fredric March. *Anatahan* (1954), never widely released, was Josef von Sternberg's final statement on the destructive power of sexuality. Don Siegel made a series of tough melodramas including *Riot in Cell Block 11* (1954), *Private Hell 36* (1954), *Baby Face Nelson* (1957), and *The Line-Up* (1958), and the masterful science fiction satire of the horror of conformity, *Invasion of the Body Snatchers* (1956); his better films of the 1960s included *Flaming Star* (1960) with Elvis Presley and *Madigan* (1968) with Richard Widmark and Henry Fonda. George Seaton's *The Country Girl* (1954), from the Clifford Odets play, gave Bing Crosby his finest role as an alcoholic actor and Grace Kelly an Oscar as his wife. Charles Laughton directed Robert Mitchum, Shelley Winters, and Lillian Gish in *The Night of the Hunter* (1955), adapted by James Agee from the novel by Davis Grubb and one of the most distinguished independent productions of the period; other major independent films included Robert Aldrich's *Kiss Me Deadly* (1955), a loose but brilliant adaptation of Mickey Spillane's novel, and Stanley Kubrick's *The Killing* (1956) and *Paths of Glory* (1957), both of which were co-scripted by novelist Jim Thompson.

Although none of them was the equal of *The Steel Helmet* or *Paths of Glory*, a number of military films did well at the box-office and included good performances: *The Caine Mutiny* (1954), *Mister Roberts* (1955), *To Hell and Back* (1955), *The Bridges at Toko-Ri* (1955), and *The Bridge on the River Kwai* (1957). James Dean played a misunderstood teenager torn between love and anger in *East of Eden* (1955), *Rebel Without a Cause* (1955), and—disguised as an adult—*Giant* (1956), before his early death in a car crash; the first of these was a loose adaptation of John Steinbeck's much better novel about Cain and Abel in the Salinas Valley, the second a loose adaptation of psychiatrist Robert Lindner's case study (notable for Nicholas Ray's widescreen color direction and for the supporting performances of Sal Mineo and Natalie Wood), and the third a relatively close adaptation of Edna Ferber's Texas saga (directed by George Stevens and starring Elizabeth Taylor and Rock Hudson, with Dennis Hopper notable in a subplot about racial tolerance), but all three films are primarily remembered for the work Dean did in them. Juvenile delinquency was forcefully addressed in Richard Brooks's controversial *The Blackboard Jungle* (1955). The interest in Italian neorealism and in the concentrated understatement of television drama contributed to a series of low-budget, well-written, and well-acted films, beginning with Delbert Mann's *Marty* in 1955. Many of the best of these were based on teleplays and screenplays by Paddy Chayefsky, including *Marty, The Catered Affair* (1956) and *The Bachelor Party* (1957); Chayefsky later distinguished himself in the genre of black comedy with his screenplays for *The Americanization of Emily* (1964), *Hospital* (1971), and *Network* (1976).

In *The Searchers* (1956), John Ford's best Western since *Stagecoach*, John Wayne created an unforgettable portrayal of the obsessive Western hero, a man whose decisions to kill or to love are sudden, silent, and unpredictable, and whose isolation is set in a profound dialectic with the equally intriguing values of home and community. Love and violence were explored with equal rigor in Ford's *The Quiet Man* (1952), set in Ireland and starring John Wayne and Maureen O'Hara; Howard Hawks thought it Ford's best film. In 1957 Mark Robson's *Peyton Place*, Alexander MacKendrick's *Sweet Smell of Success*, and Elia Kazan's *A Face in the Crowd* mixed romantic melodrama with social commentary to good effect; in them, as in Sidney Lumet's debut film, *12 Angry Men* (also 1957), it was clear that the "Hollywood happy ending" was no longer a foregone conclusion and that the battle against prejudice, evil, power, and destructive charm was an uphill one—a theme carried out by Lumet, one of the cinema's real moralists, in such later films as *Fail-Safe* (1964), *The Pawnbroker* (1965), his British-produced masterpiece *The Hill* (1965), *Serpico* (1973), *Prince of the City* (1981), and *The Verdict* (1982). The best courtroom dramas of the decade were Otto Preminger's *Anatomy of a Murder* (1959) and Billy Wilder's *Witness for the Prosecution* (1958), and the best screwball comedy was Wilder's *Some Like It Hot* (1959). Orson Welles did brilliant work before and behind the camera in *Touch of Evil* (1958), his last American film of note and one that ranks with *Chimes at Midnight* (1967) in the continuing demonstration that whether or not Hollywood chose to employ him or to trust him, there was no American filmmaker more worthy of being employed and trusted, nor any with an easier claim to the title of genius. The greatest single film of the decade was *Vertigo* (1958), notable for the performances of James Stewart and Kim Novak, for the probing directorial consciousness of its flowing camera, for the great music of Bernard Herrmann, for its masterful pacing and devastating story, and for the relentless and terrible irony of its moral consciousness. Hitchcock followed this film with *North by Northwest* (1959), and then *Psycho* (1960), the former a slick and thoroughly brilliant chase melodrama and the latter a sick and thoroughly brilliant horror film.

Isolated from that list and reserved for special discussion, the horror and science fiction films of the 1950s were extremely important, not only for the ways they mirrored the concerns of the period, but also because they were so inventive, so unpretentious, and so much fun. Their search for new monsters and dramatization of intriguing gadgets was balanced by their careful understanding of narrative formulas, and in the classicism of that balance they have proved irreplaceable. Their attention to special effects was meticulous and creative, particularly in the work of George Pal, Ray Harryhausen, and Jack Arnold, and while some worked in small format black and white, and others in 3-D, many made good use of the opportunity to work in color and widescreen. For every badly acted and badly conceived film like *Red Planet Mars* (a 1952 anti-Communist tract with a ludicrous Christian "message") or *Plan 9 from Outer Space* (1959, cruelly considered the worst film ever made), there was a carefully executed and intelligent production like *This Island Earth* (1955) or *War of the Worlds* (1953). Influenced equally by a rash of flying saucer "sightings" and by the beginnings of the space program, the first of these films dealt both with attempts to reach the stars and with speculations on what might reach us from outer space—films like *Rocketship XM* (1950), *Destination Moon* (1950), *The Man from Planet X* (1951), *When Worlds Collide* (1951), *The Day the Earth Stood Still* (1951), and *The Thing from Another World* (1951). Two characteristic films were based on stories by Ray Bradbury: *The Beast from 20,000 Fathoms* (1953), in the tradition of *The Lost World* (1924) and *King Kong* (1932–33), set a prehistoric monster loose in a modern city (a formula imitated by the Japanese in *Godzilla*, which did tremendous business in the United States in 1956), while *IT Came from Outer Space* (1953), directed in 3-D by Jack Arnold and starring the ubiquitous Richard Carlson, dramatized the excitement of confronting alien beings whose technology was superior, whose bodies were monstrous, and who had the ability to disguise themselves as cold-blooded duplicates of ordinary citizens. The theme of the alien double was turned to purposes of social commentary in *Invasion of the Body Snatchers* (1956), which was not so much about the fear of Communist agents as it was about the battle between humanism and conformity in the years of the "Organization Man."

Some of the films, like *Pharaoh's Curse* (1959) or *It! The Terror from Beyond Space* (1958), were seen only by genre enthusiasts and children, while others like *Forbidden Planet* (1956) and *The Incredible Shrinking Man* (1957) were more widely admired. Just as the frustrated, misunderstood, imaginative teenager could find an image of rebellion in *I Was a Teenage Werewolf* (1957) or of vindication in *The Blob* (1958), the patronized woman oppressed by the "feminine mystique" could enjoy the images of the competent women scientists in *This Island Earth* (1955) and *It Came from Beneath the Sea* (1955), or the monstrous revenges of *The Leech Woman* (1960) and *Attack of the 50 Foot Woman* (1958). While Stanley Kramer pondered the end of the world with a high budget in *On the Beach* (1959), Roger Corman turned out a host of low-budget films that included *The Day the World Ended* (1956), *It Con-*

*quered the World* (1956), *Not of this Earth* (1957), *The Wasp Woman* (1959), *The Little Shop of Horrors* (1960), a series of loose Poe adaptations of which the best were *The Masque of the Red Death* (1963) and *The Raven* (1964), and the bizarre fable *X—The Man with the X-Ray Eyes* (1963). Giant vermin, often symbolic of the dangers of nuclear radiation, crowded films as good as *Them!* (1954) and *Tarantula* (1955), and as run-of-the-mill as *Beginning of the End* (1957). The technique of stop-motion animation reached a rare level of distinction in *The Black Scorpion* (1957) and *20 Million Miles to Earth* (1957). The dangers and attractions of science were dramatized with real flair in *Unknown World* (1951), *Donovan's Brain* (1953), *Gog* (1954), and *The Fly* (1958). Other distinctive and creative films include *Bride of the Gorilla* (1951), *The Magnetic Monster* (1953), *Invaders from Mars* (1953), *Conquest of Space* (1955), *The Creature Walks Among Us* (1956), *Earth vs. the Flying Saucers* (1956), *Kronos* (1957), *The Monolith Monsters* (1957), *The Unearthly* (1957), *The House on Haunted Hill* (1958), *Attack of the Puppet People* (1958), *Monster on the Campus* (1958), *I Married a Monster from Outer Space* (1958), and *The Angry Red Planet* (1959).

Explicit sexuality came to the legitimate screen in two guises between 1957 and 1959, first with the American release of Roger Vadim's *And God Created Woman* (1957), starring Brigitte Bardot, and Louis Malle's *The Lovers* (1958), starring Jeanne Moreau, and then with Russ Meyer's soft-core pornography film *The Immoral Mr. Teas* (1959). All three made resounding profits. There had already been a considerable audience for foreign or "art-house" films, created in part by such films as *The Bicycle Thief, Rashomon*, and *The Seven Samurai*, and expanded by the intellectually controversial work of Ingmar Bergman, particularly *The Seventh Seal* in 1957. Together with the promise of "adult" content, this renewed interest in complex "cinematic" expression gave rise to a major market for foreign films, an audience that was primed and ready when *Black Orpheus, La Dolce Vita, The 400 Blows, Breathless, L'Avventura, Hiroshima mon amour*, and *The Virgin Spring* were all released in 1959 and 1960. "Film" suddenly became a major intellectual preoccupation, and the practice of serious film criticism, nurtured by such important writers as Otis Ferguson, Parker Tyler, Manny Farber, and James Agee, was augmented by the rising influence of such journals as *Film Quarterly*, the British *Sight and Sound*, and the French *Cahiers du cinéma*, and rendered controversial by the outspoken Pauline Kael. The film schools at USC, UCLA, and NYU began to place graduates in the industry, and the study of film history and filmmaking became respectable across America throughout the 1960s and 1970s. The search was on for an American "New Wave."

Throughout the 1960s Hollywood produced three broad varieties of films whose interest in experimentation and whose marketing strategies were closely related to their budgets: blockbusters, quality melodramas, and low-budget long shots. At the same time filmgoers were exposed to a variety of experimental films and thought-provoking imports. Although the early films of Andy Warhol (*Sleep*, 1964; *Empire*, 1964; and *The Chelsea Girls*, 1966) and Stan Brakhage (*Dog Star Man*, 1965; *Window Water Baby Moving*, 1959) never received wide commercial distribution, they were instrumental in the rise of the "New American Cinema," a highly significant upsurge of experimental and often nonnarrative art films with close ties to the earlier work of Maya Deren, Viking Eggeling, Jean Cocteau, and Luis Buñuel but which had no single program beyond that of reviving and extending the role of film as a mode of creative vision; some of the artists who came to prominence in this movement were Jonas Mekas, Ron Rice, Bruce Conner, Bruce Baillie, Robert Nelson, George Landau, Michael Snow, Ken Jacobs, Kenneth Anger, Robert Breer, Stan VanDerBeek, Ed Emshwiller, and Jack Smith. The deliberately nonstudio look of Shirley Clarke's *The Connection* (1960) and John Cassavetes's *Shadows* (1961), with their careful balance of improvisation and directorial control, reached wider audiences, and John Korty's *The Crazy Quilt* (1965) was especially appealing in its playful camerawork and wistful, loving, humorous approach to the problems of failure and idealism. While not experimental in technique, Frank and Eleanor Perry's *David and Lisa* (1962) was remarkable for its carefully researched treatment of adolescent mental illness, and their less successful *Ladybug, Ladybug* (1963) examined civil defense paranoia through the eyes of schoolchildren. All these films were expressions of a grass-roots upsurge of new talent, and by the end of the decade Hollywood was making an effort to bring some of these people, and others like them, into the industry.

On the one hand, Hollywood offered small budgets to figures like actor Dennis Hopper (*Easy Rider*, 1969) and cinematographer Haskell Wexler (*Medium Cool*, 1969), but this support was dropped when the films proved too controversial. On the other hand, directors who had proved themselves abroad, on the stage, or in television were given larger budgets and often found success in their treatment of strong material. Roman Polanski, who had studied film in Europe and had an "art-house" reputation for his Polish film *Knife in the Water* (1962) and his British thriller *Repulsion* (1965), proved a good investment with *Rosemary's Baby* (1968) and *Chinatown* (1974) even though his American films rarely reached the brilliance of his previous work. Mike Nichols made four good films in a row—*Who's Afraid of Virginia Woolf?* (1966), *The Graduate* (1967, an enormous financial success), *Catch-22* (1970), and *Carnal Knowledge* (1971, from a script by cartoonist Jules Feiffer)—but the last, his masterpiece, was also his last worthwhile picture.

The most successful recruiting effort, however, was from television, and brought to prominence Sam Peckinpah, John Frankenheimer,

George Roy Hill, Arthur Penn, Irvin Kershner, and Sidney Lumet. Peckinpah's *Ride the High Country* (1962), starring Randolph Scott and Joel McCrea, was a superb Western, but most of his later films were drastically cut by others before their release and remained in cut versions even when, like *The Wild Bunch* (1969), they did well both with critics and with audiences; he lost favor with many of those who had championed him, however, when *Straw Dogs* (1971) opened up the darker side of his investigation of the macho ethic. Frankenheimer directed two powerful political films, *The Manchurian Candidate* (1962, from the much better novel by Richard Condon) and *Seven Days in May* (1964), the excellent science fiction melodrama *Seconds* (1966), and an intense study of anti-Semitism, *The Fixer* (1968), all of which showed an interesting mix of glossy production values and experimental editing techniques, but in his later work the glossy won out. George Roy Hill, who began on a weak note with *Period of Adjustment* (1962) and later made the disastrous *Hawaii* (1966), did consistently good work when he was excited by a good script; his best films include *The World of Henry Orient* (1964), which starred Peter Sellers and was a brilliantly sensitive treatment of the friendship of two teenage girls and their relationships with their parents; *Butch Cassidy and the Sundance Kid* (1969), a comedy about the decline of the West that starred Paul Newman and Robert Redford; *Slaughterhouse Five* (1972), a New Wave-inspired treatment of Kurt Vonnegut's science fiction novel; and *The Sting* (1973), which reunited Newman and Redford in a high-energy ragtime comedy about confidence games. The most typical of these directors was Arthur Penn, who began with a psychological Western (*The Left-Handed Gun*, 1958) and a sensitive stage adaptation (*The Miracle Worker*, 1962), and then went on to explore psychological values and New Wave cutting techniques in *Mickey One* (1965) before hitting his stride with the lyrical, sophisticated, and extremely violent *Bonnie and Clyde* (1967), a film that ranked with *The Graduate* in confirming the synthesis of "movies" and "cinema" that characterized the rejuvenated Hollywood; but it also opened the door to the brutal sensationalism on which the industry came to rely in its continuing quest for the television audience.

What linked *Bonnie and Clyde*, *The Graduate*, *Easy Rider*, and *Medium Cool* was not only their violence, their self-consciously "cinematic" practices, and their role in a short-lived revival of high-quality filmmaking targeted outside the traditional middle-class market, but also the new look they took at America. Police, politicians, and corporate values were characterized as ruthless, antiromantic, intolerant, and destructive. Good characters were presented as embattled rebels, as targets for redneck shotguns (*Easy Rider*), police massacres (*Bonnie and Clyde*), governmental corruption (*Medium Cool*), and social hypocrisy (*The Graduate*). This social perspective, which had arisen in response to the war in Vietnam, focused in the hope that media exposure would lead to positive change; outside the Chicago Democratic Convention in 1968, demonstraters chanted "the whole world is watching" as police attacked them in full view of television cameras—but the world watched and nothing changed, and out of this emerged an embattled, outraged romanticism whose most characteristic fantasies were of being murdered by ignorant and intolerant men, as in John G. Avildsen's *Joe* (1970), where a redneck and a baffled father shot up a household of hippies that included his missing daughter. The belief in the value of exposure that had so highly charged documentaries like Emile De Antonio's *Point of Order* (1964), which asserted the continuing relevance of the 1954 Army-McCarthy hearings, or Peter Watkins's *The War Game* (1965), which had been commissioned by the BBC—and which they refused to show because its depiction of the aftermath of a nuclear strike was considered too vivid, even after it won the Oscar for Best Documentary in the United States—that belief became empty as the decade progressed. Of all the feature filmmakers, Arthur Penn saw this first and summed up the sadness of the hippie movement in his beautiful, painful film *Alice's Restaurant* (1969) before turning to irony and violence in his bitterly antiestablishment send up of the Ford Westerns, *Little Big Man* (1970). In concert films like *Gimme Shelter* and *Woodstock* (both 1970), as well as in stage productions like *Hair*, this romantic would-be revolution reached the peak of its enthusiasm even as it watched itself begin to die, and the stage was set for a bitter engagement of black comedy and defeatism. What Stanley Kubrick had foreseen in *Dr. Strangelove, or How I Learned to Stop Worrying and Love the Bomb* (1964)—not nuclear war, but an accommodation with insanity—was perfectly expressed in Alan Arkin's brilliant adaptation of Jules Feiffer's *Little Murders* (1971), a great black comedy about the death of hope and love. If Kubrick danced on this grave with sometimes hateful enthusiasm in *A Clockwork Orange* (1971), Robert Altman built his reputation with an ambiguous and ambivalent parade to the cemetery, so that it is not clear whether in *McCabe and Mrs. Miller* (1971) and *Nashville* (1975) he was critiquing absurdity and defeatism or embracing them as he set up his characters for their inevitable falls. In 1969 it was still possible to find, along with *Alice's Restaurant*, the dark sentimentality of John Schlesinger's *Midnight Cowboy* and the fierce energy of Robert Downey's *Putney Swope*; by 1979, when the Canadian-British *Murder by Decree*—the best of all Sherlock Holmes films—presented Jack the Ripper as a creature of the government and left the criminals unpunished, it was just another story.

As vital as these films and issues were for the new generation, for Hollywood they were more than anything else a marketing trend, and the market was in trouble. Fewer pictures were being made, and they were costing more to make. The blockbuster, which had become a standby for prestige and big receipts, was almost killed off in 1963 when *Cleopatra*—four hours long, four years in production, and given immense prerelease publicity due to the scandalous romance of its stars, Richard Burton and Elizabeth Taylor—not only failed to make back its $40 million cost but nearly ruined its studio, Twentieth Century-Fox. Not even the enormously successful *The Sound of Music* (1965) could disguise the fact that these overproduced films were going the way of the dinosaur. The decade did, however, see two distinguished and successful "big" pictures, David Lean's *Lawrence of Arabia* (1962) and Stanley Kubrick's *2001: A Space Odyssey* (1968), but both of these were primarily British productions. Realizing finally that success lay with the less expensive film of controversial or sex-and-violence content, the industry abandoned the Production Code and in 1968 adopted the Motion Picture Association of America (MPAA) system, awarding films G, M (later PG), R, or X ratings on the basis of their intended audiences; this system was discredited in 1970 when *Ryan's Daughter* was given a PG rather than the R it deserved so that its studio would not go in the red, and in later years when the X was reserved for outright pornography and for essentially unrated horror films like *Dawn of the Dead* (1979), but it remains in effect. Its most significant effect on film content has been the cutting of many films before release in order to ensure their receiving certain ratings, a practice that has in some cases been carried out *after* release, so that both *A Clockwork Orange* and *Straw Dogs* (both 1971) exist in X and later R versions.

A number of mainstream directors with established reputations responded to the opportunities of the 1960s by expanding the range of their interests—as William Wyler did in his psychological horror film, *The Collector* (1965)—or increasing the frankness of their treatment, as Elia Kazan did in his intensely romantic *Splendor in the Grass* (1961). Others continued to develop their careers more seamlessly: John Huston with *The Misfits* (1961), *The List of Adrian Messenger* (1963), *The Night of the Iguana* (1964), and *Reflections in a Golden Eye* (1967); Howard Hawks with *Hatari!* (1962), *Red Line 7000* (1965), and the cornered-jailhouse Westerns; John Ford with *Two Rode Together* (1962), *The Man Who Shot Liberty Valance* (1962), *Donovan's Reef* (1963), and *Cheyenne Autumn* (1964); Alfred Hitchcock with *The Birds* (1963) and *Marnie* (1964); Robert Rossen with *The Hustler* (1961); Robert Aldrich with *What Ever Happened to Baby Jane?* (1962), *The Dirty Dozen* (1967), and *The Killing of Sister George* (1968); Billy Wilder with *The Apartment* (1960) and *The Private Life of Sherlock Holmes* (1970); Otto Preminger with *Bunny Lake Is Missing* (1965); Stanley Donen with *Two for the Road* and *Bedazzled* (both 1967); Fred Zinnemann with *A Man for All Seasons* (1966); Martin Ritt with *The Spy Who Came in From the Cold* (1965); and Orson Welles with *Chimes at Midnight* (1967). Francis Ford Coppola made his appearance with, among

Howard Hawks's extraordinary skills as a storyteller made *Red River* (1948), with Montgomery Clift and John Wayne, one of the most tightly constructed and emotionally profound of all Westerns.

*A Streetcar Named Desire* (1951) was a drastically censored adaptation of Tennessee Williams's American tragedy, but Marlon Brando's performance was worth the price of admission.

Gene Kelly, dancin' and *Singin' in the Rain* (1952), one of the classic Hollywood musicals.

*Rebel Without a Cause* (1955), a movie that took the problems of the alienated adolescent seriously, made James Dean the brightest shooting star of the '50s.

*The Searchers* (1956) was John Ford's greatest Western in color and one of the most profound and morally ambiguous films of the period.

*North by Northwest* (1959) was Hitchcock's last great chase picture, and his last with Cary Grant. Made just after *Vertigo* and just before *Psycho*, it was a witty, elegant thriller.

Rough night at the Bates Motel. Anthony Perkins and Janet Leigh in the first and only *Psycho* (1960).

*The Graduate* (1967) set Dustin Hoffman and the music of Simon and Garfunkel against the forces of "plastic" and bourgeois corruption.

Dennis Hopper and Peter Fonda rode a vision of America to the bloody end of the line in *Easy Rider* (1969). Like *Medium Cool*, it was rated X for its radicalism as much as for "sex and violence."

An action picture with fine ensemble performances, *The Dirty Dozen* cleaned up at the box office in 1967.

John Schlesinger's *Midnight Cowboy* violated sexual taboos and was, by turns, steel-cold and sentimental. It won the Oscar for Best Picture despite its X rating.

(Right)
*2001: A Space Odyssey* (1968) charted human development from the discovery of tools through a point—shown here—where humanity is at odds with its tools, exemplified by HAL, the runaway computer.

(Left)
The cast of *The Godfather* (1972)—the greatest gangster picture since *Scarface*—poses for a "family" portrait.

Right
Roman Polanski takes a switchblade to Jack Nicholson's nose: Forget it, Jake, it's *Chinatown* (1974).

Robert De Niro and Jodie Foster in Martin Scorsese's *Taxi Driver* (1976), a disturbing look at the darker side of the night.

Robert Altman turned a fluid, wide-screen camera and 4-track Dolby magnetic soundtrack loose on the world of country and Western music in *Nashville* (1975), a black comedy of white America.

*Victor Victoria* (1982) was one of a string of adult comedies of manners in which director Blake Edwards led Julie Andrews, his wife, far from the land of Mary Poppins.

other films, *Dementia 13* (1963), *You're a Big Boy Now* (1967), and *The Rain People* (1969). John Cassavetes made his best film, *Faces*, in 1968, perfecting his slow-paced, brooding realism and his devastating intimacy in that film before going on to the wandering *Husbands* (1970) and the enormously powerful *A Woman Under the Influence* (1974). Some of Cassavetes's influence could be seen in Michael Roemer's debut film, *Nothing But a Man* (1964), one of the best films ever made about the Black American experience. While the James Bond films (beginning with *Dr. No* in 1963) did major business, such "small" films as *Faces, Nothing But a Man*, Noel Black's *Pretty Poison* (1968), Larry Pearce's *One Potato, Two Potato* (1964), and David Miller's *Lonely Are the Brave* (1962) developed considerable word-of-mouth and critical reputations, and such distinguished studio productions as *To Kill a Mockingbird* (1962, directed by Robert Mulligan from an Oscar-winning screenplay by Horton Foote (who later wrote the superior, intimate films *Tomorrow* [1971] and *Tender Mercies* [1983]) testified to an emerging and intelligent humanism, not just in film but in an America that was moving into an epoch of freedom riders and antinuclear demonstrations.

While the industry clearly kept its eye on the foreign product, as can be seen in John Sturges's Western remake of Kurosawa's *Seven Samurai, The Magnificent Seven* (1960), it still attempted to ignore the overseas work of those it had exiled during the McCarthy period. The name of Jules Dassin, for example, was usually pronounced as if it were French, and his *Rififi* (1956), however closely related to such "caper" films as Huston's *The Asphalt Jungle* (1950) and Kubrick's *The Killing* (1956), was marketed and evaluated in an entirely "foreign film" context. By the time Dassin made *Never on Sunday* (1960), many considered him a Greek, and it would still surprise many people to find that the director of *Night and the City* was responsible for the Anglo-Greek masterpiece, *A Dream of Passion* (1978), in which Ellen Burstyn and Melina Mercouri confronted *Medea* in a context influenced by Bergman's *Persona*. By the same token, Joseph Losey is today best known for his British films scripted by Harold Pinter—*The Servant* (1964), *Accident* (1967), and *The Go-Between* (1971)—as well as French films like *Mr. Klein* (1976), though it is clear enough that the grueling political commentary of *These Are the Damned* (1961) and *King and Country* (1964) is more distant in tone than in intention from *The Boy With Green Hair*. On the other hand, a self-imposed expatriate like Stanley Kubrick was courted from abroad by both studios and audiences eager to enjoy his cold-hearted and coldly beautiful satires. The bitterly superior tone of Kubrick's later work was announced in his first British film, *Lolita* (1962), which featured excellent performances by Peter Sellers and James Mason, poor work by Sue Lyon (who played a Lolita aged from the nymphet of Nabokov's far superior novel to an unimaginative teenager, for censorship reasons), and a characteristic closing shot of bullet holes in an elegant portrait. However attractive or repellent one finds this tone in *A Clockwork Orange* (1971), *Barry Lyndon* (1975), and *The Shining* (1980), it is clearly at the heart of the success of his best films, *Dr. Strangelove* and *2001*. *2001*, which opened to weak reviews and was cut by more than 20 minutes during its first month of release (footage that has never been restored), became a major hit not only because of its magnificent special effects, well-chosen music, and intriguingly cosmic philosophy (all of which made it a "must-see" for those experimenting at the time with LSD), but also because of its icepick wit, its merciless send-up of American security policies (which are responsible for the computer's destructive actions, since only the computer was deemed worthy of knowing the purposes of the mission), and its ironically sexless vision. But even *2001* pales before the ironic brilliance of *Dr. Strangelove*, the best film of the decade and one of the two or three greatest satires in film history, so intelligently written and dynamically edited that the great performances of Peter Sellers (in three roles), George C. Scott, Slim Pickens, and Sterling Hayden can only be said to have contributed to its excellence rather than to have accounted for it.

One by-product of the rise of film criticism in the 1960s was the "auteur theory," popularized by Andrew Sarris and intended to identify, among other things, the hidden "signature" of the artist presumed to be responsible for the meaning or tone of a film, usually the director. This critical tendency, while valuable for drawing attention to the career coherence of such artists as Ford, Hawks, Sirk, Hitchcock, and so on, had an unfortunate effect on such directors as Jerry Lewis (*The Nutty Professor*, 1963) who trumpeted their self-expression at the expense of their films. The auteur theory also often obscured the contributions of film artists who were not directors, and led to the denigration of directors who did not have (or flaunt) a "personal style," such as Sidney Lumet. By the 1970s it was common for people to go to "the new Altman film," to buy books not on stars but on directors, and to seek out classic films in repertory houses. Some film critics made the shift to directing, notably Peter Bogdanovich, who expressed his love for film—and particularly for Howard Hawks—in two extremely good films, *Targets* (1967, produced by Roger Corman and starring Boris Karloff in his final role) and *The Last Picture Show* (1971). While some of Bogdanovich's later films, such as *Paper Moon* (1973), proved lucrative, nothing in his later career showed the urgency and intelligence of *Targets*, the work of a young man who wanted more than anything else to *make a film* and who was in that respect like the Soviets in the 1920s, hungry for raw stock, and the *Cahiers* critics who erupted in the New Wave. One legacy of the 1960s, then, has been a new generation of filmmakers who know film history and care passionately about it, and some of them have gone on, like Coppola, Scorcese, and Lucas, to become major figures in or just outside the industry.

Of all the directors who received national attention in the 1970s, Robert Altman and William Friedkin got the best running starts, Friedkin with *The Boys in the Band* (1970) and Altman with *M\*A\*S\*H* (1970). *M\*A\*S\*H* was an extremely iconoclastic, witty, and loosely structured treatment of a medical/surgical outpost in the Korean War, chock full of reflexive tropes and dirty jokes. It insisted equally on the professionalism of the doctors and their juvenile sense of humor—hysterical in both senses of the word. *M\*A\*S\*H* appealed to a diverse adult audience and inspired a relatively sanitized and considerably more humanistic TV series that became the most successful since *I Love Lucy*. That same year Altman released another major comedy, *Brewster McCloud*, a wildly funny piece of Olympian childishness that flaunted conventional rules of narrative construction, drew equally on New Wave techniques and burlesque surrealism, parodied itself and was sarcastic about everything else, and was not as widely distributed as *M\*A\*S\*H*. His next film, *McCabe and Mrs. Miller* (1971), was more tightly structured than either of these, was admired by nearly all the critics, and showed a masterful visual sense, but was also destructively manipulative, covertly sexist, and unnecessarily violent. Although its statement was ultimately ambiguous, it stands with *A Clockwork Orange* and *Straw Dogs*, both released that same year, at the head of an apolitical and self-absorbed backlash against the concerns and concernedness of the 1960s. A self-conscious artist with a viable technique of group improvisation, a fluid and exciting sense of camera and editing and dialogue rhythm, and a sarcastic yet somehow reverent attitude toward the world, Altman was the 1970s' premier stylist (Coppola perhaps excepted). His later films were divided among experiments in cinematic subjectivity (*Images*, 1972; and *Three Women*, 1977) and sound (*California Split*, 1974), complex ensemble melodramas (*Nashville*, 1975; *Buffalo Bill and the Indians*, 1976; and *A Wedding*, 1978), and conventional narratives imbued with his characteristic style (*The Long Goodbye*, 1973; and *Thieves Like Us*, 1974). His best films include *Brewster McCloud, The Long Goodbye*, and *A Wedding*; his worst was *Quintet* (1979); and his most characteristic was *Nashville*, a beautifully acted, complexly constructed, and pretentiously vapid look at the failures of modern life.

Although *The Boys in the Band* was by no means his best film, its controversial treatment of homosexuality did bring William Friedkin to public notice as a careful craftsman able to manipulate complex material with taste and polish, and his next film, *The French Connection* (1971), won the Oscars for Best Picture, Best Director, and Best Actor (Gene Hackman). *The French Connection* and *The Exorcist* (1973) were typical of the new Hollywood both in their slick professionalism and in their frank, sensationalist brutality—the latter being responsible, almost single-handedly, for the gory intensity that came to dominate the horror genre. When Friedkin followed them with *Sorcerer* (1977), a fine, thoughtful, but expensive remake of Henri-Georges Clouzot's *The Wages of Fear* (1955), his audience appeared to be disappointed by its relative lack of violence and speed, and Friedkin has not had a major hit since *The Exorcist*, even though *The Brink's Job* (1979) was a superb caper film and *Cruising* (1980) was a profoundly controversial and daring film about homosexuality, murder, and the dark side of the problem of identity.

On the gentler side, the films of Paul Mazursky found a ready audience. *Bob & Carol & Ted & Alice* (1969) was a well-informed satire of "California consciousness," creative bonding, and group-encounter psychology. Mazursky followed it with *Blume in Love* (1973), a first-class screwball comedy, and *Harry and Tonto* (1974), a less interesting picaresque comedy about death. By the time he made *An Unmarried Woman* in 1978 Mazursky, while clearly remaining interested in the vagaries of modern bonding, had lost much of his sense of character; while *An Unmarried Woman* had a short vogue as a feminist picture, closer examination revealed that it was in fact a muddle. A similar confusion greeted two earlier films starring Jane Fonda and Donald Sutherland, Alan Pakula's *Klute* (1971) and Alan Myerson's *Steelyard Blues* (1973). The former, about a prostitute who needs to be saved by a male detective, was acclaimed for its "feminist" content, while the latter, which dealt far more authentically and creatively with similar material and which set out to teach its audience something about violence, theater, and manipulation, was ignored.

Although the American feminist movement was in full swing, there were few great roles for self-directed, intelligent, and creative heroines of the sort that had abounded in the 1940s, and when such characters did arise—as in *Billy Jack* (1972) or *The Stepford Wives* (1975)—they were often presented as victims. *The Exorcist* can be seen to critique a working mother whose daughter has to be saved by two priests who understand the importance of self-sacrifice. "The death of a beautiful woman," one of Poe's formulas, did tremendous box office in the guise of *Love Story* (1971), a treacly melodrama about a foulmouthed undergraduate whose death brings her husband closer to his father. One of the strongest and most serious films about women helping each other was in fact made for television (as were a growing number of films throughout the 1970s): Daniel Petrie's *Sybil* (1976) was a carefully researched and authentically moving case history about a psychiatrist (Joanne Woodward) and a patient with multiple personalities (Sally Field). An equally important and intelligent film about a psychic healer, *Resurrection* (1980), starring Ellen Burstyn and also directed by Petrie, hardly saw release, while the Oscars descended on a genuinely terrible film about a bad father who becomes a good mother, *Kramer vs. Kramer* (1980).

Looking back, one can see that 1967 was the critical year in the failure of the vision of marriage, when *Bonnie and Clyde* apotheosized in slow motion the union of bloody death and when *The Graduate* could stir up great audience sympathy for the union of young lovers but had no idea what to do with them after they had gotten together. The crucial feminist breakthrough came not in films-by-and-about-women like Claudia Weill's *Girlfriends* (1978), but in a French film by Jean-Luc Godard and Jean-Pierre Gorin, *Tout va bien* (1972), in which the character played by Jane Fonda looks at the camera and demands access to "another image," taking control of the film from within and critiquing not only its imagery but the way it has imaged her. While films about sensitive men were on the rise in the eighties (e.g., *Ordinary People*, 1980), many films about intriguing women seem impelled to consign them to death or isolation (e.g., *Resurrection, Sophie's Choice* [1982], *Frances* [1982]). It appears fair to say that one of the only American films to have projected a loving and viable image of marriage since *Guess Who's Coming to Dinner?* has been *Poltergeist* (1982).

Two sorts of documentary film enjoyed wide distribution in the late 1960s and early 1970s: the concert film and the low-budget cinéma vérité look at the underside of American institutions. Fred Wiseman exposed a mental hospital in *Titicut Follies* (1967) and went on to examing everything from a monastery to a slaughterhouse; one of his best was *High School* (1969). The Maysles brothers followed a salesman of expensive Bibles in *Salesman* (1969), and the Rolling Stones in *Gimme Shelter* (1970). Don Pennebaker made an excellent film around Bob Dylan, *Don't Look Back* (1967), and contributed to *Monterey Pop* (1969), a significant concert film that was eclipsed in popularity by Michael Wadleigh's ambitious *Woodstock* (1970). Cinda Firestone's *Attica* (1974) was the most accurate and careful treatment of that prison riot and was as important as any of these films in bringing the documentary back to the center of social discourse and out of Cousteau's seas and Disney's deserts. While Wadleigh never followed up *Woodstock* in its own terms, his horror film *Wolfen* (1981) revealed a continuing commitment to the value structures of the "counterculture"; Wiseman and Pennebaker have continued to make important documentaries, but their work has received less attention in recent years.

While American politics and institutions were not examined as openly or rigorously in recent features as they were in those documentaries, Hollywood did tackle the military and the police within a commercial margin of safety. Science fiction provided a useful mask for Rod Serling and Franklin Schaffner's antinuclear satire, *Planet of the Apes* (1968), a satire arguably intensified in Ted Post's sequel *Beneath the Planet of the Apes* (1970) and then abandoned in the pointless further sequels. Schaffner's *Patton* (1970, from a script by Coppola) was more a dramatization than a critique of the flamboyant general, and any implications that film might have borne about an irresponsible military or about the war in Vietnam were hastily disclaimed. Don Siegel's *Dirty Harry* (1971) made a strong statement about the conflict between the police and the law, giving Clint Eastwood free rein to urbanize the gunman type he had played in Sergio Leone's Italian Westerns and in Ted Post's *Hang 'Em High* (1968), except that "Dirty Harry" was a more emotional and frustrated figure whose violent eruptions were socially and legally problematic. When Ted Post made the "Dirty Harry" sequel, *Magnum Force* (1973), Eastwood's figure proved more centrist in relation to a conspiracy of vigilante police officers and officials, and it was appropriately Post who made the first film seriously to question the American involvement in Vietnam, *Go Tell the Spartans,* in 1978. This was followed quickly by Karel Reisz's film about a returned Vietnam veteran, *Who'll Stop the Rain?* (1978), and Michael Cimino's Oscar-winning but utterly muddled *The Deer Hunter* (1978). The only mainstream movie about Vietnam before Post's had been John Wayne's gung-ho propaganda film, *The Green Berets,* in 1968. Of all the Vietnam films, Alan Ormsby and Bob Clark's *Death Dream* (1972, released 1974), a low-budget horror film that portrayed the returned veteran as a zombie, remains the most uncompromising.

Don Siegel went on to make a number of fine melodramas after *Dirty Harry,* including *Charley Varrick* (1973), *The Black Windmill* (1974), *The Shootist* (1976, with John Wayne in his last film), *Telefon* (1977), and *Escape from Alcatraz* (1979), none of which had controversial political content. When Cimino, however, attempted to follow *The Deer Hunter* with a much more carefully thought-out Western about the evils of corrupt capitalism and the betrayal of the American dream, *Heaven's Gate* (1980) was denounced by the few critics and exhibitors who saw it in its complete version, withdrawn and shortened, released and buried. Although Godard probably put it best when he said that *The Deer Hunter* was not as good, nor *Heaven's Gate* as bad, as each was reported to be, it seems more than likely that it was the political incisiveness of the later film that denied it an adequate release, and that it was the equivocation of *The Deer Hunter* that gave audiences the impression that it spoke adequately to their ambivalence and confusion about the war. By the time Coppola released his film about Vietnam, *Apocalypse Now* (1979), it was politically uncontroversial, and most critical and public response centered around its superb montages, state-of-the-art sound track, pretentious script, and hopelessly bad performance by Marlon Brando. Perhaps the worst film about Vietnam, *The Green Berets* aside, was the highly praised *Coming Home* (1978), which was an intriguing treatment of paraplegia, an occasionally interesting study of postcombat stress, and on the whole a film that would have been controversial had it come out five years earlier but was, in late 1978, thoroughly safe in political terms and utterly hypocritical in its disposal of the maddened veteran. Among the better-realized political thrillers of the decade were Alan Pakula's *The Parallax View* (1974) and *All the President's Men* (1976), which looked carefully at corporate/ fictitious and presidential/factual corruption. The science fiction and horror genres, as usual, provided incisive and overlooked commentaries on related matters, notably Joe Dante's *Piranha* (1978) and Ridley Scott's *Alien* (1979), which turned corporate greed and governmental rapacity into merciless monsters.

A final legacy of the openness of the 1960s was a series of films that treated blacks with dramatic complexity, building as much on *Nothing But a Man* (1964) as on the heroic Sidney Poitier prototype seen in *The Defiant Ones* (1958) and *In the Heat of the Night* (1967). These films fell into three groups: those set in the South and concerned with portraying the enduring humanism of the major characters, like Gordon Parks's *The Learning Tree* (1969), Martin Ritt's *Sounder* (1972), and John Korty's TV film *The Autobiography of Miss Jane Pittman* (1974); those that cast blacks in genre roles usually reserved for whites, like Gordon Parks's *Shaft* (1971) or William Crain's *Blacula* (1972), which led to a cycle referred to as "blaxpolitation" films; and those, like Sidney J. Furie's *Lady Sings the Blues* (1973) and Gordon Parks's masterful *Leadbelly* (1976), that examined historical figures with a politically informed perspective and an apolitical eye on the box office. What the box office had shown in 1971 was that controversial subject matter and realistic treatment were inadequate in themselves to attract audiences; *The Panic in Needle Park,* Jerry Schatzberg's excellent but depressing film about white heroin addicts, did virtually no business, while *Shaft* and *The French Connection* made millions and *Love Story* four times more than both combined. Although glossy production values were clearly important, the most successful films needed to find a way to combine them with a compelling story and, as often as not, some degree of violence and sensationalism. This trend, while it meant the decline of the small experimental feature, resulted in the production of several excellent and polished major films—many of which, like *The Godfather* (1972), *Jaws* (1975), *Star Wars* (1977), and *Raging Bull* (1980), came from genres that had been considered suitable only for B-pictures and from directors who had been educated in film schools or by films. When *The Godfather* did three times the business of *Fiddler on the Roof* (1971), this trend was entrenched for the decade.

Most of the major studios had been bought by corporations with more interest in profitable returns on their investments than expertise in film production—Paramount, for example, became "A Gulf and Western Company" in 1966—and this led to a hit-or-miss attitude that drastically curtailed film experimentation. In the absence of film moguls who trusted their own judgment, like Zanuck, Thalberg, Cohn, and Selznick, producers began to rely on remaking what had worked recently; William Goldman's summary judgment on the present industry, in his book *Adventures in the Screen Trade* (1983), was that "NOBODY KNOWS ANYTHING." This is as good an explanation as any for the plethora of sequels to big hits: four *Rocky*s, four *Superman*s, at least three each of *Halloween* and *Friday the 13th*, and so on. It also explains why many pictures are constructed out of deals and tailored to fit packages of marketable talent rather than conceived whole and with thematic integrity. *Superman* (1978), one of the most expensive films ever made, had been conceived with its sequel in mind, and between Richard Donner's original and Richard Lester's 1980 *Superman II* there was an intelligent complementarity of purpose and style. But *Superman III* (1983), a film that both Lester and star Christopher Reeve seem to have disliked, was clearly put together by a producer who wanted to rely on the box-office appeal of Richard Pryor and who was willing to pay Margot Kidder a great deal of money simply to put in an appearance, and both of them proved dead weight. *Jaws* was a superior thriller, *Jaws 2* (1978) was boring and formulaic, but made money, and so *Jaws 3-D* was made in 1983, one of the least watchable films imaginable, utterly without energy or point. Although there have been fewer and fewer great films during the past ten years, the receipts from the occasional successes have been staggering, with films like *E.T.* (1982) and *Return of the Jedi* (1983) making hundreds of millions of dollars. Between these mega-hits and their clones, a scattering of superior films like Paramount's *Days of Heaven* (1978) manage to flourish while others disappear from sight and countless original works of dubious marketability are scrapped before production. The seeds of all this were planted in the 1970s, and it seems to have begun, oddly enough, with a great film and its great sequel.

Francis Ford Coppola's *The Godfather* (1972) was more than an excellent gangster film: it was a vision of the rise and fall of an American family, a critique of capitalism, and an intelligent study of twentieth-century ethics. As Don Vito Corleone, the Sicilian immigrant who became the head of a New York Mafia family, Marlon Brando had his greatest role (and an Oscar he declined to accept) and the film firmly established the careers of Robert Duvall, Al Pacino, Talia Shire, Diane Keaton, John Casale, James Caan, and others. With the masterful production design by Dean Tavoularis, cinematography by Gordon Willis, and music by Nino Rota, Coppola created a masterpiece that won the Best Picture Oscar, as did the sequel, *The Godfather, Part II*, in 1974. For the sequel, Coppola resorted to the cross-cutting techniques of Griffith's *Intolerance* (1916), carefully paralleling the rise of the young Vito Corleone (Robert De Niro) with the moral fall of his son Michael (Al Pacino). This powerful but depressing film asserted even more than the original how closely related were the values of family and honor and the moral history of America, shown here in both rise and fall. The lesson to be learned from this sequel, which the industry missed, was that the second film succeeded by improving on its original as well as by extending its story-line; the lesson it did not miss was that young directors, given a relatively free hand, could succeed both aesthetically and financially. Working closely with sound expert Walter Murch, Coppola made *The Conversation* (also nominated for Best Picture in 1974), then founded his own studio, American Zoetrope. The extravagant, ambitious *Apocalypse Now* (1979) reversed his fortunes, but Coppola continued to experiment, developing "electronic cinema" for *One from the Heart* (1982), a romantic melodrama whose financial failure eventually forced him to sell his studio. In its short life, Zoetrope released such important films as Carroll Ballard's *The Black Stallion* (1979) and—with the Images Film Archive—Kevin Brownlow's reconstruction of Abel Gance's *Napoleon* (1927). George Lucas's Lucasfilms, and his laboratory, Industrial Light and Magic (ILM), have been sustained by the *Star Wars* films and by ILM's state-of-the-art work on such films as *Poltergeist* (1982), but it remains to be seen whether this will lead to a new generation of studios or remain an isolated success.

Lucas, who began as a protegé of Coppola as Coppola had of Roger Corman, is said to have walked onto the Warner Brothers lot to begin his student internship the day Jack Warner walked off. His first feature, *THX-1138* (1971), was an expansion of a short he had made at USC; his second, *American Graffiti* (1973), based on his memories of cruising through Modesto in high school, was produced by Coppola and was nominated for Best Picture the year *The Sting* won the Oscar. The last film he directed, *Star Wars* (1977), was a similarly personal project, based on his enthusiasm for pulp science fiction and B-movies, and its phenomenal success ushered in a new era of children's pictures, many of them produced by Lucas himself. A bizarre conflation of *Hidden Fortress* and *The Wizard of Oz*, and the first film to use Dolby noise reduction throughout production and to be released in Dolby optical stereo, *Star Wars* preached an offbeat version of Zen Buddhism while appealing to the spirit of the 1940s' serials. The superior sequels both expanded its effects and deepened its characters: *The Empire Strikes Back*, directed by Irvin Kershner in 1980, had the true serial flavor and the most complex plot of the trilogy, while *Return of the Jedi*, directed by Richard Marquand, was the film event of 1983. In *Raiders of the Lost Ark* (1981), directed by Steven Spielberg, Lucas demonstrated his skill as a creative producer outside the *Star Wars* format and turned his love for the low-budget adventure films that had sustained his childhood into a high-budget adventure film that thrilled the present generation of children while giving their parents something viable—and antiestablishment—to enjoy.

Spielberg got his start with the TV movie *Duel* in 1971. Coming after *The Sugarland Express* (1973), his second theatrical feature, *Jaws* (1975), was not only successful but also well crafted on every level. Spielberg was then entrusted with an extremely high budget to match *Star Wars*, which he more than did with his 1977 film, *Close Encounters of the Third Kind,* a moving and well-researched "hard" science fiction piece that many found more satisfying than the "space opera" science fiction of Lucas. This film was rereleased in 1979 in a "Special Edition" that reflected Spielberg's original intentions better than the first studio cut, which was in itself a sign of how much power the new directors had. Even though his next film, *1941* (1979), was a mess, Spielberg came back with *Raiders* and then with two extraordinary films, *E.T.: The Extra-Terrestrial* and *Poltergeist,* released back to back in 1982. *Poltergeist,* which came out first, was properly credited to Tobe Hooper, the director of *The Texas Chain Saw Massacre* (1974) and *The Funhouse* (1981)—and the three of them are, with George Romero's *Dawn of the Dead* (1979), among the best horror films of the last ten years—but *Poltergeist* also showed the evidence of Spielberg as creative producer. Its masterful vision of the family, of heart and courage, its witty attack on television and suburbia, and its excellent screenplay and performances not only succeeded on their own terms but worked in diptych with *E.T.*'s science fiction vision of a similar suburb. While *E.T.* was by far the more popular film, *Poltergeist* was the best film in which Spielberg had had a hand since *Jaws*.

Another film school graduate, Paul Schrader, got his start with the scripts for Sydney Pollack's *The Yakuza* (1975), Brian De Palma's *Obsession* (1976)—a tribute to *Vertigo*—and Martin Scorsese's *Taxi Driver* (1976), before directing three of his own scripts: *Blue Collar* (1978), a tight and meaningful study of corruption in a labor union and the ways revolutionaries are turned against each other; *Hardcore* (1979), a less successful treatment of the pornography underworld and its impact on a midwestern Protestant; and *American Gigolo* (1980), a slick but intense film about a male prostitute who comes to understand the meaning of love. He followed these important films with a glossy and poorly conceived remake of Val Lewton's *Cat People* (1982), an entirely unnecessary film that incarnated most of what is bad about the contemporary horror film, from its literalist special effects and pointless violence to its apparently intentional sexism—flaws that had appeared in *Taxi Driver* but that had been absent from his other work.

Although it was *Taxi Driver* that first made Scorsese famous, that was neither his best film nor his first. It was his fourth film, *Mean Streets* (1973), that established his critical reputation, a tightly structured and very well written study of four Italian-American youths' coming of age in the modern city, goofing off on the one hand and struggling with religion and death on the other. Although Scorsese's work has been uneven—bottoming out in the violent *Alice Doesn't Live Here Anymore* (1975) and the overblown *New York, New York* (1977)—his skill and care were evident in the important concert film, *The Last Waltz* (1978), and he made a masterpiece in *Raging Bull* (1979), written by Schrader (with Mardik Martin) and starring Robert De Niro. Based on the life of prizefighter Jake La Motta, *Raging Bull* was the best fight picture since *The Set-Up,* and in spite of its extreme violence, its emotional painfulness was perfectly focused in a tough examination of self-destructive behavior, all of which somehow projected an imagery of religious transcendence. *The King of Comedy* (1983) was a box-office disaster of uncommon merit, a wonderful picture. It is safe to predict that Scorsese will continue to be a major creative presence in the American cinema; at this point only Coppola is his peer.

Brian De Palma began with a variety of underground New York humor that was done better by Robert Downey, moved up to the slick psychological mystery that was done better by Alfred Hitchcock, and then emerged as a clean, brilliant stylist when he turned to the horror film. His best films of the first type were *Greetings* (1968) and *Hi Mom!* (1970). His careful study of film history was evident in *Phantom of the Paradise* (1974) and *Obsession* (1976), but his real skills emerged in *Sisters* (1973), which was to *Psycho* as *Obsession* was to *Vertigo*. His 1976 adaptation of Stephen King's inferior novel *Carrie* went far beyond the level of the Hitchcock homage (though it was one) and authentically tapped the resonance of the best horror films with its solid interrelation of blood taboos, religious extremism, puberty, nightmares, and witchcraft; its shock ending, endlessly imitated, has not been bettered, and its balance of realistic acting with expressionist vision was shown not to be a fluke when his next film, *The Fury,* appeared in 1978. *Blow Out* (1981), while just as indebted as *The Conversation* to Antonioni's *Blow-Up,* achieved authentic horror at its conclusion, when a sound engineer mixes the dying scream of his lover with the cliché image of a bad actress who is being knifed in a shower, an image that in itself should put to rest any charges of De Palma's being simply a clone of Hitchcock.

Another director who has concentrated on the horror film is John Carpenter, whose *Halloween* (1978) was a highly successful mix of careful research into mythic sources, coy references to other films, and exploitative violence. Although his next horror film, *The Fog* (1980), was dull, his remake of *The Thing* (1982) was in many ways an improvement over Nyby's film, not least because it more closely followed the original story, John Campbell's "Who Goes There?" George Romero, who made his reputation with the grisly low-budget zombie film, *Night of the Living Dead* (1968), made a tongue-in-cheek picture (*Martin,* 1978) about a teenager who thinks he is a vampire and whose uncle accordingly drives a stake through his heart, before expanding the social satire of his zombie film with the marvelous *Dawn of the Dead* (1979). While John Badham revived *Dracula* (1979), the figure of the werewolf was given vivid and intelligent treatment in Joe Dante's *The Howling* and John Landis's *An American Werewolf in London* (both 1981).

A number of other directors did distinguished work in the 1970s. Michael Ritchie, who became known with *Downhill Racer* (1969), proved himself a clever satirist in *The Candidate* (1972) and a brilliant one in *Smile* (1975). Joan Micklin Silver made a great start with *Hester Street* (1974) and followed that with *Between the Lines* (1977) and *Head Over Heels* (1979). John Sayles, who wrote the scripts for *Piranha* and *The Howling,* directed his own work in *The Return of the Secaucus 7* (1980), a gentle prodding of the 1960s' radicals on the verge of middle age, and *Baby It's You* (1983), an incisive and moving story of "young love" under the mutually exclusive shadows of Frank Sinatra and Sarah Lawrence College. Robert Redford, best known as an actor, won the Oscar for Best Director on his first film, *Ordinary People* (1980). David Lynch, a major talent, went from film school to cult status with the nightmarish and depressing comedy *Eraserhead* (1978)—a film enjoyed by much the same audience as Jim Sherman's *The Rocky Horror Picture Show* (1975). The latter film is noteworthy for the grostesque carnivals it has attracted to its country-wide Friday midnight showings, in which the audiences talk back to the screen and act out most of its effects and events. Lynch's first major feature, *The Elephant Man* (1980), was a distinguished, beautiful, and extremely painful study of the relations between inner and outer being as they conflict in the person of a Victorian sideshow attraction. Robert Young's *Short Eyes* (1977) was a powerful study of life in prison. Herbert Ross, praised at the time for his Woody Allen film, *Play It Again, Sam* (1972) and his melodrama *The Turning Point* (1977), did better work in *Nijinsky* (1980) and major work in *Pennies from Heaven* (1981), both of which bombed.

Woody Allen achieved great fame as a director of incisive, often depressing comedies, the best of which were *Love and Death* (1975), *Annie Hall* (1977), *Manhattan* (1979), and *Zelig* (1983); reaction to his self-consciously "heavy" films, such as *Interiors* (1978) and *Stardust Memories* (1980), has been mixed, some wishing that he would return to the easy humor of films like *Take the Money and Run* (1969), others that he would simply stop making homages to Bergman and Fellini. The other major comic director of the decade was Mel Brooks, who used to write for Sid Caesar; his best films were *The Producers* (1968) and *Silent Movie* (1976), though both *Blazing Saddles* (1974) and *Young Frankenstein* (1974) had wonderful moments. Hal Ashby scored a cult hit with *Harold and Maude* (1971) and was highly praised for *The Last Detail* (1973), *Shampoo* (1975), and *Coming Home* (1978), but his best films were *Bound for Glory* (1976), a biography of Woody Guthrie, and *Being There* (1979), the last important film Peter Sellers made before his death. Two of the most striking directorial debuts were made by Jack Nicholson, with *Drive, He Said* (1972), and Slava Tsukerman, with the punk science fiction melodrama, *Liquid Sky* (1983)—films that at first glance have little to do with each other but were each visually exciting expressions of the states of mind of their respective countercultures. Bob Fosse emerged as a major director with *Cabaret* (1972), *Lennie* (1974), and *All That Jazz* (1979). Philip Kaufman directed a respectable remake of *Invasion of the Body Snatchers* (1978) and an honest film about the transition from the 1950s to the 1960s, *The Wanderers* (1979). Alan Parker followed his depressing study of brutality in a Turkish prison, *Midnight Express* (1978), with two brilliantly edited musicals, *Fame* (1980) and *Pink Floyd—The Wall* (1982). There were many other filmmakers, and other films by these people, but the diversity of new talent may be inferred from this brief overview.

Perhaps the best of all the directors to emerge in the 1970s, Terrence Malick made only two films: *Badlands* (1973) and *Days of Heaven* (1978). He too came from a film school (the AFI), though before that he had studied at Harvard and Oxford and taught philosophy at MIT. Both his films contrasted the voice-over narration of an uneducated young woman, baldly deflating and uncannily acute, with a magnificent visual landscape; both were indebted in oddly complementary ways to George Stevens and Martin Heidegger, though *Days of Heaven* had much to do with F. W. Murnau and *Badlands* with James Dean. Both also made brilliant use of music, from *Badlands'* "Love Is Strange" (Mickey and Sylvia) to *Days of Heaven*'s borrowed Saint-Saens and original Ennio Morricone. *Badlands* was an understated story of two young lovers on a killing spree, based on the Starkweather-Fugate case, and it is largely because of that understatement and the ways the naive voice-over undercuts even that, that *Badlands* was even better than *Bonnie and Clyde*. *Days of Heaven*, the best film of the decade—though the *Godfather* films offer close competition—was a tightly structured, precisely written, beautifully photographed fable whose apparently simple story of love and betrayal gave focus to a profound study of the range and meaning of the visual and audible world; in 70mm and six-track Dolby, it was an unforgettable experience in total cinema.

The 1970s and early 1980s also saw significant work by previously established directors. Alfred Hitchcock returned to his "Wrong Man" theme in the tense, witty, and grotesquely violent *Frenzy* (1972); his last film was the slick murder-comedy, *Family Plot* (1976). John Huston made several important films, including *Fat City* (1972), *The Life and Times of Judge Roy Bean* (1972), *The Man Who Would Be King* (1975) —a fit companion piece to *The Treasure of the Sierra Madre*— and *Wise Blood* (1979), one of the best films in his career. Fred Zinnemann made *The Day of the Jackal* (1973), an excellent thriller; *Julia* (1977), based on the early career of Lillian Hellman; and a masterful, slow-paced love story, *Five Days One Summer* (1983). Richard Rush impressed Ingmar Bergman with his *Getting Straight* (1970) and practically everyone with *The Stunt Man* (1980), a film the studios had considered too original and complex to release. Otto Preminger made several films of which the best was *Such Good Friends* (1971), and Billy Wilder began a slump with his worst film, *Avanti!* (1972). Robert Mulligan's *The Other* (1972) was a solid horror film, and his *Same Time, Next Year* (1978), whose plot was similar to that of *Avanti!*, was a gently emotional and pointedly satiric comedy of manners. Robert Wise did his best work in horror (*Audrey Rose*, 1977) and science fiction; although *The Andromeda Strain* (1971) was a bit too classically measured for its own good, his *Star Trek—The Motion Picture* (1979) was a mature, polished, and intelligent extension of the popular TV show. Even if audiences preferred Nicholas Meyer's sequel, *Star Trek II: The Wrath of Khan* (1982) for its greater fidelity to the original series, Wise's film had a beauty and intensity of its own.

George Cukor's last film, *Rich and Famous* (1981), was a strongly acted and well-considered remake of *Old Acquaintance* (1943). Stanley Donen, while not up to his usual standard, put good energy and heart into *The Little Prince* (1974) and *Movie Movie* (1978). Joseph L. Mankiewicz made a good glossy mystery, *Sleuth* (1972). Sam Fuller resurfaced with *Dead Pigeon on Beethoven Street* (1972), made the excellent World War II memoir *The Big Red One* (1980), and then found that *White Dog* (1982) could not be released as shot because of its controversial racial content. Blake Edwards, in the midst of Pink Panther comedy-mysteries, had a major hit with *10* (1979) and then made a bitter anti-Hollywood comedy, *S.O.B.* (1981); he followed these with the masterfully crafted sex comedy, *Victor/Victoria* (1982). The Czech expatriate Milos Forman made a wonderful comedy about contemporary America, *Taking Off* (1971) and an intense but flawed study of an oppressive mental institution, *One Flew Over the Cuckoo's Nest* (1975), before producing the great musical *Hair* (1979); all of these dovetail with his Czech films in their adroit sensitivity to social oppression and the dynamics of revolt. John Boorman followed *Deliverance* (1972), a violent film about male rites of passage, with three pseudomystical and self-conscious allegories: *Zardoz* (1974), a science fiction parable full of mirrors and paradoxes; *Exorcist II: The Heretic* (1977), a box-office disaster that was better than it seemed at first; and *Excalibur* (1981), a beautifully shot rendition of Malory's *Morte D'Arthur*. John Guillermin's *The Towering Inferno* (1974) was the best of a series of "disaster films" (most of which were produced by Irwin Allen), a popular but short-lived subgenre that set a *Grand Hotel* mix of characters in sudden physical danger and then made easy moralistic discriminations among them. The first of these was Ronald Neame's *The Poseidon Adventure* (1972), and a typical one was Mark Robson's *Earthquake* (1974).

Far more complex ethical questions were addressed in the films of Sidney Lumet, whose work matured during the decade from such exercises in tone as *Serpico* (1973), *Murder on the Orient Express* (1974), *Dog Day Afternoon* (1975), and *Network* (1976) to the intense, restrained, and masterful *Prince of the City* (1981) and *The Verdict* (1982). Like *12 Angry Men* and *The Hill,* his best previous films, *The Verdict* sets a quest for truth and justice in the context of corruptible institutions, but it goes beyond them in its purely cinematic authority, its understated color and efficient camera work commenting with rigor and integrity on the possibilities of spiritual redemption in a fallen world; it also gave Paul Newman the best role of his distinguished career. Sydney Pollack's better films included *Jeremiah Johnson* (1972), *The Way We Were* (1973), and *Tootsie* (1982); Alan Pakula did exceptionally good work in *All the President's Men* (1976) and *Sophie's Choice* (1982).

Richard Lester, born in America but best known for his British films *A Hard Day's Night* (1964), *How I Won the War* (1967), *Juggernaut* (1967), *The Three Musketeers* (1974), *The Four Musketeers* (1975), and *Robin and Marian* (1976), made three excellent films in America: *Petulia* (1968), *Cuba* (1979), and *Superman II* (1980), as well as the less successful *Superman III* (1983). British cinematographer Nicolas Roeg emerged as a major stylist when he and Donald Cammell directed *Performance* (1970); that and Roeg's other international productions *Walkabout* (1971), *Don't Look Now* (1973), and *The Man Who Fell to Earth* (1976), were brilliantly edited meditations on the problem of consciousness and the nature of illusion, but his American film, *Bad Timing—A Sensual Obsession* (1980), was a pretentious disappointment. Ken Russell, who made his reputation in his native Britain with *Women in Love* (1969), *The Devils* (1971), *The Music Lovers* (1971), and *The Boy Friend* (1971), made two intense American films that verged on self-parody, *Valentino* (1977) and *Altered States* (1980).

Sam Peckinpah's work was extremely uneven; only two of his later films were released uncut and both were made in Britain—*Straw Dogs* (1971) and *Cross of Iron* (1977, a German coproduction). His American films were all recut after he had finished them. While none of them appears to have been a ruined masterpiece like *The Wild Bunch* (1969), there was obviously great potential in *The Ballad of Cable Hogue* (1970) and *Junior Bonner* (1972). His other films included *The Getaway* (1972), *Pat Garrett and Billy the Kid* (1973), *Bring Me the Head of Alfredo Garcia* (1974), *The Killer Elite* (1975), *Convoy* (1978), and *The Osterman Weekend* (1983). John Frankenheimer's *I Walk the Line* (1970) and *The Iceman Cometh* (1973) were very good, but *Black Sunday* (1977) was typical of the emptily melodramatic turn of much of his later work. Orson Welles, whose last finished film was a weak adaptation of Isak Dinesen's *The Immortal Story* (1968) for French television, abandoned several projects before completion (*The Deep* in 1969 and *The Other Side of the Wind* in 1970) before collaborating on *F for Fake* (1975), a coy film well described by its title. He died in 1985. John Cassavetes made three films that saw wide release—*Minnie and Moskowitz* (1971), *A Woman Under the Influence* (1974), and *Gloria* (1980) —and two that were hardly released at all: *The Killing of a Chinese Bookie* (1976) and *Opening Night* (1978). Roman Polanski followed *Chinatown* (1974) with an excellent horror film, *The Tenant* (1976), and a glossy, mediocre adaptation of Thomas Hardy's *Tess* (1979). Louis Malle came to the United States to direct several films of which the best were *Atlantic City* (1980) and *My Dinner with Andre* (1981).

In the mid-1980s the film industry is dominated, for better or worse, by television. The popularity of the home video recorder has meant that many people see even first-run films on rented cassettes and have the option of creating home libraries of their favorite movies. Far more old films are seen on "late shows," cut and interrupted by commercials, than in revival houses in 35mm, although the rise of college film societies has encouraged the showing of many films in 16mm "nontheatrical" prints. A majority of theatrical films are presold to cable television (which usually shows films uncut, although the video image is inferior) if they are not entirely financed by such major outfits as Time-Life's Home Box Office. Often the majority of studio space is occupied with making films for commercial television. In spite of the fact that film scholarship has become a respected and major field of inquiry, that film festivals are on the rise, and that many new filmmakers are entering the industry with film school backgrounds and a good grasp of film history and theory, the uncertainty of the marketplace has led to a situation where 70mm blockbusters and cable television offer most of the production opportunities, and what used to be the standard 35mm feature is a secondary priority, though it has by no means disappeared. It was perhaps Peter Bogdanovich who put the problem in the clearest perspective in his careful study of cruelty, love, and loss, *The Last Picture Show* (1971), where an old woman, putting the popcorn machine to rest after showing *Red River* to an audience of three, blames television and a general lack of interest for the death of the theater that had once been the heart of the town's better life. Yet even if *Red River* (1948), with its assurance and energy, overwhelmed the flat and bitter look of the film that rendered it homage, there was still hope, in the very existence of that 1971 film, for the possibility of a rebirth.

## SELECTED BIBLIOGRAPHY

Balio, Tino, ed. *The American Film Industry*. Madison: University of Wisconsin Press, 1976.

Cavell, Stanley. *The World Viewed,* enlarged ed. Cambridge: Harvard University Press, 1979.

———. *Pursuits of Happiness.* Cambridge: Harvard University Press, 1981.

Dowdy, Andrew. *The Films of the Fifties: The American State of Mind.* New York: William Morrow, 1975.

Goldman, William. *Adventures in the Screen Trade: A Personal View of Hollywood and Screenwriting.* New York: Warner Books, 1983.

Haskell, Molly. *From Reverence to Rape: The Treatment of Women in the Movies.* New York: Holt, Rinehart, Winston, 1974.

Katz, Ephraim. *The Film Encyclopedia.* New York: Thomas Y. Crowell, 1979.

Kawin, Bruce. *How Movies Work.* New York: Macmillan, 1987.

Lees, David, and Stan Berkowitz. *The Movie Business.* New York: Vintage Books, 1981.

Mast, Gerald, ed. *The Movies in Our Midst: Documents in the Cultural History of Film in America.* Chicago: University of Chicago Press, 1982.

Monaco, James. *American Film Now: The People, The Power, The Money, The Movies.* New York: New American Library, 1979.

Peary, Gerald and Danny Peary, eds. *The American Animated Cartoon: A Critical Anthology.* New York: E. P. Dutton, 1980.

Rosenbaum, Jonathan. *Film: The Front Line.* Denver: Arden Press, 1983.

Rosenthal, Alan. *The New Documentary in Action: A Casebook in Film Making.* Berkeley, University of California Press, 1971.

Sarris, Andrew. *The American Cinema: Directors and Directions, 1929–1968.* New York: E. P. Dutton, 1968.

Schatz, Thomas. *Hollywood Genres.* New York: Random House, 1981.

Sitney, P. Adams, ed. *Film Culture Reader.* New York: Praeger, 1970.

———. *Visionary Film: The American Avant-Garde, 1943–1978,* 2nd ed. New York: Oxford University Press, 1979.

Spottiswoode, Raymond et al. *The Focal Encyclopedia of Film and Television Techniques.* London: Focal Press, 1969.

# YUGOSLAVIA
## Multi-Faceted Cinema:

Andrew Horton

Marshal Tito was once asked to explain the *whole* story of his life and the development of modern Yugoslavia. "You want the *whole* story?" replied Tito, "What is the whole story? How can anyone imagine he can tell it?" To attempt to survey the development of Yugoslav cinema since 1945 is likewise a frustrating search over a complex landscape. Film has captured the imagination of Yugoslavs since 1896 when the Lumiere brothers' first shorts were projected in a Belgrade restaurant before they appeared in Moscow and New York. Documentary makers such as Milton Manaki from Macedonia soon appeared along with movie theaters across the country. By the beginning of World War II, various production houses were turning out documentaries, entertainments including feature films, and some animation as well.

But in a very real sense Yugoslav cinema was born at the end of World War II. At that time film shared the struggle of Tito and his victorious partisans to form a united country composed of six republics and two autonomous provinces within Serbia (Voivodina, and the largely Albanian Kosovo), with five major languages, three major religions, and two alphabets (Latin and Cyrillic). Corroborating Lenin's dictum that cinema is the most important art, Yugoslav film has from the start reflected the diversity, complexity, contradictions, and accomplishments of this young nation with an ancient history.

There was no film industry when the war ended. Foreign and Yugoslav cameramen, most notably Žorž Skrigin, had documented some partisan engagements during the War, and Russian director Abraham Romm shot *In The Mountains of Yugoslavia* (*U planinama jugoslavije,* 1946) with future Yugoslav directors as assistants (Vjekoslav Afrić, France Štiglic), on location while the war was in progress. Finally, the occupation witnessed the creation of one of the first sound feature films in Yugoslavia, *Innocence Unprotected* (*Nevinost bez zaštite*, 1942). A crude romantic melodrama made by and starring Dragoljub Aleksić, a then popular daredevil strong man, the film was satirized and celebrated in 1967 by Dušan Makavejev in his collage film under the same title, which cross-edits scenes from the original film with collaborationist newsreels as well as newly shot footage.

From such meager beginnings Yugoslav film has become a diversified cinema with twenty-two production houses, 1,278 cinemas (few, however, have multiple daily screenings), and nearly seven hundred feature films, as well as thousands of documentaries and animations. At first film was centralized under the State Film Enterprise whose federal ambitions were reflected in the huge "cinema city," Koshutnyak, constructed outside Belgrade for a projected annual production of over fifty films a year. This Yugoslav Hollywood never came about, however, and today these large studios are used mostly for television and foreign productions. During the peak production year, 1967, only thirty-six feature films were made. Instead, as Yugoslavia decentralized politically during the 1950s, so did the film industry. According to the 1956 Film Law, each republic was to have its own film center. In fact, many companies had already formed, beginning with Avala Film in Belgrade and Jadran Film in Zagreb shortly after the war. By 1949 production houses existed in Ljubljana, Skopje, Sarajevo, and Montenegro, with other areas such as Novi Sad and Kosovo to follow later.

According to the 1974 constitution, Yugoslavia is "a socialist self-management democratic community of working people." Neither a planned economy as in the Soviet Union nor a market economy as in Western countries, Yugoslavia exists in a sense in between as a socialist market economy. This is mirrored in the film industry in which films are often financed through a complicated (and often imaginative) combination of grants from the cultural committees of each republic, funds generated at the box office, foreign investment (including coproductions), and, more recently, funds from television companies. Over the years such a half-commercial, half-subsidized system has led to the making of two distinctive kinds of films. On the one hand is a strong market at home and abroad for routine formula films, such as those celebrating the partisans of World War II or domestic social comedies. The latter are often laced with liberal amounts of female nudity and graphic violence due to the liberal restrictions on film content. The second trend is toward more personal, less commercially oriented films of high professional quality which center on personal and social relationships and tensions.

Diversity is a blessing and a curse for Yugoslav culture and cinema. The nonaligned international policy that Tito championed after his break with Moscow and the Soviet bloc in 1948 meant that socialist realism played an increasingly less important role after 1950. By the mid-1950s, modernism (sometimes called "socialist aestheticism")—a pluralistic, more open-minded approach to the arts—had won out. As the most open of Eastern European socialist nations, Yugoslavia has allowed an impressive amount of self-criticism for a country guided by one political party, the Communist party of Yugoslavia (there are, of course limits to that self expression). An enviable strength of the best Yugoslav films is honesty and openness, to a degree not possible in the Soviet Union or Warsaw Pact nations, in treating sociopolitical conflicts as well as the individual frustrations of modern life.

On the international market, however, despite numerous awards given individual films, the price of such national diversity has been a lack of "identity" for Yugoslav film. Unlike other small nations such as Poland, Greece, and Czechoslovakia, where films appear to share certain strong characteristics, Yugoslavia is, as director Srdjan Karanović notes in the title of his latest film, *Something In Between* (*Nešto izmedju*, 1983), neither East nor West, neither totally communist nor capitalistic, neither wholly modern nor traditional, but a mixture of all of these.

Documentary received attention first after World War II. By January 1945 newsreels were appearing in Belgrade, and a series, *Film News* (*Filmske novosti*) soon followed. The first postwar documentary was a tragic study of a concentration camp near Zagreb shot the day after its liberation by Kosta Hlavati and Gustav Gavrin (*Jasenovać*, 1945).

Because there were no film academies at the time, documentaries provided on-the-spot schooling for many filmmakers. Nikola Popović, who later directed features, shot *Belgrade* (1945), which is still regarded as one of the best observations of the capital city. This was followed by films such as *Triglav in Winter* (*Triglav po zimi*, 1946), by Milka and Metod Badjura, and *Youth Builds* (*Omladina gradi*, 1946), by France Štiglic, which was about youth work drives and won Yugoslavia's first international award at the Venice Festival in 1946. Other future feature directors included Rodoš Novaković whose *The New Country* (*Nova zemlja*, 1946) poignantly treats the migration of settlers from the barren region of Lika to the fertile plains of Voivodina, and Vojislav Nanović who worked with Novaković on the first color documentary, *Review of Youth* (*Smotra mladosti*, 1947).

By the end of 1950 the young filmmakers had made 270 documentaries covering subjects ranging from the war and postwar construction to various aspects of cultural and political life. With strong funding for documentaries before the development of television, more than a hundred films a year were shot between 1951 and 1956. Films also began to be made for tourist and advertising purposes. Major filmmakers of this period include: Ante Babaja with his portrait of a city, *One Day In Rijeka* (*Jedan dan na rijeci*, 1954); Boštjan Hladnik whose *Fantastic Ballad* (*Fantastična balada*, 1957) concerns the graphic art of Slovenian artist France Mihelič; Aleksandar Petrović who made special use of color in his film about the evolution of a modernist painter (*Petar Dobrović*, 1957); and Puriša Djordjević whose *The Girl on the Front Page* (*Devojka s naslovne strane*, 1958) is a recreation of the life of a young partisan woman from the provinces, based only on her photograph.

By the 1960s documentary was firmly established in each republic. In Serbia, for instance, a strong school of nonfiction film developed at Dunav Film. Krsto Škanata, a pioneer in the Belgrade school of documentary, made vivid black-and-white films about individuals in conflict with the world around them. *Soldier, Dismissed* (*Ratniče voljno*, 1967), for instance, hints at the difficulties of many Communist war heroes in adjusting to postwar civilian life. Škanata creates drama in this film by cross-cutting between the trial of a Bosnian factory executive accused of misusing his power and footage of his mountain village where interviews reveal he was a respected partisan hero. At the end of the hearing conducted by the local Communist party, this broken man votes along with the others for his own expulsion from the Party. Such documentaries are typical of the Belgrade school and served as the basis of many eminent careers. Documentarists of note who later became feature directors during the 1960s include Dušan Makavejev, Karpo Godina, Krsto Papić, and Žellimir Žilnik.

Mention of two other filmmakers will suggest the developments in recent documentary. Aleksandar Ilić films animals in his short color films in a nonromantic but metaphorical manner. In *The Mallet* (*Malj*, 1977) Ilić draws upon his memories of his four years in concentration camps to portray a Kafkaesque tale. We see a chicken-processing factory in which hands (we never see the "people") sort out baby chicks on a ceaselessly moving conveyor belt. One black chick is continually tossed into a scrap heap, but manages to escape just before it would have been crushed among the bodies of dead and dying "rejects." As in many Yugoslav documentaries, Ilić's film is all the more effective because of the absence of any voice-over narration.

Vlatko Gilić shapes carefully structured metaphorical documentaries. *Love* (*Ljubav*, 1973) combines a few stylized shots of a bridge under construction with those of a wife of one of the workers who brings a picnic lunch on a rare visit. These unadorned scenes suggest both one peasant couple's simple affection and the modern tensions (his job is one thousand kilometers away from home) that make this love so rare. One is tempted to call many of these films "nonfiction parables." Single concept films shot in a documentary manner, they imply much more than they show.

Yugoslav film has made its strongest contribution to world cinema in animation. The renaissance of animation began with the so-called Zagreb School—an interrelated, but highly individualistic group of artists and filmmakers influenced by both the classical techniques of Walt Disney and the more experimental approaches of Czech and Polish cartoonists. A first effort, *The Big Meeting* (*Veliki miting,* 1951), was a Disney imitation satirizing Yugoslavia's break with Moscow in 1948.

A lack of money and supplies led Zagreb artists to abandon classical animation methods and to develop the technique of *reduced animation,* in which only about one third of the drawings traditionally needed were used in a cartoon. Because reduced animation was cheaper and faster, and so allowed animators much greater flexibility, the technique was soon picked up around the world. While the technique now seems commonplace in American advertising, for instance, it is Zagreb that deserves the originating credit.

Zagreb cartoons are recognizable not only for the individuality of technique but also for the universality of their humanistic approach. Seldom employing spoken languge, these animations have dealt with such topics as war, unfriendly neighbors (a particularly popular theme for a country that has been attacked from numerous directions, often simultaneously, throughout history), the dangers of a consumer society, and the desire for freedom and beauty in an increasingly regulated, polluted, and militaristic world.

Dušan Vukotić has had much to do with establishing Zagreb animation. More influenced by Eastern European cartoons than by Disney, Vukotić experimented with simple lines and semiabstract comic characters, creating a satire of Westerns in *Cowboy Jimmy* (1957) with a script by Vastroslav Mimica (who wrote over twenty other animation scripts, directing nine of them). Two of Vukotić's best films are *Piccolo* (1959) which treats the unfriendly neighbor theme ironically and *Surogat* (*Ersatz,* 1961). *Surogat* deals with modern man's unsuccessful search for happiness through consumer goods, leisure time, and relations with the opposite sex. Jazz accompanies a line figure of a man who can blow up an inflatable object to create anything he desires, from air mattresses to fish, and finally, a woman. While he has control over objects, a woman is another matter. She runs off with another fellow, thus triggering our hero's wrath. He proceeds to unplug everything including the sky and sea and even the frame of the animation. Such films not only treat human foibles with a light satiric touch but also a delight in reflexive jokes on the process of animation itself (the disappearance of the "frame," for instance).

Numerous artists have since established their individual talents. Vladimir Kristl's *Don Quixote* (*Don kihot,* 1961) was the first Yugoslav animation completely controlled (conceived, drawn, and directed) by one artist. Borrowing Cervantes's knight-errant, Kristl had Quixote battling the military-industrial complex, the mass media, and consumer society, and *winning.* Aleksandar Marks and Vladimir Jutriša have worked as a team on many projects, and Zlatko Grgić has shown a flair for pure physical fun in works such as *Maxi Cat* (*Maxi, Mačka,* 1970). Zlatko Bourek from Slovenia has helped animate the popular *Professor Balthasar* series, which, since 1968, has been constructed loosely around problems that are solved by a kindly, wise, and magical professor. Bourek also animated distinctive films of his own such as *The Cat* (*Mačka,* 1971), based on Aesop's fable of a cat that changes into a young woman until a mouse appears, bringing out its true nature. Ironic yet humanistic, these works most often demonstrate a sympathy for the common man or woman caught in struggles that are both universal and contemporary.

Zagreb animators have never remained static. Many of the artists free-lance and form their own profit-sharing projects. Much animation is commissioned on a coproduction basis with companies in Europe and the United States, and some artists do work overseas. Nevertheless, Zagreb remains an international center, a fact celebrated every two years in the widely attended international Animation Festival held in Zagreb.

The growing complexity and sophistication of Yugoslav animation can be seen in such works as Nedeljko Dragić's *Diary* (*Dnevnik,* 1974) and Zdenko Gašparović's *Satiemania* (1978). Organized by theme rather than by plot, both films are much darker works than early Zagreb films, and both present a view of an Americanized megalopolis (both artists have worked in the United States) that is surrealistic, lyrical, nightmarish, and satirical. The animation used resembles the modern style of Steinberg, but both draw upon all of animation history in their work.

Talented animators have appeared in other republics as well. In Macedonia a Skopje School has evolved under the leadership of Darko Marković, Petar Gligorov, and Boro Pejčinov. Borislav Šagtinać works in Novi Sad, and in Belgrade Nikola Majdak, Zoran Jovanović, and Dušan Petričić produce respected original work. The winner of numerous international awards at Oberhausen and other festivals, Yugoslav animation has had a direct influence on animators elsewhere, as reflected in commercials and even animated features such as *The Yellow Submarine* (1968).

Feature film production in Yugoslavia falls roughly into three distinct periods. From 1945 to about 1962 the infant industry established itself, creating the beginnings of a professional cinema and exploring a variety of topics, genres, and styles in the process. The period between 1961 and 1973 saw a directors' cinema or "intimist film" (a personal cinema), a particularly fruitful period of filmmaking during which a new generation of *auteurs* came of age. It is no accident that this fertile time coincided with a sense of liberalization throughout Yugoslavia as well as with the spirit of social unrest and youth movements around the world. At that moment film was in the vanguard of Yugoslav culture as a medium of honest social expression. When pressure was brought to curb the extremes of this expression (labeled the "black cinema" by critics who felt some filmmakers, such as Živojin Pavlović and Žellmir Žilnik, overstressed negative aspects of socialist life), the film boom swiftly faded away. The most notable example of reprisal against a filmmaker at that time was the three-year prison sentence given to student filmmaker Lazar Stojanović in 1973 for his film of that year never shown publically, *Plastic Jesus*, the title being taken from an American popular song.

By 1976, however, a third phase of Yugoslav filmmaking appeared. A young generation of directors labeled the "Prague School" returned from their film studies at FAMU, the Czech film school, to fill the gap created by producers who hesitated to work with directors from the 1960s movement. This generation, which has since been joined by other talented directors, has made an impressive series of films that, while less radical and political than those of the 1960s, are nevertheless highly professional works popular with home audiences and that draw increasing international recognition.

The first Yugoslav feature film after the war was *Slavica* (1947), an epic about a young Dalmation woman, Slavica, who represents the entire span of the Yugoslav fight for liberation. Written and directed by Vjekoslav Afrić, a Dalmatian who drew upon his own experiences, *Slavica* was a propitious beginning for the young cinema. First, it combined documentary and drama for an authentic power: the crowd and war scenes were reenacted using actual locations and a public that still had fresh memories of the events depicted. Second, the film is indebted almost equally to Russian cinema (montage sequences, for instance) and American cinema (comedy and personal romantic and dramatic moments, as in Slavica's love and marriage to a young fisherman), influences which were to continue in the early years of Yugoslav film. Finally, Afrić's film anticipates many of the directions Yugoslav films were to take. The war theme and the partisan desire for a new society prefigure the partisan film. The inclusion of scenes involving collaborators points the way to much more subtle studies of civilian compliance and betrayal in films such as Lordan Zafranović's respected *The Occupation in 26 Pictures* (*Okupacija u 26 slika*, 1978), which treats the Italian occupation of the Dalmatian city Dubrovnik. Romantic, melodramatic, and comic elements of *Slavica* suggest the more popular genres that followed.

The partisan film began with the honest enthusiasm of *Slavica*, but quickly settled in to an exaggerated mythology of the good partisans winning out against the evil Germans and Italian Fascists, a genre that fulfills a role similar to that of the Western in American cinema. In literature as well as film, World War II and related events (especially those involving the Stalinist period between 1945 and 1948) became

who made worthy films in a variety of genres. Beginning with youth-oriented films such as *Blue Seagull* (*Sinji galeb,* 1953), he moved on to show the influence of a Hollywood tradition of strongly plotted films with tightly written dialogue that is close to everyday speech. His *Three Girls Called Anna* (*Tri ane,* 1959), made for Vardar Film in Skopje, is a gripping story of a father who searches for his lost daughter after the war. A director who has worked steadily, he proved a proto-type for later 1960s filmmakers with his *Face to Face* (*Licem u lice,* 1963), the first film to openly assess Yugoslavia's self-management pol-icy as it relates to the possibility for error and falsification within local Communist organizations. Bauer's straightforward narrative has much of the emotional impact of a problem drama such as *Twelve Angry Men.*

The first truly modern Yugoslav film, which heralded the coming of the 1960s cinema, was *Saturday Night* (*Subotom uvece,* 1957) by Vladi-mir Pogačić. An omnibus film in three parts (a form used by numerous Yugoslav directors), each a contemporary narrative told skillfully with psychological naturalism, the most successful being the episode "Doc" about a ruined man with a fixation on boxing. Pogačić's slice of life ap-proach was apparent from his first film, *Story of a Factory* (*Prica o fa-brici,* 1949), about a factory disrupted by sabotage.

Nineteen sixty-one inaugurated a new decade for Yugoslav film both in quantity (thirty-two features made) and quality. Slovenian Boštjan Hladnik broadened his republic's reputation for poetic cinema by win-ning the Best Film of 1961 award at Pula with his debut film, *Dance In The Rain* (*Ples na Kiši*). The following year he tested the limits of the newly emerging Yugoslav cinema with *Sand Castle* (*Peščeni grad,* 1962), a stylized film about three youths who attempt to reject society and live in their own world. Ahead of its time, it was turned down by the Pula Festival. Also of importance for the beginnings of a new Yugo-slav cinema were *Two* (*Dvoje,* 1961) by Aleksandar Petrovic and *The City* (*Grad,* 1963) by Zivojin Pavlovic, Vojislav Rakonjac, and Marko Babac, which was officially censored by a court in Sarajevo.

The new films were more modern and experimental in style and con-tent. Vatroslav Mimica, who had begun his career in animation, turned to making complex features including *Prometheus From Vishevica Is-land* (*Prometej sa otoka viševice,* 1964). Mimica was one of the first to reexamine the war experience in light of the present, some twenty years later. In the film a partisan hero, now an important executive, re-turns to the island where he had lived his war experience. The film squarely asks what has happened to the socialist ideals the partisans fought for as Mate, the protagonist, becomes disillusioned. Mimica in-tercuts war scenes with the present in a staccato, jarring rhythm that successfully approximates Mate's troubled mind.

That the 1960s were a time for reevaluation was apparent on the na-tional level as an even more decentralized constitution was put into effect in 1963. In cinema the spirit of exploration, evaluation, and more liberal expression was evident in numerous young directors, but most especially in the works of Aleksandar Petrović, Živojin Pavlović, and Dušan Makavejev.

Aleksandar Petrović, who brought to feature film work a strong background in art history and documentary films such as *Flight Above the Marsh* (*Let Nad Močvaram*, 1957), became the early proponent of an "intimate" or personalized cinema with his first feature, *Two* (*Dvoje*, 1961). In his second feature *Days* (*Dani*, 1963), a portrait of the emptiness of a young married woman's life, Petrović further explored how a film could be at once personal (a glimpse of a woman's life), Yugoslavian (a portrait of middle-class Belgrade life at the time), and universal (what urban life has become for millions in almost any city anywhere). While his work is rooted in the specific reality of Yugoslavia, Petrović succeeded in suggesting a broader dimension through his "intimate" approach.

Even more significant in terms of innovation was his third film, *Three* (*Tri*, 1965), which received an Academy Award nomination as well as first prize at the Karlovy Vary Festival. A triptych film based on three short stories by Antonije Isaković, *Three* presents three existential encounters with death during World War II. Each segment stars Bata Živojlnović, a leading actor sometimes called a Yugoslav Spencer Tracy. In the first story he *observes* the execution of an innocent stranger by restless soldiers at a country train station; in the second he is the *victim* of a tense chase across a barren landscape as German soldiers relentlessly hunt him down only to kill another partisan instead; and in the final episode he is a partisan commander who must *sentence to death* a lovely young woman despite his obvious interest in her. Petrović's film is remarkable for its economy of style and narrative in conveying complex psychological states visually and realistically. The film is also universal in its depiction of human nature under the pressure of war. Furthermore, each episode has subtle reverberations in the others, which open to the audience the many significant nuances of these taut tales.

Best known abroad, however, is Petrović's next work, *I Even Met Happy Gypsies* (*Skupjaći perja*, 1967), which was nominated for an Academy Award and which won the International Film Critics Award at Cannes. Shot in rich colors by Tomislav Pinter, a leading cinematographer, the film is a nonstop narrative of gypsy life today in Voivodina, Serbia. By turns boisterous, colorful, lyrical, and tragic, the film was important to Yugoslav cinema not just for its local color, but because of its nonromantic realism (most of the dialogue is in "gypsy" with Serbo-Croatian subtitles) in depicting an ethnic group at the bottom of the Yugoslav social ladder. Voted by Yugoslav film critics in 1983 the best Yugoslav film ever made, the work continues to exert a strong influ-

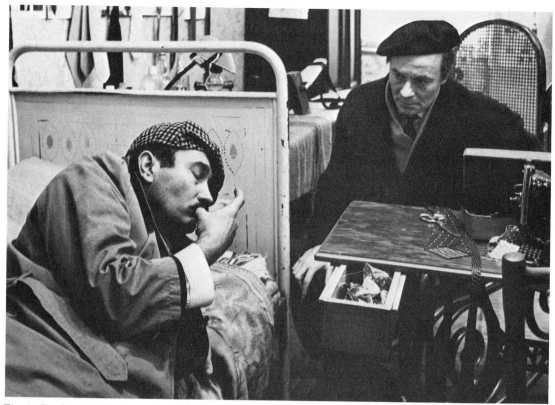

Zivojn Ravlović's *The Rats Wake Up* (1967) captured a down-and-out realism never before seen on Yugoslav screens.

*I Even Met Happy Gypsies* (1967), directed by Aleksandar Petrović, was voted by Yugoslav critics the best Yugoslav film ever.

(Right)
Dušan Vukotić's *Surogat*
(*Ersatz*, 1961) reflected
Yugoslavia's prominence
in animation by winning
an Academy Award.

(Left)
*Who's That Singing over
There?* (1980) by Slobodan
Šigan, a Serbian cross
section set in 1941,
represents new directions
for Yugoslav comedy.

(Right)
Emir Kusturica's *When
Father Was Away on
Business* (1985) won the
Best Film Award at
Cannes and was
nominated for an
Academy Award.

ence on Yugoslav filmmakers. Petrović has since worked on international coproductions including *The Master and Margarita* (*Maestro i Margarita*, 1972), based on the novel by Mikhail Bulgakov, and his innovative follow-up to *Gypsies*, *The End of the World* (*Biće Skoro Propast Sveta*, 1968) which blends a folk art camera style with Brechtian forms of narration.

Zivojn Pavlović is equally respected as an author and as a filmmaker. In his fiction and his ten feature films to date, he has unswervingly held to an austere naturalism captured in lean prose style and an equally unobtrusive camera and editing style. His territory is the margin of society, and his protagonists are basically simple people, good people, who are overcome and betrayed by their environments. In *The Rats Wake Up* (*Budjenje pacova*, 1967) the lover of the film's luckless male protagonist tells him, "I always wanted a decent life, but one slip and it all goes to hell," just before she takes all of his borrowed money and skips town. With a script by two of Yugoslavia's best known screenwriters, Goran Mihić and Ljubiša Kozomara, the film is shot, as are many of his early films, in darkly shadowed black and white to match Pavlović's dim view of human relations. Nineteen sixty-seven was a peak production year for Yugoslavia and a busy one for Pavlović, who also released *When I Was Dead and White* (*Kad budem mrtav i beo*), also written by Mihić and Kozomara. In this tale Pavlović traced the rise and fall of a selfish young vagabond whose carefree way eventually leads to his murder.

Pavlović's most ambitious film and one of the most impressive Yugoslav films to date is *The Ambush* (*Zaseda*, 1969), based on one of his own stories and one by Antonije Isaković. *The Ambush* follows the growing disillusionment of a young partisan boy with the new socialist state during the pro-Stalinist period immediately after the war. Opening and closing the film with images of Stalin and with Russian marches on the sound track, Pavlović unblinkingly examines the shortcomings of overzealous Communists during that period who, swept up in their own self-importance and power, proceeded to commit crimes similar to those of previous rulers (Turks, Nazis, Croatian Nationalists, and so on) in the belief that the ends justified the means. A prime example of the so-called black cinema, *The Ambush* is told simply yet with heavy, dark irony.

The closing scene is a good illustration. The young Communist, Ivo, leaves a village in disgust because a power-greedy Communist officer falsely claimed to have killed a leader of the Chetniks (the anti-communist right-wing nationalist organization). On a mountain road he is stopped by three other partisan soldiers who accuse him of being a Chetnik. Not bothering to check on his pleas of innocence, they execute him on the spot. But before Pavlović cuts to a final long shot of Ivo's body, Ivo calls out in close-up, "You filthy peasant trash. Some

Revolution!" The ambush is thus not for the "enemy" but for the revolution itself.

It is one of the largest ironies of Yugoslav film history that *The Ambush* received the Golden Arena Award at Pula for the Best Film of 1969 but was then never commercially released and seen only by a relatively few Yugoslavs during special screenings. Though not openly banned, *The Ambush* received minimal public exposure because of its black cinema label. Pavlović, however, unlike most of the 1960s directors who were singled out as too critical, has managed to make films on a regular basis without significantly altering his view of man and society.

Dušan Makavejev has received wide international attention because of his innovative and provocative form of collage and "compilation" cinema. Makavejev, who began his career with ironic documentaries, entered feature films with *Man Is Not A Bird* (*Čovek nije tica,* 1965), shot in *cinéma vérité*-styled black and white by the respected cinematographer Aleksandar Petković. Building on a mundane affair between a hairdresser (played by Yugoslavia's leading actress, Milena Dravić) and a factory engineer in a drab industrial town in eastern Serbia, Makavejev creates a fresh and challenging effect through his juxtaposition of documentary-like photography (much in the spirit of early Godard but with more passion) and disruptive editing (influenced by Russian montage). In one sequence, for instance, Makavejev cross-cuts continually between the hairdresser's seminude body and the factory where her lover works. Influenced by the writings of Wilhelm Reich, Makavejev interrelates personal and sexual relationships with the sociopolitical struggles in one's environment.

*The Loves of a Switchboard Operator* (*Ljubavni slučajili ili tragedije službenice ptt,* 1967) again builds from a commonplace love affair which, in this case, leads to murder. In this film Makavejev applies his techniques to a Hungarian-Yugoslav operator working in Belgrade and a Muslim rat exterminator who is also a member of the Communist party, to ironically suggest a number of sociopolitical observations.

*W.R. Mysteries of the Organism* (*W.R. misterije organiza,* 1971) was to be Makavejev's most complete synthesis of his compilation technique and also his last film made in Yugoslavia. Straining the limits of free expression in his country, he created an almost surrealistic flow of images, juxtaposing everything from Yugoslavia and the United States to sex and politics, film and life, Freud and Marx, and humor and horror in a vision that was simultaneously liberating and ironic.

As in the case of Pavlović's *The Ambush*, censorship proved subtle rather than direct. Never banned outright, enough pressure was brought to bear that Makavejev did not release the film in his homeland, and left soon after for Europe and, later, the United States. Makavejev admits that no easy lessons can be drawn from the death of the 1960s directors' cinema including the black cinema. He has said, "Even if I am a victim of this tightening of control, it is difficult for me to make a negative criticism of it without putting my own feelings in perspective." (*Film Comment* 11, no. 4 (July/August 1975): 19.) Makavejev has continued his career outside his country with films such as *Sweet Movie, Montenegro,* and *The Coca-Cola Kid* though he has received offers to make films in Yugoslavia.

An extraordinary variety of other talents emerged during the period from 1965 to 1969. Puriša Djordjević began in documentaries and then turned to making highly personal poetic features. He is especially remembered for his wartime trilogy, *Girl (Devojka,* 1965), starring Milena Dravić as a young partisan woman in a tragic but triumphant love relationship with a young soldier; *Dream (San,* 1966), which is an impressionistic view of the gap between the dreams and realities of a group of partisans fighting in Djordjević's home town, Čačak; and *Morning (Jutro,* 1967), which uses a depiction of the first day of peace after World War II as an illustration of postwar existence in which the end of fighting does not mean the end of the hostile feelings created during the war. The lyricism of his approach is clear in the conclusion to *Dream* in a scene which shows all of the partisans whose lives we have followed return after their deaths to a hillside in a glorious resurrection *as if* their dreams had come true.

Also produced in 1967 was the memorable *The Birch Tree (Breza)*, by Ante Babaja and based on a work by Slavko Kolar. This film stands alone in Yugoslav cinema as a haunting work of naive folk art shot in subtle textures and colors by Tomislav Pinter and carefully integrated by Babaja with Croatian peasant musical motifs. The beauty of nature is balanced with the destructive patriarchal behavior of the main peasant figure whose actions directly and indirectly contribute to his wife's premature death. Both man and nature are united in the closing scene of this sympathetic though unsentimental film as the husband hugs the birch tree he has always associated with his lost wife.

Želimir Žilnik is often linked with Pavlović as a leading figure in the black cinema even though he completed only one film, *Early Works (Rani radovi,* 1969), during this period. Partially improvised, his film is a political allegory shot in a breezy *cinéma vérité* style that focuses on restless youths caught at that time between the theory and the practice of Marxist socialism (the title refers to Marx's more radical early works). Coscripted by Branko Vučićević, a major contributor to a cinema of political self-examination, Žilnik's film presents a young female revolutionary named Yugoslava eventually executed by three male companions who are unable to accept her radical teachings. When his proposed second feature, *Das Kapital,* was shelved before he could edit it in 1972, Žilnik became yet another victim of the tightening of free expression in Yugoslav cinema. In 1983 he completed his second feature, *The Second Generation* (*Druga generacija*), fourteen years after his debut. This newer work suggests an interesting avenue for filmmakers wishing to combine documentary and drama, improvisation and scripted filmmaking. A story of Yugoslav youth today who have lived abroad, the film is an honest and open look at a social problem told through the narration of the young people involved (all of whom are nonprofessionals).

Krsto Papić also belongs to the period of political examination for his brutal village tragedy, *Handcuffs* (*Lisice*, 1969), coscripted by Mirko Kovač, whose talent for politically oriented scripts is seen in his other works, including *The Occupation in 26 Pictures* (*Okupacija U26 SLIKA*, 1978). Papić who has a sharp anthropological interest in documentary, combines a tough examination of the primitive dangers of provincial mentalities with a drama involving the Yugoslav Communist party's overreaction in pursuing Stalinists in the period just after the split with Moscow in 1948. Also of note was Djordje Kadijević who cowrote and directed *Holiday* (*Praznik*, 1967), a sensitive tale of two American pilots, one black and one white, who crash near a village controlled by Chetniks, the nationalistic forces that fought the Communists. The film was produced through the experimental Kino Klub of Belgrade.

Finally, several directors developed unique formalistic styles during the 1960s. Zvonimir Berković in *Rondo* (1966) constructed an intricate triangle between a married couple and the artist-husband's best friend that is based on Mozart's complicated musical forms and the precision of chess, which becomes both a game and a metaphor for the inferno finally established. In *On Wings of Paper* (*Na papirnatih avionih*, 1967), Slovenian director Matjaž Klopčić dissects the sterility of modern life and the symptomatic fear of love in a poetic but disjointed style that suggests early Godard and Antonioni, utilizing crisp images of Ljubljana and its surrounding mountains.

But even as the fertile period of Yugoslav cinema drew to a close under official and more subtle pressure, new talents were emerging. Bato Čengić working with screenwriter Branko Vučićević in Sarajevo created the challenging films *The Role of My Family in the World Revolution* (*Uloga moje porodice u svjetskoj revoluciji*, 1971) and *Scenes from the Life of Shock Workers* (*Slike iz života udarnika*, 1972). In Macedonia Kiril Cenevski appeared as an accomplished director in 1971 with *Black Seed* (*Crno seme*), an uncompromising film about the treatment of Macedonian soldiers in the Greek royal army after the end of World War II and during the Greek civil war. And Miloš Radivojević proved in *Without Words* (*Bez*, 1972) that a feature film could be made in twenty-four different scenes, each starring the versatile actor Dragon Nikolić, without the need for spoken language. Radivojević has settled for more traditional narrative approaches after this experimental exercise, making films about troubled youth in contemporary situations, such as the world surrounding an academy of music in *Living Like the Rest of Us* (*Živeti kao sav normalan svet*, 1982).

The dark period of uncertainty that ensued in Yugoslav film was broken by the arrival of the Prague School of Yugoslav directors and cinematographers who had studied in Czechoslovakia and who had begun their home careers in television. Of the group, which includes Goran Marković, Rajko Grlić, Srdjan Karanović, Lordan Zafranović, Emir Kusturica, and cinematographers Živko Zalar, Vilko Filać, and Paga Popović, it was Goran Paskaljević who first scored with an enthusiastic public in his first feature, *The Beach Guard in Winter* (*Čuvar plaze u zimskom*, 1976), a social comedy about a young man with no career and no hopes of finding a place to live with his wife-to-be. In the end he decides, like several million other Yugoslavs have, to become a "guest-worker" in Sweden. Paskaljević went on to make an offbeat road film, *The Dog Who Loved Trains (Pas koji je voleo vozove*, 1977), about misfits in a Serbian rodeo.

The Prague group brought about a new phenomenon in Yugoslav cinema. For the first time the public showed a preference for Yugoslav films in general (specific films such as Petrović's *I Have Even Met Happy Gypsies* had attracted large audiences previously). In 1978 Yugoslav films domestically outsold all foreign films, including American films, for the first time. The unusualness of this trend, which has continued and which shows no sign of reversing, can be seen if compared with attendance trends in a country like West Germany, where New German Cinema, successful abroad, drew relatively small crowds at home.

Other popular films followed. Goran Marković, the son of well-known actors, made two films about youths unable to adapt to contemporary society: *Special Education* (*Specijalno vaspitanje*, 1977) and *National Class* (*Nacionalna klasa do 785 cm*, 1979). Both are presented in a straightforward narrative manner, and both end on a dark note brightened only by the possibility of male friendship. *Special Education*, a true-life story of a young village boy sentenced to five years in a Belgrade reform school, is representative of the realistic films of the new Yugoslav cinema which have attracted a large young audience (the film resembles a tougher version of Truffaut's *400 Blows*). More recently, Marković has been in the forefront of Yugoslav directors influenced by American genre films such as *Star Wars, Raiders of the Lost Ark,* and the films of John Carpenter. Marković's *Variola Vera* (1982) is a gripping hospital genre tale of a plague that breaks out in a hospital which the authorities try to ignore, then cover up.

Rajko Grlić has proven a sensitive social critic who mixes compassion and satire in complex films such as *Bravo Maestro* (1978), which was shown at Cannes, and *The Melody Haunts My Memory* (*Samo jednom se ljubi*, 1981), which was a large popular success at home and was also screened at Cannes. Both films examine the gap between personal dreams and passions, and social (and socialist) realities. In *Bravo Maestro* a talented composer makes compromises with his wife, friends, and sociopolitical organizations in order to become famous. In a stirring conclusion, Grlić presents the young man, now unhappy with his past compromises, on stage receiving a large ovation for a composition he shamelessly copied from various sources. *The Melody Haunts My Memory* shows a young partisan war hero whose postwar life and ideals crumble in the face of an all consuming sexual passion for a young dancer. Grlić ends his film on even a bleaker note than *Bravo Maestro* as the protagonist escapes from a mental hospital where he has been incarcerated and commits suicide in the dressing room of his dancer-wife while she is on stage. Grlić does not blame the imperfections of Yugoslav socialism for his characters' downfalls. Rather, he shows contemporary life to be a confusing interplay between personal dreams and ambitions on the one hand and the multitude of social forces that demand one's attention on the other.

With his first feature, *Social Game (Društvena igra,* 1972), Srdjan Karanović caught the critics' attention as a filmmaker interested in cinema and life as a form of "play" or game. To make his debut film like no other film made, Karanović advertised in Yugoslav papers for people to write him their fantasies of what role they would "play" if chosen for the film. After four thousand letters poured in, he narrowed the lot down to about twenty-four and built his loosely constructed script around these everyday individuals who then played themselves. Such an initial film was a clear sign that Karanović intended to build his films according to his own rules. Calling his second film, *The Fragrance of Wild Flowers* (*Miris poljskog sveća,* 1977), a "documentary fairy tale," Karanović tells the story of a famous middle-aged actor who is "fed up" with his art and his life. But when he walks out of his job and marriage toward a freer existence with an old friend on a barge on the Danube, he discovers that his act becomes a media event. While he finds no peace, he triggers the admiration of hundreds of dissatisfied individuals who take his action as a sign for them to live out their own fantasies. One of the few new Yugoslav films released commercially in the United States, the film is representative of the best work of these younger directors. The haunting music is by Zoran Simjanović, who has composed unmistakably original scores for many new Yugoslav films. The camera work, which involves a television film within the film, is by Živko Zaler, a leading cinematographer, and the script is cowritten with Rajko Grlić just as many of Grlić's films have been worked on by Karanović, thus indicating the close cooperation between many of the new directors.

Karanović has continued to explore new territory with each project. His third film, *Petria's Wreath* (*Petrijin venac,* 1980), is a sympathetic adaptation of a novel about a village woman who outlives her lovers and husbands under the harshest of provincial circumstances. In his next film, *Something in Between* (*Nešto izmedju,* 1983), he experiments with mixing romantic social comedy and melodrama in a popular story of an American woman in love with two Yugoslavs. The film was shown at Cannes and other festivals.

The 1980s continue to witness quality films finding popular audiences. In Slovenia the lyrical tradition has been refined even further in *The Raft of the Medusa* (*Splav meduze,* 1980), made by cinematographer turned director Karpo Godina. Shot in stylized pastels, the film evokes an impressionistic memory of a small, intimate group of Yugoslav avant-garde artists living between the world wars. And in Sarajevo, Emir Kusturica appeared in 1981 with a charmingly poignant film, *Do You Remember Dolly Bell?* (*Sješac li se dolly bell*), about the coming of age of a teenage Moslem boy from a poor family who falls in love with a young prostitute. The film was honored at Venice and has played for long runs in Europe and Canada.

Comedy is often underestimated by Yugoslav critics, but Yugoslav comedies deserve attention. One of the best playwrights of the first half of the century, Branislav Nušić, has provided material for memorable film comedies by, among others, Puriša Djordjević, Soja Jovanović (Yugoslavia's only major woman director), and Vuk Babić, who in 1966 drew from two Nušić comedies to shape his own *Before The War* (*Pre rata*). Influenced by silent film comedy as well, Babić's film is a fine example of social caricature mixed with well-aimed farce.

Slobodan Šijan has continued in this tradition while establishing his own comic tone in his first film, *Who's That Singing Over There?* (*Ko to tamo peva,* 1980). With a screenplay by Dušan Kovačević, a contemporary writer of ironic stage comedy, the film involves a robust cross-section of Serbian country characters on a back-road bus ride to Belgrade on the eve of the German invasion of Yugoslavia in 1941. Šijan's camera observes each character's individual foibles and then frames the whole group against the Serbian landscape and as part of a country song sung by gypsies accompanying the group. Šijan followed up this film with a black comedy (again written by Kovačević) about five generations of a family of undertakers: *The Marathon Runners Run Their Lap of Honor* (*Maratonci trče počasni krug,* 1982).

In sophisticated comedy the Czechoslovakian director František Čap, who moved to Yugoslavia in 1948, is unrivaled. *Vesna* (1953) was a witty social comedy about a young female student and her friends. Directed with polished charm, the film was the winner at the first Pula Festival.

The all-time Yugoslav box-office success is, in fact, a comedy. Nića Milošević's *A Tight Spot* (*Tesna koža,* 1982) is a social satire built around a patriarchal figure, a common middle-aged man of today trying to hold together his restless family on an insufficient income from a small bureaucratic job. It is not Molière, but it is playfully up to date for

Yugoslav audiences who are also caught in an economic squeeze as the nation enters a long period of "stabilization" to bring large international debts into line. Branko Baletić's American-styled comedy *Balkan Express* (*Balkan ekspres,* 1983) follows a band of small-time crooks through battlefields and bedrooms during World War II in a light-hearted mood reminiscent of *Butch Cassidy and the Sundance Kid.* Both films are testimony to the staying power of comedy and of Yugoslav film's contemporary ability to deliver it.

Clearly a healthy indication of the growing importance of the new Yugoslav cinema was the 1985 Golden Palm award at Cannes for Emir Kusturica's *When Father Was Away on Business* (*Otac na sluzbenom putu*) along with the film's subsequent nomination for an Oscar in the United States as Best Foreign Film of 1985. Kusturica's film is in many ways an "anthology film" that reflects the influence of much of modern Yugoslav cinema in its bitter-sweet depiction of a Muslim family's struggles under the anti-Stalinist purges in Yugoslavia during the early 1950s. Kusturica's personal triumph bodes well for Yugoslav cinema.

Other aspects of the Yugoslavian film industry include coproductions and foreign productions that have made use of Yugoslavia's varied landscapes and professional facilities. Claude Autant-Lara, Gillo Pontecorvo, Sam Peckinpah, Orson Welles, Andrzej Wajda, and Alan Pakula (*Sophie's Choice,* 1982) all worked in Yugoslavia. Yugoslav film is thoroughly documented through the efforts of the Institut Za Film in Belgrade, and seven major film journals insure a steady flow of timely information about Yugoslav and world cinema. Film archives exist in Ljubljana, Zagreb, and Skopje, and the national cinemathèque in Belgrade, Jugoslavenska Kinoteka, is one of the major film collections in the world.

The future? The world economic crisis means a paradoxically bust-and-boom period for cinema. "It is a time of confusion," says one filmmaker in Yugoslavia, "but confusion can be helpful in Yugoslavia for it means that opportunities then arise for new talent to enter!" Even with tighter budgets, it seems likely that the popularity of Yugoslav films with home audiences is a good sign for the near future for these filmmakers who are influenced by East and West.

## SELECTED BIBLIOGRAPHY

### Books

Boglić, Mira, ed. *Almanac of Croatian Film 1966–1970.* Zagreb: The Association of Film Workers of Croatia, 1971. (Description of Croatian films and filmmakers.)

*Filmografija Jugoslovenskog Dugometražnog Igranog Filma 1945–1980.* Beograd: Institut za Film, 1981. (Film credits for all feature films, 1945–1980.)

Goulding, Daniel J. *Liberated Cinema: The Yugoslav Experience.* Bloomington: Indiana University Press, 1985.

Holloway, Ronald. *Z Is for Zagreb.* London: Tantivy Press, 1972. (A useful introduction to the Zagreb animators written by *Variety*'s reviewer for Yugoslav films.)

Liehm, Mira and Antonin J. *The Most Important Art: Soviet and Eastern European Film after 1945.* Berkeley: University of California Press, 1977. (Helpful survey of Yugoslav film in context of other Eastern European countries.)

Munitié, Ranko. *The Yugoslav Film from 1945 to 1979.* Beograd: *Yugoslav Survey* offprint, 1979. (Many titles and dates but little organization.)

Stoil, Michael Jon. *Cinema Beyond the Danube: The Camera and Politics.* Metuchen, NJ: Scarecrow Press, 1974. (Not as thorough as Liehm's work.)

Volk, Peter. *Istorija Jugoslavenske Kinematografije 1896–1982.* Beograd: Institut za Film, 1983. (Newly published, this is the first complete book on Yugoslav film history in Yugoslavia. Though in Serbo-Croatian, there are English summaries after each chapter.)

Articles

Horton, Andrew. "Satire and Sympathy: A New Wave of Yugoslavian Filmmakers." *Cinéaste* 11, no. 2 (spring 1982):18–22. (A survey of the Prague School directors and film trends in the new Yugoslav cinema.

———. "The New Serbo-Creationism," American Film, 11, no. 4 (January-February 1986): 24–30.

# ABOUT THE CONTRIBUTORS

WILLIAM LUHR (the editor) is associate professor of English and Film, Saint Peter's College, New Jersey. Author of *Raymond Chandler and Film* (1982) and co-author (with Peter Lehman) of *Authorship and Narrative in the Cinema: Issues in Contemporary Aesthetics and Criticism* (1977) and *Blake Edwards* (1981), he has published numerous articles and reviews on film.

DUDLEY ANDREW is professor and head of the Film Studies Division in the Department of Communication Studies as well as chair of the Comparative Literature Program, at the University of Iowa. His books include *The Major Film Theories* (1976), *André Bazin* (1978), *Film in the Aura of Art* (1984), and *Concepts in Film Theory* (1984). He is currently at work, among other projects, on a history of French film in the 1930s.

PATRICIA AUFDERHEIDE is a Washington, D.C.-based journalist on the arts, and editor of *In These Times* newspaper. She has her Ph.D. in Latin American history from the University of Minnesota and is visiting professor of International Studies, Duke University. In 1985 she toured Latin America with the *La otra cara,* an exhibit of American independent films.

PETER BONDANELLA is professor of Italian Studies, Indiana University, where he teaches Renaissance literature and Italian cinema, and president of the American Association for Italian Studies. Among his many books and articles are *Federico Fellini: Essays in Criticism* (1978) and *Italian Cinema: From Neorealism to the Present* (1983).

JULIANNE BURTON teaches Latin American Literature and Film at the University of California, Santa Cruz. She has published widely on Latin American cinema in the United States and abroad, is editor of *Cinema and Social Change in Latin America: Conversations with Filmmakers* (1986), and compiler of *The New Latin American Cinema: An Annotated Bibliography* (1983).

AYSE FRANKO was born in Turkey. She has a Master's degree in Cinema Studies from New York University, and is now post-production supervisor at Interlink Film Graphic Design in Hollywood, California.

DAN GEORGAKAS is an editor of *Cineaste,* co-editor of *The Cineaste Interviews* (1983) and of *In Focus—A Guide to Using Films,* (1980) and co-author of *Solidarity Forever* 1985), based on the 1979 film *The Wobblies.*

PIERS HANDLING, a native of Canada, taught film at Carleton University and Queen's University. Author of *The Films of Don Shebib* and editor of *Self Portrait: Essays on the Canadian and Quebec Cinemas,* he has published numerous articles on the Canadian film scene. He is now with the Toronto Festival of Festivals.

LEO HECHT is chairman of Russian Studies at George Mason University. He has published three books and numerous articles and has presented many papers on various aspects of Russian culture. He is editor of *NEWSNOTES on Soviet and East European Drama and Theatre.*

VIRGINIA HIGGINBOTHAM teaches in the Department of Spanish and Portuguese at the University of Texas, Austin. Among her publications are *The Comic Spirit of Federico García Lorca* (1976), *Luis Buñuel* (1979), and numerous articles on surrealism, Spanish theater, and film. A study of Carlos Saura, the Spanish filmmaker, is in work.

KYOKO HIRANO has a degree in journalism from the University of Tokyo and is completing her Ph.D. in Cinema Studies at New York University, where she has also taught a course on Japanese film. A contributor on Japanese film directors and films to Macmillan's *International Film/Film Directors Guides,* she is Film Program Coordinator at the Japan Society of New York.

ANDREW HORTON is professor of Film Studies at the University of New Orleans and a screenwriter who has written three feature films with Yugoslav director Srdjan Karanović. Co-editor of *Modern European Filmmakers and the Art of Adaptation* (1981), he is author of *The Films of George Roy Hill* (1985).

BRUCE KAWIN is professor of English and Film Studies at the University of Colorado, Boulder. He is the author of three books on William Faulkner's film career, including *Faulkner and Film* (1977), and of *Telling It Again and Again* (1972), *Mindscreen* (1978), and *The Mind of the Novel* (1982).

ELAINE MANCINI received her Ph.D. in Cinema Studies from New York University, was a Fulbright scholar, and has taught film in the United States and Europe. She is author of *Struggles of the Italian Film Industry During Fascism* (1985), and co-author of *D.W. Griffith and the Biograph Company* (1985).

FREDERICK J. MARKER is professor of English and Drama, University of Toronto. A director of many theater productions, he is co-editor, with Lise-Lone Marker, of *Ingmar Bergman: A Project for the Theatre* (1983).

LISE-LONE MARKER, born in Denmark, is professor of Theatrical History, the University of Toronto. She is also co-author with Frederick J. Marker of *Ingmar Bergman: Four Decades in the Theater.*

NEIL McDONALD is foundation lecturer (equivalent to professor) in Film History at Mitchell College of Advanced Education, Bathurst, New South Wales, Australia, where he has taught since 1970. He is the author of numerous articles on film and theater and contributed the entries on Australian Drama and Shakespeare and Film to the *McGraw-Hill Encyclopedia of World Drama,* second edition, 1984.

NICHOLAS E. MEYER, born in Argentina, was the Argentine correspondent for *Variety* and film and book reviewer for the *Buenos Aires Herald,* the English-language daily. After writing about the United States film scene for Argentine publications for several years from New York, he now lives near Buenos Aires.

JOHN MOSIER is editor of the *New Orleans Review,* a contributing editor for *Americas* Magazine, and associated director of the Film Buffs Institute of Loyola University, New Orleans. His writings have appeared in South America and Europe as well as the United States.

ERIC RENTSCHLER, associate professor of German and director of Film Studies at the University of California, Irvine, has written extensively on German film history. His publications include *West German Film in the Course of Time* (1984) and the anthology *German Film and Literature: Adaptations and Transformations* (1986).

ELLA SHOHAT has published in such film periodicals as *Screen* and *Film Quarterly.* She is currently writing her doctoral dissertation on Israeli cinema in the Cinema Studies Department, New York University.

ANDREW SINCLAIR is a screenwriter and director based in London, author of several novels and other books, among them biographies of Dylan Thomas and John Ford. He has lectured on history and film at universities in Great Britain and the United States.

JOSEF ŠKVORECKÝ is a Canadian novelist of Czech background. Besides many novels he is the author of *All the Bright Young Men and Women: A Personal History of Czech Cinema* (1972) and *Jiri Menzel and the History of "Closely Observed Trains"* (1982). His latest novel is *The Engineer of Human Souls* (1984). He teaches English literature and film at the University of Toronto.

ROBERT STAM teaches Cinema Studies at New York University. Co-author with Randall Johnson of *Brazilian Cinema* (1982) and *Reflexivity in Film and Literature: From Don Quixote to Jean-Luc Godard* (1985), he is a recent recipient of a Guggenheim fellowship.

CLYDE TAYLOR teaches film and literature at Tufts University. Founder of the African Film Society, he was awarded an "Indie" in 1985 from the Association of Independent Video and Film Producers for his criticism of cinema of people of color.

ROSIE THOMAS is currently completing a Ph.D. in Hindi cinema at the London School of Economics. She is a lecturer in the Department of Film and Photography at Harrow College of Higher Education and other colleges in England.

JOÃO LUIZ VIERA received his Ph.D. in Cinema Studies from New York University, and teaches film at the Universidade Federal Fluminense in Rio de Janeiro, Brazil. He is co-author of *D.W. Griffith and the Biograph Company* (1985), and has published in *Framework* and *Filme Cultura.*

DENNIS WEST teaches film and literature at the University of Idaho. His articles on Latin American cinema have appeared in *Cineaste, The American Hispanist, Caribbean Review,* and other journals.

ESTHER YAU is a doctoral candidate in the Department of Theater, Film and Television at the University of California, Los Angeles. She is currently working on her dissertation on Women and Chinese Cinema.

# Photo Credits

The stills credited below with M are used courtesy of the Museum of Modern Art Film Stills Archive, New York, N.Y.

AFRICA. All stills M.

ARGENTINA. From the author's private collection.

AUSTRALIA. *Adventures of Barry Mackenzie,* courtesy Phillip Adams and the National Film and Sound Archive. *Man from Snowy River*, courtesy Hoyts and the National Film and Sound Archive. *Breaker Morant*, courtesy South Australian Film Development Corporation and the national Film and Sound Archive. *Bliss*, courtesy Anthony Buckley. The others are from the author's private collection.

BELGIUM. All stills M.

BRAZIL. All stills M.

CANADA. Courtesy National Film, Television and Sound Archives.

CHINA. *Family, The Wild Boar Forest, Stage Sisters,* and *Boat People,* M. *A Time to Live and a Time to Die,* courtesy 24th New York Film Festival, 1986. *Yellow Earth* and *Homecoming,* collection of the author.

CUBA. From the author's private collection.

CZECHOSLOVAKIA. From the author's private collection.

FRANCE. *Forbidden Games*, courtesy French Cultural Services, New York, N.Y. *Diary of a Country Priest, Diabolique, Breathless, The 400 Blows, Last Year at Marienbad,* and *The Marquise of O.——,* M. *Just before Nightfall,* 11th New York Film Festival. Others courtesy Lorrimer Publishing Limited, London.

GERMANY. *The Murderers Are Among Us, Aren't We Wonderful?, The Thousand Eyes of Dr. Mabuse, Yesterday Girl, The Merchant of Four Seasons, The Mystery of Kaspar Hauser, Germany in Autumn,* and *Berlin Alexanderplatz,* courtesy Stiftung Deutsche Kinemathek. *I Was Nineteen* and *The Legend of Paul and Paula,* courtesy Deutsches Filmmuseum, Frankfurt. *Kings of the Road,* courtesy Gray City Films. *Bye, Bye Bavaria,* courtesy Filmverlag der Autoren.

GREAT BRITAIN. *Brief Encounter, The Third Man,* and *Saturday Night and Sunday Morning,* National Film Archive, Stills Library, London. *Kind Hearts and Coronets, Horror of Dracula, The Bridge on the River Kwai,* and *Lolita,* M. Others, courtesy Lorrimer Publishing Limited, London.

GREECE. *Electra* and *Zorba the Greek,* M. *Thanos and Despina* and *Traveling Players,* courtesy *Cineaste.*

HUNGARY. From the author's private collection.

INDIA. *Mother India* and *Pathetic Fallacy,* courtesy National Film Archive, Stills Library, London. *The Chess Players,* M. All others courtesy the author.

ISRAEL. From the author's private collection.

ITALY. *Rome, Open City, Divorce, Italian Style, Once Upon a Time in the West, Red Desert, 8½, The Conformist,* and *Seven Beauties,* M. *The Bicycle Thief,* courtesy Lorrimer Publishing Limited, London. All others from the author's private collection.

JAPAN. *Rashomon* and *Seven Samurai,* M. *Carmen Goes Home, Tokyo Story, The Human Condition, Night and Fog in Japan,* and *Tora the Tramp,* courtesy Shōchiku Co., Ltd. *Fight without Code* and *Ballad of Narayama,* courtesy Tōei Company, Ltd. *Until We Meet Again* and *Floating Clouds,* courtesy Toho Co., Ltd. *Farewell to Earth,* courtesy The Production Gunrō.

LATIN AMERICA. From the author's private collection.

MEXICO. *The Young and the Damned, Wuthering Heights, Reed: Insurgent Mexico, Letters from Marusia,* M. *Nazarín,* National Film Archive, Stills Library, London. *The Exterminating Angel,* courtesy Lorrimer Publishing Limited, London.

THE NETHERLANDS. All stills M.

POLAND. From the author's private collection.

PORTUGAL. Both stills M.

SPAIN. All stills M.

SWEDEN. *The Silence, Persona, Loving Couples,* and *Elvira Madigan,* courtesy Swedish Information Service, New York, N.Y. *I Am Curious Yellow,* and *Fanny and Alexander,* M. *Seventh Seal* and *Wild Strawberries,* courtesy Lorrimer Publishing Limited, London.

SWITZERLAND. All stills M.

TURKEY. All stills M.

UNION OF SOVIET SOCIALIST REPUBLICS. *The Battle of Stalingrad,* courtesy Soviet Archives. *Ballad of a Soldier, Ivan's Childhood, Andrei Rublev, Uncle Vanya, The Shooting Party, The Twelve Chairs,* and *An Unfinished Piece for a Player Piano,* courtesy Corinth Films. *Siberiada, Moscow Doesn't Believe in Tears,* and *26 Days in the Life of Dostoevskii,* courtesy International Film Exchange, Ltd.

UNITED STATES. *Red River, Singin' in the Rain, Rebel without a Cause, The Searchers, North by Northwest, Psycho, The Godfather, Taxi Driver, Nashville,* and *Victor, Victoria,* M. *A Streetcar Named Desire, The Graduate, Easy Rider, The Dirty Dozen, Midnight Cowboy, 2001,* and *Chinatown,* courtesy Lorrimer Publishing Limited, London.

YUGOSLAVIA. From the author's private collection.

# INDEXES

Abbreviations used in the two indexes refer to the articles as follows: Af., AFRICA; Arg., ARGENTINA; Aus., AUSTRALIA; Bel., BELGIUM; Braz., BRAZIL; Can., CANADA; Ch., CHINA; Cu., CUBA; Cz., CZECHOSLOVAKIA; Fr., FRANCE; Ger., GERMANY; GB, GREAT BRITAIN; Gr., GREECE; Hu., HUNGARY; Ind., INDIA; Isr., ISRAEL; It., ITALY; Ja., JAPAN; LA, LATIN AMERICA; Mex., MEXICO; Ne., NETHERLANDS; Pol., POLAND; Por., PORTUGAL; Sp., SPAIN; Swe., SWEDEN; Swit., SWITZERLAND; Tu., TURKEY; USSR, UNION OF SOVIET SOCIALIST REPUBLICS; US, UNITED STATES; Yu., YUGOSLAVIA

## Index of Directors

# Index of Film Titles

For reasons of space non-English titles are omitted here for languages given in romanized script in the text: Chinese, Greek, Hebrew, Indian, Japanese, and Russian. The foreign-language title is also omitted when the original is either identical to or readily identifiable with the English version. Original titles, including transliterations, are provided in the texts of the individual articles.